Printing Technology

4th Edition

J. Michael Adams, Professor and Dean
College of Design Arts, Drexel University
Philadelphia, Pennsylvania

David D. Faux, Professor
State University of New York
Oswego, New York

Lloyd J. Rieber, Associate Professor
St. Mary's University
Halifax, Nova Scotia, Canada

Delmar Publishers

I(T)P™ An International Thomson Publishing Company
Albany • Bonn • Boston • Cincinnati • Detroit • London • Madrid
Melbourne • Mexico City • New York • Pacific Grove • Paris
San Francisco • Singapore • Tokyo • Toronto • Washington

NOTICE TO THE READER

Cover photo: Gary Conner
Delmar Staff
Publisher: Robert D. Lynch
Senior Administrative Editor: John Anderson
Developmental Editor: Barbara A. Riedell
Production Coordinator: Andrew Crouth
Art & Design Coordinator: Nicole Reamer

COPYRIGHT © 1996
By Delmar Publishers Inc.
an International Thomson Publishing Company
I(T)P   The ITP logo is a trademark under license

Printed in the United States of America

For more information, contact:

Delmar Publishers Inc.
3 Columbia Circle , Box 15015
Albany, New York 12212-5015

International Thomson Publishing
Berkshire House
168-173 High Holborn
London, WC1V7AA
England

Thomas Nelson Australia
102 Dodds Street
South Melbourne 3205
Victoria, Australia

Nelson Canada
1120 Birchmont Road
Scarborough, Ontario
M1K 5G4, Canada

Delmar Publishers' Online Services
To access Delmar on the World Wide Web, point your browser to:
http://www.delmar.com/delmar.html
To access through Gopher: gopher:/ / gopher.delmar.com
(Delmar online is part of "thomson.com", an Internet
site with information on more than 30 publishers of the
International Publishing organization.)
For more information on our products and services:
email: info@delmar.com
Or call 800-347-7707

International Thomson Publishing GmbH
Konigswinterer Str. 418
53227 Bonn
Germany

International Thomson Publishing Asia
221 Henderson Bldg. #05-10
Singapore 0315

International Thomson Publishing Japan
Kyowa Building, 3F
2-2-1 Hirakawa-cho
Chiyoda-ku, Tokyo 102
Japan

1 2 3 4 5 6 7 8 9 10 XXX 01 00 99 98 97 96 95

Library of Congress Cataloging-in-Publication Data

Adams, J. Michael.
    Printing technology / J. Michael Adams, David D. Faux, Lloyd J.
Rieber. — 4th ed.
        p.   cm.
    Includes index.
    ISBN 0–8273–6907–7
    1. Printing, Practical.   I. Faux, David D.   II. Rieber, Lloyd J.
III. Title.
Z244.A515   1996
686.2—dc20
                                    95–34510
                                      CIP

Table of Contents

AUG 1996

19 Finishing Operations 513

20 Estimating and Production Control 535

21 Customer-Defined Quality Management 565

Appendixes

Introduction

When *Printing Technology* was introduced in 1977, it was one of a new generation of books that dealt with printing as a technology, rather than as merely a process. The decade before had seen a revolution in the printing industry. Computer typesetting had become a commercial reality; presensitized litho plates had been introduced; offset printing had surpassed relief in percentage of sheets printed; web presses had grown in sophistication and acceptance. The first edition of *Printing Technology* covered the printing processes, but it also addressed the printing revolution and offered an introduction to the sophistication of printing.

We are still amazed by and appreciative of the reception of that first edition. Classroom teachers and their students reacted with enthusiasm. Instructors liked the combination of concepts with practice, and students liked the understandable language and contemporary illustrations. The second edition arrived in 1982, and the third came in 1988 as a result of the encouragement of many individuals who offered suggestions for improvement. The third edition has been used at nearly every level of graphic arts education—in public, private, and industrial training—and has found wide national and international acceptance.

Preparation of the Fourth Edition

As changes were planned for the fourth edition, it became apparent the industry had experienced another revolution: The computer had entered every aspect of printing management and production and had become the overriding element that guided all changes.

In its fourth edition, *Printing Technology* has been revised and updated to present the most current procedures and state-of-the-art materials in each phase of the printing process. The content has been reorganized to give students an understanding of the historical evolution of printing, as well as knowledge about the latest equipment and processes. The fourth edition stresses computer applications in printing.

Of special note is the addition of electrostatic as one of the primary printing processes. This decision reflects a true revolution and redefinition of printing. For at least the past one hundred years, "printing" has included only relief, intaglio, screen, and, only grudgingly, lithography. Also included are several new chapters, notably an entirely new chapter on customer-defined quality (the basis of Total Quality Management).

Information about composition has been totally rewritten to stress computer image generation and assembly, including full-page make-up and desktop publishing systems. The chapters on offset press operation have been rewritten to include web printing, computer-aided press control, and registration control devices commonly used in the industry. Detailed discussions assume the reader has no previous knowledge about printing technology.

SPECIFIC CHAPTER CHANGES are as follows:

Chapter 1

- Addition of Xerography to basic printing methods

- Update on industry data
- Change in typical company organization

Chapter 2

- New illustration program with two new illustrations on pointsize comparison and dingbats
- Addition of proofreading appendix

Chapter 3:

- New illustration program
- Expanded descriptions of all classifying type
- Expanded copyfitting section

Chapter 4

- New illustration program
- Positioned "cold type" as a traditional technique that dates from the late 1960s and is the foundation for all cold type technology

Chapter 5

- This is a completely revised chapter
- New illustration program

Chapter 6

- New illustration program
- Greatly expanded narrative about f/stops
- New section on spreads and chokes
- General updating of terminology

Chapter 7

- New illustration program
- Simplified discussion on logarithms
- Expanded discussion on the differences between solid line and vignetted screens

- Focused chapter on traditional photographic methods; directed attention to the new chapter on digital halftone imaging

Chapter 8

- This is a completely revised chapter
- New illustration program

Chapter 9

- Revised to include micro separation

Chapter 10

- New illustration program
- Clarified unit as "traditional" mechanical stripping

Chapter 11

- Information about photopolymer presensitized surface plates added
- Added section on direct-to-plate systems

Chapter 12

- New halftone illustrations
- Expanded and enhanced the "systems" approach to learning press configuration
- Added a section on blanket cylinder considerations

Chapter 13

- New halftone illustrations
- Update of GATF quality control devices

Chapter 14

- Expanded discussion of fabric classification and selection
- Added explanation of mechanical stretching

Chapter 15

- New halftone illustrations
- Added metric conversions to appropriate numbers
- Technical updating throughout

Chapter 16

- New halftone illustrations
- Clarification of details in the conventional gravure process

Chapter 17

- Entirely new digital press section

Chapter 18

- Added material on papermaking and paper characteristics
- Added section on recycled papers
- Added section on calculating ink coverage
- Expanded discussion on PMS system

Chapter 19

- New illustration program
- Added section on demographic printing and binding
- Added discussion on packaging and shipping

Chapter 20

- Expanded introduction to reinforce the concept of expenses and profit
- New illustration program
- Changed basic cost diagrams to reflect current corporate priorities and realistic expenses
- Introduced computer-based management and estimating systems

Chapter 21

- New coverage of customer-defined quality management

Dedication

The Fourth Edition of Printing Technology is dedicated to three individuals. Without their loving support and encouragement this book would not have been possible.

Susan M. Adams

Jeanne C. Faux

Karen L. Rieber

Acknowledgements

Many individuals and organizations were fundamental to completion of this fourth edition of *Printing Technology*. Special appreciation must be expressed to Katie Connor who coordinated the illustration program for this edition. Her attention to detail, creative problem-solving and incredible persistence are humbly acknowledged and applauded.

The authors are grateful for the ideas, support, suggestions and action of other individuals. Of special note are the contributions of Richard Gorelick, Edward Ball, Bill Hurlburt, James Craig, Richard W. Foster, Joanne M. Frank, and Jonathan C. Oler.

Without the endorsement and support of the print community, the task of writing Printing Technology would be impossible. The following must be recognized for the critical role they played in assisting and sustaining the authors.

3M Mertle Collection, University of Minnesota
3M Printing & Publishing Systems Division
A.B. Dick Company
Acti Cameras Inc.
Advanced Process Supply/Wisconsin Automated
Agfa-Gevaert, Inc.
American Paper Institute, Recycled Paperboard Division
AM International
Apple Computers
Arcata Graphics Company, Fairfield
Art Institute of Chicago
Baumfolder Corporation
Berkey Technical
Beta Screen Corporation
Covalent Systems Corporation
Custom-Bilt Machinery, Inc.
C-Thru Ruler Company
DuPont Crosfield Electronic Imaging
E.I. DuPont DeNours
Enkel Corporation
Environmental Choice Program, Canada
Foster Manufacturing
General Binding Corporation, Northbrook, IL
Gorelick & Associates
Graphic Arts Manufacturing Company
Graphic Arts Technical Foundation
Gravure Association of America
GTI, Graphic Technology Inc.
Hagen Systems Inc.
Heidelberg Eastern
Hewlett-Packard Corporation
IBM Corporation
Indigo America
International Museum of Photography at George Eastman House
Eastman Kodak Company
Kroy, Inc.
LogEtronics Corporation
Macbeth, Division of Kollmorgen Instruments Corporation
Mackenzie & Harris Type
MAN Roland
Mead Paper

Mergenthaler Linotype Company
Morrill Press, Division of Engraph, Inc.
Micro Essential Laboratory, Inc.
Misomex North America, Inc.
Muller-Martini Corporation
NASA
Naz-Dar/KC
NuArc Company, Inc.
Pantone, Inc.
Pearl Pressman Liberty Communications Group
Rachwal Systems
Rockwell Graphic Systems, Rockwell International Corporation
F.P. Rosback Company
Scangraphics
John N. Schaedler, Inc.
Schaefer Machine Company, Inc.
Screen USA, Subsidiary of Dainippon Screen Mfg. Co., Ltd.
Smithsonian Institution
Solna Web USA, Inc.
Southern Gravure Service
Stouffer Graphic Arts Equipment Company
Texet Corporation
Tobias Associates, Inc.
Tourist Office of Spain
Ulano Corporation, Inc.
University of Pennsylvania
Vandersons Corporation
Videojet Systems International
Western Lithotech
Xerox Corporation
John Britts, Kenneth Dubois and Kevin Fogarty: CANON U.S.A., Inc.
Douglas and George Caruso, Speedway Press, Inc.
Roger Cherry, Macomb CC
Kate Crawford, Sinclair CC
Mark Doyle: Xerox Corporation
Ben Franklin Faux: Buena High School, Sierra Vista, Arizona
Kenneth Fay, HEUFT USA, Inc.
Chuck Finley, Columbus State C.C.
Kenneth Hanulec: Mitsubishi Imaging (MC), Inc.
John Henry, Mitchell Printing Company

Drew Hill and Alex McCombie: Drew Hill Graphic Design Group and New World Media
Ronald Hindmarch: Hilton High School, Hilton, NY
Gary Hinkle, Illinois Central College
Kenneth Hoffman, Michael Kleper, and Jere Rentzel: Rochester Institute of Technology, Rochester, NY
John Kallis, California University of PA
Edward Kelly: 3M Printing and Publishing Systems Division
Dennis Killian, Gregory Shambo, and Keith Fengler: Phillips & Jacobs, Inc.
Kent Kreul, Brayton Brunkhurst, Randy Flynn, and Philip Livingston: Milprint, Inc.
Arthur Lange: Langeraphic
Ling-Hsaia Lee, Central Mich Univ
Nancy and John Leininger: Clemson University, Clemson, South Carolina
Sam Mason: Advanced Color Technology
Andrew Mohr: Eastwood Litho, Inc.
William Mulvey: Geneva High School, Geneva, NY
Arthur Palermo and Jack Williams: Midstate Printing Company
Robert Poormon, Board of Cooperative Education Services, Mexico, NY
Jesus Rodriguez, Pittsburgh State Univ
Tom Schildgen, Ariz State
Mike Stinnett, Oakland Tech Ctr
Kenneth Swanson: Bowne Business Communications
Janet Zimmer, State University of New York as Oswego
Todd Zimmer, Sealright Corporation, Fulton, NY
State University of New York at Oswego Art Department: Catherine Bebout, Al Bremner, Cynthia Clabough, Nick D'Innocenzo, Thomas Eckersley, Donna Fauler, Michael Fox, John Fuller, Paul Garland, Natasha Hopkins, Sewall Oertling, Mindy Ostrow, Barbara Perry, Zabel Sarian, Jon Shishido, Lisa Shortslef, Kate Timm, Helen Zakin, and Richard Zakin

The Printing Industry

Anecdote to Chapter One

An Early Chinese Press. The press was a low, flat table solid enough to hold the form in place.
The Bettman Archives.

It is possible to trace the origins of printing to the use of seals to "sign" official documents as early as 255 B.C., during the Han dynasty in China. A ceramic stamp was pressed into a sheet of moist clay. When dry, the imprint served as a means of certifying the authenticity of the document. When paper was invented, around A.D. 105, the transition to the use of the seal with ink was a natural one.

Early documents and manuscripts were copied and recopied by hand. Frequent copying mistakes were made from one edition to the next; copies often differed significantly from the author's original. Around A.D. 175, the Chinese began the practice of cutting the writings of important scholars into stone. The stones were placed in centers of learning, and students made "rubbings," or copies, on paper from the carvings. The process was faster than hand copying, and all editions were identical to the first.

No one knows when the ideas of the seal and stone rubbings came together, but in China in A.D. 953, under the administration of Fêng Tao, a large-scale block-printing operation was set up to reproduce the Confucian classics. Block prints were generally made from slabs of hard, fine-grained wood that were carved to leave well-defined raised images. The raised portions of the block were inked, paper was laid over the block, and a pad was rubbed across the surface to transfer the ink to the paper.

During the Sung dynasty, around A.D. 1401, a common man named Pi Shêng invented movable type. Building on the ideas of block printing, Shêng cut individual characters into small pieces of clay. The clay was fired to make it hard, and the individual pieces were placed in an iron frame to create the printing form. Because the pieces did not fit together perfectly, they were embedded in a mixture of hot pine resin, wax, and paper ashes. When cold, all the pieces held together perfectly tight, and the form was inked and printed. Reheating the resin mixture loosened the pieces of type so they could be reused. Other materials, including wood, tin, copper, and bronze, were used for the same purpose.

The idea of movable type traveled to neighboring countries. In Korea, in A.D. 1403, King T'aijong ordered that everything within his reach be printed in order to pass on the tradition of information contained in the works. Three hundred thousand pieces of bronze type were cast, and printing began. Less than fifty years later in Northern Germany, Johann Gutenberg worked a similar process, only using the Roman alphabet. His efforts earned him the title "father of printing." It is interesting to speculate if Gutenberg learned of the process from visitors to Asia.

Objectives for Chapter 1

After completing this chapter you will be able to:

- Discuss the evolution of graphic symbols from prehistoric times to the modern alphabet of the present.

- List the major printing processes and describe the differences between them.

- List and describe the steps in the printing cycle.

- Rank the printing industry in terms of number of individual firms, number of employees, and "value added."

- Describe the structure and purpose of each level of a small- to medium-sized printing company.

- Compare the kinds of services provided by the different types of printing businesses.

- Describe the different ways to enter, train, and advance in the printing industry.

Introduction

Printing has been identified as the single most significant technological development in the history of the human species. Prior to the invention of printing all information and communication was transmitted verbally. Ideas survived as long as someone could remember

Figure 1.1. **An early message.** Pictured is a cave drawing (message made by prehistoric people) in the Altamira caves in Spain.
Courtesy of Spanish National Tourist Office, New York.

the concept. Little information was retained unchanged for more than three generations. Folklore and legend formed the base for all cultures. Before printing it was very difficult to communicate messages to a large number of people. The oral tradition was limited to small groups and the memory of the speaker.

Printing created the ability to record ideas so they could survive across many generations. It also allowed information to be communicated exactly to any number of people. Once ideas and information were made permanent and everyone had access to them, true science and technological development began.

The foundation, and power, of print is the ability to reproduce graphic symbols and messages in large quantities. Graphic messages are possible because lines can be made into shapes that have meanings to human beings. As early as 35,000 B.C. people were drawing messages on cave walls (figure 1.1). These were probably intended to be temporary messages, but they became permanent. They were simple drawings—merely lines—but they carried meaning

to the people of that period: "This is a mammoth," "Oh, what a feast we had," or "We hunted a great hairy beast."

Development of Pictographs

Drawings that carry meaning because they look like real objects are called pictographs (figure 1.2a). Pictographs have a one-to-one relationship with reality. To symbolize one ox (called *aleph*), draw one symbol of an ox. To represent five oxen, draw five ox symbols. It is difficult to use pictographs to communicate complex ideas, such as "I have six oxen—one brown, four white, and one white and brown." It is impossible to symbolize abstract ideas, such as love or hate, with a pictographic system.

About 1200 B.C., in a small country called Phoenicia (now a part of Syria), a group of traders began to realize the limitations of the pictographic system. They attempted to simplify the picture notations in their account books by streamlining their symbols. But no matter how they drew the lines, *aleph* still

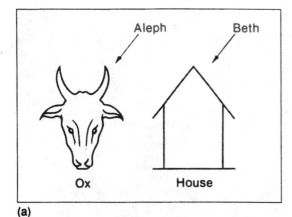

(a)

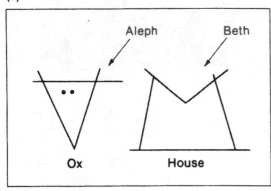

(b)

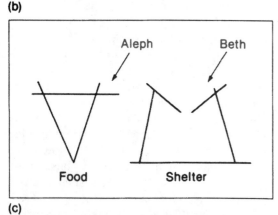

(c)

Figure 1.2.   **The development of ideographs.**
Pictographs shown here in (a) and (b) were drawn
to represent real objects. They were gradually simplified to represent general ideas and became
known as ideographs (c).

symbolized one ox and *beth* still stood for one
house (figure 1.2b).

Development of Ideographs

The next step the Phoenicians took was to
have drawings symbolize ideas. These drawings are called ideographs. With this system
aleph became the symbol for food and *beth* represented a dwelling or shelter (figure 1.2c).
Ideographs are simple drawings that symbolize ideas or concepts rather than concrete objects. They were a vast improvement over
pictographs because they could easily represent complex or abstract ideas, but they were
still clumsy. The number of symbols in an
ideographic system can be overwhelming.
Most Asian societies, such as Japan, Korea,
and China, still use ideographic symbol systems which contain over ten thousand different characters. It could take a lifetime to learn
the meaning of all the symbols.

Development of Phonetic Symbols

By 900 B.C. the Phoenicians had made another
change. Instead of the picture symbolizing the
ox or food, the picture came to represent a
sound. Whenever the readers saw the symbol,
they could make the sound that the symbol
represented. When the symbols were placed
together, whole words could be repeated. This
idea of representing sounds by symbols is
known as a phonetic symbol system and is the
basis for most modern written languages. The
Phoenicians developed nineteen such symbols, but they were traders and were not concerned with recording all words used in
everyday conversation. We form verbal symbols today by combining consonants and vowels. The Phoenician system contained no
vowels and was of little use in recording everyday speech.

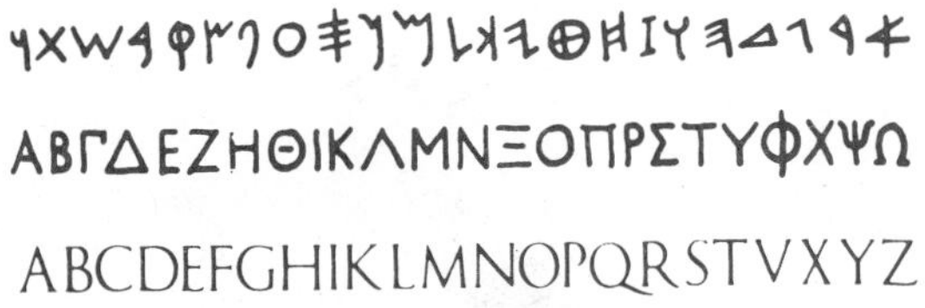

ᏎXW3ᏓᏒᎧᎧ0ᏎᎩᎽᏞᎧ1ᎧᎮᏗᏔᏞᎧ1ᎧᏔᏜ9ᎧᎧ

ΑΒΓΔΕΖΗΘΙΚΛΜΝΞΟΠΡΣΤΥΦΧΨΩ

ABCDEFGHIKLMNOPQRSTVXYZ

Figure 1.3. The development of our alphabet.
Illustrated from top to bottom are the Phoenician alphabet (900 B.C.), the Greek alphabet (403 B.C.), and the Roman alphabet (300 B.C.).

By 403 B.C. the Greeks had officially adopted the Phoenician system after adding five vowels and changing the names of the letters (figure 1.3). *Aleph* became *alpha* and *beth* became *beta*, which together form our term *alphabet*.

About one hundred years later, the early Roman empire borrowed the Greek alphabet and refined it to meet its needs. The Romans accepted thirteen Greek letters outright, revised eight, and added *F* and *Q*, for a total of twenty-three—all that were necessary to write Latin. The Roman system stood firm for nearly twelve centuries. About one thousand years ago the letter *U* was added as a rounded *V*, and two *V*s were put together to form *W*. Five hundred years later the letter *J* was added for a total of twenty-six letters that form our contemporary Latin alphabet.

There were still some problems with the consistency of rules to be worked out, however. Early Greek and Roman writing was done by scribes—all with different "penmanship." Some wrote from left to right; some wrote from right to left. Combine these differences with the lack of agreement on the use of punctuation marks or spaces between words or sentences, and the whole system could be quite a mess.

It wasn't until movable metal type was introduced by Johann Gutenberg in the mid fif-

teenth century that any true standard of punctuation or sentence structure was achieved. It took printing technology to stabilize the phonetic symbol system as we know it today. Slight changes have been made, but the basic composition of our alphabet has remained the same from the time of Gutenberg.

Printing Technology

All printing processes reproduce lines and/or dots that form an image. **Printing** is the process of manufacturing multiple copies of graphic images. Although most people think of printing as putting ink on paper, printing is not limited to any particular materials or inks. The embossing process uses no ink at all, and all shapes and sizes of metals, wood, and plastics are common receivers of printed messages.

Major Printing Processes

The following five major printing processes are used to reproduce graphic images:

- Relief printing
- Intaglio printing
- Screen printing
- Lithographic printing
- Xerography

Each of these processes is suited for specific applications, such as newspaper, book, package, or textile printing.

Relief Printing

The **relief printing** process includes letterpress printing, flexographic printing, and all other methods of transferring an image from a raised surface (figure 1.4a). Although it was once a major process in the printing industry, letterpress printing has been replaced largely by other printing processes. Most relief printing

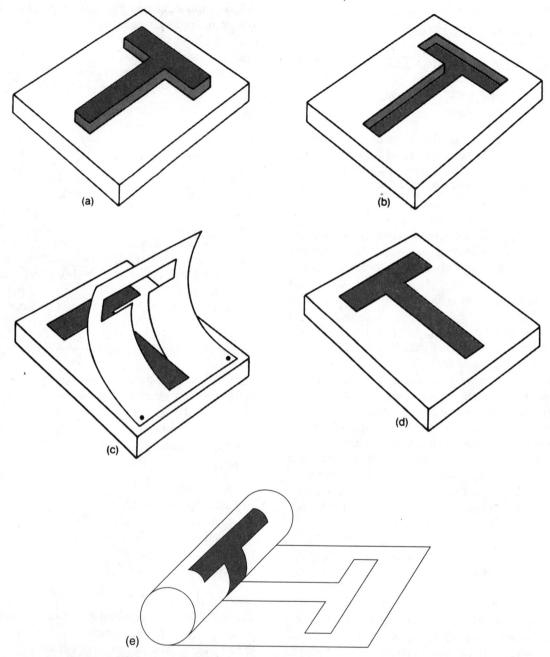

Figure 1.4.   Five main printing processes. (a) Relief printing transfers an image from a raised surface. (b) Intaglio printing transfers an image from a sunken surface. (c) Screen printing transfers an image through a stencil. (d) Lithographic printing transfers an image chemically from a flat surface. (e) Electrostatic printing transfers an image electromagnetically.

done today is done with flexography. Flexographic printing is used extensively in the packaging industry for printing on corrugated board, paper cartons, and plastic film. Flexography is also becoming a significant process for printing newspapers, newspaper inserts, catalogs, and directories.

Intaglio Printing

Intaglio printing is the reverse of relief printing. An intaglio image is transferred from a sunken surface (figure 1.4b). Copperplate etching and engraving are two intaglio processes. Industrial intaglio printing is called **gravure.** Gravure is used for extremely long press runs. Cellophane and aluminum-foil candy bar wrappers are two common packaging materials printed with gravure printing. *Reader's Digest* and *National Geographic* are but two of the many national magazines that are printed with gravure.

Screen Printing

Screen printing transfers an image by allowing ink to pass through openings in a stencil that has been applied to a screen mesh (figure 1.4c). The screen process is sometimes called "silk screen printing." Silk is rarely used to hold the stencil industrially, however, because silk is not as durable as industrial screen materials. Some of the industrial uses for screen printing include printing on plastic such as round plastic containers, printing large display signs and billboards, and printing on textiles. Another major use for screen printing is in the manufacture of printed circuit boards for electrical/electronic equipment.

Lithography

Lithography as it is known today is a relatively new process, dating from around 1798. A lithographic image is transferred from a flat surface. Certain areas on the surface are chemically treated to accept ink while other areas are left untreated so that they will repel ink. When the surface is inked, the ink remains in the ink-receptive areas, but not in the untreated areas. When a material such as paper contacts the surface, ink is transferred to the paper (figure 1.4d). This process is sometimes called planography, offset lithography, offset, or photo-offset lithography.

Offset lithographic printing is the most widely used printing process in the commercial printing industry. Its major application is for printing on paper; thus it is ideal for printing newspapers, books, magazines, pamphlets, and all other forms of paper publications.

Xerography

Xerography (or **electrostatic printing**) was invented in 1937 by Chester Carlson. It involves creating an image by electromagnetically charging areas of a special drum. As a result, the drum attracts a toner of metallic powder. The powder is then transferred and fused to a sheet of paper (figure 1.4e).

Even a decade ago Xerography would not have been classified as one of the major printing processes. However, over the last ten years a revolution has occurred. Today, nearly one-third of all image pages are reproduced on high-speed copiers, and color electrostatic reproduction is rapidly gaining acceptance. When a "copier" can deliver six thousand or more images that meet or exceed traditional ink density targets in an hour, the copier must be recognized as a printing press.

Although there are several older printing processes, such as collography, which prints from a fragile gelatin emulsion, these five major printing processes account for nearly 99 percent of all work done in the contemporary printing industry.

Printing technology has long been a powerful tool for social change. Edward George Bulwer-Lytton wrote, "The pen is mightier than the sword." But his statement assumes that the ideas the pen recorded are distributed.

Without printing, few would read the words, and the pen would be a very weak weapon.

Printers have long been the most influential individuals in the community. Early colonial printers helped to shape our country by reproducing, recording, and distributing the ideas and events of the period. Benjamin Franklin, an early American patriot, was proudest of his role as a printer. After being active in the Revolution, a signer of the Declaration of Independence, a member of the First and Second Continental Congresses, founder of the first American library, an author, an inventor, a publisher, and ambassador to France, he directed that his epitaph should read "B. Franklin, Printer."

Printing Cycle

Since the time of Franklin, the basic cycle of the printing industry has not changed much from the following procedures:

1. Identifying a need
2. Creating an image design
3. Reproducing the image design
4. Distributing the printed message

The printing cycle begins with an identified need. The need might be as simple as the reproduction of a form or as sophisticated as a poster intended to change human attitudes. It could be as ordinary as a package designed to convince a consumer to buy one brand of cereal rather than another. Whatever the need, a graphic design evolves. Special design agencies are often set up whose sole purpose is to sell ideas to clients and work closely with the printer as the design is turned into print.

The function of printing management is to be responsible for creating and controlling the reproduction process. Skilled workers must be employed and an organization created that efficiently and effectively delivers printed products. Once a job is proposed, the most efficient printing process must be identified. Such variables as the type of material to be printed, length of run, number and types of colors, time requirements, desired quality, and customer's cost limitations must all be considered. An estimate must be made for each job. A profit must be made, and yet the estimate must be low enough to attract work in a very competitive market. If the customer approves the estimate, management must schedule the job, arrange to obtain all materials, ensure quality control, and keep track of all phases of production so the job is finished on schedule.

The final test of the cycle is the method of distributing the printed message. Without an audience for the graphic images created by the artist and printer, the printing cycle is useless. Printing is mailed; handed out on busy streets; sold on street corners; and shipped to department stores, corner drugstores, and local newsstands. It is passed out in highway tollbooths, filed in offices, pasted on billboards, carried on placards, or even thumbtacked to poster boards. The purpose of all this activity is to place printed matter in the hands of consumers.

Sequence of Steps in the Printing Processes

The printing industry has historically consisted of shops identified with particular processes, such as relief printing or lithography. Craftsmen were trained and then bound by union or guild structure to a particular process. Recently it has become common for a printing establishment to use a variety of printing processes. Regardless of the printing process used, however, there is a sequence of production steps that all printing follows. This sequence consists of the following steps:

▪ Image design
▪ Image generation

- Image conversion
- Image assembly
- Image carrier preparation
- Image transfer
- Finishing

The point of a printed product is to meet a need—such as to inform, pursuade, entertain, or convince. The design must fulfill the customer's need. In the **image design** step, sketches and final layouts are made. Design variables such as type style, visual position, type size, balance, and harmony are all considered. After the customer approves the design, the image must be generated and made into a final form. Specifications developed during the image design stage are carefully followed during image generation. Traditionally, image generation was performed by hand, perhaps using photographic techniques. Advances in computer technology, however, have moved most image generation to the computer monitor and keyboard.

Most printing processes rely to a large degree on photography. Images are usually converted to transparent film in the **image conversion** step, placed in the proper printing order in the **image assembly** step, and then photographically transferred to an image carrier during the **image carrier preparation** step. The image carriers for each printing process may operate differently, but all must be prepared with the same general photographic considerations. Just as the computer revolution has affected image generation, it also has impacted image conversion and image assembly steps. Some organizations bypass traditional techniques and move directly from design to carrier preparation. No matter what technical tools are used, however, the sequence of steps remain the same.

The image must be printed onto a receiver material during the **image transfer** step. **Finishing** is the last step which combines the printed material into a final finished form that can be delivered to the customer. This may include cutting, perforating, scoring, folding, inserting, stapling, binding, or packaging.

This book is designed to reflect contemporary printing technology. Letterpress printing is presented first to give a historical overview of the development of modern printing. The discussion of letterpress also introduces new terms and concepts needed to understand the other printing processes. All of the steps in the printing sequences for the lithographic and screen processes are examined in detail. The gravure process is discussed only briefly because the complexity of image carrier preparation and image transfer for gravure printing are beyond the scope of this work. Flexography is presented in some depth because it represents a contemporary relief process and is a significant and growing part of the printing industry.

The printing industry is much larger than any one printing process. The printing industry reflects a manufacturing technology. A technology cannot be learned by examining tools or materials. A technology is mastered by understanding concepts. The first ten chapters of this text provide the fundamental concepts needed for mastering the technology of printing. The remaining chapters cover the procedures used in each of the major printing processes.

Size and Scope of the Printing Industry

The United States Department of Commerce classifies all industries in the United States by Standard Industrial Classification (SIC) numbers. In this classification system, the printing industry is part of SIC number 27 (Printing and Publishing). Department of Commerce information indicates that the United States printing and publishing industry consists of more than forty-nine thousand individual establishments that employ more than one million people. In 1994, industry yearly sales exceeded $140 billion. These figures place printing and publishing among the top five United States industries in terms of number of individual establishments and in terms of number of employees.

Economists use several measures to gauge the importance of an industry in a society's economy. The gross national product (GNP) is a figure that represents the overall annual flow of goods and services in an economy. In the United States, the printing industry is ranked among the top ten contributors to the GNP. "Value added" is a measure of the difference between the cost of raw materials and the final market price of a product. The higher the value-added figure, the more valuable the skills that went into the manufacturing of the product. Again, printing ranks among the top ten contributors to the GNP.

Printing is a major American industry, with significant career opportunities at many levels. Students seeking to enter printing as a career are typically attracted by the technology and the craft associated with the production phase—the smell of the ink; the noise of a large, high-speed press; and the excitement of creating an image. A large portion of this book is concerned with production procedures; however, it must be recognized that production is only one part of this large and complex industry. Perhaps only half of all those employed in printing actually work with the reproduction process. The other half are concerned with management, marketing and sales, accounting, and support services such as supplying equipment, paper, ink, and chemicals.

It is important to briefly examine how companies are commonly organized and classified.

Structure of Companies

The printing industry is dominated by small- to medium-sized companies that employ one to twenty-five people. There are "giants" in the industry that employ many hundreds or thousands of workers, but they account for a very small proportion (perhaps as small as 4 percent) of all the companies involved with the printing trade.

The structure of any printing company depends on many variables, including size, location, physical facilities, type of product, financing method (such as corporation or partnership), and management style. In fact, it is safe to assume that no two printing organizations are structured exactly alike. Figure 1.5 shows a possible structure for a small- to medium-sized company made up of ten to twenty-five employees. In smaller organizations one individual might serve several functions. In larger companies many workers might be assigned to one area.

Board of Directors. The board of directors represents the financial control of the company. The board might own the company or it might be an elected body, as is often the case in large corporations. The president of a company is often a member of the board of directors and acts as the board's representative to carry out its policies. The board defines the scope and purpose of the company, makes or approves major decisions, and monitors financial performance. In our economy profit is the primary driving force for all companies or corporations. The board of directors is responsible to the stockholders for delivery of a maximum return or profit based upon investment.

Management. The president or chief executive officer (CEO) of a company often delegates top-level management of day-to-day operation to a general manager. The office manager coordinates such important tasks as correspondence, record keeping, accounting, payroll, and customer billing. The sales manager is responsible for an important part of the company: managing and directing the sales team

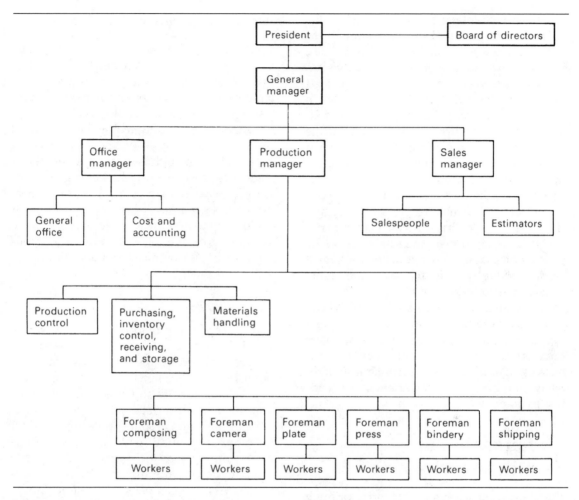

Figure 1.5. **Typical organizational structure of a small- to medium-sized (ten to twenty-five employees) printing company**

that brings customers to the company. Sales representatives contact customers who require printing services and work with skilled estimators who calculate costs. The production manager is responsible for controlling the materials, craftspeople, and equipment to deliver a printed product that meets or exceeds customer expectations. Many managerial positions in the printing industry are filled by individuals who have moved up the ranks from the craft or entry level.

Production. The production phase is generally divided into three categories:

- Production planning
- Manufacturing
- Quality assurance

One aspect of planning production is scheduling work efficiently within the limitations of time, equipment, and human skills. People in charge of purchasing, inventory control, and receiving and storage are responsible for the advance ordering of all supplies. Some firms test incoming supplies such as ink, paper, plates, and films to guarantee they meet quality standards. Costly press downtime can be avoided by assuring the quality of the materials used in the printing process. Accurate material handling ensures that supplies are delivered to the correct workstation (such as the camera room or the press room) when needed and that the finished product is removed from the last station on time. Production stations of composition, camera, plate making, press, bindery, and shipping must be directed by skilled supervisors who work to meet the schedules set by production control. The production itself must be carried out by individuals who are highly skilled in the printing crafts.

Although a worker's skill is not directly related to any form of organization or managerial control, it is important that employees understand the basic organization of their business. The efficiency of an organization directly influences the employment of everyone in the company.

Organization of Printing Services

There are several ways to categorize printing companies. One traditional way is by the kinds of services or produces the companies deliver. With this view, printing organizations can be classified into eight distinct areas:

- Commercial
- Trade shops
- Special purpose
- Quick printing
- In-plant
- Publishing
- Packaging
- Related industries

Commercial Printing

Commercial printing is done by a company that is willing to take on nearly any sort of printing job. Commercial printers can usually handle a large variety of printing jobs, regardless of sheet size, number of ink colors, length of run, or even binding requirements. Typical products produced in a commercial printing shop include small business cards, letterhead stationery, posters, and four-color glossy advertising sheets for mailing. If a commercial printer does not have all of the equipment or skilled staff to perform a whole job, parts of the job, such as die cutting, foil stamping, or binding, may be subcontracted to trade shops.

Trade Shops

Some companies provide services only to the printing trade. These are called **trade shops.** Not all commercial, special purpose, in-plant, publishing, or packaging companies can afford to own and operate all the equipment necessary to meet their total production requirements. For example, some printers may find it far more economical, when assigned a four-color printing job, to contract with another company to produce high-quality color separations. Another company might decide not to buy bindery equipment because only a small percentage of its work requires folding, collating, or binding. When the company receives a contract that requires binding, it sends it to a trade shop that specializes in binding.

Special Purpose Printing

Special purpose printing is defined by the limited type of jobs performed by a company. One printer might print only labels. The printer would purchase special equipment and accept orders for only labels. However, the printer would make labels to any size, shape,

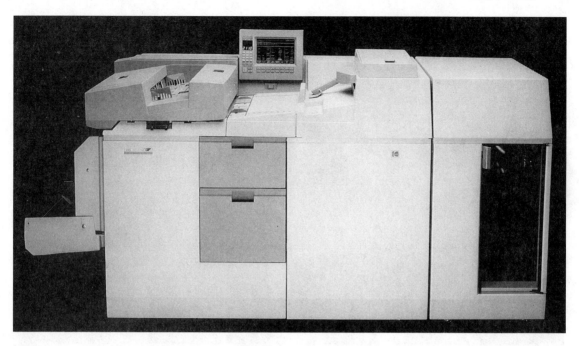

Figure 1.6.   A xerographic (photocopying) system. This 100-copies-per-minute photocopier allows users to reproduce standard sheet sizes with cover pages and wire-staple binding. All machine functions are accessed through the control panel.
Courtesy of Eastman Kodak.

number of colors, length of run, or purpose. Another printer might specialize in business forms, such as order forms, estimate blanks, filing sheets, school notepaper, or duplicate sales slips. Forms printing is an important area of the printing industry in terms of size and yearly sales. Yet another example of special purpose printing is called "legal" printing. Legal printers are concerned with reproducing pieces such as corporate stock offerings, insurance policies, or financial reports.

Quick Printing

Within the last several years, a whole **quick printing** sector of the printing industry has grown around the use of the xerographic process (sometimes called electrostatic print-

ing). More commonly known as photocopying, or simply copying, the xerographic process allows copies to be reproduced without the use of a traditional printing plate press. The explosion of quick print shops has revolutionized public access to the reproduction process. Most copy centers offer walk-in services that include copies up to 11 inches × 17 inches, spot (solid) color, full-color images, binding, computer rental time, and an array of supplies such as matching envelopes, binders, and presentation folders (figure 1.6).

In-Plant Printing

In-plant printing is defined as any printing operation that is owned by, and serves the needs of, a single company or corporation. A

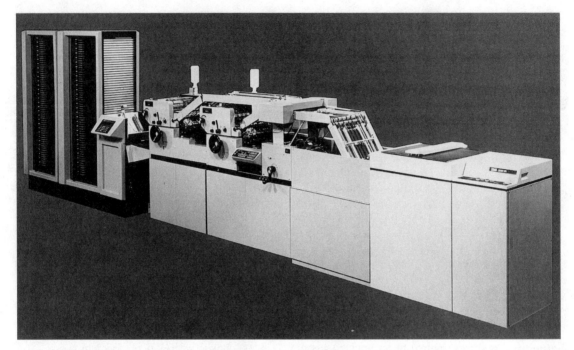

Figure 1.7. In-plant production equipment. In-plant production is often done with a "systems" approach and with equipment that automates much of the time-consuming labor.
Courtesy of Multigraphics, a division of AM International, Inc.

business might manufacture a variety of products that must each be packaged with an instruction sheet. Management could decide it is more convenient and cost efficient to set up its own shop to print the instruction sheets rather than to send the job to a commercial printer. The company would then also be able to produce in-house forms, promotion pieces, company letterhead and stationery, time cards, and almost all of its printing needs.

Many in-plant printers use the lithographic process. Equipment manufacturers are currently marketing systems with a platemaker "in line" with a press, collator, and binder. With the "systems" approach, the in-plant printer can enter original copy (such as a typed form) into an automatic direct image platemaking system, select the number of copies to be printed and the preferred binding method, and produce bound copies in a matter of minutes (figure 1.7).

Publishing

Another category of printing services that we use nearly every day is **publishing.** Within this category are the thousands of companies that produce daily or weekly newspapers, and the even larger group of companies that produces periodicals, such as *Time* and *Newsweek*, which sell to a national market. Consider also the group of businesses that produces and markets books. The publisher of this book is a private company that produces textbooks. It is important to understand that printers do not usually make decisions to publish a book or a magazine. Printers are rarely the publisher. Publishers, however, require the skills of the printer to manufacture their products.

Package Printing

Hundreds of different containers we use every day are produced by **package printing.** The idea of impulse buying (buying a product on the visual appeal of the package) has skyrocketed the demand for high-quality, multicolor packages that attract the consumer's attention. Package printers decorate and form hundreds of millions of folded paperboard boxes, flexible packages, and corrugated boxes each year. Millions of printed plastic bags are used every day in grocery stores and companies that distribute or package food. Corrugated boxes and thin plastic film are both printed by flexography. Packaging, however, is not restricted to paper or plastic. Think of all the steel and aluminum soft drink and beer containers sold every day. These packages are produced by a special process called "metal decorating."

Related Industries

The last category of services in the printing industry is called **related industries.** The raw materials of the printer are such things as ink, paper, plates, chemicals, and many other supplies. Printers also use special purpose equipment, such as presses, paper cutters, platemakers, cameras, and light tables, to produce their products. Companies that provide services to printers by either producing or selling these supplies and equipment are called related industries. Other businesses, such as consulting firms and advertising agencies that prepare designs for reproduction, might also perform a service, but they do not make or sell a physical product.

Preparing for a Career in Printing

Viewing the printing industry as made up of commercial, special purpose, quick printing, in-plant, publishing, package printing, trade shops, and related industries is only one way to look at this broad industry. The industry does not stand alone; it is carried by people. There is a need for skilled people power. There are no fixed paths to entering the printing industry, but a few general observations can be made.

Upper-Level Management Preparation

Managerial levels—specifically upper-level positions (see figure 1.5)—usually, but not always, require a college degree. There are many schools that offer degrees with extensive specialization in printing technology. Printing specialization, however, is not a requirement. Individuals with experience in such areas as art, journalism, engineering, chemistry, physics, research, data processing and computers, sales, marketing, and management are also employed in printing companies.

Middle-Level Management Preparation

Middle-level management, such as section foremen or production control people, and skilled craftspeople enter the industry by a variety of routes. There are trade high schools designed to provide high-school graduates with skills necessary for direct entrance to the industry. Other secondary school programs offer vocational or industrial arts classes combined with a cooperative work experience (where the student spends part of a day in a local printing company and part of the day in school). There are also technical printing programs offered in two-year community colleges that lead to associate degrees.

Craft-Level Preparation

Union membership may influence craft-level entrance to the industry. Printing establishments can be either closed or open shops. A **closed shop** requires union membership. An open shop does not have such a requirement. In an **open shop,** individuals can belong to a union, but they do not have to belong to keep their jobs.

Union Membership. There are several craft unions in the United States that represent the printing trades. Some reflect only one specific type of skill, such as press operators. Others extend across many craft lines. One advantage of union membership is national negotiating power for wages and benefits. Another advantage of union membership is on-the-job training. In closed union shops trainees generally receive on-the-job training through structured apprenticeship programs.

Nonunion Organizations. Even though nonunion open shop workers are not represented in national-level collective bargaining, there are organizations that provide services such as retirement benefits and health insurance to nonunion printers. The advantage of open shop work is that the wage level is not necessarily linked to union pay scales. Open shops emphasize previous skills combined with knowledge gained on the job. There is a national nonunion certification called the Master Craftsman Program, which is coordinated through the Printing Industries of America. Many open shops also provide on-the-job training.

Career Advancement

Advancement in the printing industry is based on performance. The most skillful managers and workers gradually assume more responsibility through practice and additional training. Many organizations provide continuing updating and training to the printing professions. Three examples are the Graphic Arts Technical Foundation (GATF), the Printing Industries of America (PIA), and the National Association of Printers and Lithographers (NAPL). All of these nonprofit organizations are designed to meet the research, technical, and educational needs of their members. They are supported by printers, suppliers, manufacturers, graphic-arts educators, and students. They are each involved in solving industrial problems, conducting applied research, publishing the results of their work in the form of books and audio visual aids, and conducting workshops.

Many other types of printing organizations serve both professional and social needs (See appendix C). There are several management organizations, a number of fellowship groups, and even student clubs. The printing industry is made up of a vast group of people all devoted to the goal of fulfilling the print communication needs of a technical world.

Key Terms

printing	gravure	image design
relief printing	screen printing	image conversion
letterpress	lithography	image assembly
flexography	Xerography	image carrier preparation
intaglio printing	electrostatic printing	image transfer

finishing
commercial printing
trade shops
special purpose printing

quick printing
in-plant printing
publishing
package printing

related industries
closed shop
open shop

Questions for Review

1. What is a pictograph?
2. What is an ideograph?
3. What is a phonetic symbol?
4. What are the five main printing processes?
5. What is the sequence of steps that all printers follow regardless of the printing process they are using?
6. What is the purpose of the board of directors of a printing company?
7. What is the task of the production manager in a printing company?
8. What is one job of the production-planning department in a printing company?
9. What kind of printing services do trade shops provide for the printing industry?
10. What is the difference between a closed shop and an open shop in the printing industry?
11. List the different ways to enter, train, and advance in the different levels of the graphic-arts industry.

CHAPTER 2

The Tradition of Foundry Type

Johann Gutenberg—The father of printing

The inventor of printing in the Western world is generally considered to be Johann Gensfleisch zum Gutenberg, who was born in the city of Mainz, Germany in 1397. The wealth of the Gutenberg family freed Johann for a life of leisure and pleasure during which he developed an interest in technology—primarily seal making and goldsmithing. In 1438 Gutenberg started a business that produced religious mirrors in Strasbourg. By that time he was considered a master craftsman in metalworking.

There is evidence that by 1444 Gutenberg had returned to Mainz to set up a printing shop. As a goldsmith he had cut letters and symbols into precious metals and into wax to form molds to cast jewelry. It is unknown exactly how he conceived of casting letters for printing. However, the concept of "mirror" images was common knowledge.

Gutenberg's casting process involved first cutting a letter by hand in reverse on a piece of hard metal, then punching the letter shape into a soft copper mold to form a die called a matrix.

He next needed a suitable metal to cast in the matrix. He experimented with pewter hardened with large quantities of antimony, but the mixture shrank when it cooled and pulled away from the matrix. The letters formed were imperfect.

Gutenberg's experience with lead in mirror manufacturing encouraged him to try a combination of lead, tin, and antimony. His original formula (5 percent tin, 12 percent antimony, and 83 percent lead) is used nearly unchanged in casting today. Characters can be perfectly cast with this alloy because it expands when it cools and forms a duplicate of the matrix cavity. Using Gutenberg's system, two workers could cast and dress (trim away excess material) twenty-five pieces of type an hour.

Gutenberg's most notable work, a forty-two-line-a-page Bible, was begun in 1452 and completed by 1455. Each page contained around 2,800 characters. Two pages were printed at the same time, so 5,600 pieces of type were needed to make each two-page printing. It was the practice for the next two pages to be composed during the press run of the current two, so at least 11,200 letters were needed to even begin printing. Working a normal workday (twelve hours), it took two craftsmen more than thirty-seven workdays just to prepare the initial type. At this rate, more than three years were needed to complete just two hundred copies of Gutenberg's Bible.

Much of the language of modern printing comes from the craft of foundry type composition developed by Gutenberg and his workers more than five hundred years ago. Terms such as "form," "leading," "uppercase," "lowercase," "type size," "impression," and "make-ready" originated with Gutenberg. All printers today owe the hundreds of early craftsmen who followed Gutenberg in the tradition of hand-set foundry type and gave us both a language and an art.

Objectives for Chapter 2

After completing this chapter you will be able to:

- Identify the major parts of a piece of foundry type.
- Describe the procedure for composing a line of foundry type.
- Name the advantages that line-casting and character-casting composing machines have over foundry type composition.
- Differentiate between a duplicate plate and a primary relief plate.
- Outline the procedure to lock up and print a simple relief form.
- List and describe four special letterpress applications.

Introduction

Until recently relief printing (printing from a raised surface) was the most important reproduction process. Photographic and computer technology has drastically reduced use of the relief process, however. The influence of relief printing continues despite its decline because nearly all contemporary concepts and vocabulary are based on the relief technique.

All relief printing involves printing from lead-based metal type, called **foundry type** or **hot type.** Printing from lead-based hot type is often referred to as **letterpress** printing. For more than four hundred years after Gutenberg invented casting, letterpress printing accounted for almost all of the industrial printing done in the world. With the introduction of other printing processes, particularly lithography, letterpress's share of the printing market declined. Today letterpress printing accounts for only a small share of the printing industry. Most relief printing done today is done with flexography, a process that prints from a raised rubber surface in much the same way reproductions are made from rubber stamps. Although flexography is now more common, it is important to understand the letterpress process. Much of the terminology printers use comes from the tradition of foundry type and the letterpress process. There are also applications of letterpress printing used today that cannot be accomplished by any other method.

Foundry Type Composition

Composition is the process of assembling type for printing. The methods used for hot type composition of foundry type for letterpress have changed little since the days of Gutenberg. Individual characters are cast on separate bodies by type founders. The printer composes words and sentences by placing the appropriate cast characters, symbols, and spaces next to each other in a composing stick. (See "Composing a Line of Type" page 24.)

Identifying Foundry Type

To work with foundry type, you must be able to identify the significant parts of each cast character (figure 2.1). The actual printing surface is called the "face." The sides of the character are cast at an angle (called the "beard") for greater strength. The beard slopes down to the nonprinting shoulder and counter. The "feet" are parallel to the face. The distance from the face to the feet is the "height to paper" or **type-high.** For most English-speaking countries, type-high is 0.918 inches.

All characters in a **font** (a collection of type of the same style and size) have a nick cut in the same position on the type body. When setting a line of foundry type, it is easy to glance at the row of nicks. If one nick does not line up with all the rest, the printer knows it is probably a wrong font character. The nick side is often called the "belly side." The distance from the belly to the back side is the **point size** of the piece of type. Note that the type body in figure 2.1 is larger than the character *A*. Type point size is defined by the point size of the body, not by the size of the character.

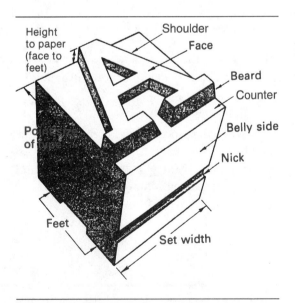

Figure 2.1.   Example of a foundry type character. Foundry type characters are cast on individual bodies.

The distance across the nick or belly side of the type is an important measure called the **set width.** The letter *m*, for example, is wider than the letter *i*. Therefore, the set width of *m* is greater than that of *i*, or, stated another way, the set width is proportional to the size of the letter on the type body. Most typewriters form nonproportional letters. This makes it possible to type the letter *m*, backspace, and type the letter *i* in the same visual space.

Special Characters

By using variations of the twenty-six letters of our Latin alphabet, many characters can be cast as foundry type to meet a special purpose. Gutenberg cast nearly 250 different characters and symbols to print his Bible. He cast that many characters because he was attempting to duplicate the variations inherent in scribe hand-lettering.

A **ligature** is two or more connected letters on the same type body (figure 2.2). The

Figure 2.2. Examples of ligatures

most common are *fi* and *fl* combinations. When any portion of the printing face extends over the body of the type, the character is said to be **kerned. Kerns** are very common in italic faces.

Another classification of special characters is called **dingbats.** Dingbats are commonly used symbols such as bullets, asterisks, outline boxes, and pointing fingers (figure 2.3).

Type Storage Systems

The earliest relief printers stored identical characters in small compartments or bins. As the number of type styles grew, each font was stored in what was termed a "case."

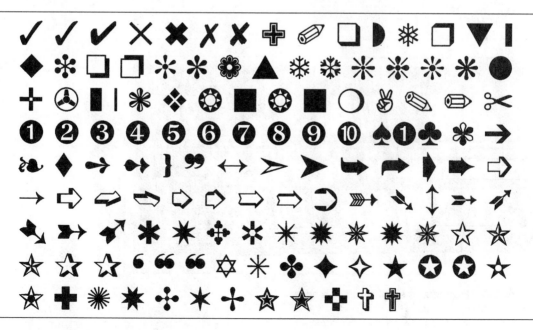

Figure 2.3. Examples of dingbats

A once-popular type storage system was the **news case.** An entire font of letters was stored in two cases: capitals were in one case and small letters were in another. The case with capitals was traditionally stored on a shelf directly over the case with small letters. Our terms *uppercase* and *lowercase* to indicate CAPITAL or small letters respectively come from the use of the news case.

The most popular type case is the **California job case** (figure 2.4). It is designed to hold one font of characters made up of upper- and lowercase letters, numerals, punctuation marks, ligatures, special symbols (such as $), and spacing material in a total of eighty-nine small boxes. Lowercase letters and symbols are assigned positions and spaces in the case according to how frequently they are used.

The Printer's Measurement System

Printers use a special system to measure almost all printed images. This system was developed from the measurement of foundry type and continues to be used today. In this system 6 **picas** equal 1 inch, and 12 **points** equal 1 pica.

Type size is almost always described in points. Common type sizes are 6, 7, 8, 9, 10, 11, 12, 14, 16, 18, 24, 36, 42, 60, and 72 points (figure 2.5). Traditionally, anything over 72 points was measured in inches (because 72 points/12 points = 6 picas = 1 inch). However, contemporary computer systems offer the option of sizing characters up to 127 points in one-point increments.

Space between lines of type is also measured in points. When a customer requests a type page to be set "10 on 12" (10/12), the printer understands that the letters will be 10 points high, with 2 points of space between each line (12 points – 10 points = 2 points).

The length and depth lines of type are specified in picas. Most newspaper columns are 13 picas wide. A 36-pica line is 6 inches long (because 1 inch equals 6 picas). Column depth

Figure 2.4.   Example of a California job case.
Courtesy of Mackenzie and Harris Inc., San Francisco, CA.

6 7 8 9 10 11 12 14 16 18 24 36 42 60 72

Figure 2.5. **Point sizes.** Common foundry type point sizes.

is measured in picas from the top of the first line on a page to the bottom of the last line of type.

Word-Spacing Material

All hot type spacing material in a given font is the same point size. Each space must match the point size of the type it is being used with and must be less than the height of the type (usually 0.800 inch or less) (figure 2.6).

Within any font size, then, is a collection of different pieces of spacing material. The basic unit of spacing material in each font is an **em quad,** sometimes called the "mutton quad." The em quad is a square piece of spacing material. Each side of the em quad is the point size of the font the em quad is from. For example, an em quad from a 12-point font of type would measure 12 points × 12 points on the face and would be less than type-high; an 18-point font would contain em quads that are 18 points in each dimension on the face (figure 2.7).

All other spacing material in a font is based on the size of the em quad. Two **en quads,** or "nut quads," placed together equal the dimension of one em quad. For example, if

Figure 2.6. **Example showing spacing material between words.** Spacing material used between words must match the point size of the type and be less than the height of the type.

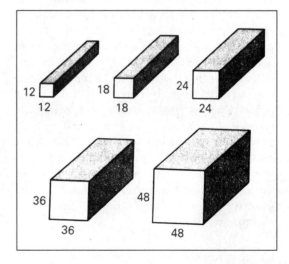

Figure 2.7. **Examples of em quads.** The em, or mutton, quad is the basic word-spacing unit in each font.

the font size is 12 points, the en quad will measure 6 points × 12 points on the face. A 3-em space (abbreviated from "three to the em") is one-third of an em quad. The smallest space typically found in a job case is the 5-em space, which is one-fifth of an em quad. Some spaces, such as the 2-em quad or the 3-em quad, are larger than the em quad.

For most composition, the em quad is used to indent the first line of a paragraph, the en quad is used to separate sentences, and the 3-em space is placed between words. Combinations of all spacing material are used to achieve equal line lengths of type composition.

There is one more class of spacing material called thin spaces. The most common measure of thin spaces is 1/2 point (generally made of copper) and 1 point (usually made of brass). Thin spaces are generally only used for spacing between letters (called "letter spacing").

Line-Spacing Material

The space between lines, called **leading**, must be controlled with line-spacing material. Line-spacing material is less than type-high and is generally cut from long strips to the length of line being set. All line-spacing material is classified according to thickness. **Leads** are generally 2 points thick, but anything from 1 to 4 points thick is considered a lead. **Slugs** are typically 6 points thick, but any piece up to 24 points (2 picas) is labeled a slug. Both leads and slugs are made from type metal. Any line-spacing material that is 24 points thick or thicker is called **furniture.** Furniture is made from type metal, wood (generally oak), or an aluminum alloy.

Composing a Line of Type

Foundry type characters are placed in a **composing stick** to form words and sentences. The most common composing sticks have slots which seat an adjustable knee to an exact pica or half-pica position. Type is always set with the right hand. The composing stick is held in the left (figure 2.8).

To set type in the composing stick, begin by adjusting the knee to the desired line length. Then place a piece of line-spacing material in the stick. The first character of the first word is always seated against the knee of the composing stick, nick up. All other characters and spaces are set in order after this first character. The thumb of your left hand applies pressure against the last character set to keep the line from falling out of the stick.

When all characters have been set, it is necessary to fill the gap remaining at the end of the line. The line must be held snugly in place within the preset line length. This is accomplished by filling the gap with spacing material. If the gap is large, begin with em quads or 2-ems until only a small space is left. Then select combinations of spacing to fill the line perfectly. Ideally, the last space will slide into place with only slight resistance, and the entire composing stick can be turned upside down without the line falling out. This process of making the line tight in the stick is called **quadding out.** To set another line of type, insert a piece of line-spacing material and repeat the techniques used to set the first line. The amount of line-spacing material added between two lines of type determines the leading of the two lines.

Because cast characters are smaller than the type body, it is possible to set type with no leading and keep the letters on one line from touching the letters on the line below. Type that has been set with no leading between lines is referred to as "set solid."

Centering a Line of Type. A printer frequently wants to reproduce a series of centered lines, one over the other. To do this, set the entire first line in the stick against the knee. Quad out the line by placing equal amounts of spacing material on each end of the line.

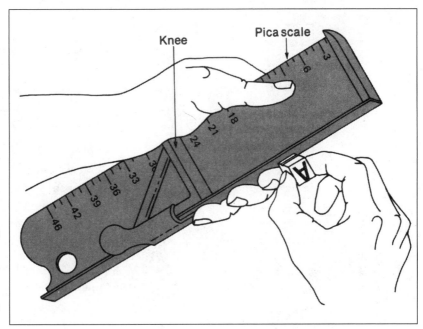

Figure 2.8. Example of a composing stick. When using a composing stick, hold the stick in your left hand and place the first character, nick up, against the knee. Always compose from left to right.

Straight Composition. Straight composition or **justification** is the process of setting type so that both the left and right margins form straight lines (figure 2.9). Hand-set straight composition involves setting each line of type against the knee of the composing stick, determining the amount of space left at the end of the line, then dividing the space equally between the words in the line. Spacing material from the case is inserted between words in the line so that the words are separated from each other by nearly equal amounts and the line is tight in the composing stick.

Storing the Form. The composition process creates what printers call a form. A **form** is the grouping of cast characters, symbols, and spaces that makes up a job or complete segment of a job (such as one page to be printed in a book). Composed forms are stored in shallow metal trays called **galleys**.

Proofing Techniques

Once set, hot type composition is difficult to read because the characters are cast in reverse. A sample print of type composition is called a **proof.** Printers check for typesetting errors by "proofing," which means comparing composed copy to the rough or manuscript copy provided by the customer. Most companies employ proofreaders to proof copy for errors. Over the past century a collection of special proofreader's marks or notes have been developed to communicate to the printer what corrections need to be made on the proof (figure 2.10). These same symbols are used when proofing foundry, photographic, or computer composition. Appendix D contains a proofreading exercise.

If the printer sets the **copy** (the original words or information supplied by the customer) exactly as provided, but the customer

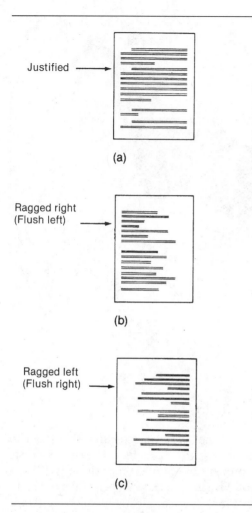

Justified

(a)

Ragged right
(Flush left)

(b)

Ragged left
(Flush right)

(c)

⊗ Defective letter	⊙ Colon
ⓓ Push down space	*bf* Boldface
# Make paragraph	9 Turn over
⤳ Take out (delete)	Two-em dash
⋀ Insert at this point	One-em dash
□ Em-quad space	// Space evenly
⊏ Move over	# Insert space
◯ Close up entirely	‖ Straighten lines
⹀ Hyphen	⊙ Period
ⱽ Quotation	⋀ Comma
⋁ Apostrophe	*no* # No paragraph
⸴ Semicolon	*lig* Ligature
wf Wrong-font letter	‿ Less space
stet Let it stand	*out-see copy* Out—see copy
tr Transpose	*spell out* Spell out
⊘ Verify	*caps* Capitals
lc Lowercase letter	*sc* Small capitals
ital Italic	*rom* Roman letter

Figure 2.10.   Examples of commonly used proofreader's marks. Proofreader's marks are used to indicate type corrections that must be made on proof sheets.

Figure 2.9.   Examples of three styles of composition. (a) Justified composition is set flush left and flush right. (b) Copy can also be set ragged right (flush left) or (c) ragged left (flush right).

makes changes to the copy, the customer pays for author's alterations—"AA's." However, if the printer makes mistakes setting the copy they are called **typos,** and corrections must be made without charge.

Galley Proofs.   A **galley proof** is "pulled" on a device called a galley proof press. It is called a galley proof because foundry type jobs are usually transferred from composing sticks to galleys. Galleys match the bottom thickness of composing sticks (0.050 inches).

The galley press is designed so that during composition the printer places the composing stick or a galley filled with forms on the bed, inks the type with a brayer, or ink roller, sets the paper on the form, and pulls the roller over the paper. Galley proofs are delivered to the printing customer before the job goes to press.

Reproduction Proofs. **Reproduction proofs** are high-quality proofs made on a reproduction proof press (figure 2.11). There are three primary considerations when pulling a reproduction proof: precision, quality type forms, and a good ink-and-paper combination.

Because reproduction proofs are designed to be photographed, they must be puffed from perfect pieces of type. Many companies reserve special fonts of foundry type to be used exclusively for "repro" proofs.

Machine Composition of Hot Type

It probably was not long after the pages of Gutenberg's first Bible were dry that printers began thinking of ways to improve the speed of hand-set composition. Many ideas were tried—even suspending a composing stick around the printer's neck by a rope so type could be set with both hands.

Machine hot type composition is a refinement of the hand-set foundry type concept. Instead of individual pieces of raised type, matrices are placed together to generate words and sentences. Molten type metal is then forced into the matrices to form the raised printing surface. When the metal cools to form a solid cast character, each matrix is returned to a storage system to be used again. Most machines use a keyboard (like a typewriter) to control the position of each matrix. After the

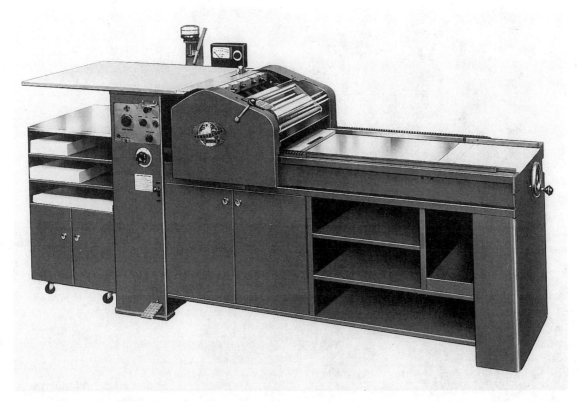

Figure 2.11. **A reproduction proof press.**
Courtesy of Vandersons Corporation, Chicago.

type has been used, it can be melted and returned to the machine to be reused.

Line-Casting Machines. On July 3, 1886, the first truly automatic typesetting machine was demonstrated in the composing room of the *New York Tribune.* The device was designed by Ottmar Mergenthaler. His invention, the **Linotype machine,** has been called one of the ten greatest in the history of the human race (figure 2.12).

The Linotype machine is based on the concept of a recirculating matrix which is continually reused in the machine. The Linotype performs the following four basic operations with the matrices:

1. Matrices and spacebands are activated by keyboard control;
2. The line is justified;
3. The slug is cast; and
4. Each matrix and spaceband is returned to its storage position.

The Linotype can be, and probably has been, set up to do nearly every typesetting function in almost every language.

A second line-casting machine (although not completely automatic) was the **Ludlow,** named after its inventor, Washington I. Ludlow. The device was designed around 1888 and could cast type from 8- through 144-point characters from hand-set matrices.

Figure 2.12.   A Linotype machine.
Courtesy of Mergenthaler Linotype Company.

Character-Casting Machines. The Monotype system was designed by Tolbert Lanston in 1889 to cast and assemble individual pieces of hot type in a line. The system was made up of two machines: a keyboard device which punched holes into a long paper tape and a casting mechanism which cast type automatically from the information on the tape.

Character sizes up to 36 points and line lengths up to 60 picas (90 picas with a special attachment) could be cast on the same Monotype machine. For small faces, up to 150 characters per minute could be cast. Because of the machine's speed and versatility, several keyboards could be constantly functioning to feed a single caster.

Relief Printing Plates

After the forms are composed, they must be assembled to make a printing plate. Historically, there are two main categories of relief plates: primary and duplicate (or secondary). While there is little contemporary use for these plates, understanding them is the foundation for understand other reproduction processes.

Primary plates serve two functions. They can be prepared to be placed directly on the printing press or they can be used only as master plates from which duplicate plates are made. Primary plates can be prepared manually by assembling composed type forms, or they can be made photomechanically as photoengravings or photopolymer (plastic) plates.

Duplicate plates are made from master forms that are not intended for use as printing surfaces. Copies or duplicates of the master are made for the actual printing operation. Duplicate plates have several advantages. They are ideal in extremely long print runs when one plate would wear out long before the job is finished. There are also instances, especially in newspaper production, where the master form is prepared in one location and duplicate plates are shipped to many plants across the country. **Stereotyping** is a very old process used to produce a duplicate relief plate. Stereotypes were once widely used in newspaper printing (figure 2.13). The procedures of preparing the relief plate to print are basically the same for both primary and duplicate plates.

Typical Lockup Procedures

Lockup is the process of locking a relief plate in a clamping frame or holding system commonly called a **chase.** The following section examines one type of lockup, the **chaser lockup**, which is used on a platen press. The procedures for any other press are similar.

Chases vary in size depending upon the press to be used. The smallest chase is 3 inches by 5 inches; some chases are as large as 6 square feet. Whatever the size of the chase, its requirements remain the same: it must be sturdy, it must fit the printing press exactly, and it must lie perfectly flat on a smooth surface without wobbling.

Figure 2.13. A cast stereotype plate

Figure 2.14.   An imposing stone or stone table

Figure 2.15.   Examples of furniture

The process of placing the relief form in the proper position in the chase so the images will be placed correctly on the final printed sheet is called **imposition.**

Lockup is done on a special table called an **imposing stone** or simply a stone table (figure 2.14). The name "stone table" comes from early imposing tables that were made from polished granite. It is extremely important that the surface of the table is perfectly flat. The granite was nicked easily so it has been almost totally replaced by steel today. The name "stone table" remains, however.

Few relief plates are as large as the inside dimensions of the chase being used. Furniture (figure 2.15) is used to fill the unused portions.

The locks that hold the form in place in the lockup are called **quoins** (pronounced *coins*). Quoins are opened and closed by quoin keys (figure 2.16).

Reglets are thin pieces of wood that are always placed on either side of each quoin in a lockup. A printer never directly lifts a foundry typeform. It must slide from place to place.

To begin lockup, slide the type form from the galley to the stone table surface; be sure there is no dust or lint under the form. Always place the chase over the type form. Never place the chase down first and try to put the form inside of it because the foundry type could spill easily. Every chase has a top and a bottom. Always place the top of the chase away from you as you stand at the stone table. Place the chase over the type form so that the form is held

Figure 2.16.   Examples of quoins and quoin keys

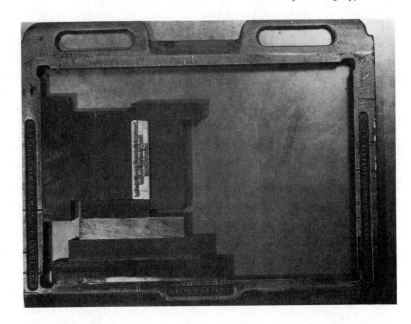

Figure 2.17. Building the chase out to the bottom and left sides. From the blocked form, first build with furniture out to the bottom and left sides of the chase.

slightly above center on the bed of the press when the chase is mounted in the press.

The next step is to block around the form with furniture. After the form has been surrounded, build furniture out to the sides of the chase from the bottom and left sides of the chase (figure 2.17). Then place quoins to the top and right of the form and build more furniture out from the form to the top and right sides of the chase (figure 2.18).

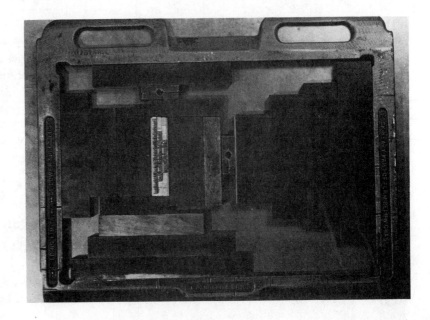

Figure 2.18. Building the chase out to the top and right sides. With the quoins in place, build the chase out to the top and right sides.

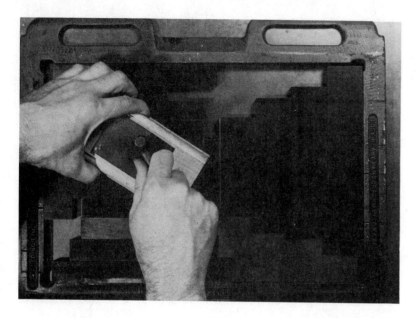

Figure 2.19.   Using a planer block. Gently place the planer block on the face of the form and tap it several times with a quoin key.

If the furniture has been properly placed, reglets should just slide into place on either side of each quoin. It might be necessary to vary combinations of furniture width in order to include the reglets, but they must be added.

The next step is very important. First insert a quoin key and tighten each quoin until slight pressure is placed on the form and the furniture. If any part of the form is not properly seated against the stone, the printing faces will not be on the same plane, and image quality will be difficult to control on the press. Then place a planer block gently on the face of the form and sharply tap it several times with a quoin key to jog each character against the table (figure 2.19). Tighten the quoins a bit more, plane the form a second time, and turn the quoins to their outermost position with light resistance. Never force a quoin. It is possible to spring a chase out of flatness or even to damage one beyond repair by applying too much pressure. Be sure never to plane a form that has been completely tightened. Damaged type will be the only result.

The last step is to check that all parts of the form have been securely clamped in place through a process called **checking for lift** (figure 2.20). Carefully lift one corner of the chase high enough to insert one part of a quoin key. With your thumb, gently press down toward the table over all parts of the form. If any portion of the form moves, the lockup is not acceptable and must be corrected. The lift may have resulted because composition techniques were poor when the original form was set, furniture positions were faulty around the form, or the quoins were not tightened enough. If the lockup passes the test for lift, the job is ready for the press.

Traditional Hand-Fed Platen Press Operations

This book does not examine the operation of all the different forms of relief equipment in detail. Its goal is to provide enough information to allow you to transfer general understanding

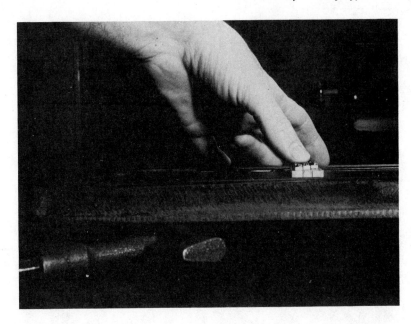

Figure 2.20.   Checking for lift. Check for lift by placing a quoin key under one edge of the chase and pressing your thumb over the form.

to specific operations with the assistance of a classroom instructor or a press operation manual. The following sections examine basic platen press techniques. The discussion is applicable to nearly any form of relief press used for letterpress printing.

Letterpress Machines

Letterpress is a common term which spans a wide range of devices and materials in the printing industry. Letterpress machines can be divided into three groups:

- ▌ Platen presses
- ▌ Flat bed cylinder presses
- ▌ Rotary presses

At one time the hand-fed platen press was the backbone of every print shop in America. Some hand-fed devices still remain, but where letterpress is still used, hand-fed machines have been replaced largely by automatic devices.

Figure 2.21 illustrates the basic components of a hand-fed power-operated platen press. The size on any platen press is determined by the inside dimensions of its chase.

The flat bed cylinder press can print larger sheet sizes than the platen press. The image is transferred to only a small portion of the sheet at any given time by the force of the impression cylinder, so much less total pressure is needed and more printing area can be covered (figure 2.22).

On a rotary press image transfer takes place as the paper passes between an impression and a plate cylinder. Rotary presses generally use cast duplicate plates (electrotypes and stereotypes).

Packing the Hand-Fed Platen Press

The platen press gets its name from the flat rectangular base that pushes the paper against the type form during the printing operation. **Packing** is the material that is clamped on the platen by the bails (figure 2.23). Packing serves

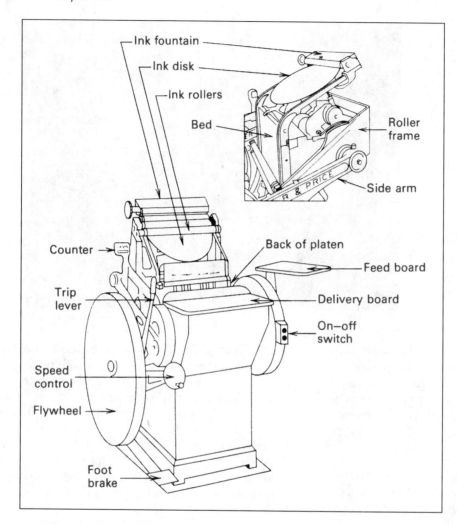

Figure 2.21.
**Diagram of the
basic components
of a hand-fed power
platen press**

two functions. First, because the distance from the platen to the type form is not easily altered, packing is the only means of controlling the overall **impression** (amount of pressure) that the press sheet receives. Second, the top sheet of the packing holds the mechanical fingers (called **gauge pins**) that in turn hold the press sheet in place during the printing operation.

If the impression is too heavy, the type will emboss the paper, or punch through it. If the impression is too light, a poor image will result. For the impression to be perfect, the form must press against the paper hard enough to reproduce characters clearly and sharply, but not so hard that the image can be felt on the back of the printed sheet.

The process of placing packing on the platen is called **dressing the press.** The first sheets to be positioned are the **hanger sheets.** The hanger sheets are cut so that they extend

Figure 2.22. Example of a traditional flat bed cylinder press design.
Courtesy of Heidelberg Platen Press.

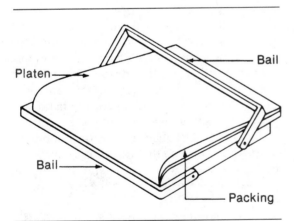

Figure 2.23.   Diagram of press platen and bails

is the pressboard, which is cut to the size of the chase and placed under the last hanger sheet but is not held by either bail (figure 2.24c). The **pressboard** is a heavy, hard paper sheet that gives a firm, flat, accurate base to the packing. With all materials in place, the tympan paper is drawn smoothly under the top bail and is clamped in place.

Inking the Press

Most power platen presses are equipped with an ink fountain that automatically adds ink to the ink disk during a long print run. When setting up the press for a short-run job, the ink disk can be easily inked by hand. The first step of the procedure is to distribute a small quantity of ink over several areas of the ink disk. Then turn on the motor and allow the press to idle at a low speed until the ink is evenly distributed over the entire disk.

Novice printers sometimes have difficulty judging the amount of ink to place on

under the bottom bail but do not reach the top bail of the platen (figure 2.24a). Next, the oil-treated manila **tympan sheet,** or drawsheet, is cut long enough to be held by both bails and is clamped with the three hanger sheets under the bottom bail (figure 2.24b). The last addition

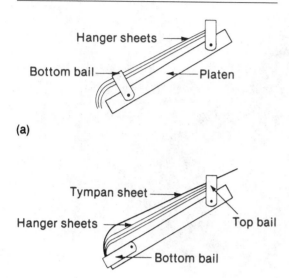

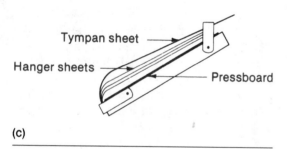

Figure 2.24.   Diagram for dressing the press.
(a) Insert the hanger sheets under the bottom, but not to the top, bail. (b) Position the tympan sheet over the hanger sheets and secure all sheets at the bottom bail. (c) Place a sheet of pressboard under the last hanger sheet.

the disk. Too little ink will produce a gray, fuzzy image. However, it is always better to start with too little ink than too much. Too much ink will plug the type form and result in a dense, blurred image. Ink can be added later if needed.

Inserting the Chase

After the press has been properly inked and dressed, it is ready to receive the chase. Turn the flywheel by hand until the platen is at its farthest position from the bed and the ink form rollers are in their lowest position. At the stone table, test the form for lift. Then move the chase to a vertical position and wipe the back of the form with a clean rag to remove any dust or lint that might prevent perfect contact with the bed of the press.

While the chase is still in the vertical position, carefully carry it to the press, place the frame against the bed, and lock it into position (figure 2.25). It is important that the chase is held firmly by the clamping device and is perfectly seated against the bed's frame.

Controlling Image Position on the Press Sheet

Because the surface of the drawsheet on the platen is perfectly flat and smooth, some device is necessary to hold the press sheet in the proper printing position during the printing operation. On automatic presses this is accomplished by mechanical grippers. On hand-fed platen presses gauge pins are used (figure 2.26). The basic challenge is to attach the pins to the drawsheet so that each press sheet will be held in the same position and so that the printed image will appear in the correct position on every press sheet.

To determine the proper gauge pin positions, the form must first be printed on the clean drawsheet. This is called pulling an impression. The press should be operated by hand for this impression. On the drawsheet, print an image that is clear enough to determine the exact position of the form.

Next draw two lines the proper distance from the printed image on the drawsheet. These two lines represent the position of the

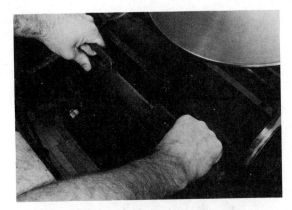

Figure 2.25.   Inserting the chase. Seat the chase in the bed of the press and lock it into place.

top and left edges of the press sheet during the printing operation (figure 2.27).

To hold the sheet on these lines attach gauge pins to the drawsheet. Place two on the lead edge (front edge) and one on the left edge (figure 2.27).

When all three gauge pins have been inserted in the tympan, check to ensure that the

grippers do not line up with any gauge pins. Then place at least one gripper in a position to catch part of the press sheet (figure 2.28). The grippers prevent the sheet from moving during the printing operation and keep the sheet from sticking to the inked form as the platen moves back to deliver the printed sheet.

The final gauge pin positions are located after a proof has been taken on an actual press sheet. Small adjustments of one or more pins are always necessary so that the image appears parallel to one edge of the sheet and is in proper printing position. Once the exact gauge pin locations are established, push the nibs, or feet, of the gauge pins into the tympan paper so the pins will not shift during production.

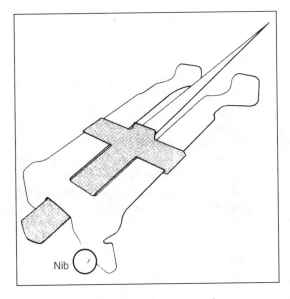

Figure 2.26.   Diagram of a gauge pin

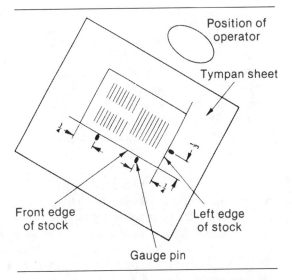

Figure 2.27.   Determining the press sheet position. Identify the position of the stock on the tympan by drawing lines to the front and left edges of the image. Place two gauge pins on the front edge of the stock at a distance of 1/4 the length of the sheet in from each edge. Place one gauge pin on the left edge of the stock at a distance of 1/3 the width of the sheet in from the front edge.

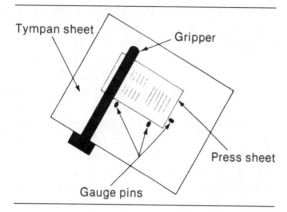

Figure 2.28. Using a gripper. A gripper is placed in line with part of the press sheet but does not touch a gauge pin.

Figure 2.29. Throw-off lever. The impression control for most hand-fed platen presses is a throw-off lever located at the side of the machine.

Final Make-Ready

Final **make-ready** is the process of adjusting the impression to obtain the best possible image quality. This is done by printing an impression on a press sheet and examining the image for print quality. On most platen presses, the operator pulls a throw-off lever to print an impression. Pulling the impression lever may be the origin of the term, "pulling an impression" (figure 2.29).

If the press is properly inked, and the overall image on the press sheet is too light, overall impression can be improved by adding press packing. If the image is light in only certain areas, overlays, underlays, and spotting up must be used. Spotting up is a procedure that uses tissue paper to build up areas where the impression is low.

Feeding the Press

Several steps can be taken to feed the power platen press smoothly and without difficulty. First, fan the pile of press paper to remove any static electricity. Then slant the pile to make it easier to lift one sheet at a time. Place the stack

on an easy-to-reach spot of the infeed table. Stand comfortably in front of the platen section within easy reach of both the paper and the platen areas.

The feeding, printing, and delivering for a platen press is a two-hand operation. The right hand feeds a sheet into the gauge pins while the left hand removes a printed sheet and stacks it on the delivery table. Inexperienced operators should practice feeding stock with the chase removed from the bed and with the press in an off-impression position. Skillful printers can feed some jobs at the rate of five thousand impressions per hour, but the novice should concentrate on consistency, not on speed.

Cleaning the Press

To clean the press, remove the chase and place it on the stone table to be knocked down or store it for future use. Then wash the ink disk with a rag saturated with wash-up solvent. Next turn the flywheel by hand until the ink rollers move to the top of the bed. With a cloth saturated with wash-up solvent, clean the rollers.

Special Letterpress Applications

Up to this point, we have discussed only the use of ink to form the image with relief presses. Several other operations can be performed with a relief press. Some use no ink to create an image and others contribute to the final image design. Some of the possible operations are perforating, creasing, embossing, die cutting, hot foil stamping, and numbering. These specialty operations help letterpress continue to play an active role in modern printing technology.

Perforating

Perforating is commonly required in jobs where portions of a piece are to be removed by the consumer (such as a ticket with a removable stub). In the perforating process, a series of very short slits are cut in the stock paper, leaving only a small bridge of paper in place. A perforating rule is a strip (generally about 2 points thick) of hardened steel that is made up of a series of equally spaced teeth. The teeth are driven through the stock by the motion of the press.

Creasing

Creasing is a process that uses a solid strip of hardened steel to crush the grain of the paper to create a straight line for folding. The process is also referred to as **scoring**. A ragged or cracked fold can occur when the printer tries to fold a heavy paper or when the job requires that the sheet be folded against the grain of the paper (see chapter 18).

Embossing

Embossing is a process that creates a three-dimensional image by placing a sheet of paper between a concave and convex (sometimes called female and male) set of dies (figure 2.30). The concave die is usually made of 3/16-inch or 1/4-inch brass and is mounted on a metal plate so that the topmost surface is type-high. The convex die is usually formed from the concave die, which has been mounted in a chase and placed on the press.

Die Cutting

Die cutting is a process that uses a razor-sharp steel rule to cut or punch various shapes (typically irregular) in press sheets. It is possible for the printer to produce basic die forms, but

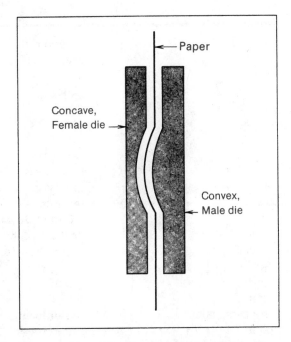

Figure 2.30. Diagram of embossing dies. Embossing creates a three-dimensional image between a male and female set of dies.

complicated designs should be prepared by commercial firms that are tooled-up to work with the hard steel rule.

Hot Foil Stamping

Hot foil stamping is a form of specialty printing that uses the platen press to its full advantage. In this process, the relief type form is locked into a special chase which can be heated while on the press. The ink rollers are removed from the press and replaced with a device that holds a plastic ribbon in front of the type form. The ribbon is available in a variety of metallic colors, including gold and silver. As an impression is made, the heated type combined with the pressure of the press during impression causes the metallic color from the ribbon to be transferred to the press sheet. Hot foil stamping is often used on greeting cards, business cards, and book covers.

Numbering

Numbering is a process that is used to print a sequential number on each press sheet. The pressure produced during each impression causes the numbering machine to advance to and print each sequential number. Rate tickets are one example of a job that can be numbered, printed, and perforated with the relief process.

Key Terms

hot type	ragged right	imposing stone
letterpress	ragged left	quoins
composition	form	quoin keys
type-high	galley	reglets
font	proof	checking for lift
set width	copy	packing
ligature	typos	gauge pins
dingbats	galley proof	impression
news case	reproduction proof	dressing the press
California job case	Linotype machine	hanger sheets
pica	Ludlow	tympan sheet
point	Monotype system	pressboard
em quad	primary plates	make-ready
en quad	duplicate plates	perforating
lead	stereotyping	creasing
slug	lockup	scoring
furniture	chase	embossing
composing stick	chaser lockup	die cutting
quadding out	platen press	hot foil stamping
justification	imposition	numbering

Questions for Review

1. Identify the major parts of a piece of foundry type.
2. What dimensions of a piece of foundry type determine set width and point size?
3. What is the point size of an en quad in a 12-point font of foundry type?
4. How thick are leads and slugs, and what are they used for?
5. What is meant by "quadding out"?
6. What are the differences between justified, centered, ragged right, and ragged left composition?
7. What is the function of lockup?
8. What does the term "imposition" describe?
9. What does the expression "dressing the press" mean?
10. How is image position controlled on a platen press?
11. What do the terms "creasing," "perforating," "embossing," "die cutting," "hot foil stamping," and "numbering" mean?

Basic Graphic Design for Printing

Anecdote to Chapter Three

On March 9, 1972, an unmanned United States rocket—*Pioneer 10*—began a one-half-billion-mile journey to the planet Jupiter and beyond. It was our country's first effort to leave this solar system. On the ship were a robot and a 6-×-9-inch, goldplated aluminum plaque attached to the rocket's antenna supports. The plaque carried a message for any extraterrestrial creatures who might encounter it. The message explained the robot's purpose and who built it.

Once the decision had been made to send a message with the rocket, the problem was deciding what to say and how to say it. If there were other creatures like us in the universe, what language would they speak—English, Russian, French? What experiences could we share with creatures who were not from Earth?

The solution was to use lines to draw the basic shapes of a man and a woman standing in front of a scale outline of *Pioneer 10*. That image could communicate our animal type and our size. A code was then devised that used the wavelength of radiation given off by a hydrogen atom (the most common element in the universe). The code described the origin of the rocket and the distance of our sun from the center of the galaxy.

Traveling at a speed of seven miles a second, it should take *Pioneer 10* more than 80 thousand years to reach the nearest star. The chances that the message will collide with an inhabited planet are slim. But that small grouping of lines and symbols stands as our first attempt to communicate with and confirm the existence of humanity to the rest of the universe.

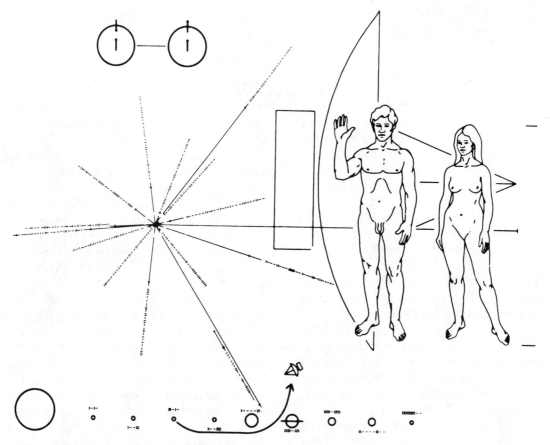

Graphic message carried on Pioneer 10.
Courtesy of NASA.

Objectives for Chapter 3

After completing this chapter you will be able to:

■ Recognize and explain the design considerations of balance, dominance, proportion, and unity.

■ Identify the common elements of alphabet design.

■ Define the terms "stroke," "stress," and "serif," and explain how they can be used to identify a typeface.

■ Discuss the six basic typestyles.

■ Measure and copyfit type.

■ Explain the three basic types of color printing, and identify tints, surprints, reverses, and bleeds.

■ List and explain the design steps used to produce a printed product.

Introduction

Printing is a manufacturing process. Printing produces multiple, identical copies of graphic images. Image design is the first step in a typical printing job. The purpose of image design is to create an image which meets the customer's need—to influence, inform, sell, or persuade. If the customer's need is not met then the printing job is useless. The purpose of printing is to reproduce an image.

An image may be created by the customer or by a professional graphic designer. It may be a simple page of text, or it may be a complex color printing job requiring several colors, scoring, embossing, and folding. Whether the job is simple or complex, the printer must provide reproductions that meet the customer's expectations and are at a price the customer can afford. Thus, the printer must be efficient and provide quality work to compete.

Efficiency and quality cannot be achieved by the printer alone, however. The printer and the graphic designer must work together. The designer must create an image that can be printed using normal reproduction techniques and provide the printer with specifications for the printing job. The printer must understand and satisfy the designer's specifications during printing. It is not necessary for a printer to be a designer, but knowing design is important for a printer. This chapter introduces some of the language, tools, and concepts of the graphic designer's art.

Design Considerations

It is impossible in a book of this nature and scope to provide more than a brief introduction to the graphic design process. Graphic design is an art and a skill; it is mastered only after years of study and practice.

A graphic designer's art is in imagining and creating a graphic image that meets a specific need. Artistic decisions about balance, dominance, proportion, and unity must be made. The purpose of the printed piece influences design decisions about the type of illustrations, paper, and binding. All of these decisions are further influenced by the budget for the piece.

A graphic designer's skill is in presenting the image design to the printer properly and with clear specifications and directions so the printer can reproduce it accurately. More printing jobs are sent back to the printer for rework due to misunderstandings between the designer and the printer than because of printing errors. Type measurement and specification, copyfitting, and the ability to prepare both type and illustrations for printing are among the many skills a graphic designer needs.

Balance

Balance is a term that describes the equilibrium and visual weight of a graphic page. The visual weight of an image on the printed sheet depends on the image's size, color, and density in relation to other images on the sheet. Designers often pretend a pin is inserted in the exact center of the page and that images have physical weight. Solid areas have more visual weight than outlines. Circular forms generally appear heavier than rectangles. Visual equilibrium is achieved when the page is perfectly balanced on the pin. Color can be used to make an image visually heavier or lighter.

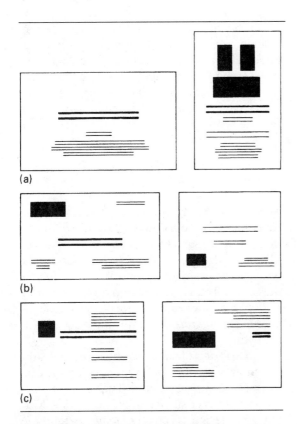

(a)

(b)

(c)

Figure 3.1.   Examples of visual balance. Examples of balance shown here are (a) formal, (b) informal, and (c) subjective.

There are three kinds of visual balance:

- Formal
- Informal
- Subjective

Formal balance (figure 3.1a) places identical visual weight on the top, bottom, and sides of a visual center. Designers often use formal balance in situations that demand dignity. Wedding and other formal invitations often have formal balance. Designs in which images create a sense of visual balance around a visual center because of their sizes, weights, and positions have **informal balance** (figure 3.1b). With **subjective balance** (figure 3.1c), design-

ers have complete freedom with image positions as the name implies, but they still seek to achieve visual balance.

Not all designs require visual balance, however. Sometimes designers purposely create images that are unbalanced to direct a reader's eyes to one spot or to communicate chaos.

Dominance

Dominance refers to the main purpose of a printed piece—to communicate a message. If a message does not dominate a piece, the reader has to search for the piece's meaning.

Dominance can be achieved by contrasting the most important parts of the message with the rest of the sheet. Some lines of type can be set larger than others. Boldface, italic, or underlining can help create dominance. Words can be printed in special colors or tints, reversed, or dropped (figure 3.2).

Good control of contrast can also direct the eye to the most important part of the message, even though it might not be the largest part. A prime example of contrast is the use of white space around densely set copy.

Proportion

Proportion is concerned with size relationships. Both the size of the sheet and the size and placement of the images on the sheet are important to proportion. A sheet that measures 1 inch × 11 inches is probably not a good page proportion (depending upon use). However, 8 1/2 inches × 11 inches is considered a good page proportion.

The idea of acceptable proportion is closely related to culture. When we see and use a particular proportion frequently it becomes appealing. For example, in most Western culture page designs the two side margins are equal, the top margin is larger than the side margins, and the bottom margin is larger than the other three (figure 3.3).

Screen tint

Drop

Reverse

Figure 3.2.   Examples of a screen tint, a drop, and a reverse

The final use of a piece must also be considered when setting margin proportions. In book design a certain portion of the page must be reserved for binding. In addition, the visual proportion of each book page is smaller than the actual page size. In practice the designer specifies the visual page size and the printer calculates the necessary or actual page size.

Unity

The idea of **unity** connects all of the design functions. It is concerned with how an entire piece flows together into a complete message. The best designs deliver one message; the worst have competing, and often confusing, messages. The classic example of poor unity design is a nineteenth-century circus poster—every act is featured and no single act attracts the eye.

This idea of unity is enhanced with the selection of appropriate typefaces and art for the message being printed. The characteristics of letterforms create feelings and moods. Mixing type designs typically creates disunity. A fundamental rule for young designers is to work with only one family of type for any given job.

Alphabet Design

Graphic designers work with the placement of images and the manipulation of white or open space. The most basic images used in graphic design are the twenty-six symbols of our Roman alphabet. Just as each individual writes in a different and distinctive style, printers reproduce the alphabet in many different **typefaces.**

Symbol Characteristics

Different letterforms are created using only five variables:

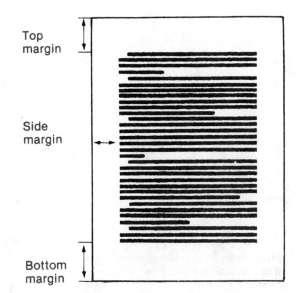

Top margin

Side margin

Bottom margin

Figure 3.3. **Margin proportions.** Margins must appear proportionally correct on the page. The top margin is usually larger than the side margins, and the bottom margin is usually larger than the top margin.

■ x-height
■ Ascenders and descenders
■ Stroke
■ Stress
■ Serifs

These variables can deliver an unlimited number of typeface designs.

x-Height and Ascenders and Descenders
Typefaces are described using a very specific vocabulary (figure 3.4). Our alphabet is made

up of uppercase (capital) and lowercase (small) characters. Both upper- and lowercase characters are formed along a common base line. The **x-height,** or **body-height,** of a typeface is the distance from the base line to the top of the lowercase letter x. The body height of a typeface can affect how large characters appear on the printed page and how easy they are to read (figure 3.5). Larger characters are easier to read. For this reason, typefaces with large body heights are often used in children's books.

Any part of a letter that drops below the x-height is called a **descender;** any letter part that extends above the x-height is called an **ascender.** Accurate recognition of words depends on the visual impact of ascenders and descenders (figure 3.6). We tend to read word-forms or word shapes rather than individual letters. As an experiment try the exercise shown in figure 3.6. Be sure to do it with someone who has not yet seen the full illustration.

Stroke
There are three major variables in letterforms: stroke, stress, and serifs. **Stroke** refers to the thickness or weight of the lines that form a

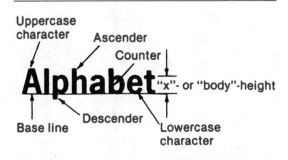

Uppercase character

Ascender

Counter

Alphabet "x"- or "body"-height

Base line

Descender

Lowercase character

Figure 3.4. **Elements of typeface design**

The x-height, or body-height, of a typeface is the distance from the base line to the top of the lowercase letter x. The body height of a typeface can affect how large or chacters appear on the printedpage and how easy they are to read.

The x-height, or body-height, of a typeface is the distance from the base line to the top of the lowercase letter x. The body height of a typeface can affect how large or chacters appear on the printedpage and how easy they are to read.

The x-height, or body-height, of a typeface is the distance from the base line to the top of the lowercase letter x. The body height of a typeface can affect how large or chacters appear on the printedpage and how easy they are to read.

The x-height, or body-height, of a typeface is the distance from the base line to the top of the lowercase letter x. The body height of a typeface can affect how large or chacters appear on the printedpage and how easy they are to read.

Figure 3.5. Comparison of body heights. These examples are all printed in Roman typefaces with the same point size and line spacing. The primary variable is x-height.

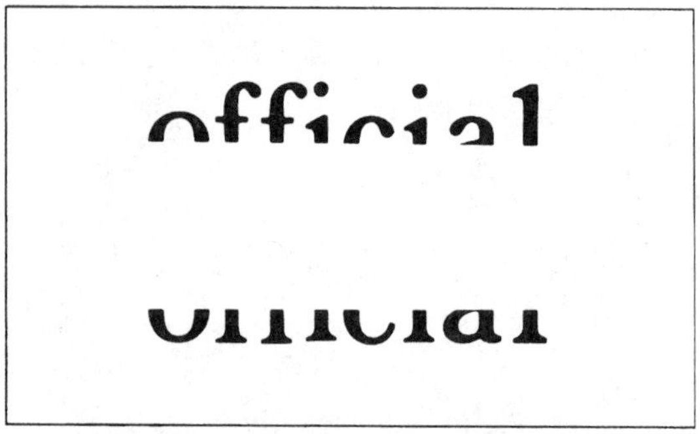

Figure 3.6. Recognizing words by their forms. Cover the top line and ask someone to read the bottom. Then reverse the procedure. Which was easier?

Stress

Stress refers to a slant of a character. Mathematically, stress is defined as the angle of a line that passes through the center of a character (figure 3.8). This can be visualized as if the os were large tires or inner tubes. If you pushed on an upright inner tube it would depress, but its base would remain in place.

Italic typefaces generally have slight negative stress. In other words, they slant a bit to the right rather than to the left. However, stress is not the only element that defines an italic

character (figure 3.7). The stroke might be uniform, as with the Helvetica typeface, or contrasting, as with the Bodoni typeface.

A scribe hand lettering manuscripts with a quill pen originated stroke variation. Today stroke can be varied with a thick felt-tip pen. Hold the pen firmly in your hand and draw a vertical line. Without changing your hand position and without lifting the tip of the pen from the paper, slowly move the pen to the right to make an arc. You will see that the line thickness varies.

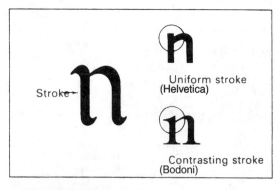

Uniform stroke
(Helvetica)

Stroke→

Contrasting stroke
(Bodoni)

Figure 3.7. Stroke. The stroke or thickness of typeface varies from design to design.

COOPER

BOOKMAN

Figure 3.8. **Comparison of stress.** The Bookman typeface has vertical stress. The *o*s in the Cooper typeface are stressed (slanted) from the upper left to the lower right.

typeface. Type designers actually modify each letter to create an italic image. For example, examine the italic letter *e* in figure 3.17. Notice that more than just stress affects its appearance.

Serifs

Serifs are small strokes that project out from the top or bottom of main letter strokes (figure 3.9). Serifs can be vertical or horizontal strokes. Vertical serifs are parallel to the base line. Horizontal letter strokes or serifs are at right angles to the base line, or slightly off 90 degrees.

A fillet is added to some letterforms. A **fillet** is an internal curve between the serif stroke and the main stroke. Fillets are generally

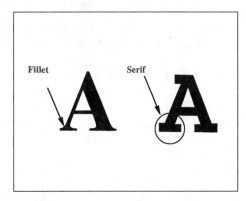

Figure 3.9. **Serifs.** Serifs are often the distinguishing feature of similar typefaces.

considered to add a sense of elegance to the basic alphabet design.

Serifs can vary in thickness and stress. Serifs can also be square or rounded. In fact, there are endless serif variations. With serifs, stress, and stroke, it is easy to see that there is no limit to the design of our Roman alphabet.

Typeface Classification

The unlimited number of variations in alphabet design makes identifying or selecting a typeface difficult for young designers. There are numerous choices, and there is no universally accepted classification system for type design. The most popular method is to organize typefaces by type style. **Type style** is defined by variations in stress, stroke, and serif. There are six basic styles in this system:

- Roman
- Sans serif
- Square serif
- Text
- Script
- Occasional

Roman

The text in this book is set in a **Roman** typeface. Body composition is set in Palatino, while figure notes use Helvetica. Ms. Nicole Reamer, the art and design coordinator for *Printing Technology*, 4e, selected these faces because "they are classic and easily read."

The Roman style is based on the characteristics of letterforms cut into granite by early Roman stonemasons. Iron chisels were used to cut horizontal and vertical lines. Where strokes did not intersect, the tool left a ragged appearance at the end of a line. A cut made with the tool straightened the unevenness. The cut was called a "serif."

The Roman typeface style is defined by two main characteristics: serifs and stroke variation.

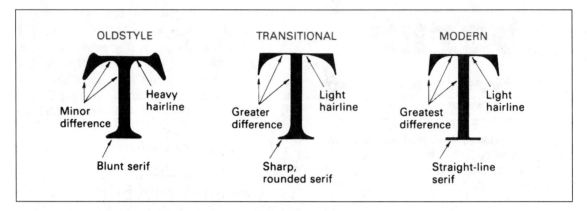

Figure 3.10.   Roman designs. Roman designs can be oldstyle, transitional, or modern.

There are three subcategories of the Roman design—oldstyle, transitional, and modern (figure 3.10). Oldstyle Roman has little stroke variation. There is usually a slight rounding of the serif base, and fillets occupy the area between main and serif strokes. A modern Roman character is formed from thick strokes contrasted with almost hairline strokes. There is generally no rounding or filleting of the serif. Between the two stylistically is transitional Roman with greater stroke variation than oldstyle but less variation than modern Roman.

Most alphabets with a Roman design are considered easy to read. Many books, magazines, and newspapers are set in Roman typefaces.

Sans Serif

Sans serif means "without serifs" (figure 3.11). Sans serif characters are typically formed with uniform strokes and with perfectly vertical letter stress. These type designs generally communicate a modern, clean visual appearance.

Square Serif

Square serif typefaces are sometimes referred to as "Egyptian" typefaces. The serifs on

Triumvirate

Avant Garde Gothic

ALDOUS VERTICAL

Figure 3.11.   Examples of sans serif typefaces

square serif typefaces are not rounded but rather appear as blocks or slabs connected to the main character strokes (figure 3.12). Square serif faces are often used in larger point sizes for display type. When set in smaller sizes, they tend to make the printed page appear dense and black.

Square serif faces generally communicate a feeling of strength or power.

Text

Text typefaces attempt to recreate the feeling of the era of medieval scribes (figure 3.13). They

Lubalin Graph Book

Figure 3.12.   An example of a square serif typeface

are generally used in very formal pieces, such as wedding invitations. Text characters are difficult to read and become almost illegible when set all uppercase (figure 3.14).

Script
Script (or cursive) designs attempt to duplicate the easy, free-flowing feeling of hand lettering (figure 3.15). As with text, script is not easy to read when set all uppercase.

Occasional
The last typeface, **occasional,** is really an "other grouping" or "catchall" category. Anything that cannot be placed in one of the other five categories is labeled occasional (figure 3.16). Some **typographers** (type designers) use the labels "novelty" or "decorative" for an occasional typeface, but whatever it is called, it has no design limits. Occasional typefaces are usually created to meet a specific design need. Companies often design and copyright a particular letterform so that consumers will associate it with their product or service.

DIANE

Figure 3.14.   An example of all uppercase text. Words in a text typeface that are set in all capital letters are almost unreadable. This word is *Diane.*

Typeface Families

Each unique combination of stress, stroke, and serif is a type style. Within each style further variations are possible. These variations define a **type family.** Just as human families are made up of various members—sisters, brothers, cousins, aunts, and so on—who have a family resemblance, type families are made up of letterform variations that have a resemblance. These variations are all based on the main type family characteristics of stroke, stress, and serif (figure 3.17).

There are thousands of different type families; each is identified by a specific name. Examples include Lubalin, Bodini, or Zapf. Others get their names from their intended use. In 1887 *The London Times* newspaper commissioned a new design. The type family used was called New Times Roman, or simply Times.

A type family variation may be created by making the characters in the basic family design bold, light, condensed, expanded, extra

Wedding Text

Figure 3.13.   An example of a text typeface

Script

Figure 3.15.   An example of a script typeface

Occasional

Comstock

Occasional

Funky

Figure 3.16.   Examples of occasional typefaces

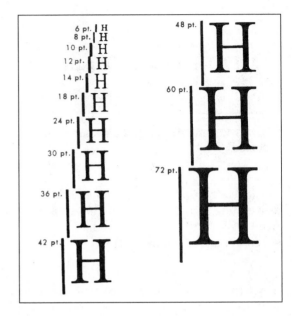

Figure 3.18.   Type size. Type size is measured in points, shown here from a small letter of 6 points to a display letter of 72 points.
Courtesy of Mackenzie and Harris, Inc., San Francisco.

bold, extra light, italic, or combinations of several variations, such as extra bold condensed. Nine different members of the Century typeface are shown in figure 3.17. The word that describes the variation—for example, bold or italic—is added to the type family name to distinguish between each member in the type family such as Lubalin bold, Lubalin italic, etc.

Century Light
Century Light Italic
Century Bold
Century Bold Italic
Century Bold Condensed
Century Bold Extended
Century Textbook
Century Textbook Italic
Century Textbook Bold

Figure 3.17.   An example of a type family. The family name of this type is Century. Its variations are combinations of different weights—light, bold, regular—and different stress.

Type Fonts

Alphabet point size is measured with the printer's measurement system explained in chapter 2. Every member (variation) of a type family can be reproduced in a range of **point** sizes (figure 3.18). A **font** is a collection of all of the characters, including punctuation marks and special symbols, of one type family variation that are the same point size. All of the characters and symbols in a font of 10-point Century Bold, for example, make up a *font* of the Century Bold variation of the Century *type family*, which is one of many type families in the *Roman* style (figure 3.19).

Graphic designers use type specimen books as their primary reference (figure 3.20). Such books typically show families of type set in sizes from 6 to 72 points. They also often display paragraph composition to show how text will appear in a job.

ABCDEFGHIJKLMNOPQRSTUVWXYZa
bcdefghijklmnopqrstuvwyxz1234567890.,
;:'"?!/!@#$%^&*()-+=—<>[]{}

Figure 3.19. **A font of type.** A font is a collection of all characters—alphabet, punctuation marks, and special symbols—for one member of a type family in one size.

Type Copy

The term "copy" is used widely in both printing and graphic design. In the most general sense, **copy** is any image or information that is part of a design or printing job. It is a noun, not a verb. The following guidelines apply:

- An author's written words that are set into type is "copy."
- A photograph inserted in an ad is "copy."
- Typeset words ready to become part of a book is "copy."
- A "copy editor" is someone who works with an author's words before final typesetting.

Type copy is all copy that will appear as type in the printed piece. Much of what is printed is type copy, which is "set into type" (see chapter 5). Designers use their knowledge of type design and typesetting to select and specify the typefaces and sizes for use on the printed piece. All type in a job is either display copy or body copy, depending on its size and function.

Display Type

Display type is typeset in a large point size—typically 14 points or larger. Uses for display type include newspaper headlines, book chapter headings, and book covers. Most printed advertisements include some display type.

Most books use display type to help organize information and make it easy to understand how ideas relate. These words are often called "A-heads," "B-heads" and "C-Heads". *Printing Technology*, 4e, uses distinct display type to help the reader:

Type Copy	A-head
Type Measurement	B-head
Measuring Type Point Size	C-head

Body Copy

Body copy is typeset in smaller point sizes than display copy—usually 14 points or less. Body composition is sometimes called "text copy." The words you are reading right now are an example of body copy. Graphic designers pick body type that is easy to read and does not detract from the author's message.

Type that is too small strains the eye and can cause headaches. Lines that are too long (line measure) and too close together (line leading) make it difficult for the eye to move easily from the end of one line to the beginning of the next. An old typesetting rule of thumb is to never set a line of type longer than the length of the line of a font's capital and lowercase letters set together (example: ABCDEFGHIJKL MNOPQRSTUVWXYZabcdefghijklmnopqrst uvwxyz). However, contemporary designers often ignore this rule if there is sufficient line spacing. The column width for newspaper body composition is selected so you can read the entire line without moving your eyes.

Some type styles are inappropriate today for body composition because they distract from the information. For example, a text typeface is hard for most individuals to read, except if they read only a few lines at a time. It simply requires too much concentration. Body type should be invisible from the information.

Times

6 pt.	ABCDEFGHIJKLMNOPQRSTUVWXYZabcdefghijklmnopqrstuvwxyz0123456789!?,"$&%{}*
7 pt.	ABCDEFGHIJKLMNOPQRSTUVWXYZabcdefghijklmnopqrstuvwxyz0123456789!?,"$&%{}*
8 pt.	ABCDEFGHIJKLMNOPQRSTUVWXYZabcdefghijklmnopqrstuvwxyz0123456789!?,"$&%{}*
9 pt.	ABCDEFGHIJKLMNOPQRSTUVWXYZabcdefghijklmnopqrstuvwxyz0123456789!?,"$&%{}*
10 pt.	ABCDEFGHIJKLMNOPQRSTUVWXYZabcdefghijklmnopqrstuvwxyz0123456789!?,"$&%{}*
12 pt.	ABCDEFGHIJKLMNOPQRSTUVWXYZabcdefghijklmnopqrstuvwxyz0123456789!?,"$&%
14 pt.	ABCDEFGHIJKLMNOPQRSTUVWXYZabcdefghijklmnopqrstuvwxyz0123456
18 pt.	ABCDEFGHIJKLMNOPQRSTUVWXYZabcdefghijklmnopqr

48 pt.

ABCDEFGHIJKLMNOP QRSTUVWXYZabcdefg hijklmnopqrstuvwxyz012 3456789!?,"$&%{}*

10/10

Lorem ipsum dolor sit amet, consectetuer adipiscing elit, sed diam nonummy nibh euismod tincidunt ut laoreet dolore magna aliquam erat volutpat. Ut wisi enim ad minim veniam, quis nostrud exerci tation ullamcorper suscipit lobortis nisl ut aliquip ex ea commodo consequat. Duis autem vel eum iriure dolor in hendrerit in vulputate velit esse molestie consequat, vel illum dolore eu feugiat nulla facilisis at vero eros et accumsan et iusto odio dignissim qui blandit praesent luptatum zzril delenit augue duis dolore te feugait nulla facilisi. Lorem ipsum dolor sit amet, consectetuer adipiscing elit, sed diam nonummy nibh euismod

10/12

Lorem ipsum dolor sit amet, consectetuer adipiscing elit, sed diam nonummy nibh euismod tincidunt ut laoreet dolore magna aliquam erat volutpat. Ut wisi enim ad minim veniam, quis nostrud exerci tation ullamcorper suscipit lobortis nisl ut aliquip ex ea commodo consequat. Duis autem vel eum iriure dolor in hendrerit in vulputate velit esse molestie consequat, vel illum dolore eu feugiat nulla facilisis at vero eros et accumsan et iusto odio dignissim qui blandit praesent luptatum zzril delenit augue duis dolore te feugait nulla facilisi. Lorem ipsum dolor sit

10/14

Lorem ipsum dolor sit amet, consectetuer adipiscing elit, sed diam nonummy nibh euismod tincidunt ut laoreet dolore magna aliquam erat volutpat. Ut wisi enim ad minim veniam, quis nostrud exerci tation ullamcorper suscipit lobortis nisl ut aliquip ex ea commodo consequat. Duis autem vel eum iriure dolor in hendrerit in vulputate velit esse molestie consequat, vel illum dolore eu feugiat nulla facilisis at vero eros et accumsan et iusto odio dignissim qui blandit praesent lupta-

Point size:	6	7	8	9	10	11	12	13	18	20	24	36
Chars/Pica:	5	4.29	3.75	3.33	3	2.73	2.5	2.31	1.67	1.5	1.25	0.83

	6	7	8	9	10	11	12	13	18	20	24	36
Cap height::	0.25"	0.5"	0.75"	1"	1.25"	1.5"	2"	2.25"	2.25"	2.5"	2.75"	3"
Approx. pt. size:	26.32	52.64	78.97	105.29	131.61	157.93	184.25	210.58	236.9	263.22	289.54	315.86

Figure 3.20.   **An example of a type specimen book page**

Specifying Copy Measurement

A designer must specify the sizes in which display copy and body copy are to be typeset. Selection of type size is a design decision, but it is based in part on the amount of space available for type matter on the printed piece. Display type for a business card, for example, probably would be too large if it were set in 72-point type; for this application 24-point type might be more appropriate. If this textbook were set in 14-point type instead of 10-point type, many more pages would be required to set the same amount of copy because fewer characters would fit on each text page.

Specifying Type Point Size

There is a difference between the actual height of a typeset character and the point size of the character. Recall from our discussion of foundry type in chapter 2 that type point size is the size of the foundry type body from the belly to the back side (figure 2.1). Thus the height of a typeset foundry type character is actually less than the point size of the lead body on which it is cast. A small amount of white space remains above and below the character when the character is typeset (figure 3.21).

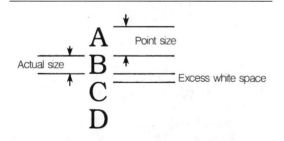

Figure 3.21. Comparison of actual size and point size. The characters above are all set in 24-point type with no leading. Their actual size is about 16 points, which leaves about 6 points of excess white space between them.

(a)

A small amount of white space remains above and below the character when the character is typeset. Thus, even if lines of type are set solid (with no extra leading between them) there will always be some space between the lines of type.

Copy set 9/9, Century Book

(b)

A small amount of white space remains above and below the character when the character is typeset. Thus, even if lines of type are set solid (with no extra leading between them) there will always be some space between the lines of type.

Copy set 12/12, Century Book

Figure 3.22. Type set solid. The first paragraph above (a) is set solid in 9-point type; the second paragraph (b) is set solid in 12-point type. The amount of extra white space between the lines depends on the point size of the type.

This extra space above and below typeset characters exists whether the characters are generated from foundry type, a computer, or phototypesetting. Thus, even if lines of type are set solid (with no extra leading between them), there will always be some space between each line of type (figure 3.22). The amount of space above and below the typeset character depends on the point size in which the character is set. A 48-point character will have more extra space above and below it than will a 24-point character.

Measurement is the only way to precisely determine the actual height of a 48-point character from a specific typeface when it is

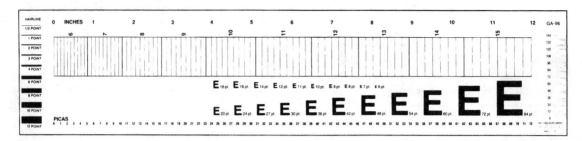

Figure 3.23. **A type rule.** *Note:* rule has been photographically reduced and is not shown in accurate scale.
Courtesy of C-Thru Ruler Company.

typeset. Transparent type rulers, like to the one in figure 3.23, aid in type measurement and specification. A display of the uppercase *E*, typeset in point sizes from 6 to 84, is printed across the face of the rule. To use a type ruler the character size display is moved over the typeset composition. A designer can compare the *E* in this rule to a typeset uppercase character in print. The number on the rule face printed next to the *E* that most closely matches the height of the typeset character gives an approximation of the typeset character's point size.

The relationship of the typeset height of a character to its specified point size can also be approximated by applying the "two-thirds rule." On average, the height of a typeset character is approximately 2/3 its specified point size. Applying this rule, an uppercase character specified at 48 points will be approximately 32 points high when typeset (48 points × 2/3 = 32 points).

Type specimen books also help the designer to determine and specify to the printer desired sizes.

Specifying Line Spacing

Line spacing is defined as the vertical distance between one base line and the next, measured in points (figure 3.24). The term **leading** is sometimes used as well.

Graphic designers typically specify type size and line space together. For example, a 9 point type set with 2 extra points of space would be specified as 9/12, read "nine on twelve."

It is sometimes necessary to measure the line spacing on existing typeset copy. The ruler shown in figure 3.23 provides a means of gauging leading. Notice the set of vertical lines above the character size display. The lines in the set of vertical lines to the far right are 15 points apart. By turning the ruler so that these lines are horizontal and by moving this portion of the transparent rule over the existing type it is possible to position each group along the type base line. When any two ruler lines fall exactly on two adjacent base lines line spacing has been determined.

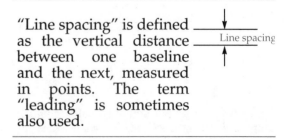

"Line spacing" is defined as the vertical distance between one baseline and the next, measured in points. The term "leading" is sometimes also used.

Figure 3.24. **Measuring line spacing**

Specifying Line Length and Depth

The length of a typeset line, called the line measure or line length, and the vertical distance that type occupies on the typeset page, called the depth, are both specified in picas. **Picas** can be converted to points by multiplying the total number by 12.

It is important to keep in mind the following basic printing measurement units:

- 72 points = 1 inch
- 6 picas = 1 inch
- 12 points = 1 pica

Conversion charts, similar to the one shown in figure 3.25, can be used to make pica-to-point conversions.

Copyfitting

Copyfitting is used to determine the space that one or more lines of type copy will occupy after typesetting. Type copy has traditionally been delivered to a designer as typewritten copy with nonproportional characters. More recently, however, many authors have begun to write on microcomputers and deliver proportional pages with back-up storage disks. Whatever the mode of transmittal, designers do much copyfitting to predict how much space the original copy will occupy when it is typeset. Without copyfitting, the designer would have no idea how much type would fit in any area of the design.

In chapter 2 we mentioned that foundry type has proportional set widths. This is also true of most laser-quality output from a microcomputer and also phototypeset type. For example, a 10-point *m* in a typeface such as Century is wider than a 10-point *i* in the same typeface. Not only does the set width of each character vary within a specific typeface, but the set width of the same character varies from one typeface to another. A 10-point *e* in the Century typeface is likely to have a different set width than a 10-point *e* in the Helvetica typeface. Variations in both the set width and point size of a typeface must be considered during copyfitting.

To copyfit, you must know the number of characters to be typeset; the measure of the typeset line; and the typeface, point size, and leading. Copyfitting involves three basic steps:

1. Count the typewritten characters or obtain a character count from a computer file.
2. Determine the number of typeset lines that will be delivered from that character count.
3. Calculate the depth that the typeset material will occupy.

For our example, we will set the copy shown in figure 3.26a in the Century Book typeface, on a 17-pica measure, in 8-point type, with 10-point leading. In other words, the line of type will be 17 picas long, the point size will be 8, and there will be 10 points from one base line to the next. A designer would specify this as "8/10 × 17."

Step 1: Count the Characters

For small amounts of copy, as might be required for a one-line headline, the total number of characters to be typeset can be determined by simply counting the characters. For larger blocks of body copy, such as a typewritten paragraph or a page, it is easier to estimate the total number of characters. It is easiest to have a computer report the number of characters from a disk file.

The paragraph in figure 3.26a contains 10 lines of typewriter copy. Note that the copy is flush left (ragged right) so each of the 10 lines is a different length. We must account for these differences in line length by identifying an

Pica-to-Point Conversion Chart											

Points ⟶

Picas	0	1	2	3	4	5	6	7	8	9	10	11
0	0	1	2	3	4	5	6	7	8	9	10	11
1	12	13	14	15	16	17	18	19	20	21	22	23
2	24	25	26	27	28	29	30	31	32	33	34	35
3	36	37	38	39	40	41	42	43	44	45	46	47
4	48	49	50	51	52	53	54	55	56	57	58	59
5	60	61	62	63	64	65	66	67	68	69	70	71
6	72	73	74	75	76	77	78	79	80	81	82	83
7	84	85	86	87	88	89	90	91	92	93	94	95
8	96	97	98	99	100	101	102	103	104	105	106	107
9	108	109	110	111	112	113	114	115	116	117	118	119
10	120	121	122	123	124	125	126	127	128	129	130	131
11	132	133	134	135	136	137	138	139	140	141	142	143
12	144	145	146	147	148	149	150	151	152	153	154	155
13	156	157	158	159	160	161	162	163	164	165	166	167
14	168	169	170	171	172	173	174	175	176	177	178	179
15	180	181	182	183	184	185	186	187	188	189	190	191
16	192	193	194	195	196	197	198	199	200	201	202	203
17	204	205	206	207	208	209	210	211	212	213	214	215
18	216	217	218	219	220	221	222	223	224	225	226	227
19	228	229	230	231	232	233	234	235	236	237	238	239
20	240	241	242	243	244	245	246	247	248	249	250	251
21	252	253	254	255	256	257	258	259	260	261	262	263
22	264	265	266	267	268	269	270	271	272	273	274	275
23	276	277	278	279	280	281	282	283	284	285	286	287
24	288	289	290	291	292	293	294	295	296	297	298	299

Figure 3.25.   A pica-to-point conversion chart

Averaging
Line ⟶

(a)

```
    This is the number of characters that will fit on

a line of type from my typewriter.  On my typewriter, I

get 10 characters per inch, because I have a "pica"

typewriter.  If I had an "elite" typewriter, I'd get

12 characters per inch.  Note that all the copy from my

typewriter is flush left (ragged right).  When I copyfit

this copy, I must account for the fact that all of the

lines of copy are not the same length.  I have to either

count all of the characters in the copy individually, or

I have to average them up.
```

(b)

This is the number of characters that will fit on a line of type from my typewriter. On my typewriter, I get 10 characters per inch, because I have a ''pica'' typewriter. If I had an ''elite'' typewriter, I'd get 12 characters per inch. Note that all the copy from my typewriter is flush left (ragged right). When I copyfit this copy, I must account for the fact that all of the lines of copy are not the same length. I have to either count all of the characters in the copy individually, or I have to average them.

Figure 3.26.   Copyfitting typewriter copy. The paragraph in (a) contains approximately 512 typewritten characters. This paragraph is typeset in (b) Century Book, on a 17-pica line typeface 8/10.

average line of copy. To do so, first find an average full line of copy and draw a line in pencil along the right side of the copy after the last character in the line. This step is not mechanical and requires only visual judgment of "average length." Then count the typewriter characters—all alphabet characters, punctuation marks, and spaces—to the left of this line to get the average number of characters in one full line of copy.

In figure 3.26a, the averaging line was drawn after the *m* at the end of the fifth line of copy. The fifth line looked to be about the average line length; some lines were shorter, some were longer. There are 54 characters to the left of the averaging line in the fifth line of copy. The first line of copy is indented, but because it will be typeset as an indented line, it counts as a full line. The last line of copy is not a full line, however, so there are only nine full lines of typewritten copy. Thus, there are a total of 486 characters in the full lines to the left of the averaging line (54 characters per line × 9 full lines of copy = 486 characters). The last line of copy has only 26 characters including spaces and punctuation. When added to the 486 characters already calculated, the total comes to 512 characters.

This estimate alone would be good enough for many copyfitting purposes. More precision can be attained by adding the number of characters to the right of the averaging line and subtracting the number of blank spaces at the end of lines that fall a few characters short of the averaging line, but this precision is seldom necessary.

This copyfitting technique can be used for manuscripts with many hundreds of pages. Simply determine the average number of characters per page and multiply that figure by the number of pages. It is not necessary to count the number of partial pages over large volumes; this technique delivers reasonably accurate results.

Step 2: Determine the Number of Typeset Lines Required

To determine the number of lines required to set the type, you must know:

▪ How many characters are to be typeset;
▪ The number of characters that will fit on a typeset line; and
▪ The leading or desired line spacing.

In step 1 we found that the job has approximately 512 characters.

Information about the number of characters that can be typeset per pica is supplied by type specimen books. Figure 3.27 is a character-per-pica chart for the typeface Century Book. This chart shows the number of characters per pica that can be typeset in four variations of the Century Book typeface for sizes from 6 points to 24 points.

This job is to be set in 8-point Century Book. Referring to figure 3.27 we find that 8-point Century Book outputs as type at an average of 3.09 characters per pica. Our line measure is to be 17 picas. To determine the number of characters that will fit on one line we multiply 17 by 3.09, or approximately 53 characters.

This job is to be set 8/10, or 8-point type on 10-point line spacing. If we divide the characters to be typeset (512) by the number of characters that can fit on a typeset line (53), we find that our copy requires 10 typeset lines (512 characters ÷ 53 characters per line = 9.66 typeset lines).

Characters Per Pica

	6	7	8	9	10	11	12	14	18	24
Century Book	4.12	3.53	**3.09**	2.75	2.47	2.25	2.06	1.77	1.37	1.03
Century Bold	4.09	3.50	3.07	2.73	2.45	2.23	2.04	1.75	1.36	1.02
Century Italic	3.83	3.28	2.87	2.55	2.30	2.09	1.91	1.64	1.28	0.96
Century Bold Italic	3.86	3.31	2.89	2.57	2.31	2.10	1.93	1.65	1.29	0.96

Figure 3.27. **Character-per-pica chart for the Century Book typeface**

*Step 3: Calculate the Depth
of the Typeset Material*

All that remains is to calculate the depth of the copy. This is done by multiplying the leading for the copy by the number of typeset lines required. In our example, the number of typeset lines required from step 2 was 10. The leading to be used is 10-point. Multiplying the leading value (10-point leading) by the number of typeset lines required (10 lines) gives a copy depth of 100 points (10 points per line × 10 lines = 100 points).

There are 12 points in 1 pica. Dividing 100 points by 12 gives a copy depth of approximately 8 picas (100 points ÷ 12 = 8.33). Thus 512 characters, set in 8-point Century Book, with 10-point leading, on a 17-pica line measure, will occupy an area 17 picas wide and approximately 8 picas deep (figure 3.26b).

Copyfitting procedures are the same regardless of the size of the job.

Dealing with Art Copy

In addition to type copy, most printing jobs include art copy. There are two basic types of art copy: line copy and continuous-tone. Line copy (figure 3.28a) is composed entirely of lines and/or dots. An illustration drawn with technical pens is a good example of line copy. The lines can be drawn in a variety of thicknesses, but all of the lines are the same tone. As a result, each line is just as dense and black as all of the others.

Continuous-tone copy consists of images in a variety of tones. One common type of continuous-tone copy is a black-and-white photograph. A black-and-white photograph has tones ranging from white and grey through black.

No printing press can print more than one tone in one ink color from a single printing plate. Thus it is not possible to print all of the tones in a continuous-tone photograph as a

(a)

(b)

Figure 3.28. **Two types of art copy.** Line copy (a) consists entirely of lines and/or dots. Continuous-tone copy (b) consists of shades from white to black and must be converted to a halftone for printing.

range of tones from white to black. To print a black-and-white, continuous-tone photograph, the photo must be converted to a **halftone.** In **halftone conversion,** all of the different tones on the original black-and-white. photograph are converted to dots. The different sizes of these dots gives the illusion of various tones. Many large dots together appear as a darker, black area in print; small dots appear as a lighter, grey area (figure 3.28b). Halftone conversion is explained in detail in chapter 7.

Cropping

Sometimes part of the image on an original photograph or illustration is not wanted on the printed reproduction. Crop marks are used to indicate the part of the original art that is to be reproduced on the printed sheet.

An example of an original illustration is shown in figure 3.29a. The cropped reproduction is shown in figure 3.29b. Crop marks are never drawn on an original. Instead, the original is mounted on a board and the crop marks are drawn on the board near the top, bottom, and sides of the original. Crop marks are also sometimes marked on a tissue overlay. Most designers measure the distance between crop marks in inches.

It is important that crop marks are dense black so that they will reproduce clearly on the film negative. For this reason, crop marks are typically made with a grease pencil, such as a china marker. Once crop marks are recorded on the negative, they provide a reference when stripping for positioning of the cropped image (see chapter 10).

Scaling Art

It is often necessary to enlarge or reduce the size of display type, illustrations, or photographs to fit certain space on the design. Enlargements and reproductions are typically

Figure 3.29.   Crop marks. (a) Crop marks are used to indicate which part of the photograph should be printed. The cropped photograph is shown in (b).

produced photographically, either as negatives, which are assembled with the type image during stripping, or as paper positives, which can be pasted up on a mechanical (see chapter 4). The industry refers to these paper positives as **photostats,** or simply **stats.** The production of stats in the diffusion transfer process is discussed in chapter 6. The process of determining the exact percentage to enlarge or reduce an original is called scaling.

Designers and printers use a **proportion scale** to determine and specify the percentage that the image should be enlarged or reduced. The camera operator sets the camera to reproduce the image at the specified percentage of its original size. To use a proportion scale, first measure an existing dimension (called the original size) of the copy to be enlarged or reduced.

Consider the example in figure 3.30. The line is 5 inches long but it must be reduced to fit an area on the copy that is only 3 1/2 inches long. Locate the original size, 5 inches, on the inside scale of the proportion scale. Then find the desired final measurement, 3 1/2 inches, on the outside scale. Rotate the wheel until the inside measurement (5) lines up with the outside measurement (3 1/2). With the original and final dimensions in line, read the percentage size difference, 71 percent, at the arrow. A stat must be made at a 71 percent reduction to reproduce this image in the correct length.

In **scaling** 100 percent is considered original size. If the example in figure 3.30 were copied at 100 percent, then the stat image would be 5 inches long. A 50 percent reduction would give an image 2 1/2 inches long. In contrast, a 200 percent enlargement would be 10 inches long.

Camera enlargements or reductions alter the size of the copy in two directions, not just in the calculated one. Figure 3.31 illustrates the **diagonal line method** of predicting two-dimensional size changes. To use this method, first affix the art work to be scaled to a drawing board. Then tape a sheet of tracing paper over the copy and draw a rectangle around the edges of the image. Draw a diagonal line from the lower left corner of the rectangle through the upper right corner and continue it across the page. Measure the desired width of the image along the base of the rectangle. From that point draw a vertical line that intersects the diagonal line. The intersection of the two lines defines the new height and width of the scaled copy. The same information can be obtained by reading the proportional scale.

Use of Color

With rare exceptions (such as embossing), all printing creates an image using ink, which is a distinct color. In fact, even a job printed in black is a one-color reproduction. However, when the term "color printing" is used the printer is generally referring to multiple colors on the same sheet. Printing with more than one color is expensive because each color requires an additional printing plate and an additional impression on the printing press. Ink and paper considerations also affect the cost of color printing (see chapter 18).

Printers classify color printing in the following three groups:

■ Fake
■ Flat
■ Process

Figure 3.30. Using a proportion scale. This job requires a size change from 5 inches to 3 1/2 inches. A 71 percent reduction is calculated by aligning the original width (5) on the inside scale with the final size (3 1/2) on the outside scale.

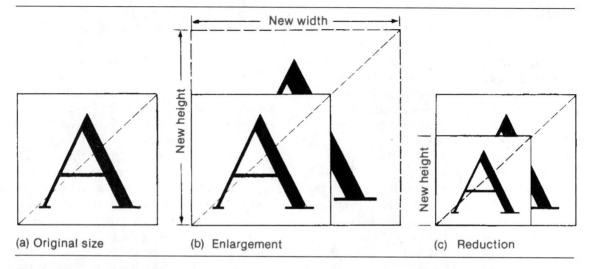

Figure 3.31.   The diagonal line method of scaling. This method can be used to predict the dimensions of the original (a) after enlargement (b) or reduction (c).

Fake Color

A one-color reproduction printed on a colored sheet is known as **fake color.** Any ink color and sheet combination could be used, but the sheet must carry only one layer of ink.

Flat Color

The inks the printer purchases or mixes for a specific job are called **flat colors.** Flat colors can be specified from a color-matching system or hand mixed to match a color submitted by the designer. A color-matching system generally employs a swatchbook with samples of ink colors printed on both coated and uncoated papers (see chapter 18). All colors are numbered, and mixing formulas are included. If the designer specifies a swatchbook number, the printer can easily mix the required color. Hand mixing of colors to match a color sample is a more difficult trial-and-error process.

Process Color

The term **process color** refers to the use of four specific colors—process blue (cyan), process red (magenta), process yellow, and black—

suspended in a translucent vehicle. Because the ink is translucent the pigment colors act as filters and blend to form other colors. **Four-color process printing** is used to reproduce continuous-tone color images, such as color photographs. Chapter 9 discusses the use of four-color process printing to create the illusion of nearly any color on the printed sheet.

Tints, Surprints, Reverses, and Bleeds

An interesting technique for creating the illusion of different tones or color hues with a single color is the use of a **screen tint.** Tints break solid areas into uniform series of dots. The size of the dot is specified as a percentage of the paper area that is covered with ink. A 60% screen tint places dots over 60% of the image area (figure 3.32).

Both **surprints** (often called overprints) and **reverses** are images positioned over another design. Surprints are reproduced as solids; reverses are reproduced as open areas. Both techniques are often used to set words over a picture or an illustration. It is important

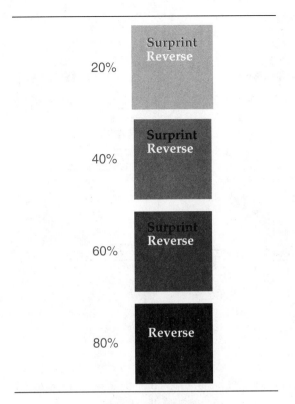

Figure 3.32. **Surprints and reverses shown on selected screen tints.** Note the effect of a dark background, such as an 80% tint, on a surprint.

to consider the density of the background area when deciding whether to use a reverse or a surprint (figure 3.32). A surprint will not show up well in a dark background, and a reverse will not show up well in a light background.

A common printing design technique is to "bleed" an image off the edge of the page. A **bleed** is a design that extends an image to the edge of the printed sheet. The technique is not difficult, but it is often confusing to novice designers. During printing, the bleed edge of an image is actually printed beyond the dimensions of the trim size for the printed sheet. When the printed sheets are trimmed to final size, the part of the bleed that was printed beyond the trim sheet size is cut away, leaving the

image printed to the edge of the trimmed sheet (figure 3.33).

Image Positions on the Printing Plate

Most presses ink printing plates with ink rollers. The rollers pick up ink from a reservoir system, pass over the plate to ink the image areas, then return to the reservoir to re-ink. Halftone images require more ink during printing than does most other type copy. If several halftone images are placed so that they fall in a line at right angles to the ink rollers, it is difficult to obtain uniform ink coverage across the printed sheet.

One common result of improper image placement, particularly on small presses, is ink depletion (figure 3.34). As the ink roller revolves over the sheet, it has enough ink to properly print the first halftone on the lead edge of the sheet, but not enough ink to print the remaining images in line with the halftone on the tail edge of the sheet. The ink becomes depleted from the ink rollers faster than it can be replaced from the ink reservoir. The result is good ink coverage on the lead edge of the sheet, but poor ink coverage on the tail edge of the sheet. Correct image position during the design stage can balance ink distribution needs to avoid ink depletion (figure 3.35).

Design Steps

The primary graphic design task is to produce an image that communicates the customer's desired message to the intended audience. The steps that designers traditionally follow to accomplish this task consist of the following:

1. Prepare a set of thumbnail sketches.
2. Prepare rough layouts based on the preliminary thumbnail sketches.
3. Prepare a comprehensive layout.
4. Prepare a final layout or mechanical.

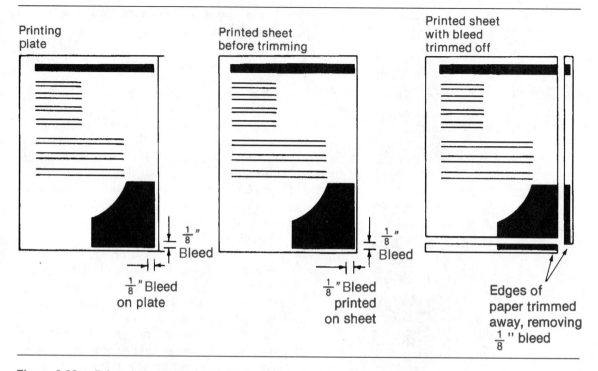

Figure 3.33.   Printed sheet dimensions larger than the bleed image. When a bleed is required, the image is printed beyond the trim size and then trimmed.

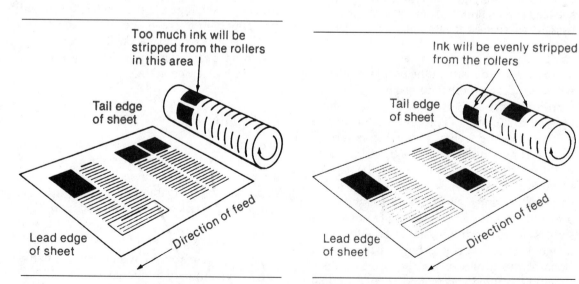

Figure 3.34.   Image position that can result in ink depletion

Figure 3.35.   Image position that will help avoid ink depletion

TYPE AND ILLUSTRATION SPECIFICATIONS
for "Role of the Artist" mailer (inside)

1. ROLE OF THE 18 pt. Spartan Book, caps (all capitals)
2. Artist 30 pt. Brush, C & C.L. (caps and lowercase)
3. Body composition Bodoni & Bodoni Bold, 9 pt.

About the speaker: (Bold) Art's formal preparation in advertising design began with a year at Pratt Institute in Brooklyn. He left Pratt to enter the army in 1952. After completing intelligence school at Fort Riley, he went to Germany with the Second Armored Division. Completing his hitch with the army in 1955, he did design drafting for Oneida Products. In 1956 Art entered Mohawk Valley Technical Institute to further his education in the area of design. He received his AAS degree in 1958 at the top of his class. While attending MVTI, Art completed his work experience program at Canterbury Press and was immediately hired by the company. Concentrating mainly in the art area, he also gained experience in single- and multicolor stripping, specification and production scheduling, estimating and full-service sales. He also became involved in the first phototypesetting establishments in Central New York. While at Canterbury Press Art increased his education by receiving a certificate in Commercial Art and Illustration from the Famous Artist School.

In 1966 Art accepted a position as an artist with Concord Studios, Ltd., of Syracuse—a subsidiary of Midstate Printing Corp. His present responsibilities include the design and preparation of commercial brochures and catalogs.

Supported by his charming wife Sheila, he became active in the Syracuse Club in 1966 and has served as rough proofs editor, table host, treasurer, second and first vice president, president, and currently is chairman of the board of governors.

We are pleased to have a talented, local craftsman make a presentation about a controversial and misunderstood area of our business.

Come witness a verbal and visual presentation of the ROLE OF THE ARTIST in the printing industry. (Bold)

4. EXCELLENT LADIES PROGRAM 9 pt. Bodoni Bold
5. at Raphaels Restaurant, (Bold) Tuesday, February 19, 1974
   State Fair Boulevard, Lakeland, New York
6. COCKTAILS 6:30   DINNER 7:30 (Bold)
7. Hot Buffet Dinner—only $5.00 (Bold)—includes tax and gratuity
   Reservations Please: To your key man or Gene Cook (472–7815)
8. Support Graphic Arts Education
   Cover by H. Rose—Student, Oswego State University
9. Halftone of artist
10. Speaker (Bold, C & L.C.)
    ART LANGE (Bold, Caps)
11. 20% background tint

Figure 3.36.   Provided job copy. Type and illustration specifications for the printer's use are marked on the copy.

To illustrate this process, let us follow each step on a typical printing assignment.

The College of Design Arts at Drexel University wants to promote a gallery opening event. The Director provided the body copy (figure 3.36). Our task is to design a mailer that attracts attention, communicates the feeling of the event, and carries all of the necessary information.

Thumbnail Sketches

The process begins with a series of **thumbnail sketches** (small, quick pencil renderings that show the arrangement of type, line drawings, and white space). They are proportional to, but always smaller than, reproduction size (see figure 3.37). Thumbnails do not necessarily carry the wording that will appear on the final product. Penciled lines are frequently used to indicate type placement. A straightedge is rarely used, and the designer concentrates only on the overall visual effect of the printed piece.

Rough Layouts

A **rough layout** is a detailed expansion of the thumbnail sketch that carries all the necessary

(a)   (b)

Figure 3.37.   Thumbnail sketches

printing information. Any printer should be able to produce the final reproduction from the directions on the rough layout. The rough layout is generally the same size as the final product and contains the actual wording of the piece, margin specifications, image placement for any line drawings or halftone photographs, and type specifications (typefaces and sizes to be used). (If there is a great deal of body copy, typewritten copy is sometimes attached and the rough indicates where it is to be placed after typesetting.) In addition, any special operations, such as folding, trimming, or perforating, to be performed, are indicated on the rough layout. The drawing is done in pencil and may be sketched, but it must be an accurate representation of the final printed sheet.

In our example several decisions were made after the thumbnail sketch was produced. It was judged most economical to produce the job as a single folded and stapled sheet with one side after the fold left blank for the mailing address. The final trim size was to be 4 1/2 inches × 6 1/4 inches. The rough layout for the cover of this job, therefore, was constructed so the image would fill only half of one side of the press sheet (figure 3.38a).

To produce the rough layout, the outline of the paper size to be run through the press was first placed on a clean sheet of white drawing paper. This outline forms the **paper lines.** It was decided to bleed the image off of three edges of the sheet, so **trim lines** were

drawn to represent where the press sheets would be trimmed after the job was printed. (An image is generally allowed to bleed into the trim area from 1/16 inch to 1/8 inch). A line was also drawn to indicate the position for the final fold. The fold line is important for this type of job because it becomes the top image limit for the cover. It must be clearly defined and all art and copy positioned with the fold line as a virtual base.

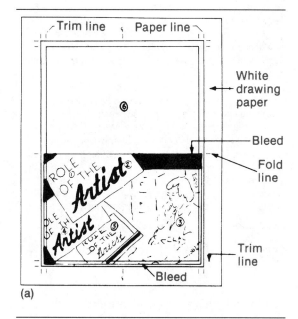

(a)

TYPE AND ILLUSTRATION SPECIFICATIONS for "Role of the Artist" mailer

1. Role of the *36 pt. Spartan Book*
2. Artist *60 pt. Brush*
3. Two-tone posterization of artist
4. Lettering to represent rough layout
5. Lettering to represent thumbnail layout
6. Space for the address

(b)

Figure 3.38.   The rough layout

After all guidelines were positioned, the thumbnail idea was transferred in detail to the rough. The wording was placed on the drawing. Although it is not necessary to duplicate typestyles when forming the rough, it is important to include style and size specifications. The complexity of this cover required numbers to indicate printing instructions and type specifications on a second sheet (figure 3.38b).

All image positions, whether type or illustrations, should be indicated accurately. Photographs are generally sketched in place and the originals are placed in a work envelope with the rough.

In addition to the rough layout, the graphic designer prepares a detailed work sheet for each job (figure 3.39). A work sheet should contain any information that is necessary to print the job.

WORK SHEET FOR "Role of the Artist" mailer
1. Type of stock: Warren, Cameo Dull Cover
2. Weight of stock: Cover 80
3. Color of stock: White
4. Finish of stock: C2S (coated two sides)
5. Basic sheet size: 20 × 26
6. Number of basic size sheets needed: 500
7. Process of production: Offset
8. Finish trim size: 5 5/8 × 7 1/2
9. Ink color: Black
10. Length of run: 4,500
11. Imposition: 1-up
12. Finishing techniques: Score for fold
13. Special processing: Trim

Figure 3.39. Job work sheet. The work sheet contains all printing and materials specifications.

Comprehensives

In most instances the customer approves the rough and the design immediately goes into production. In some cases, however, such as for expensive multicolor jobs, the customer expects to see a comprehensive layout. Most printing customers have had little experience interpreting roughs and are unable to use them to visualize the final product.

A **comprehensive** is an artist's rendering that attempts to duplicate the appearance of the final product. It is drawn to final size and carries no guidelines or printing instructions. In it display type is skillfully hand lettered or shown in a manner that resembles the actual type styles and sizes, and any illustrations are drawn in place. Figure 3.40 shows the comprehensives for the cover and the text of the printing association's meeting.

Many techniques are used to indicate detailed body copy. In figure 3.40, a razor blade was used to shave a pencil point to the x-height of the type, the line spacing was measured ac-

curately, and the lines were drawn with the chiseled pencil to represent body composition. With this method the customer gets an impression of the type weight on the page, yet the artist does not have to spend time hand lettering a great deal of body copy.

Final Layout

If the job is to be produced by hand-set foundry type or by some form of machine hot type composition method, the type form is prepared directly from the rough layout.

If the printing process relies on printing plates produced from film negatives, one or more mechanicals must be produced. The **mechanical** is a camera-ready layout, made from detailed information on the rough. A negative made from the mechanical is used to make the actual printing image. Figure 3.41 shows the camera-ready layout for the sample job. Chapter 4 deals with the process of preparing traditional, hand-produced mechanicals.

(a)

Figure 3.41.   **Camera-ready copy**

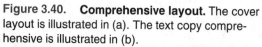

(b)

Figure 3.40.   Comprehensive layout. The cover layout is illustrated in (a). The text copy comprehensive is illustrated in (b).

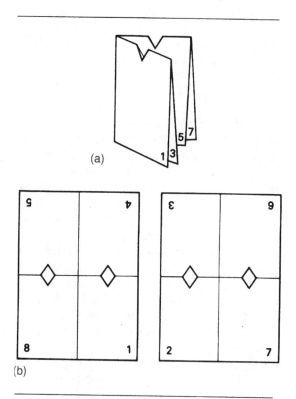

(a)

(b)

Figure 3.42.   Preparing the dummy. (a) The press sheet is folded, numbered, and notched at the top. (b) The opened sheet, which is numbered on the front and on the back, is a guide to correct positioning of the pages.

Dummy

Jobs that are made up of **signatures** formed by folding one or several press sheets can be very confusing in the final layout stage. To simplify the process, a **dummy** is usually prepared. A blank press sheet that is identical in size to the paper that will be used for the job is folded in the order that it will be folded after the press run. The sequence of folds is important and will influence page placement.

Without trimming the folded sheet, the printer numbers each page and cuts a notch through the top of the folds. When the dummy is unfolded, the notch indicates the head of each page and the pages appear in their proper order for the final layout. Figure 3.42 illustrates the dummy preparation process.

Key Terms

balance	text	scaling
formal balance	script	diagonal line method
informal balance	occasional	fake color
subjective balance	typographer	flat color
dominance	type family	process color
unity	point	four-color process printing
typeface	font	screen tint
x-height	copy	surprint
body-height	display type	reverse
ascender	body copy	bleed
descender	pica	thumbnail sketch
stress	copyfitting	rough layout
stroke	continuous-tone copy	paper lines
serifs	halftone	trim lines
fillet	halftone conversion	comprehensive
type style	crop marks	mechanical
Roman	photostats	transfer type
sans serif	stats	dummy
square serif	proportion scale	

Questions for Review

1. Define x-height, ascenders, and descenders.
2. What are the six typeface categories?
3. What can be done to a type family to produce a variation of the family?
4. Define the term "font."
5. What is the difference between display type and body copy?
6. How many points are there in 2 picas? How many picas are there in 252 points?
7. Why is a typeset character actually smaller than its specified point size?

8. Copyfit 15 lines of typewritten copy containing 840 words. The copy is to be set in 10-point Helvetica, which will average 2.62 characters per pica. The copy is to be set 10/12 on a 20-pica line measure.

9. Using a proportion scale, give the percentage reduction needed to reduce a 5 1/2 inch image to 3 1/2 inches.

10. Describe the difference between a halftone and line copy.

11. What are the difference between fake, flat, and process colors?

12. Describe a screen tint, a surprint, a reverse, and a bleed.

13. Thumbnails, roughs, comprehensives, mechanicals, and dummys are all used during image design. Discuss the purpose and preparation of each.

Traditional Cold Type Layout and Paste-Up

Anecdote to Chapter Four

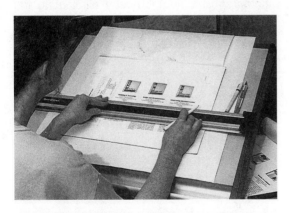

Paste-up artist working at a layout board.
Courtesy of Bill Hurlburt/Maple Glenn, PA.

Before World War II, almost all printing was done with the letterpress process using cast metal type. The growth of offset lithography after World War II forced printers to develop alternative methods of setting type. No longer were all images printed directly from raised metal type. Instead, most images were arranged on a flat paper surface and pho-

tographed to produce a film negative. The negative was then used to produce a printing plate. The name "hot type composition" had been used to describe cast type images, so it seemed natural to give the name "cold type composition" to this new photographic method of producing images.

Cold type composition has several advantages over hot type composition. One major advantage is that artists have far more flexibility and ease in producing images for printing. Almost any two-dimensional image can be photographed and printed. In addition, cold type images can be enlarged, reduced, or cropped without being recast. A second advantage of cold type composition is the speed with which images can be produced. The time-consuming step of casting the image onto a type-high lead body is eliminated with cold type. Finally, cold type makes it possible for printers to greatly expand their type libraries. Heavy type cases and banks of type cabinets have been replaced with computers that can reproduce hundreds of different typefaces at speeds impossible to achieve with cast metal type.

One early method of producing cold type images involved first composing hot type images and then pulling "reproduction proofs" on a special proof press that produced exceptional high-quality images. The reproduction proofs were then pasted up on a piece of paper and photographed to produce the cold type image. As computer-based photocomposition systems became available, however, the reproduction proof process was replaced with more direct methods of cold type image generation.

With the development of cold type composition came a new occupation in the printing industry—paste-up artist. The paste-up artist is responsible for arranging cold type images into proper printing position and pasting them up on a flat surface so that they can be photographed. Early paste-up artists used paper as a base to carry the images. However, it was soon discovered that paper was not stable.

When the temperature or humidity changed, the size of the paper would change, causing a shift or change in image position. This in turn caused registration and alignment problems for the printer, particularly when printing multicolor work. To overcome registration problems, some paste-up artists used plate glass for paste-up. Glass was stable, but it was expensive, awkward, anddifficult to handle. Modern paste-up is done on stiff paperboard or plastic sheets that are specially formulated for dimensional stability.

New developments in electronics have brought about even more changes in layout and paste-up. As you will see in chapter 5, composition systems now exist that allow an artist to electronically compose total pages—including rules, line drawings, halftones, and type—on a computer screen. Once set on the screen, the complete page can be produced as photographic output, thereby eliminating the need for layout and paste-up.

Objectives for Chapter 4

After completing this chapter you will be able to:

- Identify tools and materials for traditional layout and paste-up.
- Identify the three traditional cold type techniques for handling photographs on a paste-up.
- Describe the cold type steps when working from a rough layout.
- Describe the cold type steps for preparing a single-color paste-up.
- Describe procedures for cutting a mask.
- Describe the steps for preparing a multicolor paste-up.
- Describe the steps for preparing a reverse.
- Describe the steps for preparing a surprint.

Introduction

The goal of layout and paste-up is to bring all the different pieces of composition together into a final form that meets job specifications and is of sufficient quality to be reproduced photographically. Printers generally refer to this "camera-ready copy" as a **paste-up** or a **mechanical**.

Technology has radically changed nearly every dimension of printing production, but these changes have been especially dramatic in the preparation of camera-ready copy. This area of printing production has come to be known as prepress technology because so many traditional steps have been eliminated or compressed. **Prepress** is a new term that describes the revolutionary technological changes that have transformed the copy preparation steps traditionally taken prior to reaching the printing press. In general, it refers to computer applications of full-page composition, color separation, and color proofing.

The purpose of this chapter is to introduce the traditional cold type assembly techniques that have been used so successfully by many designers and printers. Understanding these steps and concerns establishes an excellent foundation for learning prepress technologies.

It is important to recognize that the "traditional" cold type process has enjoyed popular industry acceptance only since the late 1960s. One generation can spark a tradition and this is indeed the case with cold type layout and paste-up.

Surfaces and Materials for Layout and Paste-Up

Paste-Up Surfaces

There are two types of paste-up surfaces generally used to assemble cold type images:

- Drafting board
- Light table

The least expensive paste-up surface is the common **drafting board** (figure 4.1). The surface is usually set at an angle to eliminate light reflection from the paper or from the board and

Figure 4.1.   Drafting board. A drafting board is an inexpensive paste-up surface.
Courtesy of Foster Manufacturing Co.

to reduce back strain for the paste-up artist. Many companies cover the wooden drafting board with thick, coated paper or with a special adhesive-backed plastic. Any surface is acceptable as long as it is flat and smooth and its edges are perfectly straight.

The second type of paste-up surface is a **light table** (figure 4.2). Light tables are used during stripping to bring pieces of transparent

Figure 4.2.   Light table. A light table is also used for paste-up.
Courtesy of Foster Manufacturing Co.

film together (see chapter 10). A light table is made from a sheet of glass with a diffusion sheet beneath it. Light shines up through the glass from beneath the diffusion sheet. The main advantage of the glass is that it is hard and is not damaged when pieces of copy are trimmed with a razor blade or an X-ACTO® knife. With a light table it is possible to see through most layout paper. When preprinted layout sheets are used, it is possible to see through the copy to line up images with the printed guidelines.

Paste-Up Materials

Paste-Up Board

The industry uses several different materials for paste-up board. The most stable and most expensive material is called **illustration board.** Different manufacturers use their trade names for illustration board, but their products all have the same general characteristics. Illustration board is smooth, white, and has a finish that allows inked lines to be ruled without feathering. **Feathering** is the tendency of ink to spread on a rough, porous surface. This is undesirable because lines of uneven weight result. Illustration board is formed by laminating layers of board stock and paper. It is a thick, strong material that is not easily damaged with handling.

While many people in the printing industry use 110-pound index paper or heavier material for paste-up, an increasingly common paste-up material is 60- or 70-pound **offset paper.** The pound measure refers to paper weight and is a general description of paper thickness (see chapter 18). Sixty- or 70-pound paper is thinner than the stock used for business cards but is thicker than most office typing paper.

Companies with jobs that have the same column or page size, such as newspapers, usually print guidelines on offset paper to receive the paste-up. With **preprinted paste-up sheets,** the layout artist does not have to draw guidelines for every job.

Offset paper is a popular paste-up board material because it is inexpensive and can be used on a light table. Using preprinted sheets with a light table usually cuts labor costs because paste-ups can be produced very rapidly.

Polyester sheets or **acetate** (plastic) **sheets** are yet another type of paste-up material. Some clear sheets are used, but the most common ones have frosted surfaces. These stable-base sheets are used mainly as overlays to carry images for a second color.

A **stable-base sheet** does not change size with moderate changes in temperature and humidity. Dimensional stability is very important with jobs involving the register of two or more colors or with work that requires critical size tolerances. The Uniform Product Code (UPC) is an example of an image that must be held to exact size specifications (figure 4.3). Of the three major paste-up materials, illustration board and polyester sheets are the most stable.

Paste-Up Tools

Most tools used for layout and paste-up are common pieces of artist or drafting equipment. The three most basic tools are a **T-square,** a

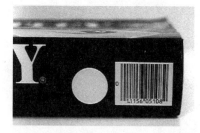

Figure 4.3. Printing the Uniform Product Code (UPC). Printing this code imposes critical size tolerances on the printer because variations in code bar thickness result in inaccurate readings at the cash register.
Courtesy of Bill Hurlburt/Maple Glenn, PA.

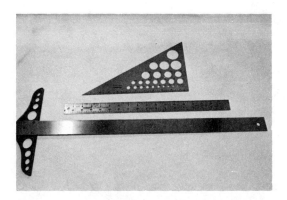

Figure 4.4. Three basic layout and paste-up tools. T-squares, triangles, and rulers are available in various lengths in both plastic and steel.
Courtesy of Bill Hurlburt/Maple Glenn, PA.

Figure 4.5. Cutting tools. X-ACTO® knives (or other stick-type cutters) and single-edge razor blades are commonly used to cut pieces of art. The blades should be replaced often to ensure clean, smooth edges.
Courtesy of Bill Hurlburt/Maple Glenn, PA.

triangle, and a **ruler** (figure 4.4). Both plastic and steel tools are commonly used. Plastic edges are easy to look through when positioning lines of type, but they are easily damaged. This is a special problem when the tools are used for ruling. A nick in a plastic edge can ruin a carefully inked line. A plastic edge should never be used as a guide for cutting. Steel tools are more expensive than plastic but are nearly indestructible under normal use. Layout rulers come with both English units (inch) and printer's units (pica).

Several different types of cutting tools are used by the paste-up artist. **X-ACTO® knives** and **single-edge razor blades** are the two most common handheld cutting tools (figure 4.5). It is always best to hold these blades as low as possible when cutting paper. This technique shears rather than stabs the paper and prevents the sheet from ripping or wrinkling. Rapid cuts can be made with a small table-model **guillotine cutter** (figure 4.6). This device is well-named—extreme caution should be taken to keep fingers away from the cutting edge and blade.

Adhesive tape is used to hold both the board and the overlay material in place during paste-up. Designers commonly use masking tape, clear cellophane tape, and white tape for this purpose. Masking tape is used to secure the board to the working surface. Cellophane tape is used to tape clear plastic sheets in place. White tape is often used to hold large pieces of copy to the paste-up board.

Burnishers are used in the layout room to adhere dry-transfer images or small pieces of pressure-sensitive materials to the paste-up board. Burnishers come in several different shapes (figure 4.7). Ball-pointed burnishers can be purchased in many styles. Some burnishers are spring loaded so uniform pressure can be applied to any surface. Straight burnishers are also available, but they are not as popular as the ball-pointed type.

Part of the layout artist's job is to add layout and image lines to the paste-up. All guidelines not intended to print are drawn with a

Figure 4.6.   A table-model guillotine cutter

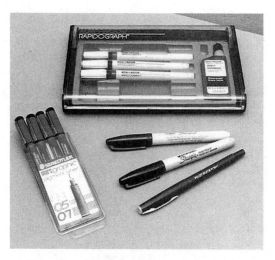

Figure 4.8.   Technical and felt-tip pens. Two devices used to create dense black lines on a paste-up are (left) technical pens and (right) reproduction-quality felt-tip pens.
Courtesy of Bill Hurlburt/Maple Glenn, PA.

light blue (nonrepro) pencil or pen. These light blue lines on the layout are not recorded on the film used to make the negative for the printing plate. Special pens are used for lines that should be recorded on the film, such as trim lines or fold marks (figure 4.8). The most common tool of this type is a technical pen with black **India ink**. India ink is especially dense and forms perfect film images. A tool gaining wide acceptance is called a reproquality (reproduction-quality) disposable drawing pen. This inexpensive, felt-tip pen is available in a variety of line widths. Most ballpoint or office-grade felt-tip pens are not acceptable for paste-up work.

Paste-Up Adhesives

The term "copy" is commonly used in the layout room. Recall from chapter 3 that this term is used in the graphic arts to describe a wide range of materials. In this chapter "copy" refers to the pieces of art and type that are applied to the paste-up.

The main goal in traditional cold type paste-up is to adhere different pieces of copy to the paste-up board in the proper printing positions for a specific job. Several different adhesives can be used to hold the images in place.

A **wax coater** (figure 4.9) is a device designed to place a uniform layer of wax material on one side of a sheet of paper. The piece of paper to be coated is placed image up on the feeder side of the machine. As the sheet pushes against the drive rollers, it is drawn through the device and against the wax drum. After the pieces of paper are coated, they may be laid aside and used at any time. The advantage of

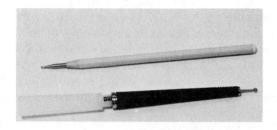

Figure 4.7.   Two types of burnishers

using a wax coater is that the adhesive can be pushed into place on the paste-up and then removed for repositioning any number of times. The adhesive continues to work as long as it remains free of lint and dirt and does not dry out. The wax coating does dry eventually, but its useful life is several weeks, well beyond normal paste-up time requirements.

Rubber cement is an inexpensive adhesive that is applied wet to the back of copy. To use rubber cement, place the copy image down on a sheet of scrap paper and, with a small brush, carefully cover the back of the copy with the adhesive. Be sure the copy does not shift and that no thick areas of cement remain on the sheet. The drying time of rubber cement is short so a cemented sheet must be used immediately.

It is not easy to remove images that have been adhered with rubber cement. The liquid is also messy. The wet cement sometimes creeps out around the edges of the paper. As it dries, it tends to pick up dirt that can form an image when the paste-up is photographed. If this happens, remember it is easier to remove excess rubber cement when it is dry than when it is wet. Use a soft eraser to rub the area of dried cement away from the paste-up.

Some designers use tube and/or stick adhesives to mount copy on the paste-up. These are available in a variety of forms. Most, however, are applied by coating the back of the paper with a liquid or paste that dries rapidly. Before purchasing, care should be taken to read the product directions and specifications. For example, one brand specifies that for permanent mounting the copy should be applied while the adhesive is wet. If the adhesive is allowed to dry before mounting, then the copy can be positioned, removed, and attached again, like a wax coating. Of course, reading labels is a must for everything you use. In this case it makes a popular consumer product

which is intended for mounting photographs in an album ideal for cold type paste-up.

Types of Art

Jobs with images for paste-up come to the layout room in several forms. As mentioned in chapter 3, **line work** (such as type, ink drawings, and clip art) and **continuous-tone photographs** are the two most common sorts of images (figure 4.10). Most paste-up jobs have black images on an opaque paper base. **Opaque** means that under normal viewing it is not possible to see through the sheet. You can read the words on this page without seeing the type on the other side of the sheet because the paper is opaque.

Clip art is camera-ready material, usually line art, that is purchased by printers and designers in forms ready for paste-up. The label "clip art" comes from the way it is used. Clip art was first only available in printed form. A large sheet would hold many images and when an image was needed it was simply

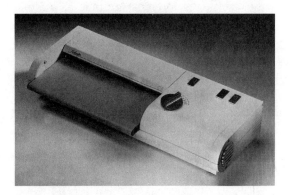

Figure 4.9. A wax coater. The drive roller pulls the paper through the wax in the wax coater.
Courtesy of Schafer Machine Company, Inc.

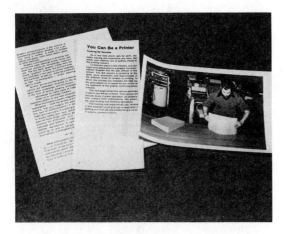

Figure 4.10.   Paste-up copy. The copy for paste-up is either line work or continuous-tone photographs.

cut out using a scissors and pasted to a mechanical. Today, clip art is available on disk or CD-ROM and can be "cut and pasted" into a variety of computer application programs.

Jobs sometimes arrive with images on a transparent base. **Transparent-based images** can be seen through the backing sheet. The images themselves might be black, red, or green. Both green and red reproduce the same way black does for most graphic arts films. These images are typically used for multicolor work.

Working with Photographs

Many jobs include photographs. Because most printing processes cannot directly reproduce continuous-tone images it is necessary to adapt the mechanical. There are three basic ways for the layout artist to handle photographs at this stage:

- Use prescreened halftones
- Form a window on the negative
- Draw holding lines

Prescreened Halftones

The idea of halftones is discussed in great detail in chapter 7. Basically, halftones are continuous-tone images that have been converted to dots. Dense, black areas of the halftone have large dots; light areas have small dots. The resulting image tricks the human eye into thinking it sees continuous tones.

It is possible to prepare an opaque halftone that can be pasted onto the mechanical and rephotographed with the rest of the job as line copy. This is called a **prescreened halftone** (figure 4.11). They are sometimes called **stats** or **photostats**. However, the terms can be used for normal line copy that has been

ut
rb
sn
tr
yh
id
vii
yg

eu
tr
ig
yg
ot
yg
sb
gh
y

Benson Franklin Faux
Agyrt skk vinoiduyuib gsd nrrb syysvgrf y frdutsnkr yi otivbufr frysukrf otubyubh ubdy ib ygr osdyr-yu. Ydyskktm s dgrry ig ytsvubh

Figure 4.11.   A prescreened print pasted on a mechanical. Random letters are used here to visualize copy applied to a typical job.

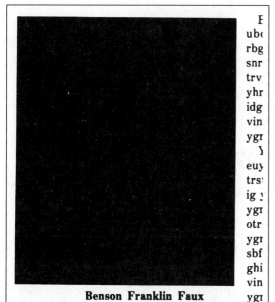

Benson Franklin Faux
Agyrt skk vinoiduyuib gsd nrrb syysvgrf yi frdutsnkr yi otivbufr frysukrf otubyubh ubdty ib ygr osdyr-yu. Ydyskktm s dgrry ig ytsvubh o

Figure 4.12. A blockout on a mechanical. When this layout is photographed, the black area will appear on the negative as a clear rectangle window into which the halftone negative will be positioned.

enlarged or reduced photographically on a paper base.

Windows on the Negative

The second way to handle photographs is to create a **window** on the negative. This is achieved by adhering a layer of red or black material, sometimes called a "blockout," to the area on the paste-up where the photograph is to appear in the final reproduction (figure 4.12). When the layout is photographed, the black or red blockout forms a clear area (a window) on the negative. A halftone negative can

then be attached under the window during stripping prior to making a printing plate (see chapter 10).

Black acetate may also be used to create a window, but the most common material is translucent red. It is possible to see guidelines through the red material and, therefore, to make a more accurate cut.

Holding Lines

The last way to handle photographs on the mechanical is to draw holding lines (figure 4.13). **Holding lines** can be simple corner marks or bold inked lines that act as a border on the final reproduction. Holding lines act as a guide

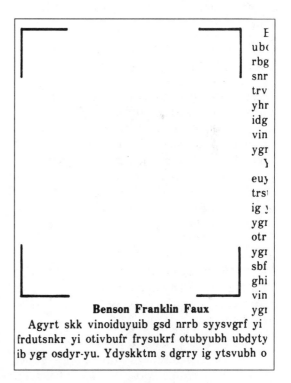

Benson Franklin Faux
Agyrt skk vinoiduyuib gsd nrrb syysvgrf yi frdutsnkr yi otivbufr frysukrf otubyubh ubdty ib ygr osdyr-yu. Ydyskktm s dgrry ig ytsvubh o

Figure 4.13. Holding lines drawn on a mechanical. These lines serve as a guide in the placement of the halftone negative.

for hand cutting windows from mechanical masking film or for positioning a halftone negative during stripping when film images are positioned together on a light table. This technique is used only when multiple flats are used during stripping (see chapter 10).

Working from the Rough Layout

The **rough layout** is the detailed guide used to identify and position every piece of art on the paste-up. Recall from chapter 3 that the rough is a sort of "floor plan" that predicts and describes the final product. It should contain all the information necessary to produce the job. Unless the final product satisfies the customer all effort is pointless. "Redo" jobs lose money for the company.

Reviewing Instructions

The first step in beginning any paste-up job is to examine the work order, special instructions, and rough layout. The goal of this step is to understand exactly the customer's expectations. Everything in the job jacket should be thoroughly understood.

The job jacket should contain several categories of information. The five most common are the following:

- Type content and specifications (such as size and style)
- Final product dimensions
- Image positions for all elements
- Finishing operations (such as folding, trimming, scoring, or perforating)
- Press specifications (including paper length of run, imposition, and ink color)

The layout artist must consider every part of the rough in addition to considering im-age positions. For example, if finishing operations such as folding and trimming are indicated on the rough, then lines that can be used in the bindery as guides for the finishing operation must be added to the paste-up. If the layout department forgets to add these lines, major problems may occur later in the production process.

The sequence of paste-up operations can vary depending on job requirements. The ability to read a rough and anticipate the order of steps is important. This ability is developed with experience.

Checking for Completeness

After reviewing the job instructions, it is important to ensure that all necessary pieces are in the job jacket. It is frustrating and costly to begin paste-up and discover that one piece of copy is missing when nearing completion. It is difficult and confusing to remove the job from the layout board, set it aside, and begin another job while waiting for the missing copy.

In addition to checking for all pieces it is also important to check the composition against the rough layout. Check that all type composition is complete and in camera-ready form. Examine the artwork and review each piece. Measure each piece and determine if enlargements or reductions are necessary.

Before beginning any work on the paste-up, make sure that everything is ready. Be sure that all instructions are clear and understood. A few minutes' delay at this point prevents problems later on.

Trimming the Copy

The last step before beginning the paste-up is to trim all pieces of art copy and type galleys to workable sizes. Use a razor or an X-ACTO® knife with a steel ruler to trim each piece to within 1/4 inch to 1/2 inch of the image size. It is better not to use a guillotine paper cutter for this operation because it is easy to make a mistake and cut through an image.

When trimming copy, always place the ruler over the nonimage area rather than over the copy. The back side of the metal might scratch a photograph or a type character. The ruler also has a tendency to carry dirt which can spot the copy. If the amount of trim is too small to support the ruler, place a piece of clean scrap paper under the ruler and over the image.

When all copy has been trimmed to size, place the pieces of copy on the layout table in the positions in which they will appear on the paste-up. This step saves time and prevents confusion. Some layout artists wax coat each piece before trimming. The hot wax has a tendency to flow over the edge of the paper, however. If enough wax becomes attached to the edge, it picks up dirt when mounted on the board and photographs as a line. Coating before trimming tends to eliminate this problem.

Preparing a Single-Color Paste-Up

Novice layout artists should begin to develop paste-up skills by working on simple, single-color jobs. Basic layout skills should be developed before attempting multicolor work or single-color jobs that require overlays. The purpose of this section is to review basic paste-up procedures. More sophisticated techniques are discussed in the following sections.

Mounting the Paste-Up Board

The first step is to select and mount the paste-up board on the layout table. If preprinted sheets are used, then the selection process is simple. If illustration board, offset paper, or a plastic sheet is used, then the material must be cut to size. Cut a piece that is slightly larger

than the press paper size. A good approach is to cut the board at least 1 inch larger in each dimension than the press sheet. For example, if the press sheet size is to be 8 1/2 inches × 11 inches, then cut the paste-up board at least 9 1/2 inches × 12 inches. Board that is a great deal larger than the job dimensions is cumbersome. A very large board is sometimes impossible to position on the graphic arts camera and is also difficult to store when the job is finished.

Be sure the layout table is clean and free of spots of rubber cement or dirt. Position the board near the head of the T-square to the left side of the layout surface if you are right-handed, to the right side if you are left-handed (figure 4.14). The position of the T-square is important because the blade of a T-square is more stable when it is close to the head than when it is out near the end of the blade. This arrangement also allows space to lay the rough and pieces of copy within easy reach. If a preprinted layout sheet is used, then position the sheet so the guidelines are in line with the T-square edge.

When the board is in position, secure it to the table with pieces of masking tape at each

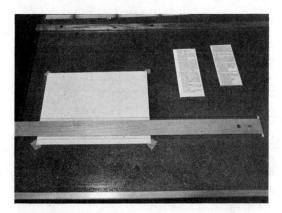

Figure 4.14. Position of the layout board and the head of the T-square. This position of the board and the head of the T-square on the left of the table is correct for a right-handed person.

corner. It is important that the paste-up board does not shift during paste-up. If the board moves in the middle of the job, then the elements will be crooked and unacceptable to the customer.

Adding Layout Lines

The next step in the paste-up process is to add layout lines to the paste-up board (figure 4.15). Preprinted layout sheets already have layout lines. When working with blank board, it is necessary to add layout lines. Begin by drawing light **center lines** for each dimension. Next add **paper lines.** Carefully measure the dimensions of the press sheet and position the paper lines the proper distances from the center lines as specified on the job ticket. Paper lines should be drawn in light blue pencil because they are not intended to print. Nonprint (nonrepro) blue lines are used by the layout artist as a guide and are not needed after the paste-up is finished.

Now add any **fold lines.** These are also drawn in light blue pencil and appear as dashed lines. Small fold lines are sometimes drawn in black on the edge of the paper dimensions as a guide for the bindery. Use India ink or a repro felt-tip pen to make fold lines on the board. These fold lines will print but are usually cut away when the job is trimmed to final size.

If the job is to be trimmed, then small black **trim lines** should be placed on the board. Trim lines are used by the paper cutter to cut the final job accurately to the desired size. Trim lines are cut away during the operation and do not appear on the sheets delivered to the customer. The lines must, however, appear on the press sheet and are therefore added to the paste-up in black ink.

Image guidelines are added to the paste-up in nonrepro blue. These lines are used by the layout artist to position pieces of copy. Measure in from the paper lines to define the

Figure 4.15.   Adding layout lines to the board. Using a triangle and a T-square, draw the dimensions of the press sheet in light-blue pencil so that the rectangle formed is centered on the layout board. Fold lines are drawn in light-blue pencil, but small black marks are added at the edge of the sheet as guides for the bindery. Trim lines must be added if the job is to be trimmed during the finishing operation. Image guidelines are drawn in nonrepro blue and are used as guides to position the copy.

image margins (sometimes called the image extremes). Always follow the specifications listed on the rough. Then add any special measurements to position the different elements of the job. If a headline is to appear a certain distance from the top of the sheet, draw a blue line to indicate its position. Do the same for the positions of all pieces of art.

Figure 4.15 shows one part of a mechanical with appropriate guidelines. Of course, blue lines do not reproduce photographically and would not normally appear.

Attaching the Copy

To attach copy, begin mounting the copy at the top of the sheet and work downward. Moving the T-square over the copy can smudge or scratch the copy. By beginning to attach copy

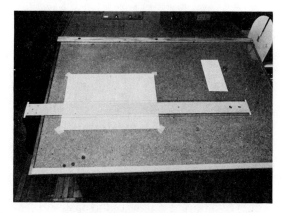

Figure 4.16.   Positioning the copy. Use the plastic edge of the T-square to position and straighten each piece of copy.

Figure 4.17.   Using a cover sheet. A cover sheet is used to protect the finished paste-up and to specify directions for the camera operator or the stripper.

from the top, each piece is positioned and then not touched again. Use blue image guidelines to position each piece. Use the plastic edge of the T-square to ensure that each piece is straight (figure 4.16). It is also wise to check image position with a triangle to make sure that both horizontal and vertical dimensions are straight and line up perfectly with all other pieces.

If the sheet has a wax coating, gently position the sheet and use the point of an X-ACTO® knife to shift it into position. Slight pressure against the T-square will then secure it in place. After checking the vertical edge of the sheet with a triangle, the sheet can be lifted and repositioned if necessary.

Some layout artists use a rubber roller to attach the copy firmly to the board. To use this technique, place a piece of clean paper over the image and move the roller firmly against the surface of the paper. The paper keeps the image clean and ensures that it will not be scratched during the operation.

The process of checking the alignment of each piece and pressing into place is used for all job elements. After each piece is positioned, carefully check its placement by referring to the rough layout.

Some layout artists add a cover sheet to protect the art (figure 4.17). Cut a piece of tissue or cover paper to the size of the layout board, but add 1 inch to the hinge. Fold the sheet at the 1-inch point and slide it over the board. Tape it on the back side of the paste-up board with masking tape. Write any directions from the rough that are important for the darkroom or stripping tasks directly on the cover sheet.

Cutting Masks

A **mask** is material that blocks light. The most common masking material used in layout is red masking film. This type of film is not light sensitive, but it does have a thick emulsion that can be cut away with a razor blade or knife to leave a clear plastic support sheet.

Masks are commonly used to cut halftone windows, to create open areas for screen tints, to drop out areas around photographs, and to create special overlay images.

To prepare a mask, cut a piece of masking film larger than the image dimensions of the

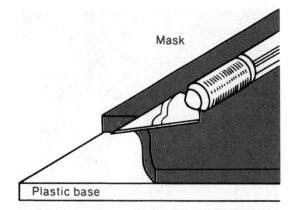

Figure 4.18. **Cutting masking material.** Cut through the emulsion layer, but not through the plastic support sheet.

job. Use an X-ACTO® knife or another sharp instrument to cut through the emulsion layer, but do not cut through the plastic base (figure 4.18). To make a shear cut, keep the blade angle low. Always cut to the center of any image line. With this technique, images overlap and "fit" together well.

After an area has been cut out and the mask has been positioned over the image, stab the emulsion layer with the point of the knife. By gently lifting the knife point, the unneeded portion of the emulsion layer can be lifted away.

After the mask is cut it can be positioned over the layout to meet job specifications. The mask is always positioned with the emulsion layer up and is taped along one edge so it can be hinged back out of the way.

Preparing a Multicolor Paste-Up

Multicolor jobs are more complex than single-color jobs but they do not need to be more difficult. In the simplest multicolor job a single-color paste-up might be converted to a two-color paste-up by specifying on the overlay that one portion of the image print in black ink and another portion print in red. As with single-color work, every multicolor job begins by setting up the paste-up board. Draw the paper lines, fold lines, and image guidelines in nonrepro blue. Place all image guidelines for each color on the same paste-up sheet. Add trim or fold marks for the finishing room in black India ink or in repro felt-tip pen.

The production process now follows the artist's directions. There are several methods of stripping this job. With one the photographer shoots two film negatives of the paste-up. The stripper then prepares two separate flats and unwanted images are simply masked out (see chapter 10). Another method is to make only one negative. During stripping masks are cut that flip back and forth to cover or uncover images. The platemaker then follows the stripper's directions to prepare two separate printing plates. These procedures are discussed in more detail in chapter 10.

Adding Register Marks

For multicolor work it is necessary to add **register marks** (figure 4.19). Register marks can be purchased commercially on pressure-sensitive tape or they can be created with a black lay-out pen.

Register marks help the press operator align one color over another in perfect register. On single-color presses, one color of a multicolor job is printed first. The paper is then returned to the press, and another color is printed. The operator adjusts the paper or printing plate so the register marks from the second color print precisely over those from the first.

A minimum of three register marks should be placed on the board to ensure good registration. Register marks should always be placed in areas that will be trimmed off after the job is finished. Some companies prefer to place register marks in the image area and to then remove them from the plate after the

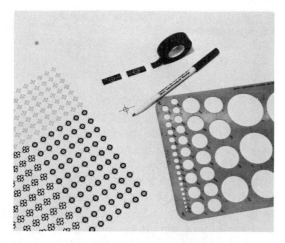

Figure 4.19.   Register marks. Register marks can be purchased in pressure-sensitive or preprinted form, or they can be created by hand with a black ruling pen.

Figure 4.20.   Adding the color overlay. Hinge a piece of plastic over the board to receive the second set of images. Be sure to cut away the areas over the register marks.

first sheets have been checked for register. Always follow shop guidelines when placing register marks.

Working with an Overlay

Position the first set of images using normal single-color procedures. Check to ensure that all pieces are straight and firmly attached. Most two-color jobs use black and some other color. Most layout artists place the color used to create the greatest number of images or to cover the greatest surface area on the illustration board or base sheet. This color is usually black.

The second-color images are placed on a special **overlay sheet.** Place a piece of clear or frosted plastic over the paste-up board. Tape one edge of the plastic sheet in several places to create a hinge (figure 4.20). It should be possible to look through the plastic sheet and see the blue pencil image guidelines for the second set of images.

Mount each piece of copy on the overlay as is done with paste-up board material.

Use rubber cement, a wax coater, or dry adhesives. Use the guidelines on the board to make sure the new images are in their proper positions and are aligned with the first images (figure 4.21).

Figure 4.21.   Mounting the second-color copy. Following the image guidelines on the first sheet, affix the second set of images to the overlay sheet.

When the camera room photographs the paste-up, two separate pieces of film are used. The first piece of film is taken of the board paste-up with the overlay hinged back out of the way. The second piece of film is taken when the overlay is hinged back and a white piece of paper is placed between the board and overlay. If the register marks can be seen clearly, they will be recorded on both pieces of film. Because the marks are in identical positions for both exposures, they will appear in the same position on both negatives. They will then appear in the correct position on two printing plates and can be used on the press to check fit, which means alignment of one image to another.

Again, check both the board and the overlay to make sure that all copy is in the correct position, is straight, and is tightly bonded, and that the whole area is free of dirt or scratches. After the tissue or cover sheet has been added, the job is ready to be sent to the camera room.

This technique can be used for three- and four-color jobs or for work that uses an overlay for several different screen tints. For each additional color, another overlay is hinged from an edge of the board.

Preparing Reverses and Surprints

Many jobs require the use of reverses or surprints to create a special image or effect. Paste-up techniques for reverses and surprints are similar.

Reverses

A **reverse** is a recognizable image created by the absence of a printed image (see figure 3.2 in chapter 3). Copy preparation for a reverse involves the following three steps (figure 4.22):

1. Paste-up
2. Film positive
3. Stripping assembly

First, the desired reverse image is prepared as if it were a normal one-color paste-up. Black or red copy is positioned on the board in the desired printing position. Second, the paste-up is sent to the camera room to be produced as a film positive. The film positive blocks the image area and creates the desired reverse image. The third step is done during stripping, when the pieces of film are assembled for plate making (see chapter 10). From directions specified by the layout artist, the film positive is positioned over another image, usually a film negative. If light passes through both the positive and the negative to the plate, the positive creates a reverse image.

Another way to prepare a reverse is with red masking film. It is possible to cut a design by hand and then use the mask in the stripping operation. The technique chosen depends on the type of image being reversed. If the image can be cut easily by hand, the masking-film method is acceptable. Reverses that involve type or special designs with complex images require the paste-up technique.

Surprints

A **surprint** is an image that is printed over another image. Surprints are commonly used to print dark type over a light area of a halftone photograph or a screen tint. The technique used to prepare a surprint is similar to that used to prepare a two-color paste-up using an overlay.

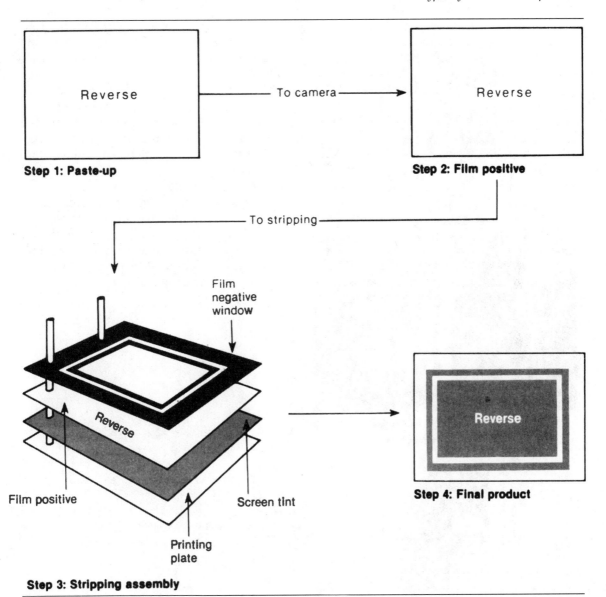

Figure 4.22. Preparing reverse copy for printing. A reverse is a recognizable image created by the absence of a printed image. In this example, a screen tint is used with a film negative window to create the reverse image.

Paste-up with overlay
and register marks

Film negative of base

Film negative of overlay

When a surprint is prepared, the base image (usually a photograph) is mounted on the paste-up board, and the surprint image (usually type) is positioned on the overlay sheet. The camera room prepares separate film images and sends the job to the stripper. Two separate exposures—the first is the base image and the second is the surprint image—are used to prepare the printing plate. These images are combined to form one image on the final printed sheet (figure 4.23).

Another method of surprint preparation is to use a clear plastic overlay sheet to hold the characters. When the job goes to the camera room, it is shot as one halftone. The first method of using separate exposures, however, is preferred because it makes a denser surprint on the final press sheets.

Final printed sheet

Figure 4.23. **Preparing surprint copy for printing.** A surprint is an image that is printed over another image. In a single-color surprint the two film negatives are exposed separately to the printing plate.

Key Terms

paste-up
mechanical
prepress
drafting board
light table
illustration board
feathering
offset paper
preprinted paste-up sheets
polyester sheet
acetate sheet
T-square
triangle
ruler

X-ACTO knife®
single-edge razor blades
guillotine cutter
burnishers
India ink
opaque
line work
continuous-tone photographs
clip art
transparent-based images
wax coater
prescreened halftone
stats
photostats

window
holding lines
rough layout
center lines
paper lines
fold lines
trim lines
image guidelines
mask
register marks
overlay sheet
reverse
surprint

Questions for Review

1. What are the three types of table surfaces used for traditional cold type paste-up?
2. What are three common paste-up board materials?
3. What is a burnisher?
4. What does the term "opaque" mean?
5. What are the two most common types of images in paste-up?
6. What is the purpose of a wax coater?
7. Why is a blockout used on a paste-up to produce a window?
8. Why is nonrepro blue used for paper lines, fold lines, and image guidelines?
9. What is the purpose of trim marks on a paste-up?
10. What is a mask?
11. When are register marks used?
12. What is the purpose of an overlay?
13. What is a reverse? A surprint?

Digital Imaging— Basic Understandings

Anecdote to Chapter Five

The introduction of the first successful typewriter—then·called a writing machine—in the fall of 1867 began a series of important changes in this country and in the world. The typewriter contributed to a revolution in the printing industry. What is considered a commonplace printing tool today was feared by printers of the 1800s.

Christopher Sholes and several associates built the first successful typewriter in Milwaukee in the summer of 1867. Sholes began as a printer's apprentice and later became a successful editor and publisher. By the time he perfected the first typewriter, Sholes had already invented several other machines that had impacted the printing industry. One was the automatic labeling-pasting machine that was the forerunner of the high-speed machines used today to address newspapers, magazines, and envelopes for bulk mailing. Another example of Sholes's inventions was a machine that could be mounted in a press to automatically number successive press sheets.

The first typewriter was a cumbersome tool that "typed" under the page. As a result, the typist could not see what had been produced until the sheet was removed from the machine. In addition, only thin tissue paper could be used because the characters, or keys, hit the paper from the back and pushed the sheet against a piece of carbon paper to form the image.

One of the first persons to purchase a commercially manufactured typewriter was printer-author Mark Twain (Samuel Clemens). Despite the typewriter's disadvantages, Twain thought it was a marvelous device, and he preferred it to handwriting. He managed to reach a typing speed of twelve words per minute.

The typewriter was not well received by all printers when it first entered the business world, however. Before the typewriter, all letters were handwritten. If more than two or three copies of a letter were required, such as by a law office or by the courts, a printer would hand set the job and make copies on a printing press. Printers feared that the typewriter would take over much of their work. In 1885, the *Inland Printer* of New York City wrote that the time might come when each printing office

An early writing machine.
Smithsonian Institution, photo No. 38–785F

would have a typewriting machine and could execute jobs on it as well as on any other printing apparatus. By the early 1900s the typewriter was so popular that several type founders cut typefaces that duplicated typewriter copy. With these typefaces, jobs could be run on the press but they would look as if they were typewritten.

High-quality typewriters that could produce dense, consistent images were once used with photography for cold type composition. Printers could "set type" by typing on a piece of paper, photographing the sheet, and transferring the image to a printing plate—all without touching a type case. Later developments in computers teamed the typewriter keyboard with photographic output in a process known as phototypesetting. The typewriter keyboard is now an important part of almost every type composition device.

Objectives for Chapter 5

After completing this chapter you will be able to:

- Discuss the major components of a computer system and explain the difference between hardware and software.

- List and describe the major classifications of computers.

- Explain the concept of digital data.

- Describe the difference between raster and vector images.

■ Discuss scanner operation and outline the scanner types.

■ Discuss CD-ROM.

■ Describe the basic concepts of image capture.

■ Discuss the procedures involved in still video photography and digital photography.

Introduction

The printing industry has undergone a revolution in the past decade. Traditional hand methods of preparing images—whether type, line drawings, or continuous-tone images—are being replaced rapidly by digital technology. The computer has become the printer's fundamental tool.

The primary advantage of generating images by computer is speed. Foundry type can be composed by a "quick" (a skilled compositor) at the average rate of 4 characters per minute. Line-casting hot type machines average 6 characters per second (CPS). An expert typist on a good day can generate 8 CPS (100 words per minute). A typical computer composition system, however, can typeset well over 1,000 CPS. Some systems can typeset over 64,000 CPS.

The computer as a prepress tool has moved far beyond basic typesetting. It can generate, manipulate, edit, and output nearly any form of monochrome or color image. It can be used to assemble full pages of type and graphic images. It can separate complex images into primary colors. It can scan and digitize type (see Concept of Digital Information, p. 99) and images prepared by hand. It can receive information from a satellite thousands of miles away or by telephone line. It can track the work in progress, compile work standards, and deliver data that was impossible to gather and monitor even a decade ago.

Chapters 5 and 8 deal with digital imaging technology. This book is not intended to provide details on the operation of any specific system or device. Manufacturers supply detailed operating procedures for their equip-

ment. If such information were included here it would be hopelessly out of date before this book was even off the press. The rate of technological change and improvement is simply too fast to do so. It is possible, however, to provide a general understanding about how digital imaging systems operate and to describe some of the functions that they can perform. This general understanding may make the manufacturer's documentation easier to follow and to apply.

Computer Operation

To understand digital imaging, you must have some understanding about how computers operate. A computer is basically an adding machine that can add and subtract at very rapid speeds. Much has been said about how simple computers are, but they are actually quite complex.

Components of a Computer System

Hardware and Software

A basic computer system is made up of hardware and software. **Hardware** (figure 5.1) is the physical apparatus such as the wires, the computer, the monitor, the keyboard, the mouse, and the disk drive. To produce a graphic product, a computer must use software. **Software** is the set of instructions that enables a computer to do useful work.

A computer system uses two types of software: system software and application software. **System software** provides instruc-

Figure 5.1. Computer hardware. Hardware is the physical apparatus of the computer such as the CPU, the monitor, the keyboard, and the mouse.

tions the computer needs to perform a system function, such as saving data to a disk, sharing a volume of the hard drive with other users, or sending a file to a printer. **Application software** provides instructions the computer needs to perform a specific function, such as word processing, illustrating, manipulating images, laying out pages, or imposing or separating files. System software and application software for the graphic arts work together to manipulate data into usable images for the printing processes.

The Logic Board

The heart of a computer is the logic board (figure 5.2). The logic board contains the central processing unit (CPU), a quartz crystal clock, parts for connecting input and output devices, memory, and a feed line from a power supply.

The Central Processing Unit

The **central processing unit (CPU)** is the brain of a computer. The rate at which the CPU processes data usually determines the cost of the computer and the computer's ability to process graphics used by the printing industry. Every instruction and graphic input to the computer is processed by the CPU before any output occurs.

The Quartz Crystal Clock

A **quartz crystal clock** emits pulses that are used to coordinate a computer's operations. It sends signals on the network at several million beats per second. Every action of the computer, such as booting up, starting up, examining memory, checking input and output ports, and looking to a special memory chip for the next set of instructions, are coordinated by the beat of the quartz clock.

Input and Output Ports

External devices plug into the logic board through **input and output ports (I/O)**. A keyboard and mouse are examples of input devices. A monitor and printer are output devices. A modem and an external disk drive can input data to, and also receive data from, the logic board.

Memory

Memory chips (figure 5.3) are placed in the logic board to store instructions and data. There are two basic kinds of memory: read-only memory (ROM) and random-access memory (RAM).

Read-only memory (ROM) chips hold permanently written instructions. These instructions are accessed by the microprocessor upon start up and prepare the computer for use. ROM chips retain their contents even when the power is turned off.

Random-access memory (RAM) stores data as you use the computer system. RAM is the computer's main memory; it stores data as long as the microprocessor needs it. As new data enters RAM cells old data is eliminated. This exchange of data slows the computer's processing, however. Processing speed can be increased by installing large amounts of RAM. This allows more application and project data to reside in active memory. To add memory to the logic board, you need to install single

1. **A Motorola microprocessor:** Runs at a clock speed of 33 megahertz.

2. **Built-in video:** Supports up to 16.7 million colors. Its video RAM can be expanded.

3. **SCSI controllers:** Transfers data at up to 4 mega-bytes per second to and from external interfaced devices.

4. **NuBus slots:** Allows the addition of hardware cards to expand the abilities of the system (e.g.: a video capture card).

5. **Processor-direct slot:** Can accept high-speed I/O cards or accelerator cards.

6. **RAM SIMM slots:**Has 16 slots for up to 64 megabytes of random access memory.

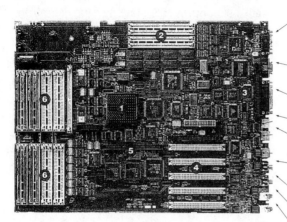

Video connector: supports color for a variety of screen sizes. Requires additional RAM to support 16.7 million colors on all monitors and requires an additional NuBus board to support 16.7 million colors on 9-inch and 21-inch displays.

Ethernet connector: For twisted-pair, thin coax, and AUI media, including thick coax and fiber-optic cable.

SCSI connector: Connects up to seven SCSI devices.

Serial Port (modem)

Serial port (Printer: Connects to a LocalTalk network.

Apple Desktop bus port: For connecting a keyboard, mouse, and other input devices.

Sound input (left and right)

Sound input: For microphone.

Stereo sound output

Definitions and Descriptions

1. Microprocessor: A chip that contains all the elements of a computer's CPU—the brain of a computer system.
2. Video: The hardware and memory on the logic board that operates and supports the monitor and the quality of its color.
3. SCSI: The letters stand for *Small Computer Systems Interface.* The SCSI connector is used to attach peripherals such as an external hard drive, CD-ROM player, or a scanner.
4. NuBus: A 32-bit bus architecture for Macintosh II computers. A bus is a set of wires for carrying signals through a computer. A Nubus slot allows the addition of hardware such as video capture cards and network interface cards.
5. Processor-direct slot: A slot that provides direct access to the CPU for the highest possible performance if an accelerator or expansion card were installed.
6. SIMM slots: Slots into which *Single Line Memory Modules* are inserted to increase the RAM of the computer.
7. Serial: A serial port processes data or instructions in sequence—one bit at a time.
8. Modem: A device that allows data to be sent over telephone lines. It is the abbreviation for "modulator/demodulator."
9. LocalTalk network: A network system used to connect computers, printers, and other devices so users can share information and output data.
10. Ethernet: A high-speed system used to connect computers, printers, and other devices so users can share information and output data. It requires specialbuilt-in hardware or the insertion of an ethernet card in an expansion slot to connect from a computer to a network.

Apple Computer, Inc. • 20525 Mariani Avenue • Cupertino, California 95014. Taken from the Macintosh Quadra promotion piece 3/92.95K.91532.V003278

Figure 5.2.   Components of a Macintosh Quadra logic board

Figure 5.3. Memory chips. These memory chips or SIMMs are RAM chips or the main memory device of the computer. When placed in the SIMM slots of the logic board RAM chips hold data as long as the microprocessor needs it.

in-line memory modules (SIMMs). SIMMs come in a variety of sizes and speeds. The SIMM size and speed needed depend on the type of computer and the complexity of the work to be done.

Computers with limited RAM can use a technique called virtual memory. **Virtual memory** divides programs and data into segments, stores them on disk, and loads them into memory when needed. This technique requires that the startup or default (scratch) drive has adequate open space. Using virtual memory is not as productive as using RAM.

The Power Supply

The **power supply** is not on the logic board but it is very important because it converts alternating current from the plug in the wall to the direct-current voltages needed to run a computer's system board. Because the current coming from the plug in the wall can fluctuate and damage the logic board, it is important to connect the logic board to a voltage stabilizer.

Classifying Computers

There are several types of computer available for prepress applications. Traditionally the types have been divided into mainframe computers, minicomputers, and microcomputers. However, increased performance and capabilities are blurring these distinctions.

Computer Types

A **mainframe computer** has traditionally been the fastest computer capable of handling large amounts of software and data. It can also serve large numbers of users simultaneously. A **minicomputer** is slower than a mainframe computer and normally has more memory than a microcomputer. A **microcomputer** has been referred to as a desktop or portable personal computer; it has a microprocessor and the memory suited for a single user. Although these classifications are still somewhat valid, they can be misleading.

For example, microcomputers made for the graphic arts industry have fast microprocessors, can be networked, can do more than one task at the same time, and can act as file or print servers for many users. Also, minicomputers today are much faster and more versatile than the mainframe computers of a few years ago.

Computer Capability

A computer's processing speed depends upon the power of its microprocessors and the orchestration of its electronic components. Microprocessors are being produced with more power than ever imagined. They are rated by three factors: the amount of memory (RAM) their chips can control, work length or bits of information they can handle, and how fast they process data (clock speed) expressed as millions of cycles per second (megahertz or MHz).

The Macintosh and the IBM PC are based on complex-instruction-set computing (CISC) microprocessors. Other computers currently used in IBM, Sun, Silicon graphics, Dec, and other vendors' faster workstations are powered by a reduced-instruction-set computing (RISC) design.

Early in 1994 Macintosh introduced computers that run on IBM/Motorola PowerPC 601 RISC processors. Changing the microprocessor or CPU architecture of these computers also required changing their operating systems and software applications. Although such changes caused major problems for hardware and software manufacturers, they provided much faster prepress systems. The 601 and 604 microprocessors are faster because their RISC architectures process instructions faster than the older 68040 CISC architecture.

Computer Terminology

Terminology and labels for microprocessors are sometimes confusing to new learners. However, they quickly become familiar through use. Macintosh Quadra, for example, uses the Motorola 68000, 68020, 68030, and 68040 microprocessors. These numbers are simply names for specific elements with unique characteristics. The IBM PC uses the Intel 80286, 80386, and 80486 microprocessors— sometimes called the "engines." When people use the term "a 486 machine," they are referring to an IBM PC with an Intel 80486 microprocessor. When people use the term "040," they are referring to the speed of the 68040 Motorola microprocessor engine in a Mac Quadra. The concept of CPU speed can be confusing because some computer names do not indicate how fast the computers operate. For example, a Mac running a 68040 Motorola microprocessor (Quadra 800) operates at 33 MHz. Its spec sheet, however, must be checked to determine that speed. In contrast, PowerPCs were introduced with CPU speeds as part of their names. The first three models to be introduced were the 6100/60, the 7100/66, and the 8100/80. The numbers *60*, *66*, and *80* represent the 60MHz, 66MHz, and 80MHz speeds at which the CPUs operate respectively.

As the quest for speed continues microcomputers will become much faster. Processing speed and storage ability are very important to digital imaging technology and high-resolution color images. In the past most microcomputers were incapable of doing high-resolution work. That problem is being resolved as the computer revolution continues.

Computer Imagesetting

Due to the improvement of the microprocessor, a microcomputer system integrated with off-the-shelf technology is highly capable of quality imagesetting. An **imagesetter** (figure 5.4) is a device used to output a computer image at an acceptable resolution onto photographic film, paper, and, in some cases, printing plates.

An imagesetting system capable of producing film, paper, and plate output can be assembled from a vast technology-parts bin offered to the graphic arts industry by a vari-

Figure 5.4.   Imagesetter. An imagesetter like the one shown here is capable of outputting images on photographic paper; film; or small, short-run offset plates.

ety of vendors. A skilled artist or craftsperson using this system is capable of producing computer-assisted design, page layout, imposition, and film or plate imaging. Because this system is capable of performing most of the processes up to and including making plates, it is called an **electronic prepress workstation** (figure 5.5). Such a workstation consists of the following basic components:

- A very fast microcomputer system loaded with memory and internal storage
- A back-up storage mechanism capable of holding large amounts of data
- Scanning devices capable of inputting data from film or print originals
- A postscript-compatible laser printer capable of producing black-and-white proofs or color comprehensives
- An imagesetter capable of outputting film, paper, and plate material at various resolutions
- A film processor capable of making consistent and uniform negatives and prints

The systems in figure 5.5 are productive black-and-white and process color workstations for medium-quality, small-size printing jobs. High resolution, large-size, process color work requires a more powerful system. By combining minicomputer or mainframe computer power with appropriate input and output devices, vendors can provide very capable **digital prepress workstations.**

The Concept of Digital Information

A computer accepts data and stores it, and software allows it to be manipulated into a message or information that is understandable to humans. This process of converting information to digital data can be done in-house or it can be sent to a **service bureau** to be done. Printed pieces cannot be computer-generated until all pictures, illustrations, and type are converted to digital data and placed onto a storage mechanism.

Creating Digital Data

The data conversion process usually begins with keyboard input. All systems use a keyboard similar to that found on a standard typewriter. The keyboard is connected to a video screen through the logic board. Each time the operator presses a key on the keyboard, an alphanumeric code for that key's character is stored in memory, and the symbol for that keystroke displays on the video screen. An **alphanumeric code** (figure 5.6) is a unique symbol made up of numbers and letters. It may also include standard punctuation and symbols such as the dollar sign ($). There is an alphanumeric code for each letter of the alphabet (both upper- and lowercase), and for each number. All data entered into the computer by the operator, and each instruction entered by the software, is converted to alphanumeric code and stored in memory as numbers. The numbers are binary (two-number) sequences of the two digits 0 and 1. Each 0 or 1 is called a **bit** (short for "binary digit"). Individual bits cause the switches in the central processing unit to turn on or off. A **byte** is a group of eight bits that represent a letter or a numeral. Information represented by a sequence of digits is said to be **digital data** or digitized information.

Line illustrations created in the computer called **object art** begin as sets of numbers. Graphics software, such as an illustration package, translates the images the artist draws into binary $1s$ and $0s$. The computer then uses the logic board's circuits to process the data at lighting speed. The artist also can instruct the illustration software to fill the created shapes with colorful hues, tints, or blends.

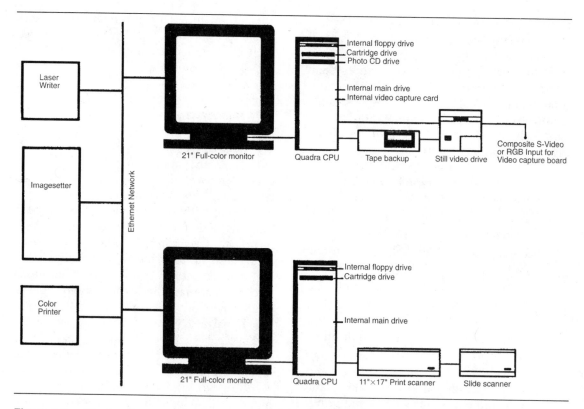

Figure 5.5. **Electronic prepress workstations.** Two computers attached to appropriate external input and output devices make a very productive prepress department for a small printing or publishing organization.

Photographs, negatives, slides, still video, and video images are examples of **analog data**. Analog data is bound to a carrier or medium such as film. When analog data is

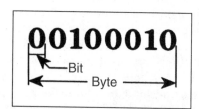

Figure 5.6. **Alphanumeric code.** There is an alphanumeric code for each capital letter, lowercase letter, point, and figure processed by the computer. Each code is broken into units called bits and bytes.

copied to another analog carrier (such as when making a Xerox copy of a Xerox copy) quality is always lost. In contrast, digital data is not bound to a carrier and can be copied any number of times without quality loss. Also, it can be transmitted, stored, retrieved, and combined on demand.

Translating Analog Data

Analog data can be translated to digital data to avoid any loss of quality and to enjoy greater flexibility. At the beginning of the analog-to-digital translation process a sensor of some type—like a densitometer (see chapter 7)—converts the image to electrical signals of varying voltages because analog data can be represented by a variable physical quantity such as voltage. Before an analog signal can be interpreted by a computer, however, it must be converted to binary language. This conversion takes place as the analog signal travels through an analog-to-digital (A-to-D) converter. The converter constantly samples the voltage and changes it to digital information.

It is often necessary to convert digital data back to analog information producing a film transparency from a computer image, for example. This is accomplished by using a reverse mechanism called a digital-to-analog (D-to-A) converter. Sending computer digital data to a standard television monitor, to a still video disk, or to video tape, (see Video Capture pg. 109) for presentation purposes are all examples of D-to-A converting. Most output devices that produce proofs, comprehensives, films, and plates for the graphic arts industry use digital output.

Figure 5.7. **Scanned line art.** Bit-mapped line art is made up of picture elements and is produced by scanning an image into an application. As is shown, the jaggedy or pixel appearance is very noticeable when these images are enlarged.

Digital Image Entry

Two types of images are created in or brought into graphics software: bit-mapped (raster) or object-oriented (vector).

Raster Images

Bit-mapped or **raster images** are created in paint type applications or by scanning (see the Scanners and Scanning section later in this chapter). Bit-mapped, **line art** images are represented by picture elements (**pixels**) that are assigned a value by the computer. Scanned line art images are assigned one bit (0 or 1) per pixel—either black or white (figure 5.7). The quality of these images depends on input and output resolution.

Resolution refers to the number of samples that a scanner or capture device makes per inch and is measured in dots per inch (**dpi**) or

pixels per inch (**ppi**). When an image is output to a laser printer or an imagesetter its resolution is described by the number of dots the output device can generate in 1 inch (dpi). The resolution at which a line image is bit-mapped and the resolution of the output device determine the quality of the image.

Assume that a 300-dpi laser printer is used. In an attempt to improve image quality a scan is made at 600 dpi. When the image is sent to the laser printer it adopts the resolution of the output device—300 dpi. Scanning at a dpi higher than the output device does not improve image quality, it just increases the file size. Figure 5.8 shows that after 300 dpi scanning input there is no real increase in image quality—only an undesirable increase in file or storage area size.

Grey-scale or continuous-tone images pose a slightly different bit-mapping problem. A grey-scale image is made up of black, white,

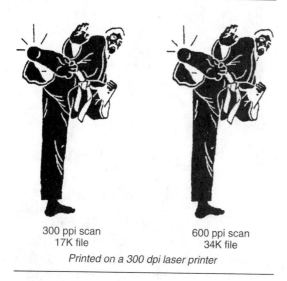

300 ppi scan   600 ppi scan
17K file   34K file

Printed on a 300 dpi laser printer

Figure 5.8.   Scanned line art. Scanning at a dpi higher than the output device does not improve quality, it just increases the file size.

and intermediate tones. One bit per pixel cannot represent a shade of grey however. It can only represent black or white. Most grey-scale images are 8 bits, which is enough to distinguish 256 levels of grey through various combinations. When scanning continuous-tone images the output device must therefore be set to make an 8-bit sample. Grey-scale images are imageset as halftones (see chapter 8), and the minimum input resolution is 1 ppi for each line per inch (**lpi**) of the halftone. The best halftone reproduction occurs if the input resolution is 1.5 to 2 times the lpi of the halftone. Therefore, if a halftone is to be printed at 133 lpi it should be scanned at 200 ppi ($133 \times 1.5 = 199.5$ or 200 lpi) (figure 5.9)

Enlarging bit-mapped images requires planning. If the image is not going to be enlarged, the optimum image can be obtained if the input resolution is 1.5 to 2 times the lpi of the halftone. When a bit-mapped image is enlarged its resolution reduces (figure 5.10). If the halftone lpi and the size of the final image are known in advance, the proper input reso-

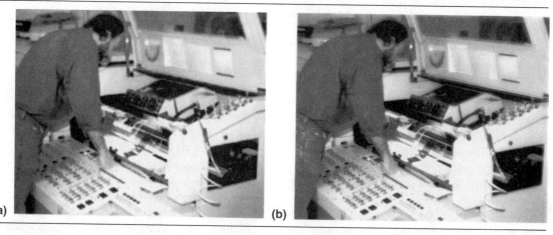

(a)   (b)

Figure 5.9.   Grey-scale images. (a) Scanned at 72 ppi. (b) Scanned at 200 ppi. Both a and b were recorded to film as 133-lpi halftones.

Figure 5.10. Grey-scale images. Image B was scanned at 1.5 × lpi (133) for a 2-inch image width. Enlarging it to 4 inches as shown here increases the size of the picture elements and destroys the image's resolution.

lution can be determined. If they are not known, a low-resolution, position-only image can be used during the layout process. The final scan can then be made after the layout is complete and all halftone lpis and sizes are known.

Vector Images

If line art is scanned into an application it is a bit-mapped, resolution-dependent image. If it is created in a paint program it is also a bit-mapped image. When it is created in an illustration or a draw program, however, it is object-oriented or a **vector image**. Vector images (figure 5.11) are made up of mathematically described paths called vectors. Vector software, such as Adobe Illustrator, does not store the lines of an image as a string of picture elements, but rather as drawing instructions or formulas that describe the directions of lines.

The addresses of two different points define a line. The outline of an alphabet character is a complex mathematical expression in a vector image.

Vector art has many advantages over raster art. It can be reshaped, rotated, enlarged, reduced, and manipulated in many other ways without sacrificing quality. Vector formats are usually smaller than raster formats and sometimes print faster. Raster images can be converted to vector images by placing a scanned file in an object-oriented application such as Adobe Illustrator or Macromedia's Freehand. Using the scanned file as a template, the image can be redrawn or automatically traced.

In addition to resizing and shaping capabilities, vector art has an advantage over raster art during output. The drawing application used to create vector art mathematically determines the shape of the object and

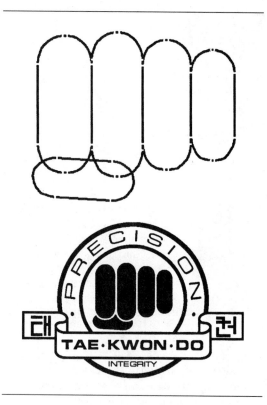

Figure 5.11. **Vector image.** The fist in the logo consists of vectors that describe the mathematical paths of the lines.

allows output at a printer or imagesetter's highest resolution. This is why vector images are said to be resolution-independent—they are not governed by the resolution of the input. Vector images are excellent for line illustrations, synthetic color illustrations, or any artwork that requires changing, resizing, or manipulating.

Once raster and vector files are created they must be saved and stored on disk. There are many different **file formats** for structuring data as it is recorded to disk. Figure 5.12 describes the characteristics of commonly used file formats. Figure 5.13 outlines the procedure

for determining file size, which is very important when working with limited disk space.

Scanners and Scanning

Scanners are input devices that convert analog information to digital information and digitize various types of copy for editing with software.

There are many different types of scanners at various levels of quality. Scanner selection is determined by the kind of input used and the quality of output desired. An inexpensive desktop scanner would be very appropriate for an office environment where the output printer is between 300 dpi and 1200 dpi resolution. A small- to medium-size printing organization reproducing quality halftones and detailed line art would require a more expensive scanner with higher resolution. A company capturing color transparencies, negatives, and color prints would require an even higher quality scanner and possibly more than one type.

Flatbed Scanners

One of the most popular scanners is the **flatbed scanner** used by desktop publishers (figure 5.14). There are many to choose from. They are capable of scanning or digitizing both monochrome (black-and-white) and color prints. Some are also capable of scanning transparent film. A scanner's price depends on its size, its ability to scan both opaque and transparent copy, its maximum scanning resolution, and its maximum color sample per pixel.

Film Scanners

Film scanners (figure 5.15) must be capable of higher resolution than print scanners because slides and negatives have more gradations from highlight to shadow and are normally smaller than prints. Some desktop film scanners are capable of sampling a 35-mm trans-

1. **MacPaint format:** Commonly used to transfer bit-mapped images between Macintosh applications. It formats black-and-white files at 72 dpi in an 8 inch × 10 inch vertical orientation. The paint format eliminates attributes such as high-resolution, grey-scale values and color.

2. **PICT file format:** Used among graphics and page-layout applications as an intermediary file format. It can hold a mixture of raster and vector objects. It can hold bit maps with resolutions greater than 72 dpi. Good for low-end line and bit-mapped art with limited color in the same file. It is the format used when cutting and copying to the clipboard.

3. **PICT 2 file format:** Defines bit-mapped or object-oriented images on the Macintosh. It supports 24-bit color. Excellent format for presentation viewed on screen. It is poorly supported by page-layout programs.

4. **TIFF (tag image file format):** Used to exchange bit-mapped images, usually scans, between applications and computer platforms. It is the best format for storing images with different resolutions, grey tones, colors. It does not store object-oriented images. Grey-scale TIFF holds 256 greys and is used in page-layout programs because it is capable of TIFF image adjustment. Color TIFF is the format for images to be color separated.

5. **EPS (encapsulated postscript) file format:** The format supported by most draw, illustration, and page-layout programs. It is the preferred format for storing object-oriented artwork. ASCII and binary are the two types of EPS formats. Object-oriented software programs save in the ASCII format. When a file is saved, a low-resolution, bit-mapped PICT preview image is also saved as a view file for page-layout programs. When manipulating EPS view files in page-layout programs, the screen image appears distorted but prints fine. Bit-mapped images are also saved in the EPS format. Binary EPS, a more compact format, uses about half the disk space of an ASCII file. Some applications may not support binary EPS files. All programs support the ASCII encoding option.

6. **Postscript file:** A text-based description of an image. Most applications allow a postscript file to be created. Once a file is created, the application that created it is not needed for printing. Postscript files created with application can be placed into another application and cropped and sized. However, they cannot be edited so it is important to keep the original version.

7. **DCS (desktop color separation) file:** Designed for separating color TIFF and PICT images into a yellow, magenta, cyan, and black channel or plate. A DCS separation consists of five files—yellow, magenta, cyan, black, and a PICT view file for screen display in a page-layout program. When the final layout is separated the page-layout application accesses the separation files and merges each file with the page negative or plate. Any image manipulation done to the PICT view file is applied during separation.

Figure 5.12.   Commonly used file formats

parency at over 5,000 ppi or dpi. This level of resolution is necessary when working with small images.

Take for example a 35-mm slide that is only 1 inch on its short side. Assume that a scan of this slide is made at 1200 dpi at 100 percent, and that the resulting image will be printed in a magazine at a dimension of 8 inches on the short side. As the image is enlarged in the page layout software, resolution decreases proportionately. At 1 inch the image has a resolution of 1200 dpi. At 2 inches the resolution reduces to 600 dpi, then to 300 dpi at 4 inches and finally to 150 dpi at 8 inches. Normally the digital halftone requires 1.5 to 2 times as many pixels as the halftone screen frequency that will be used in the final printing. Therefore, the 8-inch image at 150 dpi is adequate only to produce a quality 75–100 lpi halftone (75 lpi × 2 = 150). The magazine may require that all pictures be reproduced at 120 or 133 lpi (133 lpi × 2 = 266). A 75–100 lpi halftone may be adequate for newspaper work, but it is not adequate for a quality magazine.

The following procedure can be used to estimate file size. Here is a formula that allows you to estimate file size using your own file variables:

(tonal resolution/8) × (spatial resolution)² × (dimensions) = file size

Divide the **tonal resolution** by 8 bits to determine bytes per sample. Squaring the **spatial resolution** gives the number of **samples per square inch.** Multiply that number by the number of bytes per sample to get the number of bytes per square inch. Multiply that number by the **size of the job in square inches** to get the total **number of bytes in a job.** Divide that number by 1,024 to get kilobytes or by 1,048,576 to get megabytes.

Tonal resolution: Depth of grey-scale or color. A line art scan is only 1 bit deep because 1 bit is all that is needed to distinguish black from white. Most grey-scale images are 8 bits deep in order to distinguish 256 levels of grey. Color images are commonly 24 bits deep in order to distinguish 16.7 million different colors.

Spatial resolution: Laser printer and imagesetter resolution is only two dimensional. It is dependent on the number of dots in the horizontal and vertical directions. Scanners have horizontal and vertical directions—and also depth. Both scanners and imagesetters describe horizontal and vertical resolution in terms of dots per inch (dpi) and sometimes in pixels per inch (ppi) or samples per inch.

1. Assume that a 4-inch × 5-inch line illustration will be scanned at 300 dpi. What is the file size?
   (tonal resolution / 8) × (spatial resolution)² × (dimensions) = file size
   (1/8) × (300)² × (4 × 5) = file size
   .125 × 90,000 × 20 = file size

   225,000 bytes = file size
   225,000/1,024 = file size of 219 kilobytes

2. Assume that a 4-inch × 5-inch black and white photograph will be scanned at 300 dpi. What is the file size?
   (tonal resolution / 8) × (spatial resolution)² × (dimensions) = file size
   (8/8) × (300)² × (4 × 5) = file size
   1 × 90,000 × 20 = file size
   1,800,000 bytes = file size
   1,800,000 / 1,048,576 = file size of 1.7 megabytes

3. Assume that a 4-inch × 5-inch color photograph will be scanned at 300 dpi. What is the file size?
   (tonal resolution / 8) × (spatial resolution)² × (dimensions) = file size
   (24/8) × (300)² × (4 × 5) = file size
   3 × 90,000 × 20 = file size
   5,400,000 bytes = file size
   5,400,000 / 1,048,576 = file size of 5.14 megabytes

Figure 5.13.   Determining file size

Drum Scanners

Drum scanners (figure 5.16) are input devices for professional color reproduction applications. An illustration, a photograph, or a transparency can be fastened to the scanner's rotating drum. Drum scanners are more expensive than flatbed or film scanners; more complex than flatbed or film scanners; and require more skill to mount, scan, and use their associated software. However, they are very efficient because they have three photomultipliers (red, green, and blue) scanning the original at once and with a very accurate beam.

Drum scanners perform functions such as sharpening the focus and converting RGB (red, green, and blue) to CMYK (cyan, magenta, yellow, and black) during the input process. Images scanned using flatbed and

Figure 5.14. **Flatbed scanner.** A flatbed scanner is capable of scanning both print and film images.

Figure 5.16. **Drum scanner.** Drum scanners are efficient and accurate, but are more costly than flatbed and film scanners.

film scanners normally capture only a RGB scan. Adjusting, sharpening, and converting the image to CMYK in a flatbed or film scanner is done using image manipulation software—such as Adobe Photoshop. These image manipulations take time and slows production. The small desktop drum scanner in figure 5.16 scans up to a 9.8 inch × 13 inch (25 cm × 35 cm) original and features a 4064 dpi resolution.

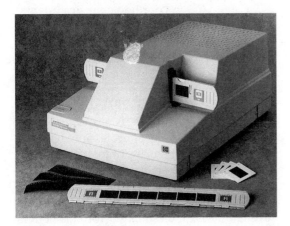

Figure 5.15. **Film scanner.** A 35-mm film scanner must sample at a higher resolution than a flatbed scanner because the image being scanned is always enlarged.

Regardless of scanner type, resolution is critical. As discussed earlier, resolution is the maximum ppi that a scanner can distinguish. More image data is captured and saved as the ppi increases. More image data keeps line art from having jaggedy edges, prevents loss of fine-line detail, and allows enlargement without losing quality. It is important to scan at the appropriate resolution.

Most inexpensive flatbed scanners digitize color images at 24 bits per pixel and black-and-white images at 8 bits per pixel. The red, blue, and green elements of a color image are each captured at 8 bits per pixel. Some scanners take three scans to capture all three elements while others capture all three elements in one pass. Some flatbed scanners and most slide scanners and drum scanners capture images at a sampling rate higher than 8 bit per pixel*(12 bits or 16 bits per color element). These scanners actually capture more information than most imaging software can handle (Apple QuickDraw uses 24-bit color for example). The additional information is eventually sampled down to 8 bits per pixel per color. Before each color is sampled down the **image gamma** (arrangement of highlight, midtone, and shadow detail) can be adjusted to obtain the optimum image.

A sheet-fed or flatbed scanner is an excellent converter for bringing typed or printed information into the system for page layout. Optical character recognition (OCR) software is needed to work with the scanner. **Optical character recognition** (OCR) is a process in which a scanner, using appropriate software, can "read" copy from book, magazine, newspaper, or typed pages. "Reading" means that the images are translated to digital data.

Today's OCR software programs are virtually automatic. They are capable of recognizing almost any type style and type size. They do this by comparing page patterns with programmed information about character shapes. Most of the advanced automatic OCR programs include page recognition software that can differentiate between text and graphics.

Entry-level automatic OCR software features a wide variety of scanners and different languages. The scanners are fast and quite accurate; they have optional programs for dot-matrix print recognition and are bit-mapped to vector conversion.

CD-ROM

CD-ROM is an acronym for "compact disc read-only memory." Nearly everyone is familiar with audio CDs because they have virtually replaced vinyl records. We have CD players in our homes, in our schools, at work, and in our cars. CD-ROMs for computers look exactly like audio CDs. In fact, a CD-ROM drive can play audio CDs.

The printing and publishing industries have been using CD and CD-ROM players for years. Type fonts, clip art, and photo collections can be purchased and are used commonly by newspaper and commercial publishers.

Early in this decade, Eastman Kodak Company introduced a new system that married traditional silver photography with digital imaging on a platter called the Kodak Photo CD Master disc (figure 5.17). **Photo CDs** are produced by a system capable of scanning slides and negatives onto special CDs. These discs contain images that can be displayed on television using a photo CD player. They can also be input into presentation or page layout software programs for graphic communication purposes. Figure 5.18 shows a Kodak photo CD imaging workstation in operation.

To make the system work, consumers take pictures as usual with their 35-mm cameras using film. When the film is sent for processing, the consumer can opt to have the film images transferred at full resolution to a Photo CD Master disc. The Photo CD Master disc is a 120-mm platter that holds about 100 images, or four 24-exposure rolls of film. The resolution of a photo CD image is sixteen times that of today's television and four times the resolution of high definition television (HDTV). It is important to note that photo CD discs cannot be read by all CD players. Special software is needed to access this data. Do not attempt to use a photo CD in your home music system.

Photo CD technology was developed for general photo consumers because they shoot billions of photographs each year. Kodak has now also developed photo CD formats, products, and applications that offer opportunities for professional photographers and publishers. The Pro Photo CD Master disc is built to meet the requirements of professional photographers and commercial printers. This system (figure 5.19) stores images from larger film formats such as 70 mm, 120 mm, and 4 inches × 5 inches, and therefore requires a larger format scanner. Because these larger formats contain more data the file sizes are also larger and fewer images can be placed on each photo CD

Figure 5.17. Photo CD Master disc. The Photo CD Master disc marries traditional silver photography with digital imaging. The disc is housed in a case that also contains an index print displaying all images on the disc.

disc. Depending on the film format, the discs can hold from 25 to 100 images.

Video Capture

Video capture or **frame grabbing** is a term used to describe the process of converting live analog video to a still digitized image. Frame grabbing is used by printers and publishers to obtain still images that are only available on video. Newspaper publishers often use video still images to meet the daily pressures presented by their type of communication.

Video Capture Hardware

Video capture requires specific hardware. A video capture card must be placed in an available expansion slot in the computer (figure 5.20). The expansion card not only converts a

video (analog) image to a digital one, it also converts a digital image back to analog. External devices such as a camcorder, a VCR, or a laser disc player can be attached to the video-in plug of the capture card (figure 5.21).

Figure 5.22 shows the types of connectors used when attaching external devices to the video capture card. The branching-type cable used to bring images into the video capture system has a 9-pin D-type connector on one end and any or all of the following connectors on the other: BNC, RCA/phone, and a 4-pin DIN (S-video). Video out requires one end of the cable to be a 9-pin, D-type male. The other end is determined by the connector required by the output device. Another 9-pin, D-type connector or four BNC connectors (one each for red, green, blue, and composite sync) are required on the other end if an RGB multiscan monitor is connected as the output

Figure 5.18.   Photo CD imaging workstation. A photo CD imaging workstation is used to write master discs.

device. A 4-pin DIN connector is required if the output device is an S-video VCR. A RCA/phono connector is required to output to any composite video device. There is a difference in the quality of video transmission between devices when various connectors are used. A composite video connection using a RCA/phone connector transfers an acceptable signal between devices; an S-video connection is better, and a RGB/sync with 4 BNC connections is the best. Red, blue, and green signals transferred separately produce a higher quality color image.

Most publishers are not interested in video out if its only purpose is to capture images for printing production. Output from digital image to analog video is only necessary to go back to video for presentation purposes.

A second, multiscan monitor is needed to view images from the video source while the capture is being made. Figure 5.23 illustrates the hookup of another monitor from the output connector of the card in the expansion slot of the CPU.

Video Capture Software
All capture cards come with their own software. Most manufacturers also supply a plug-in module for an image manipulation software program (such as Adobe Photoshop). The plug-in module is installed in the software folder and allows the open software application to acquire the capture card input and thereby digitize the selected image. Once the image is captured it is manipulated using a procedure similar to the one used to manipulate scanned images.

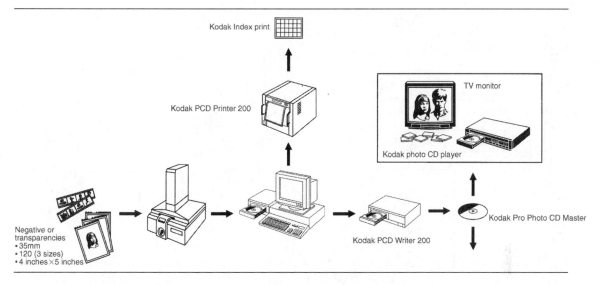

Figure 5.19. **Kodak professional photo CD imaging workstation.** This system meets the needs of professionals who work from larger film formats.

Still Video Photography

Still video combines traditional photography and video technology to produce an all-electronic system capable of producing outstanding graphics presentation images and low- to medium-resolution publishing images. The still video camera (figure 5.24) offers a higher quality image than does videotape because it is designed to capture a still image with and without synchronized flash.

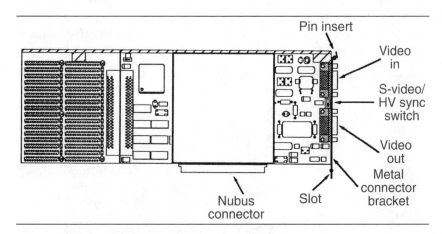

Figure 5.20. **Video capture card.** Video capture is accomplished by installing an expansion card in the logic board of the computer. Audio/video computers already have a similar card installed.

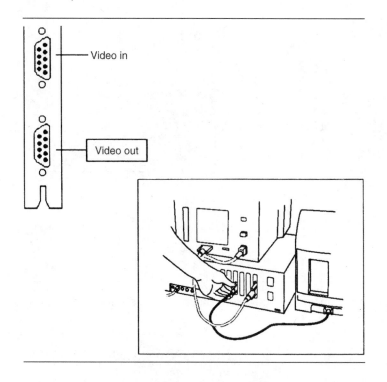

Figure 5.21. The video-in plug of the video capture card accepts composite video, s-video, or RGB video input.

During the mid 1980s major manufacturers interested in this technology met and agreed on a standard format for the video floppy disk (figure 5.25). A video floppy disk contains fifty tracks capable of storing either a **field** (medium-resolution) image or a higher resolution **frame** image on two successive tracks. In frame mode the disk can record twenty-five frame images. Video images are made up of two fields that are merged by a television receiver to make one complete frame. Alternate scan lines (odd and even) are transmitted in each field and interlace to form the image (figure 5.26).

The still video system illustrated in figure 5.27 is unique in that it has the ability to record

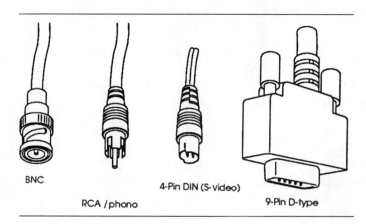

Figure 5.22.   Connectors. Bringing images into the system requires a cable with a 9-pin, D-type connector on one end to attach to the card. The other end would consist of three branching cables with S-video, composite, and RGB connectors for attaching any video source.

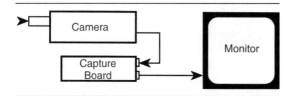

Figure 5.23. Monitor hookup. Another multi-scan monitor is necessary to view the video source while the capture is being made.

Figure 5.24. Still video camera. Still video combines traditional photography and video technology to produce an all-electronic still imaging system.

images for immediate playback to television. It can also digitize images for publishing. When a picture is taken it is recorded on a video floppy disk as an analog image. The images can be viewed immediately by playing from the camera to a normal television monitor. If the images are unsatisfactory they can be erased and the disk can be used again.

Still video images are adequate for graphic design and desktop publishing applications. These images must be digitized to be brought into the computer because all still video images are analog data. There are two basic ways to digitize still video images. The first method has already been discussed and involves using a video capture card. When using video capture cards it is important to use an S-video connector from the camera to the capture card. The S-video connector separates the luminance and color components of the video signal to produce a higher quality image.

The second, and very practical, way for publishers to digitize still images is to use an external digitizing drive (figure 5.28). When the video floppy is inserted in the drive the images are digitized in the appropriate software. This procedure frees the camera for field use.

Software is also required to complete the digitizing process regardless of what hardware method is used to digitize or capture the image. All manufacturers of capture hardware supply the necessary software. They also sup-

ply plug-in modules for popular image processing software (such as Adobe Photoshop). The capture boards are acquired through the image processing software. The image is digitized in the application for manipulation and storage. Due to current video resolution, the size at which an image can be enlarged at higher halftone screen rulings is limited. It is adequate for smaller images to be reproduced under 133 lpi.

Figure 5.25. Video floppy disk. A video floppy disk can record fifty field images or twenty-five frame images.

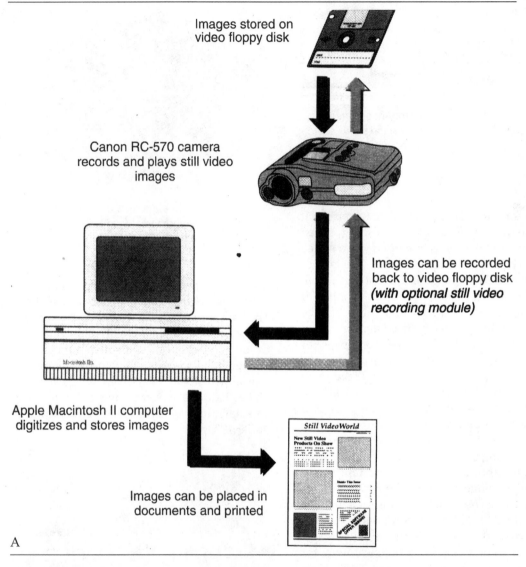

Images stored on
video floppy disk

Canon RC-570 camera
records and plays still video
images

Images can be recorded
back to video floppy disk
*(with optional still video
recording module)*

Apple Macintosh II computer
digitizes and stores images

Images can be placed in
documents and printed

A

Figure 5.26. **A. Digitizing images for publishing. B. Hook-up for viewing.** When viewing on AC power, connect the AC video-out terminal on the coupler and the video-in terminal on the TV or VCR.

The benefit of still video is obviously the speed at which images can be recorded and brought into publishing jobs. It is also a very versatile system. In addition to being used in graphic design support and desktop publishing, the system can be used for presentations, point-of-sale, training, storyboarding, real estate, medical records, engineering, and education.

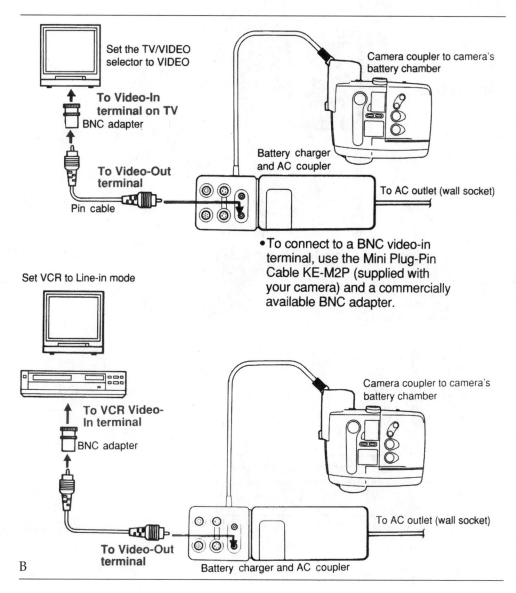

Figure 5.26. continued

Digital Photography

Digital still images offer many advantages to the printer and publisher. Images captured by a digital camera are quality images of adequate resolution. These images can be im-ported quickly into software for manipulation—defects can be removed; composite images can be produced; backgrounds can be changed; and hue, saturation, brightness, contrast, gamma, and sharpness can be improved.

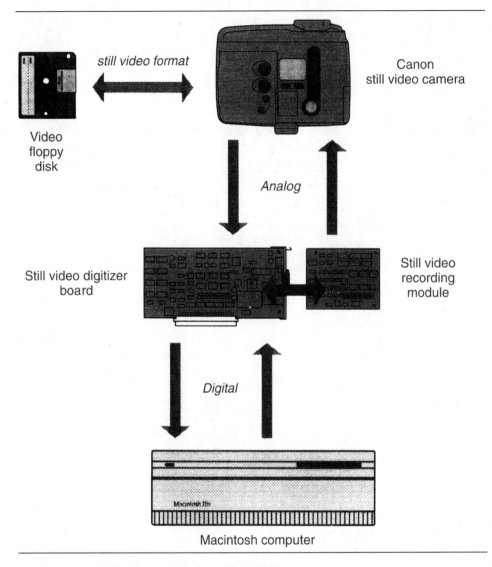

still video format

Video
floppy
disk

Canon
still video camera

Analog

Still video digitizer
board

Still video
recording
module

Digital

Macintosh computer

Figure 5.27. Still video capture board installation

Converting images to digital data within the camera system eliminates traditional silver imaging. Digital capture speeds the manufacturing process and has environmental advantages. Most vendors use a memory card to hold the picture information in RAM after the signal is converted from analog information to digital data by using a charged coupled device (CCD).

Eastman Kodak introduced a system in the early 1980s that combined a traditional Nikon camera with a camera back, a winder, and a digital storage unit. The Kodak professional digital camera system (figure 5.29) is designed to produce quality images for instant transmission to meet tight deadlines by eliminating film processing.

Figure 5.28. **Canon external digitizing drive.**
An external digitizing or video floppy drive converts the video images on the drive to digital data in an image manipulation software package.

The system is used like any traditional 35-mm camera—compose, focus, and shoot. The imaging system captures color or black-and-white digital images and stores them on a cable-connected storage unit. The digital storage unit can hold 156 noncompressed images or 400 to 600 compressed images. The storage unit also offers the opportunity to view the captured images in black and white on a built-in, 4-inch monitor.

The camera winder allows image sequences to be captured. Using 8 megabytes of dynamic random-access memory (DRAM) six images can be captured in each 2.5-second burst. A more advanced system using 32 megabytes of DRAM allows up to twenty-four images to be captured in one burst.

Kodak's professional digital camera system requires a Macintosh computer and modem to transmit images (figure 5.30). This system has built-in compression and transmission and requires only an off-the-shelf modem.

The Kodak DCS 200 digital camera (figure 5.31) is a more portable system designed for desktop application. It holds fifty images on its hard drive which is attached under the camera. It is available in both a black-and-white and a color model. The back of the storage drive contains a small computer systems interface (SCSI) port for direct downloading to a computer. Because the images are already digital there is no need for a frame grabber to make an analog-to-digital conversion.

Digital photography is a very young technology that will develop rapidly in the near future. By the time this edition of *Printing Technology* is published new hardware and software for digital imaging and processing will be available to, and affordable for, most users.

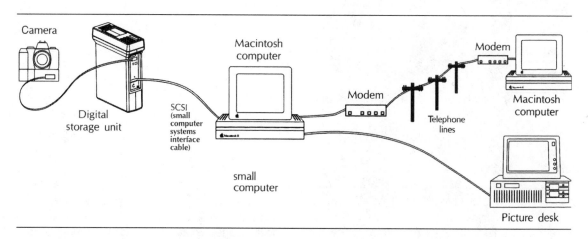

Figure 5.29. **Kodak professional digital camera system**

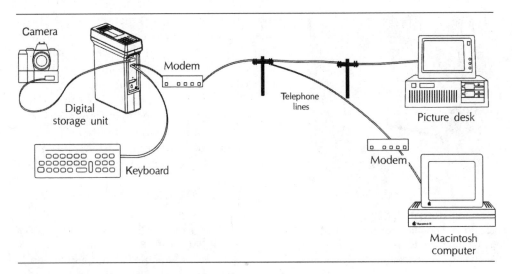

Figure 5.30.   Kodak professional digital camera system with built-in compression and transmission

Figure 5.31.   The Kodak DCS 200 digital camera. This portable system is designed for desktop applications and holds fifty images on its hard drive.

Key Terms

hardware
software
system software
application software
  microprocessor
central processing unit (CPU)
quartz crystal clock
input/output ports
read-only memory (ROM)
random-access memory (RAM)
virtual memory
power supply
mainframe computer
minicomputer
microcomputer
imagesetter
electronic prepress workstation

digital prepress workstation
service bureau
alphanumeric code
bit
byte
digital data
object art
analog data
raster image
line art
pixel
resolution
dots per inch (dpi)
pixels per inch (ppi)
lines per inch (lpi)
vector image

file format
scanner
flatbed scanner
film scanner
drum scanner
image gamma
optical character recognition
  (OCR)
compact disk read-only memory
  (CD ROM)
photo CD
frame grabbing
still video
frame
field
digital photography

Questions for Review

1. What component controls how fast a computer processes data? Where is it located?

2. Describe the two basic kinds of memory used by a computer. Which type is added by the owner to increase the computer's ability to handle larger files?

3. Classify the following components or devices as "input devices" or "output devices": keyboard, monitor, mouse, scanner, and printer.

4. Differentiate between a bit and a byte. Is the size of a floppy disk measured in bits or in bytes?

5. Differentiate between analog and digital information. List three examples of each.

6. Assume your facility is using a 600-dpi laser printer for output. At what resolution would you scan line art to obtain the best output from your printer?

7. Outline the procedure for scanning line art assuming that a 300-dpi laser printer will produce the final output.

8. Outline the procedure for scanning a black-and-white picture assuming that it will be printed in a school newspaper at 85 lpi.

9. List the major advantages vector line art has over raster line art when used as an illustration in a printing job.

10. Explain why film scanners have higher resolution capabilities than do flatbed scanners.

11. Discuss a practical application of OCR.

12. State two reasons why you would use photo CD as a method of placing a picture into a printing job.

13. Why would printers and publishers use a "frame grab" from a video source?

14. What is required to "capture" or "grab" a video image into a computer?

15. Do still video cameras capture images as analog information or as digital data?

What is the difference between a field and a frame?

16. List the advantages of using digital photography as part of the printing process.

CHAPTER 6

Line Photography

Photographers and printers have gone to great lengths to create special photographic effects. One of the early ideas was to create huge illustrations that would dazzle the layman's mind. At a photographic exhibition in Vienna in 1864, an enlargement of a flea was entered that was more than "a meter" in height. The picture startled those who saw it because they could not imagine how the print was made. Oversized prints of that time were usually made on several pieces of paper joined together. They were usually of such poor quality that elaborate retouching was necessary at the joints.

In 1899 the Chicago and Alton Railroads commissioned the Pullman Train Works to build an elaborate passenger train to celebrate the coming turn of the century. The company also wanted to exhibit a massive photograph of the train at the Paris Exposition the following year. Mr George R. Lawrence, the company's photographer, was asked to build the largest camera in the world so that the "Alton Limited" could be photographed on one negative.

J. A. Anderson of Chicago, under Lawrence's supervision, spent two and a half months building the camera. When fully extended on four 2 × 6 inch beams, the completed device was almost 20 feet long. It was constructed completely from solid cherry. The heavy rubber bellows took 40 gallons of glue to prepare. A special hinged frame on the back of the camera held the 8 × 10 foot glass negative. The two Zeiss lenses used in the camera were specially made. One was wide angle, with a 5½ foot focal length. The other was telescopic, with a 10 foot focal length. The camera with one lens weighed 900 pounds. With the plate holder and plate, it weighed over 1,400 pounds. It was so large that the front lens panel was a hinged door through which the photographer could climb into the device to clean the interior.

In the spring of 1900 the finished camera was placed in a padded van and mounted on a flatcar for a short journey to Brighton Park, where the exposition photo was to be shot. It took fifteen men to set up "The Mammoth," as

The Mammoth.
Courtesy of the Smithsonian Institution, Photo No. 72–10645.

it was officially named. A special focusing screen was hinged in the back, and the image was "focused" by several men pushing the lens forward or backward on the wooden track.

The exposure took 2½ minutes to make. It took 5 gallons of developer to process the image. Three prints were made from the 5 × 8 foot plate. One was placed on a wall in the train's grand salon. The second was given to the United States government as a gift for a new building. The third was sent to the Paris Exposition. The exposition officials found the photograph so remarkable that they required a certified affidavit specifying the details of its manufacture before they would accept it as "the world's largest photograph."

Objectives for Chapter 6

After completing this chapter you will be able to:

▪ Classify photographic films.

▪ Identify the basic parts of any camera and recall their names and purposes.

▪ List the basic line photography tools.

▪ Define "basic exposure."

▪ Recall the steps in making a basic line exposure on a process camera.

- Identify the variables in photographic chemical processing.
- Recall the steps in chemical processing for line photography.

- Explain the process of making film duplicates.
- Explain the process of making diffusion transfers.

Introduction

When we use the term "photography," we tend to think of pictures processed at our corner drugstore, school pictures, or perhaps family portraits. This kind of photography is called **continuous-tone photography** and is an important part of our world. However, the applications of photography go far beyond continuous-tone photography. Photographs taken from weather satellites plot weather patterns and provide storm warnings that save human lives. Infrared photographs taken from airplanes can predict crop production. Infrared photographs taken in hospitals detect cancer in the human body. X rays have long been used to assist in setting bones. Photography is used to produce miniature electronic circuits, and photofabrication is a growing part of the metal-working industry.

As we learned in chapters 4 and 5, most type images for printing production are generated using light-sensitive material. In addition, negative and positive film images are used to record images on the plate or image carrier. All images carriers—whether used for relief, screen, or lithographic printing—can be prepared photographically.

All of the major printing processes place one consistent layer of ink on some receiver, such as paper. This idea cannot be overemphasized. *Printers only reproduce lines.* These lines can be so big that we see them as huge ink areas or so small that we need a magnifying glass to see them, but they all have the same ink density (figure 6.1). The primary concern of this chapter is the production of line images that

can be used with the printing processes. This process is called **line photography.**

Except by using special techniques, it is not possible to print a continuous-tone photograph. **Continuous-tone photographs** have varying shades of grey called **tones**. A picture reproduced in a book or a magazine is not a continuous-tone image. Such a picture is reproduced through **halftone photography.** This process breaks the tones of a picture into small, dense dots that trick the eye into seeing what appear to be various tones. Chapter 7 deals with halftone photography.

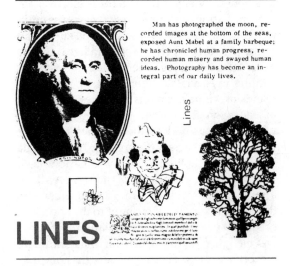

Man has photographed the moon, recorded images at the bottom of the seas, exposed Aunt Mabel at a family barbeque; he has chronicled human progress, recorded human misery and swayed human ideas. Photography has become an integral part of our daily lives.

Figure 6.1. Examples of line reproduction.
This illustration shows some different images that are reproduced by lines.

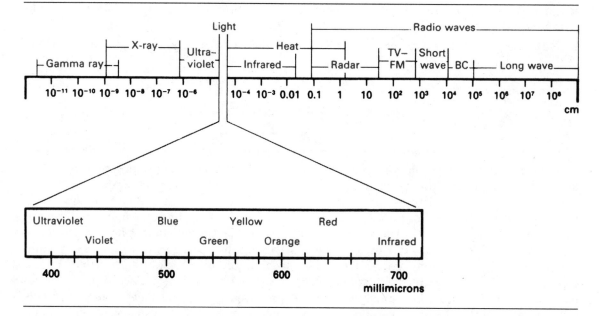

Figure 6.2.   **Wavelengths of different colors of the visible light spectrum**

The Nature of Light

It is generally agreed that light is electromagnetic radiation measured in wavelengths emitted from either a natural source (the sun) or an artificial source (such as a camera light) (figure 6.2). All electromagnetic radiation, whether gamma rays, visible light, heat, or radio and television signals, travels in waves. The effect of radiation is determined by wavelength, which is measured as the distance from one wave crest to the next (figure 6.3). The top scale in figure 6.2 shows that X-ray radiation has a very short wavelength while radio waves have a long wavelength. Figure 6.2 also illustrates the relationship of visible light to the spectrum of known electromagnetic radiation. Light has wavelengths in the spectrum that stimulate our optic nerves. These wavelengths comprise the **visible spectrum.**

Because light waves are short, they are generally measured in millimicrons (mμ)

(1 mμ = 1 billionth of 1 meter or 25 millionths of 1 inch) or in angstrom units (A.U.) (1 mμ = 10 A.U.). Each color of the visible spectrum has a unique wavelength. White light is the balanced presence of radiation from the visible spectrum.

The human eye can perceive wavelengths from about 400 mμ to about 700 mμ. In other words, if we can see it we call it "light." The shorter wavelengths (closer to 400 mμ) produce the colors on the blue end of the spectrum; the longer wavelengths (closer to 700

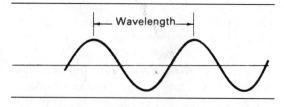

Figure 6.3.   **Diagram of wavelength**

mμ) produce the colors at the red end of the spectrum. The human eye is most sensitive to the green portion, or center portion, of the visible spectrum, between 500 mμ and 580 mμ.

The basis of photography is a chemical change caused when radiation in the visible spectrum contacts a light-sensitive material called an **emulsion**. As explained in appendix B, graphic arts photographic processes use artificial light sources that vary in the range of wavelengths of visible light they produce. Some light sources produce wavelengths high in the blue end of the spectrum; others produce wavelengths high in the red end. As will be seen in what follows, light-sensitive emulsions are formulated to record select wavelengths of light. That is, emulsions are produced that are sensitive to some colors in the spectrum but not to others.

Light-Sensitive Materials

All light-sensitive materials, whether films or plates, can be classified according to three main variables:

- Color sensitivity
- Contrast
- Film speed

Color Sensitivity
Color sensitivity describes the area of the visible electromagnetic spectrum that causes a chemical change in a particular emulsion. A **wedge spectrogram** is often used to show a film's reaction to light across the visible spectrum (figure 6.4a). Notice, for example, that blue-sensitive film (figure 6.4b) is only exposed by wavelenghts of light from the left end of the visible spectrum—from about 400 mμ to 550 mμ. The height of the graph indicates sensitivity. Wavelengths near the center of the sensitivity range—around 475 mμ—produce the fastest chemical reactions. A greater amount of

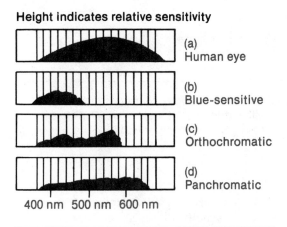

Height indicates relative sensitivity

(a) Human eye
(b) Blue-sensitive
(c) Orthochromatic
(d) Panchromatic

400 nm   500 nm   600 nm

Figure 6.4.   **Examples of wedge spectrograms.** A wedge spectrogram shows a film's reaction to light across the visible spectrum.

light is needed from the 400 mμ or 550 mμ ends to obtain the same film exposure.

There are three basic types of light-sensitive emulsions: blue-sensitive, orthochromatic, and panchromatic materials.

Blue-sensitive materials are often called "color blind" because they react to only the blue end of the spectrum (figure 6.4b). On a negative they record high densities from blue light, but they record very little from the green or red end of the spectrum. Roomlight film, which can be used outside the darkroom, is blue-light sensitive.

Orthochromatic material is not red-sensitive, but it is sensitive to all other portions of the visible spectrum (figure 6.4c). Because they are not sensitive to red light, "ortho films" can be safely handled under a red darkroom safelight.

Most film manufacturers provide a wedge spectrograph for each of their films. Figure 6.5 illustrates the sensitivity of one type of ortho film. The most efficient and accurate

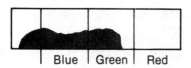

Figure 6.5.   Wedge spectrogram for Kodak Ko-dalith Ortho film 2556, type 3 (ESTAR base).
Courtesy of Eastman Kodak Company.

photographs are obtained when the peak sensitivity of a film's spectrograph corresponds to the peak output of a light source (See appendix B).

Panchromatic material is sensitive to all visible colors and is approximately as sensitive as the human eye (figure 6.4d). Because they are sensitive to all of the colors that humans see, "pan films" can be used to record variations in tone and are ideally suited for continuous-tone photography. Being sensitive to all wavelengths of light also means that a panchromatic emulsion is exposed by any visible light that strikes it. Therefore, pan films must be processed in total darkness.

Contrast

Contrast, the second variable that can be used to classify light-sensitive materials, is a term that describes the compression or expansion of the shades or tones of original copy on the film or plate. (Refer to figure 7.4 in chapter 7 for a comparison of normal and high contrast pictures.)

Contrast is described by a film's **characteristic curve,** also called a "log E curve," "H & D curve," "Density-log E curve," "D-log E curve," or "sensitometric curve" (figure 6.6).

Film manufacturers provide characteristic curves for each of their films. Figure 6.7 illustrates the curves for Kodak's Ortho 3, an extremely high-contrast film. These curves reveal that a very slight change in exposure pro-

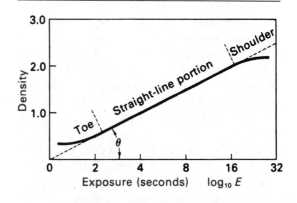

Figure 6.6.   Example of a film's characteristic curve. The toe of the curve is a gradual incline because a light-sensitive material does not produce a predictable density when exposed by a small amount of light. In other words, a predictable amount of density is not developed until a specific exposure time is reached. The straight-line portion represents an expected density development for each exposure. Eventually, the curve shoulders off even as exposure is increased—that is, the film fails to produce an expected amount of density as the exposure increases. The film fails to reciprocate.

vides a rapid jump in film density. This quality is ideal for printing production because the film records sharp, clean lines between image and nonimage areas of the original copy.

Film Speed

Film speed is the third main variable that can be used to classify light-sensitive materials. Each film or plate material requires a different amount of light to cause a chemical change in the emulsion. Emulsions that require little light are called "fast" while those that require a lot of light are called "slow." Because there are so many different emulsions requiring different amounts of light, the concept of "fast versus slow" is meaningless, however. For that rea-

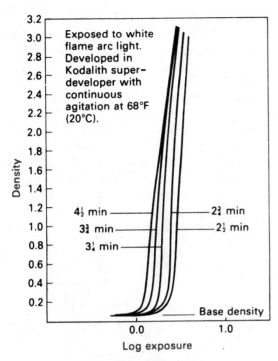

Figure 6.7. Characteristic curves for Kodak Ortho 3 film.
Courtesy of Eastman Kodak Company.

Table 6.1. Exposure indexes for meters marked for "ASA" speeds or exposure indexes

White-Flame Arc	Tungsten or Quartz-Iodine	Pulsed-Xenon*
10	6	10

*This value indicates the relative speed of this material to pulsed-xenon illumination as measured by a conventional time-totalizing device.

Note: Example of exposure—When making a same-size (1:1) line reproduction under average shop conditions, with two 35-ampere arc lamps about 48 inches from the copyboard, expose for about 10 seconds at *f* 32.

Source: Eastman Kodak Company.

son, an **exposure index** is assigned to each film by the manufacturer. The ASA system (developed by the American National Standards Institute) applies a number scale to relative film speed—the higher the number, the faster the film. For example, a film with an ASA rating of 25 requires twice as much light to create the same image density as does a film rated at ASA 50. Exposure index is assigned as a function of the type of light source used to expose the film. Table 6.1 lists the ASA ratings assigned to Kodak's Ortho 3 film under different lighting conditions.

It is important to understand that color sensitivity, contrast, and film speed are unrelated variables that cannot be compared directly. It is possible to produce films that exhibit any combination of these three characteristics.

Film Emulsions

All photographic films use some type of light-sensitive material called an emulsion to record an image. The characteristics of the light-sensitive emulsion, as well as the quantity and type of light reaching that emulsion, determine the sort of image recorded on the film. Most film emulsions are formed from silver halide suspended in a gelatin compound (picture fruit suspended in a bowl of gelatin). The most common film emulsion component is silver bromide ($AgBr$), which reacts rapidly and predictably. Silver iodide (AgI) and silver chloride ($AgCl$) are less common emulsion components and are almost always used with silver bromide to produce different film characteristics.

Despite their chemical differences, all films are structured in the same general manner (figure 6.8). The emulsion is bonded to a base material by an adhesive lower layer. Glass was long used as base material because it is transparent and extremely stable. Most materials change size or shape when the temperature changes. It is very important in graphic arts photography that the base supporting the

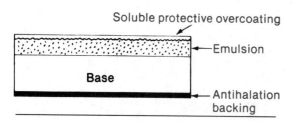

Figure 6.8.　A typical film structure

emulsion not change size. If it does, an image may distort or fail to fit exactly in the desired location on the printed page.

Glass is still used in some topographic mapping and electronic circuitry—fields in which perfect registration (image location) is critical and in which the size of the film must not change with humidity, temperature, or age. In contrast, graphic arts films are usually made from a cellulose-ester- or polystyrene-based material. The advantage these materials have over glass is that they are flexible and much less expensive. Several patented flexible bases, such as Cronar, have been developed for this purpose. These materials compete with glass in dimensional stability.

In addition to the stability problems of base materials, there are stability problems caused when the emulsion and the base are laminated because each part is affected differently by the environment and by age. For many years film was formed from only the base and the emulsion material. This type of film had several problems, however. During exposure the light would pass through the camera lens, strike and expose the emulsion, and then pass through the base material. It would reflect from the back of the base material and again pass through the emulsion, re-exposing it (figure 6.9a). To prevent this effect, an **antihalation dye** is now placed over the back of the film base. Instead of being reflected, the light is absorbed by the dye and exposes

the film only once (figure 6.9b). The antihalation dye also serves as an anticurl agent with flexible base films. The antihalation dye dissolves during chemical processing.

Another problem a film made of only a base and an emulsion had was the gelatin material in the emulsion was frail. To overcome this weakness, the emulsion is blanketed with a transparent protective layer called overcoating (figure 6.8). This **overcoating** protects the gelatin material from fingerprints and adds an antistress factor during handling. Like the antihalation dye, the overcoating dissolves during chemical processing.

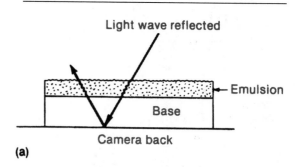

(a)

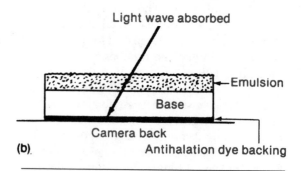

(b)

Figure 6.9.　Comparison of light rays through two types of film structure. Without the antihalation dye layer (a) light reflected from the back of the film base reexposes the emulsion. The antihalation dye (b) absorbs the light rays and prevents reexposure.

Camera Fundamentals

Line photography is also called "process photography," "reproduction photography," or "high-contrast photography." Whatever label is applied, the goals are the same: to make precision enlargements and reductions, and to critically control line dimensions with a process camera.

Process cameras vary in type, size, complexity, and cost. Regardless of their differences, all process cameras provide four basic services:

- A place to mount the light-sensitive film and the orginal image
- A means of focusing an image on the film
- A system to enlarge or reduce the original image on the film
- A system to control the amount of light that reaches the film emulsion

Process Camera Concepts

To understand how a process camera works first build a general understanding of how any photographic system operates. Then move on to how line photography uses the same approach. All that is required for process photography is a light source, a light-tight box to hold the film, a way to focus an image on the film, a way to control the amount of light that reaches the film, and, of course, something to photograph.

Whatever the light source, it should be directed at the object to be photographed because film records reflected light. It is easy to position an artificial light source so that all areas of the object receive the proper amount of light. If we use natural light (the sun), we have to position the object to get the proper illumination. In line photography, artificial light is always used to illuminate the image because uniform illumination across the image is required.

Process Camera Controls

Process cameras all have the same controls. There must be some sort of opening through which to pass and aim light. This is called the **lens.** It is necessary to be able to move the lens so the light reflected from the object is sharp and clear on the film. This movement is called **focusing.** If the image is not in focus, a blurred picture results.

After the image is focused, there must be a way to control the amount of light that passes through the lens. This is important. If too little light reaches the film, no image is recorded. If too much light strikes the film, then the film is completely exposed. The two ways to control this passage of light are by controlling:

- The size of the lens opening
- The amount of time the lens is open

A simple way to understand how light is controlled is to think of a camera lens as a water faucet and of light as the water that passes through the pipe. First, consider the size of the pipe. It seems logical that a 2-inch pipe will pass nearly twice the amount of water as a 1-inch pipe in the same amount of time. If we run water through the 1-inch pipe for twice as much time as through the 2-inch pipe, the same amount of water should pass through each pipe. This example is not mathematically accurate in terms of the amount of water passed, but it does show the importance of the relationship between time and area. Actually, the amount of water—or light—that passes through an opening is a function of the area of the pipe, not the diameter.

The light controls for a camera operate like the water faucet. We can accurately control the amount of time the lens or "pipe" stays open with the **shutter.** This amount of time is called **shutter speed**. It is also possible to vary the size of the lens opening. This opening is called the **aperture**. The aperture is controlled by the **diaphragm.** The size of the aperture is based on the f/stop system (figure 6.10).

The **f/stop system** is based on the ratio of the aperture diameter to the focal length of the camera lens. **Focal length** is the distance from the node, or center, of the lens to the film board when the lens is focused at infinity (maximum reduction for graphic arts cameras). The for-mula to determine an f/stop number is:

f/number = focal length/diameter of the aperture

For example, if the lens has an 8-inch fo-cal length, a 1-inch aperture is assigned the f/stop value of f/8 (8 ÷ 1 = 8). A 1/2-inch aperture is f/16 (8 ÷ 1/2 = 16). In theory it is possible to create any f/stop number. An aper-ture diameter of 3/8 inches produces f/21.33 (8 ÷ 3/8 = 21.33). However, lens manufactur-ers have agreed upon a sequence of the most efficient f/stop numbers or ratios. The num-bers are f/1.4, f/2, f/2.8, f/4, f/5.6, f/8, f/11, f/16, f/22, f/32, and f/64. Graphic arts process cameras generally use ratios from f/8 to f/64.

All of these numbers—or ratios—differ by a factor of 2 in the amount of light they pass. In other words, moving from one f/stop to an-other either doubles or halves the amount of light. Notice in figure 6.10 that the larger the f/stop number, the smaller the aperture. Changing the f/stop from f/32 to f/22 doubles the aperture. Moving from f/16 to f/22 halves it. This is an especially powerful tool in deter-mining equivalent exposures.

The diaphragm and shutter work to-gether. Each f/stop either doubles or halves the cross-sectional area of the preceding f/stop. Therefore, the shutter speed can be halved or doubled to correspond with a one-step di-aphragm change. (Remember, changing the f/stop actually changes the diameter of the aperture.) For example, if the film were being exposed correctly at f/16 for 40 seconds, an **equivalent exposure** could be made at f/8 for

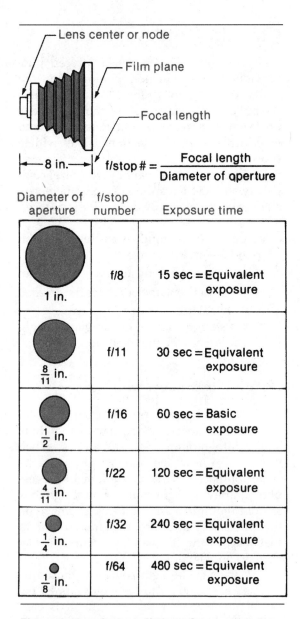

Diameter of aperture	f/stop number	Exposure time
1 in.	f/8	15 sec = Equivalent exposure
8/11 in.	f/11	30 sec = Equivalent exposure
1/2 in.	f/16	60 sec = Basic exposure
4/11 in.	f/22	120 sec = Equivalent exposure
1/4 in.	f/32	240 sec = Equivalent exposure
1/8 in.	f/64	480 sec = Equivalent exposure

Figure 6.10.   Camera f/stops. Camera f/stops are the relationships between focal lengths and lens opening sizes. In this figure, the focal length is always 8 inches but the lens opening sizes vary from 1 inch to 1/8 inch. The basic exposure time is 60 seconds (f/16). Equivalent exposure times are given for the remaining f/stops.

10 seconds (f/16 @ 40 sec = f/11 @ 20 sec. = f/8 @ 10 sec.) The same amount of light would hit the film, and the film record would be the same. An understanding of this relationship is a powerful tool for any photographer. A camera operator often seeks to reduce the exposure time to save time and camera lights which, like any artificial light source, wear out with use.

Because f/stop numbers result from mathematical formulas that are based on focal length and aperture diameter, information can be accurately compared between different cameras. In other words, f/16 on a 35-mm camera and f/16 on a large process camera pass the same amount of light.

Process Camera Classifications

The process camera is large—as large as a printing plate—because it must be able to hold large sheets of film, but it is really nothing more than a sophisticated light-tight box. The film end of the camera opens to show a **filmboard** (figure 6.11), which holds the film in place during the exposure. A vacuum-back filmboard is generally used to hold the film flat on the filmboard and ensure that it does not shift during exposure. The filmboard hinges closed and is parallel to the copyboard at the opposite end of the camera. The **copyboard** is simply a glass-covered frame that holds the copy to be photographed. There are general guidelines on both the film and the copyboard that, if followed, ensure that the image records in the center of the film.

Process cameras have an artificial light source that directs light at the copyboard. Most light systems are controlled by the camera shutter. When a timer opens the shutter, the lights go on. They automatically shut off when the timer closes the shutter.

One great advantage of the process camera is that it can enlarge and reduce original copy. Size changes are referred to by the percentage of the original that is to be recorded

on the film. A 100 percent or 1:1 reproduction exposes an image on the film that is the same size as the original copy. A 25 percent reduction exposes an image that is one-quarter the original size. A 200 percent enlargement exposes an image that is twice the size of the original copy. The percentage of enlargement or reduction is controlled by changing the positions of the camera lens and the copyboard. On some cameras this adjustment is made manually by lining up percentage tapes (see figure 6.12) or by following guide numbers provided by the camera manufacturer. Newer cameras, such as the one shown in figure 6.11, have digital readout devices that can be used to set the lens and copyboard automatically through the camera console.

The amount of light necessary to produce a quality image on the film is calculated at a 100 percent (or same-size) reproduction called "basic exposure" (see the Basic Exposure and Camera Operation section later in this chapter). Whenever the positions of the lens and copyboard are changed for enlargement or reduction, the distance the reflected light must travel from the copyboard to reach the film changes, and thus the amount of light that reaches the film also changes. Whatever the percentage of enlargement or reduction, the quantity of light reaching the film must remain the same as for a 100 percent reproduction to produce an acceptable exposure. Most process cameras have a **variable diaphragm control** that increases or decreases the amount of light reaching the film. This control changes the f/stop (aperture) to correspond to the percentage of enlargement or reduction. For example, if a 67 percent reduction is being made, the diaphragm control is moved to align with 67 percent. With this method, the exposure time remains the same and only the aperture opening varies to provide the correct exposure.

A more accurate tool to control film exposure is a **light integrator** (figure 6.13). A light integrator uses a photoelectric cell. This cell is

Figure 6.11.   A horizontal process camera.
Courtesy of ACTI Products, Inc.

connected to a device that measures the units of light reaching the film. With a light integrator, the camera operator simply dials the desired amount of light. The lens automatically closes when that quantity of light has reached the photoelectric cell. Any variation in light, such as changes in the voltage of the power source that operates the camera lights, are automatically accounted for.

Process cameras can be classified according to where they are intended to be used or according to their basic shapes. A **galley camera** is designed to operate in normal room light, so the film has to be loaded in a darkroom and

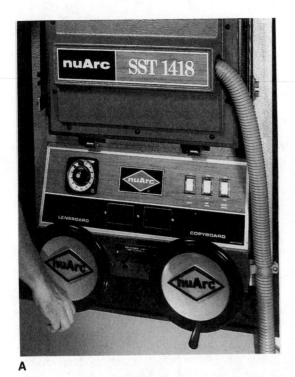

A

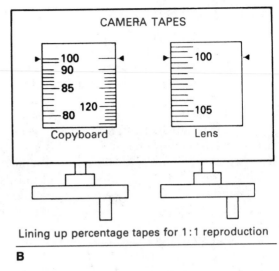

B

Figure 6.12.   **Adjusting the distance between the camera lens and the copyboard.** (a) Before exposing the film, the operator must adjust the camera to achieve the correct size of the final image. (b) On some cameras, this is done by moving the percentage tapes until both are set at the desired reproduction size. Courtesy of nuArc Company, Inc.

then carried in a light-tight container to the camera. A **darkroom camera** is designed to operate in a safelight situation, so the photographer can load the film in the camera without leaving the darkroom.

Process cameras can also be classified in terms of their design. A **horizontal process camera** (figure 6.11) has a long stationary bed. The film end is usually in the darkroom and the lights and lens protrude through a wall into a normally lighted room (figure 6.14). A **vertical process camera** is a self-contained unit that takes up little space in the darkroom (figure 6.15).

Figure 6.13.   **A light integrator.** This machine automatically controls the amount of light used to expose the film in the camera. Courtesy of Graphic Arts Manufacturing Co.

Basic Exposure and Camera Operation

In general, **basic exposure** is the camera aperture-and-shutter speed combination that produces a quality film image of normal line copy with standardized chemical processing. The basic exposure will differ from one camera to the next depending on many variables, such as energy level of the light source, color temperature (see appendix B), processing chemicals, temperature control, rate of agitation, copy characteristics, and, especially, type of film. Whenever one of the variables changes, however slightly, the basic exposure must be recalculated. Once the basic exposure has been determined, it can be used to accurately predict new exposure times for any change in reproduction size or copy characteristics. The procedures for determining basic camera exposure are explained in detail in appendix A.

Let us work through the concept of basic exposure using a typical line exposure exam-

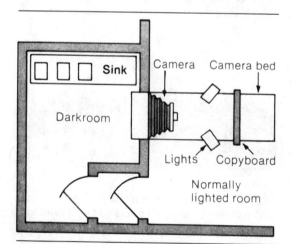

Figure 6.14.   A horizontal process camera installed between two rooms. The diagram shows a horizontal process camera with the copy end in a normally lighted room and the film end in a darkroom.

ple. Assume that our task is to produce a high-contrast negative, such as the copy shown in figure 6.1, which can be used to expose a printing plate. Remember: high contrast means two tones—image or no image, ink or no ink. In order to meet job specifications, we are told to provide a 53 percent reduction. Our process camera is a horizontal model with a basic exposure of f/16 for 22 seconds. (The explanation that follows can also be applied to a vertical camera.)

Mounting the Copy

Begin by mounting the copy in the copyboard. Swing the copyboard to a horizontal position and open the glass cover. Spots of dirt or dust can interfere with image quality, so the glass should be thoroughly cleaned on both sides before each use. There is usually some sort of guideline system on the copyboard that allows the original to be placed nearly perfectly in the center of the copyboard (figure 6.16). The copyboard guidelines align with guidelines on the filmboard. Because the camera lens reverses the image, place the copy so that it will be upside down when the copyboard is in a vertical position. If fine focusing is necessary, seeing the image right-side-up is less confusing.

A graphic arts **step tablet** or **grey scale** is a tool used by camera operators to aid in judging the quality of a film image (figure 6.17). With every exposure, the camera operator places the grey scale on the copyboard next to the material being photographed (figure 6.18). The exact position of the grey scale does not matter, but it is important that it does not cover any line detail. It should also receive the same amount of light as the copy and be in a position so it is recorded on the film. When the film is developed, both the copy image and the grey scale are visible. As individual density steps on the scale darken and fill during development, they serve as visual cues that indicate the stage of film development. After development, the

Figure 6.15. A vertical process camera.
Courtesy of nuArc Company, Inc.

grey scale image on the film serves as a means of judging the film's usability.

When the copy and grey scale are in position, close the glass over the copyboard and turn on the vacuum pump. Again check for lint or dust in the image area, and make sure that the copy has not moved. Swing the copyboard into a vertical position so that it is parallel to the filmboard.

Focusing

Enlargement and reduction on our horizontal process camera are controlled by percentage tapes. By moving the tapes, the relative positions of the lens and copyboard can be changed so that the image is in perfect focus and is reproduced in the required size at the same time. To make a 53 percent reproduction, both tapes are positioned at 53 percent.

Some cameras have ground-glass screens that can be used to check both image position and focus. Swing or place the ground glass into focusing or viewing position. When the camera lights are turned on, the reflected image projects through the lens onto the inside layer of glass and it is possible to use a magnifying glass to check the focus.

Figure 6.16.   Mounting copy in the copyboard. The copy is centered on the copyboard guidelines and positioned to be upside down when the frame is in the vertical position.
Courtesy of nuArc Company, Inc.

It might be necessary to adjust the camera lights to achieve even illumination across the image. It is generally recommended to set the lights at 45-degree angles from the copyboard frame (figure 6.19). The ground-glass image can be used to judge the evenness of intensity across the image. Some types of reflection densitometers (see chapter 7) can be used to make the same, but more precise, measurement.

Setting the Aperture and Shutter Speed

Next, prepare the aperture and shutter speed timer controls. Set the timer for the basic exposure time. For our example this is 22 seconds. Because we are making a 53 percent reduction, move the variable diaphragm control arm to 53 percent on the f/16 scale (figure 6.20). This setting automatically adjusts the lens opening (aperture) for the proper quantity of light at a 53 percent reduction.

It is important to understand that when the variable diaphragm control is moved along this scale, the f/stop setting changes to correspond to the basic camera exposure. The f/stop setting for the basic exposure is determined at a 100 percent (same-size) exposure. In this example, a 53 percent reduction is being made. When the percentage tapes are set at 53 percent, the relative positions of the lens, filmboard, and copyboard are different from what they would be at a 100 percent reproduction (figure 6.21). Thus, the intensity of the light striking the film will be different as well. An adjustment has to be made to either the exposure time or to the aperture to allow the proper amount of light to reach the film. If the exposure time is kept the same, the variable diaphragm control can be used to change the aperture. Without a variable diaphragm control, a new calculation for exposure time has to be made each time an enlargement or reduction is made. This calculation compensates for

Figure 6.17. A grey scale.
Courtesy of Stouffer Graphic Arts Equipment Co.

the light intensity change at the filmboard which results from each change in lens and copyboard position. The variable diaphragm control provides a scale with the calculations already computed.

Digital Control

On cameras with digital control, it is often unnecessary to manually adjust the copyboard or filmboard, or to manually set the aperture opening. Instead, the camera operator keyboards in the required enlargement or reduction information. A microcomputer in the camera automatically makes the camera adjustments. The most sophisticated digital cameras have memory and can remember the basic exposure times and conditions used for producing a variety of exposures. With these cameras, the operator needs only to enter enlargement and reduction information, then call for the appropriate exposure program by entering a keyboard code. The microcomputer sets the camera according to preprogrammed information.

The preceding first steps of setting up the camera for making a line exposure can be performed in normal room light; the following last steps cannot.

Mounting the Film

The process darkroom is normally equipped with a dual lighting system—normal room light and a **safelight** that does not expose the film. Recall figure 6.4. Safelights are selected according to the film emulsion sensitivity being used. When working with high-contrast, orthochromatic film use a red safelight (figure 6.4c). Use a white light for preparatory work only.

With only the red safelight on, carefully open the film box, remove one sheet of film, and replace the cover. A common error for new photographers is to forget to close the box until after the camera exposure has been made. With some darkroom designs, most of the film in the box has been ruined by that time.

Handle film only by the outside edges. If a wet or even moist finger touches the emulsion, a fingerprint can appear on the developed film and ruin the image's usability.

Center the sheet of film on the guidelines on the filmboard with the emulsion side up (so that it faces the copyboard when the filmboard is closed). There are rare instances when the emulsion side is placed face down, but in

Figure 6.18.   Using a grey scale. Place a graphic arts grey scale next to the copy, but do not allow it to cover any image area.
Courtesy of R. Kampas.

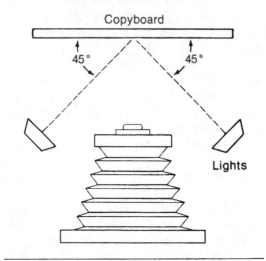

Figure 6.19.   Position of camera lights. The camera lights are usually positioned at 45-degree angles from the copyboard.

general the film is exposed through the emulsion. Even in the red light of the darkroom it is easy to identify the emulsion side of the film.

There are three basic ways to identify the emulsion side of a piece of film. The easiest way is to look at the sheet. The darker side is the antihalation dye layer, and the lighter side is the emulsion (figure 6.22). This is easy to remember because the antihalation dye is dark to absorb the light that passes through the film.

A second way to identify the emulsion side is by remembering that most films tend to curl into the emulsion side. Be careful, however, because the heat of your hand can cause curling in either direction. The third method of identifying the emulsion side of a piece of film works only for film that is intended for use in total or nearly complete darkness. On such film, the manufacturer uses a notching system. Each type of film has a unique pattern of notches so that the photographer can identify different materials in the dark by using only a fingertip (figure 6.23). The notches also serve to identify the emulsion side. If the sheet is held so that the notches are in the upper

Figure 6.20. **Setting the aperture control.** Adjust the aperture by moving the diaphragm arm to the reproduction percentage size to align with the f/stop size for the basic exposure.
Courtesy of nuArc Company, Inc.

right-hand corner, the emulsion is facing the photographer.

In most cameras, the film is held in place on the filmboard by a vacuum system. It is necessary to adjust the filmboard so that vacuum pressure is applied uniformly over the entire area of the film sheet and does not lose holding power by pulling air where there is no film. Individual cameras are adjusted differently, but most are designed to accommodate the most common film sizes.

With the film in place, turn on the vacuum pump and carefully roll the film with a roller to remove any air pockets that might be trapped under the sheet (figure 6.24). Be extremely careful; the emulsion is very fragile and is easily scratched. To eliminate the possibility of air pockets, many photographers turn on the vacuum and then roll the film into position.

Exposing the Film

The last step is to make the exposure. Swing the filmboard so that it is parallel to the copyboard, and lock the frame into place. When you push the timer control button, the camera lights automatically go on and the shutter opens. When the preset exposure time has been reached (22 seconds for this example), the shutter closes and the lights go off. Open the camera back, turn off the vacuum, and remove the film. The film appears no different than it did before the exposure, but it now carries an invisible, or latent, image (see the following

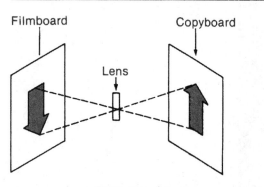

100% Reproduction

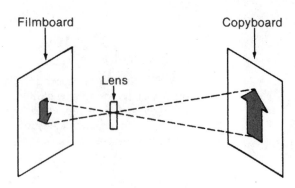

50% Reduction

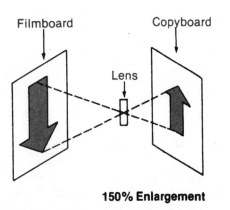

150% Enlargement

Figure 6.21. **Adjustments for enlargements or reductions.** The relative position of the filmboard, lens, and copyboard change for enlargements and reductions. This change affects the intensity of light striking the filmboard. To maintain the intensity of a 100 percent reproduction, adjustments must be made to exposure time or aperture opening.

section called Chemical Processing). Chemical processing is necessary to make the latent image visible and permanent.

Chemical Processing

The purpose of film development during chemical processing is to change the latent or invisible image on a sheet of exposed film to a visible and permanent image.

Figure 6.22. **Identifying the emulsion side by its color.** The emulsion side, or lighter side, of the film is placed face up on the filmboard.

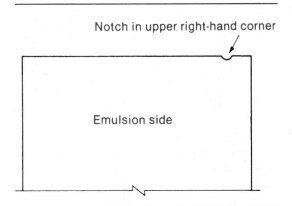

Figure 6.23. **Using notches to identify the emulsion side.** When the film notches are in the upper right-hand corner, the emulsion side is up.

Figure 6.24. **Removing air pockets from the film.** After positioning the film on the filmboard, turn on the vacuum and carefully roll the sheet to remove any trapped air.
Courtesy of R. Kampas.

Processing Chemicals

When light of the proper quantity and quality (wavelength and intensity respectively) strikes the light-sensitive silver halide emulsion on the film, a change takes place. It is a subtle change in the chemical structure of the halide crystals, a change that cannot be detected by the human eye. Because this change is invisible, an exposure is said to produce a **latent image.**

Light passes through the lens to the film and selectively alters portions of the emulsion according to the amount of light reflected from the copy on the copyboard. The white areas of the original copy (generally nonimage areas) reflect a great deal of light, which causes many halide crystals to blacken. The black or pigmented areas of the original (generally the image areas) absorb most of the light, reflecting little back to the film and thus changing very few or no halide crystals. These crystals do not blacken. This is a very important concept. Photography depends on light reflected from the original copy to record a reverse (or negative) image on a sheet of film (figure 6.25).

To reiterate, where light is reflected from the original copy, halide crystals change. Where halide crystals change, the film is black after processing. This is the film record image of the white (nonimage) areas on the

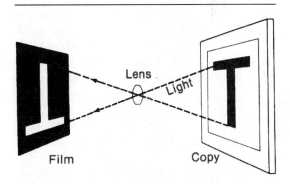

Figure 6.25. **Film exposure.** The light reflected from the nonimage or light portions of the original copy exposes the film and results in a negative image where the reflected light was not absorbed by the film.

photographed copy. Where light is not reflected from the copy halide crystals do not change. The film in these areas is clear after processing because the unchanged halide crystals wash away during processing. The clear areas on the film are the film record of the dark (image) areas on the copy. This is why a film image is a "negative" of the original copy—the dark and light areas of the copy and the film are reversed.

Processing Steps

For lith or orthochromatic films, at least three chemical solutions and a water bath are used during film processing. The steps in film processing are as follows:

1. Developing the film
2. Stopping the development
3. Fixing the image
4. Washing away the chemical residue

Developing the Film

The **developer** is a complex solution designed to make the latent image visible. It has three weaknesses, however. The solution contains an organic compound, called the developing agent, dissolved in water. The developer changes each exposed silver halide crystal to a grain of black metallic silver (which is why exposed areas of the film blacken during processing). The change takes place very slowly, so an activator (usually sodium hydroxide) is added to speed the process. In addition to being very slow, the developing agent oxidizes (loses its ability to work when exposed to air). When a developer turns brown, oxidation has broken down the activity level of the developer and no film can be processed in it. A preservative, usually sodium sulfite, is added to the developer solution to delay the effects of oxidation.

The third and final weakness of the developer is that it is "infectious." When all of the

exposed silver halide crystals have been changed to black metallic silver, the solution begins to work on the unexposed crystals. If the process were allowed to continue, the entire sheet of film would be a solid layer of black silver and it would be unusable. This is why lith film must be removed from the developer as soon as the exposed silver halide crystals have changed to black metallic silver.

An unexposed area of film that does not appear clear is called "fogged." Fog can result from accidental exposure to light or to developing agents. To prevent fog, a restrainer, generally potassium bromide, is added to the developer solution.

Although developers differ in the characteristics of the chemical emulsion of the film, they are all made of the following five parts:

1. Solvent (water)
2. Developing agent
3. Activator
4. Preservative
5. Restrainer

Developer manufacturers always recommend development procedures for their chemicals. It is critical for both personal safety and predictability of results to always follow these specifications exactly. Manufacturers also recommend the maximum number of square inches of film that should be processed in a quantity of developer solution before new developer should be mixed. Most developer solutions are designed to function at exactly 68°F (20°C). Any temperature fluctuation decreases the predictability of the results.

Stopping the Development

Once the desired level of development has been reached, the developing action must be halted immediately. Plunging the film from the developer (a base) into an acid solution stops developer activity. This acid solution is called the **stop-bath** or **short-stop.** It is usually made of a small amount of acetic acid combined with a large amount of water. The stop-bath really serves two functions:

- To halt the film development
- To extend the life of the third solution, the fixer

Fixing the Image
After development is stopped, the image on the piece of film is visible but not permanent. The silver halide crystals that were not exposed are still in the emulsion and are visible as cloudy areas in the clear areas of the film. These unexposed crystals are still sensitive to light. The fixing bath removes all of these unexposed silver crystals and makes the film image permanent.

The **fixing bath** is a chemical solution that is nearly as complex as the developer. As with all photographic chemicals, its main solvent is water. Water does not dissolve unexposed halide crystals, but a compound called sodium thiosulfate or **hypo** does. This is such an important ingredient of the fixing bath that "hypo" is often used interchangeably with "fixer." Acetic acid, the primary ingredient of the stop-bath, is also added to the fixing bath to neutralize any developer that the film might still carry. The acetic acid, however, has a tendency to render the hypo useless as a fixing agent by turning it into small pieces of sulfur. To combat this reaction, a preservative called sodium sulfite, which combines with the sulfur and changes it back to hypo, is added to the fixing bath.

During development, the gelatin of the film emulsion swells because it absorbs the water. To reharden the gelatin, a hardener, such as potassium alum, is added to the fixing bath. A pH of 4 must be maintained (pH is a measure of acidity of a solution) if a hardener is used. To accomplish this step in the process, a buffer, such as boric acid, is used.

After development and the stop-bath, the unexposed portions of the film negative appear milky white under red safelight conditions. This milk-white color is actually the unexposed silver halide crystals that remain in the clear areas of the film. Fixing time is generally determined by leaving the film in the hypo twice the amount of time required to remove these unexposed crystals and make the film clear.

Washing Away the Chemical Residue
The fourth step for all photographic processes is to wash away all traces of the processing chemicals. During chemical processing, some of the processing solutions become attached to the film base and emulsion material. If the solutions are allowed to remain on the film, they can yellow or gradually begin to fade the image. Over a long storage time, they can also cause acid burns that eat through the base.

Because water is the main solvent for all of the processing solutions, a simple running-water bath removes all objectionable chemicals. Depending on the rate of water exchange, 10 minutes in a strong water flow should be sufficient to clean films; 30 to 45 minutes suffices for any other photographic materials, such as photographic paper prints.

Controlling Chemical Processing

There are many processes to store and work with the chemical baths, such as shallow-tray, deep-tank, or automatic. Whatever process is used, three variables must be controlled:

- Agitation
- Time
- Temperature

Agitation
Agitation refers to the flow of the chemical solution back and forth over the film during processing. If the film were allowed to sit

undisturbed in the solution, the chemicals in contact with the emulsion would quickly become exhausted. Agitation during development ensures that new chemicals continually flow over the film for constant chemical action. The rate of agitation is not important, but the consistency of the motion is.

By being consistent, the photographer can duplicate results for every piece of film that is processed. If the right and left pages of this book were made from two different pieces of film, and the piece of film that recorded the right page had been agitated more frequently or more rapidly than the piece of film that recorded the left page, the images on the right page would appear lighter than would the images on the left. This would be true even if both pieces of film were agitated for the same length of time. This is because the film for the right page, which had been agitated more frequently, would be overdeveloped, and the images would "fill in" (some of the unexposed silver halide crystals in the image areas would turn to black metallic silver). All of the images on the right page would appear thinner and smaller than would the images on the left.

Time and Temperature

Like agitation, time and chemical temperature in processing must be controlled. Several different types of darkroom timers are available to assist photographers in controlling processing times. If the temperature of a chemical is within 1/2 degree of the optimum (68°F or 20°C), the temperature is usually considered "in control" for line photography. Temperature control sinks are generally used to control chemical temperatures.

The film's manufacturer provides recommended processing times. For example, Kodak recommends that with the shallow-tray method, its lith film should be developed for 2 3/4 minutes with 10 seconds in the stopbath. It should be fixed twice as long as it takes to clear the film.

Shallow-Tray Chemical Processing

The following steps are used for chemical processing with the shallow-tray method (figure 6.26). All of these steps, except washing and drying, are carried out under safelight conditions.

1. Before placing the film in the developer, set the timer for the recommended developing time (usually 2 3/4 minutes). Place the dry, exposed film from the camera in the developer with the emulsion side up and cover the film completely with the liquid. (The film is placed emulsion side up in the developer so that you can inspect the image as it becomes visible during development. You could see the image develop if the film were emulsion side down in the developer, but because you would be looking through the dark antihalation backing, the image would appear to be developing more slowly than it is.) Remember to handle the film as little as possible; touch it only along the outside edges. As soon as the film is covered by the developer, turn on the timer and start agitating the film. Keep the agitation as consistent as possible. As the film develops, the latent image becomes visible. As soon as you can see the image, look for the image of the grey scale.

Visually inspecting the grey scale on the film as it develops allows you to correct for slight variations in time, temperature, agitation, or copy during development. For normal line copy, a solid step 4 should usually be obtained on the grey scale. Extremely fine-line detail should be developed less (steps 2 or 3); bold lines could be developed much more (steps 5 or 6) (figure 6.27). If for some reason the development time has reached the recommended length and normal copy shows only a solid step 3 on the scale, then the processing should be extended because optimal results have not yet been obtained. This could happen if the developer was old and almost exhausted. Development should not be extended much beyond the recommended time, however. If the

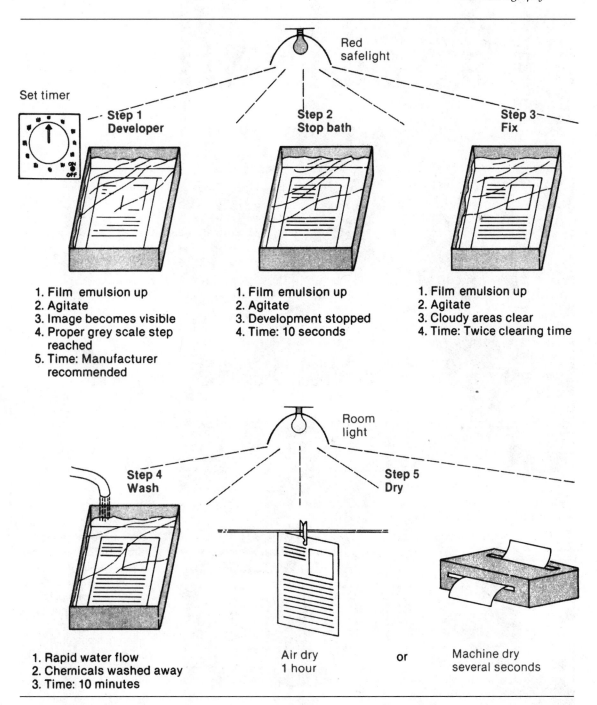

Set timer

Step 1
Developer

Step 2
Stop bath

Step 3
Fix

Red
safelight

1. Film emulsion up
2. Agitate
3. Image becomes visible
4. Proper grey scale step reached
5. Time: Manufacturer recommended

1. Film emulsion up
2. Agitate
3. Development stopped
4. Time: 10 seconds

1. Film emulsion up
2. Agitate
3. Cloudy areas clear
4. Time: Twice clearing time

Room
light

Step 4
Wash

Step 5
Dry

1. Rapid water flow
2. Chemicals washed away
3. Time: 10 minutes

Air dry
1 hour

or

Machine dry
several seconds

Figure 6.26. **Shallow-tray method of developing film**

Figure 6.27. Using a grey scale to gauge film development. Grey scales can be used to gauge the stage of development for a piece of film. Different types of copy are developed to different steps. In this example, normal copy is developed to step 4, fine-line copy is developed to step 3, and heavy copy is developed to step 6.

recommended time is 2 3/4 minutes and a solid step 4 has not been reached with normal copy after 5 minutes, discard the film and expose a new sheet. You may need either to increase the exposure time because some variable is not in control or to mix new developer.

2. When the correct grey scale step appears on the film, move the film to the stop-bath. To do this, lift the film out of the developer by one corner and let it drain briefly over the developing tray. Then place it in the stop-bath. Agitate the film in the stop-bath at the same consistent rate it was agitated throughout development. Leave the film in the stop-bath for at least 10 seconds.

3. Again pick the film up by one corner and let it drain into the stop-bath. Then move it to the fixer. Again, the film should be placed in the fixer emulsion side up. Watch the cloudy areas on the film as you agitate it in the fixer. Make a mental note of the length of time that it takes the cloudy areas to clear completely. Agitate the film in the fixer for twice the amount of time that it takes for the unexposed areas to lose their cloudy appearance. If it takes 20 seconds for the unexposed areas to clear completely, a 40-second fixing bath with constant agitation should suffice.

4. When the film has been fixed for the proper amount of time, lift it out of the fixer, let it drain, and put it in a running-water bath. Ten minutes of strong water flow should wash all remaining chemicals from the film.

5. After the film is washed, either hang it up to air dry or put it through a film dryer. Complete air drying usually takes up to 1 hour. Automatic film dryers can reduce this time to less than 1 minute.

Automatic Film Processing

In automatic film processing a continuous belt or roller system passes the film through a developer, a stop-fixer combination bath, a washing tank, and a dryer (figure 6.28). With deep-tank chemical storage, there is little problem with oxidation because there is little surface area of the liquid exposed to air. Long periods of disuse will cause some activity change. Chemical exhaustion as a result of film processing is controlled by adding a small quantity of replenisher after each piece of film enters the machine. The amount of replenisher that is generally added is a function of the area of the sheet of film being processed. When replenishers are used, the chemical solutions generally need to be removed from the tanks only several times a year for machine maintenance.

Automatic film processing is an attractive alternative to shallow-tray processing. Most automatic film processing units (figure 6.29) are designed for dry-to-dry (operator touches no liquids) delivery in 4 to 5 minutes. This is a tremendous advantage over shallow-tray processing because the photographer never gets wet hands and is free to make another exposure in the camera room while a sheet of film is processing. In addition, automatic processing provides accurate time, temperature, and agitation control and reduces production costs through faster processing. However, automatic processing should not be viewed as a solution for all production problems. It can, in fact, cause more problems than it solves.

There is no single chemical solution that can process all photographic materials a printer might use. If material that was not designed for use with the developer passes through the automatic processor, the material will not develop properly, and the chemical balance of the processor may change. Further, adding replenisher to the developer to keep the activity level correct is not simple. With most automatic processor machines, huge quantities of replenisher must be added after even an overnight shutdown when there is no second or third shift. **Control strips**

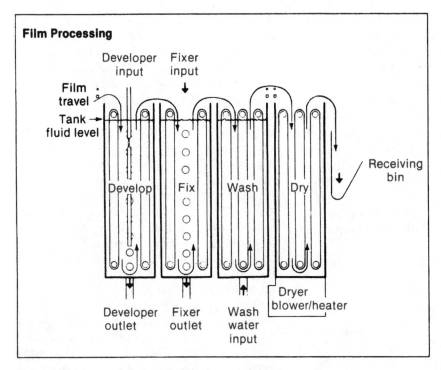

Film Processing

Figure 6.28.   Side view diagram of a typical automatic film processor.
Rollers move the film from tank to tank.

(pre-exposed film strips) are used to measure developer activity. Depending on the use level, the camera operator must feed a control strip through the machine to check the developer several times a day. If the strip is overdeveloped, the processing activity is too high. If the strip is underdeveloped, the processing activity is too low. Activity that is too low is corrected simply by using the automatic replenishment system. An activity level that is too high, however, is a larger problem. The

Figure 6.29.   An automatic film-processing unit. A unit like this machine provides greater accuracy and control of agitation, time, and temperature than is possible with manual processing methods.
Courtesy of Log E/LogEtronics, Inc.

general technique for reducing a high processing activity level is to expose several sheets of film to room light, send them through the automatic processor without replenisher, and then process another control strip. While all this is going on, no productive processing is taking place, film is being wasted, and the cost of the day's processing is mounting.

Whether shallow-tray or automatic processing is used, the problem of controlling chemical processing is a primary concern. If the camera operator is not aware of all the processing variables and the ways to control them, consistent high-quality results become impossible.

Film-to-Film Processes

While much graphic arts photography involves making transparent negatives from opaque positive originals, it is often necessary to produce film positives or negatives from film materials (when using positive-acting plates). Two common film-to-film processes are used in the industry:

- Camera copying from a back-lighted copyboard
- Contact printing

Back-Lighted Copyboard

Process cameras can have two types of copyboards. The first type was discussed previously and is called **solid-back copyboard**. This type is typically covered with black material. As was also discussed earlier, when a film negative is produced from positive, opaque copy mounted in a solid-back copyboard, light is reflected from the opaque copy, passes through the camera lens, and exposes a sheet of film.

The second type of copyboard is called **back-lighted copyboard.** With this type of copyboard, a transparent film negative or positive is placed in the copyboard over a sheet of frosted glass (figure 6.30). Lights behind the frosted glass project through the open (nonemulsion) areas of the transparent material to make the exposure. If a positive is placed in the copyboard, and a negative film is used in the camera, a negative is produced. A negative transparency placed in the copyboard produces a positive on the film. With this method, producing a duplicate negative from an original negative requires two steps. The operator must back light the original negative to produce a positive, then back light the positive to produce a new negative.

Duplicating Film

Duplicating film is designed to either produce film negatives from original negatives or film positives from original positives. Duplicating film can also be used to produce film positives from opaque originals. By using duplicating film, it is possible to produce a duplicate negative or duplicate positive in one step.

Contact Printing

Contact printing is the process of exposing a sheet of film (or other light-sensitive material) by passing light directly through a negative or a positive to an unexposed sheet of film. To make a contact positive from a negative, the emulsion side of a film negative is placed against the emulsion side of an unexposed sheet of film (figure 6.31). The two sheets are then pressed together, usually in a vacuum frame, until there are no air gaps between them. Light is projected through the open image areas in the negative to the emulsion of the unexposed film. Light is blocked by the emulsion in the nonimage areas on the negative. Thus, the image produced on the contact printed film is a positive. Contact printing can also be used for making negatives from positives by passing the light through a positive

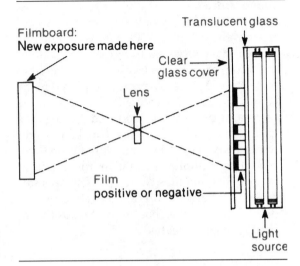

Figure 6.30.   Diagram of a back-lighted copyboard. A back-lighted copyboard is needed to photograph transparent negative or positive film.

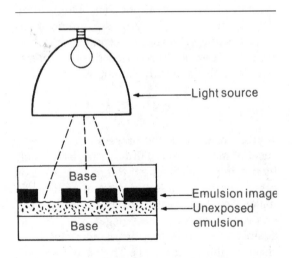

Figure 6.31.   Contact printing. This diagram shows the proper placement of the film negative against a fresh sheet of film to make a contact positive. Note that the two pieces of film are placed emulsion to emulsion.

film image, or for making duplicate images in one step with duplicating film.

A grey scale is usually not used with contact printing, so there is no visible guide to film development. In general, films that have been contact printed are processed in the same manner as camera-produced films and follow manufacturer recommendations for time, temperature, and agitation. However, film made with a contact printer has a wider latitude (less crucial development conditions) during development than does film made with projection exposure. This is due in part to the fact that, with contact printing, there is no possibility of light reaching the film from a nonimage area during exposure because the exposed and unexposed film are in "intimate contact" (pressed tightly together). Thus a grey scale image is not required to control development.

Lateral Reverse

A transparent film negative that has been exposed correctly in a process camera is **right reading** through the base side. In other words, as the printer looks at the film with the base

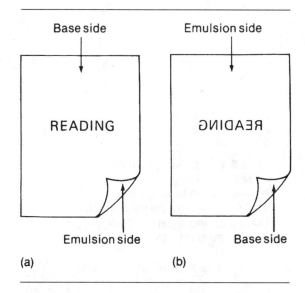

Base side   Emulsion side

READING   ᴮᴺᴵᴰᴬᴱᴿ

Emulsion side   Base side

(a)   (b)

Figure 6.32.   Right-reading transparent film. (a) Transparent film that has been correctly exposed in a process camera is right reading through the base side and (b) wrong reading through the emulsion side. The positive produced in figure 6.31 will be right reading.

side up, the copy reads from left to right (figure 6.32a). Right-reading film images are required for most printing operations. There are, however, several situations, such as photo-engraving for relief printing, preparation of screen printing stencils, and some printing plates, that require exposures made through film positives. These situations often require the film to be **wrong reading**. In this case the copy does not read from left to right through the base (figure 6.32b).

Changing a right-reading sheet of film to a wrong-reading sheet of film or vice versa is called a **lateral reverse.** This can be accomplished on the camera by reversing the right-reading sheet on the back-lighted camera copyboard. A lateral reverse can also be produced through contact printing by placing the base side of the right-reading film against the emulsion side of the new sheet (figure 6.33). The light spreads slightly between the two sheets of film because of the gap between emulsions, but it is expected and can be diminished by compensating for the spread when preparing the original film negative.

Spreads and Chokes

A common design technique is to print one solid color around an image such as type. Preparing these images for printing is not so easy. The process is to "drop" or eliminate the type from the surrounding color image, and then print the type exactly in the open area. The problem is trying to fit the two images exactly together on the press—there is almost always some white area showing. The solution is to enlarge the type slightly and shrink the background opening slightly. Then, when the images are printed, they will overlap slightly and there will be no obvious white space.

This technique is called **spreads and chokes**. Spreads, or thicker lines, are made from film negatives; chokes, or thinner lines, are made from film positives. The amount of spread and choke is determined by using transparent spacers and a "spread and choke target" which, when developed, provides a quantitative and visual measure.

The process starts by making a film positive from the orginal film negative. To make a choke, place spacers between the film positive

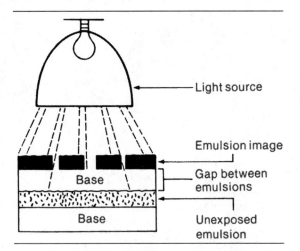

Figure 6.33.   Making a lateral reverse. This diagram shows the placement of the base side of the exposed film against the emulsion side of an unexposed sheet of film for producing a lateral reverse.

and the duplicating film in a contact frame (figure 6.34). During exposure the spacers cause the light to creep around the image and make the overall image slightly smaller.

To make a spread, sandwich the spacers between the original film negative and the duplicating film in the contact frame (figure 6.35). During exposure the spacers cause the light to expand and make the overall image slightly larger.

The duplicate films are then used to produce the printing plates. When printed the two images slightly overlap.

Rapid Access Processing

Up to this point we have been discussing traditional graphic films and processing. These films are commonly called **lith films**, and the

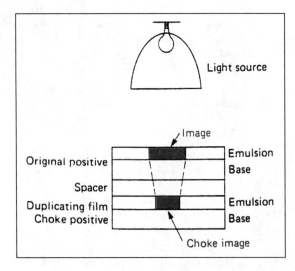

Figure 6.34.   Choke diagram

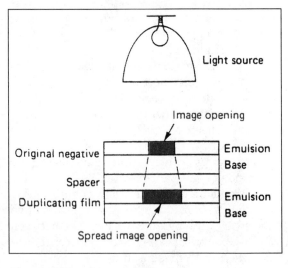

Figure 6.35.   Spread diagram

developers used with them are called **lith developers**. The primary disadvantage of lith processing is the lack of latitude during development. Development time, temperature, and agitation have to be critically controlled. If all of these conditions are not "in control," then it is impossible to predict results exactly. For large-line images, there is generally not a problem. However, much production time can be lost trying to obtain an acceptable film image with any other type of original copy.

Rapid access nearly eliminates dependence upon time, temperature, and agitation controls. Rapid access processing offers much wider latitude than lith, which gives it several advantages. Development requires only one solution and the fixer is simpler in chemical composition than that used for lith. Thus, whether shallow-tray or automatic processing is used, no replenisher is needed. The camera operator need only keep the developer and fixer "topped off" to the appropriate levels. In addition, because of the differences in developer chemistry, the developer is not easily exhausted through oxidation. Although rapid access developer eventually becomes exhausted from processing film, it can be left in the development tray and exposed to air for a day or more without becoming exhausted through oxidation.

The latitude for rapid access processing is also increased because the three major development variables (time, temperature, and agitation) are far less crucial than they are for lith development. If properly exposed, film developed in rapid access chemistry almost completely stops developing at the proper point. As a result, there is almost no chance of over- or underdevelopment. The exposed emulsion moves rapidly to maximum density and then slows to almost no chemical activity.

Most rapid access chemistry requires a minimum development time of 90 seconds. However, the film will not overdevelop if it is left in the developer for far longer. Because the film stops developing at the proper point, development time does not need to be controlled for copy variations. A piece of film used to record fine-line detail can be developed for the same length of time as a piece of film used to record normal detail. Another advantage of rapid access is that it can be used to process a range of film materials, including process camera films, contacting films, duplicating films, and even some typesetting papers.

All of these advantages add up to processing simplicity and productivity in the camera room, particularly with automatic processing. Critical chemical replenishment and monitoring through control strips is not needed with a rapid access film processor, and the processor can be used to process a wide range of film materials without changing chemistry. The speed of development time also increases productivity. Automatic processors can process rapid access materials from dry-to-dry in two minutes or less. Many automatic processors designed for lith processing can be converted easily for rapid access processing.

When they were first introduced, rapid access materials and chemistry proved excellent for line work but not for halftone reproduction. Within a few years manufacturers introduced halftone screens specially designed for use with their rapid access materials. Halftones produced with these screens and developed in rapid access chemistry are acceptable for a variety of applications where reproduction quality need not be the highest possible.

To meet the need for high-quality halftones, manufacturers have introduced a new product called **high-speed lith** that is a cross between traditional lith and rapid access. High-speed lith is said to offer the same high-quality development available with traditional lith, but at much faster speeds and with simpler processing procedures.

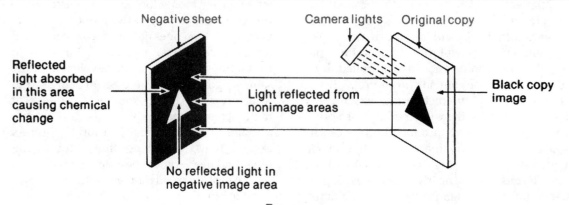

Exposure

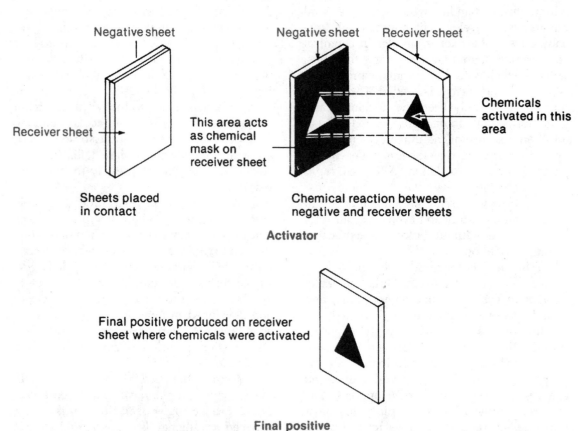

Final positive

Figure 6.36.   **The diffusion transfer process for producing an opaque positive from a positive original**

Diffusion Transfer

Diffusion transfer is a photographic process that produces quality opaque positives from positive originals. Diffusion transfer has widespread applications for printing production in such areas as copy preparation, proofing, and lithographic plate making.

Diffusion transfer basically involves using a light-sensitive negative image sheet and a chemically treated receiver sheet that is not light sensitive (figure 6.36). The negative sheet is exposed to the camera copy through normal line photography techniques. Wherever light is reflected from the camera copy (the nonimage areas of the copy), an image is recorded on the receiver sheet. Wherever light is absorbed by the camera copy (the black image areas of the copy), no image is recorded on the receiver sheet. After exposure, the negative sheet and the receiver sheet are placed in contact and pass through a processor that contains an "activator" solution. The image recorded on the negative sheet from the nonimage areas of the copy acts as a chemical mask and prevents any image from being transferred to the receiver sheet in these areas. Where no image was recorded on the negative sheet (that is, the dark areas of the copy where no light was reflected from the copy to the negative sheet), the activator or developer bath causes an image to be transferred to the receiver sheet. In this way a positive image is produced on the receiver sheet. In other words, wherever chemicals are transferred, an image is formed; where no chemicals are transferred, no image is formed.

Several characteristics of diffusion transfer material should be mentioned. Because it is a transfer process, the camera exposure results are reversed from a direct line photograph. To increase the density of the image on the receiver sheet, decrease the exposure time; to decrease density, increase the exposure time. When processing the materials, place the negative sheet under and before the receiver sheet

with the emulsions of the two together. The sandwich is then inserted into the processor, where it is passed between a separator rod, through the activator bath, and into intimate contact with two pressure rollers. The transfer actually takes place in 5 to 7 seconds, but the sheets should not be separated for at least 30 seconds (figure 6.37). Once the transfer has taken place, the negative sheet cannot be reused and should be discarded. The receiver sheet is still chemically sensitive and can be reused any number of times if multiple images are required, but it must be washed in running water for several minutes after exposure to prevent a slight yellowing from age.

Diffusion transfer materials can be used to produce stats during copy preparation to enlarge or reduce headlines, copyfit text material, clean soiled original copy, convert color line material to black-and-white copy, make reverses, and, with special screens, prepare halftones. Diffusion transfer materials can also be used to make reflex proofs (contact proofs from opaque paste ups). Lithographic printing plates and transparent films that accept a diffusion transfer image have also been developed.

Figure 6.37. Example of diffusion transfer sheets. The sheets that have been through the activator bath can be separated after 30 seconds.

Key Terms

continuous-tone
photography
line photography
continuous-tone
photograph
tones
halftone photography
visible spectrum
emulsion
color sensitivity
wedge spectrogram
blue-sensitive material
orthochromatic material
panchromatic material
contrast
characteristic curve
film speed
exposure index
antihalation dye
overcoating
process camera

lens
focusing
shutter
shutter speed
aperture
diaphragm
f/stop system
focal length
equivalent exposure
filmboard
copyboard
variable diaphragm control
light integrator
galley camera
darkroom camera
horizontal process camera
vertical process camera
basic exposure
step tablet
grey scale
safelight

latent image
developer
stop-bath
short-stop
fixing bath
hypo
agitation
control strips
solid-back copyboard
back-lighted copyboard
duplicating film
contact printing
right reading
wrong reading
lateral reverse
spreads and chokes
lith film
lith developer
rapid access
high-speed lith
diffusion transfer

Questions for Review

1. What common characteristic of all printing processes forms the primary concern of line photography?

2. What is the basis of photography?

3. What determines the effect of electromagnetic radiation such as light?

4. What colors is panchromatic film sensitive to? What colors is orthochromatic film sensitive to?

5. What does film speed tell about a film emulsion?

6. What is the purpose of the antihalation backing (or dye) on any piece of film?

7. What is the change in quantity of light passed through the lens when the aperture is changed from f/16 to f/22?

8. What is the difference between a galley camera and a darkroom camera?

9. Why are process cameras so large?

10. What does "basic exposure" mean?

11. What is the purpose of a camera light integrator?

12. Why is it important to clean any dirt or dust from the glass cover of a camera copyboard when making an exposure?

13. What is the purpose of a graphic arts step tablet (sometimes called a grey scale)?

14. What happens to the film emulsion during exposure?

15. What is the purpose of each of the chemical baths—developer, stop, fixer, and wash—used in processing film?

16. What three major concerns does the photographer always try to control during chemical processing?

17. What is the importance of agitating photographic chemical baths in film processing?

18. Describe the process of contact printing.

19. What is the difference between a right-reading film image and a wrong-reading film image?

20. How does rapid access processing differ from lith processing?

21. Describe the diffusion transfer process. For how many seconds should developed film remain in the stop-bath?

22. How long should film remain in the fixer?

23. What effect does longer exposure time have on the density recorded on diffusion transfer materials?

Halftone Photography

Anecdote to Chapter Seven

The first commercial halftone illustration reproduced in a mass circulation publication appeared in the March 4, 1880 issue of the New York *Daily Graphic*. It was a picture of a scene in Shantytown, New York. As the picture's cutline advertised, it was a "reproduction direct from nature." Even before it ran the first halftone illustration, however, the New York *Daily Graphic* was a startling venture in both design and manufacture. An editorial in the *Daily Graphic* from the same period observed that "the boldness of the experiment, when it was proposed to start and maintain in the city of New York a daily illustrated newspaper, was well fitted to take away the breath."

Before halftones, the only way to add illustrations to a printed piece was to include line drawings by artists. It was the day of the "sketch artist," or the "artist on the spot," as many newspapers advertised. The task of providing enough artists' illustrations to fill twelve pages of newspaper was a mammoth undertaking.

The person responsible for the *Daily Graphic's* success was a young man named

Stephen H. Horgan, then twenty-six years old. As early as 1875 Horgan conceived of a method to make the density gradations of a photographic negative into lines, and the halftone illustration was born.

Horgan's first commercial halftone was made with a negative screen formed from a series of fine rulings, all slightly out of focus. A print was made by projecting the original photographic negative through the negative screen. The result was then treated exactly like a line drawing by the production workers.

Horgan's early work was with single-line screens. In other words, the gradation lines from opaque to transparent on the screens ran parallel. The resulting reproductions looked, to many printers, somewhat like the artists' drawings that they had been working with for many years. The single-line screens were coarse and well suited to reproduction on fast letterpress equipment using inexpensive paper.

The single-line illustrations were all right, but there was room for improvement. The next challenge was to print cross-line halftones.

The first commercial halftone illustration.
Courtesy of Smithsonian Institution, Photo No. 73–5138.

Every press operator, however, said only a fool would suggest that a cross-line halftone could be printed without looking like a "puddle of mud."

The "foolish" ideas of people like Stephen Horgan have contributed to the growth and refinement of halftone photography, the subject of this chapter.

Objectives for Chapter 7

After completing this chapter you will be able to:

■ Differentiate between density, tone, and contrast.

■ Discuss the purposes of reflection, transmission, and dot area densitometers.

■ Discuss the significance of a grey scale in the photomechanical process.

■ Explain the difference between a halftone screen and a screen tint.

■ Explain how a halftone screen produces dots of varying sizes.

■ List standard screen rulings.

■ Explain how to determine appropriate highlight and shadow dot sizes.

■ Discuss the differences between various types of halftone screens.

■ Identify continuous-tone copy.

- Identify highlight, midtone, and shadow areas of continuous-tone copy.
- Select the proper instrument for measuring highlight and shadow densities.
- Describe the data needed to calculate halftone exposures with a halftone computer.
- Discuss the concept of "contrast" and explain how contrast is controlled in the halftone process.
- Explain the purpose of main, flash, and bump exposures.
- Identify the characteristics of a quality halftone negative.

Introduction

Much discussion has been devoted in this book to the idea that the major printing processes work exclusively with lines. Lines can have meaning, depending on how they are drawn. The lines that form the words on this page communicate information to you. The lines on a $100 bill communicate another sort of message.

You learned in chapter 6 that high-contrast photography is well suited to line work. A line negative either passes light (in the image area) or blocks the passage of light (in the nonimage area) to a printing plate. If all images that needed to be reproduced were made only of lines, then simple line exposures would meet all printing needs. There is, however, a large group of images that do not have line characteristics—continuous-tone images.

A continuous-tone image is not made up of lines. It is formed by a combination of varying shades of grey. The typical photograph, which is a continuous-tone image, is made up of a gradation of tones ranging from "paper white," through grey to the darkest black. Examples of other continuous-tone images are ink-and-brush washes, charcoal sketches, watercolor paintings, soft-pencil drawings, and oil paintings. If we attempted to reproduce a continuous-tone print on high-contrast film, we would lose "information" or detail that is contained in the midtones (figure 7.1).

To reproduce such a print using one of the major printing processes, it is necessary to change the print into a special type of line image called a **halftone.**

The microcomputer has radically changed long-standing attitudes and techniques in nearly every dimension of the printing industry. These changes have been especially radical in halftone preparation.

This chapter describes how to prepare halftones by traditional photographic means. It is divided into two sections. Section 1 is an introduction to the basic ideas of halftones. Section 2 examines halftone procedures in detail and discusses methods of evaluating halftone negatives. The computer as a tool in halftone imaging is discussed in detail in chapter 8.

SECTION 1

Density, Tone, and Contrast

In chapter 6 we discussed how to make a line photograph from a high-contrast image. Before proceeding to a discussion of halftone photography, it is necessary to establish a basic understanding of the terms "density," "tone,"

Figure 7.1. **A high-contrast reproduction of a continuous-tone image.** There are only black-and-white areas in this type of print. There are no grey tones.

and "contrast," and to determine what they mean to the graphic arts photographer.

Density

In the most general terms, **density** describes the ability of a material to absorb or transmit light. It is well known in the construction industry that a house with a white roof is much cooler in the summer than one with a black roof. The white shingles reflect a great deal of light and, consequently, heat. The black shingles absorb the light and store the sun's heat in the house. In the tropics, light-colored clothing is much cooler and more comfortable than clothing that is dark because it reflects light and heat.

In printing production, the density of the copy, film emulsion, and printing plate emulsion are all important. In printing, a film negative is used to either pass or absorb light. If

properly exposed and processed, the film negative passes light in the image areas and blocks light in the nonimage areas to expose a light-sensitive printing plate. In other words, the film emulsion must be more dense in the nonimage areas than in the image areas. Thus, the density of the film emulsion in the nonimage areas directly influences the quality of the printed piece.

While photographers are standing over the washing sink examining wet negatives, however, they are hard pressed to make accurate judgments about the density of the emulsion on the film. It is a safelight environment, viewing a transparent material through a liquid. A negative can be examined with a magnifying glass on a wet light table (a water-proof viewing area). If the copy were grossly over- or underprocessed, the photographer might be able to detect the problem (figure 7.2). However, the film could appear acceptable and still yield the best possible printed results. The

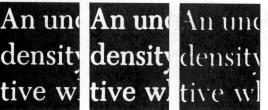

Correct exposure	Underexposure	Overexposure
This segment was exposed correctly. The negative areas are either clearly transparent or densely opaque. Edges are sharp, and detail proportions are true to the original.	This segment was underexposed. Although transparent areas are clear, the dark areas have low density. A positive made from a negative of this type shows thickening of all detail.	This segment was overexposed. Although dense areas are opaque, density appears in some areas which should be clear. A positive made from a negative of this type shows loss of fine detail.

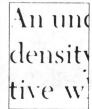

Figure 7.2. Examples of correct exposure, underexposure, and overexposure. It is possible to judge underexposure or overexposure by comparing the reproduction with the original copy.

photographer has several tools to ensure that a negative is of truly acceptable quality and will faithfully reproduce the original copy. The grey scale used during the development of a line negative, which was discussed in chapter 6, is one such tool. When photographers watch the grey scale during film development and wait for a step 4 to go solid, they are actually waiting for the film emulsion to reach a specific level of density.

Reflectance and Transmittance

The printer is concerned with both the density of the image on the original copy and with the density of the emulsion on the piece of film. The density of the image on the copy is defined by the term **reflectance.** The density of the film emulsion is defined by the term **transmittance.**

Reflectance is a measure of the percentage of direct light, or **incident light,** that is reflected from an area of the copy. Transmittance is a measure of the percentage of directed light that passes through an area on a piece of film. For example, if 100 units of light are directed from the camera lights to the copy and only 50 units of light are reflected back from an area on the copy to the camera lens, reflectance for that area of the copy is 50 percent. If 100 units of light are directed at an area on a piece of film and only 50 units of light pass through that area of the film, transmittance in that area of the film emulsion is 50 percent. See figure 7.3.

Tone and Contrast

Up to this point in the discussion of line photography, we have been concerned only with copy that is either all black in the image areas or all white in the nonimage areas. Our object has been to reproduce every area with no density (every nonimage area) on the copy as an area of density on the film emulsion, and every area with density (every image area) on the copy as an area with no density on the film emulsion. In chapter 6 we examined the use of the grey scale during processing to determine proper development. When the grey scale is a solid step 4, the nonimage areas on the film are dense enough so that they do not pass light when the negative is used to produce a printing plate.

Halftone copy such as a snapshot is not composed of only black-and-white areas. Halftone copy is made up of white, black, and grey areas. These differing shades from white through grey to black are called **tones.** Different tones have different densities.

Line copy that is either all black or all white is called **high-contrast copy** because the two tones of the copy (black and white) are very different in appearance. **Contrast** is simply a measure of how different the tones on a

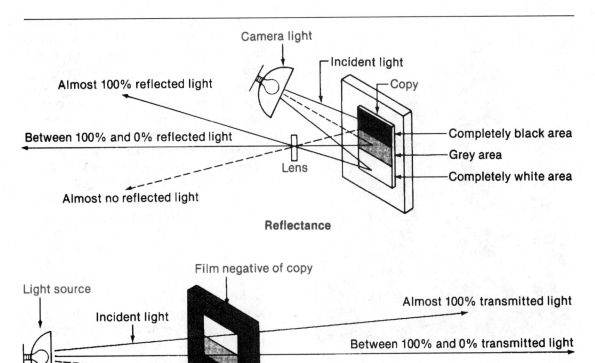

Figure 7.3.   **The relationship between incident light and reflectance or transmittance.** From the diagram we can see that there is an inverse relationship between the light that is reflected from the original image area and the light that is transmitted through the negative. That is, almost no light is reflected from the black area of the image. However, in the corresponding area of the negative, almost 100 percent of the light is transmitted.

piece of copy are in appearance. Two tones on line copy can be called discontinuous if they are very different.

Halftone copy is called **continuous-tone copy** because all (or most) of its tones are on a continuum from white to black. Each of these tones has a different density on the copy. In fact, the differing densities in these tones give the copy contrast and detail (figure 7.4).

Recall from chapter 6 that high-contrast film is used in graphic arts photography. When exposed and processed, high-contrast film emulsion has only two tones or areas of density. The emulsion is either clear and transmits light or it is black and transmits no light.

Graphic arts film has to be high contrast because printing presses cannot print varying tones. A printing press puts ink density in the

(a)

image areas and no ink density in the nonimage areas. The printer's problem when dealing with a continuous-tone photograph is how to record a continuous-tone image on a high-contrast film. In fact, it cannot be done. What can be done, however, is break a high-contrast image into a series of dots of varying shapes and sizes (but all of the same density) to give the illusion of tone variations. The dot patterns are produced by using a special screen. The resulting dot formation is called a **halftone.** The screen used to produce halftone dot patterns is discussed later in this chapter.

Densitometry

Measurements of density belong to an area called **densitometry.** Reflectance and transmittance can be expressed algebraically as follows:

$$Reflectance = R = \frac{I_r}{I_{rw}}$$

where:

R = reflectance
I_r = intensity of light reflected from copy
I_{rw} = intensity of light reflected from white paper

$$Transmittance = T = \frac{I_t}{I_i}$$

(b)

Figure 7.4. Comparison of a normal-contrast picture and a high-contrast picture. (a) A normal-contrast picture shows shades or tones from white through grey to black. (b) A high-contrast picture shows only two colors, white (no ink) and black. Thus, more visual information is contained in (a) than in (b).

where:

T = transmittance

I_t = intensity of transmitted light

I_i = intensity of incident light

As discussed earlier, transmittance is a measure of the light that passes through film; reflectance is a measure of the light that reflects from copy.

These formula describe the examples in the reflectance and transmittance section of this chapter: A light source is directed at a piece of copy. 100 units of light are reflected back from the white or nonimage area of the paper (I_{rw}) and 50 units are reflected back from an image or tone (I_r), reflectance is 50% (50 ÷ 100 = 0.5 or 50%). We could use percentages for I_{rw} and I_r, but nothing in life functions as perfectly as mathematical examples in textbooks. In reality, I_{rw} might be measured at 112.76 units and I_r as 48.89. Doing the arithmetic (48.89 ÷ 112.76) we find that reflectance equals 43.357573608%. Such a long number has little meaning. Is 43.400000000% significantly denser than 43.357573608%? Can we really perceive the difference—probably not—but is it denser than another material? The problem is that the numbers simply become too large for us to understand and interpret. The solution is logarithms.

Logarithms are a way to express large quantities by using small numbers. Logarithmic information is readily available from tables in any mathematics book. Table 7.1 shows some common transmittance and density relationships. Although in theory there is no maximum density reading, realistically, for printing, there is no need to measure an optical density much greater than 3.0.

A density reading is nothing more than a logarithmic scale ranging from 0.0 to around 3.0 that equates a numeric value to the relative ability of a material to absorb or transmit light. The higher the density reading, the denser the

Table 7.1. Some common transmittance and density relationships

Transmittance	Density
100%	0.0
10%	1.0
1%	2.0
0.1%	3.0
0.01%	4.0
0.001%	5.0
.	
.	
.	
0.0000001%	9.0
.	
. and so forth	

material. Remember that dark areas on a piece of copy are denser than light areas.

So now you understand the mathematics of densitometry. You can use densitometry to gain information about a photograph or a film negative without using mathematical formulas, however. Printers do not have to be able to manipulate logarithms in order to work with optical density. Densitometric tools read transmittance and provide readings that are already translated to logarithmic numbers. A variety of tools measure transmittance and reflectance using logarithmic scales.

Densitometers

Density is measured by a tool called a **densitometer.** The first densitometers, called **visual densitometers,** use human judgment to compare tonal densities visually (figure 7.5). The device has a set of known density wedges. The printer inserts the material to be measured in the densitometer and visually compares it to the previously known densities. After identifying a wedge that is identical in density to the test material, the printer records the

Figure 7.5.   A visual densitometer. Visual densitometers allow the operator to compare copy, which is placed under the probe, to labeled densities that are seen through the viewing element.

logarithmic value printed on the wedge. To determine the density of another image, the printed standards are compared to the area by eye. When a known area is judged to match the unknown area, the printed value is assumed to be the density.

A **photoelectric densitometer** operates on the logarithmic measure of incident light. A controlled beam is projected onto the material to be tested, and the machine measures the transmittance or reflectance. Most photoelectric densitometers have readout devices that immediately report the logarithmic density.

Visual densitometers are less expensive and more rugged than photoelectric densitometers, but they depend too much on the operator's judgment. Most individuals become tired after twenty to thirty single tone visual measurements. Color densities are even more difficult to perceive than densities on visual densitometers. For these reasons, visual densitometers are almost never used today in the printing industry. In contrast, photoelectric densitometers are independent of the operator's judgment, provide extremely consistent

results, and usually have color heads that accurately read primary color densities.

Photoelectric densitometers are classified according to the type of materials they are designed to measure: opaque or transparent. Any ink or emulsion on a solid base (such as paper) that is not designed to pass light is called opaque copy. Examples of opaque materials are drawings, paste-ups, continuous-tone paper photographic prints, or sheets of paper from a printing press. The density of opaque materials is measured using reflected light with a device called a **reflection densitometer** (figure 7.6). Before any reading is taken, the device is always calibrated to the same reading

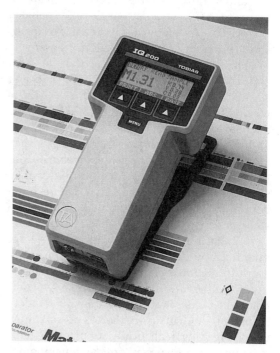

Figure 7.6.   A reflection densitometer. The reflection densitometer is placed over a specific area of copy. Light is projected from the densitometer and reflects back into the densitometer probe. This reflected light is measured and displays digitally as density units.
Courtesy of Tobias Associates, Inc.

(usually 0.0, but some devices calibrate to 0.10) using of a standard white opaque wedge to ensure accurate measurements. This calibration process is called **zeroing.** After zeroing, the reflection densitometer directs a narrow, controlled beam of light at a 45-degree angle onto an area of the opaque material. The amount of light that is reflected is measured photoelectrically and is then translated to a logarithmic number.

Any ink or emulsion that is on a clear base (such as glass) and is designed to pass light is called transparent material. Graphic arts film is one example of transparent material. Another example is a color photographic slide. The density of transparent material is measured by light passing through the base with a device called a **transmission densitometer** (figure 7.7). A transmission densitometer passes a narrow beam of light at a 90-degree angle to an area on the transparent film. The amount of light that passes through

the film is measured and then translated to a logarithmic number. Care must be taken when zeroing a transmission densitometer. The base material of all transparent film has some small amount of density, sometimes called fog. The device should be zeroed on a clear area of the piece of film being measured. This subtracts density that is unrelated to the image density.

Grey Scale and Density

It is important to understand that the graphic arts grey scale discussed in chapter 6 is simply a visual illustration of the logarithmic density scale. Each step on the grey scale is an area of specific, measurable density. The number of steps is arbitrary, however. Most printers use 10-, 12-, or 21-step grey scales. Grey scales are available commercially in opaque or transparent forms. The opaque scale can be used as a crude sort of visual densitometer, but it is best used to indicate film density during and after chemical processing.

Examine the grey scale in figure 7.8. It only approximates a 12-step grey scale (an opaque scale could not be reproduced here because it is made up of different tones), but it illustrates the usefulness of the tool. Each of the evenly divided twelve steps of the scale represents an increase in density from around 0.00 (no density) to 1.65. Printed next to each step are the manufacturer's density values in increments of 0.15. Figure 7.8 shows an uncalibrated grey scale. Uncalibrated grey scales can be measured with a reflection densitometer.

From the scale it can be seen that step 4 represents a density of 0.45. If this small scale were placed on a copyboard and photographed, the light reflected by step 4 would be the same as the light reflected by any part of the copy having a density of 0.45. *This is the key to this tool.*

The white nonimage areas for high-contrast copy such as line copy all have about

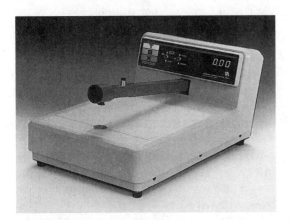

Figure 7.7.   A transmission densitometer. A negative or positive film image can be placed between the densitometer probe and the densitometer table. Light is passed (transmitted) through the film to the densitometer probe. The amount of light transmitted through the film is read and recorded on the densitometer display.
Courtesy of Tobias Associates, Inc.

Figure 7.8.   A 12-step grey scale. This scale is divided into twelve steps representing densities from 0.00 to 1.65.

Courtesy of Stauffer Graphic Arts Equipment Co.

the same density. This density is 0.45 or less. When determining the basic exposure for line shots on the process camera (see appendix A), we select an exposure time and aperture that causes step 4 on the grey scale to fill (go solid) with controlled development conditions. In doing so, we ensure that all white nonimage areas on the copy record as solid black areas on the film negative when a solid step 4 is reached during film development. Any images on the copy (lines, dots, or even fingerprints and smudges) with density greater than 0.45 (darker than a step 4 on the opaque grey scale) record as clear areas on the film negative when the film is developed to a solid step 4.

Understanding the grey scale steps as specific blocks of density is a powerful tool for the graphic arts photographer. With it the pho-

tographer can predict how different camera apertures or shutter speeds will affect the density of the film emulsion.

Graphic arts photographers have learned that a change of one f/stop number on the camera produces a 0.30 density shift on a sheet of film. For example, assume that after processing a line negative, a solid step 2 with a density of 0.15 was produced from an exposure of f/16 for 20 seconds. If a solid step 4 (density of 0.45) was desired for normal copy, changing the exposure one f/stop to f/11 for 20 seconds (or f/16 for 40 seconds) would add 0.30 density to the film (0.15 + 0.30 = 0.45). This one f/stop change in exposure will produce a solid step 4 which is appropriate for normal copy.

This concept of a predictable density shift as a result of exposure was discovered last century and can be used in all phases of photography, whether continuous-tone, line, halftone, special effects, or color separation.

The Sensitometer

A sensitometer extends the concept of a grey scale a bit further. A **sensitometer** is an instrument that accurately exposes a grey scale of density from 0.0 to 3.0 in increments of 0.30 or 0.15 density. The device has its own calibrated light source and its own shutter. In practice, the unexposed edge of a sheet of film is inserted under the cover and an exposure is made. Two separate images record on the emulsion where the film is covered during exposure—a sensitometric step image and the reproduced camera image.

During processing the sensitometer can be checked to judge the stage of development. The advantage of this technique is that if the film is processed to the same step each time, the processing conditions will always be the same and the results on the film will be absolutely consistent. This is not the case for a camera-exposed grey scale because the grey scale's density is a function of the camera exposure—the smaller the exposure, the longer the development necessary to produce the same density step. The sensitometer is ideal for processing images that require absolutely consistent development, such as halftones or color separations. A sensitometer can also be used to produce control strips for checking the activity level of automatic film processors. Sensitometers are used almost exclusively in graphic arts photographic research and are not generally considered production tools.

Halftone Screens

Halftone screens are the tools used by the graphic arts photographer to convert continous-tone images to halftone images that can be reproduced on a press. This section reviews the terminology and classifications of these basic tools.

Halftone Screen Rulings

The most common method of printing a continuous-tone photograph is to convert the image to line copy by a process called **halftone photography**. With this method, the continuous-tone image is broken into a series of dots of varying size but equal density. The dots combine in such a way as to trick the eye into believing that the picture is still continuous tone (figure 7.9). This illusion is accomplished by placing a ruled halftone screen between the copy and the film in a process camera (figure 7.10). On the camera, light is reflected from the white highlight areas of the copy and is absorbed by the black shadow areas. (See the Areas of Continuous-Tone Print section later in this chapter for more about highlights and shadows.) The middle tones (grey areas) absorb light to varying degrees, depending on their densities. The reflected light then passes through the openings in the halftone screen and forms dots on the halftone negative. The size of each dot is controlled by the amount of light that passes through the screen, which is in turn controlled by the amount of light reflected from the different areas on the copy.

It is perhaps easiest to understand a halftone screen by picturing crossed solid

Figure 7.9. Halftone reproduction. A halftone photograph is a series of lines or dots so small that they trick the eye into seeing a continuous-line image. Note that the dot pattern is visible in the detail enlargement on the left of the halftone. Courtesy of Chris Savas.

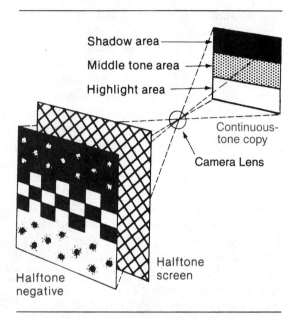

Shadow area

Middle tone area

Highlight area

Continuous-
tone copy

Camera Lens

Halftone
screen

Halftone
negative

**Figure 7.10.   Diagram of halftone screen
use.** A halftone screen is placed between the
continuous-tone copy and the film when exposing
the film to break the continuous-tone copy into dots
of varying sizes and shapes. White or highlight areas of the copy produce big, black dots on film.
Middle tone areas produce intermediate-size dots,
and black or shadow areas produce small dots.

lines—like the texture of a window screen used
to keep insects out of your home. The openings
between the lines pass light; the lines themselves do not. If we were to count the number
of parallel lines in 1 inch of the screen, we
would have a rough idea of the size of dot that
would be produced with that screen.

The more lines per inch of screen, the
smaller the average dot produced. This measure is referred to as **screen ruling.** Figure 7.11
shows the same image produced using a 65-
line screen (there were 65 parallel lines in any
given inch in the screen that produced the
halftone negative) and a 133-line screen (there
were 133 parallel lines in any given inch of

the screen). It is apparent from this figure that
the finer screen ruling (133-line screen) produces a more natural appearing picture.

Three variables help decide what screen
ruling to use for a halftone photograph:

- Normal viewing distance
- Process of reproduction
- Type of base material

Normal Viewing Distance

A halftone photograph appears to have continuous tone because the eye cannot detect minute
line detail at normal viewing distance. "Normal viewing distance" varies with the function
of the printed piece. This book is intended to be
read at about 14 inches (or 36 centimeters) from
your eyes. Therefore, the normal viewing distance for this book is 14 inches. A billboard you
might see along a busy highway is designed to
be read from approximately 300 yards (or 275
meters). Three-hundred yards, then, is the normal viewing distance for the billboard. The best
halftone screen ruling for a billboard might be
as coarse as 10 lines per inch. As viewing distance gets smaller so too must the screen ruling.
Screen rulings range from the huge dot size of
a billboard to the fine dots produced from a
300-line screen.

Process of Reproduction

The method and material of reproduction also
influence the selection of screen ruling. For example, with current technology, a 300-line
halftone is much too fine to be used with screen
printing; stencils cannot be made that will adhere to any support fabric. For some printing
methods, a 300-line screen ruling is possible,
but it becomes a test of sophisticated reproduction control.

Type of Base Material

The ink-absorbing characteristics of base materials in printing vary widely. Newsprint
rapidly absorbs ink and tends to spread or

Figure 7.11. Examples of 65-line and 133-line screen halftones.
Notice that you can actually see 65 line dots with the naked eye, but 133
lines per inch require magnification to detect.

increase dot size. A 300-line screen printed in your newspaer would probably look like a puddle of black ink as a result. Clay-based or coated papers, such as those used for most popular magazines, do not absorb or spread ink and can hold fine detail with little trouble.

For most processes and paper characteristics, screen rulings of 65, 85, 100, 120, 133, and 150 lines per inch are the simplest to manipulate and are the most widely used.

Halftone Screen Structure

Although the crossed-solid-line pattern of a halftone screen is easy to visualize, it is not an accurate image of how the most commonly used screens are made. The dots formed by the clear openings between solid line rulings in screens would all have the same shape and size. To produce a halftone, however, we need dots of varying shapes and sizes and therefore openings of varying sizes in the screens.

There are solid-line screens, called **screen tints,** but they are not used to produce halftone photographs. The typical halftone screen is constructed using a photographic emulsion to form a **vignetted screen pattern.** Figure 7.12 is an artist's rendering of what the intersection of two crossed lines in solid-line screen and vignetted screen areas might look like greatly magnified.

Screen tints are used for many purposes. The most common is to create the illusion of two colors when really only printing one color. If a 30-percent screen tint is with a solid red, the tint appears pink. The job can then have areas of solid red and other areas of pink, but only one color is printed on press. Notice that screen tints have rigidly controlled openings (figure 7.12a). Screen tints are classified according to the amount of light they pass to the piece of film. A 40-percent screen tint passes 40 percent of light through its openings and blocks 60 percent by its solid lines. Figure 7.13 shows the range of typical screen tints. The lines in some

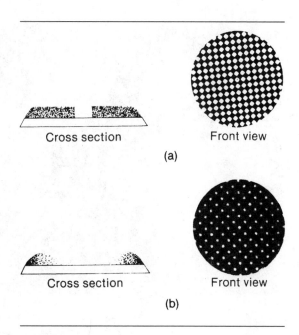

Figure 7.12.   Comparing a solid-line screen to a vignetted screen. (a) A solid-line screen with evenly shaped and sized openings is used to produce an even tone tint. (b) A vignetted screen produces variations in the sizes and shapes of the dots which result in the continuous-tone appearance of halftones.

solid-line screens do not cross. These screen patterns are generally referred to as "special effect screen tints" (figure 7.14). Screen tints and solid-line special effect screen tints are not used to produce halftones (although special effect halftone screens do exist). Solid line screen tints produce dots of uniform size. Halftone dots must be of different sizes.

As mentioned earlier, to appear continuous, a halftone must be formed from dots of varying shapes and sizes. Figure 7.12b illustrates the structure of the vignetted screen that produces these variations. The center portion of the screen opening (the area between the intersection of two dots) is clear, but the density of the screen's photographic emulsion

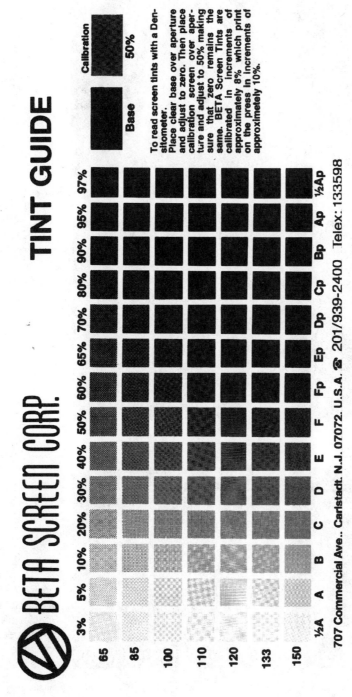

Figure 7.13. **Screen tints.** In this screen tint guide, the horizontal rows show screen ruling and the vertical columns show dot size.
Courtesy of Beta Screen Corp.

Mahogany

Mezzotint

Circleline

100 Straightline

Wavyline

50 Straightline

Figure 7.14. Examples of special effect tints. Special effect screen tints can be used to create different impressions with the same image.

Courtesy of James Craig, Production Planning.

increases as the diameter of the opening grows larger. Visualize this as a pile of sand, high and deep at the center, but gradually decreasing in depth until there are no grains of sand.

When light reflected from the copy passes through the vignetted screen opening, a dot the size of the clear part of the opening forms on the film immediately. As the quantity of light reaching the screen increases, more light penetrates the denser portion near the outer edge of the opening and the dot recorded on the film becomes larger. Within any halftone photograph, there is a wide range of individual dot size. These variations are related directly to the amount of light reflected from the copy and focused through the camera lens onto the halftone screen. The more light that is reflected from the copy, the more light that penetrates the denser portions of the vignetted dots and the larger the dots recorded on the film.

All of this makes sense if you remember that more light is reflected from the white highlight areas of the copy and less light is reflected from the dark shadow areas. You would want larger dots in the highlight areas on the film negative to block more light from reaching the printing plate. If more light were blocked, small dots would be produced on the plate. These small dots would print as small dots on the final page, thereby providing white highlight areas that have little density because little ink is printed in them.

Dot Size and Shape

To control individual dot size variation, it is necessary to identify and measure dot size (the area the dot covers on the printed sheet). Dot size is measured in terms of percentage of ink coverage. Thus, a printer speaks of a printed halftone as having a 5-percent or 10-percent dot in the highlight area, and a 90-percent or 95-percent dot in the shadow area. What is meant is that 5 percent of the highlight area is covered by dots and 95 percent of the shadow area is covered by dots.

Dot size varies according to screen ruling. A 20-percent dot produced from a 65-line screen is larger than a 20-percent dot produced from a 133-line screen. This presents no problems for the printer, however, because a 20-percent dot produced from a 65-line screen covers 20 percent of the printed area with ink. Likewise, a 20 percent dot from a 133-line screen covers 20 percent of the printed area with ink. One dot would be smaller than the other, but the percentage of ink coverage produced in each area would be the same. Comparing dot size between different lined screens is done only when printers select a screen for a job. Comparing dot percentage sizes produced by the same screen, however, is done whenever printers attempt to assess the results of a halftone they have made, decide whether they have put the correct-sized dot in the highlight and shadow areas of the negative, or determine if they printed the correct-sized dot in the highlight and shadow areas of a halftone reproduction.

Traditional halftone screens are designed to produce one of two different types of dot structure:

- Square
- Elliptical

Square Dot Structure
Figure 7.15 illustrates the typical range of dot sizes for a conventional "square dot structure." Although the square dot screen is commonly used, it has some problems. In the area of the 50-percent dot there is a sudden visual jump in dot size that does not reproduce the original photograph accurately (figure 7.16).

Elliptical Dot Structure
Figure 7.17 shows the elliptical dot size range that was developed to overcome the square dot's limitations. Notice that in the 50-percent

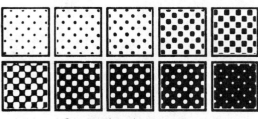

Conventional square dot

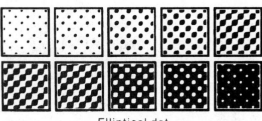

Elliptical dot

Figure 7.15.   Examples of square dot sizes. A typical range of dot sizes for a square dot screen is from 5 percent to 95 percent.

Figure 7.17.   Examples of elliptical dot sizes. Shown is a typical range of dot sizes (5 percent to 95 percent) for an elliptical dot screen.

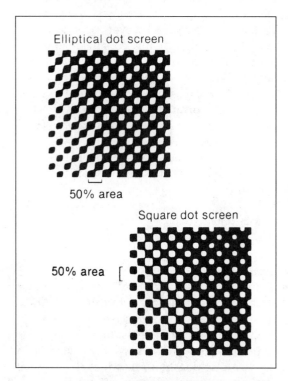

Figure 7.16.   Comparing a square dot screen to an elliptical dot screen. The 50-percent area of the square dot screen jumps suddenly. The elliptical dot screen has a slower visual shift in the same area.

Courtesy of Eastman Kodak Company.

area the elliptical dot structure provides a smooth transition to where one dot finally touches another on all four sides.

Measuring Dot Area

Both square and elliptical dots are produced using a halftone screen in exactly the same manner. Whatever dot structure is used to produce the halftone, there are two techniques printers use to measure dot area:

- Visual inspection
- Dot area meter

Visual Inspection

It is possible to use a **linen tester** or magnifying glass to view dots of any size (figure 7.18). Using this tool to compare figure 7.15 or 7.17 with a halftone negative, we can approximate dot size. This is done less by comparing the actual size of the dot to the illustration than by comparing the configuration of an area of dots. As was mentioned previously, the 50-percent dot is easy to recognize. If a square dot screen was used to reproduce the negative, a 50-percent dot is found on the negative in an area where the dots just start to touch on all four corners. If an elliptical dot screen was used to produce the negative, the 50-percent

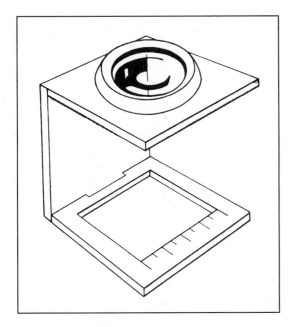

Figure 7.18. **A linen tester.** A linen tester is used to view dot structure.

Figure 7.19. **Example of a dot area meter.** This transmission dot area meter measures dot sizes on transparent materials.

dot is found in an area on the negative just before the dots start to touch on two corners. By viewing the amount of white space around a printed 10-percent dot, it becomes easy to identify an area on a negative that will produce a 10-percent dot.

Visual dot size identification is not as complicated as it may seem. When graphic arts photographers make halftones, they are mainly concerned with the dots that will reproduce the highlight areas of the copy (typically around 5-percent to 10-percent dots, depending upon the printing method) and the dots that will reproduce the shadow areas of the copy (typically around 90-percent to 95-percent dots). Some practice is required, but an experienced printer can at least estimate highlight and shadow dot size visually. However, this becomes somewhat of a subjective problem. Is a dot 9-percent, or 11-percent, or 13-percent? As much as a 7-percent variation in

visual judgment, even among experienced camera operators, is possible.

Dot Area Meter

Although printers can work with this inaccuracy, one solution is to use a **dot area meter** (figure 7.19). This device "integrates" or averages the amount of light passing through a selected area on a halftone negative and equates that measure to a dot area reading.

It is also possible to adapt the information from a transmission densitometer to measure dot area, although there is some slight loss in accuracy. With this technique, density reading of the target area on a halftone negative is made using the transmission densitometer. The density number is then located on

Table 7.2. Conversion from density readings to percent dot area

Integrated Halftone Density	Percent Dot Areas	Integrated Halftone Density	Percent Dot Areas
0.00	0	0.36	56
0.01	2	0.38	58
0.02	5	0.40	60
0.03	7	0.42	62
0.04	9	0.44	64
0.05	11	0.46	65
0.06	13	0.48	67
0.07	15	0.50	68
0.08	17	0.54	71
0.09	19	0.58	74
0.10	21	0.62	76
0.11	22	0.66	78
0.12	24	0.70	80
0.13	26	0.74	82
0.14	28	0.78	83
0.15	29	0.82	85
0.16	31	0.86	86
0.17	32	0.90	87
0.18	34	0.95	89
0.19	35	1.00	90
0.20	37	1.10	92
0.22	40	1.20	94
0.24	42	1.30	95
0.26	45	1.40	96
0.28	48	1.50	97
0.30	50	1.70	98
0.32	52	2.00	99
0.34	54		

a density-dot area conversion table (table 7.2). However, it is preferable and more accurate to use a dot area meter.

Halftone Screen Preparation

There are several basic methods for preparing halftone negatives from continuous-tone originals. The earliest technique used a glass ruled screen. Parallel lines were first etched on two sheets of glass. The sheets were then cemented with their sets of lines at right angles to create dot-forming openings. To produce a halftone, the cemented glass screen was placed a predetermined distance from the film in the camera. The camera image was then focused on the screen and finally refocused on the film.

The size of the predetermined distance was critical in this method. It was a measure of the ratio of the lens-to-copy and copy-to-screen distance. Halftone negatives produced with such screens were traditionally thought to be of the highest quality. However, the high cost of the screens, combined with the high level of sophistication required to use them and the development of high-quality vignetted contact screens, have resulted in their decline.

The simplest method of halftone preparation uses "prescreened film," which allows halftone negatives to be produced without a halftone screen. A piece of prepared film, simply exposed and processed, gives an acceptable halftone reproduction. The screen is, in a sense, "built into" the prepared film. Prescreened film is ideal for simple exposures. Halftone exposures can be produced without a vacuum frame holding system, and the film can be used in any portable camera (such as a press camera) to make halftones of three-dimensional scenes. However, chemical processing control limitations on this method restrict the use of prescreened film. It cannot be used for high-quality halftone reproductions.

Contact Halftone Screens

Contact halftone screens have revolutionized the printing industry. They are inexpensive and simple to use, and they require no sophis-ticated equipment or manipulation. Contact halftone screens form dots using a vignetted screen pattern (see the Halftone Screen Structure section of this chapter). All further discussion of halftone production assumes a contact screen in used.

Types of Contact Halftone Screens

The two basic types of contact screens are classified according to the color of dye used to produce the screen emulsion. The two colors are magenta and grey. Within each category are special purpose screens. Table 7.3 outlines these variations and defines the use intended for each. In general, any contact screen may be used with any sort of copy. However, best results will be obtained if the appropriate screen is used for a specific job.

Magenta Screens

Magenta screens are designed to work with monochromatic (black-and-white) originals. Filters may be used to change the basic density range of the screen (see the Understanding Halftone Exposures section for more about basic density range), but the process is cumbersome and rarely used. Magenta nega-

Table 7.3. A classification of vignetted contact screens for halftone photography

Magenta	
Negative	Camera negatives from positive black-and-white originals
Positive	Contact positives from continuous-tone separation negatives
Photogravure	Intermediate halftone negatives for the gravure process
Grey	
Negative	Halftone negatives from positive color originals (transparency or print)
Diffusion Transfer	Opaque camera positives (stats) from black-and-white positive originals using the diffusion transfer process

tive screens are used on a process camera to produce halftone negatives from opaque (paper) positives. Magenta positive screens are designed to make halftone positives in a contact printing frame from continuous-tone negative transparencies. Magenta photogravure screens are structured for the special requirements of the gravure printing process (see chapter 16).

Grey Screens

Grey screens are popular for reproducing black-and-white photographs and are also designed to work with colored continuous-tone originals. Grey screens do not respond to filter control of the basic density range of the screen. Grey negative screens are intended to be used to make halftone negatives from either opaque or transparent copy. Grey diffusion transfer screens are designed to make positive opaque halftones from positive opaque originals by using the diffusion transfer process.

Whatever the type of contact screen used, the basic processing steps are the same.

SECTION 2

Section 1 outlined some basic ideas about halftone photography. Now our attention turns to deeper understanding of more specific halftone procedures. This section examines some terminology, shows how exposures can be determined, and provides enough information so that you will be able to produce an acceptable halftone negative.

Areas of a Continuous-Tone Print

There are three areas that both printers and photographers identify as the most significant measures of the quality of a continuous-tone print (figure 7.20):

- Highlight area
- Shadow area
- Middle tone area

The **highlight area** is that portion of a picture that contains detail but has the least amount of density. The darkest areas of the print are called the **shadow areas**. All the shades of grey between the highlights and the shadows are called the **middle tone areas**. Middle tones contain the most pictorial detail or information.

There is a special kind of highlight, called a **spectral highlight**, that has no detail or density. Examples include the gleam of the chrome on an automobile or the pinpoint iris of a model's eye. Spectral highlights contain no detail and should not carry a halftone dot.

It is possible to compare the density of these three areas of a print with the density of the steps on any graphic arts grey scale. We can also equate these densities to the size of halftone dots on the film negative and on the final printed sheet. For example, in figure 7.20:

1. The highlight detail begins in step 1, or with a density near 0.05. The highlight dots begin with the smallest reproducible dot (generally about 5 percent) and extend to about a 20-percent or 25-percent dot.

2. The shadow detail ends in step 10, or with a density of about 1.45. The shadow dots extend from about 75 percent or 80 percent to the largest reproducible dot (generally about 95 percent) before solid black is reached.

3. The middle tone area for this photo is roughly from step 3 to step 7, but it is not a definite range. Middle tone dots typically range from about a 25-percent dot to a 75-percent dot.

Figure 7.20. Areas of a continuous-tone print. In this continuous-tone print, the highlight areas correspond to steps 1 and 2 on the grey scale. From the grey scale, we see that the middle range is from 3 to 7. The shadow area ranges from 8 to 11 on the grey scale.

Several things need to be emphasized with respect to this comparison. Printers do not typically measure a particular highlight, middle tone, or shadow density. They are primarily concerned with density extremes (the density difference from the lightest highlight to the darkest shadow). This measure is called the **copy density range (CDR)** of the photograph. The CDR is the shadow density minus the highlight density. This is an important relationship to remember. The CDR of figure 7.20 is 1.40 (1.45 − 0.05). The typical continuous-tone photograph has a CDR of approximately 1.70.

Comparing the dot size and the grey scale tonal area should not be taken to mean that a certain dot size should be formed in any particular part of the grey scale for every halftone negative. Printers are concerned that the smallest dot appear in the highlight step and that the largest dot appear in the last shadow step. The

placement of any dot sizes between these two extremes controls the contrast of the halftone and depends on the photograph being reproduced. There is no rule that states in which step any dot should be placed.

Understanding Halftone Exposures

Two simple exposures are generally used to produce a halftone negative photographically from a vignetted contact screen:

- Main
- Flash

They both are relatively straightforward and easy to understand.

Main Exposure

The initial exposure is called the **main exposure.** Sometimes referred to as the "highlight exposure" or the "detail exposure," the main exposure is simply an exposure on film made through a contact screen using a process camera. The main exposure controls where the smallest highlight dot is placed on the grey scale and in the corresponding areas of the negative.

Just as each continuous-tone photograph has a different CDR, so does each halftone contact screen have a different density range. The **basic density range (BDR)** of a halftone screen is the density range that is reproduced on the film with one main exposure through the halftone screen. This density range is also called the **screen range.**

Figure 7.21 illustrates three different main exposures of the same grey scale. Each grey scale shows dots throughout the range of steps. Notice that increasing the exposure moves the highlight dot down the scale, but that the BDR recorded on the grey scales remains the same—only it moves down the scale. The only difference between the three scales is in the placement of the highlight dot. The highlight dot moves downward with increasing exposure. As mentioned earlier, the main exposure controls the placement of the smallest highlight dot.

Assume that we have a halftone screen that produced a highlight dot in the density value of 0.05 and a shadow dot in the density value of 1.05. The BDR of this screen would be 0.90 (1.05 – 0.05 = 1.00). This simply means that our screen can record no more than a BDR of 1.00 with only a main exposure. If the CDR of the photograph we are shooting is smaller than the BDR of the screen we are using, one main exposure will reproduce the original. If the BDR of the photograph is larger than that of the screen, however, the image will not be accurately reproduced. As was already mentioned, the

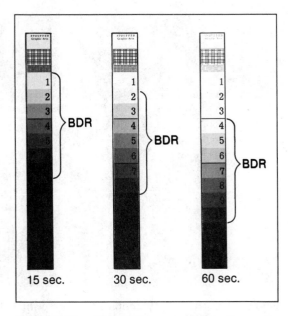

Figure 7.21.   Three main exposures of a grey scale. Three different main exposures were made of the same grey scale. Notice that the basic density range does not change as the exposure is increased; it just moves down the scale.

typical continuous-tone photograph has a density range of 1.70. This difference between CDR and screen density range is called **excess density.** It must be handled with a flash exposure.

Flash Exposure

The **flash exposure** is a nonimage exposure on the film through the contact screen. Light may be flashed through the lens, but a special flashing lamp is typically used. Nearly all the identifiable detail of a continuous-tone photograph is found in the highlight to middle tone areas. One main exposure will record most of the detail of a typical photograph. However, there is still some detail in the shadow areas; this shadow density affects the contrast of the final product. Most halftone screens are not equipped to record the entire range of shadow density and detail. Because shadows usually absorb more light than they reflect, the film records shadow detail long after any reflected highlight detail has been recorded. The main exposure typically cannot form reproducible shadow dots on the film and still reproduce the highlight detail faithfully. The function of the flash exposure is twofold:

- It adds density to the weak shadow dots, bringing them to reproducible sizes.
- It adds uniform exposure to the entire negative by increasing the size of all dots, especially those representing the shadow areas.

The flash exposure is needed to make the final halftone reproduction match the density range of the original print as closely as possible. This is not difficult to understand if you remember the vignetted dot pattern on the halftone screen. The highlight areas of the copy reflect the most light back to the camera lens. In just a few seconds of main exposure, the light reflected from the highlight areas of the copy passes through the clear areas in the center of the elliptical dot and produce a dot on the film emulsion. As the main exposure continues, light reflected from the highlight areas penetrates the denser portions of the vignetted dot, and the highlight dots grow in size. At the same time, some of the middle tone areas reflect enough light to penetrate the vignetted dot and they, too, record an image. However, the dark shadow areas of the photograph absorb most of the camera light and reflect back only a small amount. During the main exposures, this small amount of light reflected from the shadow areas may penetrate only the very center of the vignetted dot, which is clear. The dots produced by the light reflected from the shadow areas during the main exposure are so small that they cannot be printed.

The flash exposure is made directly through the halftone screen and does not rely on light reflected from the copy. Therefore, an equal amount of light passes through all parts of the screen. The flash exposure increases the size of all the dots recorded during the main exposure, but it has more of an effect on the shadow dots than on the highlight dots. This is because the highlight dots, having been formed from the reflection of the white camera light, are about as large as they can get. Enough light penetrated the vignetted screen dots in the highlight area to almost completely expose the film emulsion in the highlight areas. The yellow flash light does not have much effect in these areas; there just are not many unchanged silver halide crystals left to change. However, the flash exposure greatly affects the shadow area because the shadow area was not affected much during the main exposure. The small dots made in the shadow area during the main exposure enlarge during the flash exposure. This is why the flash exposure is said to control the placement of the shadow dot.

Figure 7.22 illustrates three different flash exposures of a grey scale made using the same main exposure. Notice that the position of the highlight dot does not significantly change, but the shadow dot moves down the scale as the flash exposure increases. The length of the flash is calculated from the amount of excess density of the print (CDR of print−BDR of screen). The goal is to print a 95-percent dot (or largest reproducible dot) in the darkest shadow area containing detail.

Controlling Halftone Contrast

The placement of the middle tone dots in a halftone photograph affects contrast. The term "contrast" is bantered about frequently by both printers and photographers, but what

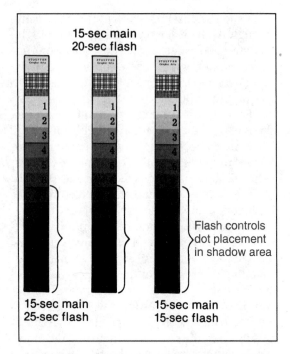

15-sec main
20-sec flash

1
2
3
4

Flash controls
dot placement
in shadow area

15-sec main
25-sec flash

1
2
3
4

1
2
3
4

15-sec main
15-sec flash

Figure 7.22.   Three flash exposures of a grey scale. Three different flash exposures of the same grey scale were made using the same main exposure. In steps 9 to 7, notice that the shadow dot moves up the scale with increased flash exposure.

does it really mean? Figure 7.23 is an example of a "contrasty" print. Figure 7.24 shows a normal print. Examine each reproduction. Figure 7.23 has fewer visible tones than figure 7.24. Also, figure 7.23 has a greater shadow density with no detail. In other words, a high-contrast photograph usually has a compressed tonal range and little detail in the highlights and shadows. The compression or expansion of tones defines contrast.

We can control contrast on the final printed sheet when we produce a halftone. By compressing or expanding the tonal range, we shift the middle tone dots up or down the scale. The two ways of controlling contrast are by using:

■ A filter
■ A special camera exposure

When using a magenta contact screen, it is possible to shorten or lengthen a tonal range by using a yellow or magenta filter. The filter is placed in front of the camera lens during the main exposure. The filter actually changes the screen's BDR. The following list shows how a screen's BDR is changed using different filters. They symbol "CC" stands for "color correcting filter", "M" represents a magenta filter and "Y" represents a yellow filter. The numbers 50 or 10 are a numerical designation of color intensity.

Filter	Adjusted BDR
■ CC-50M	1.15
■ CC-10M	1.35
■ Without a filter	1.40
■ CC-10Y	1.45
■ CC-50Y	1.60

Notice that if a screen has a BDR of 1.40, but is exposed through a CC-50M filter, the BDR is reduced to 1.15.

The most frequently used technique to increase contrast is to use a **bump exposure** or a no-screen exposure. With this technique, a second, image-forming exposure is made on the camera without the contact screen in place. This exposure must be made either before or after the main and flash exposures, but not between the two. The actual exposure time is expressed as a percentage of the main exposure. Figure 7.25 illustrates two different bump exposures of a grey scale using the same main and flash exposures. The bump compresses the screen range and therefore increases contrast. Figure 7.26 shows how using a bump exposure can improve a previously flat image.

Again, a bump exposure is not difficult to understand if you think about what is actually being recorded on the film. After the main and

Figure 7.23. **A contrast print.** A print or its reproduction is considered to have contrast when there is very little detail in the highlights and shadows and when there are few intermediate tones.
Courtesy of R. Kampas.

Figure 7.24. **A normal print.** A normal print or reproduction has highlight detail, shadow detail, and a range of intermediate tones.
Courtesy of R. Kampas.

flash exposures, the highlight areas on the film are almost completely filled in, and the shadow areas have recorded printable dots. The bump exposure is made without the contact screen using light reflected from the copy that is in the exact location it was in during the main exposure. Unlike the flash exposure, however, the bump exposure affects the highlight areas of the film. These areas have been almost completely exposed during the main exposure and require only a small additional exposure to completely fill in. The shadow areas are relatively unaffected by the small additional amount of exposure.

A bump exposure is very short. As the small burst of light strikes the copyboard, it is immediately reflected by the extreme highlights and is almost completely absorbed by the shadows. When the reflected light passes through the lens to the film, the dots in the highlight areas close, but the dots in the shadow areas are not affected. When the film is

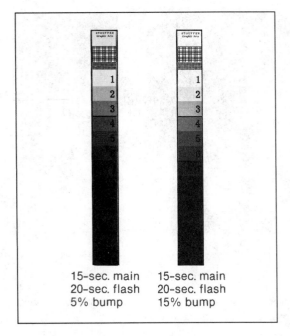

15–sec. main   15–sec. main
20–sec. flash   20–sec. flash
5% bump   15% bump

Figure 7.25.   Two bump exposures of a grey scale. Two different bump exposures of the same grey scale were made using the same main and flash exposures. Notice that a 5-percent bump produces detail from steps 1 through 8. A 15-percent bump produces detail from steps 2 through 7. An increase in bump exposure eliminates two tones from the grey scale—steps 1 and 8. Instead of eight tones there are now six. Contrast has been increased.

Figure 7.26.   A print enhanced using a bump exposure

processed, the bump exposure has compressed the tones of the original by reducing the number of density steps between the highlight and shadow areas.

Understanding Halftone Dots

The density variations in a continuous-tone original are represented in a halftone reproduction as dots of various sizes. The size of

these dots in any area of the halftone negative is determined by the amount of light reflected from the original to that area during the main and bump exposures, as well as by the amount of exposure produced by the flash. Halftone dots communicate information or detail from the original. Where there are no dots on a printed halftone, there are either completely open, inkless areas or completely filled in, inked areas.

The object of making a halftone is to produce a printed piece that reflects the tonal range of the original through variations in dot size and placement. The more closely the halftone approximates the tonal range of the original, the more closely it shows the detail of the original.

Printable Dots

It is impossible to observe all of the dot sizes on a halftone negative during film development to check for accurate dot size. Instead, printers use "aim points" that are typically at either extreme of the original's density range. They try to place the smallest dots or aim points that can be printed in the detail highlight areas of the original to show highlight detail in the print; the largest dots that can be printed are placed in the detail shadow areas. Thus, the positions of the smallest and largest printable dots on both the negative and the printed piece are important.

Remember that on the negative, the *smallest* printable dots appear as small, clear openings surrounded by black, exposed emulsion (density). During platemaking, these small openings expose only small dots on the printing plate. These small dots transfer small dots (highlight dots) to the printing paper and reproduce detail in the highlight area of the printed piece.

The *largest* printable dots appear on the negative as small areas of density surrounded by large, clear openings. During platemaking, these large openings expose large dots on the printing plate, which transfer large dots to the printing paper. These large dots (shadow dots) reproduce detail in the shadow area of the printed piece.

A press operator refers to a dot that is printable as a dot that the press can "hold," or as a dot that can be "held" on press. A 5-percent to 10-percent highlight dot can be held with most offset presses (see chapter 13). Dots that are smaller are too small to print accurately and consistently; some may not print at all. The largest printable shadow dot that can be held with most offset processes is a 95-percent shadow dot. On press, these dots appear as tiny, unprinted areas surrounded by ink. Shadow dots larger than 95 percent tend to fill in on press and go solid.

The smallest and largest printable dots are of concern to the camera operator. If the highlight dots on the negative (small, open areas surrounded by density) are too small, they will not pass enough light during platemaking to expose printable dots on the printing plate, and detail will be lost in the highlight areas. If the large, open areas on the negative that produce shadow dots in the print are too large, they may fill in during platemaking and become plugged with ink on press.

To make an acceptable halftone, the camera operator must know something about printable dot size. The correct size of a printable dot (such as 5 percent, 10 percent, 95 percent) is determined through knowing about the printing process to be used, the working conditions in the printing plant, and the ink and paper (or other substrate) to be used for printing. This information is given to the camera operator before the halftone is made.

Dot Gain

One very important consideration when determining printable dot size is **dot gain**. Halftone dots tend to grow in size during platemaking and when on press. Critical exposure and development control is needed during platemaking to reproduce the dot structure on the negative accurately. Improper plate exposure or processing produces dot sizes on the plate that differ in size from those on the negative. If the dots recorded on the printing plate are larger than those on the negative, larger dots will be printed and detail will be lost.

Even if the dots' sizes are recorded on the plate accurately, dot gain can still occur on press. In the offset printing process, improper ink and water balance can cause dot gain or loss. The type and condition of the press can also affect dot gain, as can the paper-and-ink combination being printed. Uncoated papers, such as bond or newsprint, absorb ink (see chapter 18). A dot printed on uncoated paper tends to spread and grow larger—ink is absorbed and spreads into the paper like water into a sponge. Small highlight dots get bigger; large shadow dots fill in. Coated paper has better "ink holdout." It does not absorb as much ink, and dots do not spread as much as they do on uncoated paper.

Dot size is inspected visually with a magnifying glass or a dot area meter. The sizes of the smallest and largest dots that can be reproduced (plated and printed) are determined by comparing dot size on the negative to the actual printed dot size. Through this comparison, a historical record of expected dot gain for a variety of processing and printing conditions on a variety of paper-and-ink combinations can be developed. Equipped with this knowledge, camera operators can recognize the smallest and largest printable dots for particular processes and working conditions, and they can place them in the correct density areas on the negative.

If no information is known about dot gain, shop tests must be run. One common test is to plate the negative made during the main test (see the following section), print it on a number of paper types commonly used in the plant, and measure for dot gain. In practice, a variety of control devices are available to the camera operator, plate department, and press operator to monitor and control dot gain.

Camera Calibration for Halftone Exposures

It is possible to produce a halftone negative by trial and error. In other words, we can guess at the main and flash exposures, produce a halftone, evaluate the results, and then try to compensate for any limitations on the negative by changing the exposures. The problem with a trial-and-error method is that it leads to a great waste of both film and time. Every original photograph is likely to have a slightly different CDR than the next. Likewise, each halftone screen will have a slightly different BDR than every other. Even if we could use trial and error to come up with main, flash, and bump exposure times that would produce acceptable halftones for the majority of our continuous-tone originals, there would always be problem photographs (such as especially flat or contrasty originals) that our trial-and-error exposure times would not reproduce correctly. That is, our results would not be predictable.

Predictable results are required in halftone photography to both control quality and reduce waste in the camera room. To achieve predictable results, we must have densitometric information about our working conditions and about our original copy. Information about our working conditions— the BDR of our screen and the effects on film density recorded during the main, flash, and bump exposures—is gathered during camera calibration for halftones. Information about the original copy—the CDR and the actual densities of the highlight and shadow areas— is read from the original photograph with a densitometer.

Through camera calibration we determine the following:

- The BDR of the halftone screen we are going to use
- The minimum flash required to record density in the shadow areas on the negative
- The effect that a bump exposure of a specific duration has on the highlight areas of the negative

These three pieces of information are determined from three tests, one each for the main, flash, and bump exposures. During these tests, only exposure changes. All other darkroom conditions, including camera lighting and chemical and film processing control, are kept

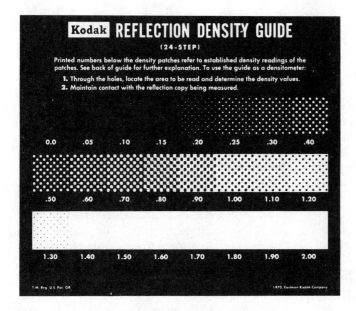

Figure 7.27. **The 24-step reflection density guide.** The main exposure test shows a range from 20 to 1.20, or a BDR of 1.00 with a 30-second exposure.
Courtesy of Eastman Kodak Company.

as consistent as possible. If shallow-tray processing is used, it is advisable to mix fresh developer after each test to keep a consistent level of developer activity.

Main Test

The main test is used to determine the BDR of the halftone screen. This test requires a visual grey scale with steps of known density, such as the 24-step reflection density guide shown in figure 7.27. In addition, a basic knowledge of camera operation is needed (see chapter 6).

1. Place a step-calibrated grey scale in the center of the copyboard.

2. Set the lens for an aperture that is two f/stops smaller than the largest possible f/stop opening on the camera.

3. Place an unexposed sheet of film on the filmboard, emulsion side up.

4. Place a halftone screen over the film, emulsion side down.

5. Set the camera exposure for a test exposure. A 30-second test exposure is generally a good starting point.

6. Develop the negative according to the manufacturer's recommendations, keeping processing conditions absolutely consistent.

7. Look for the smallest printable highlight dot on the negative. For this test, the smallest printable dot should fall between the 0.00 density step and the 0.30 density step on the negative image of the grey scale.

8. Observe the density step on the negative image of the grey scale that contains the smallest printable highlight dot. Read the corresponding density of this step on the calibrated grey scale. In figure 7.27, the smallest printable dot was produced in the fifth step, representing 0.20 units of density. Record your results.

9. Now examine the remaining steps in which dots were recorded on the grey scale negative. Note and record the density step that carries the largest printable shadow dot. For figure 7.27, the dots recorded in the 1.30

density step appeared too large to be printable; those in the 1.20 step were slightly too small. We determined that the largest printable dot would be recorded at about a density step of 1.25.

10. Obtain the BDR of the screen by subtracting the density reading in the density step that contains the smallest printable dot (highlight) from the density reading in the density step that contains the largest printable dot (shadow).

The BDR of the screen we tested was 1.05:

Shadow density	1.25
Highlight density	−0.20
Basic density range (BDR)	1.05

A screen BDR of 1.05 means that if we make an exposure through that screen, in the camera that was used to test the screen, with the same film, under the same processing conditions, from a continuous-tone original that has a copy density range of 1.05, then all of the image density—from the whitest white, through midtones, to black—can be recorded with only a main exposure. Most continuous-tone originals have a wider density range than 1.05. Using the tested screen, a flash will be required to accurately reproduce the detail displayed in the complete tone range of any continuous-tone original that has a CDR greater than 1.05.

Main Test Adjustments

When making a main test exposure we are most concerned with recording the highlight dot in a step between 0.00 and 0.30 as viewed on the film. The second, and equally important, goal is to record the full CDR.

If the first printable dot was recorded in the 1.40 step of the negative grey scale, and the screen BDR was 1.05, the shadow

dot would appear in the 2.45 density step (1.40 + 1.05 = 2.45). Most reflection density guides, such as the one shown in figure 7.27, do not have density steps this high. If we cannot see the highlight and shadow dot placement, then we cannot determine the screen BDR.

This would be the case if an extremely long trial main exposure were used—long main exposure would move the highlights down the scale. An overly short trial main exposure would have the opposite result, and a midtone dot, larger than the highlight dot, would appear in the 0.00 density step of the negative grey scale. Again, the screen BDR could not be determined because the highlight dot would not show on the grey scale.

If a dot larger than the smallest printable dot is recorded in the 0.00 step, rerun the test with an increased exposure time. Increasing the exposure moves the dot sizes recorded in each step up the scale toward 0.30. If the smallest printable dot is recorded above the 0.30 density step, decrease exposure time. Decreasing the main exposure moves the dot sizes recorded in each step down the scale, toward 0.00.

If the first test exposure did not place the smallest printable dot in the 0.00 to 0.30 density range, it is possible to predict a new test exposure: *Doubling the main exposure shifts all halftone dots up the scale 0.30 units of density. Halving the main exposure shifts all halftone dots down the scale 0.30 units of density.* Thus, if the smallest printable dot is found in the 0.40 density step, exposure with the same aperture but for half the exposure time will place this dot in the 0.10 density step. This is an extremely important concept. It applies to all photographic exposures, no matter what type of camera, film, or intended product use.

Repeat the main test until the required highlight dot placement is achieved.

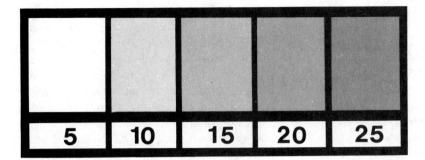

Figure 7.28. Flash exposure test. The negative produced during the flash exposure test shows that a reproducible shadow dot was obtained at 10 seconds.

Flash Test

Results from the flash test are used to calculate the amount of flash exposure needed to extend the density range in the shadow area of the negative by an amount consistent with the shadow detail density range on the original. To make this calculation we must determine the minimum flash required to produce a printable shadow dot on the negative. The flash test is made with a step exposure. Use the same type of film and the same screen used in the main test.

1. Position the screen and the film emulsion-to-emulsion on the filmboard, under the flash lamp. Turn on the vacuum.

2. Cover most of the sheet of film with an opaque sheet of paper (such as cardboard), leaving about one-fifth of the sheet uncovered.

3. Expose the uncovered area for 5 seconds.

4. Without moving the film or the screen, shift the opaque paper so that it uncovers another one-fifth of the sheet of film and expose for another 5 seconds.

5. Continue this process until the whole sheet of film has been uncovered and exposed for 5 seconds.

6. Process the film using standard conditions and methods.

7. Examine the negative for the largest printable dot, and record the flash exposure needed to produce it.

The results of our flash test are shown in figure 7.28. Five steps were used. The first step was exposed 5 times for a total of 25 seconds; the last step received only one 5-second exposure. For our test, a printable shadow dot was produced with 10 seconds of flash exposure. Dots were produced with the 5-second exposure, but these dots were too large and would fill in during plate making and printing.

Flash Test Explanation

Recall that the flash exposure extends the density range recorded on the negative by increasing the density apparent in the shadow area, the area which received the least light reflected from the copy. Density is added in the shadow area during the flash by making an exposure with a flashing lamp directly through the negative onto the film emulsion. During the main exposure, the highlight areas of the copy reflect a great deal of light. Thus, the amount of light added to the negative highlight dots during the flash produce almost no further exposure, and the flash has little effect on the highlight dots. However, only a small amount of light is reflected from the shadow areas of the original during the main exposure. Therefore, the amount of light received in the shadow areas during the flash produce much more exposure in these areas on the film. This is why the flash extends density mainly in the shadow areas: it increases dot size mainly in shadow areas, which were the least affected by the main exposure.

When exposure calculations are made for a halftone, a balance is struck between the exposure times such that the main exposure produces the smallest printable dots, which reproduce highlight detail in about the same density as the highlight detail on the original, and the flash extends density only in the shadow areas.

The main exposure produces the highlight dots and continues producing midtone dots up the scale until the BDR of the screen is reached. The BDR of the screen in our example was 1.05, which means that the density range of the original will be reproduced only up to 1.05 units of density. Density over this amount will appear as completely open, unexposed areas on the negative. Thus, these areas will not be reproduced with dots on the print and will appear on the printed piece as a solid ink mass. If the copy has a CDR of 1.70, and the screen has a BDR of 1.05, there are 0.65 units (1.70–1.05) of "excess density" which will not be reproduced by the main exposure only. Without a flash to extend the density range in the shadows, a print with a very short density range would be produced.

This idea of extending the recorded image range should not be confused with the BDR of the screen. A flash exposure adds density in the shadow areas of the recorded halftone image, and thereby "extends" the image density range. It does not, however, affect the BDR of the screen in any way.

Bump Test

We have now seen that a flash is used to extend density into the shadow areas when the CDR exceeds the screen density range. There are oc-

casions, however, when the screen BDR exceeds the CDR. When the screen BDR exceeds the CDR, it is impossible to produce both an acceptable highlight dot and an acceptable shadow dot with a single main exposure. If the exposure produced an acceptable highlight dot, the shadow dot would be too large. If an acceptable shadow dot were produced, the highlight dot would be placed too far down the grey scale. A bump exposure is required in these situations, to increase exposure in the highlight areas. This has the effect of compressing the screen BDR to more closely match the CDR.

Another use of the bump exposure is to improve the appearance of an unacceptable original photograph. By compressing the CDR, the bump increases contrast, giving the image what is often called "more snap." "Snap," it should be noted, is not a characteristic that can be measured accurately. The bump exposure tends to close the small negative highlight halftone dots; the result is a more appealing image.

The bump is a no-screen exposure, generally made after the main and flash exposures. The bump is a very short exposure during which light reflected from the copy exposes the negative. The shadow and midtone areas of the copy reflect very little light during this short exposure. Thus, the bump has no effect on the shadow areas of the negative, and little effect on the midtones. The highlight areas, on the other hand, reflect the most light and are most affected by the bump.

Use the same screen and processing conditions for the bump test that were used in the main and flash test.

1. Place a sheet of film emulsion-to-emulsion with the contact screen on the filmboard.

2. Position a calibrated grey scale on the copyboard.

3. Expose the film through the lens using the main exposure time that was determined during the main test to give the correct highlight dot location (0.00 to 0.30).

4. Keeping the vacuum on and being careful not to shift the film, open the camera back and remove the halftone screen. Then close the camera back.

5. Expose the film through the lens for 5 percent of the main exposure (10% if a grey positive halftone screen is used). Neutral density (ND) filters can be used instead of varying exposure for the bump. Use a 1.3 ND filter for a 5 percent bump; use a 1.0 ND filter for a 10 percent bump.

6. Process the negative.

7. Locate the smallest printable highlight dot on the negative, and record the density of the step in which it appears.

8. Compare this density with the density step in which the smallest printable highlight dot occurred during the main exposure test, and record the difference between the two densities.

The difference between these two numbers is called the "highlight shift," because it represents the shift in highlight density up the density scale, that results from a no-screen, bump exposure. Accurate information about the highlight shift is needed when calculating halftone exposures for a given piece of copy.

Bump Test Adjustments
Bump exposure time is expressed as a percentage of main exposure, and can range from about 3 percent to about 10 percent or more of the main exposure. If a halftone required a 40-second main exposure with a 10-percent bump, the bump exposure would be 4 seconds (40 seconds × 10 percent = 4 seconds). An exposure this short can be reproduced accurately on cameras equipped with light-

Table 7.4. Neutral density (ND) filters for selected bump exposures

Percent Bump	Neutral Density Filter
3%	1.50
5%	1.30
10%	1.00
15%	0.80
20%	0.70

Use this table to select the proper neutral density filter for the bump.

integrated exposure systems—systems in which the actual amount of light striking the film is used to control exposure—rather than timers. Cameras not equipped with light integration often require that neutral density (ND) filters are fitted in front of their lenses during the bump. These filters reduce the intensity of the light passing through the lens, thereby increasing bump exposure times. Recommended ND filters for a range of bump exposures are shown in table 7.4. The correct filter allows you to use the same f/stop and main exposure. Bump exposure time is increased by the filter factor, which is determined by the amount of exposure the filter blocks. The more exposure the filter blocks, the higher the filter factor.

Calculating Halftone Exposures

Exposure calculations must be made for every halftone produced to determine the correct main, flash, and bump (if required) exposures needed to reproduce the original. As previously mentioned, during exposure calculation, a balance is struck between all exposure times. This balance assures that correctly sized dots will be placed in all areas of the negative to accurately reproduce the densities found in the corresponding areas of the original. Correct dot placement almost always requires adjustments to exposure times for individual copy.

For example, even though the flash exposure has little effect on dot size in the highlight areas of a halftone, it can be sufficient to increase the effect of the main exposure, producing overexposed highlight areas. To compensate for this effect, the main exposure must be decreased by the correct amount so that the total exposure (main exposure plus flash exposure) will not overexpose the highlight dots and cause them to fill in on the negative. There is also an interaction between the bump and main exposure times. If a bump exposure is used, the main exposure must be reduced to compensate for the effect that the bump will have on the dots produced by the main.

These calculations can be made mathematically. However, several halftone computers have been developed that make halftone calculation a relatively simple process. All that is needed for halftone calculation are the results from the halftone calibration tests (main, flash, and bump exposures) and readings of the CDR—the detail highlight and the detail shadow density readings from the original. The halftone computer adjusts all exposures for shop conditions using the results of the calibration tests, then adjusts these exposure times for particular copy requirements.

The first step in halftone calculation is accomplished by calibrating the computer for shop conditions. During calibration, the computer is supplied with information from the calibration tests—the BDR of the screen and the effect on density of the flash and bump exposures. After calibration, the computer can predict the required exposure times for any original, based on information that the operator enters about the CDR of the original.

A manual halftone computer is shown in figure 7.29. This device displays a number of scales which revolve around a central pin. The computer is calibrated and information about the CDR is entered by selecting and rotating the appropriate scales. This manual computer is inexpensive and comes supplied with thorough directions for calibration and use. However, it does have some disadvantages. It is not as accurate as modern, digital devices because it is hand manipulated and relies on visual readings. In addition, manual computers of this type can only be calibrated for one set of working conditions (screen and processing) at a time. They must be recalibrated each time the camera-screen combination changes. Some companies calibrate a separate manual computer for each different screen in common use.

Small, handheld digital halftone calculators, similar in operation to pocket calculators, are also available. These devices offer the advantage of more accurate readings than can be obtained with manual computers, but they generally rely on correct operator entry of information. For each halftone produced, the operator must take accurate density readings from the original and accurately enter them and calibration information into the calculator.

Microcomputers built directly into the camera are also used for halftone calculation (figure 7.30). While these devices are more expensive than handheld manual or digital calculators, they offer several advantages. All of these advantages are related to the microcomputer's ability to store information and to process it quickly. Most microcomputers programmed for halftone calculation have memory storage that allows them to store information about several sets of working conditions. A computer might be able to store information about two to forty or more different camera-screen combinations. Thus it could be used for making a variety of halftones without recalibration. The operator would simply call up the correct calibration for the camera-screen combination to be used, then enter information about the CDR of the original to be reproduced. Advanced systems can apply CDR

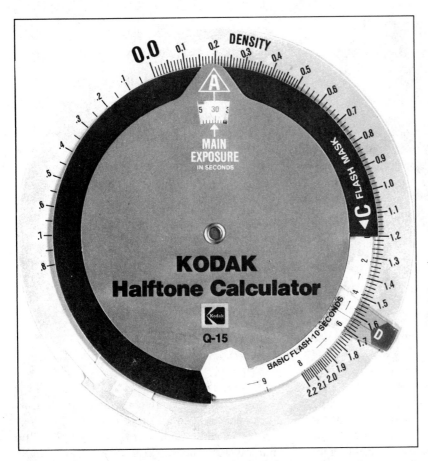

Figure 7.29. The Kodak Halftone Negative Computer, Q–15. This computer indicates precise exposure times for making halftone negatives from photographs, artwork, or other reflection copy.
Courtesy of Eastman Kodak Company.

readings to information about ink-and-paper combinations, press, and other process conditions, as well as camera-screen combinations. All of this amounts to a reduction of waste and an increase in accuracy, predictability, and quality control. Calculation speed is increased as well; on most computers, final exposure settings can be determined in a matter of seconds.

The most recent improvements in halftone computers have led to the development of microcomputers that can accept density read-

ings directly from the original copy without the need for operator entry. Such devices connect a densitometer directly to the computer through a serial interface. The interface consists of a port (socket) on the computer into which a plug from the densitometer can be inserted. Densitometric readings are passed directly from the densitometer head to the computer memory for use in exposure calculations. The densitometer can be positioned manually by the operator on the detail highlight and

Figure 7.30.   Microcomputers for halftone calculation. This vertical camera has a built-in microcomputer for halftone calculations. The operator keys in information about the highlight and shadow densities of the original. This information is used with preprogrammed information to calculate exposure for a particular screen and film material.
Courtesy of Agfa-Gevaert, Inc.

shadow areas of the original, or a scanning densitometer can be used to read and record original copy densities.

Often the densitometer is built right into the darkroom camera (figure 7.31). This configuration eliminates the need for the operator to enter any density readings. The microcomputer receives density readings directly from the densitometer. Exposure adjustments are made automatically based on information supplied to the camera console from the microcomputer.

Processing Considerations for Halftone Photography

General film processing was explained in detail in chapter 6. Here we will only emphasize the importance of being able to repeat every processing step exactly from one negative to the next. With simple line negatives, the extent of development can be judged visually, making it possible to compensate for a slight variation in time, temperature, or agitation and still produce a usable negative. Such visual judgment is difficult when processing halftone negatives in trays.

Automatic processors provide the greatest consistency in development. Unfortunately, such processors are not always available. There are several important considerations when processing halftones in trays.

A major problem with shallow-tray and traditional lith development is chemical exhaustion. Once the two parts of the high-contrast developer have been joined, the exhaustion process begins. Even if the developing mixture is not used, it becomes exhausted in a matter of hours. This is partly a result of solutions being combined and partly a result of

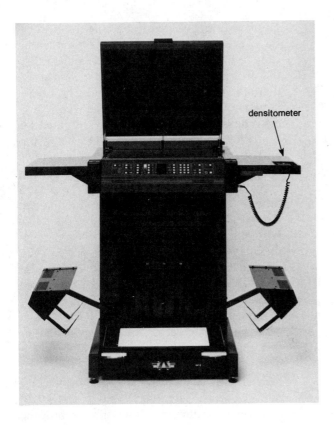

densitometer

Figure 7.31.   A process camera with a densitometer. This process camera features an on-line densitometer, which can pass density readings directly to the camera computer.
Courtesy of Agfa-Gevaert, Inc.

the surface of the chemicals coming into contact with room air (aerial oxidation). The developer also becomes exhausted through use because it reacts with the emulsion of the film, and both the developer and the film change chemical structure. Chemical exhaustion radically affects the quality of the final halftone.

Rapid access chemistry has eliminated the exhaustion problem with lith formulations. However, shallow-tray development for halftones remains problematic. The three tyrants of time, temperature, and agitation challenge predictability.

Even the most experienced darkroom professionals cannot control the amount of tray developing time exactly. The process of flooding the entire surface of the film simulta-

neously and moving the developed halftone to the stop bath can never be the same. Even a few seconds' difference between tests can produce radically different results.

Exact temperature control is also almost impossible to achieve. Recent tests conducted at Drexel University, in Philadelphia, found as much as a 6-degree temperature variation in normal darkroom tray chemistry. The primary cause for the variation was the heat introduced by the technician's hands. Even a 1-degree difference can result in extreme halftone variation.

The final consideration is the rate of tray agitation. Still development—a technique discussed in chapter 6 that uses no agitation—does not apply to halftone work. With halftone negatives, the technique softens contrast on the negative and produces a softer, less defined dot. A mechanical tray technique leaves streaks in halftone negatives because currents of chemicals flow in the same paths over the film.

The goal is to agitate in at least three directions at a consistent rate, and thereby replace fresh chemistry on the surface of the film continually. The actual speed is not significant, only that the rate is the same for every piece of film. Watching the second hand sweep on a darkroom timer is helpful. Some photographers even use a metronome to ensure a consistent rate. However, across an entire day of halftone production, few photographers can deliver exactly the same agitation for every image.

Even with these frustrations, successful halftones can be produced by shallow-tray processing techniques. Careful attention must be given to controlling all variables.

Typical Halftone Procedures

Let us tie the information of this section together by following the typical procedures for making a halftone negative from a continuous-tone original using a manual or digital hand-held computer.

1. With a visual or reflection densitometer, determine the highlight and shadow densities of the original. Be sure to measure the lightest area with detail for the highlights and the densest area (whether there is detail or not) for the shadows. With that information, determine the main and flash exposure times from a halftone computer. If a bump exposure is necessary, identify the time with the same tool.

2. Set up the process camera by using the procedures described in chapter 6. Clean the copyboard glass, center the original photo-

graph and grey scale on the guidelines, close the frame (turn on the vacuum system if the camera has one), and move the copyboard so that it is parallel to the film plane. Adjust the diaphragm control to the percentage of enlargement or reduction desired at the f/stop opening that the computer was calibrated for (the photographer generally writes the f/stop on the computer as a reminder). Then move the percentage tapes so that they are balanced at the correct reproduction size. Set the camera timer at the main exposure time. Then adjust the flash timer to the flash exposure time. It is wise to check for even illumination by viewing the image through a ground glass screen. Aim the camera lights if necessary. Check for correct image position and camera focus. Adjust the vacuum system on the filmboard to the size of the contact screen, not to the size of the piece of film. (The contact screen must always be larger than the piece of film being used.)

3. To make the halftone exposures, first turn off the normal room lights so the darkroom is under safelight. Remove a sheet of high-contrast film from the storage box (be sure to close the box immediately because this is a good habit to develop) and mount the piece of film on the camera filmboard, emulsion side up. If both the copy and the film are centered on the guidelines, there is little chance of ruining a sheet because the image missed the film. Next position the halftone contact screen over the film so that the emulsions of the two pieces are touching (figure 7.32). Turn on the vacuum system and carefully roll out any air pockets that are trapped between the film and the screen. A loss of detail will occur if an air gap between the emulsions is allowed.

Close the camera back and turn on the timer to make the main exposure. When the shutter closes, open the camera back and, without touching the film or screen, make the flash exposure (figure 7.33). If a bump exposure is to

Figure 7.32.   Adding the halftone screen to the film sheet. Place the emulsion of the contact screen in contact with the emulsion of the film. Courtesy of nuArc Company, Inc.

be made, reset the camera timer, remove the halftone screen carefully so the film does not shift, close the camera back, and make the through-the-lens bump exposure.

4. Remove the exposed film from the camera and process it by standard shop procedures. When the film is dry, evaluate the grey scale and image areas for usability. In the most general terms, the negative should carry a printable highlight dot in the same area of the image that was measured on the densitometer for highlight detail and a printable shadow dot in the corresponding shadow area. Increasing the main exposure will move the highlight dot farther up the grey scale.

Evaluating the usability of halftone images and making knowledgeable changes to correct defects in the halftones are the most important parts of the photographer's job. The following section takes a closer look at these processes.

Figure 7.33.   Making the flash exposure. After making the main exposure, open the camera back, turn on the flashing lamp, and make the flash exposure.

Evaluating Halftone Negatives

The major variables involved in photographic halftone production have now been introduced. The central purpose has been to deal with the basics of the process. The ultimate goal has been, of course, to be able to produce the best possible halftone from any continuous-tone image. We have talked about aim points (highlights and shadows) and suggested that the placement of middle tone dots was an important control of contrast. However, no concrete method of interpreting the true usability of a halftone or of correcting inaccuracies was presented. This interpretation is vital.

It should be obvious that there are problems with any visual interpretation of a halftone. Most people have difficulty judging negative image and sometimes become confused between shadow and highlight dots. Another problem is that the actual picture is made up of dots of random shape and size that can usually be viewed only through a magnifying glass.

The solution to these problems is not to deal with the individual dots as they appear in the image itself but rather to be concerned with their positions on the grey scale that was photographed with the continuous-tone photograph. As mentioned earlier, the grey scale is simply a numeric measure of density; each step can be equated easily to a corresponding area of density on the print, so interpretation becomes much easier. The actual technique is to compare the grey scale that was photographed with the continuous-tone print to the print itself.

Assume that when the original density readings from the continuous-tone print were taken, they were 0.10 for the highlight area and 1.40 for the shadow area. On the grey scale in figure 7.8, 0.10 density lies somewhere between step 1 and step 2; the density of 1.40 lies in about step 10. (If you do not have a calibrated grey scale, you can calibrate the one you have with a reflection densitometer by simply reading the density in each step.) If your halftone negative (and, consequently, your printed halftone positive) is going to have the same density range as your continuous-tone original, you would expect to see the grey scale almost completely filled in at step 1 or step 2 and almost completely clear at around step 10.

Actual dot size in these steps can be determined by looking at the dots with a magnifying glass. Again, the key is not to look at individual dots but to look at an area of dots. An area of dots on the negative film image of the grey scale that will produce 10-percent highlight dots on the printed piece will appear mostly black with a uniform pattern of small, clear openings. An area of dots on the negative film image of the grey scale that will produce 95-percent shadow dots on the printed piece will appear clear with a uniform pattern of small black dots. If the placement of your shadow and highlight dots on the film image of the grey scale corresponds to the density recordings of the shadow and highlight areas from the original photograph, you can have some confidence that your final printed halftone will represent the continuous-tone original accurately. This should be the case if the halftone negative computer was calibrated and used accurately and all exposure and processing steps were carried out correctly.

Correcting Defects

What if the dots fall in the wrong place? This is where the concept of a predictable density shift discussed in section 1 of this chapter becomes important. Let's assume for the previous example that the highlight dot did not fall in step 2 but instead appeared in step 3. You know that the highlight dot placement is controlled by the main exposure. If the highlight dot was recorded in step 3, you must have had too long a main exposure. The question is "How much too long?"

If you were using the calibrated grey scale in figure 7.8, you would see that the density difference between step 3 (where the highlight dot appeared) and step 2 (where you want the highlight dot to appear) is approximately 0.15 (0.32 − 0.14 = 0.18). How much must we adjust the main exposure to move the highlight dot 0.15 units of density up the grey scale?

You know that a change of one f/stop on the camera produces a 0.30 density shift on the film emulsion. You know further that halving or doubling the shutter speed is the same as changing the f/stop one stop up or down.

In this example we want to reduce the exposure by one-half an f/stop, but depending upon the camera system, this is not usually possible. Therefore we must adjust the exposure time. Halving the time will shift the dot 0.30 units up the scale. While it is not a direct linear relationship, taking half of the half exposure—that is reducing the exposure by 1/4—will shift the dot approximately 0.15 up the scale (one-half of 0.30).

By making this exposure adjustment and reshooting the picture with all other conditions (f/stop, flash, chemistry, and processing conditions) equal, you can shift the highlight dot up approximately one step.

A halftone negative computer should eliminate the need to reshoot to produce perfect results. But even a halftone computer cannot account for differences in individual processing techniques and conditions. Visual inspection of the grey scale is one method of correcting for improper dot placement. But when you reshoot the photograph, you must vary only the shutter speed and keep all other darkroom conditions constant.

It is worth noting here that a very accurate measure of the dot size on the actual halftone negative can be achieved with a dot area meter or a transmission densitometer. As mentioned in section 1, a dot area meter (figure 7.19) reads the dot coverage in an area of a piece of transparent film material. By measuring the dot area on the halftone negative that corresponds to the areas you identified as the highlight and shadow areas of the continuous-tone original, you can establish whether you have placed the correct-sized dots in the proper locations. Measures taken with a dot area meter can be used directly. Measures taken with a transmission densitometer (figure 7.7) can be converted as shown in table 7.1.

Key Terms

halftone	photoelectric densitometer	highlight area
density	reflection densitometer	shadow area
reflectance	zeroing	middle tone area
transmittance	transmission densitometer	spectral highlight
incident light	sensitometer	copy density range (CDR)
tones	halftone photography	main exposure
high-contrast copy	screen ruling	basic density range (BDR)
contrast	screen tints	excess density
continuous-tone copy	vignetted screen pattern	flash exposure
densitometry	linen tester	bump exposure
densitometer	dot area meter	dot gain
visual densitometer		

Questions for Review

Section 1

1. Name several examples of continuous-tone images.
2. In general terms, what does the term "density" mean?
3. What does the term "contrast" describe about tones on a piece of photographic film?
4. What is the difference between a transmission densitometer and a reflection densitometer?
5. What does the term "screen ruling" mean?
6. To what does the term "normal viewing distance" refer?
7. What is the difference between a vignetted screen structure and a solid-line screen structure?
8. Which will produce a larger dot on the printed page, a 40-percent or a 60-percent screen tint?
9. What is the purpose of a dot area meter?
10. Name the two basic types of contact screens.

Section 2

1. What three areas of a continuous-tone photograph are considered the most significant measures of print quality?
2. What is meant by the basic density range (BDR) of a photograph?
3. What two types of halftone exposures are almost always used to reproduce a continuous-tone image?
4. What is the purpose of a bump exposure?
5. What is the major problem when using shallow-tray development to process halftone images?
6. Briefly outline the typical procedures when making a halftone negative from a continuous-tone original.

CHAPTER

Digital Imaging— Working With Data

Anecdote to Chapter Eight

Many electronic innovations of the 1950s and 1960s were a result of institutional and corporate military research projects. The *Time-Life* book on *Computer Images* (1991 edition) describes how computer graphics was introduced to the public through a Navy project that was underway at the Massachusetts Institute of Technology (M.I.T.). M.I.T. engineer Jay Forrester introduced the Whirlwind computer to the public in December 1951 on the Edward R. Murrow television show. During the television program Jay Forrester and his computer produced a graph representing the fuel consumption, trajectory, and velocity of a military rocket. To pose a problem to a computer, have it calculate data and produce a graphic on its monitor, almost instantly, was an awesome feat in 1951.

The Whirlwind digital computer was developed as part of a Navy flight trainer project.

Forrester and his group were working on the computer component of the project. The success of this project led to the development of a new digital computer laboratory at M.I.T. which was used to focus on military air-traffic control projects. Further development of the Whirlwind computer, in this new facility, led to the development of the semi-automatic ground environment (SAGE) system. SAGE was an interactive graphics system which was used between 1958 and 1983 to monitor air traffic in 22 U.S. sites or air-defense sectors.

Today's desktop computer operates more than 100 times faster than the 1950s Whirlwind computer. The power of today's desktop computer allows us to produce media or any combination of text, graphics, sound, animation, and video (multimedia) limited only by the imagination and creativity of the operator.

Objectives for Chapter 8

After completing this chapter you will be able to:

- Discuss two basic local area networks (LANs) and identify the best solution(s) for moving graphic files.
- Describe the procedure for creating a small computer systems interface (SCSI) chain.
- Differentiate between primary, removable, and back-up storage devices.
- Identify an appropriate monitor based on workstation requirements.

- Discuss how printer resolution (dpi) affects line and tone reproduction.
- Identify three types of color printers and discuss how they differ.
- Describe the purpose of a raster image processor (RIP) and an imagesetter.
- Discuss differences between application, system, and resource software.
- Identify and discuss types of application software commonly used in the electronic prepress area.

Introduction

This chapter continues the discussion started in chapter 5.

The printing industry has seen a revolution in the past decade. Traditional hand methods of preparing images—whether type, line drawings, or continuous-tone images—are being replaced rapidly by digital technology. The computer has become the printer's fundamental tool.

Chapter 5 laid a foundation of understanding computers as fundamental prepress tools. It introduced basic computer systems and terminology and reviewed digital image entry methods.

Chapter 8 continues that discussion. The following pages look at moving and storing data, image output techniques, and software applications.

As has been mentioned in a previous chapter, it is the intention of this book to provide details for the operation of any specific system or device. Manufacturers supply docu-

mentation giving detailed operating procedures for their equipment. If we included such documentation it would be hopelessly out of date before this book was even off the press—the rate of change and improvement is simply too fast to do so. It is possible, however, to provide a general understanding of how digital data is stored, moved, manipulated, and output.

Moving and Storing Data

As electronic prepress becomes more sophisticated and images become more complex, file sizes grow larger. Moving these files from computer to computer, storing them, and transmitting them from computer to output device are key concerns.

Networking

The basic system used to move data between input and output devices is called a local area network (LAN). Two common LAN systems are LocalTalk and Ethernet.

LocalTalk

LocalTalk is a hardware/software system that allows communication between computers and other networkable devices. LocalTalk capability is built into the computer. Every Macintosh has had built-in LocalTalk capability since the first one was made in 1984. Many computers and/or printers can be networked by plugging a LocalTalk connector (figure 8.1) into the computer's printer port. The speed of LocalTalk is adequate for moving non-graphic and small

Figure 8.1. LocalTalk connector. A LocalTalk connector attaches to the printer port of the computer.

graphic data such as word processing, database, spreadsheet, low resolution raster graphics, and small vector files. The disadvantage of LocalTalk is its inability to transmit large files rapidly. LocalTalk's data transmission rate is not fast enough to handle extensive file sharing of large 24-bit color images at publishing resolutions.

SneakerNet

Most publishers use a combination of Sneaker-Net and Ethernet to move large files through the prepress area. **SneakerNet** involves the manual transfer of removable drives from workstation to workstation. Large amounts of data can be moved faster by an operator carrying them to the next workstation than they can by sending them over a network electronically. This system works well when workstations are in the same room, floor, or building. Storage devices to accomplish this task are discussed in the Storing Data section of this chapter.

Ethernet

Ethernet is a 20-year-old solution to networking that transmits data 5 to 10 times faster than LocalTalk. Ethernet has a speed rating of 10 megabits (millions of bits) per second. Using a combination of Ethernet and SneakerNet, prepress departments have been able to solve the movement of large files.

There are three Ethernet specifications for cable—10BASE–5, 10BASE–2, and 10BASE–T. The number *10* stands for a transmission rate of 10 megabits per second. *BASE* indicates baseband transmission, which carries one signal per cable, as opposed to broadband transmission, which carries multiple signals per cable. The numbers *5* and *2* represent the distance in meters that a signal can travel through the cable. A signal can be carried 500 meters on 10BASE–5 cable and 200 meters on 10BASE–2 cable. The *T* in 10BASE–T cable stands for "twisted-pair telephone wiring," which is limited to about a distance of 100 meters.

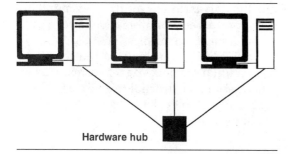

Figure 8.2.   Hardware hub. A star configuration makes trouble shooting easier because a break in one link affects only the connected workstation.

Figure 8.3.   Ethernet connection. A computer that is not Ethernet ready requires a card and an appropriate adapter.

The differences among the three Ethernet cables are in their thicknesses, shielding, and signal transmission specifications. Thick Ethernet, or 10BASE–5, is best used over long distances such as when connecting different areas of a building or when connecting different departments to the same imagesetter (see the Imagesetters section of this chapter). The 10BASE–5 and 10BASE–2 Ethernet normally daisy chain, or connect, computers in a series. Because of the limited physical characteristics of 10BASE–T (twisted-pair), the computers are placed in a star or parallel configuration. In this configuration all computers are connected directly to a hardware hub (figure 8.2). This setup is popular because network problems are easier to troubleshoot—a broken links affects only the connected workstation.

Apple has its own Ethernet cabling system which uses a 14-pin Apple attachment-unit interface (AAUI) port. With the appropriate adapters it can connect to all three cable types. Ethernet connects to the computer with a card (figure 8.3) that plugs into an internal slot or to a small computer systems interface (SCSI) port with an external adapter. (See the following section for more about SCSI.)

A network using Ethernet cable can be established to allow any workstation to communicate with another workstation, laser printer, modem, color proof printer, image-

setter, or direct image platemaker. In many cases, where large high-resolution files are common, Ethernet is too slow to transmit data and SneakerNet is impractical. A solution in this situation would be to use fiber-optic cable, which is capable of handling many signals at the same time and moves data much faster than Ethernet.

The SCSI Chain

Entering and storing digital data involves devices such as a scanner, a CD-ROM drive, a still video drive, and external storage drives. It is often necessary to connect more than one of these devices to a workstation to form a chain. The unit that connects these devices to the CPU is called a **small computer systems interface (SCSI)** (pronounced "scuzzy") port (figure 8.4). The SCSI port, which is on the back of the computer, connects the devices using a SCSI system cable that has a 25-pin male plug on one end and a 50-pin male plug on the other (figure 8.5). This cable allows one external device to be connected to the CPU. If more than one device will be connected to form a SCSI chain, a different cable is required. This is called a SCSI peripheral cable. A SCSI periph-

Figure 8.4.   The SCSI port. A SCSI port connects an external device to the computer's logic board.

Figure 8.6.   The SCSI peripheral cable. A SCSI peripheral cable is used to connect up to five external devices to the first device in a SCSI chain.

eral cable (figure 8.6) has a 50-pin male connector on each end. These cables allow up to five external SCSI devices to be attached to a CPU through the first external device.

Never connect or disconnect a SCSI cable to a device with the power on. The cable carries voltage that could damage the SCSI device or computer. Also, each SCSI device in the chain must be numbered. No two devices can have the same number. Six numbers are used. The numbers *0* and *7* cannot be used because Apple has assigned the number *0* to the internal hard drive, and the number *7* to the CPU. This leaves numbers *1* through *6* that may be assigned to SCSI chain devices.

Once the SCSI chain is established it must be terminated properly. A SCSI terminator (figure 8.7) shuts off and prevents the signal (electrical current) from going back through the chain and interrupting communication. Normally, SCSI devices are terminated at each end of the chain. Because internal drives are always terminated, it is only necessary to terminate the last device in the SCSI chain. Some external devices may also be terminated internally, however. To avoid terminating the signal too early, these devices should be last in the chain or their internal terminators must be removed or turned off. Read the device's user manual to determine if it is terminated internally.

Storing Data

Storing alphanumeric symbols and pictures is a major concern of printers and publishers. Type does not require massive storage, but

Figure 8.5.   The SCSI system cable. A SCSI system cable connects the first external device to the logic boards 25-pin plug.

Figure 8.7.   The SCSI terminator. A SCSI terminator is placed on the last device in a SCSI chain if it is not terminated internally already.

black and white and color photographs do. A basic 18 inch × 24 inch poster with twelve color photographs and some type, and two (EPS) files could easily exceed 150 megabytes in size if it were designed to print at 133 to 150 lpi. In addition to storing projects in progress, the internal hard drive must store the operating system, fonts, and applications. Often storage space on the internal hard drive is inadequate and additional storage is necessary.

In addition to being concerned about proper and adequate storage, printers and publishers are concerned about the possibility of losing or damaging files and realize that they need to back up all work. They also realize it is important to be able to move or transport large amounts of data from site to site or from workstation to workstation when networking or telecommunication is not practical.

To simplify the discussion of storing digital information, we will assume that there are three basic types of storage devices—primary, removable, and back-up.

Primary Storage Device

A **primary storage device** is the hard drive traditionally purchased with the CPU. It is a good idea to purchase the largest hard drive you can afford, since there never seems to be enough storage space for project work.

There are three basic types of hard drive mechanisms that are used as primary storage devices: 2.5-, 3.5-, and 8.25-inch. Small, portable hard drives and those used in some laptop computers are 2.5-inch devices. Their storage capacity is limited by the physical size of their hard drives. Most computers are purchased with internal 3.5-inch hard drives with storage capacities of up to 1 gigabyte. There is never enough room on the primary storage device when working with graphics because graphics require a lot of room. As a result, it may be necessary to use a larger 8.25-inch unit for fast primary storage when manipulating and separating process color files.

The primary storage device normally contains the system folder, the applications, and all other resources necessary for daily production. It is very productive to leave enough space for work in progress and for virtual memory when RAM is exceeded during image manipulation procedures.

Removable Storage Device

Most major jobs require the skills of more than one person; parts of the job are completed at different workstations or are sent to a service bureau for film output. **Removable storage devices** are used to transport parts of the job from place to place. If this is the case, a **removable cartridge drive** (figure 8.8) is appropriate. If the job is less than 80 megabytes in size, an 88-megabyte removable cartridge drive that also reads and writes to the popular 44-megabyte cartridge may solve the compatibility differences between stations. More than one cartridge would be required if work in progress exceeds 30 megabytes; a 105 megabyte, a 200 megabyte, or a 210 megabyte cartridge drive and cartridge also could be used.

With a removable cartridge drive at each workstation, data can be moved instantly. It can also be set aside and used later without occupying space on the primary drive. Car-

Figure 8.8. Removable cartridge drive. This removable cartridge drive reads from and writes to both 88-megabyte and 44-megabyte cartridges.

tridges themselves can be exchanged with operators, customers, and service bureaus while the cartridge drive is storing new data on another cartridge. Once the job is complete, the cartridge can be erased and reused or stored if no other back-up system is available.

The cartridge drive system is currently the most popular removable media device. It works much like a primary storage device, except that it uses a single metal storage disk. This disk is stored in a plastic case that can be inserted and ejected from the cartridge drive much like a floppy disk is handled in its disk drive.

There are two types of removable cartridge drives. The type of drives just discussed, the 44/88-megabyte cartridge drives, are magnetic media as are floppy drives and primary storage devices. The other type of drives are called magneto-optical. **Magneto-optical drives** provide inexpensive storage for publishers dealing with large files. These drives are also fast enough to use as second hard drives. The 3.5-inch magneto-optical drive currently has two cartridge sizes: 128- and 256-megabyte.

For administering a network or storing or transporting huge files, a 8.25-magneto-optical drive may be required. This removable device stores up to 1.3 gigabytes of data. Magneto-optical drives write information by heating a specific area of the disk with a laser to erase the area and electromagnetically create 0s. Laser pulses then reheat the disk and an opposite polarity is created to write 1s. Optical sensors in the drive then read the differences in the light reflecting from the magnetized metal surface of the disk as the 0s and 1s that constitute digitized data.

Back-up Storage Device
Saving work in a safe place requires a reliable **back-up device** and established procedures. Very basic work can be stored on floppy disks using a software program that compresses similar data into a smaller space. Removable cartridges and optical drives are also very capable of backing up basic work. When storing or duplicating hefty publishing projects, however, a tape back-up device might be most appropriate. **Digital audiotape (DAT)** (figure 8.9) is currently the most cost-effective media for back up and storage. The small DAT cartridge is a cross between audio technology and helical-scan video technology—the recording tracks are diagonal rather than longitudinal. Because DAT drives must wind slowly through tape to find files, they are not used as primary storage devices.

There are many strategies and procedures for backup. The best strategy is to save and back up regularly. When working with image manipulation and illustration/draw and page layout programs, the operator should save frequently. It is also important that the operator back up important files temporarily during daily production. A full backup is probably the most important save. This requires that every file is backed up daily and a copy is made and stored in a safe place. The tape cassette should be labeled properly with the date and file names.

Figure 8.9. Digital audiotape. Digital audiotape is currently the most cost-effective media for storing or backing up large publishing projects.

Outputting Images

Normal procedure in the desktop publishing cycle is to:

- Develop the idea using thumbnail and/or rough sketches.
- Complete the layout by constantly evaluating the overall design on a monitor.
- Output to an inexpensive laser printer for proofing during production.
- Present a color comprehensive for client approval.

During the early stages of design and layout, an output device (the monitor or the printer) gives the designer constant visual feedback. An output device allows an opportunity to share designs and layouts with fellow workers and is an excellent tool for producing a final comprehensive. Once the comprehensive is approved, a high-resolution output device produces the films or plates necessary to print the job.

Because the monitor is an output device, it is added to the discussion of monochrome printers, color printers, and high-resolution imagesetters.

Monitors

Monitors are first divided into two basic groups: monochrome and color. These groups can be further divided into subgroups.

Monochrome Monitors

Monochrome monitors are divided into black-and-white and grey-scale types. Because we live in a color world, we might question the purchase of a monochrome monitor. The only time to purchase a monochrome monitor over a color model is when all work on a particular system is in monochrome. There are advantages of doing black-and-white and grey-scale work on a monochrome monitor, however. First, monochrome monitors are less expensive than their color counterparts. They are also sharper and clearer than color monitors.

A **black-and-white (B/W) monitor** is the least expensive of the monochrome monitors. A B/W monitor is used by operators producing type, numbers, and high-contrast line images. It is not capable of displaying any grey tones between black and white. If production includes viewing continuous tone art (photos or blends), or color art in monochrome, a grey-scale monitor is necessary. **Grey-scale monitors** are capable of displaying 256 shades of grey when connected to an 8-bit video card or a built-in 8-bit video.

Monochrome monitors are either tall or wide. Tall devices are called portrait monitors and wide devices are called two-page monitors. **Portrait monitors** (figure 8.10) are designed for users constantly viewing letter-size (8.5″ × 11″) pages. They display an image that is 640 pixels × 870 pixels. Because most monitors display at 72 ppi, the monitor image is 8.88 inches wide (640 ÷ 72 ppi) and 12.08 inches high (870 ÷ 72 ppi).

A **two-page monitor** (figure 8.11) is ideal for anyone who constantly works with two facing pages. It is very important for the graphic designer to be able to evaluate the design of facing pages in a publication. Two-page monitors is usually either 19- or 21-inch diagonal size. Neither size is capable of displaying two full pages at once so some page cropping occurs. A 19-inch monitor normally displays a 1024 pixel (14.22 inch) × 768 pixel (10.66 inch) image. A 21-inch monitor displays a 1152 pixel (16 inch) × 870 pixel (12.08 inch) image. As just mentioned, the conversion from pixels to inches is based on a 72 ppi or dpi display. The dpi rating of the display is called pixel density. The **pixel density** of a screen can range from 72 dpi to 80 dpi. As the pixel density of a screen increases, the viewing image becomes more condensed.

Figure 8.12. **Color monitor**. A color monitor powered by a 24-bit video card provides full color viewing.

Figure 8.10. **Portrait monitor**. A portrait monitor is capable of displaying an 8.5 inch × 11 inch page at full size.

Figure 8.11. **Two-page monitor**. A two-page monitor is necessary when designing and laying out facing pages.

Color Monitors

Desktop publishing has allowed printers and publishers the opportunity to offer more color products to their clients. Making spot color and process color decisions and manipulating color continuous-tone images require a color monitor. **Color monitors** (figure 8.12) are classified and sized much the same as monochrome monitors. The major consideration when adding a color monitor to a system is the number of colors required by the work under production.

Color Quality

There are three major levels of color quality—**8-bit color quality**, **16-bit color quality**, and **24-bit color quality**. The 8-bit color quality represents an image made from 256 colors, 16-bit color quality creates an image from 32,768 colors, and 24-bit color quality is capable of creating an image from 16,772,216 colors. Some computers have built-in video that can be expanded from 256 colors to 16,772,216 colors by adding more video RAM (VRAM). As the monitor size gets larger, a plug-in video card becomes necessary to obtain full color viewing.

In monochrome mode, images are redrawn very quickly on the screen since less data manipulation is involved. Screen redraw is slower when there are 256 colors. Activate 24-bit color when manipulating a high-resolution, continuous-tone image and the very slow redraw can become frustrating and time consuming. The computer's CPU must process many megabytes of information to produce a full-color image on a large monitor. Only the fastest computers can handle files with many megabytes. Even the fastest microcomputer requires an accelerated video card. An **accelerated video card** contains a separate microprocessor and onboard RAM for storing image data. This separate microprocessor handles screen redraw and frees the CPU to work with the application. This arrangement is necessary when producing high resolution process color work.

Laser Printers

Laser printing marries the technologies of xerographic printing and the computer. The word *laser* is an acronym for the phrase "light amplification by stimulated emission of radiation." Simply stated, a laser is a concentrated beam of light. The beam can be made so small that it is capable of microscopic precision. The main feature of the laser light source in xerography is that it can be controlled by digitized information sent from a computer.

A **laser printer** operates exactly like a xerographic printer except when exposing. That is, a laser printer employs the six basic xerographic steps of charging, exposing, developing, transfering, fixing, and cleaning. The exposure step, however, is accomplished in laser printing by imaging the photoconductor with a laser light source rather than by reflecting from an original (figure 8.13).

Great strides have been made recently in low-cost PostScript laser printers. A PostScript printer includes a processor that converts all incoming data into one language—PostScript—that its imaging system can use to produce output. Apple introduced the first 300-dpi PostScript printer in 1986. It was an impressive imaging device and was responsible for beginning the desktop revolution. Even though 300-dpi resolution was adequate for business purposes and low resolution publishing, it was not acceptable output for quality print reproduction.

Higher-Resolution Laser Printers

Today 600-dpi resolution is inexpensive and is accepted as normal business quality. The printer revolution continues as **800-dpi**, **1,000-dpi**, and **1,200-dpi resolution** PostScript printers become more common. An excellent output device for proofing and preparing camera-ready copy would be a true PostScript, 1,200-dpi printer capable of bleeding, or running an image off the edge of, an 11 inch $\times$ 17 inch page (figure 8.14).

The advantage of higher-resolution laser printers is the ability to produce better halftone or picture output. The number of tones a laser printer produces depends on its resolution. Normally, 300-dpi laser printers have a halftone screen default of 53 lpi. The number of greys or tones between white and black is the printer's resolution (300 dpi) divided by the halftone's lpi (53-lpi) squared:

$$(300 \text{ dpi} \div 53 \text{ lpi})^2 = \text{number of tones}$$

$$300 \div 53 = 8.66$$

$$(8.66)^2 = 32 \text{ tones}$$

If a printer's resolution is increased to 800 dpi, a much better halftone is produced:

$$(800 \text{ dpi} \div 53 \text{ lpi})^2 = \text{number of tones}$$

$$800 \div 53 = 18.09$$

$$(18.09)^2 = 227.7 \text{ tones}$$

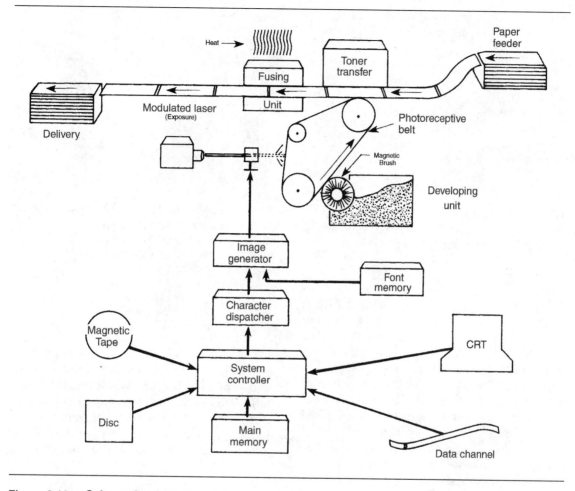

Figure 8.13. Schematic of a laser printer

Although increasing the number of tones eliminates a high-contrast look, the halftone is still composed of 53 dpi. To make the image look less coarse, the lpi could be increased to 85 lpi, and a 1200-dpi printer could be used.

$$(1200 \text{ dpi} \div 85 \text{ lpi})^2 = \text{number of tones}$$

$$1200 \div 85 = 14.1$$

$$(14.1)^2 = 198.8 \text{ tones}$$

At a halftone resolution of 85 lpi, 198 tones looks much better than 32 tones at 53 lpi. In fact, 85-lpi resolution is adequate for newspaper and some in-plant printing needs.

Color Printers

It is very important to consider a PostScript printer when adding a color device to a Macintosh network. A problem occurs when a desktop publishing job includes encapsulated

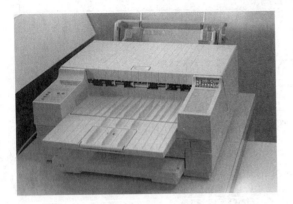

Figure 8.14.   Laser printer. A high-resolution laser printer produces very good typography and reasonable prescreened halftones.

Figure 8.15.   Canon color laser copier system. A color laser copier such as Canon's CLC 550 is a unique graphic system. It is capable of producing multimedia products, electronic prepress proofs, and short-run color. As a stand-alone copier, the color laser system offers the graphic communicator quality color and flexible features. Because copies very closely reproduce the quality of the originals, counterfeit protection is built into the system.

PostScript images from programs such as Adobe Illustrator, Aldus FreeHand, or Adobe Photoshop. These images must be translated to raster formats or to dots that make up the printed job. This translation requires either a hardware raster image processor (RIP) or a software RIP such as ColorAge's Freedom of Press Professional. (See the Imagesetters section of this chapter for more about RIP.) The disadvantage of using a software RIP is that the power of a productive workstation must be used to do the PostScript translation.

In addition to short-run color laser copiers (figure 8.15), there are three major groups of color printers that are used by the printing industry to produce color comprehensives and proofs, mock-ups and prototypes, scanned and captured images, and presentation transparencies. The three printer groups are thermal wax, ink jet, and dye sublimation. In most cases these color printers are less expensive than color laser copy systems because they are not designed for heavy-duty repetitive imaging.

Thermal-Wax Printers

The **thermal-wax printer** has been the most popular color desktop printer for publishing and especially for producing bright presentation transparencies. This printer creates 300-dpi images by transferring wax from a yellow, magenta, cyan, or sometimes black ribbon onto a special substrate using a thermal printing head.

Ink-Jet Printers

Ink-jet printers offer liquid and solid ink imaging technology. Traditional ink-jet printers (figure 8.16) utilize water-based dyes stored in yellow, magenta, cyan, and black cartridges. During imaging a fine spray of ink is released from the cartridges through tiny nozzles.

Phase-Change Solid Ink Printer

Phase-change solid ink printer technology is based on the use of dye-impregnated wax which changes state during the printing process. Before the wax is transferred to the sheet, it is melted to liquid form and then hard-

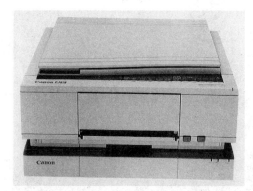

Figure 8.16. **Color printer.** Thermal-wax, ink-jet, and dye-sublimation printers are popular for making comprehensives for printers and transparencies for presenters. Pictured here is Canon's CJ10 ink-jet printer, scanner, and copy machine.

Figure 8.17. **Dye-sublimation printer**. A dye-sublimation printer is a continuous-tone imaging system capable of achieving photograph-like quality.

ened to the sheet as it cools. The advantage of this technology is in the variety of plain paper weights on which it can print. This process produces brilliant images of very good quality and is more inexpensive than thermal-wax transfer.

Dye-Sublimation Printers

Dye-sublimation printers (figure 8.17) are capable of achieving photograph-like quality. They do not use the dithering process used by ink-jet and wax-thermal printers, which is the technique of using a noncontinuous pattern of yellow, magenta, cyan, and black dots to create the illusion of tone. A dye-sublimation printer is instead a continuous-tone imaging system that transfers colored dyes from a plastic ribbon to a special plastic sheet. Continuous tones are created when the dyes from the ribbon are vaporized by heat and then absorbed into the special sheet. Instead of producing a specific number of dpi, the dye-sublimation printer transfers vaporized dyes to "areas per inch," blending them seamlessly.

The near-photographic quality of a dye-sublimation printer makes it ideal for presentation graphics and for proofing publications containing continuous-tone color. It is also the printer of choice for producing prints from analog and digital cameras because of its near photographic quality. The disadvantages of dye-sublimation proofs are fuzzy type, high initial cost, and high cost per proof.

Imagesetters

The term **imagesetter** is used to describe an output device that records processed data to photographic paper, film, or plate material. Several companies produce imagesetting devices that record at various resolutions and onto a variety of film sizes. The smaller, less sophisticated, devices are less costly than the high-resolution, large-film-size, color-separation-capable systems.

There are three major components involved in producing film from computer data—a hardware or software raster image processor (RIP), a film imager or recorder (imagesetter), and a film processor.

The Raster Image Processor

The **raster image processor (RIP)** (figure 8.18) converts PostScript and raster data to the machine bitmaps the recorder can process. This

Figure 8.18.   Raster image processor. A raster image processor converts various types of digital data to machine bitmaps understood by the film recorder to which it is attached.

conversion process is very labor intensive and requires a highly productive RIP. It is important that a basic RIP have a fast microprocessor, quality screening hardware, sufficient font storage, and Ethernet capability.

The Film Imager or Recorder
The film imager **recorder** (figure 8.19) exposes the single-color, spot-color, or process-color separations on a light-sensitive substrate. Most midrange imagesetters offer a variety of resolutions up to 3,000 ± dpi. This resolution range ensures quality output with a full range of tones at commonly used halftone screen rulings (133 lpi to 150 lpi). Midrange imagesetters are designed for service bureaus, printers, magazine publishers, or any manufacturer processing and recording computer-generated illustrations or graphics as color separations.

Figure 8.19.   Imagesetter. An imagesetter or recorder receives bitmaps from the RIP and translates them to an image by exposing film or plate material.

The Film Processor
The **film processor** develops, fixes, washes, and dries exposed light-sensitive output from the imagesetter. A processor with adequate developer storage and control is necessary to produce film negatives or positives with appropriate maximum densities. It is recommended to discuss these requirements with the imagesetter and film manufacturer before purchasing a processor.

A calibration procedure is needed to orchestrate all of these devices into one productive system. **Calibration exposure tests** are produced and measured with a densitometer. If the calibration films do not meet specifications, software and hardware adjustments must be made until quality output is achieved.

Software

The first step toward getting a computer system up and running is to connect all hardware components properly. The next step is to install the software. There are four basic kinds of software–system, resource, application, and utility.

System Software

System software manages the operation of the computer. It communicates with all hardware components, creates and tracks files, and orchestrates all information processed within the system. When you purchase a computer with an internal hard drive, the system software was most likely installed by the distributor. The system should operate when properly connected, and positive images and messages should appear on the monitor.

If your internal hard drive requires the installation of an operating system, or if you are upgrading an old system, be sure to follow the procedures called "Installing System Software" in your computer's reference manual.

Resource Software

Resource software for the Macintosh computer consists of various software programs known to the computer's operating system. The major resources that must be installed in the System folder are fonts and desk accessories. When properly installed these resources are used by the operating system or an application as needed. Resources are stored in folders inside the System folder. If the latest operating system is used with resource management software, such as Fifth Generation's Suitcase, it is not necessary to place all resources in the System folder. If desk accessories will be accessed through the Apple menu, they must be placed in the Apple menu folder which is inside the System folder.

Fonts

Fonts are usually the first resource that graphic communicators consider because they are ex-

pensive and constitute the major image in printing and publishing. The three methods used to create fonts are Bitmap, TrueType, and PostScript.

Bitmap fonts are created by dots or bits of information. Geneva, used as the labeling font on the Macintosh, is very readable at approximately 72 ppi on the monitor or when printed on a non-PostScript printer. Bitmap fonts are not commonly used for professional typesetting purposes because of their dot or jagged edge construction.

TrueType fonts are Apple's answer to quality typography use with its new operating system. TrueType's outline font technology has eliminated the jagged appearance of the Bitmap font structure. A TrueType font file is used with the operating system to draw or produce any size letter on the monitor or from a printer.

PostScript fonts are by far the most popular and frequently used. They consist of both screen and printer fonts. The screen font is bitmapped and is necessary to produce the font image on the screen. The printer font file contains the information that draws the sharp outline image seen on the screen or on PostScript printer output. PostScript fonts do not appear as sharp outline images on the screen unless the software program Adobe Type Manager is used with the screen Bitmap font and the outline printer font.

Desk Accessories

Desk accessories (DAs) are small programs such as calculator, chooser, fast find, key caps, or scrapbook that appear under the Apple menu. They respond much like applications when chosen from the menu. Other desk accessories are alert sounds and FKEYs. Alert sound software, such as the "beep" when a mistake is made, allows the operator to select which alert is used. FKEYs are programs designed to perform specific tasks. An example of an FKEY is the frequently used SHIFT + COMMAND + 3 combination which captures the screen image as a MacPaint (bitmapped) document. Alert sounds and FKEYs can be stored in the System file or outside the System file in a resource folder.

Application Software

Application software are programs written to perform specialized tasks such as scanning, image manipulation, drawing and illustrating, and page layout. The applications on the computer determine the kind of work that can be done by the CPU. Applications for printing and publishing are normally large and require formal installation procedures. Read the installation procedures first, have all application disks and serial numbers ready, and then insert the disk recommended by the procedure. The operating system takes over; usually you must simply follow screen messages to complete the installation. Some applications do not require a computer-controlled installation. Installation may only require that the program be copied from the floppy onto the hard drive. The method of installation depends on the application's size.

There is no doubt that continuous-tone imaging for publishing and commercial photography is rapidly becoming an electronic process. Scanner and photo CD technologies have become accepted quality methods of converting silver photographs (analog data) to usable digital data for image manipulation and processing. Digital photography is revolutionary in that images are converted to digital data and stored as they are captured through the lens and converted by the internal hardware of the camera.

Scanning Software
Scanned or **digitized images** are raster or bitmapped images meaning that they are composed of "pixels" or "picture elements." To prevent jagged edges or visible pixels, 1-bit black and white art must be scanned in at the output resolution—input resolution to output resolution must be a 1:1 ratio. To prevent visible pixels, black and white pictures (8-bit grey scale) and color pictures (24-bit color) should be scanned at 2 times the lpi ruling of the halftone screen used for the press run.

Image Manipulation and Processing Software
Image manipulation and processing software such as Adobe Photoshop offers the electronic prepress operator the ability to complete quickly tasks that were traditionally very time consuming. Once photographs are either scanned and stored, scanned and written to a photo CD, or photographed with a digital camera and stored on the camera's hard drive, they are ready for some of the following manipulations or processes:

- Cropping, sizing, and establishing appropriate resolution
- Adjusting highlight, shadow, and intermediate tones between black and white
- Adjusting hue, saturation, brightness, and contrast
- Adjusting or correcting color balance
- Sharpening images
- Removing scratches, blemishes, or unwanted images
- Restoring damaged or incomplete image sections
- Creating composite images from more than one original
- Creating special effects or altering images to better communicate ideas
- Removing and/or creating backgrounds to improve picture meaning or quality
- Controlling under-color removal, grey component replacement, and dot gain

- Encapsulating or embedding screen ruling and tone value adjustments
- Color separating an image into yellow, magenta, cyan, and black channels
- Compressing data
- Saving an image as separations in the appropriate format

When the manipulated and processed images are saved in the proper format on the hard drive or removable storage, they are ready in most cases to be placed in a page layout software program such as Adobe PageMaker or QuarkXPress. (See the next section on page layout software.) Before that, however, these images may be placed into vector or **object-oriented software** programs such as Macromedia FreeHand or Adobe Illustrator to manipulate or add line art and type.

Drawing or Illustrating Software
Draw or illustration software produces vector or object-oriented art and type. Object-oriented software programs use the graphic capabilities of the PostScript language to manipulate that art and type. PostScript handles these images well because they are mathematically based. PostScript objects are created by establishing and manipulating vector or control points with a variety of drawing tools. When an image is created, each line or curve is assigned its own mathematical definition. In other words, as the operator draws lines the direction is mathematically computed by the software, and vector points are established by the software. The lines are called **Bezier curves**. These curves are defined by the control points placed by the operator. Because PostScript language instructs the printer about the shape created by vector points, the shapes are resolution independent. This means that output from object-oriented programs adopts the resolution of the output device. This means that the higher the resolution of the output de-

vice the sharper the image. This also means that these images can be enlarged, reduced, or manipulated without losing detail or quality.

When saved or exported for use in a page layout program, object-oriented images become **encapsulated PostScript (EPS) files**. When a file is saved in EPS format, it is written in the PostScript language that contains the code necessary for printing. PostScript images, whether separate or integrated with text in a page layout program, must be converted to bit maps before they are printed. The conversion process for interpreting PostScript to bit maps is called **rasterizing**. This is accomplished with a **Raster Image Processor** (RIP). A **RIP** converts the object-oriented and bit-mapped images from any graphics software to pixels or bit maps that the printer or imagesetter understands. RIPs can be stand-alone devices or they can be incorporated into all PostScript printers.

Page Layout Software
Page layout software programs such as Aldus PageMaker and QuarkXPress allow designers, typesetters, layout artists, advertisers, editors, and anyone who communicates using hard print products the opportunity to assemble an attractive product. Aldus launched the desktop publishing revolution in 1985 when it introduced its page layout program called PageMaker. Using a page layout program on a 1 megabyte Macintosh Plus limited the operator to mainly typographic layouts. It was not until the early 1990s that hardware and software allowed text and graphics, which included high-resolution line art, grey scale images, and 24-bit color images with special effects, to be integrated.

Today, inexpensive high-speed workstations, quality scanners, and fast imagesetters have allowed all members of the graphic communication community to access personal prepress technology.

Traditionally, prepress operators use thumbnail sketches, rough layouts, and comprehensives to achieve customer approval. Using thumbnails and roughs to develop an idea before going to a page layout program is not a bad idea. Establishing the size and format of a piece is very helpful to get off to a quick start. Also, knowing approximate picture sizes, image-resolution requirements, type sizes, and column lengths allows operators to work smart by keeping file sizes as small as possible.

Establishing the product format on the computer as soon as possible has many advantages. While a prepress person develops the design or layout, a comprehensive is being developed. In fact, the final mechanicals, films, or plates are also being created at the same time. Job progress can be shown easily to fellow workers and clients at any time and changes can be made on demand.

Integrating photographs with text can be a problem during the early stages of product development, however. Continuous-tone images, when scanned at appropriate resolutions for production, create large files. When high-resolution images are placed in a layout during the early stages of development, screen redraw and overall operating speeds are adversely affected. It is recommended that after scanning continuous-tone images at the proper resolution, they be stored temporarily, and low-resolution, "position only" files be created for use during the design stages. Once the final layout is approved, the low-resolution position images can be replaced easily with the appropriate image at the exact size and resolution. This procedure increases production and eliminates storage problems.

Electronic prepress procedures from design through platemaking have many advantages. They can also be very demanding. Knowing the entire prepress process, knowing all printing concerns, understanding computer operation and maintenance, having design and layout abilities, knowing telecommunications, and using a service bureau require a capable, well-prepared individual. This may be the case in the thousands of small establishments typical of the printing and publishing industry. In larger organizations an appropriate division of labor can be established, and prepress specialists with clearly identified job descriptions can be identified.

Once the job is completed in the page layout program, it is ready to be imageset. If the job will be placed on removable storage and delivered to a service bureau for output, it is suggested that a test print be made to a laser printer on site. The job can also be reduced slightly to include all printer's marks on the laser printer's paper size. Assuming that the laser printer has adequate memory to handle the job, the printing process will prove that all files are present and properly named and linked. This procedure may also be a good idea even if an in-house imagesetter is available.

Electronic prepress page layout has many advantages for the graphic communicator:

- The ability to produce design variations
- The ability to make changes to the final layout
- Local control of image input and manipulation
- Inexpensive, low-resolution proofing
- Film and/or plate output directly from the computer
- Quick turnaround on customer alterations, proofs, films, and overall production
- The ability to keep the entire printing cycle in house

Utility Software

Think of utilities as tools for the toolbox that keep your computer running and aid in solving nagging, everyday problems.

It is best to start building your utility toolbox by acquiring a major utility program. A

utility software program is a starter set of maintenance tools all in one box. It is likely that other, smaller tools or programs will be added to your utility folder toolbox as unique problems are encountered. It is difficult to discuss specific utilities because they change as rapidly as systems and system software do. There are, however, general concerns that a user must be sensitive to in order to maintain a system.

It is not as difficult to maintain one system as it is to maintain a network of old and new computers using different versions of system software. Regardless of the complexity of the system, the utility programs used should together have the ability to:

- Locate, identify, and eradicate virus infections
- Recover erased, crashed, lost, or corrupted files
- Test a drive for defects
- Repair damaged files and folders
- Optimize and defragment disks and drives
- Make quick copies of files and drives

- Handle and manipulate fonts and accessories
- Save the screen from "burn-in damage"
- Tune a drive to operate at its most efficient level
- Secure disk data with password protection
- Format a drive of any type
- Load drivers on removable media drives automatically
- Mount drives that do not mount during start up
- Provide detailed information about a drive
- Protect and unprotect files

Although this list is incomplete, it covers the major problems that need to be dealt with on a daily basis. The users of electronic prepress hardware and software must be concerned with technical issues that are traditionally dealt with by skilled craftspeople. It is recommended that utility software manuals be required reading for those who maintain the computer systems.

Key Terms

LocalTalk	portrait monitor	imagesetter
SneakerNet	two-page monitor	(RIP) raster image processor
Ethernet	pixel density	recorder
(SCSI) small computer systems interface	color monitor	film processor
primary storage device	8-bit, 16-bit, and 24-bit color quality	calibration exposure test
removable storage device	accelerated video card	system software
removable cartridge drive	laser printer	resource software
magneto-optical drive	800-dpi, 1,000-dpi, and 1,200-dpi resolution	Bitmap font
back-up device	thermal-wax printer	TrueType font
digital audiotape (DAT)	ink-jet printer	PostScript font
monochrome monitor	phase-change solid ink printer	desk accessories (DAs)
black-and-white (B/W) monitor	dye-sublimation printer	application software
grey-scale monitor		digitized image
		image manipulation and processing software

object-oriented software
draw or illustration
    software

Bezier curve
encapsulated PostScript
    (EPS) file

rasterizing
page layout software
utility software program

Questions for Review

1. Which LAN allows the fastest communication between computers—LocalTalk or Ethernet? Explain the meanings of 10BASE–5, 10BASE–2, and 10BASE–T.

2. Explain how to set up a SCSI chain consisting of a computer, an external CD-ROM player, and a scanner.

3. An internal hard drive is considered a _____ storage device; an 88-megabyte cartridge drive is a _____ storage device; and a digital audiotape drive would make a good _____ storage device.

4. Which type of monitor would you select to view an 8.5 inch × 11 inch facing page layout that includes color pictures? Why?

5. Describe how a laser exposure unit operates.

6. List the three major groups of color printers. Which type would you use to print a photograph captured with a digital camera? Why?

7. Why is a chemical processor required when using an imagesetter?

8. _____ software manages the operation of the computer. Fonts are _____ software known to the computer's operating system. Apple's answer to quality typography is called _____. PostScript fonts consist of both _____ and _____ fonts.

Color Separation

In 1862, Louis Ducos du Hauron sent a letter to M. Lelut of the Academie de Medecine et Sciences in Paris describing his ideas for a "Physical Solution of the Problem of Reproducing Colors by Photography." Du Hauron said:

> The method which I propose is based on the principle that the simple colors are reduced to three—red, yellow, and blue—the combinations of which in different proportions give us the infinite variety of shades we see in nature. One may now say that analysis of the solar spectrum by means of a glass which passes only one color has proved that red exists in all parts of the spectrum, and the like for yellow and blue, and that one is forced to admit that the solar spectrum is formed of three superimposed spectra having their maxima of intensity at different points. Thus one might consider a picture which represents nature as composed of three pictures superimposed, the one red, the second yellow, and the third blue. The re-
> sult of this would be that if one could obtain separately these three images by photography and then reunite them in one, one would obtain an image of nature with all the tints that it contains.[1]

Du Hauron's ideas were responsible, in part, for the later development of successful additive color plates and film.

A man named Frederick E. Ives was a journeyman printer who became interested in photography. He was familiar with Hauron's ideas about color reproduction and worked to refine them. In 1880 Ives moved from Ithaca, New York, to Philadelphia. From that time on he only did research in color photography and photomechanical printing.

By the end of 1881, Ives had received two United States patents for a specialized halftone printing process and was beginning to spend most of his energy on color. In 1885, at the

---

[1]Louis W. Sipley, *A Half Century of Color* (New York: Macmillan, 1951), p. 22.

Philadelphia "Novelties Exhibition," he exhibited a process of photographing colors and a photomechanical method for reproducing them.

In May of 1892, Ives was invited to present a paper outlining his ideas before the Society of Arts in London. At that time he displayed the Photochromoscope camera he had invented. Using a single exposure, the device recorded a three-color image on three separate plates. The transparent separations could then be viewed through red, green, and blue color filters.

Ives produced the illustration on page in 1893 with his tricolor process. It is perhaps the first photomechanically printed color image. It is uncertain whether it was reproduced by using a relief plate or a gravure cylinder, but the halftones were certainly made from cross-line screens.

By the turn of the century, almost all printers and photographers understood the color separation process, and national publications such as the *National Geographic* had begun to use full-color picture printing.

Objectives for Chapter 9

After completing this chapter you will be able to:

- Define "process color photography."
- Explain additive color theory.
- Discuss how subtractive colors relate to additive colors.
- Explain how a color filter works.
- Explain the reason for concern about screen angle on process color separation negatives.
- Discuss how four black-and-white halftones can produce a full-color reproduction.

- Briefly describe the purposes of a mask.
- Differentiate between direct and indirect color separation methods.
- Explain the purpose of dot etching.
- Explain the four primary steps in electronic color separation, including scanning, analysis and modification, storage and image editing, and exposure.
- Differentiate between traditional electronic separations and achromatic separations.

Introduction

Around 1454 Johann Gutenberg printed his famous 42-line Bible. He printed almost all of the lines of type with black ink. The initial letter on opening pages, however, was hand painted in multiple colors by special artists called "illuminators." By painting the opening letters, Gutenberg was attempting to duplicate the work of scribes who illustrated their finest work in decorative colors.

For nearly three centuries after Gutenberg, most printing was done in one color—black. Although by the nineteenth century color plates and inserts in books had become more common, they were only done in flat color. Flat color refers to a solid ink purchased or mixed for a specific use.

By the beginning of this century, printers and photographers clearly understood the color separation process, and they were printing "color photographs" in a wide number of publications. However, these color images were not the process color common today at every newsstand, book store, or grocery store. Process color is the use of ink with a translucent base that allows for creation of many colors by overprinting only four (cyan, magenta, yellow, and black).

Since the end of World War II, there has been an accelerated increase in the use and sophistication of printed color images. Color printing has now become an expectation rather than the exception. There are literally thousands of weekly or monthly magazines with color illustrations on every page. Every major metropolitan newspaper features process color in its Sunday edition, and there is even a national daily newspaper printed in four colors.

As people become accustomed to color illustrations, their demands for more and higher-quality color reproductions increase. It no longer suffices that a page merely carries several colors. Now the goal is to eliminate printing defects such as poor fit, inaccurate color balance, or insufficient ink density, and to produce a perfect color reproduction that matches or enhances the quality of the color original.

Within the last decade there have been major advances in color separation, color correction, and color reproduction technology. The purpose of this chapter is to introduce the basic concepts of color separation, discuss the significant use of scanners, and explore the potential of color correction and color editing.

Basic Color Theory

It is important to establish a firm foundation of basic color theory understanding. This section introduces key concepts and terms.

Light and Color

Isaac Newton demonstrated the hues of the visible spectrum by passing a beam of light through a glass prism (plate A). He not only produced a rainbow of color, he passed the rainbow through a second prism and reconstructed the original beam of light. Newton therefore proved that color is in light and that what we see as white light is really a mixture of all colors.

The idea of wavelength was introduced in chapter 6. Recall that the visible spectrum is that portion of electromagnetic radiation from approximately 400 mμ (millimicrons) to around 750 mμ (figure 9.1). Every distinct color in the spectrum, from blue at one end to red at the other, has a unique wavelength. However, we rarely see just one wavelength color; we more commonly perceive the effect of combinations of different wavelengths. For example, sunlight is natural white light made up of relatively uniform amounts of each wavelength in the spectrum.

Recall also the difference between reflected light and transmitted light. If you look up at the sun, you see transmitted light—light that is directed at you from a light source. If you hold a color slide between you and the sun, you see the image on the slide by transmitted light. Light passes in a straight line from the sun, through the slide, and to your eye.

If you were to look down from the sun at any object, you would see by reflected light. White light travels from the sun to an object; that light would bounce back or reflect to your eye. Every object absorbs or reflects different wavelengths of light and in different quantities.

For example, an apple might appear a strikingly bright red or a dun red. When white light strikes an apple, the apple absorbs most of the wavelengths below around 600 mμ on the visible spectrum and reflects most wavelengths above 600 mμ (figure 9.2). This combination of reflected wavelengths creates the color impression humans see as "red." The brightness of the color depends on the quantity of wavelengths that are reflected. The reflected

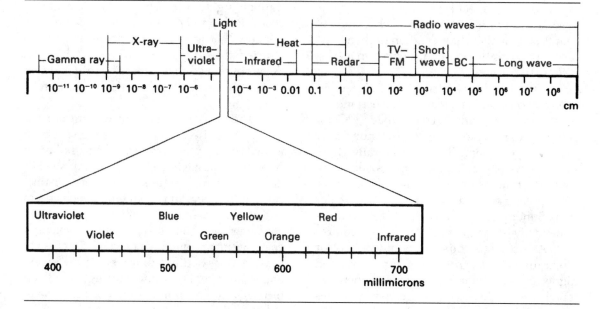

Figure 9.1.   Plot of the visible spectrum (lower bar) compared to the electromagnetic spectrum (upper bar)

wavelengths define color; the quantity of reflected wavelengths defines color intensity.

Additive Primary Colors

The visible spectrum is often described as being made up of three colors: blue, green, and red. Actually, these colors are combinations of wavelengths in each third of the spectrum. Red, green, and blue are called the **additive primary colors** because they can be combined to form every other color of light in the spectrum. Figure 9.3 shows the plot of reflected light for each of these primary colors. It is very important to understand this fundamental idea: Objects display color by absorbing and reflecting different wavelengths of light in the visible spectrum. In the case of transmitted light—looking through the color slide—the idea is the same. We perceive color because portions of the slide absorb certain wavelengths of light and pass (transmit) others.

Subtractive Primary Colors

The three **subtractive primary colors** are cyan, magenta, and yellow. They form when two of the additive primary colors combine. For example, a banana appears yellow because it absorbs wavelengths at the blue end of the visible spectrum and reflects light at the middle (green) and red ends (figure 9.3). Yellow light is therefore a combination of green and red light (plate B).

In a similar manner, when an object absorbs red light but reflects green and blue, the color cyan forms ([figure 9.3][plate F]). When green light is absorbed but blue and red light are reflected, the color magenta forms (plate F).

Plate F is an important visual to understand. It shows what happens when the three additive colors of light overlap. Where all three of these colors overlap, white light forms. Where any two of the colors overlap, one of the subtractive primaries forms. Printers use ma-

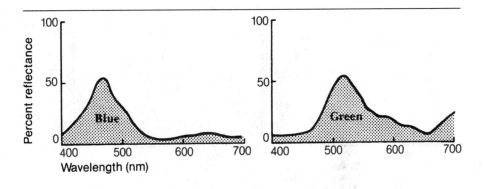

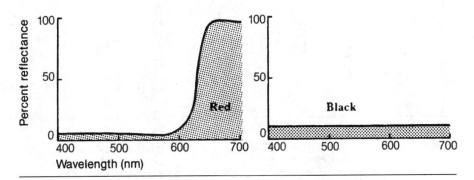

Figure 9.2.   Typical spectral reflectance curves for blue, green, red, and black objects. An apple appears red because it reflects wavelengths of light in the 600 to 700 nm range and absorbs wavelengths in the 400 to 600 nm range. Black objects absorb all wavelengths of light; white objects reflect approximately equal amounts of all wavelengths.

genta, cyan, and yellow inks to create the re-flected colors of the spectrum. These are called **process inks.** Process inks are specially formu-lated to be somewhat translucent. "Translucent" means that they both transmit and reflect light.

Plate C illustrates that when white light hits cyan ink, the ink reflects blue and green light (blue and green light create cyan) but ab-sorbs red. Plates D and E show similar relation-ships for magenta and yellow inks respectively. Process inks are translucent, which means that there is an additive effect if two process colors are printed one over the other. If equal amounts of magenta and cyan process ink overlap, the

visual effect is blue. Look at plates C and D. Compare what light each ink absorbs and re-flects. Only blue light is reflected by both ma-genta and cyan. Therefore, blue is the only color you see. If less magenta ink is printed than cyan, then the result will be a greener blue (see plate B). By controlling the amounts of cyan, magenta, yellow, and black, printers can create the illusion of any color of the visible spectrum.

Basic Separation Theory

The task, then, of color separation is to separate the hues of a continuous-tone color original

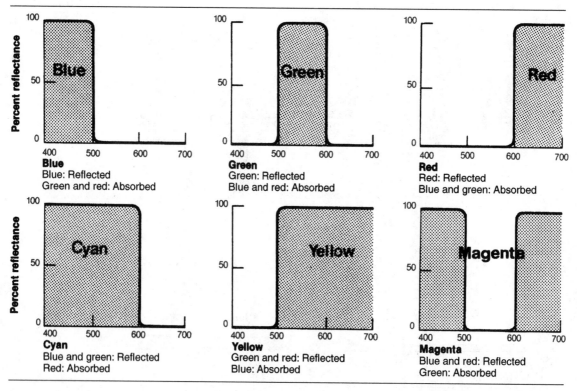

Blue
Blue: Reflected
Green and red: Absorbed

Green
Green: Reflected
Blue and red: Absorbed

Red
Red: Reflected
Blue and green: Absorbed

Cyan
Blue and green: Reflected
Red: Absorbed

Yellow
Green and red: Reflected
Blue: Absorbed

Magenta
Blue and red: Reflected
Green: Absorbed

Figure 9.3.   Additive and subtractive primary colors. The additive primary colors (top row) each reflect about one-third of the wavelengths of light in the visible spectrum and absorb the other two-thirds. The subtractive primary colors (bottom row) each reflect about two-thirds of the wavelengths of light in the visible spectrum and absorb the other one-third.

into four negatives to prepare cyan, magenta, yellow, and black printing plates. Figure 9.4 illustrates the basic concept of color separation.

When viewing this figure, it is important to keep two ideas firmly in mind:

- A color filter transmits only its own color and absorbs all other colors.
- Light that reaches the film exposes the emulsion and becomes nonimage area; the reproducible image is that area of the film that has not been exposed to light. This unexposed area of film is a record of the two additive primary colors that were absorbed by the filter.

In the color separation process, the additive primary colors—red, blue, and green—are used as filters to prepare the cyan, magenta, and yellow separation negatives. The separation process begins with a color original. The light from the original is directed through a red filter to produce the cyan separation negative (figure 9.4). Because a red filter (plate F) transmits only red color, the red patch is the only area of the original to expose the emulsion and form density on the film. The unexposed areas then represent the combination of blue and green light that was absorbed by the red filter. We see this color as cyan. The magenta separation negative is

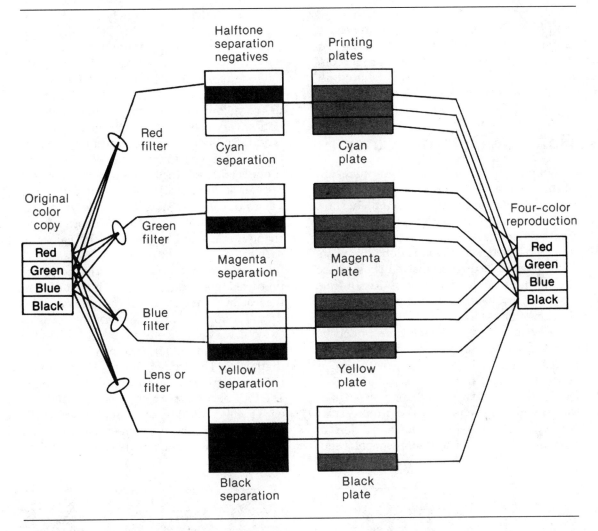

Figure 9.4. **A diagram of basic color separation**

made by using a green filter (plate G). The wavelengths reflecting from the green patch of the original transmit through the green filter and expose the film. Red and blue light, however, are absorbed by the green filter and do not expose the film. The red and blue light combine to form the magenta color we see. The blue filter (plate H), which transmits only blue light, produces the yellow separation neg-

ative by exposing the negative in all but the red and green areas (figure 9.4). The black separation negative is exposed in such a way that shadows or dark areas of the original do not record on the film. The primary hues, however, record as density on the black negative. In other words, information or image detail from each primary color is used to create the black negative.

After the negatives are exposed to printing plates, the clear areas on the film become areas of density on the plate. When the four plates are printed together in their proper combinations on one sheet, the results should duplicate the range of colors of the original copy.

Halftone Dots and Color

Although figure 9.4 is a good conceptual view of the color separation process, it only represents flat color and does not accurately show how the full range of colors is produced on the final printed sheet.

Most color separation is done from continuous-tone color originals that must be screened during the reproduction process. Recall from chapter 7 that halftone photographs create the illusion of tones by using dots of varying sizes. For example, 15-percent dots surrounded by 85-percent white space appears as light grey; correspondingly, 35-percent dots with 65-percent white space appears to be a darker grey. That same dot structure produces a range of values within a given subtractive primary color for process color reproduction. The dots of varying sizes from the four different color sep-

arations overlap to accurately reproduce the color original. It is possible to illustrate this concept with a set of color proofs (plate M).

The yellow proof in plate M is actually a halftone represented in one color (yellow); it consists of a limited range of values. These values of yellow are produced by many halftone dots of varying sizes. When the magenta proof is added to the yellow proof, additional colors and values become noticeable. When the cyan proof is added to these two proofs, the image appears to be complete. All of the colors and values of colors seem to be visible. Adding a black proof, however, increases density in the shadow areas and strengthens the values of each color.

Because the various values of each color are produced by overlapping dots, it is important that each halftone separation be prepared with dots at differing screen angles. If these angles are not controlled properly, an objectionable moiré (pronounced *more-ray*) pattern can be formed (figure 9.5). The problem is caused by individual dots overlapping at an inappropriate angle. The typical contact screen, whether solid line or vignetted halftone, has a built-in 45° angle. When overprinting two screen patterns, you must angle the second screen 30° from the first.

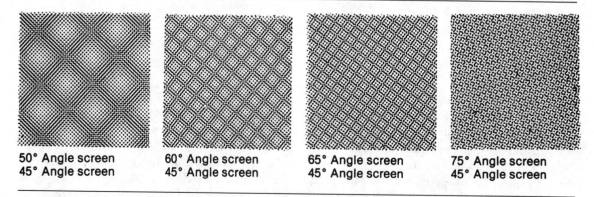

| 50° Angle screen | 60° Angle screen | 65° Angle screen | 75° Angle screen |
| 45° Angle screen | 45° Angle screen | 45° Angle screen | 45° Angle screen |

Figure 9.5.   Moiré patterns. The moiré patterns were formed by a 33-line screen at approximately 20% tone value.

Halftone screens used to make color separations anticipate the problem and build in special angles. For example, the cyan separation is typically made at a 45° angle, the magenta at 75°, the yellow at 90°, and the black at 105°. Angle control is discussed later in this chapter.

Color Masking

Color masking has three distinct goals in color reproduction:

- To compress the density range of the color original (called **tone correction**)
- To compensate for color deficiencies in process inks (called **color correction**)
- To enhance the detail of the final reproduction (called **sharpness enhancement**)

While electronic color separation has a built-in masking function, the term "masking" is still widely used, and describes what continues to be an important photographic process. Traditionally a color mask was made by exposing a color original to **pan masking film** (a continuous-tone film) through a special filter. The mask was then physically placed over unexposed film during the separation process. However, electronic color scanning is doing the masking step electronically today. A computer can be programmed to adjust the final separated digital images before they are output onto film or printing plates. Whether a physical film mask is used or electronic adjustments are made, the three goals of masking remain the same.

Tone Correction

Color transparencies typically have a maximum density of around 2.60, and color prints may reach a density of 2.00 (refer to chapter 7 for a discussion of density measurement). Although four layers of ink on a printed sheet of paper can match a 2.00 reflection density, the 2.60 density of a transparent image cannot be reproduced on the press. A mask allows the tonal range of the image to be compressed to a usable range without causing color imbalance.

Color Correction

A second goal in color masking is to compensate for the inherent limitations of printing inks. Although color theory says that cyan ink is a combination of blue and green pigments, in practice it is impossible to manufacture cyan ink without some red pigment as well. Figure 9.6 shows plots of each process ink color. Each segment of the figure compares the ideal ink with the real ink. If cyan ink absorbs green and blue pigments, as expected, but also a bit of red pigment, then it is necessary to reduce both the magenta and yellow separation negatives in areas where cyan is printed on the final reproduction. These types of interactions occur between all colors. The process of masking (whether photographic or electronic) reduces select areas of the separation negatives in an attempt to compensate for the deficiencies of process inks.

Sharpness Enhancement

The third purpose of color masking is to enhance the detail of the individual separation. A blurry or "unsharp" photographic mask produces a sharp separation. Such a photographic mask is produced by placing a diffuser sheet (generally frosted acetate) between the original and the pan masking film during the mask exposure. The diffused mask then slightly increases the contrast of the edges of the images, which in turn gives more detail to the reproduction. In the electronic version of the process, the computer exaggerates the density difference (contrast) of the image edges.

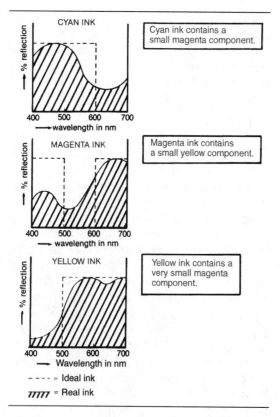

Figure 9.6.   Comparison of real inks with theoretically ideal inks.
Courtesy of D.S. America.

Methods of Producing Color Separations

There are three basic methods of making color separations. They are:

- Direct screen photographic color separation
- Indirect screen photographic color separation
- Electronic color separation by scanner

There is also a new color separation technique that is known as achromatic color or grey component replacement (GCR).

Direct Screen Color Separation

The **direct screen color separation** method produces color separation halftones in one step. In other words, the halftone and the color separations are made at the same time. This method has both cost and time advantages. Because the color-separated halftone is produced in one step, fewer pieces of film are exposed, and operators spend less time producing a set of separations. Figure 9.7 illustrates the basic steps involved in the direct screen color separation method. This method can be used with a contact system, separation enlarger (see figure 9.10), or a process camera.

The first step in any photographic separation process is to produce the color masks. Two masks are made for direct screen separations. Figure 9.8 shows how each of the three systems—contact, enlarger, and camera—is set up to produce masks. These setups will be discussed in detail later in this chapter.

The next step in the photographic separation process is to make the halftone and color separations using light that comes from the original and passes through the color separation filter, the mask, the halftone screen, and onto the halftone film (figure 9.9). The order in which the light passes through the items depends on what type of equipment is used. In the final step the plates are made from the stripped negatives and are run on the press.

Direct Screen Method—Transparent Copy
Using the direct screen method to make separations from transparencies is very popular. This process is popular because the equipment is inexpensive and frees the process camera for other production work. The separations can be made in one of four ways with this method: using a contact system, an enlarger, a camera, or a scanner. The contact process requires only a point light source with filter capability, filters, grey contact screens, and a vacuum frame or easel with a simple register system.

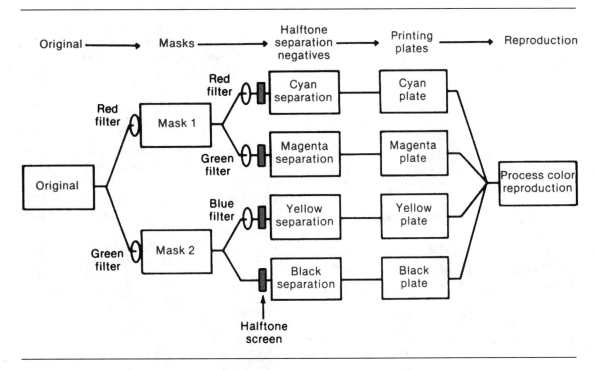

Figure 9.7.   Diagram of direct screen color separation

With both the contact and the enlarger methods of direct screen color separation only a single two-color correcting mask is needed. The mask is created by contact printing from the transparency (figure 9.10a). The final halftone separation negatives are made on high-contrast panchromatic film by sandwiching the color transparency, the mask, and the grey halftone screen with appropriate filtration (figure 9.10b). This process is described in detail in the last half of this chapter.

The projection technique of the direct screen method is generally used when a change from the original size of the copy is desired (figure 9.10c). The procedure is very similar to the contact method except that an enlarger projects the masked transparent image to the proper size through the halftone screen onto the film. An industrial enlarger is shown in figure 9.11 (see p. 237).

If a change in the size of the copy is necessary and no projection system is available, a duplicate transparency can be made to the proper size from the original and then separated by the contact technique. Several transparencies can be ganged together and separated at one time with the contact system, whereas only one image can be handled at a time with the enlarger.

Direct Screen Method—Reflection Copy

A process camera must be used to prepare color separations of reflection copy. (A scanner may be used, but this concept is discussed separately.) Unlike the direct screen method of making separations from transparencies, the direct screen method of making separations

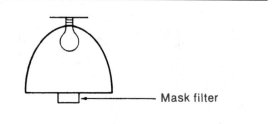

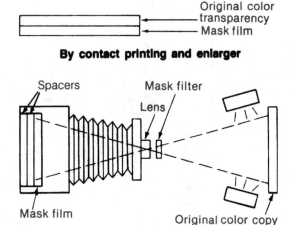

Figure 9.8.   Making the color separation mask

from reflection copy with a process camera is not popular. With this process, the copy is placed in the camera copyboard and color masks are produced to the desired sizes (figure 9.12a). Each halftone negative is made in one step by exposing a sandwich, which consists of the mask, the halftone screen, and film through the appropriate filter (figure 9.12b). The main disadvantage of this method is that the process camera cannot be used for any other purpose until the entire set of separations is produced and approved. If the camera were moved, it would be impossible to reset it to the exact enlargement or reduction ratio. Due to size or di-

mensional considerations, some jobs require the use of a process camera for color separations. Such cameras are either computer controlled or use dial micrometers to ensure an exact return to size if necessary.

Indirect Screen Color Separation

The **indirect screen color separation** method first produces a continuous-tone separation negative (figure 9.13). Next, the continuous-tone negative is screened to produce a halftone positive. The screened halftone positive is then contact printed to make the final separation negative. Advantages of the indirect method are that the negatives can be retouched or enlarged. The opportunity to enlarge, for the second time, during the separation process allows the printer to produce large posters and display work.

Each color mask for this method is made exactly like direct screen separation color masks are made (figure 9.8). The difference in making masks with the indirect screen method is that usually four masks, one for each separation negative, are made. Two masks are made for direct screen separations. After the masks are made, the indirect method differs completely from the direct method.

A continuous-tone separation negative is first made from the original by using the appropriate mask and separation filter (figure 9.14). The continuous-tone separation negative is contacted or projection printed to produce a halftone positive. The halftone positive can be made with a contact system or with a process camera (figure 9.15). An enlarger is usually not used to produce the halftone positives because the continuous-tone negative is too large to fit in the enlarger's negative carrier.

Indirect Screen Method—Transparent Copy
One of the oldest techniques of making color separations is with transparencies on a back-lighted process camera copyboard. Size

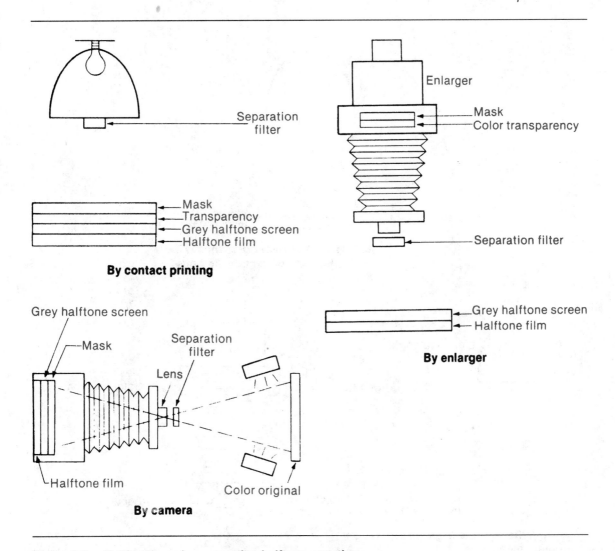

Separation filter

Mask
Transparency
Grey halftone screen
Halftone film

By contact printing

Enlarger

Mask
Color transparency

Separation filter

Grey halftone screen
Halftone film

By enlarger

Grey halftone screen

Mask

Separation filter

Lens

Halftone film

Color original

By camera

Figure 9.9.   **Making the color separation halftone negative**

changes can be made with an enlarger or they can be accommodated by the process camera. First, masks are made with the proper filter by transmitting light through the transparency, through the mask filter, and onto the mask film (figure 9.16a). **Spacer film** is used between the mask film and camera back to move the mask material away from the camera vacuum board a distance equal to the thickness of separation film. When the actual separations are made, the spacer film is replaced by film material. In this way, there is no size or focus distortion in the final product. Next, separation negatives are made by exposing continuous-tone film through the proper filter and mask (figure 9.16b). The separation negative is then placed on the copyboard and exposed to orthochromatic film through a halftone screen (figure

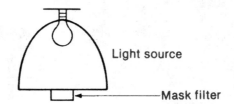

Light source

Mask filter

Color transparency
Mask film

**(a) Making the two-color mask:
Contact and projection methods**

Light source

Separation filter

Enlarger

Mask
Color transparency

Separation filter

Mask
Color transparency
Grey halftone screen
Halftone film

**(b) Making the halftone negative separation:
Contact method**

Grey halftone screen
Halftone film

**(c) Making the halftone negative separation:
Projection method**

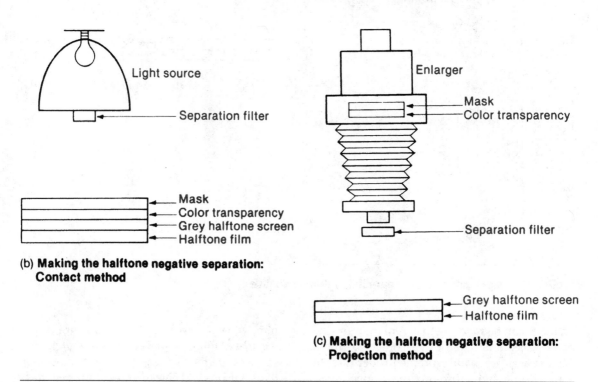

Figure 9.10.   Contact and projection methods of direct screen color separation. When the original copy is a transparency and the size of the reproduction is the same as that of the original, the contact method of separation is used. When the original is a transparency, but its size changes in the reproduction, the projection method of separation is used.

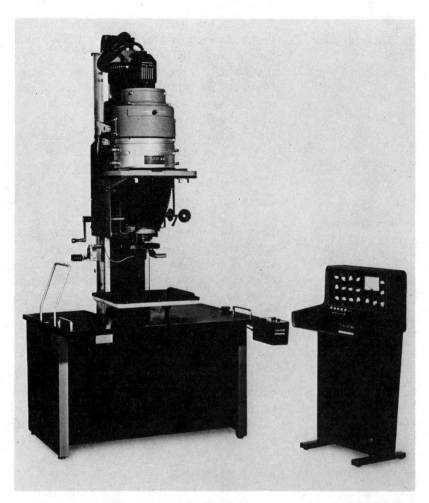

Figure 9.11.   An industrial projection enlarger and color separator.
Courtesy of Berkey Technical.

9.16c). The separation positive is then contacted to produce a halftone negative. Again, this technique requires that the camera be maintained at the required size during the entire process.

Indirect Screen Method—Reflection Copy

This technique is very similar to the indirect screen method for color separating transparent copy. Masks are exposed by light reflecting from the copy (figure 9.17a). Spacer film is placed behind the mask film so that the mask is in focus when it is placed in front of the separation film in the following step. In this next step, continuous-tone separation negatives are made by photographing the original through the appropriate filter and mask (figure 9.17b). Positives can be made by contact printing or by placing the positives in the back-lighted copyboard (figure 9.17c). The final halftone negative separations are made by contact printing (figure 9.17d).

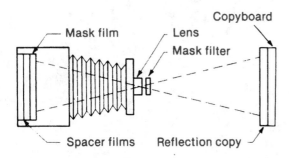

(a) Making the mask

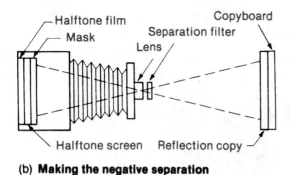

(b) Making the negative separation

Figure 9.12.   Direct screen color separation from reflection copy

Direct and indirect color separation can be done with a variety of equipment (such as a process camera, an enlarger, a contact printing system, or even an electronic scanner). A process camera can be used to separate either reflection copy, such as a color print or transparencies (with a back-lighted copyboard). An enlarger or a contact printing system can be used only to separate transparent copy. A scanner can be used to separate either transparent or reflection copy.

Several variables need to be considered when selecting the method and equipment to use for color separation. Typical considerations include available money, type of copy to be sep-

arated, the required enlargement-reduction factor, and ultimate use for the separations. Fewer steps are involved with the direct method, so it is obviously faster than the indirect process. However, the additional steps of the indirect process can be advantageous for color correction and proofing. Because indirect separations are contacted to produce the halftone negatives, they produce a better dot structure.

Electronic Color Separation

Electronic color separation is commonly called color scanning. A **scanner** (figure 9.18) is a device that electronically measures color densities of a color original (such as a slide, photograph, or painting), stores those measurements as digital information in computer memory, manipulates or alters the digital data to obtain the best printing results, and uses the new information to create four film separations.

The original concept of an electronic color scanner dates to 1937, but it was not until 1949 that the first successful scanner was actually put into commercial operation. Until recently, industrial acceptance of scanners has been slow. The industry's general feeling was that photographic color separation methods and color scanners were about the same in terms of final quality and cost. Also, scanners required a substantial initial investment.

American printers have not accepted the scanning concept as readily as has the rest of the world. However, scanning is rapidly becoming the standard method for producing screen separation negatives directly from original color copy. Scanning's acceptance is due to several factors. Computers are one. Computer systems have grown increasingly sophisticated and powerful in the last decade. In many instances these gains have come with accompanying reductions in costs. A widespread cultural acceptance and use of computers has helped change attitudes about scanners. In

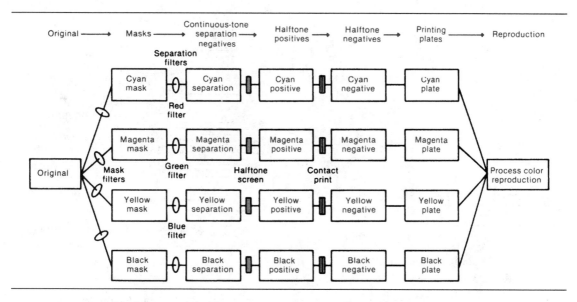

Figure 9.13. Diagram of indirect screen color separation

printing, computers are commonly used to measure and control ink densities on a printing press. When printers have the ability to measure the strengths and weaknesses of each press, they can use that information to make sets of separations that deliver maximum quality. Scanners can individualize results for any printing press. Finally, the development of powerful color editing systems has led to increased scanner use. Color editing requires and uses the data that can only come from a digital color scanner.

Basic Scanner Operation

Figure 9.19 is a simplified schematic of a scanner. The color transparency is mounted on a rotating drum. Most of the drum is clear glass or plastic. An unexposed sheet of film is mounted on the other end of the same drum. As the drum spins, a narrow beam of light passes through the transparency to a computer measuring device inside the drum. The computer takes color

and density readings and electronically stores data for cyan, magenta, yellow, and black separations. Simultaneously, the computer directs a beam of light at the unexposed sheet of film. The film is exposed in direct proportion to the density of the area being measured on the original, but for only one separation.

This is a very simplified explanation of complex and sophisticated technology. It is possible to have many variations of this basic approach. Four sheets of fresh film can be mounted on some scanners so the cyan, magenta, yellow, and black separations are produced at one time. Another method uses one large sheet of film, and the scanner records each separation at different positions on that one sheet. The computer can also store the data for output on a separate machine after color editing.

Both color transparencies and color prints can be scanned. Although the rotating drum form is the most common scanner design, an alternative is the flatbed scanner design. The

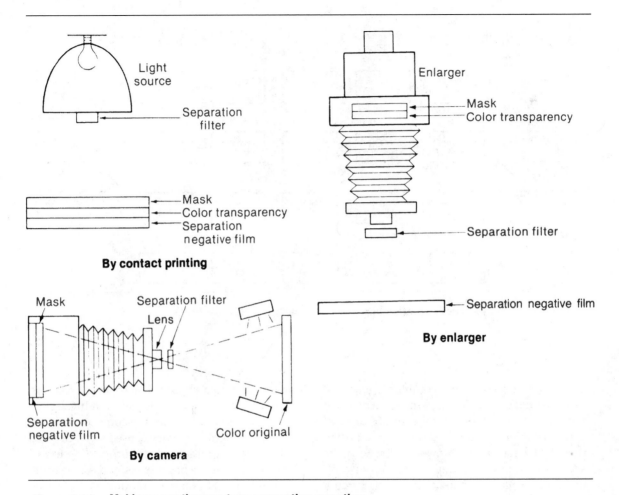

By contact printing

By enlarger

By camera

Figure 9.14.   Making a continuous-tone separation negative

flatbed design is especially useful for originals that cannot be curved around a drum.

The color scanning process involves four steps:

- Scanning
- Analysis and modification
- Storage and image editing
- Exposure

The following discussion describes scanning a color transparency. Although the procedures are slightly different for reflection copy, the basic concepts are the same for either type of original. This is a generalized explanation that does not apply to any specific manufacturer's machine.

Scanning

The color transparency is first mounted on the transparent revolving drum. Some devices have a vacuum system for this purpose, and others use a plastic sheath, but it is most common to simply secure the sheet in place with

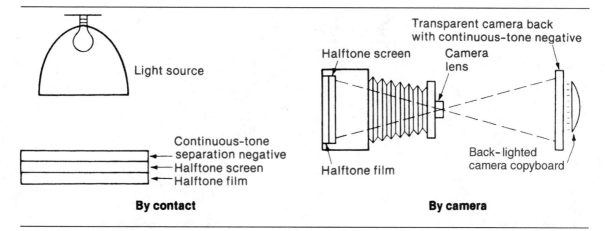

Light source

Continuous-tone
separation negative
Halftone screen
Halftone film

By contact

Transparent camera back
with continuous-tone negative

Halftone screen   Camera
lens

Halftone film

Back-lighted
camera copyboard

By camera

Figure 9.15.   **Making a color separation halftone positive**

clear cellophane tape. Although the position of the transparency is not crucial, it is important that the transparency does not move or shift as the drum rotates.

Next, a narrow beam of light passes through a condenser lens and is deflected by a mirror which is set at a 90-degree angle to the drum surface. The lamphouse of the scanner contains the light source and lenses. The two most common light sources are high-pressure xenon or tungsten-halogen lamps. The light from the mirror passes through the color transparency and is split into four light paths by microscopic optics. Each light path enters a **photomultiplier tube (PMT).** The PMT is the most important element of the scanner because it has the ability to change light to an electrical signal. The PMT can send a signal that varies in strength according to variations in the light it receives.

Three of the PMTs in the scanner are covered with red, green, and blue filters respectively. The amount of light passing into any *single* PMT is proportional to the density of a primary color from a spot on the color transparency. The PMT sends the computer a signal that controls the amount of light used to ex-

pose the separation film at the other end of the rotating drum (figure 9.20).

The red-, green-, and blue-filtered PMTs provide the computer with information to expose the cyan, magenta, and yellow separations. The fourth light path enters a PMT to provide unsharp masking information. That masking data is used by the computer to control the exposure of the final film sheets. The black separation is created by the computer using information from the cyan, magenta, and yellow signals. This entire operation occurs as the transparency drum rotates at high speed.

The lamphouse and the PMT units must be in perfect synchronization with each other. A common design is to connect the lamphouse on the inside of the drum with the analyzing unit on the outside of the drum via a U-shaped rod. As the drum rotates, the light and analyzing units move across the transparency horizontally in what is known as the scan rate.

Scan rate is typically two numbers, one over the other, such as 70/150. The first number is the number of seconds it takes to scan 1 inch. In this example, the light source and the PMTs would have moved horizontally 1 inch in 70 seconds. The second number refers to

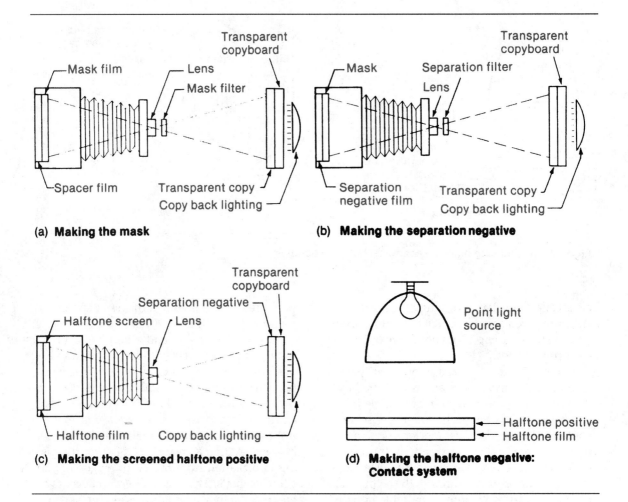

(a) **Making the mask**

(b) **Making the separation negative**

(c) **Making the screened halftone positive**

(d) **Making the halftone negative: Contact system**

Figure 9.16.   **Indirect screen color separation from transparent copy**

scan pitch. Scan pitch is the number of exposing lpi. Exposing lines is not comparable to the more familiar halftone dot screen rulings, also measured in lpi. Scan pitch describes the degree of detail the computer measures. The choice of precision depends more on enlargement requirements than on halftone ruling.

Most scanners allow for information overlap. While scan pitch refers to the actual number of scan lpi, in reality each scan both gathers new information and confirms a portion of the previous pass. This allows the computer to expose a continuous-film image rather than an image that would appear as distinct visual lines.

Analysis and Modification

The electronic signals from the PMTs must pass through the computer control system. At this point the operator can control the output variables directly. The most common areas of

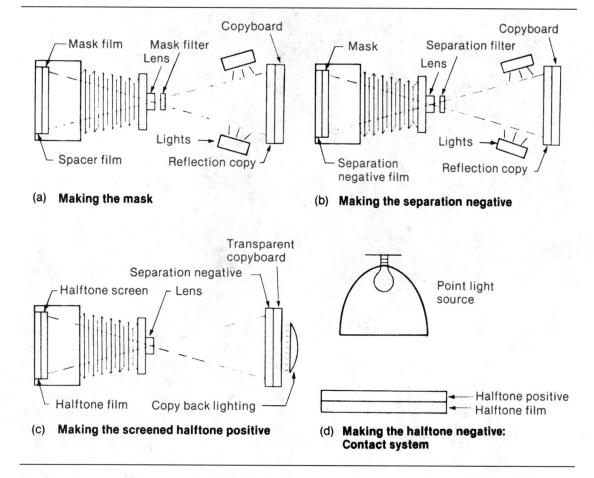

(a) **Making the mask**

(b) **Making the separation negative**

(c) **Making the screened halftone positive**

(d) **Making the halftone negative: Contact system**

Figure 9.17. **Indirect screen color separation from reflection copy**

concern are color correction and undercolor removal (UCR).

One purpose of masking, as discussed in the previous section, is to adjust for the differences between ideal and real printing inks. For example, ideal cyan ink absorbs red light and reflects blue and green light. In reality, while cyan ink does reflect most blue and green light, it also absorbs some blue and green light. This makes the ink appear contaminated with magenta and yellow inks. The solution is to reduce magenta and yellow ink wherever cyan is

also printed. The computer is ideally suited to automatically make such adjustments for all color interactions. Once the operator has set the machine for the actual press conditions, ink, paper, and press printing characteristics, the computer can take information from the color transparency and modify the data to produce the best possible set of separations.

Another reason for color correction is intended use. A printed sheet looks different depending upon its viewing situation. For example, supermarkets always place warm

Figure 9.18. An electronic rotating-cylinder color scanner.
Courtesy of Crosfield Electronics, Inc.

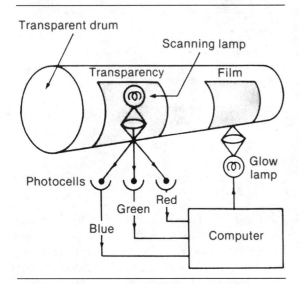

Figure 9.19.   A schematic of scanner operation.
Courtesy of Eastman Kodak Company.

(slightly red) lights over their meat counters. Customers tend to buy more meat when it appears rich red at the point of purchase. If a package with a process color image is to be placed in or near the meat counter (such as a box of frozen shrimp), then the color separations should be adjusted to reduce the magenta printer. However, an adjustment in the magenta printer affects every other color separation. Therefore, the cyan and yellow printers must also be corrected where the two overlap with magenta. The scanner's computer can be set up to make such corrections and, with the operator's direction, can produce a set of four appropriate printers.

The operator may also make adjustments to improve the color balance of an inferior color original. The system may be used to adjust for the type of paper to receive the image. The separations used to print a color image on newsprint should be different from those used for a high-quality, coated offset paper (see chapter 18).

Undercolor removal (UCR) is the process of diminishing the amount of cyan, magenta,

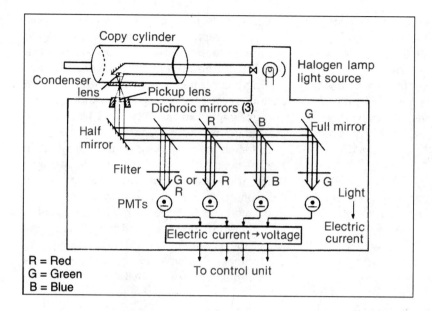

Figure 9.20. Pickup head schematic.
Courtesy of D.S. America.

and yellow ink printed in the shadows, while increasing the amount of black ink in the areas of the original where the three primary subtractive colors have been removed. Equal amounts of cyan, magenta, and yellow create a neutral grey. The basic idea is to remove equal amounts of the three colors to the extent that each individual color's clarity is retained, but to diminish neutral grey, which adds nothing to the image (figure 9.21).

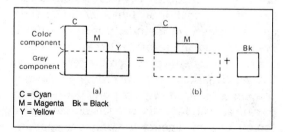

Figure 9.21. Equivalence of three-color grey and black.
Courtesy of D.S. America.

The results of UCR are the prevention of ink buildup, which tends to cause picking (see chapter 13), and increased detail in the shadow areas because of added density in the black printer. The goal of UCR is increased image quality, but one important side result is the savings gained by reducing use of expensive color inks and replacing them with relatively inexpensive black ink.

Because the scanner makes UCR adjustments electronically, and in proportion to the actual data received from the color original, it tends to give more control than is possible with any photographic process.

Storage and Image Editing

Not all scanned images are stored in computer memory. Only scanners that use video display terminals store entire transparencies. Most systems store only one scan line of data at a time. The data is modified and directed to the exposure unit (Figure 9.18). For example, on the first revolution of the drum, one scan line is recorded. As the second scan line begins, the computer adjusts the first line's digital data to the specifications the operator has set. After modification, the information is removed from computer memory and sent to the exposure unit to expose the film separations. Data from the second scan line then replaces data from the first line in computer memory. The process continues until the entire transparency has been scanned and the last line has been removed from memory and sent to the output exposure unit.

If there are few changes from the original photographic image, this approach works very well. The photograph is reproduced exactly as created and with the best possible separations given the printing conditions. However, few printing jobs have ideal printing conditions.

For example, a contact lens sales representative may want a photograph modified to give the model in the photo one green eye and one blue. Another client may want an image of King Kong climbing a building in Chicago. A company in Virginia may decide that the image of a lawn in its annual report should appear gold because of a very successful financial year. All of these changes are possible by traditional photographic printing processes, but are extremely time consuming and, therefore, very costly.

Image editing and **color editing** are relatively new terms that describe the ability to store and then electronically modify an original image using a video display terminal and a computer. Image editing refers to adding or subtracting content from a digitized photograph. Color editing means adjusting or altering color from the original. The computer storage requirements for even an 8 inch × 10 inch color photograph are immense. This decade has seen advances in storage media that make full-page color and image editing possible.

Plate N shows an example of color editing. Two unrelated images have been combined electronically to create an illustration that has never existed in reality. With color editing, any color image may be modified to meet a cus-

tomer's needs. Even if such changes were possible photographically, the effort involved would require far more time and resources than most people could afford. Electronic color and image editing has created an environment in which customers can specify major and minor changes, and designers can move beyond what can be created in the studio or in the real world.

One interesting outgrowth of image editing has been the creation of a new term—synthetic art. **Synthetic art** describes any image electronically created that was either developed by the artist/operator from imagination and, therefore, never existed in reality, or any image that combines several real images to create an image that never existed before. Plate N is a clear example of synthetic art.

Exposure

Color scanners may be classified by type of output. There are three basic methods of electronic image output: continuous-tone, contact screen halftone, and dot-generated halftones.

All early electronic scanners produced continuous-tone separations. The final printable separations were converted to screened halftones on a process camera. In general, continuous-tone separations require a finer scan pitch than any other method. The continuous-tone scanned image is most practical where it is necessary to produce the same image in different sizes. The continuous-tone negatives are mounted on the camera where they are enlarged or reduced to meet design needs. Consider a situation in which an advertising agency has set up a studio photograph for a breakfast cereal product. The agency wants the same image to appear on the cereal box in the supermarket, on billboards, on discount coupons, and in newspaper ads. Rather than paying to scan four distinct sets of sized color separations, the agency has only one continuous-tone set made. The separation halftones are then enlarged or reduced to meet the agency's needs.

A

IVES EARLY TRICOLOR EXPERIMENT

Original proof of tricolor halftone reproduction made by Frederic E.Ives about 1893. Perhaps the first three-color illustration ever produced with a crossline halftone screen.

Courtesy of 3M Company, from the Joseph S. Mertle Collection.

B

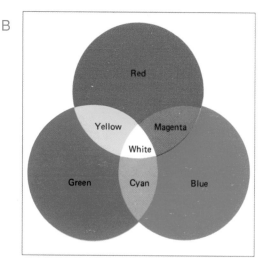

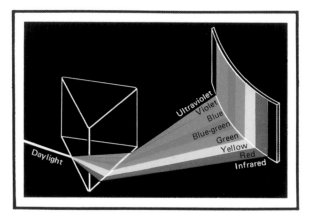

C
PRISM

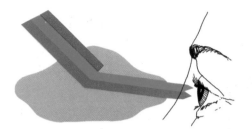

D CYAN INK
  absorbs Red
  reflects Blue
  reflects Green

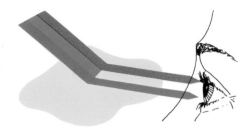

E YELLOW INK
  reflects Red
  absorbs Blue
  reflects Green

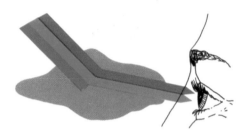

F MAGENTA INK
  reflects Red
  reflects Blue
  absorbs Green

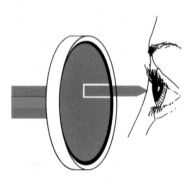

G RED FILTER
  transmits Red
  absorbs Blue
  absorbs Green

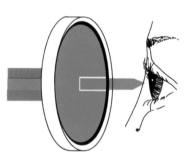

H BLUE FILTER
  absorbs Red
  transmits Blue
  absorbs Green

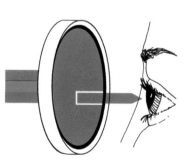

I GREEN FILTER
  absorbs Red
  absorbs Blue
  transmits Green

Yellow

Magenta

Yellow plus Magenta

Cyan

Black

Yellow, Magenta, plus Cyan

J
SEPARATIONS (left and center)
PROGRESSIVE PROOF (right)

From The Metropolitan Museum of Art, the
Michael Friedsam Collection, 1931. (Detail)

Yellow, Magenta, Cyan, plus Black

BEFORE

K
EXAMPLE OF ELECTRONIC
IMAGE EDITING

THE BOOK STORE
UNIVERSITY OF PENNSYLVANIA 1990–91

AFTER

Continuous-tone scanners are the least expensive devices for initial purchase. They, however, only produce continuous-tone separation negatives. Halftone's must be made separately.

Contact screen scanners, in theory, only add a physical contact screen between the unexposed film and the exposing unit. The contact screen used on a scanner is less dense than the traditional halftone contact screen. The same screen can be used to produce either halftone positives or halftone negatives. There is little output change between a continuous-tone scanner and a contact screen scanner. The light output of the contact screen scanner must be adjusted to the spectral sensitivity and intensity requirements of lith or rapid access film rather than a continuous-tone emulsion.

Dot-generating scanners are equipped to take the electronic signal that has been modified from the PMTs and form a computer-designed halftone dot pattern on the unexposed lith film. The terms **electronic dot generation** and **laser scanning** are sometimes used to describe the same output system. The dot pattern and screen angle are controlled by the computer. The specific dot shape is described mathematically by the original software program (figure 9.22). The computer can form round, elliptical, square, or rectangular dots.

Dot-generated halftones tend to produce hard, well-defined, individual dot patterns. This output resembles the sharp edges of a contact dot (contacting a halftone negative to produce a halftone positive gives sharp edges), rather than the more common soft-edged patterns exposed through a contact screen.

Achromatic Color

A new color separation technique that is unique to the modern electronic color scanner is **achromatic color**. The technique is also known as **grey component replacement (GCR).** The GCR process is an extension of UCR (undercolor removal). While UCR only removes cyan, yellow, and magenta in the darker neutral grey areas of the separation, GCR replaces cyan, yellow, and magenta wherever they overprint to produce a neutral grey, even in the highlights. Traditional electronic separations produce a black (ghost) separation that prints from the midtones into the shadows. The GCR process produces a more full-range black. With GCR, the black printer is responsible for producing a full range of neutral grey tones from highlight to shadow. The result is that the process inks—cyan, yellow, and magenta—only print where necessary to produce the color portion of the image. Where black is required, black prints, rather than building the color black with equal parts of each process color as is done with traditional separations. The press is now able to lay down a heavier film of the process inks without the possibility of upsetting the grey balance of the separation. In addition, much of the more expensive process ink is replaced by the less expensive black ink.

Dot Etching

It is frequently necessary to alter individual separations to emphasize or de-emphasize individual sections of color. The need for changes does not necessarily imply frequent errors or inexact processing controls, but rather is often done to specifications defined by the customer after seeing color proofs. **Dot etching** is a process that changes dot sizes on color separations with a liquid etch (a combination of potassium ferricyanide and sodium thiosulphate). The liquid etch reduces the developed silver of the film emulsion. There are two basic dot etching techniques: wet dot etching and dry dot etching.

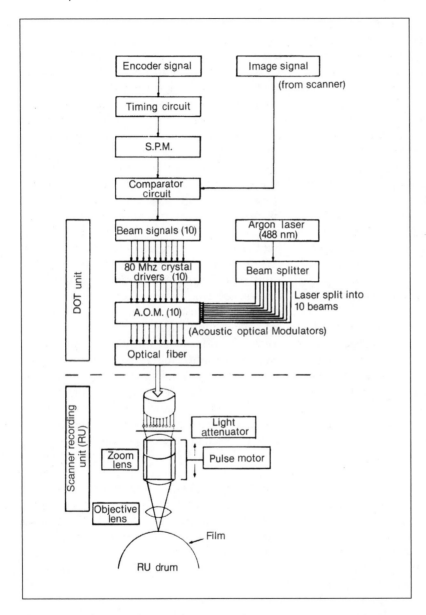

Figure 9.22. Dot generator block diagram.
Courtesy of D.S. America.

Wet Dot Etching

With **wet dot etching,** both halftone and continuous-tone separations can be dot etched. Due to the shape of the halftone dot, the etch first affects the outer edges of the dot. Etching continuous-tone separations changes tonal values on the separation in order to obtain the desired dot size on the resulting halftone reproduction. A diluted etch must be used because continuous-tone emulsions reduce rapidly.

Stain, a thin black liquid, is often used for adding highlight and shadow detail in small areas on continuous-tone images. Stain can also be used to reduce color on negatives or to add color on separation positives. **Retouching pencils** are used to add fine line detail or to repair damaged film.

Once halftone positives are made, a set of proofs indicates any necessary corrections. The areas needing correction are then marked. If the color needs to be increased in an area, a **staging solution** (or an **etch resist**) is applied with a brush to all other parts of the film. To reduce the unstaged area, the film is immersed in a tray of etch solution (start with one-quarter potassium ferricyanide, one-quarter hypo, and one-half water).

Occasionally an area becomes over-etched. It is possible to restore an etched dot by an intensification process. The process requires two solutions: a bleach and a developer. First the bleach is applied to the dot area needing intensification. The developer is then applied to the bleached area, and the original dot structure becomes visible.

Dry Dot Etching

Dry dot etching has several advantages over wet dot etching. Dry dot etching is nondestructive to the original separation films. It is also generally a faster process that requires less artistic skill of the etcher. The disadvantage of dry dot etching is that the process can be more time consuming, especially when a small change in only one area of the film is required. Dry dot etching is a two-step process that requires a contacting station and a pin register system. This process can add or reduce color locally or overall. Prior to contacting, a cut-and-peel mask must first be made which is open only in the areas to be etched.

Color Reduction

The percentage of color in an area can be reduced by first placing the original separation film emulsion to emulsion with contact (reversal) film for a normal contact exposure time. This produces a normal positive, wrong reading through the base, of the entire separation film. After the normal positive is processed, a second contact is made from this positive.

Place the normal positive in the contact frame with the mask on top of the positive and the unexposed contact film below. Again, the films must be emulsion to emulsion. Expose this second contact for an exposure time that will produce the degree of reduction required in the color. This exposure time is expressed as the number of times greater than a normal contact exposure. For instance, a minor color change may only require a 1.5-times exposure. A major change may require as much as twelve times the normal exposure. The amount of change per increase in exposure is determined through a series of test exposures. The number of times beyond the normal exposure is determined by the color evaluator. Personal judgment determines the amount of change needed.

After the additional exposure is made, the mask is removed and a normal exposure is given to the film. This exposure transfers the rest of the color information, which is to receive no color change, to the contact film. After processing, this film contains all the original information plus the reduced dot size required in the masked area.

Color Addition

Adding color or increasing dot size in a specific area is similar to color reduction. The difference, however, is that the mask is used in the first step when the contact positive is being exposed. The second step produces a normal contact of the positive, which received the color addition, because of the mask. A right-reading film negative is then produced.

Key Terms

process color photography
additive primary colors
subtractive primary colors
process ink
color masking
tone correction
color correction
sharpness enhancement
pan masking film
direct screen color
   separation
indirect screen color
   separation

spacer film
electronic color separation
scanner
photomultiplier tube (PMT)
scan rate
scan pitch
undercolor removal (UCR)
image editing
color editing
continuous-tone scanner
contact screen scanner
dot-generating scanner

electronic dot generation
laser scanning
achromatic color
grey component
   replacement (GCR)
dot etching
wet dot etching
stain
retouching pencil
staging solution
etch resist
dry dot etching

Questions for Review

1. What are the additive primary colors?

2. What are the subtractive primary colors?

3. When using subtractive primary inks, what color results from a combination of yellow and magenta?

4. What is the purpose of adding black ink if a combination of three subtractive inks approximates all colors?

5. What are the three main goals of masking in color separation?

6. What are the three basic methods of making color separations?

7. What is the advantage of the direct screen contact technique of color separation?

8. What several advantages does color separation by electronic scanning have over other techniques?

9. What is scan pitch and how does it relate to final print quality?

10. The GCR process is an extension of what masking function of the electronic color scanner?

11. What is the purpose of dot etching color separations?

12. Outline the steps to add color density in a specific area of a separation using the dry dot etching method.

CHAPTER 10

Image Assembly: Mechanical Stripping and Proofing

Anecdote to Chapter Ten

"Stripping" refers to the process of preparing and positioning a piece of film for exposure to a printing plate. The term originally described a process, used commonly as recently as the 1950s, in which a wet emulsion was removed from a special "stripping film." Stripping film was cumbersome to work with when compared to today's flexible, stable-base photographic materials, but at the time it was considered an efficient, simple material.

The stripper could use a variety of techniques when stripping. One of the most common was to manufacture the film from existing materials in the darkroom. The process started with the careful cleaning of a sheet of glass. The glass was then polished with a soft rag and a powder called "French chalk." Next, a substratum of rubber solution or egg albumen solution was poured on the glass,

Stripping film on a light table.
Courtesy of Kingsport Press, an Arcata National Company.

followed by a layer of rubber and naphtha. The final layer to be applied was a light-sensitive stripping emulsion.

While the emulsion was still wet, the plate was rushed to the camera and an exposure was made of the image to be reproduced. The plate was then taken to the developing area and processed. The wet plate then went back to the stripper, who immersed it in an acetic acid-water bath.

When the emulsion began to lift from the plate, the stripper started at one corner and actually stripped the membrane from the plate. While this was going on, another worker prepared a new glass plate by covering it with a small pool of gum Arabic solution. The wet emulsion was positioned on the second plate

and finally squeegeed into place. Depending on the printing process used, the emulsion could be placed on the plate either right reading or wrong reading. If a halftone or new piece of line art needed to be added, the stripper used a sharp knife to cut away the unwanted area and put a new wet piece in its place.

Even though wet strippers would probably not recognize the materials used today, it would take little retraining for them to function at a contemporary light table. The task of positioning film images remains the same. Even assembly on a digital computer requires the same criteria, language, and attention to detail that was required when wet sheets of emulsion were "stripped" from a glass sheet.

Objectives for Chapter 10

After completing this chapter you will be able to:

■ Understand the purpose of stripping and proofing in the printing process.

■ Recognize the equipment and supplies used in mechanical stripping and proofing.

■ Recall and explain the basic mechanical stripping steps.

■ Describe several methods of multiflat registration that include common edge, snap fitter and dowel, and punch and register pin.

■ Recall and explain the basic methods of preparing single-color proofs.

■ Describe the basic concepts of opaque and transparent color proofs.

Introduction

This chapter is divided into two main sections. The first section describes the sequences of steps used to work with film prior to making a printing plate. This operation is called mechanical stripping. The second section deals with methods of checking the quality and the accuracy of the position of the

stripped film images. This process is called mechanical proofing.

Emerging digital computer technology also allows assembly and proofing of images. However, the purpose of this chapter is to review traditional mechanical techniques as a foundation of understanding.

Stripping Transparent Materials

After the final layout has been completed and converted to transparent film, the film image must be transferred photographically to the printing plate. Although the type of plate used will differ according to the method or process of reproduction (relief, lithography, screen, or gravure), mechanical stripping and proofing steps from the darkroom to the plate room are basically the same.

The Purpose of Stripping

Mechanical **stripping** is the process of assembling all pieces of film containing images that will be carried on the same printing plate and securing them on a masking sheet that will hold them in their appropriate printing positions during the platemaking process. (For more about masking sheets, see the next section.) The assembled masking sheet with pieces of film attached is called a **flat.** After the flat is stripped, it is generally tested on some inexpensive photosensitive material to check image positions and to ensure that no undesired light reaches the plate. This process is called **proofing.** If the proof is approved by the customer, the flat is placed in contact with a printing plate, light is passed through the film, and the plate is exposed.

Most printers view the stripping process as the most important step in the printing cycle. The stripper can often correct or alter defects in the film image by etching away undesired detail. The stripper also directly controls the position of the image on the final page. If the film is not stripped square in the masking sheet, the image will appear crooked on the printed page. However, the stripping process cannot correct poor work that started on the mechanical or in the darkroom, no matter how skillful the stripper.

Stripping Equipment and Supplies

The stripper uses a variety of tools that center around a quality T-square and triangle. Tools made of plastic or other easily nicked materials are not used because the tools must serve as cutting edges for razor blades or X-ACTO® knives when trimming pieces of film or masking sheets. Most printers use one quality steel T-square and one steel 30-degrees by 60-degrees by 90-degrees triangle.

Measurements can be made with an architect's scale and an engineer's scale. Stainless steel straightedges with fractional gradations to one one-hundredth of an inch are also commonly used. For greater accuracy, an ordinary needle or a special purpose etching needle is used to mark the masking sheet when laying out a flat. The etching needle can also be used to remove unwanted emulsion from a film negative or a film positive.

Detail is added to a piece of film with a brush. Most strippers have an assortment of red sable watercolor brushes on hand. Start your collection of brushes with #0, #2, #4, and #6 brushes. In addition, your stripping area should have such things as a pair of scissors, a supply of single-edge razor blades, a low-power magnifying glass (10X), pencils (# 2H and # 4H), erasers, and several felt-tip marking pens for labeling flats.

Almost all stripping is done on a glass-topped light table (figure 10.1). One side of the glass is frosted, and a light source (generally fluorescent) is located under the glass so that the surface is illuminated evenly. When a film negative or positive is placed on the lighted glass, it is easy to view the image and to detect any film defects. A variety of light tables are available. Most are equipped with accurately ground straightedges on each side so that if a T-square is placed on any side, lines will always be at right angles to each other. More sophisticated models, called **mechanical line-up tables** (figure 10.2), come equipped with

Figure 10.1.　A glass-topped light table. On this light table, negatives for a 32-page signature or section are being assembled and stripped.
Courtesy of Pre-Press Co., Inc.

Figure 10.2.　A mechanical line-up table.
Courtesy of nuArc Company, Inc.

rolling carriages, micrometer adjustments, and attachments for ruling or scribing parallel or perpendicular lines.

Several types of supplies are needed for the stripping operation. For negative stripping, **masking sheets** that do not pass light to the printing plate must be used. The most common material is "goldenrod paper," which blocks **actinic light** (any light that exposes blue light- and ultraviolet light-sensitive emulsions) because of its color. For jobs that require greater dimensional stability, orange colored (sometimes red) vinyl masking sheets are typically used.

Special "red" translucent tape can be used to secure film negatives during stripping. This tape blocks actinic light. **Opaque** is a liquid material used to cover pinholes and other unwanted detail on film negatives. Red opaque is easier to apply than black opaque, but black colloidal-graphic opaque is thinner and thus more efficient for extremely small areas, such as when retouching halftones. Both water- and alcohol-based opaques are available.

When positives are stripped, the masking sheet and film must pass light in all but the image areas. Most positive stripping is done on clear acetate support sheets, although some special function shops use glass plates. In most positive stripping, tracing paper is used for the initial image layout. Transparent tape is used to secure the film to the flat.

All tools and supplies should be located near the center of the light table so the stripper can reach any item easily. If each item is located in a particular spot and is always returned there after use, much time can be saved. Disorder causes wasted motion and, over a period of time, increases the cost of each job.

Imposition

Imposition refers to placing images in the correct positions on the printing plate so they print in the desired locations on the final printed sheet. Several types of imposition are commonly used. The type of imposition used depends on several factors:

- The design of the printed piece (whether it is multicolor, process color, or single-color; whether one or both sides of the sheet are to be printed; whether one or several duplicate images are to be reproduced on the same sheet; and the type of finishing operations that are required, such as folding, trimming, and binding)
- The type and size of the press to be used (whether the press is sheet-fed or web-fed, and if the job is ganged, the size of the press sheet, and whether to use a large sheet or a single unit)
- The type of paper to be used during printing (whether image position in relation to grain direction will affect folding operations)

Types of Imposition

In general, the best imposition is the one that produces a quality job with maximum efficiency, minimum press time, minimum amount of paper, and minimum time in the finishing operations that follow. Without careful planning in the stripping operation, a job could be stripped, plated, and run on the press only to discover that it cannot be folded correctly.

One-Side Imposition

The simplest form of imposition is one-side imposition. In one-side imposition, one printing plate is used to print on one side of the sheet as it passes through the printing press. This type of imposition is common in small, offset press operations.

Sheetwise Imposition

Two printing plates are used in sheetwise imposition. One printing plate is used to print on one side of a press sheet. A second plate containing different information is then made, the sheets are turned over, and the sheets are printed on the other side from the second plate.

Ganged Imposition

Often the job to be printed is smaller than the press can handle, or it is so much smaller than the standard press sheet size that printing only that one job on each press sheet would be a very inefficient use of equipment. For example, it would be impossible to print 2″ × 3½″ business cards on an 11″ × 17″ press. To overcome this problem, several jobs are often "ganged" together, reproduced on a large sheet, and then cut to their final trim sizes with a paper cutter (figure 10.3). When a press sheet carries only one job, it is called "1-up" imposition. When more than one job is run on the same sheet, it is called "2-up," "3-up," "4-up," and so on, depending on the number of final jobs run on each press sheet. It makes no difference if the same or different images are printed; the same terms are used.

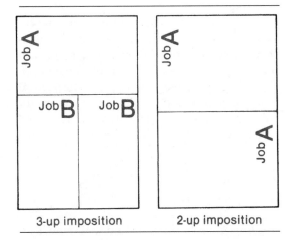

Figure 10.3. Ganged imposition. Images or pages are ganged on the press sheet for more efficient use of materials and equipment.

Signature Imposition

A large single sheet is frequently passed through a printing press and then folded and trimmed to form a portion of a book or magazine. This process is called **signature imposition.** Four-, eight-, twelve-, sixteen-, twenty-four-, and even forty-eight-page signatures are common press runs (figure 10.4). The printer must impose the pages in the proper positions so they will be in the correct sequence when folded in the final publication.

Work-and-Turn Imposition

Another common form of imposition is the work-and-turn. **Work-and-turn imposition** employs one printing plate to print on both sides of a single piece of paper (figure 10.5). The sheet is first printed on one side, the pile is turned over, and the sheet is fed through the press again with the same **lead edge** (first edge that enters the press).

Work-and-Tumble Imposition

Work-and-tumble imposition also uses one plate to print on both sides of one piece of paper. On the second pass through the press, however, the pile is tumbled (or flopped) so that the opposite edge enters the press first (figure 10.6). Both work-and-turn and work-and-tumble techniques are more efficient than sheetwise imposition because only one printing plate is prepared. Work-and-tumble imposition is generally not used where fit (critical image position) is desired—such as in multicolor jobs—because using two different lead edges requires additional press adjustments.

Elementary Stripping Techniques

It is important to keep in mind that there is no single "correct" way to strip a flat. In fact, it sometimes seems that there are as many different stripping methods as there are strippers. The techniques presented in this section are

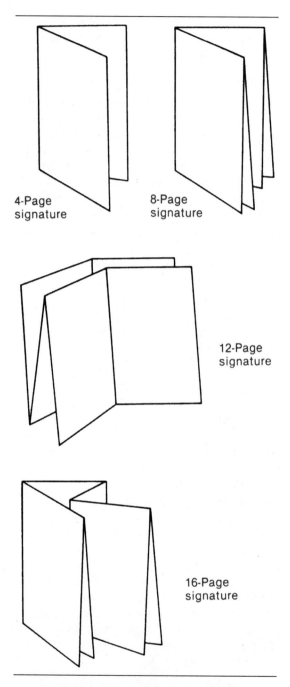

Figure 10.4. Folded signatures. A folded signature of several pages is the result of signature imposition. The number of pages that are folded is predetermined.

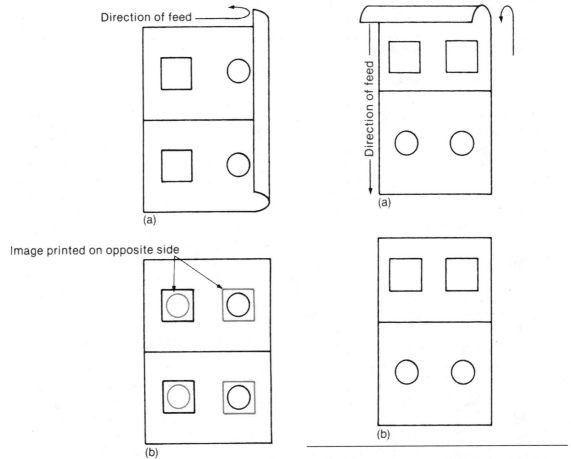

Direction of feed

(a)

Image printed on opposite side

(b)

Direction of feed

(a)

(b)

Figure 10.5. Work-and-turn imposition. (a) On the first run through the press, the first side of the sheet is printed. (b) The back of the sheet is printed on the second run through the press.

Figure 10.6. Work-and-tumble imposition showing first run (a) and second run (b)

intended to introduce some basic stripping procedures, but it should be understood that they represent only one approach.

Prestripping Considerations

Several things must be considered before the actual stripping operation begins. Most jobs arrive at the stripper's in a job jacket with a work order attached. The work order has been completed from information contained on the rough layout and from the printing customer when the contract was awarded. The rough layout should provide detailed specifications for all phases of production, but the stripper is concerned only with such things as the process of reproduction, plate size, paper size, final trim size, image position specifications, and a detailed list of all pieces of film to be stripped.

The stripper should check the contents of the job jacket against the list on the work order and examine each piece of film for quality. If the stripper has nearly completed a flat and then discovers that a piece of film is missing or is of inferior quality, the resulting delay is expensive.

The more complex the stripping job, the more important it is for the stripper to plan the stripping operation. Often it is the stripper's responsibility to make or request the various film images that may be required for a job. In addition, the stripper must plan the contents of each flat so that the minimum number of flats are used for the job.

Masking Sheets

The position of the images on the printing plate is determined by the film positions on the masking sheet. Thus the masking sheet "represents" the printing plate and must be at least the same size as the printing plate. Care must be used in placing the film images on the masking sheet to ensure that they are in the correct printing positions and are parallel to the lead edge of the masking sheet. Identifying the following four areas on the masking sheet helps to position the film images accurately in their correct printing positions:

- The cylinder line
- The gripper margin
- The point where the image begins on the printed piece (figure 10.7a)
- The plate center line

The **cylinder line** represents the masking sheet area used to clamp the lithographic plate to the press cylinder. Most offset lithographic plates are flexible and wrap around a press cylinder, which is called the **plate cylinder.** The lead edge and tail portions of the plate are covered by the clamps that hold the plate in place, so no image can be printed from these areas (figure 10.7b). The **gripper margin** is the area of the press sheet held by the mechanical fingers that pull the press sheet through the printing unit (figure 10.7b). Because these fingers cover part of the paper, it is also not possible to print an image in the gripper margin.

The top of the uppermost image on the printed piece dictates how far down from the bottom of the gripper edge the film image is stripped onto the masking sheet. Information on this dimension should be included on the rough. The center line of the masking sheet is used to line up the center of the film image area so that it is exposed squarely in the center of the lithographic plate and consequently prints in the center of the press sheet. (There are instances when an image is to be printed off center on the final press sheet; for these images, too, however, the center line of the masking sheet must be identified in order to position the film correctly.) Once these four areas are marked on the masking sheet, film can be stripped onto the sheet with confidence that the images will appear in the correct locations on the printing plate and the final press sheet.

The stripper's job is to create a flat by positioning the film on the masking sheet so that the plate transfers images in the required locations on the final press sheet. Press adjustments to change image location are possible, but they are time consuming and costly. Press adjustments for image location are also limited. For example, it is difficult, if not impossible, for a press operator to salvage a plate that has an image above the cylinder line. Often an incorrectly stripped flat must be completely re-stripped, and a new plate must be made. This wastes both time and money. The situation becomes even more critical when several flats are used to expose images on the same plate (see the Multiflat Registration of this chapter).

Masking sheets can be purchased with or without preprinted guidelines. Preprinted masking sheets are typically made in specific

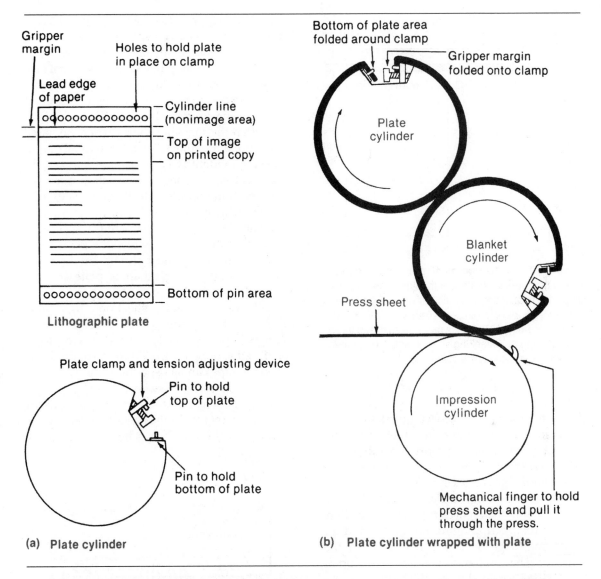

Figure 10.7. **Diagram of printing plate and plate cylinder.** The printing plate is wrapped around the plate cylinder and held in place on the top and bottom with clamps.

sizes for specific presses. For example, pre-printed masking sheets can be purchased for an 11 inch x 17 inch offset duplicator. These numbers indicate that the press can print a page up to 11 inches wide and 17 inches long. The plate for such a press would be about 11

inches wide and slightly more than 17 inches long. The plate is longer than 17 inches to allow space to clamp it to the plate cylinder.

Preprinted masking sheets of this type are generally made only for small duplicator presses (images up to 11 inches by 17 inches).

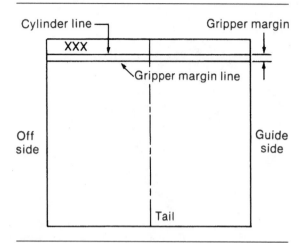

Figure 10.8.   Marking blank masking sheets. Many strippers lay out blank masking sheets using the specifications for a particular press. The cylinder line, gripper margin, and plate center line are located carefully. All layout is made from these three lines. Preprinted masking sheets, which have these guidelines provided, are also used.

Stripping for larger presses requires the use of unlined masking sheets. Whether or not the masking sheets have preprinted guidelines, the stripper's tasks remain the same: identify the cylinder line, plate center line, gripper margin, and top image distance, and strip the images into their correct printing positions (figure 10.8). Stripping for both lined and unlined masking sheets are discussed in this chapter. The discussion starts with stripping procedures for lined masking sheets.

Laying Out a Preprinted Masking Sheet

To begin the discussion, let us pick a simple one-color, single-flat stripping job: one image must be printed on 8½ inch × 11 inch paper using an 11 inch × 17 inch duplicator. For this example, we will strip a negative film image.

The stripper's first job is to select the correct masking sheet. There is no problem if there is only one size of press sheet in the shop. However, if the shop has several different size presses, careful masking sheet selection becomes necessary. Our job requires a preprinted masking sheet for an 11 inch x 17 inch duplicator. Often the masking sheet carries the name of the press manufacturer and a symbol or size marking to identify for which press the masking sheet is designed. If your shop does not have masking sheets with this information, a simple measurement will help locate the correct sheet; or you can compare the sheet to a plate from the press on which the job is to be run. The masking sheet should be the same size as or slightly larger than the plate that will be used with it.

Place the masking sheet on a light table and line up one edge of the sheet with a T-square. Tape the sheet securely in two places on the edge opposite the T-square (figure 10.9). Masking tape can be used for this purpose.

Our masking sheet is prelined in a ¼-inch grid. This grid can be used as a rough indicator of measurements on the sheet, but exact measurements should always be made carefully

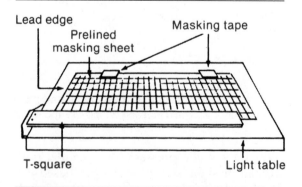

Figure 10.9.   Placing the masking sheet on the light table. Line the masking sheet up against the edge of a T-square and tape it on one side.

with a ruler. Not only is the ¼-inch grid not perfectly accurate, but we taped the masking sheet in place based on the location of the edge of the sheet against our T-square, not the printed grid. There is no reason to assume that the grid printed on the masking sheet is parallel to the edge of the masking sheet. It may be close, but it is probably not perfectly parallel. Using the T-square and ruler for all image location ensures that the images end up positioned correctly and perfectly straight on the sheet.

After the masking sheet is taped in place, look it over carefully. As shown in figure 10.8, the cylinder lines, gripper margin, and center line should be clearly identified. It is often a good idea to draw a line over the bottom of the gripper margin line and down the center line on the masking sheet. This helps you refer back to these locations as you lay out the sheet.

Now check the rough layout to determine top margin: the distance from the top of the paper to the top of the image on the printed piece (figure 10.10). A line representing the top of the image should be drawn across the masking sheet, below the bottom of the gripper margin; lines representing side and bottom margins should also be drawn (figure 10.11).

For this example, there is only one film negative. Lay it emulsion side down near the masking sheet on the light table. Examine the negative carefully. Corner marks that indicate image extremes or center lines (or both) should be recorded on the negative (figure 10.12). These marks help you position the film negative in the proper location under the masking sheet.

Attaching Film Negatives

With rare exception, all printing plates are exposed with the emulsion side of the plate against the emulsion side of the film. Recall from chapter 6 that negatives are right reading through the base. In other words, if the piece of film is placed on the light table so that the im-

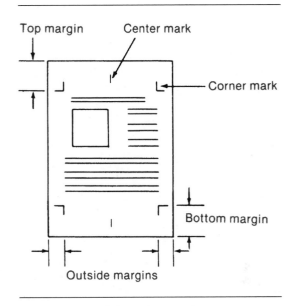

Figure 10.10. **Rough layout with margins identified**

age can be read from left to right, the base side is up and the emulsion side is against the glass. If there is any question about which is the emulsion side of the film negative, the emulsion side can be identified in one of two ways: by comparing the finish of the two sides of the film or by scratching the film edge. If the film is folded over on itself, the emulsion side is the duller of the two sides. Also, the emulsion side of the film can be scratched. A small pin scratch on the edge of the film outside the image area quickly identifies the emulsion side of the film.

Begin by placing the negative emulsion side down on the masking sheet in its appropriate position, with the images roughly falling in place with the image margins. If there is more than one negative in a job, never allow the pieces of film to overlap on the flat. If the overlap is near an image area, there may be some distortion when the plate exposure is made. With the negative in place, mark where any pieces overlap. If possible, cut any overlapping

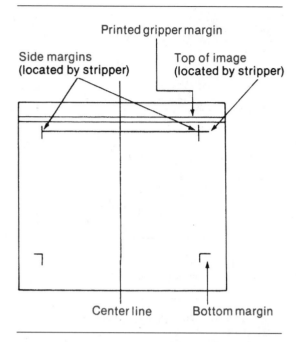

Printed gripper margin

Side margins
(located by stripper)

Top of image
(located by stripper)

Center line   Bottom margin

Figure 10.11.   Diagram of a masking sheet. Lines representing the top, side, and bottom margins are drawn first on the masking sheet. The top image margin should always be below the gripper margin.

sheets to within ½ inch of any film image. If, because of imposition (image location on the final press sheet), the cut must be less than ½ inch from an image area, delay trimming the film until both pieces have been attached. This procedure is discussed in this section. After trimming, all negatives should be removed and set aside until they are needed again.

Because the masking sheet is translucent, it is possible to see through the material to the glass surface below. With right-reading stripping, untape the masking sheet and set it aside or flip it back out of the way. Place the negative, emulsion side down, on the light table. Accurately align the image margins or "tick marks" with a T-square and triangle, and tape the film in place on the light table (figure 10.13).

Next, replace the masking sheet over the film and move it until its image lines are positioned with the image margins on the negative. It should be easy to see both sets of marks line up as you look down through the flat. Use a T-square to ensure that the margins and type lines run parallel to the edge of the masking sheet.

After the negative is in place, smooth the masking sheet and cut two small, triangular openings in the masking sheet over the negative in the nonimage areas (figure 10.14). It is important that you cut only through the masking sheet and not into the film. Practice several times on a scrap sheet. Still holding the film in position under the masking sheet, place a small piece of red tape over each triangular opening and apply pressure. This temporarily attaches the negative to the masking sheet and forms the flat.

Before untaping the flat from the light table, again check all film images for position and squareness. Improper image placement at this stage reflects throughout the rest of the job.

After the negative has been attached temporarily and checked for accuracy, release the flat from the light table by removing the tape, and carefully turn it over. Now secure the negative to the masking sheet at each corner with a small piece of cellophane tape (figure 10.15). Be sure to smooth the negative as the tape is applied to ensure that there are no buckles in the film. Once the film is taped securely to the masking sheet, turn the masking sheet over again (lined side up) and recheck the image placement.

If two pieces of film overlap, it is necessary to cut the negatives so they butt against each other. To do this without cutting into the masking sheet, insert a piece of scrap film or acetate beneath the overlapping portions of film and use a steel straightedge and a single-edge razor blade or frisket knife to cut through both pieces of film (figure 10.16). Do not remove the straightedge until you are certain

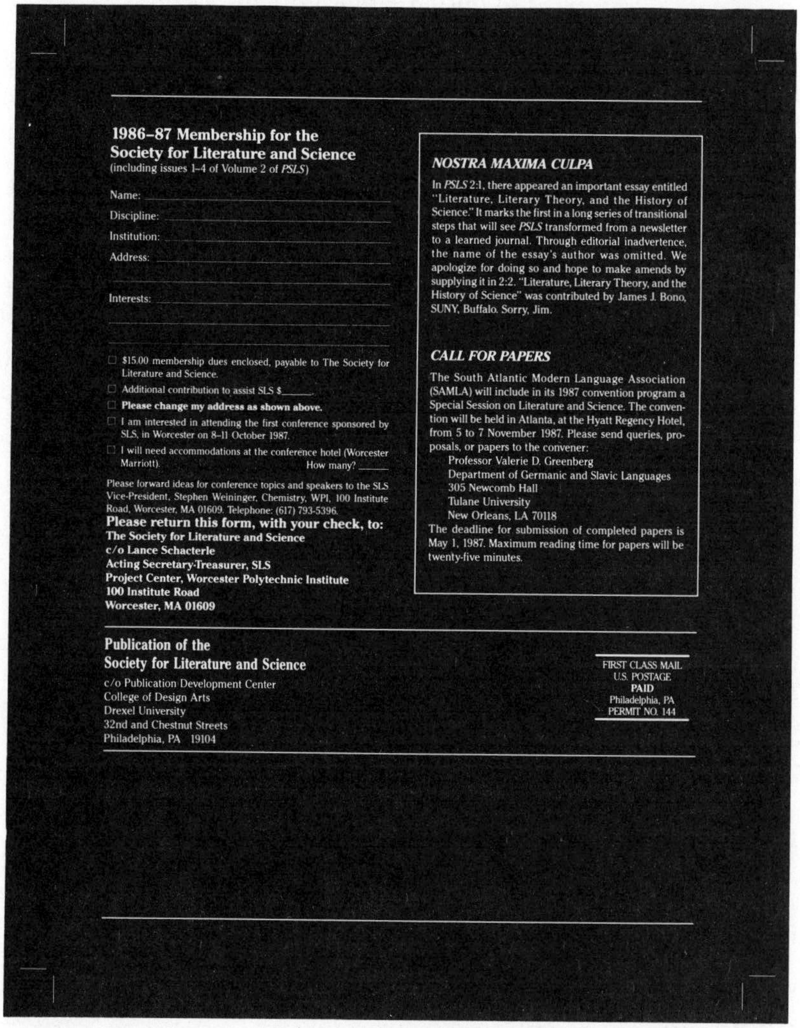

Figure 10.12. **Example of a negative with corner marks.** If corner marks are placed on the paste-up board, they appear as images on the film negative. These negative corner marks can then be lined up with the top, side, and bottom margins on the masking sheet.

that you have cut completely through both sheets of film. Remove the loose pieces and the scrap film, and tape the negatives to the masking sheet on the nonimage edges only. Do not put tape over the image areas on a negative.

After all the negatives have been located and taped in place on the masking sheet, turn the masking sheet over again so that the film emulsion is against the light table. Now cut away the masking sheet in the image areas.

Some strippers slide a piece of scrap plastic between the masking sheet and the film during this operation to ensure that only the masking sheet is cut. With practice and a sharp cutting tool (a single-edge razor blade or frisket knife), however, a plastic insert is not needed. The masking material should be removed to within ⅜ inch of the image areas. The less nonprinting area that is exposed, the better (figure 10.17).

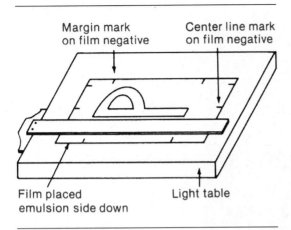

Margin mark on film negative

Center line mark on film negative

Film placed emulsion side down

Light table

Figure 10.13. Positioning the negative on the light table

Opaquing and Etching the Flat

Although theoretically the flat is now ready to be sent to the plating room, in actuality there are usually small defects that must be corrected. The most common defects are **pinholes.** These are small openings in the emulsion that pass light. They may be caused by dust on the copyboard when the camera exposure was made or by dirty original copy. Pinholes ultimately appear as ink on the final press sheet. Pinholes are undesired images and, therefore, must be blocked with opaque.

Most opaques are water based. Alcohol-turpentine- or petroleum-based materials are also available. These opaquing materials dry more rapidly than water-based opaques.

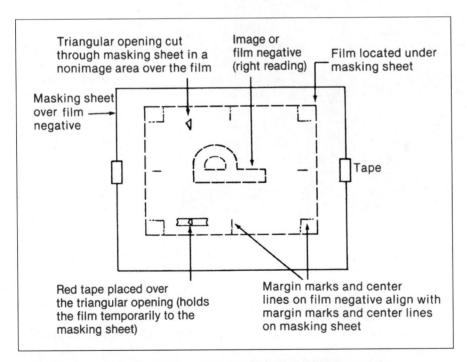

Triangular opening cut through masking sheet in a nonimage area over the film

Image or film negative (right reading)

Film located under masking sheet

Masking sheet over film negative

Tape

Red tape placed over the triangular opening (holds the film temporarily to the masking sheet)

Margin marks and center lines on film negative align with margin marks and center lines on masking sheet

Figure 10.14. Cuffing triangular openings. Looking down through the masking sheet to the film negative below, cut two small triangular openings in the masking sheet covering a nonimage area in the film. Tape over these openings with red tape to temporarily hold the film to the masking sheet.

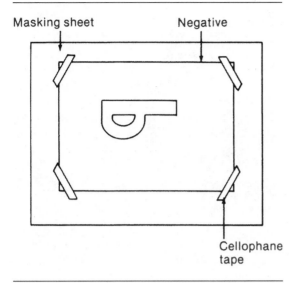

Figure 10.15. **Taping the negative to the masking sheet.** Turn the masking sheet over and tape each corner of the film negative with cellophane tape. For larger films, tape the long edges at their centers.

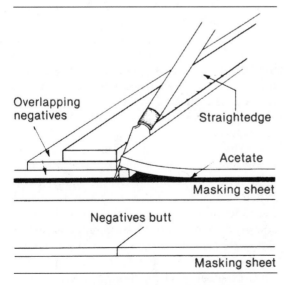

Figure 10.16. **Cutting overlapping negatives**

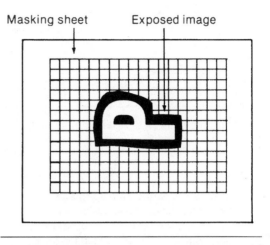

Figure 10.17. **Exposing the image area.** The masking sheet is cut away to expose the image area of the film negative.

Opaque should be applied in as thin a coat as possible yet still block light through the negative. If properly mixed, water-based opaques dry on the film in 15 to 30 seconds. Although some printers place opaque on the emulsion side of the film, we recommend opaquing only on the base side. The emulsion of any film is frail and cannot stand a great deal of manipulation. If opaque is mistakenly placed over a desired image on the base side of the film, it can be washed off or scratched away with a razor blade without damaging the film emulsion. Such scratching on the emulsion side of the film would destroy the emulsion. Also, opaque on the emulsion side of the film contacts the plate emulsion, thereby producing thick areas that could hold the film emulsion away from the plate emulsion during plate making and introduce image distortion (figure 10.18).

A film's emulsion fragility can be an advantage, however. There are frequently situations when detail needs to be added to a negative. Images can be created in the film

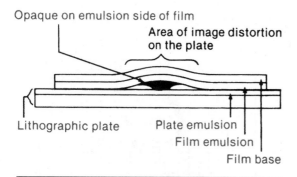

Opaque on emulsion side of film

Area of image distortion on the plate

Lithographic plate   Plate emulsion
Film emulsion
Film base

Figure 10.18.   Opaque-caused image distortion. Opaque on the emulsion side of the film can hold the film away from the plate emulsion during exposure and thereby distort the image.

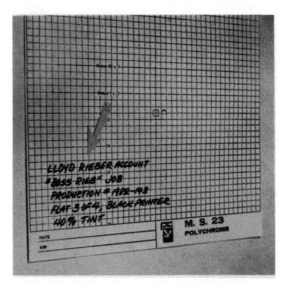

Figure 10.19.   Identifying the film flat

emulsion by scraping away the emulsion with an etching tool.

Novice strippers often have trouble deciding whether or not to opaque an area. As a rule of thumb, when someone standing over a light table looking straight down at an eye-to-flat distance of about 2 feet can see light through a pinhole, then the pinhole probably passes enough light to expose the plate.

The final step, after all opaquing and etching are complete and checked, is to label the flat. The platemaker typically handles many flats in a single day, so each must be identified. Place all information in the trailing edge of the masking sheet, out of the paper limits. The notations depend on the individual shop, but such things as the name of the account, job title or production number, sequence of the flat, ink color, or any special instructions such as the inclusion of a screen tint are all commonly included (figure 10.19).

Attaching Film Positives

There are several advantages to stripping film positives instead of negatives. Because the pos-

itive image is a black emulsion on a clear film base, it is easier to position the film on the support sheet and to register additional pieces of the film to the first piece for multicolor work. It is also possible to work with many small pieces of film, which would be difficult with negatives and goldenrod masking sheets. Finally, a positive halftone produces a higher-quality printing plate than a negative halftone. This is because a negative halftone, when made with a vignetted contact screen, produces a ghost image around each dot. When a negative is contacted to a new piece of film to make a film positive, a well-defined, hard dot is produced.

The initial layout of all guidelines is made on a piece of tracing paper instead of a goldenrod or yellow vinyl masking sheet. When complete, the tracing sheet is turned over and mounted on the light table with the T-square. A clear sheet of transparent base material is then taped in place over the reversed layout. The film positive is placed on top of this support sheet. A clear, stable plastic, such as vinyl, acetate, or a polyester-based material, is typically used. Notches are cut to indicate the plate limits to aid in placing the flat on the plate in the platemaking department.

All film positives must be adhered emulsion side up and in reverse on the support sheet so that all images are exposed emulsion to emulsion in the platemaker. The emulsion of a positive is right reading when produced by contact printing from a film negative. For that reason, it is necessary to laterally reverse the image during contacting so that the final stripped flat is emulsion to emulsion with the plate during platemaking. The Duplicating Film Materials section of chapter 6 outlines this process in detail.

Trim the positive to within ⅜ inch of the image, position it on the support sheet in line with the margin marks, and tape it in place with clear cellophane or polyester tape. The tape should not extend over any image area. When the film is too small or is too close to another piece of film to allow for taping, rubber cement can be used to secure the positive to the support material. To do this, position the positive and then lift one corner. Place a small quantity of rubber cement on the base side of the film and press the corner back into position. Repeat the operation with each corner of the positive. Be sure to use the cement sparingly and avoid any contact with the film emulsion. As with negative stripping, individual pieces of film should not overlap.

Stripping Halftones

Several techniques for adding halftone images to printed materials were discussed in chapter 4. One method suggested including a red or black pressure-sensitive material on the paste-up that would reproduce on the film negative as a clear, open window. A halftone negative could then be added to the window later in production. It is the stripper's responsibility to combine the halftone negative with the neg-

ative holding the window on the flat. This must be done in such a way that the halftone appears in the proper position on the final printed sheet and the added piece of film carrying the halftone image does not interfere with the existing images on the negative that has the window.

To add a halftone negative to a window in a main negative, first prepare the masking sheet; add the main negative(s); and complete all cutting, opaquing, and etching. Then turn the flat over on the light table so that the film is emulsion side up. Trim the halftone to be stripped into the window so that it is larger than the window opening and yet does not overlap any image detail near the window. Position the trimmed negative over the window emulsion side up, in line with the rest of the image detail on the flat, and tape it in place with clear cellophane tape. The halftone must be mounted in this position because the emulsions of both the main negative and the halftone negative must contact the printing plate when the plate exposure is made (figure 10.20).

Check to be sure that the halftone image completely fills the window. Any open area

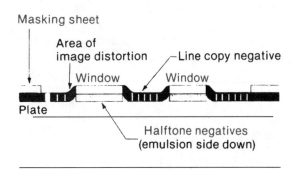

Figure 10.20. Positioning the halftone negatives. The emulsions of both the line copy and the halftone negatives must contact the emulsion of the printing plate.

around the edges of the window prints as a solid line on the final reproduction.

When you are stripping positive flats, treat a halftone exactly as you would treat all other pieces of film. Cut it to size and secure it in place with clear tape or a thin layer of rubber cement.

It is often not possible to add a halftone negative to an existing flat without overlapping image detail and creating an area of image distortion. This happens when two halftones butt together on the final printed sheet or the halftone window is too close to other image detail. In such cases, the stripper cannot work with the halftone on a single flat. The solution is to use two **complementary flats.** One flat carries the main printing detail; the second holds the halftone image (figure 10.21). If properly stripped, each flat can be exposed successively in the platemaker to combine the two

images in their proper positions on one printing plate (figure 10.22). The Multiflat Registration section later in this chapter is concerned with the problem of controlling the positions of film images that are mounted on more than one flat.

Laying Out Masking Sheets for Larger Presses

Masking sheets for offset presses larger than 11 inches by 17 inches are generally unlined. However, the stripper is still concerned with the four major areas on the masking sheet: the cylinder line, the gripper margin, the top of the image area, and the plate center line. All images are positioned from these four guidelines.

The initial layout lines are located from specifications provided by the printing press manufacturer. Table 10.1 shows the specifications for the Harris LXG offset lithographic press. The following example assumes the Harris press is used, but the process applies to any printing process or printing press.

Begin by cutting the masking sheet equal to or slightly larger than the plate size. If you are stripping positives, cut a piece of tracing paper instead of goldenrod masking sheet. Tape the sheet securely in place in the center of the light table; use a T-square to line up the top edge of the sheet accurately. Be sure that there are no buckles or loose portions in the sheet that will cause inaccurate line rulings.

Mark the edge closest to you with three Xs to identify the lead or gripper edge of the plate. Label the off (left), tail (back), and guide (right) sides (figure 10.23). From the press specifications (table 10.1), measure the position of the cylinder line from the lead edge of the sheet, and prick the goldenrod with a needle or an etching tool. Then draw a line through the point (figure 10.24). From the same specification list determine the amount of gripper margin (or bite). Mark the distance

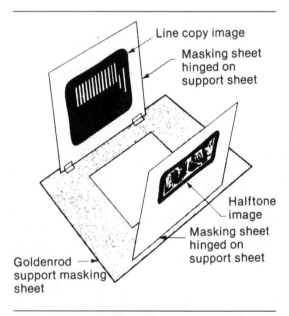

Figure 10.21.   Complementary flats. In this example of complementary flats, the two masking sheets hinge on a larger support sheet.

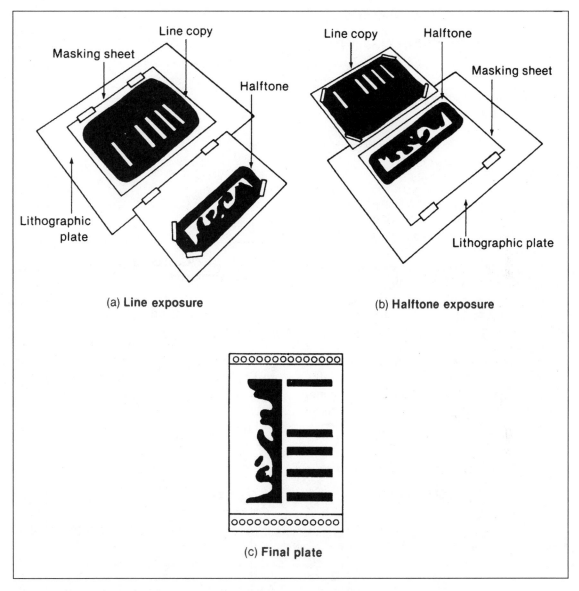

(a) **Line exposure**

(b) **Halftone exposure**

(c) **Final plate**

Figure 10.22.   Using complementary flats for double exposures. (a) The complementary flat uses one exposure to record the line copy and (b) one exposure to record the halftone. (c) The final plate carries both images.

Table 10.1.   Harris LXG Press Specifications

Maximum printing area	22⅝ × 30
Maximum sheet size	23 × 30
Minimum sheet size	9 × 12
Plate size	27 × 30
Distance from lead edge of plate to cylinder line	1¹³⁄₁₆
Gripper margin	⁵⁄₁₆

from the cylinder line to the bottom of the gripper margin, and draw a second line parallel to the first (figure 10.25). The area between the cylinder and gripper line represents the gripper margin. This area varies from press to press, but the width is generally from ³⁄₁₆ inch to ⅜ inch. It is important to remember that the gripper margin represents nonprinting area and can carry no printing image. The last initial layout line is a vertical line drawn in the center of the masking sheet (figure 10.26). All vertical measurements will be made from this center line, and all horizontal measurements will begin from the cylinder line. With these

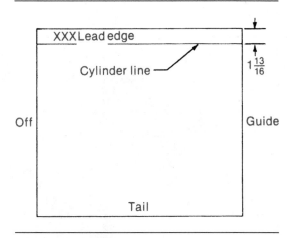

Figure 10.24.   Goldenrod masking sheet with labeled cylinder line

guidelines there is little chance of error in image placement.

Assume for this example that a 20½ inch × 24¾ inch sheet will be fed through the Harris LXG. From the center line, measure one-half the length of the plate in either direction, then cut notches in the masking sheet as illustrated in figure 10.27. The lead edge of the masking

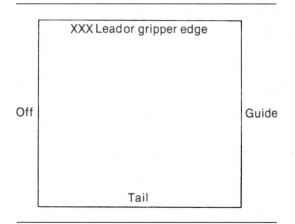

Figure 10.23.   Goldenrod masking sheet with labeled edges

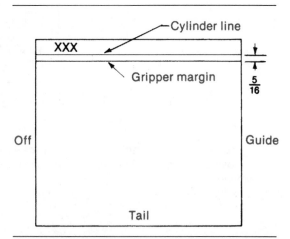

Figure 10.25.   Goldenrod masking sheet with labeled gripper margin

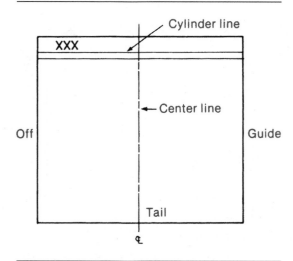

Figure 10.26. Goldenrod masking sheet with labeled vertical center line

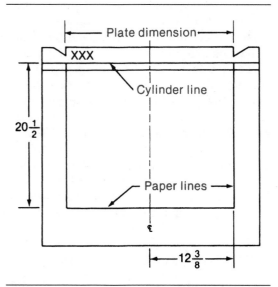

Figure 10.27. Goldenrod masking sheet with paper dimension added

sheet and these two notches serve as guides when the flat is placed on the printing plate during plate exposure.

The next concern is to define the press sheet area. The work order should identify the paper size and the way in which the sheet is to be fed through the press. If a sheet is to be trimmed after printing and a choice is possible, lay out the masking sheet so that the lead or gripper edge of the paper is trimmed. The lead edge is pulled through the press exactly parallel to the cylinder, which ensures the image is exactly square to that edge. Position any register marks (for multicolor registration) or test scales in the trim area. Measure 20½ inches from the cylinder line (the width) and 12⅜ inches on each side of the vertical center line (one-half of plate length), and draw the paper lines (figure 10.27). You must position all film images within this area. Do not extend them into the gripper margin.

When there are large sheet presses but small final printed sheet sizes, most companies gang several jobs on the same flat with the intention of cutting the paper pile after printing. In large companies the ganging positions are decided by the planning section; in most small organizations the stripper makes all of these decisions. Figure 10.28 illustrates the ganging of several smaller printed sheets on one larger press sheet. Notice that parts of the same job are identified by the same number and that image margins are defined by the use of corner ticks. Again, measuring from the cylinder and vertical center line, the stripper places all final paper lines within the large press sheet paper lines and marks the margin marks for each sheet (figure 10.29). After one check of all dimensions is made, the masking sheet is ready to receive the film negatives.

Most industrial stripping is done with the film negative emulsion side up, facing the stripper. Begin by turning the masking sheet over on the light table. Accurately position the cylinder line with a T-square and tape the

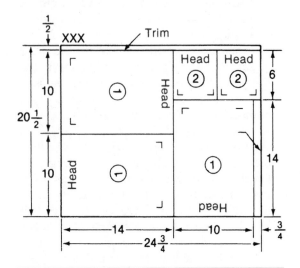

Figure 10.28.　A press sheet layout

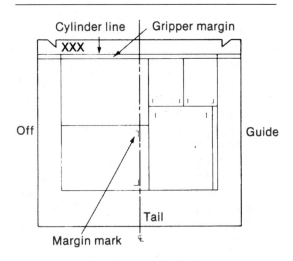

Figure 10.29.　A flat layout from the press sheet layout in figure 10.28

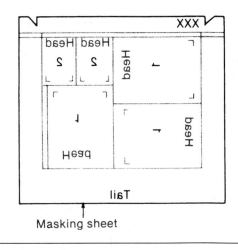

Figure 10.30.　Layout lines as seen through the base of the masking sheet

sheet in place. Check to be sure you can see the layout lines through the masking sheet (figure 10.30).

After checking the rough layout, position the first negative in the correct area, emulsion side up. Place the side margins and top image of the negative in line with the head and side guidelines on the flat. Use the T-square to ensure that the image is parallel to the cylinder line. Then tape each corner of the negative with cellophane tape. Repeat the same procedure for each remaining negative (figure 10.31).

When all negatives have been attached and checked for accurate position, turn the flat over and cut windows through the masking sheet to expose the film image openings. Opaque and etch the flat as necessary.

Multiflat Registration

It is important to realize that almost all printing plates can be exposed from five or six different flats before the sum effect of light

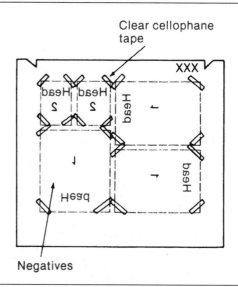

Figure 10.31. Positioning negatives on the masking sheet. Position negatives emulsion side up in line with head and side guidelines. Secure the negatives with cellophane tape.

leading through the goldenrod or yellow vinyl masking sheets begins to expose the plate emulsion in nonimage areas.

The problem of multiflat exposures is registration. The stripper must place the separate film images on each flat and then control the placement of the images from each flat on one plate. When the plate is processed, all images must appear in their proper printing positions relative to each other and to the limits of the printing press. Some form of mechanical punch or guide is generally used to aid in the multiflat registration process. These techniques are discussed shortly.

The Purpose of Registration Systems

Many situations besides complementary halftone flats require the stripper to use the multiple flat process. Commonly the stripper must print two separate screen tint values in the

same color using the same plate. It is possible to place both images on one negative and to use folding masks to make the plate exposure (figure 10.32). Two separate exposures would be made with a screen tint between the flat and the plate during each exposure. Only the desired areas would be opened for each exposure, and the proper screen would be placed between the flat and the plate each time the plate was exposed. If images are extremely close together, however, or if many different areas are spread over the entire flat, this technique is not usable. It is then necessary to place all images of common screen tint values or sizes on separate flats. With proper multiflat registration techniques, these images can be assembled on one plate in the proper tint values, screen angle, and position (figure 10.33).

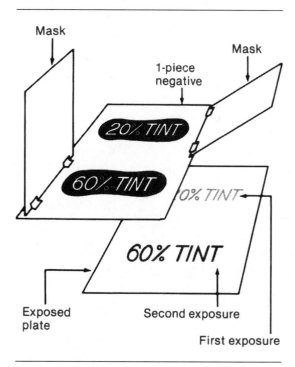

Figure 10.32. Using folding masks to control multiple plate exposures

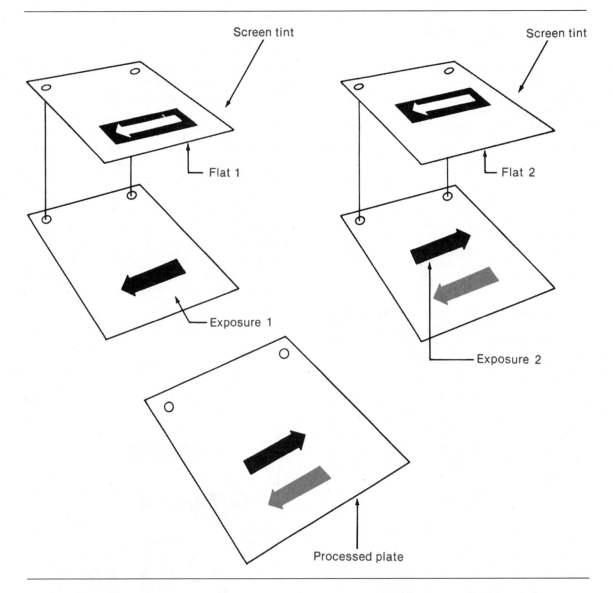

Figure 10.33.   Using multiflat registration techniques to assemble different screen tints on the same plate

Surprints and reverses were introduced in chapter 3 as a part of the design phase, but they are actually assembled by the stripper. Figure 10.34 illustrates how two flats with two separate exposures are used to produce a surprint on a single plate. Figure 10.35 shows the registration of a positive image to create a reverse in an area during a single plate exposure. Multiple flats are often used to provide a mask or frame for a larger image (figure 10.36).

Certainly multiflat registration techniques are most commonly applied in the area of process color reproduction. The four primary flats, representing cyan, magenta, yellow, and black detail, must be stripped so that the plates, when placed on the printing press, can be adjusted to "fit" the four colors together

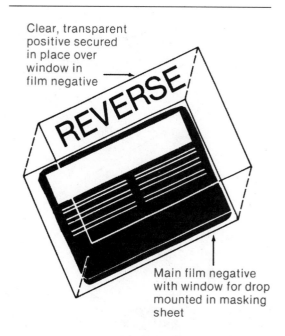

Clear, transparent positive secured in place over window in film negative

Main film negative with window for drop mounted in masking sheet

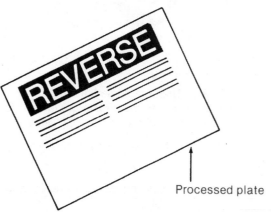

Processed plate

Figure 10.35. **Film positive positioned over a window in a flat to create a reverse**

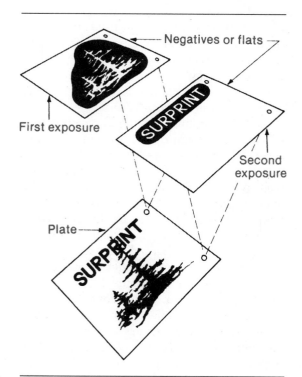

Negatives or flats

First exposure

Second exposure

Plate

Figure 10.34. **Using multiflat registration to place a surprint on one plate**

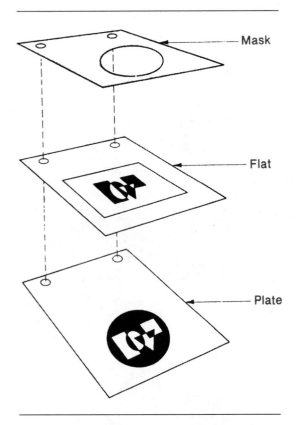

Figure 10.36.   Using multiple flat registration to create a mask or frame for a larger image. The mask is registered in place over the film positive. Only one exposure is made.

on the printed sheet, reproducing the original as closely as possible.

Basic Registration Methods

Several methods are used for multiflat registration. The ones discussed here include:

- The common edge method
- The snap fitter and dowel method
- The prepunched tab strip method
- The punch and register pin method

Common Edge Method

The simplest multiflat registration system is the **common edge method.** With this method the flat containing the greatest amount of detail is stripped first using ordinary layout and assembly procedures. This first flat is called the main or **master flat.** All remaining flats are aligned with it. The second negative (or set of negatives) is then placed in position over the completed master flat and are attached to a second masking sheet. It is important that both flats have at least two edges (generally the top and right sides or the gripper and guide sides) that line up perfectly. Any number of flats can be registered with this method as long as each image on each flat is registered to the master flat and the masking sheets have a minimum of two common edges. When the plates are exposed, the top and right edges of each flat are placed in line with the top and right edges of the plate. This method is only used for the most simple work. Understanding the technique, however, forms a good understanding of multiflat registration.

Snap Fitter and Dowel Method

A second technique of multiflat registration is the **snap fitter and dowel method.** With this system the main or master flat is stripped as usual. At the tail edge of the masking sheet, well away from any image or paper limits, two openings are cut and plastic snap fitters are taped into place (figure 10.37). The flat is then positioned on the light table with a T-square, and soft, adhesive-backed pins (dowels) are pressed through the snap fitter openings onto the glass table surface (figure 10.38). The flat can then be removed, but the dowels remain in place on the light table. When the snap fitters are inserted over the dowels a second time, the flat returns to its same previous position. To register additional flats, new snap fitters are cut into separate masking sheets and are stripped so that image detail registers to the first master flat (figure 10.39).

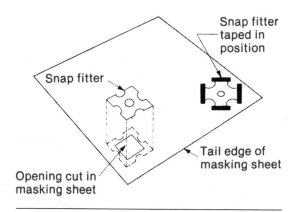

Figure 10.37. **Using snap fitters on a masking sheet**

Prepunched Tab Strip Method

Another way of controlling multiflat registration is the **prepunched tab strip method.** Most companies that employ this technique save their scrap or discarded sheets of film material and cut them into tabs that are approximately 3 inches wide and as long as their masking sheets. Three holes are then punched into each tab with a special mechanical punching device (figure 10.40). Special register pins that are generally metal are then taped to the light table so that the punched tabs fall perfectly in line with the pins (figure 10.41). After the master flat has been stripped, a punched tab is taped to the tail edge. All subsequent flats are stripped in register to the main flat while it is secured to the register pins. Tabs are added to the tail of each additional flat to hold it in register with the master.

Punch and Register Pin Method

The most efficient way of controlling registration is to apply the **punch and register pin method** from the camera to the press. With this method the camera operator uses a mechanical punch on each piece of film, as well as register pins to hold the film in position on the camera

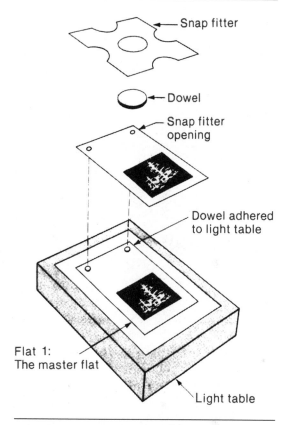

Figure 10.38. **Positioning a flat using snap fitters and dowels.** The snap fitter slides over the dowel and controls flat position.

back. This is especially effective for process color separation work where the copy does not move between exposures. Once the film is processed, the stripper works opaques and etches the film, and then mounts the film on a punched masking sheet if necessary. When the total system approach is used, the printing plate is also punched to line up with the film or masking sheet holes before plate exposure, and register pins are placed on the printing press to receive a punched plate. If used throughout the process, the technique results in printed images that line up perfectly with few press

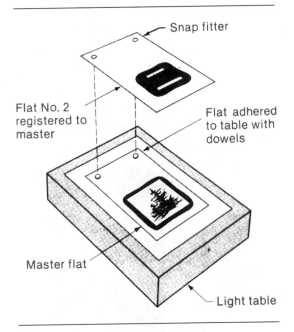

Figure 10.39.   Registering additional flats using snap filters and dowels

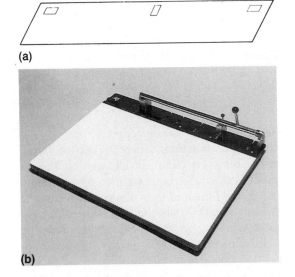

Figure 10.40.   Example of a punched tab (a) and a mechanical tab (b).
Courtesy of Dainippon Screen Mfg. Co., Ltd., distributed by DS America, Inc.

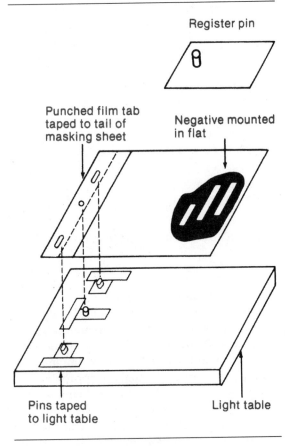

Figure 10.41.   Using register pins to secure a flat to a light table. Register pins are taped in place on the light table in line with the holes in the punched film.

adjustments. This significantly reduces costs in all areas.

Multiflat Stripping for Process Color Work

This section is concerned primarily with the specific techniques involved in stripping for four-color process printing. The general procedures apply to all other multiflat stripping, whether it is flat color, more than four colors (such as topographic mapping where five are used), or single color (where several flats are used to generate one plate).

It is generally accepted that registration for process color work is too critical to employ the common edge registration method. Some form of pin or dowel register system must be used. The most accurate method of positioning multiple flats is to use some type of master image stripped into a master flat as a guide for all subsequent images and flats. There are two basic approaches: blueline flat and single master flat.

Blueline Flat Method

With the **blueline flat method** a special flat is prepared. This flat is generally assembled using negatives and holds any detail needed to position all film images for the job, as well as all necessary registration marks. After it is assembled, the blueline master flat is exposed to a special light-sensitive solution that has been coated on a piece of clear plate glass or plastic. The processed emulsion produces a blue image that does not expose a printing plate if the clear base is used for positive stripping. If negatives are used for stripping, you can use the blueline image as a guide to register all flats. For positives, prepare a laterally reversed blueline for each flat. Then take the master flat apart and strip all pieces of film with their appropriate color.

Single Master Flat Method

The most common registration technique for color negative stripping is the **single master flat method** in which the single master flat acts as a guide for all other flats in the job. For flat color, the master flat is generally the flat that carries the greatest amount of detail. For four-color process work, the cyan, magenta, or black separation negative can be used, depending on which color carries the greatest detail. Four-color stripping with a master flat is covered here.

Prepare the master flat using common stripping techniques. After opaquing and etching the flat, apply some type of pin register device and turn the flat over on the light table with the emulsion side of the film facing you. Apply the pin system to a second masking sheet and position it over the first flat. Then place the second set of negatives, emulsion side up, in register with the first image.

Recall from chapter 9 that register marks are placed with the original during the color separation process. Each piece of film carries duplicate halftone and register mark images for each of the four color separations. The register marks are your first guides. As you impose the second negative over the first, the register marks on the negatives line up. With four-color reproductions made up of halftone images, the alignment is critical. If you view register marks on any but a 90 degree angle, the thickness of the film might cause a distortion that will put the two images out of register. To eliminate the possibility of this type of error, some strippers use a **sighting tube** to view the register marks (figure 10.42).

After all register marks are in line, hold the negative in place with some weighted

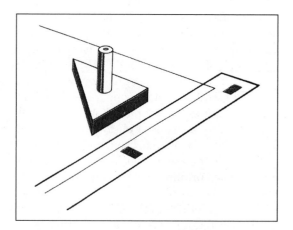

Figure 10.42. Example of a sighting tube

material (a leather bag filled with lead pellets is often used) and examine the detail registration in the halftones themselves.

If the job is made up of only four flats to print as four different colors, all flats are registered individually to the master flat. If there are more than four flats to be reproduced with only four colors (such as when using two different screen tint percentages in the same color, or when line copy falls too close to a halftone image to include it on one flat), the sequence of flat registration is important. Examine each color grouping. For each color, the flat that contains the greatest amount of image detail becomes the key flat for that color. Register each key color flat to the master flat and register all other flats in the color group to the key (figure 10.43).

A method of color stripping that produces high accuracy is stripping with clear mylar. Mylar stripping improves accuracy for two reasons:

1. Clear mylar is easier to see through than orange masking sheets.
2. Mylar is very stable and thus is affected very little by changes in temperature or humidity.

Clear mylar allows the stripper to work on top of the flat with the film pieces emulsion side up. Each mylar flat is punched and registered to the key flat. Because the process films are stripped to a clear base, a mask must be made to block unwanted light in the nonimage areas during plate exposure. For example, a page of text that contains one four-color illustration requires a mask that allows only the illustration to be exposed on the printing plate for the yellow, magenta, cyan, and black negatives. Each of these images is in the same location on each printing plate, so one mask can be used for all exposures. This mask is sometimes called a **traveling mask** because it is placed over each flat for each color as the flat is exposed to the plate. After exposure, it "travels"

to the next flat for exposure on the next plate. If the type on the page were to be printed in black, the plate for black ink would be exposed twice. The first exposure would be made with the traveling mask to produce the black negative for the four-color illustration. In the second exposure a flat would be produced that blocked exposure in the illustration area but allowed the type to be exposed.

Proofing Transparent Materials

After the job has been stripped and checked, it is ready to be converted to some form of plate or image carrier after another step—proofing each flat or job—occurs.

The Purpose of Proofing

It is difficult to interpret the image on the flat. Both printers and printing customers are distracted by such things as the masking sheet, tape, opaque, notations, or instruction marks. Moreover, the image on the flat is often a negative. It is also not possible to fold a flat to check for accuracy of image position for a work-and-turn or a signature job. The function of proofing is to check for image location and quality, and to obtain the customer's final approval to run the job. There are two basic ways to proof transparent materials: by using press proofs and by using photomechanical proofs.

Press Proofs
Press proofs are made using the same types of ink and paper that are used on the final job. Press proofing has the disadvantage of high cost. The customer must assume the costs of press time (set up, make-ready, actual running time, and clean up) and materials in press proofing. Therefore, press proofing is reserved for extremely high-quality, long-run jobs.

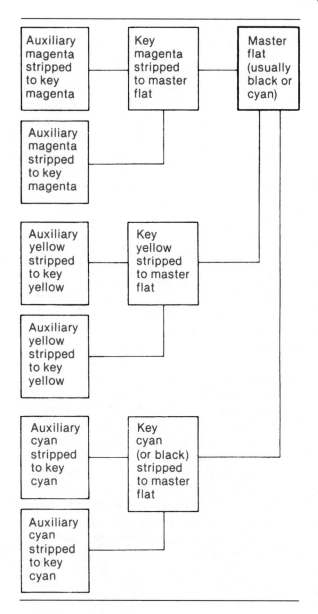

Figure 10.43.   **Example of a sequence of color flat registration for more than four flats.** A four-color reproduction may require more than four flats if two different screen tint percentages are specified in the same color or if line copy falls too close to a halftone image to be included in one flat.

A "press check" is when a customer comes to the plant to give final approval while the job is being run. With press proofing the customer can see how the final job will look (including the final colors). However, if changes must be made, the cost is very high.

Press checks are usually conducted not to check accuracy of words or image position, but rather to approve colors on the final printed sheet. The customer rarely stays for the entire press run—only to approve the first images.

With some reproduction methods, the job is actually mounted on a press and a few hundred images are produced as a proof. This is common with gravure printing (see chapter 16). Where the plate cylinder is exceptionally time consuming and costly to prepare in gravure printing, a press proof is safe insurance for both the printer and customer.

Photomechanical Proofs

Unlike press proofs, **photomechanical proofs** require no large investment in special proofing equipment and generally use existing platemaking equipment (see chapter 11). Most photomechanical proofing systems use a light-sensitive emulsion coated on some inexpensive carder, such as paper or plastic, which is then exposed through the flat in the same way the plates are exposed. The emulsion is next processed chemically to produce an image that represents the final press sheet. Contrary to what many proofing manufacturers claim, no photomechanical proof matches the quality and color of a press proof. However, the low cost of photomechanical proofs vastly outweighs this disadvantage. Photomechanical proofs are generally classified as either single color or multiple color.

Single-Color Photomechanical Proofing

Single-color photomechanical proofing is the least expensive of the proofing systems. Most methods use a vacuum frame to hold the flat in contact with a light-sensitive coating on a sheet of paper and a light source to expose the emulsion. This equipment is discussed in detail in the following section of this chapter. Single-color proofs do not show the actual ink color of the final press run. They are used only to check such things as imposition, image position, and proper masking and opaquing. Three common types of materials used for single-color proofs are blueprint, diazo, and instant image proof papers.

Blueprint Paper

Blueprint paper is a low-cost material that produces positive images from transparent film negatives. Blueprint paper is coated with an organic iron compound (potassium ferricyanide) that changes structure when struck by light. The proof is developed in water and hung up to air dry. Unfortunately, blueprint paper is not dimensionally stable (which means that it changes size easily). In addition, the image recorded on the blueprint tends to lighten with age.

Diazo Paper

Diazo paper produces a positive image when exposed to transparent film positives. Its exposed emulsion develops when placed in contact with a special liquid or gas (generally ammonia fumes). This paper has the advantage of relative dimensional stability because it is not moistened with water during development.

Instant Image Proof Paper

Instant image proof paper produces dry image proofs without processing equipment and chemicals. One example is DuPont's Dylux papers, which are exposed with ultraviolet (UV) light and produce a visible image without chemical processing. The resulting proof can be fixed, or deactivated, by bright white light exposure. Typical exposure light sources are Sylvania BLB lamps, pulsed xenon with an ultraviolet filter, mercury vapor with a UV filter, or carbon arc with a UV filter. Dylux papers are coated on one or two sides, with either a blue or near-black image. The paper can be handled under normal room light for several minutes. Different colors can be proofed for fit by using different screen tint values to represent each color.

Blueprint, diazo, and instant image proofs can all be used to check imposition for jobs that involve image alignment on both sides of a press sheet. Most papers can be purchased from the manufacturer with both sides sensitized. The first flat to be proofed is positioned on the paper, small notches that line up with the center lines of the flat are cut—or the proofing material is punched with the same punch system used for flats—and an exposure is made. The proofing paper is then turned over, the center lines of the second flat are placed in line with the small notches, and the second exposure is made. Once processed, the proof can be folded or cut to approximate the final job. If paper that is sensitized on both sides is not available, two separate sheets can be glued together for the same effect.

Multiple-Color Photomechanical Proofing

It is possible to proof some types of multicolor jobs, such as jobs requiring flat color (see chapter 3), on a single-color photomechanical proofing material by varying the exposure time for each color. The intensity of the image recorded varies with exposure time. Thus, if each color is exposed with a different exposure time, each color records as a different shade. Similar effects can be achieved by using various screen tint values to expose each color on a single-color proofing material. Both of these techniques for showing color are acceptable for checking registration and the fit of one image with another. They are not widely used, however, because the customer usually prefers seeing proofs in color.

While registration and fit are important to the printer, the designer or customer is interested primarily in what the job will look like after printing. Thus, multicolor proofing is typically used to proof the job in color so the printer and the customer can predict how the colors—whether flat or process—will appear on the final press sheet. Therefore, the proofing system's ability to produce an image that is as close as possible to the image that will print on the final press sheet is important. A press proof can provide a nearly exact reproduction of the image that will print during the press run. Photomechanical color proofs cannot do this because they are rarely made from the paper that is used in the press run and because they use colored emulsions or colored toners, rather than process inks, to produce colors. Photomechanical color proofing materials can be classified as either transparent or opaque based.

Transparent Color Proofs

Transparent color proofs are generally formed from separate sheets of clear-based plastic (each carrying one color image) that are positioned one on top the other so that the total effect approximates the printed job. Many companies produce transparent proofing materials. One commonly used product is Color-Key, which is manufactured by the 3M Company. Color-Key sheets are negative or positive acting. They produce transparent colors on a clear polyester backing. The sheets are exposed to a high-intensity light source with the emulsion of the negative or positive proofed against the base side of the proofing sheet. The image is processed with a special 3M Color-Key developer, rinsed in water, and allowed to air dry (figure 10.44). When used for proofing four-color process negatives, the exposed and developed sheets are sandwiched yellow first, then magenta, cyan, and black last. Each sheet is placed in register with the previous sheet and is fastened on one side to hold all of the sheets in register. One advantage of transparent proofs is that the potential press sheet can be placed under the transparent sandwich of colors to approximate the appearance of the final job. One disadvantage of this type of proofing system is that the proof takes on a color cast from the polyester backing.

Opaque Color Proofs

Opaque color proofs are generally prepared by adhering, exposing, and developing each

1. Place Color-Key in exposure unit.

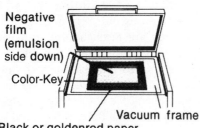

Negative film (emulsion side down)

Color-Key

Vacuum frame

Black or goldenrod paper

2. Expose solid 4 to 5 step on grey scale.

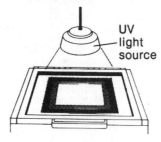

UV light source

3. Place exposed pad around special on level glass.

Glass should feel slightly cool (surface temperature of 70°F to 80°F)

4. Wrap Webril proof pad around special Color-Key developing block.

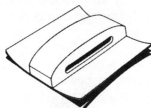

5. Pour negative Color-Key developer smoothly.

Spread immediately with light, sweeping motion.

6. Begin development.

Use light, figure-8 motion to remove *most* background coating.

7. Turn fresh side of pad out.

8. Finish development.

Use moderate pressure and tight, circular motion.

9. Rinse both sides.

70°F to 80°F

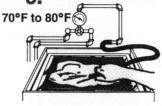

Firmly squeegee uncoated side.

10. Blot dry with newsprint or other absorbent paper.

Figure 10.44.   Processing steps for 3M Color-Key negative material.
Courtesy of Printing Products Division, 3M Company.

color emulsion on a special solid-based sheet successively. A typical product is Cromalin, which is manufactured by the DuPont Corporation. The Cromalin system uses a patented laminator to apply a special photopolymer to the proof stock. The laminated sheet is then exposed through a film positive by using a conventional platemaking system. After exposure, the top mylar protective layer is removed and the entire sheet is dusted with a color toner, which is accepted only by the exposed areas. The dry toners are available in a wide variety of colors and usually can be mixed to match any press ink color. After all surplus toner powder has been removed, the proof sheet can be relaminated and exposed to additional flats to produce other color images on the same sheet.

It is important that all color proofs be viewed under a common light source. Any variation in color temperature, light intensity, amount of reflected room light, evenness of illumination, or surrounding color environment changes human judgment concerning color values. Many problems result when the printer and the customer use two different light sources or viewing situations to view color proofs. In the industry 5,000° K color temperature emitted from an artificial source is generally accepted as the standard for color viewing. Several companies have developed color viewing systems that meet the industry's specifications (figure 10.45).

Digital Proofing

Digital proofing is a relatively new development in color proofing that promises to overcome some of the limitations of transparent and opaque color proofs. With **digital proofing,** digitized color separations are sent electronically from a color scanner or a graphics workstation to a proofing mechanism that makes a color proof directly from the digitized infor-

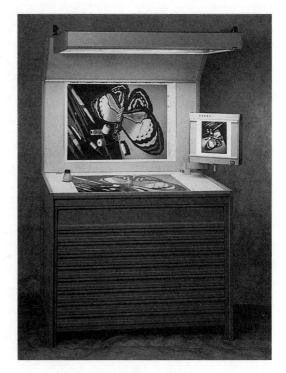

Figure 10.45. Example of a color viewer.
Courtesy of GTI Graphic Technology, Inc.

mation (figure 10.46). The device operates by recording the digitized image as electronic charges on an image carrier, which is typically a chrome drum. The charged areas of the drum then cause a liquid color solution to be transferred to a sheet of paper in a process similar to xerography (see chapter 1).

Digitized proofing can provide process color proofs for four-color process printing that are remarkably similar in color to those that are produced during the actual press run. As just mentioned, they have several advantages over transparent or opaque proofing materials. The liquid color solution can be formulated to duplicate process colors produced by press inks, and the sheet of the paper that the job is proofed on can be the same stock that is used in the final press run. As a result, color fidelity is quite

Figure 10.46.   Digital color proofing. This digital color proofing system can produce up to four 30 inch ×
40 inch proofs an hour.
Courtesy of Eastman Kodak Company, Graphic Imaging Systems Division.

high. That is, the colors on the proof are "true" to the colors that are produced on the press. In addition, because digital proofing requires no camera work, this process is faster than any photomechanical proofing process when several proofs have to be made.

Key Terms

stripping	work-and-turn imposition	master flat
flat	lead edge	snap fitter and dowel method
proofing	work-and-tumble imposition	prepunched tab strip
mechanical line-up table	cylinder line	method
masking sheets	plate cylinder	punch and register pin
actinic light	gripper margin	method
opaque	pinholes	blueline flat method
imposition	complementary flats	single master flat method
signature imposition	common edge method	sighting tube

traveling mask
press proof
photomechanical proofs

blueprint paper
diazo paper
instant image proof paper

transparent color proofs
opaque color proofs
digital proofing

Questions for Review

1. What is the task of the industrial stripper?

2. What is the purpose of the masking sheet when preparing a negative flat?

3. What does the term "imposition" mean?

4. What is a signature?

5. What does the cylinder line represent on a flat?

6. Why can no image be printed in the gripper margin?

7. What is the purpose of opaquing a film negative?

8. What is the purpose of etching a film negative?

9. What are some advantages stripping film positives has over stripping film negatives?

10. Why must a halftone negative be mounted in a window on the flat so that the halftone emulsion is facing in the same direction as the emulsion on the negative that carries the window?

11. What are complementary flats?

12. Briefly describe how to use the punch and register pin technique to control registration from the camera to the press.

13. What are the two basic approaches of multiflat stripping for process color work?

14. Differentiate between a key flat and a master flat for multiflat stripping for process color work.

15. What is the purpose of proofing?

16. What are two common types of single-color, photomechanical proofing?

17. What are the two basic groups of multicolor photomechanical proofs?

CHAPTER

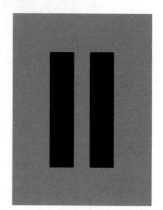

Offset Platemaking

Anecdote to Chapter Eleven

In 1789 a law student at the University of Ingolstadt in Bavaria, Germany, named Alois Senefelder, wrote a play entitled *Die Maedchenkenner* and had it published. After all printing costs were subtracted, Senefelder made a sizable profit from his play and became convinced he would make his fortune on the stage. Senefelder is little known to us today as a playwright, but he is widely recognized as the inventor of lithography.

After *Die Maedchenkenner,* Senefelder's plays were not well received, and he lost money. He was convinced, however, that it was not the quality of his writing but rather the high cost of the printing that strained his finances. After viewing printers at work one day, Senefelder decided printing was a simple task and resolved to learn the craft so he might write, print, and publish his own works. The printing process common where Senefelder lived was copperplate engraving. In this process, the images to be printed were carved in reverse into soft copper plates with a flexible steel tool.

Senefelder purchased the necessary tools and materials and began to learn the printer's craft. He soon learned that it was not as simple as he had assumed. He made many errors, which required him to purchase new copper plates. The number of errors and the cost of replacement copper were so great that Senefelder was driven to invent a correction fluid to fill in his mistakes. (The fluid was made from three parts wax and one part soap which were mixed with a small quantity of lampblack and dissolved in rain water.)

Unfortunately, Senefelder's skills and finances were so small that he could not afford to continue practicing on actual copper plates even with his correction fluid. He tried inexpensive tin as a substitute, but his resources continued to dwindle.

By chance Senefelder learned of a material called Kellhein stone—a limestone quarried at a local site. Kellhein stone had the unique quality that slabs of nearly any thickness could be cut easily. Kellhein stone, unlike copper, could be polished to a perfect surface

Alois Senefelder.
Courtesy of Smithsonian Institution, Photo No. 10577A.

with little effort. Senefelder resolved to practice writing in reverse on Kellhein stone to develop the skill necessary to be able to return to copper. The stage was set for a discovery. Senefelder relates in his book:

> I had just succeeded in my little laboratory in polishing a stone plate, which I intended to cover with etching ground, in order to continue my exercises in writing backwards, when my mother entered the room, and desired me to write her a bill

for the washerwoman, who was waiting for the linen; I happened not to have even the smallest slip of paper at hand, as my little stock of paper had been entirely exhausted by taking proof impressions from the stones; nor was there even a drop of ink in the inkstand. As the matter would not admit of delay, and we had nobody in the house to send for a supply of the deficient materials, I resolved to write the list with my ink prepared with wax, soap, and lampblack, on the stone which I had just polished, and from which I could copy it at leisure.[1]

An idea resulted from that experience. Making a border of wax around the Kellhein stone, Senefelder allowed an acid solution to stand on the entire stone surface for a short period of time and thereby etch away the limestone in any areas on which he had not drawn an image. The wax writing solution resisted the acid. After Senefelder removed the acid from the stone, he found that the coated, or image, areas were raised about 1/10 inch above the rest of the stone. By carefully rolling ink over the surface, he could ink only the image area and easily transfer this ink to a sheet of paper with a little pressure.

Senefelder had invented an adaptation of the relief process—printing from a raised surface. Because of the low cost of the stone, the ease of creating an image, and the simplicity of transferring the image to paper, Senefelder felt he could compete easily with local printers for jobs. He contracted with several people, notably music sellers, to produce musical scores, and he continued to experiment with his invention.

Senefelder called his invention "lithography," based on the Greek words *lithos*, meaning stone, and *graphein*, meaning to write. Although his discovery was a significant

---

[1]Alois Senefelder, *A Complete Course of Lithography,* reprint of 1819 edition (New York: DeCapo Press, 1968), p. 9.

advance beyond copperplate engraving or even hand-set relief type, Senefelder's greatest contribution was refining what he called "chemical lithography."

After several years of experimentation, Senefelder observed that a solution of gum (gum arabic) and water, when coated over the stone, would clog the pores in the stone and repel ink. As long as the gum-water mixture remained moist, an ink brayer rolled over the entire stone surface would deposit pigment only in the image area on the stone. By alternately moistening and inking the stone, Senefelder could build up a layer of pigment sufficient to transfer a perfect image to a sheet of paper.

It is this concept that moisture and ink repell each other that is the basis for all contemporary lithographic printing.

Objectives for Chapter 11

After completing this chapter you will be able to:

- Describe the basic components of a platemaker.
- Explain what is meant by actinic light and tell why platemakers produce this type of light.
- Explain how a sensitivity guide can be used to calibrate a platemaker.
- Explain why offset plates are grained.
- Explain the basic components of light-sensitive coating for offset plates.
- Differentiate between negative-acting and positive-acting plates.
- List the steps involved in processing an additive lithographic plate.
- List the steps involved in processing a subtractive lithographic plate.
- Describe the construction of a deep-etch plate.
- Explain how a diffusion transfer lithographic plate is exposed and processed.
- Discuss the processes used to make projection plates.
- Explain the operation of a step-and-repeat platemaking system.
- Describe the on-press, direct-to-plate process.

Introduction

The preparation and printing of most modern metal plates used in lithographic printing is based on the original concepts of stone printing developed by Senefelder nearly two hundred years ago. Senefelder's invention was intended and used as an industrial process. Printers used this technique to reproduce images such as advertisements, business forms, maps, and many other printed products.

Lithography developed a reputation as a fine arts process in America through the products of the Currier and Ives Company that operated from 1835 to 1895. Today, stone lithography remains an art process. Historically it has formed the foundation for a major portion of the commercial printing industry. A brief review of the steps taken by a stone lithographer will help you better understand contemporary industrial techniques.

A slab of lithographic stone (generally limestone) is first cleaned and ground to a perfectly flat surface using a smaller stone and water mixed with carborundum. This process is called **graining.**

Once the stone is grained and dry, the artist-printer begins to draw on its surface with a lithographic grease crayon (a refinement of Senefelder's original correction fluid). This process forms the printing image. Graining creates a slight tooth, or texture, which makes it easier to draw on the stone with the grease crayon. The grease absorbs slightly into the pores of the stone.

A gum arabic solution (generally mixed with a small quantity of nitric acid), called an **etch,** is then worked into the entire stone surface. The gum absorbs into the nonimage areas of the stone and solidifies the grease, or image, areas in a process called etching. **Etching** seals the open parts (nonimage areas) of the stone against grease but keeps these open parts receptive to water. After the crayon residue is removed with turpentine, the stone is ready to print.

A roller of ink is prepared, and a layer of water is wiped on the stone with a damp cloth. The water is repelled by the grease crayon image areas, but it remains in the nonimage or open areas. As the ink roller moves over the stone, the film of water acts as a buffer that repels ink. Wherever there is no water (as on the crayon image), the ink remains.

If a prepared piece of paper is positioned carefully over the stone and pressure is applied, the image on the stone will be transferred to the sheet. A skillful stone lithographer can prepare a stone and pull one print every ten minutes.

Contemporary printers do not print from lithographic stones. Rather than a litho stone, printers use thin aluminium plates. The basic concepts are the same, however, whether using a stone or plate. One important difference is that early lithographers had to create reversed images on the stone, since the paper came directly into contact with the stone surface. Reversing the image on the stone made it right-reading on the paper. Modern lithography creates a right-reading image on the plate. On the press, the plate image is transferred to a blanket (which reverses or offsets it), which then transfers the image to the paper (reversing it again)—hence the term "offset lithography" (see chapter 13).

Equipment for Proofing and Plating

This section introduces the basic equipment used to prepare proofs and offset lithographic plates.

Exposure Systems

Most proofing materials and most offset plates contain photoemulsion surfaces that form images when exposed to light. During platemaking, light passing through a transparent image carrier, such as a film negative or a film positive, strikes the plate or proofing material emulsion. The areas of emulsion that are affected by the light become the image or the nonimage areas, depending upon the type of photoemulsion used on the proofing or plate material. Most proofing materials and offset plates can be exposed in the same type of exposure unit.

Whether exposure systems are used for platemaking, proofing, or daylight-handling film exposures, they are usually referred to as **platemakers.** The simplest exposure system is made up of a vacuum frame and some high-intensity light source. The vacuum frame holds the film or flat in contact with the proofing material, film, or plate; the light source provides

Figure 11.1.   A flip-top platemaker.
Courtesy of nuArc Company, Inc.

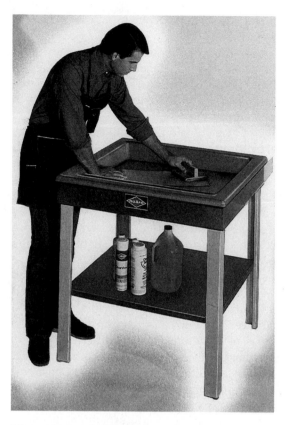

Figure 11.2.   A platemaking sink.
Courtesy of nuArc Company, Inc.

the light needed for exposure. Some platemakers have the vacuum frame and light source set within a cabinet (figure 11.1). In other systems the frame and lights are on rolling stands that can be moved closer together or farther apart, or they can be used as an overhead light source.

Most proofing and plate photoemulsions have peak sensitivity in the blue and ultraviolet end of the visible spectrum and little sensitivity in the remaining areas of the spectrum (see the Light Sources section of Appendix B). Light in the blue and ultraviolet end of the visible spectrum is referred to as **actinic light.** Because most proofing, daylight film, and plate photoemulsions are primarily sensitive to actinic light, they must be handled in a special environment. Most facilities use a yellow filter to block actinic light from normal illumination sources.

The most efficient light sources for exposing proofing materials and offset plates produce light that is high in the actinic end of the spectrum. The two most commonly used light sources for platemaking are metal halide and pulsed xenon. Carbon arc lamps are also sometimes used. However, carbon arc lamps emit fumes and dirt that must be removed from the plateroom with a ventilation system; this is a major disadvantage of carbon arc lamps.

Processing Systems

The equipment for processing printing plates varies. The simplest type of equipment is a

Figure 11.3.   An automatic plate processing unit.
Courtesy of Western Litho Plate and Supply Company.

smooth, slanted, hard surface set in a sink with a water source (figure 11.2). This type of equipment , called a **platemaking sink,** is generally used for hand processing lithographic plates, but it can also be used for developing several types of photomechanical proofs.

Many large companies use automatic processing units that produce plates ready for press without any hand finishing (figure 11.3). Although the specific configuration varies from unit to unit, all automatic systems accept the exposed plate for insertion at one end; use automatic drive rollers for uniform feeding; and deliver a finished, gummed, and dried plate at the other end.

A variety of special purpose platemakers and processing units are designed for use with specific processes (such as an electrostatic platemaker for the electrostatic platemaking process).

Light Source Calibration

Exposure is the most important variable in the plating and proofing processes. The simplest form of platemaker control has a toggle switch that can be plugged into an automatic timer or controlled manually by an operator with a watch. The problem (as with line photography) is that accurate exposure is not necessarily related to time. Variables such as line voltage, light source position, and the age of the lamp can influence exposure. The most accurate tool for controlling exposure is a **light integrator** (figure 11.4). With a phototube sensing unit mounted on the platemaker vacuum frame, the integrator automatically controls the units of light reaching the plate or proof and alters exposure time with any line or light source variation. Such a system ensures that there is no more than a 0.5-percent difference in the amount of light that strikes the plate from any two exposures made at the same time setting.

Whether you use a simple toggle switch system or an integrated system, the initial problem is to determine the quantity of exposure needed to produce a quality plate or proof image. Most plate or proofing material manufacturers provide recommended exposures for general lighting situations. However, the actual exposure differs for each working situation. To calibrate or to determine this actual exposure, you must use a transparent grey scale or sensitivity guide (see chapter 6 for more about grey scales).

The Sensitivity Guide

The **sensitivity guide** is a continuous-tone density scale. (Remember it is a transparent grey scale.) The density of each step on the guide increases from around 0.0 density at step 1 to generally around 3.0 density at the last step. There is generally a 0.15 density difference between steps. The guide passes progressively less light to the plate or proof as the step numbers increase.

In addition to suggesting an exposure, plate or proofing material manufacturers will also indicate which specific step reading the exposure should record on the sensitivity guide.

To determine the actual exposure for a specific working situation, place a test sheet of

Figure 11.4.   A light integrator.
Courtesy of Graphic Arts Manufacturing Co.

the plate or proofing material in the plate-maker, with the emulsion positioned as specified by the manufacturer. Place a sensitivity guide over the sheet with the right-reading side of the transparent grey scale facing the exposure lamp. Mask all other areas of the emulsion with a masking sheet. Make an initial exposure according to the manufacturer's recommendations. Then process the plate or proofing material with appropriate procedures and controls. If the resulting image shows a step reading that is less than required, increase the exposure. If a higher step is recorded, decrease the exposure and run another test. Continue using this trial-and-error technique until the desired step is reached. The exposure that produces the desired step density becomes the actual exposure for that specific material.

For greatest consistency of results, a sensitivity guide should be stripped into the flat in a nonimage area for every plate. Another alternative is to test the exposure with the guide daily. If variation occurs, either each processing step should be reexamined for any variation, or the entire system should be recalibrated. Of course, the test should be rerun every time a new type of plate material is used.

Lithographic Printing Plates

The basis of all industrial lithography today is a combination of photographic principles and Senefelder's original observation that oil and water do not mix. Almost all modern lithographic presses employ the offset principle and use a thin paper, plastic, or metal sheet as an image carrier , called a **plate,** which can be wrapped around the plate cylinder. When prepared for printing, the plate surface consists of two areas: image areas, which repel water (and thus remain dry and accept ink), and nonimage areas, which accept water. Therefore, the basic requirement of almost all lithographic printing plates is the ability to produce a plate surface that has "hydrophobic" image areas; that is, they repel water. The nonimage areas of the plate must be "hydrophilic"; that is, they must accept water. Offset plates differ largely in the methods they use to separate the image from the nonimage areas.

Base Plate Materials

The great majority of plates used in offset lithography are made of thin metal sheets. Metal plate thicknesses range from 0.005 inch to around 0.030 inch, depending on the size of the plate and the type of press. The entire plate must be of uniform thickness, however. It is generally held to a gauge tolerance of 0.0005 inch. Most metals for plates are cold rolled to the final plate gauge or thickness to produce a hard printing surface.

Zinc was the standard plate material of the industry for years, but it has been replaced almost totally by aluminum for all but special purpose plates. Some types of plates are made from materials such as steel, stainless steel, chromium, copper, and even paper, but aluminum enjoys the most widespread use.

Just as Senefelder had to prepare, or grain, the stone surface before an image could be added to it, modern lithographic plates must also be grained. The term "graining" is actually misleading because relatively little roughness is imparted to the surface. On metal surface printing plates, graining is a roughening process that must be performed so that a uniform layer of photoemulsion will adhere to the plate. All graining processes can be classified as either mechanical or chemical.

Mechanical Graining

The simplest form of **mechanical graining** of the plate surface is accomplished by placing the plate in a rotating tub filled with steel ball bearings, water, and some form of abrasive material. Assembly-line techniques have been applied to the process so that a continuous row of plates passes under a series of nylon brushes with a spray of water and pumice. Sandblasting has also been used, but this procedure presents some problems because small pieces of abrasive become embedded in the metal plate surface.

Chemical Graining

Chemical graining of lithographic plates is similar to Senefelder's first trial acid etch of a piece of stone. The plate is submerged in an acid bath that creates surface roughness. One chemical graining technique uses an electrolytic reaction in a solution of hydrofluoric acid to create surface roughness on the plate. Almost all presensitized surface plates (see following sections) are formed from anodized aluminum. The surface is treated chemically and then sealed. The anodized surface is unaffected by almost all acids but remains water receptive.

Coating Materials

All photosensitive lithographic metal plates have a photoemulsion surface consisting of some form of light-sensitive material combined with a collodion coated on a grained metal surface. A **collodion** is an organic compound that forms a strong, continuous layer. When mixed with the light-sensitive solution and then exposed to light, the **colloid** or emulsion becomes insoluble and forms a strong, continuous coating on the printing plate. Gum arabic is a collodion commonly used in many emulsions. It is also used for a variety of other purposes in the lithographic process, such as in press fountain solution (see chapter 13) and as a protective coating over finished plates.

Ammonium bichromate combined with egg albumin was used previously as the photoemulsion in the photolithography process. Albumin has been replaced gradually by other solutions, however, until now it is very nearly obsolete. Popular industrial coatings today are polyvinyl alcohol (PVA), diazo, and photopolymers.

Classifying Lithographic Plates

Lithographic plates can be classified in several ways. The most common method is to group them according to structure and action.

Lithographic plate structure can be described as surface or deep etch. **Surface plates** can be visualized as being formed from a colloid sitting on the surface of the metal (figure 11.5). **Deep-etch plates** are formed when the colloid material bonds into the plate surface (figure 11.6). There are, of course, special purpose plates that defy classification.

A second way to classify lithographic plates is by action. Almost all industrial lithography uses the photographic process to produce the image area on the plate. Plate emulsions can be formulated for use with either film negatives or film positives. When the plate image is formed by passing light through the clear or image areas of a negative, the plate is called **negative acting**. When a positive is used to expose the plate, the plate is called **pos-**

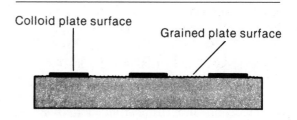

Figure 11.5.   Cross section of a lithographic surface plate

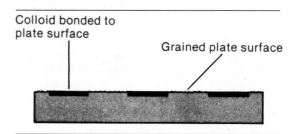

Figure 11.6.   Cross section of a lithographic deep-etch plate

itive acting. Plate action is not necessarily associated with plate structure, however. Surface plates can be designed for use with either film negatives or film positives, but only film positives can be used with deep-etch plates.

Surface Plates

Direct Image Nonphotographic Surface Plates

The **direct image nonphotographic surface plate** is the closest remaining industrial link to the original Senefelder craft. Most current direct image base materials are either paper, acetate, plastic-impregnated paper, or thin aluminum foil adhered to a paper base. Whatever the base, however, almost all of these types of plates have surfaces that are treated chemically to be especially grease receptive. For that reason, dirty or moist fingers that touch these plates reproduce fingerprints or smudges on the printed sheet.

Any oil-based substance can adhere to the surface of a direct image plate. Images may be hand drawn with a lithographic crayon, a pencil, a pen and brush, or even a ballpoint pen. Probably the most common process is to type directly on the plate using the carbon ribbon in an electric typewriter.

When the direct image plate is actually run, it is placed on the press and a special liquid etch is rubbed into its surface. The etch serves to make the image areas somewhat permanent and the nonimage areas water receptive.

The quality of direct image nonphotographic plates ranges according to the potential length of run of the plates. The most inexpensive plates are projected to yield a maximum of fifty press sheets before the plate image begins to break down. The highest-quality plates produce up to five thousand quality copies.

Direct image plates do not enjoy widespread industrial use because of their frailty and the manual preparation required.

Wipe-On Surface Plates

The **wipe-on metal surface plate** is a refinement of the early attempts to sensitize a lithographic stone with a photographic emulsion. To make this type of plate, an emulsion is hand or machine coated onto a pregrained plate immediately prior to plate exposure.

The base material in this process usually is either aluminum or zinc. All wipe-on surface plates are supplied to the printer with a fine-grain surface and are treated with a protective coating that acts as a link between the future emulsion coating and the base metal. The emulsion is generally mixed in small quantities shortly before it is applied to the pregrained plate. All current emulsions are formed by mixing a dry diazo powder and a liquid base.

There are two techniques for coating the light-sensitive emulsion onto a wipe-on surface plate: by hand or with a mechanical roller. With the hand process, the emulsion is applied with a damp sponge (or cheesecloth). The goal is to place a fairly uniform layer of emulsion over every portion of the plate surface.

The mechanical roller approach for wipe-on plates employs a dual roller device (figure 11.7). As the plate passes between the two rollers, a perfectly uniform layer of emulsion is distributed over one side of the plate. The gap between the rollers can be adjusted to apply the desired thickness of emulsion on the plates. There is no problem with coating consistency or streaking with this process, two major difficulties with the hand process.

Almost all lithographic plates now used for production are negative acting (some positive-acting plates are currently used as image carriers for press proofing). Most wipe-on surface plates are exposed through a film negative, using a vacuum frame and a high-intensity light source. Specific exposure times vary according to the individual plate and emulsion combination and the working environment. Manufacturers' specifications should always be followed.

Wipe-on plates are processed by one of two methods. The first technique involves two steps. A pool of desensitizer gum is first poured onto the wipe-on plate and is rubbed into the entire plate surface with a damp sponge. The gum solution serves the dual function of removing any unexposed emulsion and making the nonprinting area water receptive. Any excess gum solution is removed. A second solution, made primarily of lacquer, is then rubbed over the entire plate. Finally, the plate is washed with water.

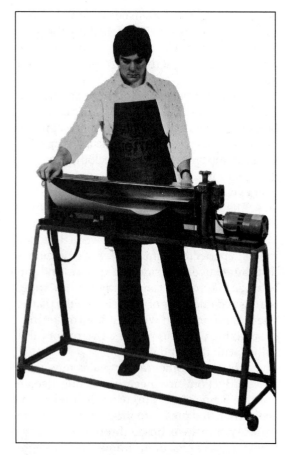

Figure 11.7.   Coating a wipe-on surface plate with a mechanical roller.
Courtesy of Western Litho Plate and Supply Company

The image area of the wipe-on plate, which hardened during exposure, would theoretically accept ink and could be used on the printing press. However, adhering a layer of lacquer to the exposed areas of the wipe-on plate greatly increases the number of copies that can be made from the plate. The lacquer strengthens the image bond to the plate. With the two-step process, a final layer of desensitizer gum is generally buffed into the entire

surface of the plate until it is dry. This last step serves to protect the plate until the job is run on the press and also ensures that all unexposed emulsion is removed.

The second alternative wipe-on processing technique involves one step in which a lacquer developer removes the unexposed emulsion while the lacquer adheres to the image areas. After the plate is washed with water, it is buffed with a coating of gum arabic until its entire surface is dry.

Presensitized Surface Plates

Presensitized surface plates are by far the plates most widely used for commercial offset lithography. These plates are called "presensitized" because they are supplied from the manufacturer with the emulsion surface already coated on the metal base. The first presensitized metal plates were introduced by the 3M Company in 1950. Since that time, many other manufacturers have developed similar plates.

Presensitized plates offer several advantages. Because they are precoated with a photoemulsion, the platemaker need not be concerned with mixing and wiping on the emulsion, or using and maintaining emulsion-coating equipment. Presensitized plates are used by the platemaker directly from the manufacturer's wrapper with no surface preparation. In addition, the plates are processed with ease, have reasonably long shelf lives (generally up to six months), and can be produced for high-quality, long-run press situations.

The base material for presensitized plates can be paper, aluminum foil laminated to paper, or a sheet of aluminum. Paper and foil plates are generally used only for very short-run jobs. As discussed previously, the presensitized metal plates are typically grained and then anodized. Aluminum plates can be sensitized on one or both sides.

Almost all presensitized emulsion-coating materials used today contain diazo. The specific makeup of the solution varies from manufacturer to manufacturer, but the primary ingredient of all solution types is nitrogen. When the plate emulsion is exposed to a sufficient quantity of light, the nitrogen is released from the solution and the material becomes insensitive to additional light. The insensitive emulsion then can readily accept dyes that become the printing, ink-receptive surfaces.

Presensitized plates are available in a wide range of capabilities, from plates that handle short runs of less than 1,000 copies to emulsions that can easily produce as many as 300,000 impressions. With their anodized metal surfaces, diazo emulsions, and mass production techniques, presensitized plates compete easily in quality and cost with other types of surface plates.

In addition to being either negative or positive acting, presensitized plates can also be classified as additive or subtractive. Recall that for wipe-on plates a lacquer is adhered to the image areas to increase the plate's potential life. The lacquer, then, is the surface that actually accepts the ink. The same concept is used when preparing the image areas for presensitized plates. When the printer applies a lacquer-like material to the image areas during plate processing, the presensitized plate is **additive.** When the printing surface is built into the emulsion by the manufacturer and the printer merely desensitizes the unexposed areas, the plate is **subtractive.**

Processing Additive Plates

Additive plates can be processed with a two- or a one-step technique. With the two-step technique, the plate, after exposure, is first desensitized with a gum-acid solution. The chemical is distributed over the plate with a moist sponge to remove the emulsion and/or make the unexposed emulsion area water receptive. The entire plate is then rubbed with a gum-water-lacquer mixture (plate developer) to build up the image areas. Finally, the plate is washed, squeegeed, coated with a light layer of gum arabic, and buffed dry (figure 11.8). With the one-step technique, the desensitizer (the gum-acid solution) and lacquer-developer functions are combined. The plate is developed with that single solution and is then washed, squeegeed, gummed, and buffed dry.

Processing Subtractive Plates

Negative-acting presensitized emulsions are exposed by light passing through the open or image areas of a film negative. With negative-acting subtractive plates, only one developing step is taken. After exposure, a special developer that is supplied by the plate manufacturer is used to remove the unexposed lacquer emulsion that was added during the presensitizing process. Again, the plate is washed and squeegeed. Often, a special subtractive gum must be used to coat and protect the plate for storage (figure 11.9).

Positive-acting presensitized plates are exposed by light passing through the open or nonimage areas of a film positive. As mentioned earlier, positive-acting presensitized plates can be classified as either additive or subtractive. In general, after exposure, the exposed emulsion of a positive-acting additive plate is removed by wiping it with a special developer supplied by the manufacturer. The unexposed or image area remains in place. The developing action is then halted by a fixing agent. As with negative-acting additive plates, lacquer is rubbed into the positive-acting plate. The lacquer adheres to the image areas and increases the potential length of the press run. After the plate is washed and squeegeed, it is coated with gum arabic and buffed dry. Positive-acting subtractive plates are processed in a similar manner, but without the lacquer step.

When using both sides

1 Expose both sides.

2 Clamp plate over pad of paper.

3 Desensitize plate.

Scrub entire surface.

4 Sponge off excess.

A thin film should remain.

5 Pour developer required.

Soak developer into pad.

6 Rub up image.

Use *firm* circular motion over *entire* surface.

7 Sponge off excess developer.

8 Apply final gum.

Polish dry with disposable wipe.

9 Replace paper beneath plate.

Turn plate over.
Repeat processing steps 2 through 8 for second side.

10 Store plate in hanging position.

If stacked, slip–sheet to prevent scratching or contamination.

Figure 11.8.   Processing additive lithographic surface plates.
Courtesy of Printing Products Division 3M Company.

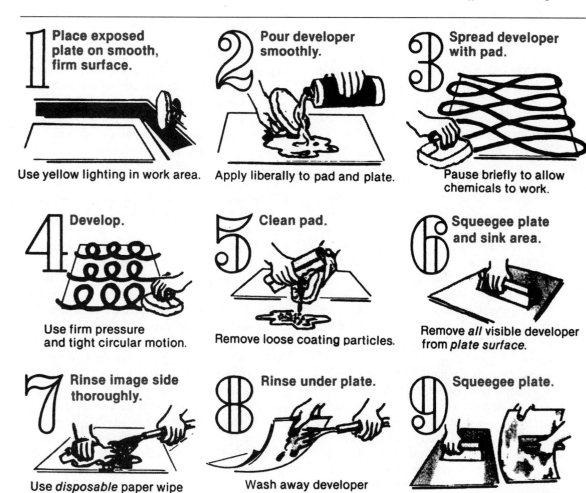

1 Place exposed plate on smooth, firm surface.

Use yellow lighting in work area.

2 Pour developer smoothly.

Apply liberally to pad and plate.

3 Spread developer with pad.

Pause briefly to allow chemicals to work.

4 Develop.

Use firm pressure and tight circular motion.

5 Clean pad.

Remove loose coating particles.

6 Squeegee plate and sink area.

Remove *all* visible developer from *plate surface*.

7 Rinse image side thoroughly.

Use *disposable* paper wipe to mop surface while rinsing.

8 Rinse under plate.

Wash away developer and sensitizers.

9 Squeegee plate.

Face   Backside

10 Gum plate.
- Place plate on dry surface.
- Dry plate if still wet.
- Pour on liberal amount of gum.
- Spread with disposable wipe.

- Buff dry with fresh disposable wipe.
- Turn plate over on clean dry surface.
- Dry backside with wipe.

Storage – Slip-sheet processed plates to prevent scratching or contamination.

Figure 11.9. Processing subtractive lithographic surface plates.
Courtesy of Printing Products Division 3M Company.

Presensitized Photopolymer Surface Plates

One disadvantage of presensitized surface plates that have diazo emulsions is that they cannot be used for extremely long press runs. Until the development of presensitized **photopolymer plates,** only deep-etch or bimetal plates (bimetal plates are no longer popular and are not discussed in this chapter) could be used for offset press runs of a million or more copies. When exposed and processed properly, photopolymer emulsions on presensitized plates produce image areas that are extremely hard and wear resistant, which means that they can be used for press runs that are much longer than plates with diazo emulsions. At the same time, the exposure and development process for photopolymer emulsions is far less involved and less time consuming than that for deep-etch or bimetal plates.

Negative-acting photopolymer emulsions consist of molecules called **monomers.** When exposed to actinic light, these monomers link and cross-link with each other chemically to form polymers. **Polymers** can be thought of as complex chains of monomers that are linked so strongly that they behave as one hard, wear-resistant molecule. Photopolymer plates are developed in a manner similar to presensitized diazo emulsion plates. The developer removes the unexposed plate coating but leaves the exposed coating (image area) on the plate.

Positive-acting photopolymer plates can be baked in large ovens for a specific time, at a specific temperature. The baking firmly adheres the image to the plate surface, as well as adheres a special baking gum to the nonimage portions of the plate. Plate life of more than one million impressions is possible. Newer, negative-acting photopolymer plates are now available that reach this plate life without the need for baking.

Deep-Etch Plates

The basic concept of the deep-etch plate is that of a stencil formed on the plate that covers the nonimage areas with a resist but leaves image areas as open base metal that can be etched with a special solution. A resist is a chemically inert material that protects nonimage portions of the plate from acid. Two types of coating materials are commonly used to form the stencil: a bichromate gum solution and a bichromate PVA formulation. The gum compound provides greater exposure latitude, but the PVA is easier to process.

The base material for deep-etch plates can be aluminum, zinc, or even stainless steel. The plate is fine grained by a mechanical or a chemical process. Some manufacturers have refined techniques that can use an anodized aluminum plate surface. Some types of deep-etch plates can be regrained after one use and used a second time with no decrease in image quality.

After the base plate is coated with the light-sensitive emulsion, a right-reading film positive is registered with the carrier in a vacuum frame and a high-intensity light source is projected through the clear, or nonimage, areas on the positive. The actinic light hardens the emulsion in the nonimage areas. In the image areas, however, no light reaches the plate and the coating remains soft.

There is basically only one category of deep-etch plates. The emulsion areas of all deep-etch plates are bonded or etched into the base metal—unlike surface plates, where the emulsion is merely adhered to the plate surface. This characteristic permits a deep-etch plate to hold more ink than any other type of lithographic plate. The result is a greater ink density on the printed sheet. Halftones appear more brilliant and with superb tonal range representation.

Deep-etch plates are unrivaled for high-quality, extremely long run press jobs. Runs of 500,000 impressions are common, and longer editions have been printed on quality machines run by experienced craftspeople.

Special Purpose Lithographic Plates and Platemaking Systems

Not all classification systems are all inclusive. This section discusses plates that do not fit into previous categories.

Diffusion Transfer Plates

Diffusion transfer plates are formed from a light-sensitive coating on an intermediate carrier that is exposed and then transferred to the actual printing plate.

Recall from chapter 6 that the diffusion transfer process is used to produce quality opaque positives (either enlarged, reduced, or same size) from positive opaque originals on a process camera. The copy is positioned on the copyboard and the reproduction size and camera exposure are adjusted. A sheet of diffusion transfer negative material is placed on the filmboard and an exposure is made. A sheet of receiver paper is then positioned emulsion to emulsion with the negative and both are passed through an activator bath. After a short period of time the sheets are separated. A positive image forms on the opaque receiver sheet and the sheeet is ready for paste-up.

The advantage of the diffusion transfer plate technique is that the usual film and stripping steps are bypassed because the intermediate sheet can be exposed in a process camera or contact print frame, or even on a special purpose electronic scanner. Several types of transfer systems are available commercially. The PMT (photomechanical transfer) Metal Litho Plate by the Eastman Kodak Company is one example.

In the diffusion transfer platemaking process, an aluminum plate can be substituted for the paper receiver sheet. The fine-grained plate need only be fixed and gummed before it is placed on the press. The plate can produce up to 25,000 press copies with a quality that rivals a medium-run presensitized metal plate.

Electrostatic Plates

The process of making **electrostatic transfer plates** is based on the concept of xerographic image reproduction. The idea is commonplace in the office copier now marketed by the Xerox Corporation and others. The basic electrostatic platemaking procedure involves light striking a photoresponsive surface that has been charged with static electricity (hence the name "electrostatic") to form an image.

In practice, some type of material is coated (selenium and zinc oxide compounds are two patented coverings) on the electrostatic plate and the material is then positively charged. When light (generally reflected light through a type of process camera) strikes the plate, the positive charge is lost in the nonimage areas, which leaves only the image area positively charged. The remaining charged image area is then dusted with negatively charged resin powder. The powder, which clings only to the image area, is then fused to the plate to be run on lithographic presses (figure 11.10).

One interesting feature of the electrostatic system is that corrections can be made directly on the plate. The negative pole of a magnet is used to remove the resin powder from unwanted areas before the powder is fused to the plate. Resin powder can also be added in areas where it was not deposited during the initial process.

Several manufacturers have developed plate materials that can carry the photoresponsive surface directly. One such manufacturer, the Addressograph-Multigraph Corporation,

Photosensitive lithographic
plate, positively (+) charged

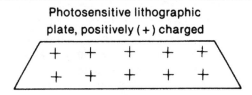

Reflected light

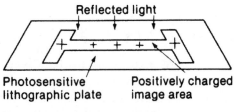

Photosensitive
lithographic plate

Positively charged
image area

Exposure

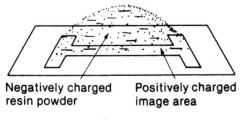

Negatively charged
resin powder

Positively charged
image area

Dusting

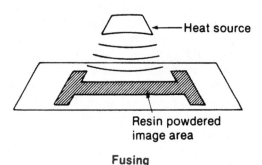

Heat source

Resin powdered
image area

Fusing

Figure 11.10.   Electrostatic printing process.
Electrostatic printing uses a positively charged image to attract negatively charged resin powder. The resin powder is then fused in place with heat.

Figure 11.11.   A lithographic printing system with an electrostatic platemaker.
Courtesy of Multigraphics, a Division of AM International, Inc.

has linked an electrostatic platemaker to an offset lithographic press. The original copy is inserted in the copier, and the plate is prepared automatically and delivered to the plate cylinder by a belt delivery system that attaches it to the press. The press automatically runs the required number of sheets, removes the plate, cleans the blanket cylinder, and turns the whole system off (figure 11.11).

The electrostatic process is receiving widespread acceptance for automatic systems in the printing industry. Although intended for low- to medium-quality short runs (up to five thousand copies), the low cost of the electrostatic system makes it a viable platemaking alternative for many printers who print one color of ink, usually black, on standard sheet sizes (8 1/2 inches × 11 inches or 8 1/2 inches × 14 inches).

Recent developments have linked a computer and page-description software to an electrostatic platemaker. This topic is discussed later in this chapter.

Projection Plates

There are two basic types of **projection platemaking** devices in common use.

Small Projection Plate Systems

Small projection platemaking systems are often used in quick-print or in-plant operations to reproduce one original on one printing plate for short-run applications. Small projection platemaking systems are intended for work where short-run, low- to medium-quality copies are to be run on presses set up for a standard paper size. Most projection plates for these systems are designed to receive an image directly from a positive original by using a special camera-platemaker. In practice, an opaque, camera-ready original is mounted on the copyboard. Light reflected from the original passes through a lens which can enlarge or reduce the copy size. Most systems store the plate material in roll form and automatically advance and cut the required plate length prior to exposure. Plate development is accomplished automatically in the camera-platemaker.

The camera lights for projection plates do not produce the intense actinic light characteristic of platemakers. As a result, projection plates contain silver halide emulsions that react to light more quickly than do the diazo or bichromate solutions used for most plate photoemulsions. Small projection plate systems often use paper or plastic as the plate base material. Plastic is generally used for projection plates requiring higher resolution capabilities or longer press runs than paper bases provide.

A typical projection speed plate is structured with four separate layers: the bottom base material, a developer emulsion layer, a sensitized emulsion layer, and a top fogged emulsion layer. The reflected light passes through the top emulsion layer and exposes the sensitized emulsion layer. Where light does not reflect from the copy (the image areas), the emulsion remains unexposed. The plate is then passed through a bath that activates the bottom chemical layer and causes the developer to begin to travel toward the top fogged layer. The exposed portions of the second, sensitized emulsion layer exhaust the developer, and the process halts in the nonimage areas. Where the sensitized emulsion in the second layer was not exposed, the developer is allowed to pass to the top fogged area where it changes the fogged layer to black metallic silver. Finally, the plate is delivered through a stop-bath, which halts the entire developing process.

The top surface of the plate, then, is made up of a hardened image area that is ink receptive and an undeveloped, nonimage area that is water receptive. Most direct image photographic plate systems are totally automatic, self-contained units that deliver finished plates within seconds after the exposure has been made.

The advantages of this technique are speed and low cost. The entire film-stripping operation is eliminated because no film is made. The position of the original on the exposure unit determines the position of the image on the plate.

Larger Projection Plate Systems

A second type of projection platemaking system is designed to expose metal-based projection plates. These systems are used in book, newspaper, and directory work where single-color page images must be imposed into signatures of several pages. These projection platemaking systems combine stripping, imposition, and platemaking in one operation. Rather than photographically reproducing each original directly on a single plate through a camera lens, these systems record a number of opaque originals onto photographic film from which the images are exposed in the

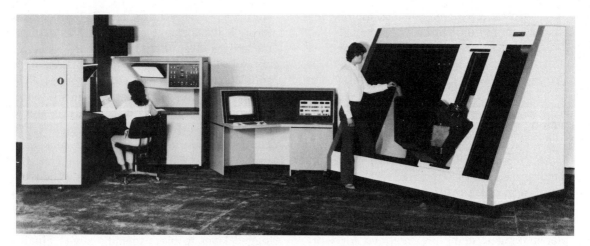

Figure 11.12. **A projection platemaker.** This direct-to-plate projection system eliminates mechanical make-up and stripping. With this system copy can be plated up to 90 percent faster than through traditional operations. Courtesy of Rachwal Systems.

correct imposition onto a plate to make up a signature. In practice, opaque originals of each page in a job are photographed as individual frames on a roll of photographic film. As each original page is photographed, a code is included with each frame to indicate the sequence of the frame in the job. The film is then processed and loaded into a projection platemaker, where it is exposed one frame at a time, directly onto a printing plate. In most systems the plate exposure unit is mounted on a carriage that moves across the plate. A computer is used to control image placement so that the correct frames are exposed on the plate in the correct imposition (figure 11.12).

Because projection platemaking combines stripping and platemaking in one operation, it greatly increases the speed with which images can be plated. A typical newspaper page, for example, can be assembled and plated in a few minutes. In addition, because image placement is controlled by computer, image location and imposition problems can be virtually eliminated.

Step-and-Repeat Platemaking

Often a number of identical images must be placed on a single printing plate. One solution is to prepare a separate mechanical layout for each image and gang them all on one illustration board. A second method is to prepare only one original image but produce a film conversion for each desired plate image. All pieces of film can then be stripped onto one flat. Unfortunately, both of these methods would take far too much time. To meet the need of identical, multiple-plate images, the industry has developed the step-and-repeat platemaker (figure 11.13).

With **step-and-repeat platemaking**, one paste-up and film conversion is prepared. The single negative (or positive) is then masked and fitted into a special frame or chase. When the chase is inserted in the step-and-repeat platemaker, the device can be manually or automatically moved to each required position on the plate where an exposure is made. During each exposure, all areas of the plate except

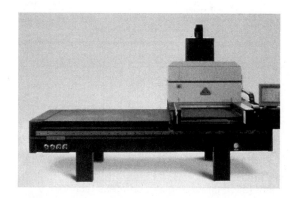

Figure 11.13.   **A step-and-repeat platemaker.**
Courtesy of Rola Zenith Corporation.

the portion under the chase are covered and receive no light.

Image exposure and placement is computer controlled on most modern step-and-repeat platemaking systems. With computer-controlled systems, information about plate and press sheet size and the number and positions of images to be repeated is preprogrammed into a computer. The computer causes the carriage that carries the chase to automatically position the chase, make the exposure, then reposition the chase in the next required location. Step-and-repeat operations are used typically to print labels and for other printing jobs where the printing of several duplicate images on a single press sheet is the most efficient procedure.

Direct-to-Plate Systems

Chapter 10 spent a great deal of time discussing the stripping process. For years the stripping department was where every job came together. The stripper assembled the work of the designer, the typesetter, the mechanical paste-up person, and the photographer into the exact position and sequence

required for the press. Film negatives (or positives) were laboriously positioned and prepared for platemaking.

Stripping is still widely employed. However, microcomputer applications have diminished its use. A number of companies have developed **direct-to-plate systems** that eliminate much of this labor-intensive step. The goal is to reduce the possibility of error, speed the process, and eliminate traditional darkroom and light table operations.

Off-Press Systems

Laser plate exposure systems are ideally suited for exposing plates from digitized information contained in computer memory. A relatively common practice has been to electronically scan a traditional mechanical paste-up into the computer. The digital data is then fed back to a **laser platemaker** to create the plate. System software controls image position on the plate and, therefore, on the final printed sheet.

This process can be done in two separate steps, or it can be combined into one operation. The single-step system contains two laser beams, one of which reads the copy. The other exposes a printing plate simultaneously. During operation, the "read laser" scans across an opaque original, projecting light onto the copy. Areas that reflect light back from the copy are treated as nonimage areas; areas that absorb light are treated as image areas. The read laser then passes this scanned information to the computer as digitized input. The computer uses this digitized information to activate a "write laser" which exposes the plate.

A more recent application eliminates all mechanical preparation. Chapters 4 and 5 introduced page description languages and raster image processing. It is relatively simple to substitute a printing plate ·for paper or film in an imagesetting-type system. Images created on the computer can be assembled, positioned, and passed to a platemaker without any mechanical work.

On-Press Systems

An even newer development is a proprietary computer-driven, direct-to-plate system that creates the plate while it is mounted on the press. Developed by Presstek Inc., the Pearl™ Imaging System offers several significant advantages over traditional methods:

- Because the plate is mounted on the press before exposure, there are almost no registration problems.
- The system significantly reduces press make-ready time.
- The plate uses a waterless technology, which is more stable and allows greater ink densities than water-based lithography.
- Material costs are competitive with traditional systems, but the process saves as much as 60 percent in craftworker time.

Plate Design

The basis of this technology is in the plate design (figure 11.14). The plate is built in three layers. The polyester base provides the strength and stability to hold the two other layers and also remain in place on the press. The polyester is also "ink-accepting," meaning that ink readily adheres to it.

The top layer is a silicone compound. Silicone is naturally ink-repelling. The basic approach is to remove the silicone in the image areas, but leave it where no image is desired (the nonimage areas). As ink rollers are applied to the plate, ink is repelled by the silicone areas, but attaches to the polyester. In this way, the plate functions without the traditional ink-water balance problems (see chapter 13).

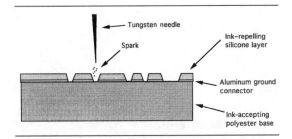

Figure 11.14.   Plate design of first generation direct-to-plate, on-press technology. First-generation direct-to-plate, on-press technology employed a plate built from three layers: an ink-repelling silicone layer, an aluminum ground connector layer, and an ink-accepting polyester base.

In the first design, the middle layer was an aluminum ground connector. Current technology uses an infrared-absorbent material (see the following).

Plate Exposure

The original Pearl system used a **spark-erosion approach** for plate exposure (figure 11.15). Sixteen closely spaced tungsten-needle electrodes were used to carve tracks in the plate cylinder as the cylinder rotated. A spark would be projected at the plate surface. The aluminum ground connector layer completed the electrical path. In addition to burning away the silicone, the spark also vaporized the aluminum, exposing the bottom polyester layer of the plate. The resulting dust was removed by a small, rotating brush.

Second-generation technology replaces the tungsten-needle electrodes with laser diodes. Instead of an aluminum-based middle layer, the plate employs an infrared-absorbent material at its center which matches the laser's output wavelength. The material vaporizes when struck by laser light and therefore loosens the top silicone layer, which can then be wiped away by the press operator. With this new system, image resolutions of 1,016, 1,270, 2032, and 2,540 dpi are possible.

The Process

In a production environment this process is relatively straightforward. The press operator mounts a blank plate on each plate cylinder of the press. The press is turned on, but without ink and paper feed. A RIP job (see chapter 8) is fed to the press controller and then to the individual laser diodes contained in the recording head (figure 11.15). The stream of bits from the RIP are translated into pits on the surface of each plate.

All plates are exposed simultaneously. In other words, on a four-unit press, all four plates are exposed at the same time. Total elapsed time is from 12 minutes to 20 minutes. There is an inverse relationship between resolution and the amount of time it takes to burn a plate—the finer the resolution the longer it takes to prepare the plate.

While the plates are being prepared, the press crew is involved with normal procedures, such as loading paper, checking the ink fountain, and preparing the area.

The RIP can send information to the press's computer-controlled inking system, and actually adjust individual key settings for the specific job.

Once the plates are exposed, the operator turns off the press and cleans each plate. The press is then started, ink rollers are dropped

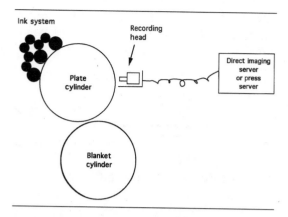

Figure 11.15. The spark-erosion approach. A PostScript file is sent thorough a RIP which renders the page directly onto a proprietary plate system. A laser is used to blast away the surface covering.

onto the plate, and the paper feed begins. After the first few impressions, full color or ink intensity is reached, and the job is run.

On-press, direct-to-plate systems will gain acceptance and use over the next several years. An even newer technology, called a "digital press," moves the direct-to-plate concept even further by creating a new plate image with each rotation of the plate cylinder. Digital presses are discussed in greater detail in chapter 17.

Key Terms

lithography
graining
etch
etching
platemaker
actinic light
platemaking sink
light integrator
sensitivity guide

plate
mechanical graining
chemical graining
collodion
colloid
surface plate
deep-etch plate
negative-acting plate
positive-acting plate

direct image non photo-
   graphic surface plate
wipe-on metal surface plate
presensitized surface plate
additive plate
subtractive plate
photopolymer plates
monomer
polymer

diffusion transfer plate
electrostatic transfer plate
projection platemaking

step-and-repeat
    platemaking
direct-to-plate system

laser platemaking
spark-erosion approach
laser diodes

Questions for Review

I. What is the basis of all industrial lithography?

2. Describe the basic components of a platemaker.

3. What is meant by actinic light? Why is actinic light important in platemaking?

4. How is platemaker exposure calibrated for plate production?

5. What is the purpose of lithographic plate graining?

6. What are the three most basic types of lithographic plates?

7. What is the difference between a negative-acting plate and a positive-acting lithographic plate?

8. How is a direct image nonphotographic plate prepared?

9. Describe two methods of preparing a wipe-on surface plate.

10. How do presensitized surface plates differ from wipe-on plates? What are the advantages of presensitized plates?

II. What is the difference between an additive plate and a subtractive plate? How is each plate processed?

12. Describe how deep-etch plates differ from surface plates.

13. How are diffusion transfer lithographic plates made?

14. What is the advantage of electrostatic plates?

15. Describe the operation of two types of projection platemaking systems.

16. How does a laser plate exposure system work? What are the advantages of this type of system?

17. Describe the process of step-and-repeat platemaking. Give two examples for the use of this process.

18. Why is direct-to-plate processing considered an important technical development?

19. Describe the basic on-press, direct-to-plate process.

Printing Presses: An Overview

Anecdote to Chapter Twelve

The first high-speed printing press was designed around 1450 by Johann Gutenberg in Germany. Gutenberg tried several different designs, but he settled on the basic form of a wine press. He placed the bed of the press so that it could be rolled out from under the plate, activated the screw by a lever, and added a frame, or tympan, to hold the paper. With this device Gutenberg printed his famous forty-two-line Bible (called the Gutenberg Bible). It took him just over three years to print two hundred copies.

Gutenberg's press worked so well that three hundred years later Benjamin Franklin used a similar design (see illustration). Two men were needed to operate Franklin's press. The type was locked in place on the bed of the press, the raised portions of the type were inked, and the paper was positioned on the tympan frame and swung into place over the type. The bed was then rolled under the platen and the lever (a pressure plate) was activated to press the sheet against the type. The press was then opened, the printed sheet was hung on a line to dry, and the entire process was repeated. Using this method, two press operators could make about three hundred impressions in a single twelve-hour work-day. The basic steps of feeding the paper, registering the paper to the form, printing, and finally delivering the sheet remain in printing today. Modern processes, however, are more accurate and more rapid than the modified wine press.

A replica of Benjamin Franklin's press.
Courtesy of Smithsonian Institution, Photo No. 17539-B.

Objectives for Chapter 12

After completing this chapter you will be able to:

- Recall the four units that make up any printing press.
- Discuss the development of press designs from platen presses to rotary presses.
- Explain the principle of offset printing.

- Diagram the cylinder configuration of an offset perfecting press.
- Explain how the feeder unit, registration unit, printing unit, inking unit, dampening unit, and delivery unit operate on an offset lithographic press.
- Give a general description of the operation of a web offset press.

Introduction

A **printing press** is a machine that transfers an image from a plate or an image carrier to a substrate, such as paper. It is certainly possible to transfer images from a plate without using a machine—consider a rubber stamp or a stencil—but printing presses are much faster and print more accurately than hand methods.

Gutenberg's version of the wine press could be operated at the then fantastic rate of one copy every three minutes. Contemporary automatic presses operate at a medium speed of around 125 copies each minute (6,000 to 8,000 copies per hour). When the paper is fed from a continuous roll (called "web feeding"), the paper can pass under a printing plate as rapidly as 1,800 feet per minute.

The design of Gutenberg's original press has been refined a bit, but modern presses still perform the same basic operations of feeding, registering, printing, and delivering that Gutenberg's press performed more than five centuries ago. It is important to understand that every printing press—relief, gravure, screen, lithographic, and Xerographic—is built from four basic units (figure 12.1):

- Feeding unit
- Registration unit
- Printing unit
- Delivery unit

The actual buttons and switches that cause a press to run differ from machine to machine. However, every press has these four fundamental elements regardless of size, manufacturer, complexity, or cost. If you first learn the basic tasks of each unit and then how the units function together you will always have the skills to advance and adapt in the printing industry. It is easy to learn buttons and switches—the individual who understands systems will be able to operate any press.

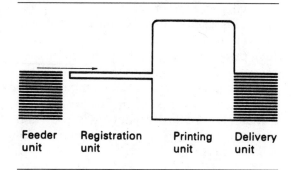

Feeder unit   **Registration unit**   **Printing unit**   **Delivery unit**

Figure 12.1.   **The four units common to all presses**

The goal of the **feeding** unit is to feed stock into the press rapidly and uniformly. The **feeding** unit can be as simple as a human hand picking up a sheet of paper or as complex as an air-vacuum device that automatically fans the top sheets of a paper pile and lifts a sheet with mechanical fingers.

The **registration** unit is designed to ensure that the press sheet is held in the same position for each impression. It is important that the printed image appear in the same spot on every sheet. Registration is especially important for color printing, which requires two or more impressions on each press sheet. The different colored images made during each impression would not line up if the position of the paper were not controlled during printing.

Once the sheet is held firmly in the proper position, the image is transferred from the plate to the press sheet in the **printing unit.** The placement of the plate or image carrier might vary with the type of printing (relief, screen, gravure, or lithography), but there are general similarities between all presses.

After printing, the completed sheet must be removed from the press by the **delivery unit.** Five centuries ago, Gutenberg picked up each printed sheet and hung it on a wire line to dry. Modern presses generally deliver a uniform stack of sheets that can be easily folded, collated, packaged, or cut.

This chapter discusses the development of printing presses and the operation of the four press systems. Much of this discussion centers around the systems used on offset lithographic presses because offset lithographic printing is the printing method used most commonly in industry. Gravure, screen, and flexographic presses are discussed in more detail later in the text.

Press Development

Since Gutenberg developed his first printing press, major improvements have been made in press design. These improvements have increased both the speed and the quality with which work can be printed. Modern press designs are the result of changes in the method used to move paper through the press and in the method used to transfer an image. A brief look at press development will help you understand the operation of a modern offset press.

Platen Press

If it were in operation today, Gutenberg's converted wine press would be labeled a **platen press.** On this type of press, the paper is placed between the type form and a flat surface called a **platen** (figure 12.2a). The type form and the platen are then brought together, and an image is transferred to the press sheet (figure 12.2b). Although the feeding, registration, and delivery units have now been automated, the basic problems inherent in the platen press design remain. The paper must be inserted, held in place, and printed, and it must remain in place until the platen opens sufficiently for the sheet to be removed. The process is slow.

In addition to being slow, the platen press process is limited to the page size that can be

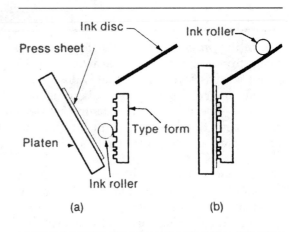

Figure 12.2.   Diagram of a platen press. (a) A press sheet is positioned on a platen when the platen press is open. (b) The image is transferred when the press is closed.

printed. The platen press requires 175 pounds of pressure per square inch (psi) to transfer ink from the type form to the press sheet. A press capable of printing an 11 inch × 14 inch image must be able to produce 26,950 pounds of pressure. (This is why early wooden printing presses were built in the basement or first floor of a two-story building. The press was the main support for the floor above.) Speed and size were the two factors that led to the development of the flat bed cylinder press.

Flat Bed Cylinder Press

An improvement over the platen press, the **flat bed cylinder press** is constructed so that the press sheet rolls into contact with the type form as a cylinder moves across the press (figure 12.3). Mechanical fingers, or **grippers,** hold the press sheet in place during the cylinder's movement and automatically open at the end of one rotation. Ink rollers are usually attached to the cylinder assembly so that as an image is being printed, the form is also being reinked.

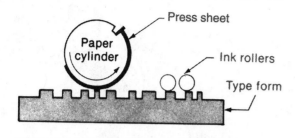

Figure 12.3. Diagram of a flat bed cylinder press. A flat bed cylinder press rolls the press sheet over the plate carrying the image.

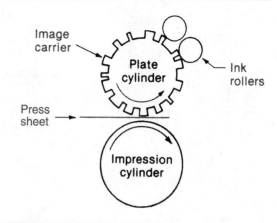

Figure 12.4. Diagram of a rotary press. A rotary press moves the press sheet between two cylinders—the plate cylinder, which holds the image carrier, and the impression cylinder, which pushes the press sheet against the type form or image carrier.

After each impression, the cylinder raises automatically and rolls back to the starting point to receive another sheet. On some models the cylinder is stationary and the type form moves.

One advantage of the flat bed cylinder design is that, because only a very narrow portion of the sheet is being printed at any given instant, much less pressure is required to transfer the image than is required for the platen design. A slight modification is to place the type form in a vertical position so that the bed and the cylinder rotate in opposite directions. This cuts the printing time in half because the cylinder makes only a 180-degree turn for each impression. However, motion is still wasted when the cylinder and/or the type form return to their original positions and no image is being transferred.

Rotary Press

The **rotary press** is formed from two cylinders. One cylinder called the **plate cylinder,** holds the type form while the other cylinder acts as the **impression cylinder** to push the press sheet against the type form (figure 12.4). As the cylinders rotate, a press sheet is inserted between them so that an image is placed in the same position on every sheet. Ink rollers continually replace ink that has been transferred to

the press sheets. The impression cylinder can usually be moved up or down to adjust impression pressure for the weight or thickness of the material being printed.

The rotary press is efficient. Because one impression is made with each cylinder rotation, there is no wasted motion. The rotary press is the only press design that can transfer an image to a continuous roll of paper. This process is called **web printing.** The rotary configuration can also be easily adapted to multicolor presswork. One common rotary press of this design places several plate cylinders around a single impression cylinder (figure 12.5). All modern offset lithographic presses are rotary presses.

Offset Press

The term "offset" is generally associated with the lithographic process, but the offset principle can be applied to a variety of printing

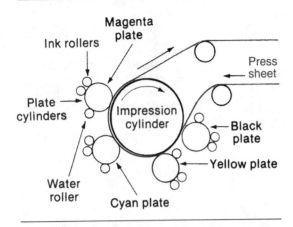

Figure 12.5.   Diagram of a multicylinder rotary press. A rotary, web-fed press can be adapted to place several plate cylinders around a single impression cylinder for multicolor work.

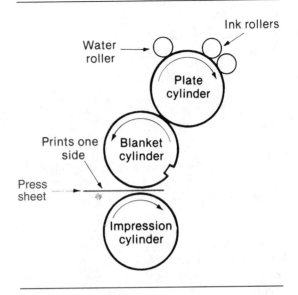

Figure 12.6.   Diagram of an offset rotary press. Using the offset principle, the offset press transfers an image (or offset) from the plate cylinder to the blanket cylinder, which reverses the image. The reversed image is then passed to the press sheet as it moves between the blanket and impression cylinders.

processes. An **offset press** transfers (or offsets) an image from an inked printing plate cylinder to a rubber **blanket cylinder**. The blanket cylinder reverses the image. The blanket cylinder then transfers the reversed image to the press sheet (figure 12.6).

Transferring an image from a blanket cylinder to the press sheet, rather than transferring the image directly from the plate cylinder to the press sheet, has several advantages. Paper has an abrasive effect on printing plates. If the paper were allowed to contact the printing plate throughout the press run, the plate would soon become too worn to print properly. Having the plate contact the rubber blanket cylinder instead of the printing press sheet, lengthens the life of the plate cylinder. In addition, whenever an image is transferred from one carrier to another, the symbols are reversed (recall that foundry type is cast in reverse). When a blanket cylinder is used on an offset press, the characters on the printing plate must be right reading. The characters will print in reverse on the blanket cylinder,

then be reversed again (back to right reading) on the press sheet. Right-reading characters are more convenient for people to work with and assemble during the composition and stripping processes. A rubber blanket cylinder also tends to diminish unwanted background detail or "scum" that might accumulate on the printing plate.

A **perfecting press** can print simultaneously on both sides of the press sheet as it passes through the printing unit (figure 12.7). The most common perfecting presses use the rotary configuration and can be designed for either sheet-fed or web-fed reproduction. (See the Feeder Unit section of this chapter for more about sheet-fed and web-fed reproduction.)

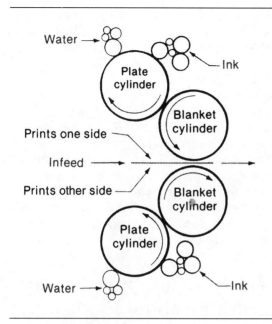

Figure 12.7. **Diagram of a blanket-to-blanket perfecting press configuration**

Understanding Offset Press Operation

Offset lithographic presses, which are presses that can feed sheets larger than 11 inches × 17 inches, can be classified and described in many different ways. For example, one press might be labeled a "five-unit, perfecting in-line web." Another might be called a "single-color, sheet-fed" press. The terms are meaningful to experienced printers, but they are foreign to new students in the field. Whenever people move to learn something in a new field, they have to learn the field-specific language.

The purpose of this section is to describe in some detail the process and vocabulary of basic press operation. Of course, it would be possible to write volumes about each category of operation. However, you must understand the main controls and variables within each press unit before you begin the process of printing. This description provides that understanding. Once you are proficient in this content, you can move to the volumes of advanced technical manuals on printing presses and their operation.

Classifying Offset Lithographic Presses

Offset lithographic presses are classified most simply as either duplicators or presses. These types are based on the maximum size of press sheet the press can print.

Offset Duplicators

Duplicators are any offset lithographic machines that can feed a maximum press sheet size of 11 inches × 17 inches. A duplicator is assumed not to have the degree of control found on a larger offset press, but the feeder, registration, printing, and delivery units are always present in a duplicator.

Tabletop duplicators are designed for short-run work and can be operated by office personnel. Most models have friction paper feed, control registration by positioning of the paper pile, and use a simple gravity delivery system. Figure 12.8 shows a common pedestal-type duplicator. Pedestal duplicators are usually more rugged than tabletop duplicators and have a few more sophisticated controls than the tabletop devices.

An offset duplicator can do any job a larger press can handle, but each handles a different sheet size. (See the following section.) Modern duplicators can print on a variety of paper stock thicknesses at speeds of 5,000 to 10,000 impressions per hour. They are also available with a web-fed design and multiple-printing units for efficient multicolor printing.

Duplicators are versatile machines that meet the short-run demands of the printing industry. They have the same basic controls as offset presses yet are significantly less

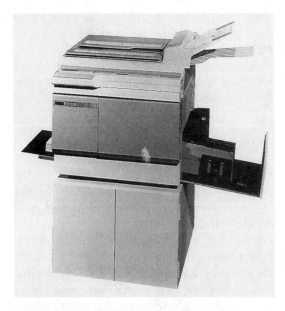

Figure 12.8.　A common pedestal type duplicator.
Courtesy of Multigraphics, a Division of AM International, Inc.

expensive. Duplicators are commonly used for introductory press training because of their similarity to larger offset presses.

Offset Presses

A true offset press can feed a sheet size greater than 11 inches × 17 inches. Sheet-fed offset presses (see the Feeder Unit of this chapter) can print press sheets from 12 5/8 inches × 18 inches to 54 inches × 77 inches. Figure 12.9 shows a common lithographic offset press.

Although presses and duplicators are technically different, the word *duplicator* is rarely used. Rather, both duplicators and larger presses are referred to as "presses" in everyday use.

The Systems Approach to Learning about Presses

It is critical to keep firmly in mind that all presses are designed and built using four basic units: feeding, registration, printing, and delivery. The following material describes the printing process as a sheet of press paper goes from one end of the press to the other. It is also

Figure 12.9.　A lithographic offset press.
Courtesy of Miller Printing Equipment Corp.

critical to always remember the simple visualization presented in figure 12.1. If you think of the overall system while learning the specifics, you will ultimately become a more skillful press operator.

Finally, remember that while this discussion focuses on offset lithographic presses, these concepts apply to every other printing method. If you understand how the four units of an offset press function, then you could walk up to a flat bed relief press, and with brief instruction on buttons and switches, probably run it. This approach of classifying units, looking at specifics, and transferring learning to other applications is called the systems approach. It will serve you well throughout your life.

The Feeding Unit

One method of categorizing presses is by the form of the material sent through the feeding system. When a roll of paper is placed in the feeding unit, the press is classified as **web fed** or, simply, web (figure 12.10). When the feeding unit picks up individual press sheets from a pile, the press is classified as **sheet fed.** Our primary concern in this discussion is sheet-fed presses. Web presses are discussed later in this chapter.

The feeding unit for a sheet-fed offset press must separate the top sheet of paper from the infeed pile, pick it up, and deliver it to the registration unit. This process must be done consistently for each sheet in the pile. Only one sheet can be fed at a time, and each sheet must reach the registration unit at a precise moment to be registered and sent to the printing unit.

Loading Systems

The simplest and most common sheet-feeding system is **pilefeeding** (figure 12.11). With this system a pile of paper is placed on a feed table while the press is turned off. The table is then raised to a predetermined feeding height and the press run begins. As each sheet is removed from the pile, the press moves the table up

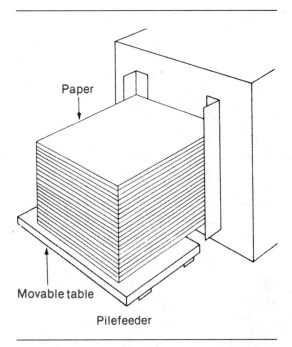

Figure 12.11. **Diagram of a press with a pile feeder**

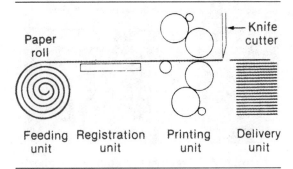

Figure 12.10. **Diagram of a web-fed press**

so that the top of the pile remains at a constant height.

Pilefeeding presents no difficulties when all the sheets for a single job can be placed in one pile. However, when the press must be stopped and started several times during an extremely long run to add more paper, problems are often encountered. When a job is first set up on a press, a certain amount of paper is spoiled during **make-ready** (preparation work) to obtain a quality printed image. During a steady press run, it is relatively easy to maintain consistent quality. Whenever the press is stopped, however, not only is production time lost, but more paper wastage could occur before a quality impression is obtained again.

Continuous sheet feeding provides a means of adding sheets to a feeding system without stopping the press in the middle of a run. There are two common continuous-feed designs. The older of the two designs generally has a feed table located over the registration unit (figure 12.12). The printer fans the paper, and the pile is spread on the infeed table. A continuous belt then moves the pile around and under the feed table to the registration unit. Additional paper is fanned and added to the moving pile as needed.

The second continuous sheet-feeding system provides continuous feeding by loading new paper under an existing pile while the press is running (figure 12.13). Before the pile has run out, temporary rods are inserted between open channels in the table, and the fresh pile is elevated into feeding position. The rods are then removed, and a single stack of paper is again in the feeding unit.

Types of Feeders
The most common type of mechanical feeder is the **successive sheet-feeding system** (figure 12.14). Mechanical fingers pick up one sheet from the top of the paper pile and direct it into the registration unit.

Usually, an air blast is used to separate the top press sheet from the rest of the pile. This blast can be adjusted for papers of different weight and for different atmospheric con-

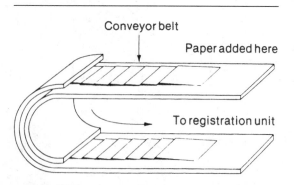

Figure 12.12. Diagram of a continuous sheet-feeding system

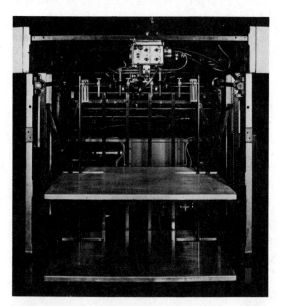

Figure 12.13. Example of a continuous sheet-feeding system that uses dual tables.
Courtesy of Miller Printing Equipment Corp.

Figure 12.14. **Diagram of a successive sheet-feeding system**

ditions. On dry days, when press sheets tend to cling together because of static electricity, the air blast can be increased. Heavy papers require a stronger air blast than light papers. Coated papers, too, generally require a stronger air blast than uncoated papers. The air blast must be strong enough to "float" the top piece of paper above the pile at a specified height below the sucker feet.

The **sucker feet** are small vacuum tubes that grab the floating top sheet and send it down the registration board where the registration unit takes over. (The registration board consists of conveyor belts and a registration system.) The amount of vacuum in the sucker feet can be adjusted for the weight of paper being printed. Heavy papers generally require more vacuum than light papers. The object is to adjust the vacuum so that only one piece of paper is picked up by the sucker feet and delivered to the registration unit.

In actual operation, the sucker feet grab the top press sheet from the pile and move it forward a short distance to where it is picked up by pull-in wheels (or some other device) that put it squarely on a conveyer belt system on the registration board. The press automatically controls the precise moment when the sucker feet grab the top sheet, as well as movement of the sheet toward the registration board and the precise moment when the vacuum is cut off and the sheet enters the registration unit.

As the press removes paper from the infeed table, the height of the paper pile decreases. However, the paper pile must be main-

tained at a constant distance from the sucker feet. This requirement is accomplished automatically by the press. As the press removes paper from the infeed pile, the infeed table automatically moves up, which moves the infeed pile closer to the sucker feet.

The feeding system must be adjusted for air blast, vacuum, paper pile height, and upward movement of infeed table as the paper is used.

The paper feed must be synchronized with the printing unit—each time an impression is made, the feeder must be ready to insert a fresh press sheet. In high-speed presses with successive sheet-feeding systems, the paper literally flies through the registration unit to keep up with the printing unit. It is not easy to hold accurate registration when high-speed printing with a single sheet feeder. The paper may misalign as it enters the registration board due to the high rate of speed.

In contrast to a successive sheet feeder, a **stream feeder** overlaps sheets on the registration board and slows the rate of sheet movement significantly (figure 12.15). With a stream feeder, sheets move through the registration unit at a fraction of the speed of the printing unit. This makes accurate registration control less difficult.

Automatic Feeder Controls
Whatever the method of paper loading or feeding, there are common feeder system controls on all sheet-fed presses. When the paper pile is loaded into the feeding system, it is

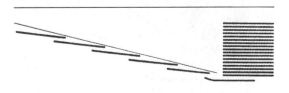

Figure 12.15. **Diagram of a stream-feeding system**

centered on the press. A scale is usually provided somewhere on the feeder to ensure accurate paper position. Once the pile has been centered, movable side and back guides are positioned to just touch the paper so that the pile will not shift position during the press run (figure 12.16).

The height of the pile can usually be adjusted and maintained automatically by the press. Usually some type of sensing bar touches the top of the pile immediately after a sheet has been fed and directs a gear-and-chain pile height control. The pile height that is required depends on such factors as the paper weight, environmental conditions, and feeding method. The top of the pile must be as level as possible for consistent feeding. This is usually a problem only with large press sheets. Wedges or blocks are often placed under a pile of large press sheets to keep the sheets level.

To ensure that only one sheet feeds into the registration unit at a time, the top sheet must be separated from the rest of the pile. Various mechanisms are used on different machines, but they are all called **sheet separators.** The most common is a blast of directed air, which was just discussed. Blower tubes, which can be directed at the front, side, or rear of a pile, place a blanket of air under the first few press sheets (figure 12.17). Another common approach is to combine a blast of air with a mechanical **combing wheel,** which curls one edge of the paper above the rest of the stack (figure 12.18). With either technique, a sucker foot moves to the top sheet, applies suction, and forwards it into the registration unit. (Sucker feet were discussed in more detail in the previous section.) Most sheet separators have at least two sucker feet. Both the volume of air to separate the top sheet and the amount of vacuum pull in the sucker feet can be adjusted for different paper characteristics.

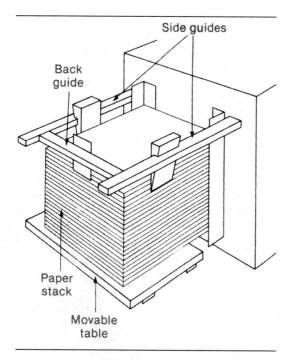

Figure 12.16. Diagram showing movable guides. The movable side and back guides hold the pile in position.

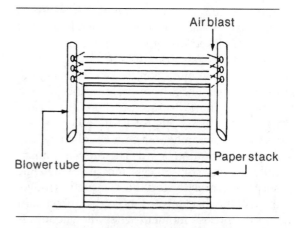

Figure 12.17. Diagram showing blower tubes. Blower tubes force a blanket of air under the first few sheets of paper and float them above the rest of the pile.

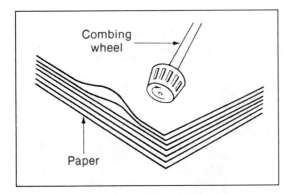

Figure 12.18. **A mechanical combing wheel**

The final consideration is to ensure that only one sheet feeds into the press from the feeder to the registration unit at a time. Multiple sheets can jam the press, give poor image impression, fail to be held in register, and even damage the printing unit. Most presses have **double-sheet detectors** (figure 12.19) to check for multiple sheets. These devices either eject double sheets from the registration system or stop the press when double sheets are detected. Usually a double-sheet detector merely gauges the thickness of the passing paper us-

ing a sensing switch. The gap from the switch to the paper can be set to any thickness. When the allowable gap is exceeded (there are double sheets and the paper is too thick), the switch is tripped and the double sheets are ejected. On some presses, the paper feeder shuts down when a double sheet is detected. If all paper-feed adjustments have been made properly, the feeder should rarely feed multiple sheets.

The Registration Unit

Importance of Registration
Registration is the process of controlling and directing a press sheet as it enters the printing unit. The goal of registration is to ensure consistent image position on every sheet printed. When one color is to be printed over another on a single sheet, the image will not fit on the sheet unless all sheets are held in register throughout the press run. The ideas of registration and fit are often confused. **Fit** refers to the image position on the press sheet. This term is often used when discussing flat color work. Two colors that are printed adjacent to each other in the proper positions are said to have proper fit. Fit can be affected by a variety of factors, including the original mechanical, the camera operations used to reproduce that mechanical, and the stripping of the job. **Registration** refers to the consistency of the position of the printed image during printing. An image that has the proper fit in stripping can be made to register properly. However, if the fit was wrong in stripping, no amount of adjustments on press will bring the image into correct register.

Typical Registration Designs
After leaving the infeed pile, the press sheet is moved along the registration board toward the registration unit. As mentioned earlier, the registration board consists of a conveyer belt

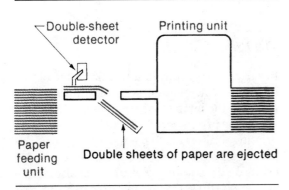

Figure 12.19. **Diagram showing a double-sheet detector**

system and some type of registration system. The paper is carried along the conveyer belts until it reaches the registration unit, where it is stopped momentarily and squared to the plate cylinder along its top edge by a headstop. A **headstop** is a mechanical gate that stops the paper on the registration unit. At the same time the paper is being aligned by the headstop, it is either being pushed or pulled slightly sideways and placed in the proper printing position. It is important to understand that before each press sheet is printed, the registration unit places it in exactly the same position as the preceding sheet. This position determines where the image will print on the press sheet. The registration unit must be adjusted for paper width as well as image location.

The actual registering of the press sheet is performed just before the sheet enters the printing unit. There are only two basic types of sheet-fed automatic registration systems: three-point guide and two-point pull rotary.

In a three-point guide system, the press sheet advances along the registration board and halts against the headstops (figure 12.20). Next, side guides push the sheet into the proper printing position, the front guides move out of the way, and the sheet moves into the printing unit. There is a tendency for heavy paper stock to bounce back as it contacts the headstop. In contrast, extremely lightweight materials buckle easily with this push system. Either condition can lead to misregistration.

The two-point pull rotary system reduces the possibility of the press sheet misregistering (figure 12.21). With this system the headstop still swings into position at the head of the registration board, but one side guide is locked into position and does not move. As the press sheet meets the headstop and comes to rest, a finger or roller lowers against the sheet. The sheet is then pulled by a rolling, or rotary, motion against the stationary side guide or "pull

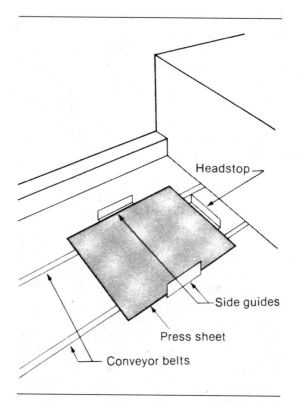

Figure 12.20.   Diagram of a three-point guide system

guide." Once the sheet is in register, it moves into the printing unit.

The Printing Unit

In offset lithography the printing unit places ink and a water solution on the printing plate, transfers the image to the press sheet, and forwards the press sheet to the delivery unit. The printing unit must be adjusted so that the proper amount of ink and water solution deposits on the printing plate. It must also be adjusted so that the image transfers to the printing paper accurately, evenly, and consis-

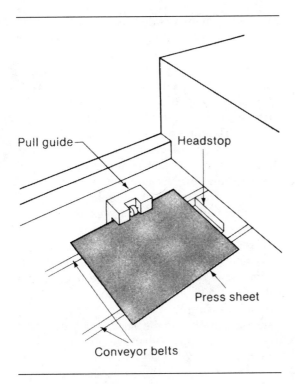

Figure 12.21. **Diagram of a two-point pull rotary system**

blanket cylinder during the printing process. The plate cylinder generally has some form of clamping system that holds the plate squarely and firmly in place. Ink and water **form rollers** contact the plate while it is attached to the plate cylinder, thereby causing the image areas on the plate to be inked. The plate image is then transferred to the blanket cylinder, and the image is reversed. Next the press sheet passes between the blanket cylinder and impression cylinder, and the image is offset back to right-reading form on the press sheet. The impression cylinder applies the pressure that is needed to transfer the image from the blanket cylinder to the press sheet.

Figure 12.22 shows one common plate, blanket, and impression cylinder configuration called the **three-cylinder principle.** Notice that because the blanket cylinder is above the impression cylinder, the press sheet travels in a straight line from the feeder to the delivery unit. Note also the direction of rotation of each

tently. Every offset printing unit is made up of the following three systems:

- The cylinder system
- The inking system
- The dampening system

Each system serves an important function in the total image transfer process and thus each is examined in detail.

Cylinder System Configurations

The cylinder system for any offset press has three functioning parts: a plate cylinder, a blanket cylinder, and an impression cylinder. The function of the plate cylinder is to hold the plate and revolve it into contact with the

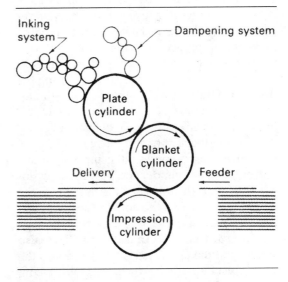

Figure 12.22. **Example of a three-cylinder configuration**

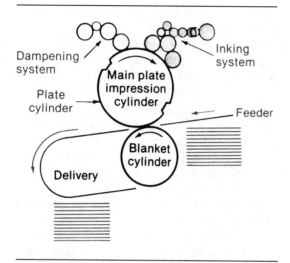

Figure 12.23.   Example of a two-cylinder configuration

cylinder and the logical placement of the dampening and inking systems. Remember that the plate must be moist before it is inked.

Figure 12.23 illustrates an alternative cylinder configuration called the **two-cylinder principle.** With this design the functions of the plate and impression cylinders are combined on one main cylinder that has twice the circumference of the blanket cylinder. During the first half of the main plate/impression cylinder rotation, the image is offset from the plate section of the main cylinder to the blanket cylinder. During the next half of the revolution, the press sheet passes between the impression section of the main cylinder and the blanket cylinder. Because the blanket cylinder is beneath the impression cylinder, the delivery system must flop the press sheet to have the printed image face upward on the outfeed table. This also means that the press sheets being fed into the press must be placed on the infeed table facing downward.

While the three-cylinder configuration is commonly found on both duplicators and presses, the two-cylinder design is never used on contemporary offset presses because it is too slow.

Impression Cylinder Adjustments

The gap between the blanket cylinder and the impression cylinder affects the final image quality. The pressure must be sufficient to transfer a dense ink image but not so great that it smashes the blanket cylinder or the press sheet. Controlling this gap is referred to as adjusting **impression.** Each time the thickness of the paper being printed changes, the impression must be readjusted. Heavier papers need a wider gap than lighter papers.

On most duplicators, the impression cylinder can be raised or lowered by a simple set-screw arrangement. On most presses, impression is controlled by adding or removing packing from behind the blanket cylinder or by a cam adjustment which moves the impression cylinder closer or nearer to the blanket. On some presses, both the impression cylinder and the blanket cylinder require packing.

Blanket Cylinder Concerns

An offset press blanket cylinder is consumable. Blankets wear out and must be replaced. Remember that one of the advantages of the offset technique is that paper never touches the plate cylinder. Paper is abrasive and greatly reduces plate life if allowed to contact the plate cylinder during priming. Moreover, paper often carries lint, which can be carried back into the ink and dampening systems.

Most blankets are made from a vulcanized rubber, which is bonded to a fiber support base. Blankets can stretch around cylinders and they can also deform—just like automobile tires wear unevenly, develop cracks, form bubbles, and grow brittle with age. With proper care, however, a blanket can be used for many hundreds of thousands of impressions.

When it is time to replace the blanket, clamps on the cylinder are loosened and the old blanket is removed. A new blanket is inserted under the clamps and stretched around the cylinder. Blankets are purchased according to press specifications and are sized to exactly match a specific cylinder circumference.

The Inking Unit

The goal of any inking unit is to place a uniform layer of ink across every dimension of the printing plate. The lithographic process is unique in that it requires the ink form rollers to contact the nonimage areas of the plate without transferring ink to them.

Inking Unit Configurations

All lithographic inking units are made up of four main sections:

- Ink fountain and fountain roller
- Ductor roller
- Ink distribution rollers
- Ink form rollers (figure 12.24)

The ink fountain stores a quantity of ink in a reservoir and feeds small quantities of ink to the rest of the inking system from the fountain roller. The ink distribution rollers receive ink by movement of the ductor roller, and work it into a semiliquid state that is uniformly delivered to the ink form rollers. The ink form rollers then transfer a thin layer of ink to the image portions of the lithographic plate.

Inking Unit Operation

The ink **fountain** (figure 12.24a) holds a pool of ink and controls the amount of ink that enters the inking system by feeding small amounts of ink from the **fountain rollers.** The most common type of ink fountain consists of a metal blade that is held in place near the fountain roller. The gap between the blade and the fountain roller can be controlled by adjusting screw keys to vary the amount of ink on the fountain roller. The printer adjusts the screw keys in or out as the fountain roller turns to obtain the desired quantity of ink. If the image to be printed covers only half of the plate, half of the screw keys are closed. If the plate image covers the whole plate evenly, all of the screw keys are

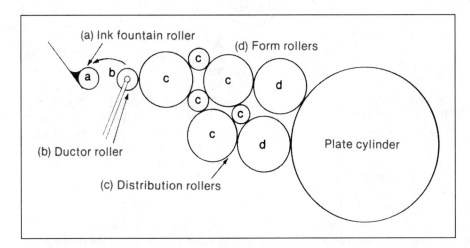

Figure 12.24. Example of a typical inking unit. A lithographic inking system consists of the ink fountain (a), the ductor rollers (b), the distribution rollers (c), and the ink form rollers (d).

moved to place a uniform layer of ink on the fountain roller.

The ink is transferred from the fountain to the ink distribution rollers by a **ductor roller** (figure 12.24b). The ductor roller is a movable roller that flops back and forth between the fountain roller and the distribution rollers. As the ductor roller swings backward and contacts the fountain roller, both rollers turn and the ductor roller is inked. The ductor roller then swings forward to contact a distribution roller and transfers ink to it. The rate of rotation of the fountain roller and the gap between the fountain blade and the fountain roller control the amount of ink added to the ink distribution system.

The ink **distribution rollers** spread the ink out to a uniform layer before it is placed on the plate (figure 12.24c). There are two general types of distribution rollers: rotating distribution rollers and oscillating distribution rollers. **Rotating distribution rollers** rotate in one direction. **Oscillating distribution rollers** rotate and also move from side to side.

The rollers that actually ink the plate are called form rollers (figure 12.24d).

A simple indication of the quality of a printing press is its number of distribution and form rollers. The greater the number of distribution rollers, the more accurate the control of ink uniformity. It is difficult to ink large, solid areas on a plate with only one form roller. With three form rollers (generally the maximum) it is relatively easy to maintain consistent ink coverage of almost any image area on the plate.

The Dampening Unit

Recall that most lithographic plates function on the principle of water- and ink-receptive areas. In order for ink to adhere only to the image areas on a plate, a layer of moisture must be placed over the nonimage areas before the plate is inked. The dampening unit accomplishes this by moistening the plate consistently throughout the press run.

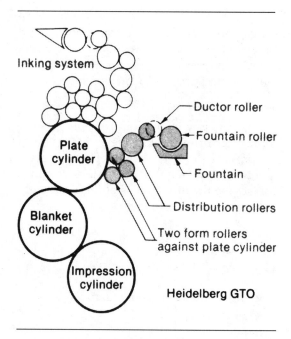

Figure 12.25.   Diagram of a direct dampening unit

Dampening Unit Configurations

There are no radical differences between the basic designs of most conventional, direct dampening units (figure 12.25). Like inking units, dampening units all contain some form of fountain, a fountain roller, a ductor roller, distribution rollers, and one or more form rollers.

Not all manufacturers use direct dampening systems where the ink and dampening rollers are separate, however. An indirect dampening system, such as the "aquamatic system" found on A.B. Dick duplicators, combines the ink and dampening rollers and carries the water solution to the plate on the ink-covered form rollers (figure 12.26).

Dampening Unit Operation

In a direct dampening system, the dampening fountain roller sits in a pool of fountain solution stored in the dampening fountain. As the press runs, the dampening fountain roller

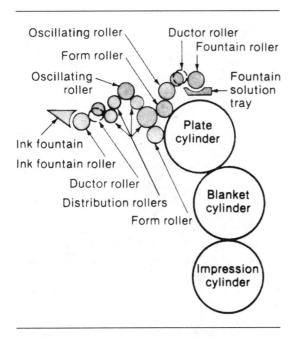

Figure 12.26. **Diagram of an indirect dampening unit**

turns, picking up fountain solution from the fountain and holding it on its surface. A ductor roller jogs back and forth from the fountain roller, where it picks up fountain solution, to a dampening distribution roller. The distribution roller takes the fountain solution from the ductor roller to the dampening form rollers, where the fountain solution is transferred to the plate.

As just mentioned, in an indirect dampening system, the dampening distribution and form rollers are also the inking distribution and form rollers. In this type of system, all the rollers in the ink and water train are first inked. Then fountain solution is added to the fountain. Because the dampening fountain roller and every other roller in the roller train is inked, the fountain solution literally rides on the surface of the inked rollers and is carried to the plate.

In both systems, the rate at which the dampening fountain roller rotates in the fountain can be varied. The faster the fountain roller turns, the more fountain solution it delivers to the dampening system. By changing the rotation speed of the fountain roller, the quantity of moisture reaching the plate can be adjusted.

The Delivery Unit

The delivery unit takes the paper from the printing unit and places it on an outfeed table. There are two common designs for sheet-fed press delivery units: gravity delivery and chain gripper delivery. **Gravity delivery** is the simpler and less dependable of the two designs. As the press sheet leaves the printing unit, it drops into a delivery pile. The basic limitation of this system is that paper cannot be delivered faster to the pile than gravity can pull it into place. With lightweight papers, air resistance reduces the possible press speed even more. For these reasons, gravity delivery is usually found on only the smallest, least expensive duplicators.

The most popular design for delivery units is **chain gripper delivery** (figure 12.27). With chain gripper delivery, the press sheet can be either pulled through the printing and delivery units by the same chain system or it can be transferred from the mechanical fingers or **grippers** on the impression cylinder in the printing unit to a different set of grippers on the chain of the delivery unit.

As the press sheet leaves the printing unit, a set of grippers grabs the leading edge of the sheet and pulls it out of the printing unit. The gripper bar is attached to a continuous chain that moves the printed sheet to a paper pile, releases it, and moves the grippers back to receive another sheet. The chain moves at the same rate and in synchronization with the feeding, registration, and printing units. As

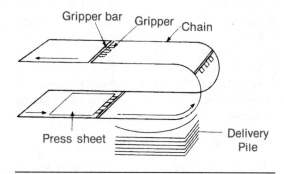

Figure 12.27. Diagram of a chain gripper delivery system

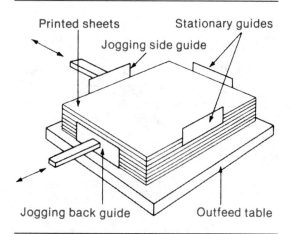

Figure 12.28. Diagram showing jogging side and back guides

one sheet is being delivered to the paper pile, another sheet is being placed on the registration board. Presses with chain gripper delivery systems can print at high speeds because the gripper chain moves the press sheet and does not depend on gravity to remove the sheet from the printing unit.

Delivery Pile Controls

Ideally, the delivery unit forms a perfectly neat stack of paper on the outfeed table. If a perfect pile forms, the printer can easily move it back to the feeding unit to print another color; can stack it in a paper cutter to trim it to a finished size; can collate it with other sheets; or can punch, drill, fold, or package it.

Jogging side and back guides are usually used to control the outfeed pile (figure 12.28). As a sheet drops onto the stack, the guides are open. As the sheet drops into position on the stack, the guides begin to close until they gently push the sheet into place. Most pile control systems are designed so that the two stationary guides can be adjusted to the paper extremes. The jogging guides are adjusted to touch the remaining two paper sides on their innermost motion. As the press operates, the delivery pile is continually touched by all four guides. This keeps the stack straight. The entire outfeed

table typically lowers automatically as the height of the delivery pile increases.

A static electric charge frequently builds on a press sheet as it passes through the printing unit. Charged sheets tend to cling to each other and often do not stack properly in the delivery unit. The most common **static eliminator** is a piece of copper tinsel attached to a thin copper wire. The tinsel is stretched across the delivery unit so that each press sheet must brush against it. The wire is grounded through the press and removes the static electricity from the sheet.

Multicolor Sheet-Fed Presses

The demand for multicolor printing is constantly increasing. In an effort to meet this demand, press manufacturers have developed many types of multicolor presses. **Multicolor sheet-fed presses** operate in the same manner and with the same functional units as single-color sheet-fed presses, but they are equipped with two or more color printing units arranged in a line one following the other. Each color printing unit is capable of delivering one color of ink to the press sheet.

Multicolor Press Design

Most multicolor presses are designed with two, four, five, or six printing units. Two-color presses are ideal for jobs that require spot color, such as a page of text in which the words are printed in one color and the display type or graphic elements (rules, boxes, decorative borders, or illustrations) are printed in another color. Four-color presses are designed especially for four-color process printing. A five- or six-color press (figure 12.29) increases printing possibilities even further by allowing a press sheet to be printed with four process colors followed by a flat color, a match color, or a var-

nish. Varnish is a clear, ink-like substance that changes the reflectance characteristics of the printed piece where it is applied. A varnished area stands out visually and has a different texture than the rest of the press sheet.

The primary advantage of a multicolor press is that more than one color can be printed in a single pass through the press. Without a multicolor press, the press sheet would have to be printed with one color, then replaced on the infeed table and run through the press again for each additional color. Not only is this a time-consuming operation, but it can lead to registration problems. As has been mentioned, paper is not dimensionally stable. When press paper passes through the press, each piece is subjected to both ink and water. Moisture from the dampening system tends to make the press sheet stretch; the sheet then shrinks as it dries. Absorption and drying of ink on the printed

Figure 12.29. **A five-color, sheet-fed offset press.** Five color printing units are arranged in line on this press. Note the press controls on the infeed table that make it possible for the operator to control the press from the infeed end. These controls can be used to adjust paper feed and a variety of other press operations.
Courtesy of Miller Printing Equipment Corp.

sheet can have a similar effect. Further, when a single-color press is used for a multicolor job, some time elapses before the press sheet is put through the press for the next color. During this time, the press sheet may shrink, stretch, or warp slightly due to humidity and other environmental conditions in the printing plant. The overall result of all these effects is that on the second pass through the press, the press sheet is not exactly the same size as it was on the first pass through the press. This makes critical registration, such as is required for process color work, difficult and sometimes impossible. A multicolor press can reduce this problem.

One additional advantage of a multicolor press is that press operators can judge the quality of the printed sheet immediately when it comes off the press, and they can make press adjustments based on their evaluations. When printing process color, all four colors must be printed with the correct press settings if the colors on the final job are to be correct. When a single-color press is used to print process color, improper press adjustments during the printing of the first color may only be discovered as the fourth color is being printed. By this time, all of the sheets have been printed with three colors, and it is too late to make any corrections. The whole job would have to be scrapped and reprinted.

Perfecting Transfer

To increase press flexibility, the multicolor press shown in figure 12.29 is equipped with a perfecting transfer system. The perfecting transfer system on this press is designed and patented by the Miller Printing Equipment Corporation, but other press manufacturers offer perfecting presses that operate on a similar principle. A schematic of a two-color press equipped with a perfecting transfer system is shown in figure 12.30. With this system it is possible for a two-color press to print two

colors on one side of the press sheet, or one color on each side of the press sheet, in one pass through the press. A four-color press equipped with the perfecting transfer system has even greater printing flexibility. It can print four colors on one side, or three colors on one side and one color on the other side, or two colors on each side. Five- or six-color presses can also be equipped with a perfecting transfer system, which again increases printing flexibility.

The perfecting transfer system introduces several additional cylinders to the press which work in conjunction with the impression and blanket cylinders commonly found on an offset press. As shown in figure 12.31, the Miller perfecting transfer system uses two transfer cylinders and one perfecting cylinder. Together these cylinders can pass a press sheet from one printing unit to another so that the press sheet reaches the second printing unit with either its printed side facing the second blanket cylinder (multicolor mode) or with its unprinted side facing the second blanket cylinder (perfecting mode). The cylinders are especially designed so that freshly printed ink does not smear when the printed side of the sheet presses against them.

In perfecting mode, the printed sheet passes from the first impression cylinder to the first transfer cylinder. At this point the printed side of the sheet is against the face of the first transfer cylinder. The first transfer cylinder then passes the sheet to the second transfer cylinder, printed side away from the face of the second transfer cylinder. The perfecting cylinder is equipped with two sets of grippers. In the perfecting mode, the perfecting cylinder grips the *tail* edge of the sheet using one set of grippers, and passes the sheet to the second impression cylinder, printed side against the face of the second impression cylinder face, using the second set of grippers, to be printed on its unprinted side. Thus, the sheet leaves the press printed on both sides. In the multicolor (nonperfecting) mode all of the cylinders still

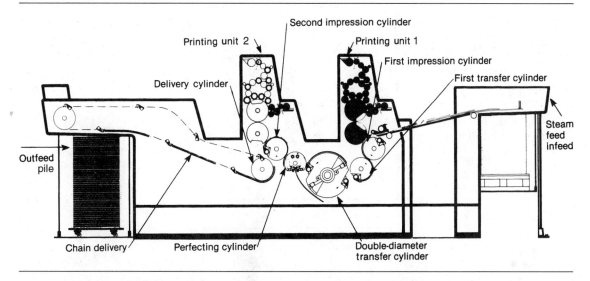

Figure 12.30.   A two-color, sheet-fed offset press equipped with a perfecting transfer system. The two transfer cylinders and the perfecting cylinder in this press allow for printing one color on each side of the press sheet or two colors on one side of the press sheet.
Courtesy of Miller Printing Equipment Corp.

handle the press sheet, but only one set of grippers is activated on the perfecting cylinder. In this mode the perfecting cylinder grips the printed sheet on its *lead* edge and passes it to the second impression cylinder printed side away from the face of the second impression cylinder. Thus, the sheet is printed with two colors on the same side.

Multicolor Press Monitoring and Control Systems

It is relatively easy for one operator to control infeed, registration, ink and water balance, and outfeed on a single-color press. However, as the number of color units in the press increases and registration becomes more critical, press control becomes a bigger problem. Until recently, the answer to this problem has been to provide each press with enough operators to monitor all press functions. Thus, a six-color press might require four to six operators. Even with the required number of operators, press control still presented problems, not the least of which was the inability of the press operators to react quickly enough to make needed press adjustments without a great deal of paper spoilage.

The use of computers has reduced this problem and has greatly improved the quality of printed products while at the same time has reduced make-ready time and spoilage. A typical, automated, multicolor press control system is shown in figure 12.32. This system involves the use of a plate scanner and a press console.

The Plate Scanner
The **plate scanner** (figure 12.33) is typically installed in the platemaking room. After a plate is made, it is scanned by the plate scanner. The scanner moves across the plate, optically

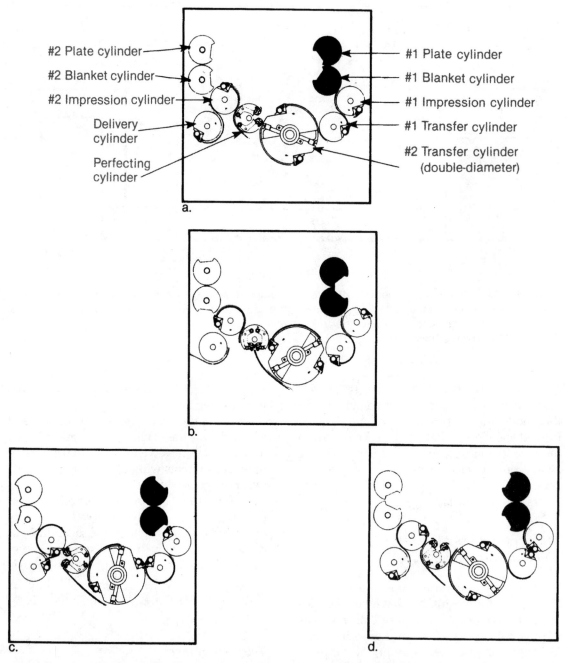

#2 Plate cylinder
#2 Blanket cylinder
#2 Impression cylinder
Delivery cylinder
Perfecting cylinder

#1 Plate cylinder
#1 Blanket cylinder
#1 Impression cylinder
#1 Transfer cylinder
#2 Transfer cylinder (double-diameter)

a.

b.

c.

d.

Figure 12.31. Schematic of the Miller perfecting transfer system, perfecting mode. Note the two-gripper system on the perfecting cylinder which grips the sheet by its tail edge with one gripper (a), then passes the sheet to the second gripper (b and c), and on to the second impression cylinder (d).
Courtesy of Miller Printing Equipment Corp.

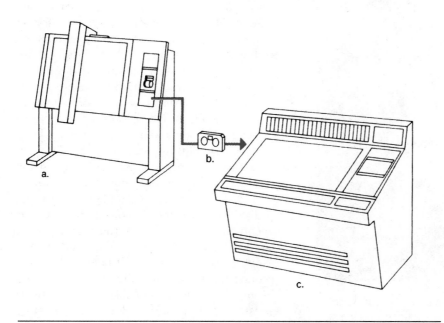

Figure 12.32. Schematic of a typical, automated, multicolor press control system. The plate scanner (a) scans the plate and prints information needed to set the press ink system on cassette tape (b) for automatic system setting through the press console (c).
Courtesy of Miller Printing Equipment Corp.

measuring the image area of the plate, and calculates the settings needed on the press ink keys and the amount of **roller stroke** needed (the stroke length required on the ink fountain roller). This information can be stored on cassette tape, digital computer disk, and/or on a printout. The data is then passed with the plate to the press room. On fully automated systems, information from the storage medium can be fed directly to the press from the press console. Adjusting the ink system is done automatically when the press reads the information on the tape. When the press is not equipped with this fully automatic feature, the press operator can use the information on the printout to preset the ink system. A plate scanner significantly reduces both make-ready and spoilage because presetting produces almost the final ink settings required for the job with the first sheet off the press.

The Press Console

The **press console** is really the heart of an automated press system (figure 12.34). At the start

Figure 12.33. A plate scanner. Note the printout tape in the center of the control panel and the slot for cassette tape at the top of the panel. The plate scanner is built into the vertical bar positioned over the plate.
Courtesy of Miller Printing Equipment Corp.

of a job, the press operator enters parameters about the job into the press console. These parameters include ink density and other job specifications. While the job prints, the operator pulls sample press sheets from the outfeed table and places them on a scanning densitometer which reads a **color bar** printed on each press sheet (figure 12.35). Color bar images can be seen recorded on the plate shown in figure 12.33. From the color bar, the console computer gathers information about density values, register, dot gain, doubling, ink trapping, and print contrast (see chapter 13). This information can be used by the console to correct press problems automatically, or to alert the operator

to problems through the cathode ray tube (CRT) screen for manual press adjustments.

More sophisticated designs mount a densitometer directly on the press that continuously reads densities from the color bar as each sheet prints. The operator then monitors a computer screen and makes adjustments accordingly. The machine-mounted densitometer can also be linked directly to the inking system to make automatic corrections.

Automated press systems offer several major advantages. Not only do they reduce spoilage during make-ready, but they keep spoilage down throughout the job by allowing for fast, accurate press adjustment. Because the press console is preprogrammed with parameters for each job, printing problems can be recognized instantly and the job can be returned quickly to the quality standards established on the "OK sheet" (the sheet approved by the printer or press operator). It takes only a few seconds for a press operator to scan a press sheet at the computer console and make press adjustments. Even if the adjustments must be made manually, they can be made from the computer console. This is an additional advantage because fewer operators are required to run the press. As a result, the printer can deliver more acceptable quality faster and at lower cost. This makes the printer more competitive in a highly competitive printing market.

Although the introduction of automated press operations means that fewer press operators are required to run a press, computer systems have not reduced the number of press operators required in the industry overall. Instead, computers have increased the amount of quality color printing being done, and therefore the number of printers needed, and they have greatly increased the knowledge needed and the type of skills required by press operators.

Most educational institutions are equipped with manual presses because the knowledge gained from manual press operations is still valuable. No matter how automated press sys-

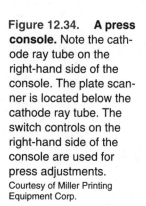

Figure 12.34. **A press console.** Note the cathode ray tube on the right-hand side of the console. The plate scanner is located below the cathode ray tube. The switch controls on the right-hand side of the console are used for press adjustments.
Courtesy of Miller Printing Equipment Corp.

GATF COMPACT COLOR TEST STRIP

Figure 12.35. **One type of color bar.** Colors printed on this test strip can be read by a scanning densitometer and used to monitor press operation.
Courtesy of Graphic Arts Technical Foundation

tems become, there will always be a need for skilled press operators who understand the basics of press operation and the concepts of print quality. This type of knowledge is gained during manual press operation, and it provides a firm foundation on which to build the skills needed to operate an automated press.

Web Offset Presses

An in-depth description of web offset press operation is beyond the scope of this text. However, the growth of web offset printing—particularly for printing books, newspapers, business forms, magazines, directories, and packaging—has made the process a major part of the commercial printing industry. The following is a brief introduction to the web offset process and to the types of web presses and auxiliary equipment commonly used in the industry.

Sections of the Web Offset Press

As mentioned earlier, web printing is printing on a continuous roll of paper (or some other substrate) rather than printing on individual sheets. The method of image transfer in web offset is not the same as the offset printing method used for sheetfed work. In both methods the image is transferred from a printing plate to a blanket cylinder, and from a blanket cylinder to a printing substrate. However,

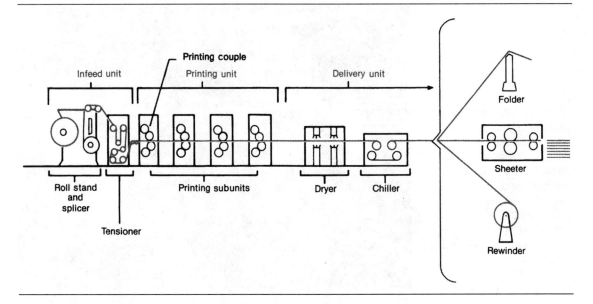

Figure 12.36.   **Major units of a web offset press**

because the substrate is wound on a roll in web printing and travels continuously through the press, the feeding, registration, and delivery units on web presses differ from those on sheet-fed presses. The major sections of a typical web press are the infeed unit, the printing unit, and the delivery unit (figure 12.36).

Infeed Unit

The infeed unit delivers paper to the web press. The infeed unit typically contains a **roll stand,** which holds the paper rolls; a **splicer,** which automatically splices the end of one web to the beginning of another web; a **web-steering device,** which controls the **sidelay** (side-to-side position) of the infeeding web; and a **tensioner,** which maintains the proper tension on the web as it enters the press.

Printing Unit

The printing unit of the web press is made up of one or more printing subunits. Each printing subunit contains one or more printing couples.

A **printing couple** contains an inking system, a dampening system, a plate cylinder, a blanket cylinder, and an impression cylinder. Each printing couple prints one color of ink.

Delivery Unit

The first major component of every delivery unit is an ink drying device. After the ink dryer, the delivery unit can consist of a variety of devices ranging from a simple **sheeter,** which cuts the moving web into sheets of the required size, to a combination sheeter and folder, which both folds the web into final signatures and trims the signatures to size. Where no folding or cutting is required, the delivery unit can contain only a rewinder, which winds the web into a roll for later processing.

Types of Web Presses

The most popular web presses for commercial printing are the blanket-to-blanket and the common impression cylinder (CIC) presses. In-line presses are also common.

Blanket-to-Blanket Web Press

A **blanket-to-blanket web press** uses two printing couples to print on both sides of the web simultaneously. Thus, it is a perfecting press. However, as you will note from figure 12.37, each blanket cylinder serves a dual function; it serves as the blanket for one printing couple and as the impression cylinder for the other printing couple. As a result, impression pressure develops between two blanket cylinder surfaces, rather than between a blanket cylinder and an impression cylinder.

Common Impression Cylinder (CIC) Web Press

Common impression cylinder (CIC) web presses use one large, central impression cylinder in conjunction with a number of printing couples (figure 12.37). The web travels around the common impression cylinder and passes under one or more of the blanket cylinders, which are each part of a printing couple. The advantage of a CIC press is that the paper or other substrate has uniform stretch around the large impression cylinder. This uniformity makes obtaining proper register, and keeping register consistent, much easier than it is on a blanket-to-blanket press.

In-Line Web Press

In addition to blanket-to-blanket and CIC web presses, in-line web presses are also common, particularly for printing forms (figure 12.38a). The major feature of an **in-line web press** is that each printing unit consists of only one blanket cylinder and one impression cylinder combined with an inking and dampening system (figure 12.28b). Thus, in-line presses are not perfecting presses and are used mostly for work that needs to be printed

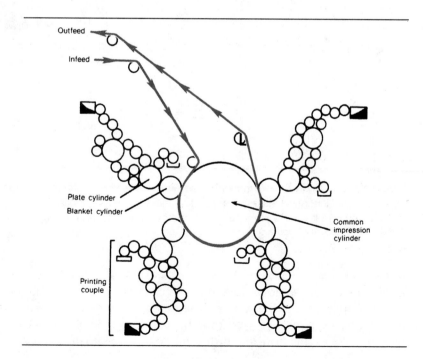

Figure 12.37. Schematic of a common impression cylinder web press

(a)

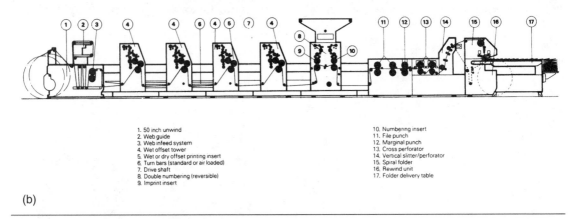

1. 50 inch unwind
2. Web guide
3. Web infeed system
4. Wet offset tower
5. Wet or dry offset printing insert
6. Turn bars (standard or air loaded)
7. Drive shaft
8. Double numbering (reversible)
9. Imprint insert

10. Numbering insert
11. File punch
12. Marginal punch
13. Cross perforator
14. Vertical slitter/perforator
15. Spiral folder
16. Rewind unit
17. Folder delivery table

(b)

Figure 12.38.   An in-line forms web press. (a) This press is specially designed for printing business forms, checks, lottery tickets, envelopes, data mailers, and other direct mail applications. (b) Equipped with four printing couples and a rewinder, this press can print from one to eight colors.
Courtesy of Müller-Martini Corporation.

on one side only, such as business forms and labels. However, some in-line presses can print on both sides of the web by inserting a **turn bar** between printing units (number 6 on figure 12.28b). The turn bar turns the web over so that the remaining units can print on the back side of the web. Typical in-line presses can print two to four colors on one side of the web or one to two colors on both sides of the web.

Components of a Web Press

The major components of the printing couple for offset printing (the plate cylinder and blanket cylinder, and associated ink and water systems) have already been discussed. The Web Offset Presses section touched upon the components unique to a web press. The following discussion focuses in more detail on those components of a web press that are not typically found on a sheet-fed offset press.

Roll Stand

The roll stand holds one or two webs of paper, and it meters or measures the paper feed into the press. On most web presses, the roll stand is placed in line with the printing couples. However, it is possible to place the roll stand to one side of the press or beneath the press to conserve space or to keep paper roll-handling operations out of the press room (figure 12.39).

Many presses are equipped with auxiliary roll stands so that more than one web can feed to the press at once (figure 12.40a). This provides great flexibility on a multiprinting unit web press because one paper web can be printed by up to four or more printing couples (figure 12.40b). Thus, on a six-color web press, a two-color job can be printed by two printing units while a four-color job is being printed on the remaining four printing units.

A **dancer roller,** operating in conjunction with a brake on the roll stand, controls the web as it unwinds from the roll stand and enters the printing unit. The infeeding web wraps around the dancer roller, which actually rides on the moving web and presses its weight against the moving web paper. The dancer roller is free to move up and down; this up-and-down movement controls the brake on the roll stand (figure 12.41). As shown in figure 12.41, if the web feeds too rapidly, the paper

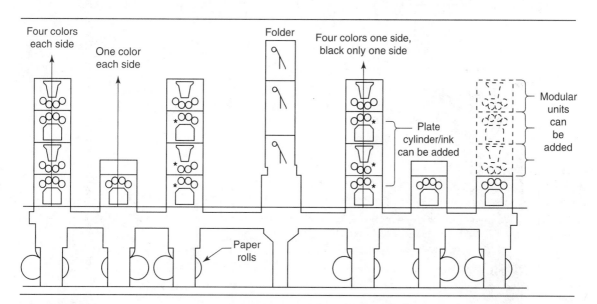

Figure 12.39.   Web press flexibility. This multiunit web press is supplied with four base units to which other vertical printing couples can be added. With a modular unit design such as this, the press can be configured for the type of job to be printed, and press flexibility is greatly increased. Note that the paper is fed from rolls beneath the press room floor.
Courtesy of Graphic Systems Division, Rockwell International Corporation.

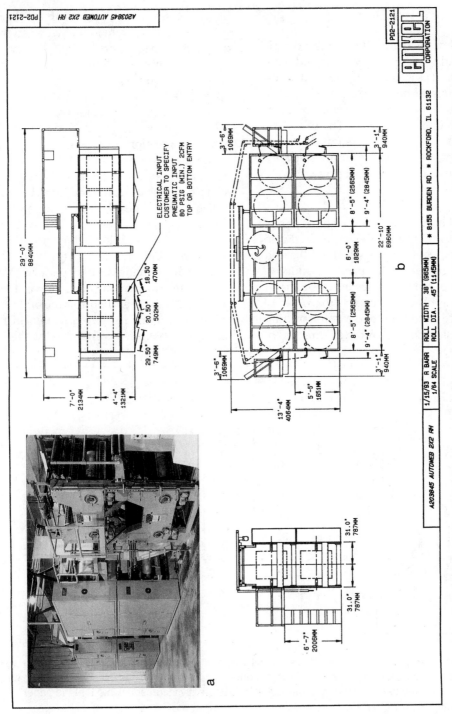

Figure 12.40. **Roll stands.** (a) This web press is equipped with four roll stands to increase press flexibility. (b) This schematic shows roll-stand configuration.
Courtesy of Enkel Corporation.

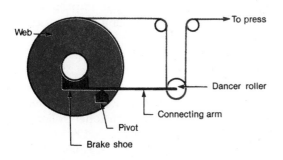

a) Normal position of dancer roller

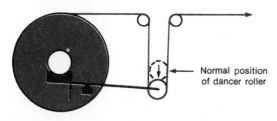

b) As dancer roller drops, brake is applied

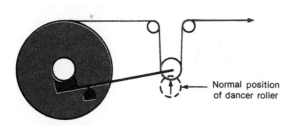

c) As Dancer roller rises, brake is released

Figure 12.41. Schematic showing operation of dancer roller and roll stand brake. Up or down movement of dancer roller controls the brake on the roll stand.

under the dancer roller becomes slack and the dancer roller drops, which automatically applies the brake to the roll stand and slows paper feed. If the web feeds too slowly, just the opposite occurs. The paper under the dancer roller becomes taut and lifts the dancer roller, which releases the brake on the roll stand and allows the web to feed more rapidly.

Splicer

In addition to the dancer roller, it is common for a roll stand to include a splicer, sometimes called a "paster." The splicer automatically positions a new web for infeed and splices the lead end of the new web to the tail end of the web being printed. There are two types of splicers: flying splicers and zero-speed splicers. Both operate automatically, and both use adhesives to connect the two webs. The difference between them is that a **flying splicer** connects the two webs while each web rotates at press speed. It does so by pressing both the adhesive lead edge of the new web and the tail edge of the printing web against a splicing arm (figure 12.42). The **zero-speed splicer** uses a **festoon,** which consists of several rollers. A festoon is a mechanism built for multiple-web rollers; the unit raises or falls. As shown in figure 12.43, the festoon holds enough paper to feed the press during the splice. As a result, the splice can be made while both the old and new web are stationary and the press is running.

Web Tensioner

Although the roll stand and dancer roller work together to meter the web as it enters the printing units, they cannot control web tension completely. Several factors, such as the tension with which the web was rolled at the mill, the type of the paper or other substrate on the web, and the configuration of the press itself, affect web tension during printing. The dancer roller and brake mechanism cannot compensate for all of these factors to maintain adequate and proper web tension. Web tension is critical.

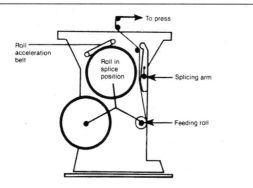

a) Splice in preparation, new roll accelerated, and splicer arm in position

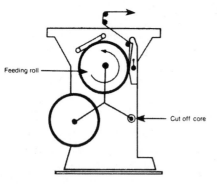

b) Splice is made, new roll feeding and old roll cut, leaving core

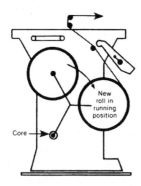

c) New roll moved into running position; splicer arm and acceleration belt moved aside

Figure 12.42.   A flying splicer. After the splice is made, the core is removed and a new web is mounted.

Improper tension can lead to improper image registration. In the worst case, improper tension can break the web, forcing the operator to shut down the press.

Most presses employ a tensioner to maintain consistent web tension (figure 12.44). The **tensioner** consists of a series of rollers over which the infeeding web passes. As the infeeding roll passes over the tensioner rollers, it "recovers" from the tension with which it was wound at the mill and is regulated to the proper, even tension for the press run. Many tensioners consist of a series of variable speed rollers, followed by a second dancer roller. This configuration ensures proper web tension and minimum variation.

Dryer and Chill Rolls

The **dryer** and the **chill rolls** work together to ensure that the ink on the printed sheet is dry and set when it comes off the web. If the web were allowed to leave the press with wet ink, ink setoff would be a problem, and the wet ink would almost certainly smear as the web passed through the folder, cutter, or rewinder. Most web printing inks are heat-set inks. A web printed with heat-set ink passes from the last printing unit through a dryer, which brings the moving web up to a temperature of about 300°F in a few seconds. This temperature is high enough to evaporate most of the ink solvent. It also softens the resin that binds the ink pigments together during chilling. Chilling immediately follows drying. Chilling is accomplished by passing the web over a series of water-cooled chill rolls. During chilling, web temperature is reduced to about 90°F, which is cool enough to set the binder and pigment and produce a dry print.

Folding and Cutting

Because of the nature of web press work, most web presses are equipped with one or more folders that fold the webs into signatures as they leave the press. The type of folder

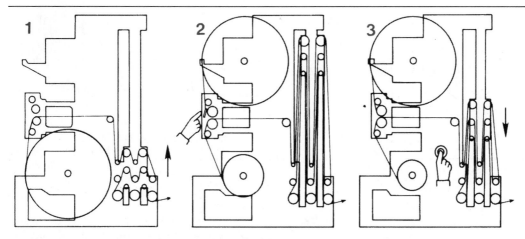

(1) The roll is feeding into the press, and the festoon has begun rising. (2) The festoon has expanded to store a full 80 feet of paper; a new roll has been mounted, and its lead edge has been prepared for the splice. (3) The expired roll has been stopped, and paper feeds into the running press from the collapsing festoon. The lead edge of the splice roll has been placed close to the surface of the expiring web.

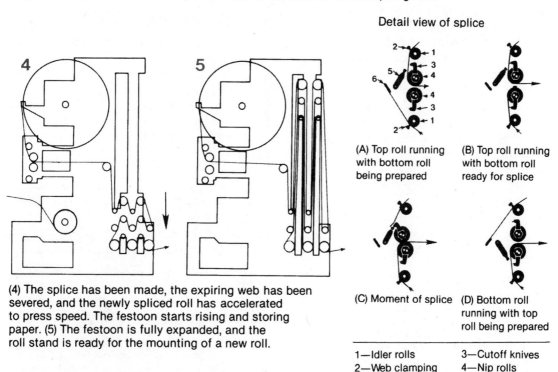

(4) The splice has been made, the expiring web has been severed, and the newly spliced roll has accelerated to press speed. The festoon starts rising and storing paper. (5) The festoon is fully expanded, and the roll stand is ready for the mounting of a new roll.

Detail view of splice

(A) Top roll running with bottom roll being prepared

(B) Top roll running with bottom roll ready for splice

(C) Moment of splice

(D) Bottom roll running with top roll being prepared

1—Idler rolls	3—Cutoff knives
2—Web clamping brushes to hold severed web	4—Nip rolls
	5—Cutoff brush
	6—Vacuum blade

Figure 12.43.   **Splicing on a zero speed splicer**

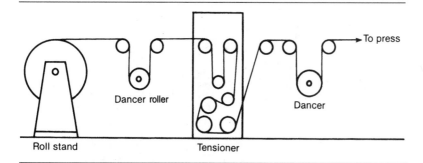

Roll stand   Dancer roller   Tensioner   Dancer   To press

Figure 12.44.   **A web tensioner.** Dancer rollers placed before and after the tensioner help maintain proper web tension.

required depends largely on the type of work being printed on the web press. There are three basic types of folders: former folders, jaw folders, and chopper or quarter folders. Often, all three folding devices are incorporated into a combination folder, as shown in figure 12.45.

A **former folder** folds the web by pulling it over a triangular-shaped former board. This action makes one "with-the-grain" fold by folding the web along its length. Folds made after the former fold are made with jaw and chopper folders. A jaw folder folds the web across its width (across its grain) by allowing it to travel around a cylinder equipped with a tucker blade. The tucker blade forces the paper into a jaw (opening) on an opposing cylinder. After passing through the folding jaw, the web is automatically cut into individual signatures and, if necessary, passes to a chopper folder. In the **chopper folder** each signature is forced between two rotating fold rollers that make the final with-the-grain fold.

Press Console

Most modern web presses print on a moving web at speeds up to 1,800 feet per minute. Much paper would be wasted if the press operator had to examine printed signatures while the press was running in order to determine if press adjustments were needed, and then had to go to the appropriate printing unit and make the required adjustments. High-speed web presses are equipped with press consoles sim-

ilar to those used on automated sheet-fed presses. Press consoles provide electronic control for register and image quality on the moving web (figure 12.46). Information such as web sidelay, register, color consistency, and

Figure 12.45.   **A combination folder.**
Courtesy of Solna, Incorporated

Figure 12.46. **A web press console.** This web press console is designed for complete press control in a single location. Note the CRT graph display of operating conditions, and color-balanced overhead lighting. The web drying unit is located behind the console.
Courtesy of M. A. N.-Roland, ISA, Inc.

backup (the position of the image being printed relative to the top and bottom of the web) is computer controlled. Press adjustments can be made "on the fly" (as the press is running at printing speed). Settings for each printing unit or couple—such as ink and dampening settings and horizontal and vertical register—can be made directly from the console. Once the press operator has the press set properly, computers continually monitor press performance and make adjustments to maintain those initial settings. The press operator monitors the console and, if necessary, makes press adjustments by adjusting switches on the console, which in turn causes the appropriate adjustments to be made on the press itself. The console greatly reduces wastage by reducing the amount of misprinted material and by reducing the amount of press downtime. Some presses even have automatic blanket washing units that are controlled from the press console. Consoles also reduce the number of people required to operate the press.

Key Terms

printing press	flat bed cylinder press	offset press
feeding unit	grippers	perfecting press
registration unit	rotary press	offset lithographic press
printing unit	plate cylinder	duplicator
delivery unit	impression cylinder	web-fed press
platen press	web printing	sheet-fed press
platen	blanket cylinder	pilefeeding

make-ready
continuous sheet-feeding
   system
successive-sheet-feeding
   system
sucker feet
stream feeder
sheet separators
combing wheel
double-sheet detector
registration
fit
headstop
form rollers
three-cylinder principle
two-cylinder principle
impression
fountain
fountain roller

ductor roller
distribution roller
rotating distribution rollers
oscillating distribution rollers
gravity delivery
chain (gripper) delivery
grippers
static eliminator
multicolor sheet-fed press
perfecting transfer system
plate scanner
roller stroke
press console
color bar
roll stand
splicer
web-steering device
sidelay

tensioner
printing couple
sheeter
blanket-to-blanket web press
common impression
   cylinder (CIC) web press
in-line web press
turn bar
dancer roller
flying splicer
zero-speed splicer
festoon
dryer
chill rolls
combination folder
former folder
jaw folder
chopper folder

Questions for Review

1. What four units are common to all presses?
2. How does a platen press differ from a flat bed cylinder press?
3. Why is the rotary press design efficient for printing?
4. Explain the offset principle.
5. Draw the cylinder configuration for a blanket-to-blanket perfecting press.
6. Differentiate between an offset duplicator and a true offset press.
7. How does a successive sheet-feeder feed paper to a press? What controls are available on this type of feeder?
8. What is the difference between registration and fit?
9. How is registration controlled on a sheet-fed offset press?
10. Describe the three- and two-cylinder configurations used on offset presses.
11. Why must control impression be adjusted?
12. Describe the roller train for the inking and dampening systems on a press equipped with a conventional direct dampening system.
13. Explain the operation of a chain delivery system.
14. What are the major units of a web offset press?
15. How does a common impression cylinder press differ from a blanket-to-blanket press?
16. How do the roll stand and dancer roller control web travel?
17. Why are a dryer and chill rolls needed on a high-speed web offset press?
18. Describe the three types of folders commonly found on a web offset press.
19. What is the purpose of a press console?

Offset Press

Anecdote to Chapter Thirteen

Alois Senefelder, the inventor of lithography, designed the first lithographic press sometime between 1798 and 1800 by borrowing the basic idea of a press that was used to reproduce copperplate engravings using a relief process. Senefelder took what was basically a flat bed cylinder design and added a tympan frame and frisket to hold the paper, a flexible blade instead of a roller to apply the pressure, and a lever-counterweight system to control the blade tension.

During production, two workers operated Senefelder's device. The workers first drew a design by hand on a slab of limestone with a grease crayon-like material and placed the "plate" on the movable bed of the press. They next covered the stone with a water and gum arabic solution. The liquid flowed off of the greasy image but covered the nongreasy stone surface. Then the workers vigorously rolled an ink-covered leather roller back and forth over the stone. The ink was repelled by the water film but attached to the grease image. The stone was ready to print after the workers care-

fully wiped it with a clean cloth to remove any excess moisture.

The workers then moved to the press where they mounted a sheet of previously dampened paper on the tympan, closed the frisket to hold the sheet in place, and lowered the frame into contact with the processed stone. Then they lowered the blade against the back of the tympan. One worker stood on the pressure lever while the other slowly turned a wheel to slide the bed under the blade. This scraping pressure caused the ink to transfer from the stone to the sheet of paper. There was always danger that the blade would apply too much pressure and the stone would break or that the sheet would slip under the scraping action. After one pass, the workers released the blade, hinged the tympan frame out of the way, and hung the sheet on a line to dry. Then they repeated the whole process.

Senefelder's press was considered a marvel of its time. In an average twelve-hour day, two craftspeople could produce perhaps fifty acceptable copies using his press. Senefelder's

Original drawing of Senefelder's lithographic press design

later designs included an automatic dampening and inking system and a lever scraper blade that moved across the stone instead of the stone moving under the blade.

Although steam power was applied to a lithographic press around 1866, Senefelder's basic design was not changed until the offset press was introduced in 1907.

Objectives for Chapter 13

After completing this chapter, you will be able to:

■ Recall the most common inking unit configuration and describe its setup operations.

■ Recall the most common dampening unit configuration and describe its setup operations.

■ Describe the basic steps in setting up and operating an offset lithographic press.

■ Recall press concerns when printing process color on sheet-fed offset lithographic presses.

■ Describe several quality control devices commonly used in offset printing.

■ Recall common roller and blanket problems and solutions, and describe mechanical adjustments that are possible on most presses.

■ Recall common press concerns.

■ Recognize a troubleshooting checklist and be able to use it to suggest solutions to press problems.

■ List common press maintenance steps.

Introduction

There are so many different offset presses on the market today with so many minute operational differences that it is easy to become bogged down trying to learn press operation by the "which-switch-does-what" method. The problem with this method is that the operator is lost if moved to another type of machine.

An operation manual prepared by the press manufacturer is unparalleled for teaching "switches." Such a manual can provide more detailed on-the-job information for a production situation than any textbook could provide. The purpose of this chapter is not to serve as a "general operation manual," but rather to deal with fundamental understandings that will enable you to run any offset duplicator or sheet-fed press after reviewing the manufacturer's operation manual.

This chapter is divided into two sections. Section 1 covers the information necessary to run an offset press. Section 2 gives important information on troubleshooting press concerns.

SECTION 1

As just mentioned, the purpose of this section is to examine the general operation of any sheet-fed offset press or duplicator. Refer to a machine's operation manual for details on operating that specific machine.

Offset Press Operation

In an industrial situation each press is usually assigned one operator or group of operators. The operator assigned to a press knows the press's characteristics and typically runs only a few standard sheet sizes. Experienced press operators typically set up the ink and water sections of the printing unit before adjusting the paper feed. Novice printers, however, do not have the advantages of being familiar with the press, knowing the sheet size run previously, or being confident around a machine as complicated as an offset press. For these reasons, it is recommended that students adjust the paper feed before adding ink or fountain solution to the printing unit when learning press operation. When the press sheets pass through the press consistently and without jamming or misfeeding, students can direct their attention to obtaining proper ink-water balance.

Feeding the Press Sheet

It is important that the press sheets are cut accurately to the same size, are the same thickness (paper weight), and are not wrinkled or stuck together. To feed the paper, begin by fanning the pile of press sheets to remove any static electricity that might be holding the individual sheets together (figure 13.1). Place the pile slightly off center in the feeder unit of the press. When the press sheet is momentarily

Figure 13.1.   Fanning the press sheets. The press sheets are fanned to remove any static electricity.

Figure 13.2.   Adding paper to the feeder unit. Seat the pile of press sheets squarely against the front plate of the feeder.

held in place in the registration unit—just before it enters the printing unit—the paper is generally jogged or pulled ⅛ inch to ³⁄₁₆ inches into final position. It is this action that causes "registration." For this reason it is important to load the pile in the feeder unit just a bit off center.

Push the pile forward so that it is seated squarely against the front plate of the feeder when held by the side and back guides (figure 13.2). The top of the paper pile must be perfectly level and parallel to the registration board. If the pile sags, place a heavy board (such as a binder board cut slightly smaller than the paper size) under the pile. If the pile curls, insert wedges at several points in the pile to make the surface level (figure 13.3).

Next, adjust the pile height below the feeder mechanism (figure 13.4). Pile height is generally measured from the sucker feet. Heavy paper must be closer to the sucker feet than light paper. To set the pile height, turn the press on and allow the automatic pile height control to raise the pile to its previously set position. When the pile is in position, turn the press off and check the distance between the pile and the sucker feet when the feet are in their lowest position. If the distance is not between ⅛ inch and ¼ inch, lower the pile manually, readjust

Figure 13.3.   Using wedges to level the paper. Push wedges into the pile of paper to level the surface of curled stock.

the pile height control, and allow the press to rerun and lift the paper pile to the new setting. Feeding problems will result if the pile height is not set properly. If the paper pile is too high, the sucker feet will pick up double sheets, or jamming will result because the air and vacuum system is not allowed to do its job. If the pile is too low, no sheets will be picked up or misfeeds will occur.

As mentioned in chapter 12, the purpose of the air blast in the feeder unit is to float the

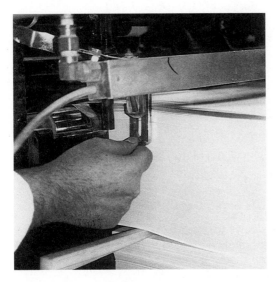

Figure 13.4. **Adjusting the pile height**

Figure 13.5. **Adjusting the air blast**

top few sheets of the pile above the rest of the pile on a blanket of air. The amount of air blast needed varies depending on the weight and size of the paper being printed. In general, the air blast should be adjusted so that the press sheets do not vibrate and the topmost sheet nearly contacts the sucker feet (figure 13.5). Too much air causes the top sheets to press together rather than separate. The vacuum should be sufficient to draw the top sheet the short distance into contact with the sucker feet but not enough to pick up more than one sheet.

Before allowing the feeder mechanism to send a press sheet to the registration unit, the pull-in wheels (not on all machines) and the double-sheet detector must be set. Adjust the pull-in wheels to a uniform pressure so that they pull each sheet squarely from the feeder onto the registration board. Double-sheet detectors either open a trap door and eject multiple sheets to a tray below the registration board or they mechanically (or electronically) cause the press to stop when a double sheet is detected. Set the detector to allow the thickness of

one sheet to pass but to trip the press if more than one sheet is fed.

Registering the Press Sheet

Next, allow the press to feed a press sheet into the registration unit until the press sheet contacts the headstop (figure 13.6). The paper is moved along the registration board by moveable conveyer tapes, straps, or skid rollers that

Figure 13.6. **Adjusting the registration unit.**
Adjust the registration unit by allowing a sheet of paper to contact the headstop. Then position the sheet jogger or pull guide.

move the tape to align with the sheet size. Then adjust the sheet jogger or pull guide to push or pull the sheet about ⅛ inch. The press sheet should lie flat in the registration unit without binding or curling. Inch the sheet into the grippers that pull it between the impression cylinder and the blanket cylinder and allow it to be transferred to the delivery unit. Heavier paper is more difficult for the sheet jogger to move and should be closer than ⅛ inch.

Delivering the Press Sheet

Before the sheet is released from the chain grippers, adjust the delivery table side guides (figure 13.7). Allow the press sheet to drop onto the delivery table and position the table end jogger.

In order to check the entire printing system, start the press and allow paper to pass from the feeder to the delivery unit. The sheets should feed smoothly and consistently to the registration board. Each sheet should be registered and transferred uniformly to the printing unit. The delivery unit should remove each sheet and stack a perfect pile on the outfeed table. Final adjustments for image registration are made after the printing unit has been

Figure 13.8.   Using make-ready sheets. Notice that a marker is placed between the make-ready or scrap sheets and the clean press sheets on the infeed table.
Courtesy of SUCO Learning Resources and R. Kampas

inked and the first few printed sheets have been checked.

It is wise to place some make-ready or scrap sheets on top of the press sheet pile. Make-ready sheets can be used for initial press setup. Be certain, however, that the make-ready sheets are of the same weight and surface finish as the final sheets (figure 13.8).

Preparing the Printing Unit

Recall from chapter 12 that two basic systems are used to put water solution and ink on the printing plate: the direct system and the indirect system. In the direct system, moisture is transferred to the plate directly from a dampening form roller. In the indirect system, the water is transferred to the plate from the ink form rollers. The major difference in preparing the printing unit for these two system is that with the indirect system, the fountain solution cannot be added to the water fountain until the press is inked completely. In the direct system, however, the ink and fountain solution can be put into the ink and water fountain during the same step. It is important to keep in mind

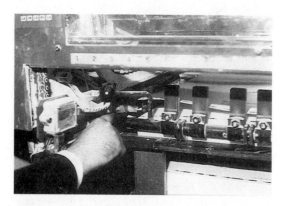

Figure 13.7.   Adjusting the delivery unit side guides

Figure 13.9.   The ink fountain. The ink fountain holds a pool of ink that is passed to the inking system. The amount of ink that is passed is controlled by ink fountain keys.

with which system you are working as you read the following.

Adjusting the Ink System

Ink is transferred from the ink fountain reservoir by a ductor roller that contacts the fountain roller. The consistency of the ink layer over the fountain roller directly influences the amount of ink fed to the distribution unit.

Many ink fountains are set up with ink fountain keys that allow the press operator to adjust the ink feed to allow for variation in ink coverage needed on the plate (figure 13.9). If large solids or halftones cover one section of the plate, it is necessary to feed additional ink to that section of the plate (figure 13.10).

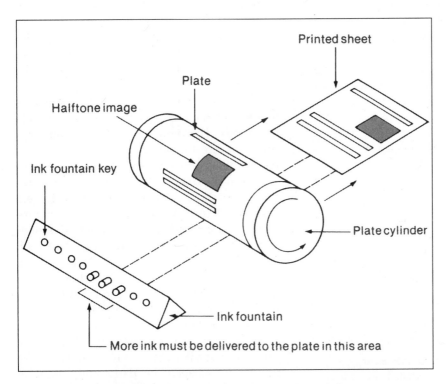

Figure 13.10.   Adjusting the ink fountain. The ink fountain keys must be adjusted to deliver more ink to areas where large halftones or other kinds of dense copy will print from the plate.

When setting up an ink fountain, assume that the ink feed needs adjustment. Begin by loosening all of the ink fountain keys. This brings the ink fountain doctor blade out of contact with the fountain roller (figure 13.11). Reverse the process by gently tightening each fountain key until you feel blade pressure against the fountain roller. Then move the fountain keys out slightly to allow a small gap between the doctor blade and the fountain roller.

When the doctor blade is straight and parallel to the fountain roller, you can add ink to the ink fountain. To check for uniform ink distribution, manually rotate the press until the ink ductor roller touches the ink fountain roller. Then turn the ink fountain roller and observe the ink coverage on the ductor roller. If the surface of the ductor roller is covered evenly, the fountain keys are set properly. If heavy or light areas are noticeable across the ductor roller, adjust the fountain keys until the ink layer is consistent. If some areas of the plate require more ink than others, open

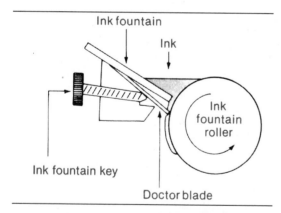

Figure 13.11.   Diagram of an ink fountain key. As the ink fountain key is adjusted, it moves the doctor blade either toward or away from the ink fountain roller, and thereby decreases or increases the amount of ink that is deposited on the roller.

the fountain keys that are in line with those sections.

Once the first rough ink adjustments have been made, and without bringing the water or ink form rollers into contact with the plate cylinder, turn the press on and allow the systems to ink up. As the distribution rollers work the ink to a fine layer, make small adjustments to ensure ink train uniformity. Do not overink the system. It is easier to add ink to the system than it is to remove it.

Adjusting the Dampening System
Fountain solution is added to the dampening fountain of most presses and duplicators from a storage bottle that works by gravity feed. This bottle should be placed into position at this time. Remember, if you are operating an indirect dampening system, the fountain solution should not be added until the whole roller train is inked. In contrast, the fountain solution can be added to a direct dampening system before, after, or during ink adjustments.

None of the ink and dampening rollers in indirect dampening systems have covers or sleeves. The dampening ductor and form rollers in direct dampening systems generally have cloth or fiber covers. If the dampening covers in the direct system are extremely dry (this may occur after a long period of press shutdown), turn on the press, bring the dampening ductor roller into contact with the fountain roller, and turn the fountain roller by hand to add extra fountain solution to the dampening ductor roller. This action speeds the dampening process. Be careful not to soak the ductor roller, however, as soaking overdampens the press.

Another way to speed the dampening process is to soak a cotton wipe in the fountain tray and squeegee the dampening solution onto the ductor roller. The form roller cover should be damp to the touch, but it should not be dripping wet. Once the dampening unit is

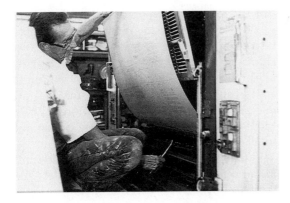

Figure 13.12. Mounting the plate on the press

inked and moistened adequately, stop the press and insert the plate.

Attaching the Plate

Mount the plate on the press by inserting the front edge of the plate in the lead clamp of the plate cylinder, and tighten the plate into position (figure 13.12). If packing is required to help control impression, select and cut the appropriate packing material, and position the packing material between the plate and the cylinder. Then rotate the cylinder forward so that the plate curves into contact with the plate cylinder. When the rear plate clamps become exposed, insert the tail edge of the plate and tighten the clamp. The plate should be tight around the cylinder, but it should not distort or stretch.

Starting Up and Proofing

Most lithographic plates have some form of gum preservative coating to protect the plate surface between development and press placement. Moisten a sponge with plain water or fountain solution and wipe the entire plate to dissolve this coating. If a direct image plate is being used, a special etch or starter solution must be used at this point.

Inking the Plate

If you are operating an indirect system, start the press and allow it to operate for a moment. Then move the form rollers into contact with the plate. The plate should pick up ink in its image areas and no ink in its nonimage areas. If no ink is picked up anywhere on the plate after several press revolutions, check to make sure that the form rollers are contacting the plate. If there is contact, you must either cut back on the moisture or add ink until the image appears on the plate. To determine which adjustment is necessary, stop the press and observe the plate. If the plate is moist with only a thin film of fountain solution (not dripping), more ink is probably needed. If the plate is overdampened, adjust the water fountain to deliver less moisture.

If you are operating a direct dampening system, start the press, let it operate for a moment, and lower the dampening form rollers into contact with the plate. Release the form rollers, stop the press, and check the plate. The surface of the plate should be moist, but dampening solution should not drip from it. If the plate is not moist, adjust the fountain system to deliver more moisture and repeat the processes of dampening and checking. Once the dampening form rollers are delivering enough moisture to the plate surface, lower the ink form rollers into contact with the plate. Ink should transfer only the image areas of the plate. If ink deposits in nonimage areas, there is probably a lack of moisture. If ink appears in nonimage areas, called scumming, place additional fountain solution onto the dampener form roller in that area.

Press Proofing

Once the plate is properly inked, place the press "on impression" (lower the plate cylinder into contact with the blanket cylinder) and allow several make-ready sheets to pass through the printing unit.

The only initial concern is image position, not image quality. Examine the first few printed sheets for consistent image placement, and compare the image placement with the proofs or layout specifications for the job. All offset presses allow the image to be raised or lowered on the sheet by moving the position of the plate image on the blanket cylinder. On most presses you can skew the plate on the plate cylinder or the paper on the registration board to square the image on the press sheet. Before final side-to-side and up-and-down adjustments of the image are made, the image must first be square to the lead edge of the press sheet. The side-to-side image position can then be adjusted by moving the registration system.

After obtaining the desired image position, start the press, lower the dampening and ink form rollers into plate contact, and begin the run with the make-ready sheets. As the sheets pass through the press, assess the image quality and make appropriate adjustments to the ink or dampening system and the impression cylinder. As the first clean sheets begin to feed, set the press sheet counter to zero and begin the press run. A counter automatically counts each sheet as it passes through the press.

Achieving Proper Ink-Water Balance

The ink-water balance is crucial in offset printing. If not enough moisture is on the plate, the image scums on the press sheet. If too much moisture reaches the plate, the image appears light and washed out (not dense enough) on the press sheet. Adding ink to an overdampened plate does not correct the ink-water balance problem. In fact, it makes matters worse because when the correct amount of moisture is finally delivered to the plate, the press will be overinked.

It is important to remember that small changes made at the fountain rollers take time to work through the distribution and form rollers and to the plate. Most fountain rollers are adjusted by a ratchet. A lever along the ratchet is moved forward or backward so many "clicks" to make the fountain roller turn faster or slower. Often the lever has a scale printed next to it. This scale does not refer to any specific quantity of ink or moisture, but rather relates to the rate of fountain roller rotation at any given time. Moving the lever up the scale makes the fountain roller rotate more rapidly. Moving the lever down the scale causes the roller to rotate more slowly.

The water fountain roller alone controls the amount of moisture placed on the plate. On the inking system, however, both the opening of the ink fountain keys and the rotation rate of the ink fountain roller control the quantity of ink reaching the plate. To achieve proper ink-water balance, the ink fountain keys, the ink fountain roller rotation rate, and the water fountain roller rotation rate must all be adjusted properly. When these elements are adjusted properly, and the press can run through several thousand impressions without the press operator touching the ink or water adjustments, the ink and water systems are said to be "in balance."

Ink-water balance can be achieved only while the press is actually printing. An inexperienced press operator may have to print many make-ready sheets to achieve this balance. Even experienced press operators allow up to 6-percent spoilage for a run of one thousand sheets. In other words, the experienced operator expects to print up to sixty press sheets to get the press to feed properly and to reach the correct ink-water balance. These spoiled sheets, called the "spoilage allowance," are added to the one thousand sheets needed for the final run and are paid for by the customer as part of the job.

The ink and water settings necessary to achieve proper ink-water balance differ with each printed job. One job may have large, dense image areas and require more water and ink than another job. When colors are printed, whether process color or flat color, proper ink-water balance must be achieved for each color. As a result, the spoilage allowance increases for color work.

The mark of an experienced press operator is the ability to get the press feeding and reaching ink-water balance with the least amount of spoilage. This takes practice and familiarity with a particular press. Novice printers do not have this experience. However, the following considerations may make achieving ink-water balance a bit easier for the novice:

1. Remember that the gauge of any printing job is the press sheet. Experienced press operators watch the outfeed table and pull every twenty-fifth, fiftieth, or one hundredth press sheet to compare with the first acceptable press proof. A quick check of the press sheet shows density inconsistencies across the image area, scumming or ink in the nonimage areas, and **set-off** (an image printed on the back of the press sheet). Checking the ink rollers and registration board will not help determine whether the printed image is acceptable, however.

2. On direct system presses, the ink and water form rollers can be lifted from the plate separately. It is always a good idea to raise the form rollers from the plate when the ink or dampening system is being adjusted. This will help keep the plate from becoming overdampened or overinked.

3. Most ink and water fountain rollers can be stopped without stopping the ductor roller or the distribution rollers. If the press appears too dry, but the ink quantity seems right, stop the paper feeder, lift the form rollers, and turn off the ink fountain roller before adjusting the water fountain roller. It may take fifty to one hundred press revolutions for a small change in the ink fountain roller adjustment to work its way to the plate. If the press is inking all this time and no paper is being printed, the ink will build up on the ink rollers. Once the water system is properly adjusted, the press will be overinked.

4. Feed jam-ups are frequent problems for inexperienced press operators. Generally a jam-up can be corrected in a short time simply by shutting off the press and removing the jammed paper. Occasionally, however, jam-ups take longer to clear. If the press is shut down for much more than two minutes during a run, the ink-water balance has to be reachieved before final sheets are printed again. Unless new make-ready sheets are placed on the infeed table after the jam-up is cleared, spoilage increases.

Remember that all the time the press is shut down, the dampening rollers are drying. If the shutdown is lengthy, it may take several press revolutions before the dampening system is back to proper moisture level. After a long press shutdown, it is best to run the press for a few minutes with the inking system off, the form rollers off of the plate, and the dampening system on. Once the dampening system is back to proper moisture level, the dampening form roller(s) can again be engaged to moisten the plate, the press can be stopped briefly, and the plate can be examined for moisture content.

Cleanup Procedures

With the availability of rubber-based inks, many small job shops clean their ink and water systems only once a week. Some operators only cover their presses with a cloth to keep dust out; others spray the ink fountain and rollers with a commercial antiscum material that coats the ink with a thin layer of lacquer and, in effect, forms a seal that prevents the ink from drying. The disadvantage of all these approaches is that paper lint and other impurities in the ink and water systems eventually build up and affect production quality. Therefore, the most effective cleanup procedure is to clean the entire printing unit thoroughly at the end of each workday.

First, however, before the inking system is cleaned, the water fountain is generally drained. A tube leading from the water fountain is used for this purpose.

The ink cleanup systems on all but the smallest offset duplicators are almost totally automatic. One common system moves a doctor blade or squeegee against an ink roller (figure 13.13). If the wash-up solution is applied to the press while it is running, the ink dissolves and passes across the squeegee into a sludge tray.

There are specific procedures to follow when cleaning the inking system. First, remove as much ink as possible from the ink fountain. Next, remove the ink fountain itself and clean it by hand with ink solvent. On most presses, the rest of the inking system is cleaned almost automatically. While the press is off, attach or engage the squeegee or other transfer roller cleanup device. Then start the press and apply press wash-up solution to one side of the distribution rollers (figure 13.14). Most of the ink rollers are driven by friction against two

or three geared rollers. If solvent were applied across the entire system, friction would be reduced and not all the rollers would turn. Apply wash-up solution until half of the system becomes clean and dry. Then apply the solvent to the remaining inked portion. Continue the procedure of applying solvent to one side of the system at a time until the entire system is clean.

The cleanup attachment of the press functions more efficiently if the leading edge of the squeegee blade is wiped clean after each use. If ink dries and hardens on the blade, the blade will not contact the roller properly. Some cleanup attachments are removed completely from the press after cleanup. Others merely hinge out of contact with the press rollers.

An alternative to the mechanical cleanup system is a blotter pad. Blotter pads are absorbent paper sheets that are cut and punched to the exact plate size for the press being used. To clean the inking system using a blotter pad, mount a blotter pad on the plate cylinder, turn on the machine, and lower the ink form rollers into contact with the pad (take special care to raise the water form roller out of contact with the plate cylinder). Apply solvent much the same as you would when using a mechanical

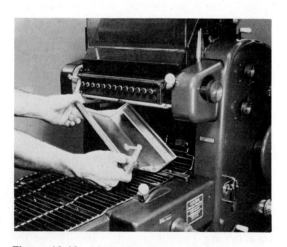

Figure 13.13.   A doctor blade

Figure 13.14.   Applying wash-up solution

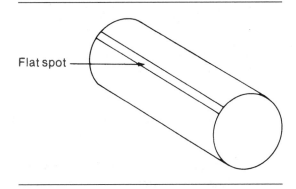

Figure 13.15. A roller with a flat spot

cleaning device. With this approach, however, the dissolved ink transfers to the blotter pad.

Many presses and duplicators have systems (often called "night latches") that separate the distribution rollers when the press is shut down. If the rollers are left in contact during lengthy shutdown periods, they develop "flat spots" where they rest together (figure 13.15). Flat spots can cause uneven ink distribution throughout the roller train. Consult the operating manual for the press that you are running to determine whether there are night latches that should be set after the press is cleaned.

Printing Process Color on Sheet-Fed Offset Presses

Most offset lithographic presses can be used to reproduce quality process color work as long as good separations, plates, paper, ink, and, most important, a skilled operator are available.

Press Concerns

The concerns when working with four-color, process printing are the same as for any quality single-color job: the sheets must be fed, registered, printed, and delivered. However, it is important when printing process color to hold accurate and consistent registration throughout the entire press run.

There is a simple method to check registration controls prior to printing a four-color job. First, set up the press for the most consistent feeding and registration and print a different job that includes both line and halftone copy. Without changing the press settings, remove the printed sheets from the delivery system and move them to the feeding system to be fed through the press a second time. The goal is to print a second layer of ink—both halftone dots and line copy—over the first image with **dot-for-dot registration.** If, after two printings, only one sharp image is observed, quality registration is being held. If the image is blurred or if there is a double image, however, either the system is not properly adjusted or the press is incapable of quality color reproduction.

When a single press is used to reproduce four-color work, color contamination between runs is always possible. Even though an ink unit is cleaned thoroughly, residual ink may interfere with the purity of the next color. This is more of a problem when a dark color, such as black, is followed by a light color, such as yellow, because impurities are more evident in a light color.

One solution is to ink the press first with a small quantity of the new ink and, after a uniform ink layer is obtained on all rollers, wash the press. The press is then reinked with the same new color in proper quantities for the production run. With this procedure the press actually gets cleaned twice, and there is little chance for color contamination. This technique, called a "color wash-up," is unnecessary when a light color is followed by black.

Sequence of Colors

Recall that process color involves overprinting four separate images in a combination that approximates the appearance of nearly any color in the visible spectrum. During printing, the sequence of colors can vary depending on the type of ink, paper, or press or on the preference of the operator. There are, however, several common sequences.

The sequence of cyan, then yellow, magenta, and finally black is used often. Yellow, magenta, cyan, and black is another frequent color order. The cyan image generally resembles a normal halftone reproduction. In other words, if process cyan is the first color placed on the sheet, detail is usually carried across the sheet wherever the final image appears. Using progressive color proofs, it is possible to compare press sheets with each color to match density and detail positions, and it is relatively easy to fit all colors into their proper positions after cyan is printed. One disadvantage with printing cyan first is a large quantity of ink is laid down on the press sheet the first pass through the press. With so much ink detail on the press sheet, all colors following cyan tend to dry rather slowly because the paper has already absorbed ink over much of its area. There is also the possibility that as the paper becomes more ink saturated with each added color, adhesion can build up between the sheet and blanket cylinder.

Many printed jobs have process color on the same page as line copy such as headlines or paragraph composition, which must appear in black. Often the color position on the page is defined by the location of this black copy. In these situations, it is necessary to print the black copy first and then fit all of the other colors in their correct positions on the sheet. The typical color sequence is black, yellow, magenta, and cyan. This approach has the added advantage of reducing the adhesion between the press sheet and the blanket cylinder because the colors that typically carry the least amount of ink detail are printed first. In instances where progressive proofs are not available, this sequence also enables the press operator to correct any color deviations on the first three colors by adjusting the cyan printer.

Quality Control Devices

Although visual inspection of the press sheet can be used effectively to determine print quality of single-color line images, the quality of halftone images, or images which require critical registration, is best determined with quality control devices. Many companies have developed quality control devices that can be stripped, plated, and printed in nonimage areas of the press sheet. Under magnification, these devices can aid the press operator in determining overall press sheet image quality and in making press adjustments. In the following section, we discuss only a few of the many quality control devices available. All of the devices discussed here have been developed by the Graphic Arts Technical Foundation (GATF), which for years has been at the forefront of research and development in the graphic arts. Readers who desire further information about these and other quality control devices can write to GATF directly at 4615 Forbes Avenue, Pittsburgh, Pennsylvania 15213. Please note that the following reproductions of GATF quality control devices are for illustration only. When supplied by GATF, these devices are of extremely high quality and fine line detail. The reproductions here in no way reflect the original film images provided by GATF.

The GATF T-Mark

The GATF **T-Mark** consists of a configuration of thin, accurately ruled lines that are used to identify image centers, folds, trims, and bleeds during printing production (figure 13.16). The T-shaped center lines signify final trims, folds, or the center-of-image points. During stripping, the cross stroke of the *T* is positioned ⅛ inch (3 mm) outside of the final image area so that is trimmed off after printing. The set of outer marks indicate standard bleed or trim allowances. In negative form, these marks provide accurate references for film assemblers when cutting masks for bleeds. When printed

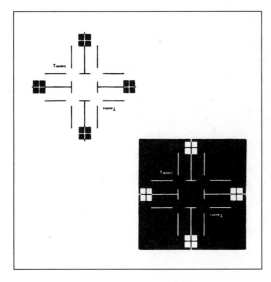

Figure 13.16.   GATF T-mark for trims, centers, and bleeds.
Courtesy of GATF.

Figure 13.17.   Image of the GATF Star Target shown in same size it appears on a press sheet.
Courtesy of GATF.

on the press sheet, these marks guide the press operator in image fit and aid bindery operators when trimming press sheet signatures before folding. The reverse image cross marks that appear in the small squares at the end of the T-marks indicate vertical and horizontal center-of-image points on film sheets. These cross marks are especially useful for aligning images during step-and-repeat operations.

In addition to the previous aids, film negative T-mark images can be positioned on master flats during four-color stripping so that they reproduce in identical locations on each of the plates used to print the job. During printing, the press operator checks to see that these marks line up for each press sheet color. These checks are an aid in achieving initial color register and in monitoring register during the press run.

The GATF Star Target

The GATF **Star Target** is a small, circular pattern of solid and clear pie-shaped wedges (figure 13.17). When printed on a press sheet,

the Star Target gives the press operator a quick and effective measure of the following:

- **Ink spread:** Spreading in all direcctions of the edges of ink dots and lines on the press sheet beyond their corresponding areas on the plate
- **Slur:** Smearing of the trailing edges of dots, resulting in ink film tapering into the white areas
- **Doubling:** Printing of a double image, which consists of a full solid and a weak second image, slightly out of register with the full solid

In practice, the Star Target is stripped into the flat so that it plates in the trim areas at each corner of the trailing edge of the press sheet. These corner areas are usually the most sensitive in showing any ink slur or doubling. The image of the Star Target on the press sheet shows the amount of ink spread and its direction by the way the center wedges of the target fill in with ink. Figure 13.18a shows a press sheet image with very little ink spread. Note that the wedge-shaped images are open almost to the white center. Compare this figure to figure 13.18b, in which ink spread has caused the wedges to fill in and create a central disk of considerable darkness and size.

Slur is recognized in a Star Target when image spread is not uniform in all directions. In figure 13.19 note that the ink spread in the center of the target is greater in one direction, producing an oval-shaped center. Doubling of an image is clearly shown in figure 13.20 where

(a)

(b)

Figure 13.18. **Photomicrographs of Star Target images on press sheets (6x).** Target (a) shows very little ink spread. Target (b) shows considerable ink spread.
Courtesy of GATF.

Figure 13.19. **Photomicrographs of Star Target image showing slur (6x).** Press slur in vertical direction has caused the center of the target to spread to an oval shape.
Courtesy of GATF.

Figure 13.20. **Photomicrographs of Star Target image showing doubling (6x).** Note weak double image adjacent to full printed image in target.
Courtesy of GATF.

Figure 13.21. **10x enlargement of a segment of a GATF QC strip.**
Courtesy of GATF.

each wedge shows a double, and the center of the target forms an oval or a figure eight.

The GATF Quality Control Strip

The GATF **Quality Control (QC) Strip** is a patterned device that helps the press operator control print quality throughout the press run (figure 13.21). The QC strip is stripped and plated to print parallel to the gripper edge (figure 13.22a). The press operator follows standard procedures to produce a properly printed sheet, which is called the "OK sheet." During the press run, the operator pulls inspection sheets from the outfeed pile, compares the QC strip printed on the OK sheet to the QC strip printed on the inspection sheet, and looks for a perfect matchup. As shown in figure 13.22b, when enlarged the QC strip provides a quick and

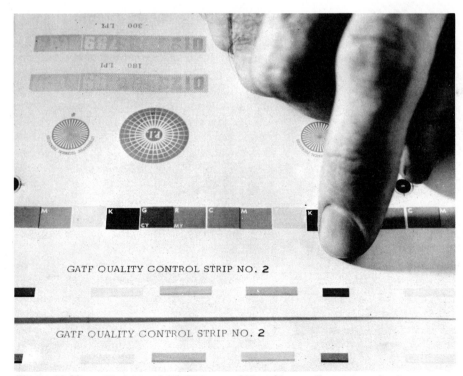

Figure 13.22a. **Closeup of QC Strips on OK and inspection press sheets.**
Courtesy of GATF.

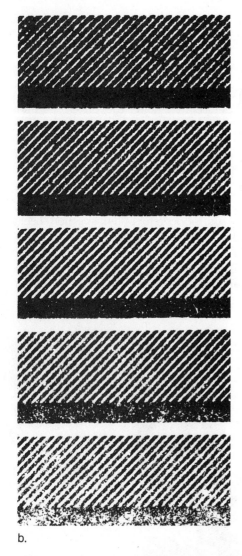

b.

Figure 13.22b.　10x enlargements of a QC Strip segment used to compare five different press sheets.
Courtesy of GATF.

effective method of comparing image quality on the inspection press sheet to image quality on the OK sheet. If the images on the two sheets do not match, press adjustments are made until an inspection sheet is produced with a QC image that matches the OK press sheet image.

The GATF Dot Gain Scale and Slur Gauge

The GATF **Dot Gain Scale** is used to determine if the dot areas of printed halftones match the dot areas on the halftone negatives or positives used to produce them. Fine screen tints are more sensitive to dot gain than coarse screens. The GATF Dot Gain Scale is designed to give numerical values to any dot sharpening (uniform loss in dot size) or dot gain (uniform gain in dot size). The scale is made up of ten 200-line screen tint steps which are graduated in density. These steps form numbers from *0* to *9* on a uniform background of 65-line tint density. When reproduced with halftone copy, some of the numbers appear darker than the background, and some appear lighter. Because the density differences from one number to the next are small, there is usually one number that is about as dense as the background. This number, therefore, is visible to the naked eye on the OK press sheet. The press operator uses the Dot Gain Scale to compare the numbers on the inspection sheet to those on the OK sheet to make sure that the same number remains invisible throughout the press run. If, for example, the number *3* were invisible on the OK sheet, but it began to appear during the press run, the press operator would be alerted to a dot gain condition and could make adjustments accordingly (figure 13.23).

Dot gain causes a dot to grow in all directions. It can result from improper exposure or development in platemaking, excessive cylinder pressures on press, too much ink, or a variety of other press factors. However, slur or doubling, which are directional, can also appear as dot gain. GATF has developed a **Slur Gauge** to help the press operator determine whether slur is occurring (figure 13.24). The Slur Gauge consists of fine horizontal lines that form the word *SLUR* on a vertical line background. Because the horizontal and vertical lines have the same density value, the word *SLUR* is in-

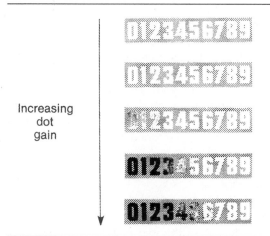

Increasing
dot
gain

Figure 13.23. GATF Dot Gain Scales showing increasing amounts of dot gain.
Courtesy of GATF.

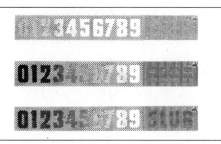

Figure 13.25. Combined Dot Gain Scale and Slur Gauge. The top scale is sharp, the second scale shows dot gain without slur, and the bottom scale shows dot gain caused by slur.
Courtesy of GATF.

visible when all lines are printed with equal thickness. When slur occurs, however, the horizontal or vertical lines thicken, and the word *SLUR* appears darker than the background, alerting the operator to the slur and the slur direction. Because slur can often be confused with uniform dot gain, GATF has combined its Dot Gain Scale with its Slur Gauge (figure 13.25). This combined scale allows the press operator to determine the cause of apparent dot gain quickly so that the problem can be corrected with minimum paper waste.

SECTION 2

This section covers some common press problems and concerns. Like all machines, presses need occasional adjustments to operate correctly. It is impossible to achieve proper ink-water balance or to print a quality image on a press that is not adjusted correctly.

Roller and Blanket Problems and Adjustments

Press operators often encounter several roller and blanket problems. Many of these problems

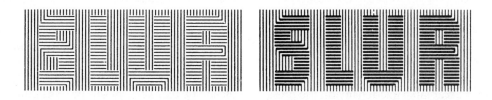

Figure 13.24. Enlarged GATF slur gauge. Image on left shows no slur; image on right shows slur.
Courtesy of GATF.

can be corrected by relatively simple adjustments. Others require roller or blanket replacement. A press operator should be familiar with the adjustment procedures for most of the rollers in the roller train and be able to recognize solutions for many of the more common roller and blanket problems.

Blanket Considerations

As discussed in chapter 12, most offset blankets are formed from vulcanized rubber bonded to a fiber support base. A wide range of blanket quality is available within these basic materials, however. There are special purpose formulations designed to be used with specific materials, such as ultraviolet drying inks or coated stock, for example. Most printers do not change blankets every time a different ink or paper is fed through the press, but the importance of blanket and special materials compatibility must be stressed. Lithographic suppliers are prepared to identify the appropriate blanket for any press situation.

Blanket Problems

There are two common problems that occur with offset blankets that the press operator must be able to recognize and correct: glazing and smashes.

Glazing

Blankets become glazed because of long periods of improper cleaning or age. A very smooth, hard, glossy surface is created when the pores of the blanket fill with ink, ink solvent, and gum known as **glaze**. A glazed blanket loses its ability to transfer enough ink to produce an acceptable ink density on the press sheet. Commercial deglazing compounds are available to clear blanket pores, but the best measure to take to prevent glazing is to wash the blanket properly after each press run.

A good technique for keeping the blanket clean is to dampen the blanket with water and to use a good blanket wash while the blanket is still wet. The water loosens any dried gum that is not dissolved by the blanket wash, and the blanket wash removes dried ink. A properly washed blanket should look like smooth velvet.

Smashes

Blankets become smashed when more material passes between the impression and blanket cylinders than the gap between the two permits. Each time the press sheet wrinkles or folds as it travels through the printing unit, the blanket becomes smashed or creased. If enough pressure is applied to the blanket, the smashed areas of the blanket push in too far to receive ink from the plate cylinder and are unable to transfer images to the press sheets. If a smash is small, a commercial "blanket fix" is available to fix it. When this fix is painted over a smashed area, it causes the surface of the blanket to swell. Do not apply fix to a blanket in a halftone or tint area, however. The swelling caused by blanket fix is not uniform and will not print a uniform halftone or tint pattern. In these situations, the blanket should be replaced. The blanket should also be replaced if there are tears in the surface of the blanket. If a large blanket area has been smashed but there are no visible breaks, it might be possible to return the blanket to usable condition by removing it from the press and soaking it in a water bath for several days.

New blankets should not be stored near excessive heat. If a blanket is exposed to high temperatures, the rubber may lose its "give" or elasticity. Blankets should be stored in flat positions with cover sheets to protect their surfaces from damage.

Plate-to-Blanket Packing and Adjustments

When the paper being printed passes between the impression cylinder and the blanket cylinder, the amount of pressure among these three elements must be uniform and sufficient to transfer ink. At the same time, this pressure cannot be so great that it is abrasive to the plate when the image is offset from the plate to the blanket.

The uniformity of the plate-to-blanket pressure can be checked easily by the operator. Turn off the dampening system and ink the entire surface of a used plate that is mounted on the press. Stop the press and lower the plate cylinder into contact with the blanket cylinder ("on impression"). Separate the two cylinders and inspect the ink band that was transferred to the blanket. If the band is approximately ⅛ inch wide across the entire width of the blanket, the system is aligned properly. If the image is light, heavy, or irregular, consult the press manual for specific recommendations.

On most offset duplicators, plate and blanket cylinder pressure is either controlled automatically by spring pressure or it can be changed by a manual screw adjustment.

On presses, plate-to-blanket pressure is usually adjusted by placing packing under the blanket and/or the plate. Packing press cylinders improperly could cause serious registration problems. Press manufacturers specify appropriate packing for their equipment. Refer to the press manual for detailed plate-to-blanket packing procedures.

Glazed Ink Rollers

Even with the most efficient cleanup procedures, ink rollers can eventually become glazed with dried ink. As mentioned earlier, **glaze** is a buildup on the rubber rollers that prevents the proper adhesion and distribution of ink. Commercially prepared deglazing compounds are available that can be used easily to remove any dried ink from the rollers. One common technique is to apply a pumice compound to the rollers in the same manner as ink is applied. Allow the pumice to work into the rollers by running the press for 5 to 10 minutes. Then wash the system with a liquid deglazing solution. Both the compound and the solution can then be removed by using wash-up solution and standard cleanup procedures. Many press operators deglaze their rollers regularly as part of a preventive maintenance system.

Dampening Rollers

Water does not adhere readily to smooth roller surfaces. Therefore, several dampening rollers are covered with some material that carries usable quantities of the water fountain solution to the plate easily. The ductor roller and form rollers are covered typically with two types of dampening covers: molleton covers and dampening sleeves.

Molleton Covers

Molleton covers are thin cloth tubes that slip over the rollers and are tied or sewn at each end. It is important that the molleton covers the entire roller uniformly. If the ends are tied so tightly that a taper forms in the roller, insufficient moisture is delivered to the plate and the outside edges of the plate scum with ink. A new molleton cover placed on a roller should be broken in. Soak the cover with water and squeeze out any excess water by rolling the covered roller over a sheet of uncoated paper. The breaking-in process removes any lint or loose threads from the cover.

Thin cloth sleeves can be used to cover badly inked molleton covers. Thin cloth and fiber sleeves react more readily to operator adjustments and make maintaining consistent moisture control easier than with the traditional molleton cover.

Dampening Sleeves

Dampening sleeves are thin fiber tubes that, when dry, are slightly larger in diameter than the roller. To apply the dampening sleeve, slide the dry sleeve over the clean roller and soak both with warm water. Within minutes the fibers in the sleeve shrink into position on the roller and the roller is ready to be installed on the press. Dampening sleeves are generally used only on form rollers. Because the sleeves are exceptionally thin compared to molleton covers, the rollers must be oversize compared to those usually supplied with the press. Despite this inconvenience, dampening sleeves are lintless and are easy to install and easy to keep adjusted to the plate cylinder.

Cleaning Dampening Rollers

At the end of each workday, remove the dampening solution from the water fountain tray. If the metal fountain roller becomes coated with ink, it can be cleaned with pumice powder and water. Coating the fountain roller with any commercial desensitizing etch occasionally ensures continued water transfer during the production day.

Cloth and fiber dampening covers and sleeves can be cleaned with a commercial dampening roller cleaner. To clean the covers and sleeves, first saturate them with water so the cleaner soaks into the fabric and not the fibers. Then scrub the surface of the covers and sleeves with a stiff brush and roller cleaner. Rinse the covers and sleeves with water and allow them to dry.

It is best to have two sets of dampening rollers for each press so a clean, dry roller is always available for use. If the press has only one set of rollers and a roller is needed immediately after cleaning, roll the needed roller against a blotter pad or cleaning sheets until all water is removed. Covers should not be cleaned daily; they should only be cleaned as necessary. They should, however, be changed when the cover material no longer accepts water.

Distribution Roller Adjustment

All distribution rollers in the ink and dampening systems must contact each other uniformly to achieve proper ink and water distribution. Most rollers are adjustable in at least one direction and are relatively simple to move.

A common method for adjusting distribution rollers involves using strips of 20-pound paper. Cut six pieces of paper, 8 inches or 9 inches long. Four of the pieces should be approximately 2 inches wide and two should be 1 inch wide. To check for uniform pressure between the two rollers, roll a set of three strips (two that are 2 inches wide and one that is 1 inch wide) between a set of rollers at each end of the rollers and then gently pull the middle pieces out (figure 13.26). The strips should slide with slight uniform resistance, but they should not tear.

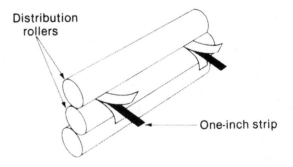

Distribution rollers

One-inch strip

Figure 13.26.   Adjusting the distribution rollers. Distribution roller adjustment can be checked by placing a set of three pieces of paper between rollers and then gently pulling the middle strips. The strips should slide with slight, uniform resistance.

Form Roller Adjustment

The ink and water form rollers must all be adjusted so that they touch the plate with the correct amount of pressure and have uniform pressure across the width of the plate. Form rollers all have some type of easy adjustment for skew and pressure.

Dampening Form Roller Adjustment

If the dampening roller is not parallel to the plate cylinder, moisture will not be distributed evenly across the plate. If all portions of the plate surface are not moistened uniformly, ink scumming occurs on the plate. The need to adjust and align the dampening form roller and plate is often indicated when one side of the plate scums and the other side does not. This adjustment must be made with the dampening form roller in place on the press.

Cut two 1-inch-wide strips of 20-pound bond paper and place one under each end of the dampening form roller (figure 13.27). Lower the dampening form roller into position against the plate cylinder. Slowly pull each paper strip to check for uniform resistance. If unequal resistance is observed, the dampening form roller is not parallel to the plate cylinder and must be reset. Both duplicators and presses have adjustments to control this form roller-to-plate alignment.

Ink Form Roller Adjustment

Ink form roller-to-plate pressure is critical. Too much pressure results in a blurred or enlarged image. Too little pressure transfers no ink. Proper adjustment requires not only that you have the proper amount of pressure, but that the pressure be even across the width of the plate. Ink form roller pressure is checked by first inking the press and then turning the press off in such a way that the plate cylinder is beneath the form rollers. With the plate cylinder in this position, bring the form rollers

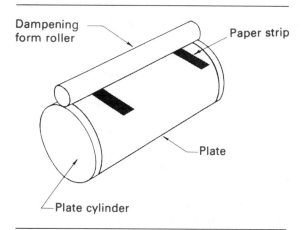

Figure 13.27. Checking the dampening form roller adjustment. Dampening form roller adjustment can be checked by placing two strips of paper under each end of the dampening form roller and comparing resistance.

into contact with the plate by moving the press to the "print" mode. Immediately bring the press off ink and rotate the plate to where you can examine the ink tracks left on it by the form rollers (figure 13.28). As shown in figure 13.29, the first roller to contact the plate should have the heaviest ink line (⅛ inch to ³⁄₁₆ inch) while the last roller should have the lightest ink line (³⁄₃₂ inch to ⅛ inch). All rollers, however, should transfer a uniform width of ink across the plate. Figure 13.30a shows proper form roller positions against a plate cylinder. Figures 13.30b and 13.30c illustrate two possible adjustments that diminish image quality on the final sheet.

Common Press Concerns

Many concerns are common to all press designs or models. This section does not contain an exhaustive list, but it should help you understand some basic press problems.

Figure 13.28.   Examples of test strips to check for ink form roller-to-plate pressure. The top two test strips show rollers that contacted the plate with uneven pressure. The third strip indicates too much pressure. The last strip is uniform and not too wide, which indicates correct pressure.

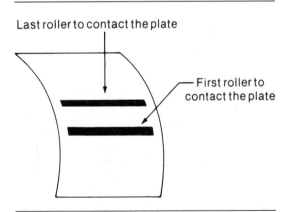

Last roller to contact the plate

First roller to contact the plate

Figure 13.29.   Examples of different tracks left by the first and last roller. The ink track left on the plate by both rollers should be even across the width of the plate. The track of the first roller, however, should be slightly wider than the track of the last roller.

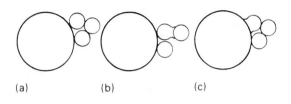

(a)   (b)   (c)

Figure 13.30.   Diagram of ink form roller adjustment. The proper adjustment of form rollers is shown in (a). Misalignment of form rollers is shown in (b) and (c).

The Dampening Solution and pH

The moisture applied to the surface of a lithographic plate actually serves two functions. First, moisture in the nonimage areas repels ink. If only pure water were used as the dampening solution, however, the action of the ink would rapidly cause the nonimage areas to become ink receptive. The second purpose of the moisture, then, is to ensure that the nonimage areas of the plate remain water-receptive. Alois Senefelder recognized the dual role of the moisture layer on the stone and used a solution made from a combination of water, acid, and gum arabic.

Ready-mixed dampening solutions are available from a commercial supplier or they can be purchased as separate components and mixed. Most dampening solutions are now made from an acid concentrate, gum arabic, and a gum preservative.

For lithographers, the most meaningful measure of dampening solution usability is its level of acidity. The numeric scale that measures acidity in a range from 0 (very acid) to 14 (very alkaline or basic) is called the **pH scale** (figure 13.31). The midpoint of the scale, 7, is considered neutral. Plate manufacturers recommend a pH level to be used with their plates. A reading between 5.5 and 4.5 is acceptable for most plates.

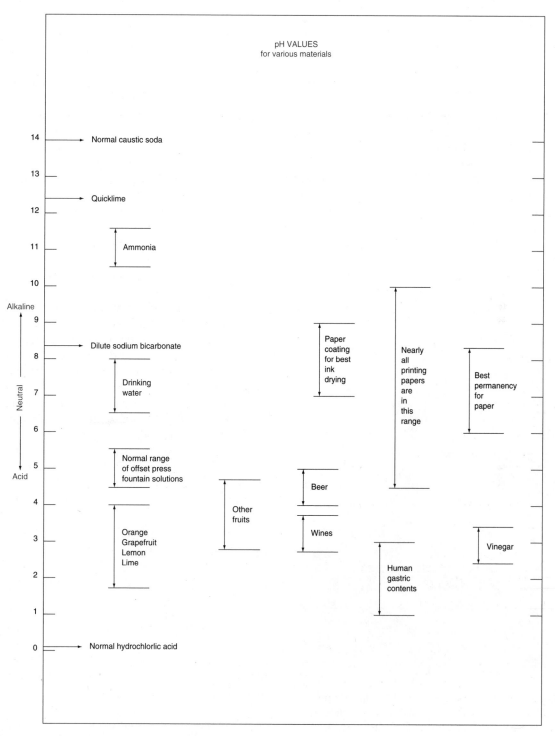

Figure 13.31. The pH values for various substances.
Courtesy of Mead Paper.

The printer can measure pH in several ways. Litmus paper pH indicators are available from printing suppliers and give acceptable readings of the acidity levels of most production situations (figure 13.32). To perform a test, remove a small piece of litmus paper from the roll and dip it into the fountain solution. The wet paper changes color and can be matched to color patches supplied with the roll of litmus paper. A pH number identifies each color patch. If the pH of the fountain solution is not in the recommended range, remix it.

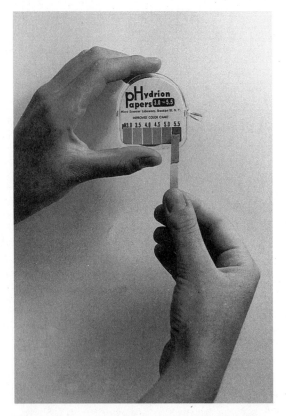

Figure 13.32.   Example of a litmus paper pH indicator. Litmus paper pH indicators are used to check the water fountain solution in most working situations.

Courtesy of Micro Essential Lab., Inc.

Some presses have built-in sensors that monitor the pH level of the dampening solution continually. With these sensors, the required pH is dialed into the unit, and the device automatically compensates for any variation in pH by adding water or acid concentrate.

A variety of problems can occur when a fountain solution is too acidic (pH reading from 1 to 3). A strongly acidic fountain solution can greatly shorten plate life. The acid tends to deteriorate the image area of all surface plates and can eventually remove the plate emulsion. When this happens, printers say the image "walked off the plate." When humidity in the press room is high, the action of the acid on the ink causes drying problems on the press sheets (especially high-acid content press sheets). A high-acid bath also breaks down the ink. In this case, the high acid content of the fountain solution attacks the ink, and the ink becomes paste like, or **emulsified.** The rollers appear glazed, and no quantity of ink that is added to the system will correct the problem. The rollers must be cleaned and the unit must be reinked.

If the acid level of the dampening solution is too low (pH reading from 7 to 14), the action of the moisture layer on the nonimage areas decreases water receptivity, and the plate scums with ink.

Ink and Paper Considerations for Lithographic Printing

Ink and paper are probably the two most common ingredients of any printing job. The customer does not want to be concerned with the details of production problems, but the printer must live with ink and paper problems on a day-to-day basis. Some characteristics of these two important ingredients of offset litho press operation are worth examining.

Working with Lithographic Ink
Ink is affected by the paper on which it is put. Many printers add materials, such as a drier or

an extender, to their ink indiscriminately at the beginning of each workday and believe that they are improving the ink in so doing. There is a trend in ink manufacturing to supply inks that require no special mixing and that match each different type of press sheet and job characteristic. Under no circumstances should additives be mixed with any ink without consulting an ink supplier.

Troubleshooting Ink Difficulties
Beyond mechanical problems caused by inexact press adjustments, there are often difficulties resulting from ink characteristics that can be corrected easily with appropriate additives. Three common problems are tinting, picking, and slow drying.

Tinting is identified by a slight discoloration over the entire nonimage area—almost like a sprayed mist or the pattern created by a 5 percent or 10 percent screen tint. Generally, the situation is caused by a reaction between the ink and the water fountain solution. If the ink is too water soluble, it bleeds back into the water fountain through the dampening system. If tinting occurs, both the ink and the dampening systems should be cleaned. A different ink formulation should also be used.

Picking is similar in appearance to small hickies over the entire image area of the press sheet (figure 13.33). A **hickey** can result from linty or poorly coated paper, but it more commonly results from ink that is too tacky. Small particles of paper tear from the surface of each press sheet and feed back into the inking system to cause the hickies. If picking is observed, the inking system should be cleaned and the ink should be mixed with a small quantity of reducer or nonpick compound.

Solving the problem of slow ink drying can be elusive unless all possible causes are recognized. Simple drying problems can generally be eliminated by adding a drier compound to the ink, but too much drier compound can actually increase drying time. Overinking a

Figure 13.33. Example of a printer's hickey. Hickies are defects in a printed image caused by small particles of ink or paper attached to the plate or blanket.

coated (nonabsorbent) stock can significantly increase drying time. On humid days, too high an acid content in the dampening solution (low pH) can cause difficulties. This combination of problems is almost impossible to solve without moving the press sheets to a humidity-controlled environment. Delayed drying can be a special problem when the press sheet must be flopped or turned to receive an image on the second side.

Paper Acid Content
In general, uncoated papers will not dry properly in a humid atmosphere if the pH of the paper is below 5 (see figure 13.31). Most coated papers have a pH of above 7.5. Coatings with a pH between 6 and 7 would also cause ink-drying problems when combined with high humidity.

Testing the pH of papers can be a cumbersome and time-consuming process. Acid content information for any paper lot is available from the manufacturer. If the room humidity is high and ink drying is a problem, consult the paper supplier for testing or information.

Paper Grain

Paper grain direction is an important characteristic that is related most closely to the ability of the individual sheets to be run through a sheet-fed lithographic press. Most paper forms when cellulose fibers combine and interlock. As paper forms on the moving wire belt of the papermaking machine, a majority of the cellulose fibers turn parallel to the direction of travel. Press sheets are defined as **grain long** when most of the paper fibers are parallel to the longest dimension of the sheet. **Grain short** means the paper fibers are at right angles to the longest dimension of the sheet.

A distinction should be made between feeding and printing as they relate to grain direction. In grain-long feeding, the grain direction is parallel to the direction of travel through the press. In grain-short feeding, the grain direction is at a right angle to the direction of press travel (figure 13.34). Grain-long printing occurs when the paper grain is parallel to the axis of the plate cylinder. Grain-short printing occurs when the paper grain is at a right angle to the plate cylinder axis.

The Mead Paper Corporation suggests that cellulose fibers expand as they absorb moisture. This expansion can be up to five times as great across the width of a fiber as along its length. This fact should suggest to lithographers that the direction of grain feed could present significant registration problems when multicolor runs are printed on a single sheet-fed offset press. In other words, on a lithographic press, press sheets contact moisture from the fountain solution. The individual cellulose fibers in the paper sheets can then change size, with the greatest increase being in the dimension across the grain. If the sheet has

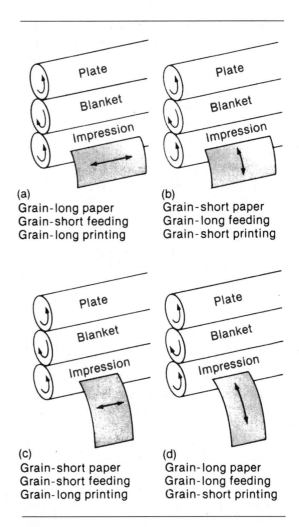

(a)
Grain-long paper
Grain-short feeding
Grain-long printing

(b)
Grain-short paper
Grain-long feeding
Grain-short printing

(c)
Grain-short paper
Grain-short feeding
Grain-long printing

(d)
Grain-long paper
Grain-long feeding
Grain-short printing

Figure 13.34. Grain direction in printing

to be run through the press several times to receive different ink colors, each pass can add more moisture to the fibers and can cause different changes in sheet size. These changes can make it extremely difficult to fit one color image to another.

Almost all offset paper is supplied grain long. It is to the printer's advantage, when involved with multicolor runs, to print with the paper grain parallel to the axis of the plate cylinder. For most presses, the printing plate is longer across the cylinder dimension than it is around. If the greatest paper expansion is going to take place across the grain, it is wise to feed the sheet so that the greatest change takes place across the smallest plate or image dimension. Also, on most presses, it is far simpler to make registration adjustments by rotating the printing cylinders than it is by moving the infeed pile.

It is important to understand that not all lithographic press work is done with grain-long printing. Grain is of little importance for simple, single-color runs or for multicolor images that do not have critical registration requirements. There are also instances when a multicolor job *must* be printed short grain. For example, when printed sheets are to be folded, grain direction is very important. Such jobs must generally be printed so that the fold is parallel to the paper grain.

Surface Texture

A wide variety of textures can be formed on the surface of all papers. This texture is generally referred to as **finish.** Because lithography transfers an image from a flat printing plate, it is difficult to print a detailed design on a very rough paper surface. Ink would never reach the valleys of rough textures. For this reason, almost all offset materials are relatively smooth. Lithographers are concerned with two main classifications of papers: coated and uncoated.

Almost all papers form by the interweaving of cellulose fibers. The surface of **uncoated paper** is made up of nothing more than these raw, interlocking fibers. Although the fibers can be polished by **calendering** (pressing the fibers between rollers or plates to smooth or glaze them), the ink image sits on, and is often absorbed into, the fibers. A **coated paper** surface has an added layer of pigment bonded to the original cellulose fibers to smooth the rough texture of this natural material. Coated papers generally carry more printed detail and produce a better finished image, but they are more

difficult to print than uncoated papers. Coated papers are available coated on one side (C1S) or coated on both sides (C2S). Both types of paper are made in at least two grades, and the surface appearance can vary from a dull to a high gloss.

There are several areas that lithographers have learned to watch when printing coated stocks. Most jam-ups occur because of static electricity between the coated sheets on the infeed table. The pile of paper should be fanned *carefully,* and the feeding should be adjusted with start-up sheets before the actual run begins. The blanket should be checked carefully for quality—specifically for glaze buildup. Glaze has a tendency to pick and split or tear coated paper. Ink quantity is more critical with coated materials than with uncoated ones. Too much ink causes **set-off** (the transfer of an image from the printed face of one sheet in the pile to the bottom face of the next sheet in the pile) of the image in the delivery pile. Overinking could also cause the paper to stick to the blanket cylinder and generally increases drying time. Roller and cylinder alignment is also more critical with coated stock and should be checked carefully.

A Troubleshooting Checklist

In theory, press setup and operation are simple. Unfortunately, difficulties may develop in every situation and prevent a quality image from printing on the final press sheets. The true craft of printing is identifying and correcting these problems. This process is called "troubleshooting." The following sections identify common press and duplicator difficulties and outline probable causes and solutions.

Scumming

Scumming is a condition in which nonimage areas accept ink.

Too Much Ink

If the press is overinked, the ink system rollers appear highly textured and a hissing sound is often heard from the rollers as the press idles. To remove excess ink without a wash-up, turn the machine off and manually roll scrap sheets of paper between two of the upper ink distributing rollers. Repeat the procedure until the required amount of ink is removed.

Dampening System Difficulties

Scumming can also be caused by insufficient moisture, dirty dampening covers, dampening covers tied too tightly, light dampening form roller pressure to the plate, or low acid level of the fountain solution.

First, study the pattern of the scum carefully and trace its position back to the dampening form roller. If the scumming covers the entire plate, it could be the result of overall lack of moisture (increase the fountain feed), poor form roller pressure (readjust), or a dirty dampening form roller cover (clean with a commercial dampening roller cleaner or replace). If the scumming pattern is on the outer edges of the plate only, the form roller cover could be tied too tightly or the ductor roller cover may have slipped (retie or replace covers). If the plate is scumming in a band that extends around the circumference of the cylinder, that area of the dampening form roller might be inked and may not be allowing the moisture to pass to the plate (clean the form roller). Scum on the plate can also be caused by improper platemaking or gumming.

Blurred Copy (Double Image)

Loose Blanket

As blankets are broken in, and during press runs, they press against the plate cylinder and tend to flatten or stretch out. If the blanket is new, immediately check for tightness.

Excessive Impression

Too much impression tends to roll the blanket ahead of the impression cylinder and causes a set-off from the press sheet back to the blanket. This in turn results in a blurred image (back off or reduce impression).

Too Much Ink

Refer to the solution under the previous Scumming section.

Grey, Washed-Out Reproduction

Too Much Moisture

If moisture is dripping off the plate or spraying onto the press sheets, water is flooding into the image areas and the plate cannot accept sufficient quantities of ink. Turn off the fountain ductor roller, lower the dampening form roller into contact with the plate, and allow the press to run. This process allows the excess fountain solution to coat the plate and evaporate. If an extra set of dampening form rollers is available, it could replace the overmoistened set. The rollers could also be removed from the press and rolled against clean, absorbent paper.

Not Enough Ink

If the inking system is carrying too little ink, a dense image cannot be transferred to the press sheet. Check the appearance of the ink coating and increase the ink feed if necessary. However, always check for too much moisture before increasing ink feed.

Incorrect Plate-to-Blanket Pressure

If the blanket image is light but the plate is inking well, the plate-to-blanket pressure is insufficient and should be readjusted, or the packing should be increased.

Incorrect Impression-to-Blanket Pressure

If the ink and dampening systems are set correctly and the blanket is receiving a good image, the impression cylinder position should be checked. Increase impression until a dense, sharp press sheet image is obtained.

Grey, Washed-Out Reproduction and Scumming

Glazed Ink Rollers

If the inking system rollers appear shiny and hard, glazed ink rollers are interacting with the moisture system and passing inconsistent or inadequate amounts of ink to the plate. Use a commercial deglazing compound to clean the inking system.

Glazed Blanket

If the blanket surface appears shiny and hard, clean it with a commercial deglazing compound.

Too Much Form Roller Pressure

If the ink and/or dampening form rollers are set too close to the plate cylinder, then sufficient ink or water solution transfer will not take place. Readjust the form roller pressure.

No Reproduction on Press Sheet

Check for insufficient ink form roller pressure (readjust), not enough plate-to-blanket pressure (reset), not enough impression (increase impression), or too much moisture and glazed blanket and ink rollers (decrease moisture and deglaze blanket and rollers).

Printer's Hickey

As mentioned earlier, hickeys are caused by small particles of ink or paper attached to the plate or blanket (figure 13.33). Stop the press and clean the plate and blanket.

Press Maintenance

Unfortunately, maintenance is often viewed as an activity that takes place after a prob-

lem occurs. Manufacturers always provide recommended maintenance programs for their machines. However, several general areas of concern should be considered for every press.

The motor that provides motion for the press is often concealed in a position that would seem to challenge a professional contortionist's skills. Because the motor is out of sight does not mean it is unimportant. Check for lubrication points and examine the belt and pulley systems often.

Chains on infeed and outfeed tables need to be kept greased and free of paper pieces or dirt. Infeed rollers become smooth from use. A piece of fine-grit, abrasive paper can be used to roughen and remove any dirt from the roller surface. Vacuum pumps usually have an oil reservoir that should be kept filled. The pump itself should be flushed several times a year.

All roller and cylinder bearings must be lubricated, usually daily. Some presses have a single oil reservoir that delivers lubrication to bearing surfaces continually.

The importance of a consistent maintenance schedule cannot be overstated. It is far cheaper to spend time each day doing preventive maintenance than to wait until a major malfunction takes place and the press is "down" for several days awaiting new parts.

A printing press is a machine that is controlled by humans. Some printers claim that each press has a distinctive personality and assign human names and characteristics accordingly: "It's Monday and Harold is kind of sluggish" or "Jane is mad at me today—she's throwing paper all over the place." However, a mechanism cannot perform "tricks" beyond what a human programs it to do. Every press problem has a cause and a solution. The printer works with a press, but it is the printer, not the machine, who controls each situation.

Key Terms

set-off
dot-for-dot registration
T-Mark
Star Target
ink spread
slur
doubling
Quality Control (QC) Strip
Dot Gain Scale

Slur Gauge
glaze
molleton covers
dampening sleeves
pH scale
emulsified
tinting
picking

hickey
grain long
grain short
finish
uncoated paper
calendering
coated paper
scumming

Questions for Review

1. Discuss the steps and procedures for setting up the paper feed on an offset press.

2. Explain how the printing unit is prepared for printing, including adjustments for ink and water for both direct and indirect dampening systems.

3. Describe the method for achieving proper ink and water balance.

4. How is press cleanup accomplished?

5. What is one way to solve possible color contamination when running process colors on a lithographic press?

6. Describe the T-Mark, Star Target, QC Strip, Dot Gain Scale, and Slur Gauge produced by GATF, and tell what quality control checks can be made with each.

7. What causes a lithographic blanket to glaze?

8. What is the purpose of dampening covers in the dampening system of a lithographic press?

9. Why is accurate alignment of form rollers against the image carrier (printing plate) so important?

10. How are printing inks formed?

11. What does the term "pH" mean?

12. What generally causes tinting on a lithographic press sheet?

13. What is the difference between grain-short and grain-long press sheets?

14. What are two possible causes of scumming on a lithographic press?

Screen Printing Stencils

Anecdote to Chapter Fourteen

Japanese stencil.
Courtesy of the Art Institute of Chicago.

It is possible that observing insects eating holes through leaves suggested the idea of stencil printing to primitive people. Examples of this idea can be seen in the early work of Polynesian Island natives. Designs were cut into green banana leaves, and dyes were forced through the leaf openings onto bark cloth, or "*tapa.*"

In Asia, the earliest stencils were produced during the Sung dynasty (A.D. 960–1280). Many examples of stencil printing that date from the same period were found in Japan. The Japanese have been extremely skillful in cutting detailed stencils from specially treated rice paper. It was easy to cut large open areas in the paper, but problems arose when the artist wanted to block out a portion of the open area. One solution was to glue center pieces or loose parts of the stencil with strands of human hair. These strands were called "ties" because they tied the different parts of the stencil together.

Fine pieces of silk fiber later replaced human hair because they were stronger.

In England during the late 1700s, stencils were used to decorate wallpaper, which had become popular in upper-class homes. European screen printers still used ties to hold the stencil pieces together, and it was difficult to create especially intricate designs.

During the early years of our country's history, the stencil was a well-guarded secret. Traveling teachers often sold the idea to local printers and signmakers. The price of the stencil depended on what the market would bear, but most printers were happy to pay almost any price for a process that was low cost and could be used to reproduce nearly any size image without being limited by the size of the available type or printing press.

In 1907, Samual Simon of Manchester, England, was granted a patent on his revolutionary new concept called a "tieless stencil." Simon's design used a piece of coarsely woven silk fabric to hold the stencil pieces in place.

With the silk as a base, extremely intricate designs could be cut and then glued to the fabric. When ink passed through the openings in the design, it flowed around the fabric threads and left an image of the opening on the print.

It was not until the outbreak of World War I that Simon's method became a significant industrial process. It was ideal for rapid, high-quality, short-run signs and illustrations. With the development of photographic stencils, the stenciling process has been used for almost every conceivable application from printing tiny microcircuits in electronics to labeling cardboard cartons and even reproducing halftone photographs.

What began as a simple stencil more than thirteen centuries ago has moved into a position of significance in the printing industry. Many labels have been applied to this process—stencil printing, silk screen serigraphy, and even mitography—but the term "screen printing" is now commonly accepted as the proper name.

Objectives for Chapter 14

After completing this chapter, you will be able to:

- Explain the basic concepts of screen printing.
- Classify types of screen stencils.
- Classify types of screen fabrics.
- Describe methods of stretching screens.
- List the steps in preparing and mounting hand-cut stencils.
- Describe the steps in preparing and mounting indirect photographic stencils.
- Describe the steps in preparing and mounting direct photographic stencils.
- Describe the different techniques of masking stencils.
- Select the appropriate type of stencil, screen, and ink for different screen printing jobs.

Introduction

Of all the major printing processes, screen printing is undoubtedly the oldest. The process was shrouded in mystery for centuries and remained a well-guarded secret until the first part of the twentieth century.

Screen printing is one of the five basic printing processes. The concept is to transfer an image by allowing ink to pass through openings in a stencil that has been applied to a screen mesh (refer to figure 1.4c). Although such terms as "silk screen," "mitography," "seriography," and "selectine" might be classified within this framework, "screen printing" is the label the industry recognizes and uses.

Basic Concept and Classification of Stencils

The Stencil

The basic concept of screen printing is simple and is based on the idea of a stencil. By taking a piece of paper, drawing some outline or sketch of an object, and then cutting out the sketch, we can make a **stencil** (figure 14.1). By placing the stencil over another sheet of paper, it is possible to paint, spray, or otherwise force ink through the stencil opening (figure 14.2). When the stencil is removed from the paper, all that remains on the printed sheet is a reproduction of the opening on the stencil (figure 14.3). This process can be repeated as long as the original stencil holds its shape.

Today the advantages of screen printing are impressive. It is ideally suited for low-

Figure 14.2.   Spraying ink through a paper stencil

Figure 14.1.   Paper stencil cut with Ulano swivel knife

Figure 14.3.   A stenciled image

cost production of high-quality, short-run printed materials. Screen printing is extremely versatile. It is possible to print on nearly any surface, texture, or shape. The process is limited only by the size of the screen frame. Fine line detail and even halftones may be reproduced by screen printing. Many types of ink, from acid etches to abrasive glues, are available with this process. Ink densities on the printed page are such that any color may be overprinted (printed over another color) without the first color showing through.

Types of Stencils

Stencils can be classified into three groups:

- Hand-cut
- Tusche-and-glue
- Photographic

As the name implies, **hand-cut stencils** are prepared by removing the printing image areas manually from some form of base or support material. **Tusche-and-glue,** an art process, involves drawing directly on the screen fabric with lithographic tusche (an oil-based pigment) and then blocking out nonimage areas with a water-based glue material. **Photographic stencils** are generally produced by using a thick, light-sensitive, gelatin-based emulsion that is exposed and developed either on supporting film or directly on the screen itself. Only hand-cut and photographic stencils are used in commercial printing.

Fabric and Frame Preparation

Screen printing preparation involves selecting and controlling screen fabrics, screen frames, fabric stretch on the frame, fabric treatment to accept a stencil, stencil preparation, and stencil masking. As with all printing processes, it is critical to control every variable to produce a quality image on the final sheet.

Screen Fabrics

There is no one fabric that can be used for all screen printing applications. The type of ink to be screened, the fineness of image line detail, the quality of the paper or base material that is to receive the image, the number of impressions, and the type of stencil must all be considered when selecting the screen fabric.

Screen fabrics are made from either natural fibers, such as silk, or man-made fibers, such as polyester, rayon, or nylon. They are also classified as either multifilament or monofilament materials. **Multifilament screens** are made up of strands of fibers twisted together into threads (figure 14.4). Silk is a multifilament fabric. **Monofilament screens** are woven from single round strands (figure 14.5). Nylon is a monofilament fabric.

As was mentioned in the chapter anecdote, silk was the first fabric used to carry screen printing stencils. Multifilament silk strands provide greater cross-sectional area than monofilament strands and allow for the

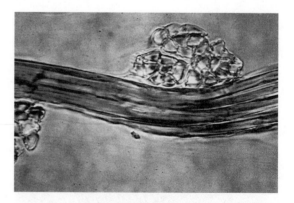

Figure 14.4. Magnified view of cross section of multifilament strand. Notice that the multifilament strand is made up of individual fibers.
Courtesy of J. Ulano Company, Inc.

Figure 14.5.   Magnified view of cross section of man-made monofilament strands.
Courtesy of J. Ulano Company, Inc.

Figure 14.6.   Magnified view of stencil applied to silk fibers.
Courtesy of J. Ulano Company, Inc.

strong adhesion of nearly any hand-cut or photographic stencil (figure 14.6). However, silk is not dimensionally stable, which means it changes shape and size with changes in temperature and humidity. This makes it unsuitable for work requiring critical control of registration and color fit. Moreover, many special purpose inks, such as abrasives or chemical resists, can quickly destroy silk fibers.

Although man-made multifilament fibers, such as multistrand polyester, do not have the natural coarseness of silk, they are stronger and can be woven more uniformly. Polyester is useful for critical registration work because it is dimensionally stable, can withstand many abrasive materials, and can pass a uniform layer of ink.

Monofilament fabrics, such as single-strand polyester, nylon, or wire cloth (copper or stainless steel), have uniform weaves and pass pigments freely through mesh openings. However, because monofilament fabric is so smooth, it can be difficult to adhere a stencil. For this reason, it is generally necessary to treat or roughen the monofilament surface to obtain good stencil adhesion (figure 14.7).

Each fabric type has its own characteristics. Nylon tends to absorb moisture and reacts

to changes in room humidity. Metal screens absorb no moisture but react to temperature changes and pass nearly any abrasive pigment with little difficulty. Monofilament polyesters have low moisture absorption rates, stabilities, and strengths. Because they are also less expensive than most other screen materials, they are rapidly becoming the main material for commercial screen printing work.

Screen fabric is purchased by the yard. Two systems are used to classify screen fabric. Silk and multifilament polyesters are classified

Figure 14.7.   Magnified view of stencil applied to monofilament fibers.
Courtesy of J. Ulano Company, Inc.

according to the ratio of open or link-passing area to thread area per inch. Numbers ranging from 0000 to about 25 are assigned to fabrics accordingly. The smaller the number, the larger the percentage of open area per inch. These fabrics are also assigned a strength indicator. A 12XX fabric is stronger than a 12X fabric. Most other fabrics, such as nylon and metal cloth, are classified according to the number of threads per inch. These fabrics are available in a range from about 60 threads per inch to a maximum of around 500 threads per inch. The two classification systems can be compared to identify equivalent opening sizes (table 14.1).

Specific recommendations cannot be made here about the type of fabric and mesh count to use in a given situation. Many variables can influence that decision. To decide which fabric type and mesh count to use, identify the type of ink to be used and consult the manufacturer's data for the screen material the manufacturer suggests is used with that ink. Manufacturers specify minimum screen mesh sizes based on the maximum pigment particle sizes in the ink (the particles, which are suspended in the liquid "vehicle," must be able to pass freely through the screen openings). Manufacturers also indicate whether the ink vehicle will interact with any commercial screen fabrics. If the vehicle is a liquid that dissolves polyesters, for example, then the printer must avoid polyester fabrics.

The next step in deciding which fabric type and mesh count to use is to consider the fineness of the line detail of the image to be screen printed. A coarse screen mesh passes a heavy layer of ink, but it does not hold a fine line stencil. In general, use a 12XX (or equivalent number) fabric for hand-cut and indirect photographic stencils with normal images and

Table 14.1.   A Comparison of Mesh Classification Systems

XX system used for silk and multi- or monofilament polyesters	Silk	Multifilament polyesters	Nylon	Monofilament polyesters	Stainless steel	Silk	Multifilament polyesters	Nylon	Monofilament polyesters	Stainless steel
6XX	74	74	70	74	70	47	43	45	34	55
8XX	86	86	90	92	88	45	32	42	42	48
10XX	109	109	108	110	105	40	20	43	39	47
12XX	125	125	120	125	120	32	28	45	30	47
14XX	139	139	138	139	135	30	26	47	35	47
16XX	157	157	157	157	145	31	25	41	24	46
18XX	166	170	166	175	165	31	31	38	34	47
20XX	173	178	185	—	180	28	29	43	—	47
25XX	200	198	196	200	200	23	26	44	32	46
			230	225	230			42	42	46
			240	245	250			39	38	36
			260	260	270			36	35	32
			283	280	—			37	34	—
			306	300	—			34	29	—
			330	330	325			30	27	30
			380	390	400			22	18	36

a 14XX (or equivalent number) or finer fabric for photographic stencils containing images with fine line detail. Multifilament fibers are generally not suitable for halftone or extremely fine line reproduction.

Organdy is often used for short-run situations where bold line detail is required, but organdy is not an industrial fabric and is not recommended for fine detail.

Screen Frames

One of the great advantages of screen printing is that there is no standard size or shape for a screen printing frame. The screen frame must hold the screen fabric without warping, be deep enough to hold the quantity of ink being printed without spilling, and be at least 4 inches wider and 4 inches longer than the largest stencil to be reproduced.

Commercially constructed frames are available, but they are not required. Frames that are custom made by the printer to meet individual needs are often just as acceptable as their commercial counterparts. Most custom-made frames are made from wood because wood is inexpensive, fairly stable, and easily cut to any dimension. The high tension that develops when modern synthetic fabrics stretch on a frame warps wooden frames constructed with common butt joints. As a result, the joints must be constructed such that the frame cannot spring in any direction (figure 14.8).

Wooden frames are not recommended for close registration work because wood has a tendency to swell and shift when damp. When exact registration is required, as in printed circuits or color process reproductions, steel or aluminum is a preferable frame material.

Fabric Stretching Techniques

Fabric manufacturers recommend the amount of tension that should be placed on their fab-

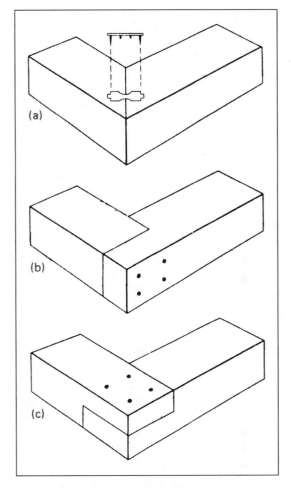

Figure 14.8.   Common wooden frame joints. Common joints used for custom-made wooden screen frames are a reinforced miter joint (a), a rabbet joint (b), and an end-lap joint (c).

rics. Generally, silk should be stretched 3 percent to 4 percent of its original dimensions in two directions. Nylon should be stretched from 4 percent to 7 percent; and polyesters should be stretched from 1 percent to 4 percent. Most suppliers recommend using a mechanical stretching system. With this system it is easy to control the exact amount of tension for any frame.

Mechanical Stretching

The basic process of **mechanical stretching** is straightforward and relatively simple. The fabric is cut to the size of the screen, but with an additional amount in each dimension that is sufficient to clamp the fabric into the stretching device. The empty screen frame is then centered in the stretching system, and the fabric is clamped into place.

The fabric is then stretched to the desired percentage. Next, the material is stapled to the frame, the pressure is released, and the excess fabric is cut away. An optional last step is to seal the staples and fabric to the frame with glue or epoxy, which provides a stronger bond.

This same basic technique is used when stretching fabric over commercial metal frames except that a cord and clamp are used instead of staples.

Hand Stretching

The easiest method of attaching screen fabric is by tacking or stapling the material to the underside of a wooden frame. It is not possible to control for tension percentage with this approach. However, for small-run jobs with coarse line detail, many printers find it acceptable.

Use number 4 carpet tacks or ¼-inch staples in a general purpose industrial staple gun. Space the tack or staples approximately ½ inch (1.27 cm) apart in two rows. Start by placing the loose fabric over the frame so that the strands are parallel to the frame edges. The rough-cut fabric should be at least 2 inches (5.08 cm) larger in each dimension of the frame. Next, place three fasteners in the upper right-hand corner of the fabric. Pull the fabric diagonally and fasten a second corner in place. Then stretch and fasten the upper left-hand corner and, next, the lower right. Now begin at the center of any long frame edge and begin spacing a row of fasteners completely around the frame. As you fasten, pull the material with fabric pliers to remove all warps from the screen surface. Go back to the starting point

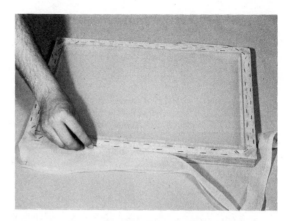

Figure 14.9. Cutting away surplus fabric

and alternate a second row of fasteners around the frame just inside the first. Finally, cut the surplus fabric from the frame with a sharp razor blade and mask the staples with gummed tape (figure 14.9).

An alternative method for hand stretching fabric on a wooden frame is a starched cord and groove technique. Cut a single notch partially through each frame side with a saw (figure 14.10). An inexpensive piece of ³⁄₁₆-inch woven clothesline will nearly perfectly fill the

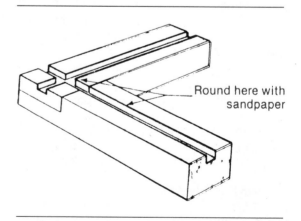

Round here with sandpaper

Figure 14.10. Wooden frame with sawed notch

groove left by a standard table saw blade. The inside groove may have to be rounded to prevent cutting the fabric, however. By carefully working from one corner, you can stretch the fabric by forcing both the clothesline and the fabric into the groove (figure 14.11). Special tools have been developed to insert the clothesline in the groove (figure 14.12), but any device that will not tear the cloth is ac-

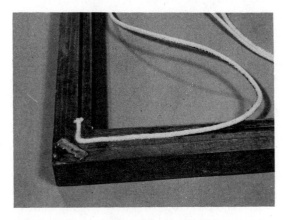

Figure 14.11. Clothesline forced into the notch to secure the screen

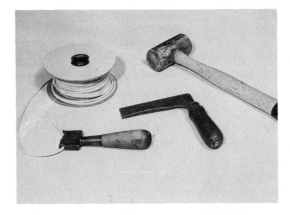

Figure 14.12. Tools used to insert clothesline into notch

ceptable. Whatever method is used, the fabric should be "drumhead" tight, without warps or tears.

Fabric Treatment

As mentioned earlier in the chapter, monofilament fabric, such as nylon or polyester, must be treated before a stencil can be adhered. A **tooth** must be produced on the smooth monofilament fibers so the stencil can be held in place.

To produce a tooth, slightly dampen the monofilament fabric with water and pour half a teaspoon of 500-grit silicon carbide for each 16 inch × 20 inch (40.64 cm × 50.8 cm) area on the back, or stencil, side of the screen. Carefully scour the fabric with a wet rag for 2 to 3 minutes. Make sure to scrub the entire screen surface. Then thoroughly rinse both sides of the screen with a strong water spray. The 500-grit silicon carbide will not clog even the smallest mesh screen opening. This operation must be repeated each time the screen receives a new stencil.

Some printers use a very fine waterproof silicon carbide paper (sandpaper) to produce a tooth on monofilament fabrics. When using this paper, wet the screen and lightly rub the entire surface of the stencil side for 4 to 5 minutes. Then thoroughly rinse both sides of the screen with a strong water spray. This technique is recommended only if no alternative method is available because the sandpaper could destory the screen if applied too roughly.

All fabrics, whether new or used, must be cleaned and degreased to ensure proper film or emulsion adhesion. If the screen is old, be sure that all ink has been removed and no foreign particles are clogging the mesh openings (figure 14.13). Ink manufacturers recommend the proper degreaser for their products. To clean and degrease a screen, first wet the screen with cold water and sprinkle both sides with powdered trisodium phosphate. If trisodium phosphate is not available, use a

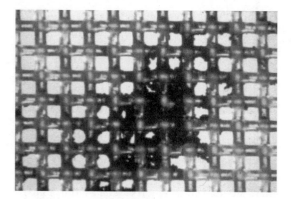

Figure 14.13.   Magnified view of a clogged screen.
Courtesy of J. Ulano Company, Inc.

commercial nonsudsing automatic dishwashing detergent. Then thoroughly scrub both sides with a soft bristle brush. Next, rinse the screen with a powerful water spray. Allow the screen to drain and dry, but do not touch the fabric—skin oils on the fibers might prevent stencil adhesion. Do *not* use commercial abrasive cleansers like Ajax because the cleanser particles can clog the screen on fine mesh fabrics and cannot be removed with the water spray.

After the fabric has been cleaned, it is ready to accept the stencil. It is important not to store the clean screen for a long period before attempting to adhere the stencil. Air carries impurities and dirt that could clog a clean screen.

Hand-Cut Stencil Methods

The hand-cut process was the earliest method used to make screen stencils. Originally, pieces of thin paper were cut and glued to the underside of a screen to make stencils. This process was tiring and time consuming, and it offered

the printer only a limited number of impressions before the paper stencil simply wore out. Later, the paper was coated with shellac or lacquer to increase its durability, but the process was still slow and had a limited run length.

In the early 1930s Joseph Ulano (founder of J. Ulano Company, Inc., now a leading screen printing supplier) made an interesting observation. He found that if a layer of lacquer was sprayed over a hard surface and was allowed to dry, a thin sheet of lacquer could be pulled from the surface in one piece. This lacquer could then be coated onto a support sheet and cut away to leave a thin, clean stencil on the sheet. The support sheet could be pulled away and the lacquer stencil could be applied to a screen. This method is the basis for nearly all hand-cut stencils in the industry today. It has the advantage of speed combined with sharp, crisp fine detail.

New materials, other than lacquer, have been developed to create hand-cut stencils. The most popular types are water based. With these materials, the stencil adheres to the screen with water, is impervious to nearly any ink vehicle, and can be removed from the screen with hot water and cleaner when the job is done.

The basic process of creating a hand-cut stencil is relatively simple. It involves only three steps:

1. Hand cutting the stencil
2. Adhering the stencil to the screen
3. Removing the support sheet

Cut-film stencils are made of two layers: a support sheet and a lacquer- or water-based emulsion. The problem in hand cutting is to cut away the emulsion without embossing or cutting the support sheet. As with all stencils, only the areas to be printed are removed from the base material.

Hand Cutting the Stencil

Place a line drawing of the desired image or design under a piece of cut-film material. Be sure that the emulsion side of the stencil material is up and that there are at least 2 inches of stencil film around all edges of the image. Tape the corners of the image and the cut-film material securely in place.

A variety of tools are used in the industry to cut the film in the next step. An X-ACTO® or frisket knife is the cheapest and the most popular. Other useful tools are a swivel knife, bicutters (for cutting parallel lines), and a beam compass (figure 14.14).

Several general techniques ensure success with a hand-cut stencil. First, a razor-sharp blade is very important. The extra pressure needed with a dull blade rounds the film edge by forcing it down into the emulsion. A round film edge will not adhere to the screen properly. To cut the film, place the stencil material on a hard, flat surface. Apply light pressure to the

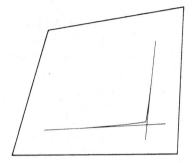

Figure 14.15.   Overlapping cuts

blade while holding it at a nearly right angle to the film. The lower the angle of the cutting blade, the greater the danger of rounding the edges of the stencil material.

Before cutting final film, practice on a piece of scrap film. Cut only through the emulsion. A cut in the base material holds excess adhering solvent during the adhering step. This excess solvent could dissolve part of the stencil material. Also, cut every line in a single stroke becauase it is extremely difficult to recut a line. Where lines meet, always overlap cuts (figure 14.15). This measure produces sharp corners on the final print and overlapping cuts always fuse together when the stencil is applied to the screen. Remove the emulsion as each image area is cut. Do not wait until all lines have been cut. The easiest method to remove an unwanted layer of cut emulsion is to stab it with the point of the cutting tool and lift it away. Remember to remove the emulsion only in the areas where ink is to appear on the final print.

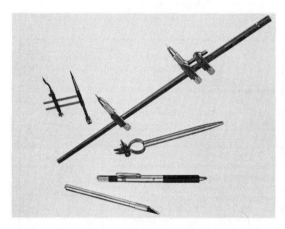

Figure 14.14.   Common cutting tools. From bottom counterclockwise: X-ACTO® knife or frisket knife, Ulano swivel knife, parallel bicutters, and beam compass cutters.

Adhering the Stencil to the Screen

Adhering Water-Soluble, Hand-Cut Stencils
There are two methods of adhering water-soluble, hand-cut stencils to screens. The first

method (figure 14.16a) uses a buildup board that is smaller than the inside dimensions of the screen frame. To begin, place the hand-cut stencil emulsion side up on the center of the buildup board. Position the screen over the stencil and the buildup board so that the screen fabric is against the emulsion side of the stencil. Then saturate a sponge or cloth with water and slowly wipe the screen fabric in overlapping strokes until the entire surface of the screen is wet. Do not rub the stencil with the sponge. Allow only enough contact to moisten the stencil emulsion. With the frame still flat, dry the emulsion through the screen with a cold-air fan. To reduce drying time, excess moisture can be blotted out of the stencil with newsprint. When the emulsion is dry, the base material of

the stencil may be peeled away. (See the Masking the Stencil section later in this chapter.)

The second method of adhering water-soluble, hand-cut stencils (figure 14.16b) involves first wetting both sides of the screen thoroughly with a clean sponge dampened with water. Then roll the emulsion side of the stencil against the bottom of the wet screen. Using light pressure, move the wet sponge over the entire surface of the base material of the stencil to adhere the stencil to the fabric of the screen. With the frame flat, dry the emulsion with a cold-air fan. To reduce drying time, again blot excess moisture with newsprint. The base material of the stencil can be peeled off when the emulsion is dry. (See the Masking the Stencil section later in this chapter.)

Traditional Adhering Technique

1. Preparation. Place the cut stencil, film up, on your buildup board, which is smaller than inside measurement of the frame. Position the prepared screen, squeegee side up, over the film.

2. Adhering. Saturate a sponge with water. Move the sponge slowly in one stroke over the fabric from the squeegee side. Slightly overlap the strokes until the entire surface is adhered. *Do not rub with the sponge.*

3. Drying. With the frame flat, dry the film from the squeegee side with a cold-air fan. To reduce drying time, excess moisture may be removed by blotting with newsprint before drying with the fan. Peel off the backing sheet when the film is dry. The adhesive will remain on the backing sheet.

(a)

Alternative Adhering Technique

1. Preparation. This technique requires a clean, well-stretched screen. Using a clean sponge, thoroughly wet both sides of the fabric with water.

2. Adhering. Place the film side of cut stencil against bottom of the wet screen. Using light pressure, move the wet sponge over the entire surface of the plastic backing to adhere the film to the fabric.

3. Drying. With the frame flat, dry the film with a cold air fan from the squeegee side. To reduce drying time, blot excess moisture with newsprint before drying with the fan. Peel off the backing sheet when the film is dry. The adhesive will remain on the backing sheet.

(b)

Figure 14.16. Adhering water-soluble, hand-cut stencils.
Courtesy of J. Ulano Company, Inc.

Adhering Lacquer-Based, Hand-Cut Stencils

Lacquer-based, hand-cut stencils use a commercial adhering fluid to soften the lacquer emulsion just enough to allow the stencil to adhere to the screen. The adhering fluid should match the specifications provided by the stencil manufacturer.

To adhere a lacquer stencil to a screen, first place the stencil emulsion side up on a buildup board. Position the screen over the stencil and the buildup board so that the screen fabric is against the emulsion of the stencil. Then place several weights on the frame to keep the stencil from shifting or, if possible, clamp the frame in place.

Next, take two clean, soft cloths and roll one into a tight ball. Moisten the cloth ball with a small quantity of adhering fluid. The cloth should not be so wet that the fluid drips from the ball. Begin in one corner of the screen with the wet cloth and moisten about a 4-inch square over the stencil. Use a blotting motion to saturate the screen area and then immediately wipe the area dry with the second cloth. The moistened area should darken. That darkened area of the screen is now adhered to the stencil. Continue blotting and drying 4-inch squares of screen over the rest of the stencil. Be extremely careful not to dissolve the lacquer of the stencil with too much solvent, but use enough lacquer so that the screen over the entire stencil is one uniform color. Lacquer-based materials dry rapidly. When the stencil is completely dry, its backing sheet may be peeled away. (See Masking the Stencil section later in this chapter).

Photographic Stencil Methods

The primary reason for the explosive growth of the screen printing industry has been development of the photographic stencil. The idea of photographic stencils is not new, however. The basic process was developed in Great Britain in 1850 by William Henry Fox Talbot. Actually, Talbot was concerned with developing a continuous-tone negative/positive process. He found that certain materials, such as gelatin, egg albumin, and glue, when mixed or coated with a potassium bichromate solution, hardened when exposed to light. The unexposed areas remained soft and could be washed away readily. It was not until 1914 that someone applied Talbot's work to the screen printing industry. Today, photographic emulsions far more sophisticated than egg albumin are available through commercial suppliers.

In photographic screen printing, printers expose light-sensitive material through a positive transparent image. After processing, unhardened areas on the stencil are washed away. The stencil is fixed, or made permanent, masked, and then printed.

The primary advantage of photographic stencils is the possibility for intricate and high-quality line detail. Step-and-repeat images, halftones, exact facsimile reproductions, and high-quality process color stencil prints are all possible and commonplace. The introduction of photographic screen printing allowed the screen printer to enter the field of packaged product illustration. A color image can be screen printed with nearly any ink on nearly any surface shape (flat, cylindrical, or irregular) with this process.

All photographic stencil processes are divided into three types:

- Indirect or transfer image method
- Direct image method
- Film emulsion or direct/indirect image method

Indirect Process

The **indirect process** uses a dry emulsion on a plastic support sheet. The stencil emulsion is

sensitized by the manufacturer and is purchased by the printer in rolls or sheets. The
stencil film is exposed through a transparent,
right-reading positive and is then treated with
a developer solution. The areas that light
reaches (the nonimage areas) harden during
exposure. The remaining areas are washed
away with a warm-water spray to form the image or printing areas. The stencil is adhered to
a clean screen while it is wet from the spray,
and the support sheet is removed after the
stencil dries (figure 14.17).

Direct Process

The **direct process** uses a wet emulsion that is
coated directly on a clean screen. The emulsion
is exposed through a transparent positive to
harden the nonimage areas. The image areas
are washed away with a warm-water spray.
When the emulsion is dry, the stencil is ready
to print (figure 14.18). Direct emulsions have a
limited shelf life when compared to indirect
materials which are basically unlimited because they are stored in an inactive form.

Direct/Indirect Process

The **direct/indirect process** combines the indirect and the direct photographic processes. An
unsensitized film material is placed under the
stencil side of the screen on a flat table. The
stencil emulsion is stored in two parts, a liquid
emulsion and a sensitizer. When the two are
mixed and coated on the screen, they become
light sensitive and coat through the screen to
the film support. When the emulsion is dry, the
backing sheet of the stencil is removed and
normal direct exposure techniques are carried
out (figure 14.19). The main advantage of the
direct/indirect process is the uniform emulsion thickness. Because the direct/indirect
process uses the procedures of both the direct

and the indirect stencil methods, it is not discussed in detail in this chapter.

Determining Photographic Stencil Exposures

Most photographic stencil emulsions have a
spectral sensitivity that peaks in the ultraviolet
to blue region of the visible spectrum (see
Light Sources in appendix B). Because the stencil emulsion must be exposed through a transparent positive, good contact is important to
ensure accurate line detail. Vacuum frames are
generally used to hold the stencil and film in
place during exposure.

Proper exposure is also important for
photographic screen stencils. An underex-
posed stencil produces an emulsion that is too
thin. A thin emulsion is difficult to adhere to
the screen material and can possibly pass ink in
a nonimage area. In contrast, an overexposed
stencil results in an emulsion that is too thick.
A thick emulsion closes the fine line detail of an
image and, if on an indirect photographic stencil, might not adhere to the fabric properly.

A commercial **step wedge** manufactured
by the J. Ulano Company, Inc. (figure 14.20,
p. 398) can be used to calibrate correct stencil
exposure. An alternative calibration device is
a transparent positive made up of normal
and hard-to-reproduce copy. The step wedge
is preferable because it contains identified
line weights.

In practice, a series of exposures is made
through the step wedge to the photographic
stencil. If an indirect stencil is used, the emulsion must be exposed through the base material (figure 14.21). If a direct stencil is used, the
transparent positive is exposed through the
bottom side of the screen (figure 14.22).

Most stencil manufacturers recommend
exposure times, but it is best to calibrate the
exposure to the specific working conditions.
Begin with the manufacturer's recommended

1. Exposure
No light strikes the photographic screen emulsion under the image areas on the transparent positive.

2. Development
Areas exposed to light during exposure harden during development.

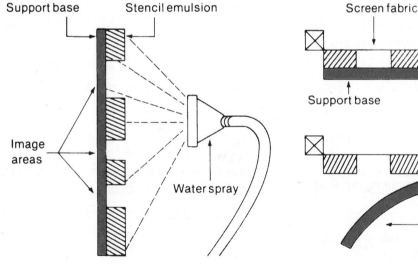

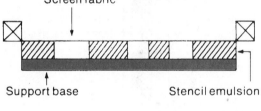

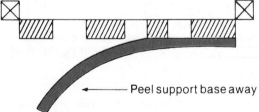

3. Wash
Unhardened areas (image areas) are washed away leaving open areas in the stencil.

4. Adhesion
The stencil emulsion is adhered to the screen fabric, let dry, and the support base is peeled away.

Figure 14.17. **Indirect screen stencil process**

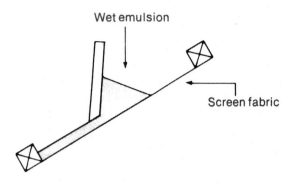

1. Coating
A wet emulsion is coated onto a clean screen.

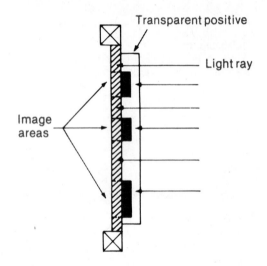

2. Exposure
Areas where light strikes the emulsion
(nonimage areas) harden during exposure.

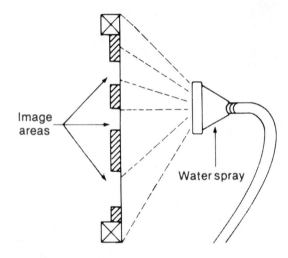

3. Wash
Unhardened areas (image areas) are washed
away leaving open areas in the stencil.

Figure 14.18.   Direct screen stencil process

exposure time for the specific light source and distance. If no time is recommended, start with 60 seconds. From the recommended time, determine exposures that are 50 percent, 75 percent, 100 percent, 125 percent, and 150 percent. For example, if 60 seconds is the recommended

exposure time, then five separate exposures would be made through the step wedge: 30 seconds (50 percent of 60 seconds), 45 seconds (75% of 60 seconds), 60 seconds (100 percent of 60 seconds), 75 seconds (125 percent of 60 seconds), and 90 seconds (150 percent of 60 seconds).

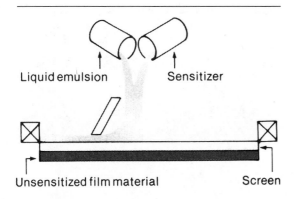

1. Coating
The two parts of the stencil emulsion are mixed and coated on the screen material. Note the piece of insensitized film material under the screen.

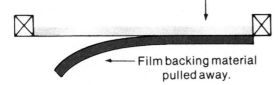

2. Removing the backing
The film backing is removed after the emulsion has dried.

Figure 14.19. Direct/indirect screen stencil process

A test exposure is easy to make if these time percentages are used. Place the transparent positive in contact with the stencil. First, expose through the positive for the shortest exposure time. For this example, the shortest exposure would be 30 seconds. Then mask one-fifth of the step wedge with opaque paper or masking film and expose the remaining uncovered portion for 15 seconds. (See the Masking the Stencil section later in this chapter for more on masking.) Move the masking sheet to cover two-fifths of the wedge and again expose

the uncovered area for 15 seconds. Continue masking an additional one-fifth of the wedge and exposing the uncovered area until the entire step wedge has been masked and exposed. Develop and wash the stencil. (See the following sections outlining the specific procedures for each type of stencil.)

Mount the stencil on the screen that will be used in the shop, allow it to dry, and make a print with the desired ink. Examine the image in detail. First identify the step that has reproduced the original line detail most faithfully. Consider the narrowest line that was reproduced, then select the exposure that has the thickest emulsion but has held that line dimension. If no step appears ideal, expose another stencil with smaller percentage difference (such as 80 percent, 90 percent, 110 percent, or 120 percent of the recommended time).

Indirect Photographic Stencil Process

The indirect photographic stencil process is known by several different names in the industry: "transfer," "carbon tissue," and "pigment paper" are a few. The process is also identified by several trade names representing indirect stencil material that is supplied by individual dealers.

The **indirect photographic stencil** is exposed through a transparent film positive. Where light strikes the stencil (nonimage areas), the emulsion hardens. Where light does not strike the stencil (image areas), the emulsion remains soft and can be washed away. Logically, the better the film positive, the better the reproduction. Chapter 6 provides detailed information on the production of positive film images.

An indirect photographic stencil is the easiest screen stencil to produce. It involves the following six steps:

1. Exposure
2. Development

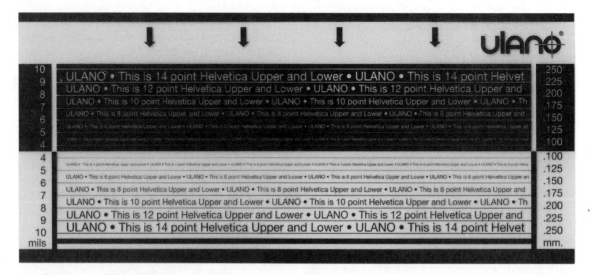

Figure 14.20.   Ulano step wedge. The Ulano step wedge is a precision tool that can be used to determine the correct exposure time for any type of photographic stencil. The illustration shown is only an approximation and in no way attempts to duplicate the quality of the original instrument.
Courtesy of J. Ulano Company, Inc.

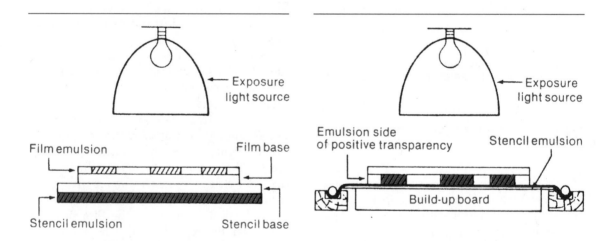

Figure 14.21.   Exposing indirect stencils. Indirect stencils must be exposed through the base side of the stencil material.

Figure 14.22.   Exposing direct stencils. A direct stencil is set up to be exposed through the bottom of the screen.

3. Washing
4. Application of the stencil to the screen
5. Drying
6. Removal of the base material

Exposure

All indirect emulsions are coated onto a transparent support sheet by the stencil manufacturer. It is always necessary to expose the stencil through the support material. Some sort of contact frame is generally used to bring the positive into contact with the presensitized stencil. It is important that the right-reading side of the positive be against the base side of the stencil. Place the positive on a tabletop so that the image reads exactly as it would on the final print. Place a sheet of stencil material over the positive so that its emulsion side is up. Be sure that the stencil extends at least 1 inch (2.54 cm) beyond all image extremes (figure 14.23). Then pick up both pieces and turn them over. To expose the stencil, the light must pass through the clear areas of the positive. Place the two sheets in the contact frame and expose the stencil for the time that was determined from the test exposure.

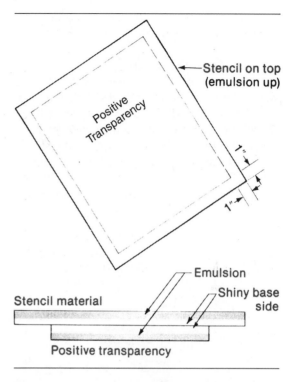

Figure 14.23. Positioning the positive transparency. The right-reading side of the positive must be placed against the base side of the stencil.

Development and Washing

The developing process removes all areas not hardened by exposure to light (all image areas). Any area covered by the positive image is washed away. Depending on the type of emulsion, indirect stencils are developed by one of two techniques: a hydrogen peroxide bath or plain water.

Some emulsions require a hydrogen peroxide bath to harden their exposed areas. These stencils are placed in the bath emulsion side up and are agitated constantly for 1 to 3 minutes, depending on the manufacturer's recommendations. The stencils are then re-

moved and sprayed with warm water (95°F to 105°F). The spray washes away the unhardened stencil areas, leaving a stencil outline of the image areas.

Other emulsions are developed in plain water immediately after being removed from the contact frame. A cool-water (70°F) spray is directed over the entire emulsion surface until the image areas wash away.

With both developing methods the concern is with stopping development as soon as the image areas are clear. Excess warm-water spray removes the hardened emulsion and can create a thin stencil. All indirect stencils are fixed by a stream of cold water (gradually decreasing the temperature).

Application of the Stencil
Indirect stencils adhere very easily to the screen fabric. Place the chilled stencil emulsion side up on a hard, flat buildup board (figure 14.24). Position the clean screen over the stencil so that the clear printing area of the stencil is in the center of the screen frame (figure 14.25). Do not move the screen once it has contacted the stencil and do not use excessive

Figure 14.26.   Removing excess moisture

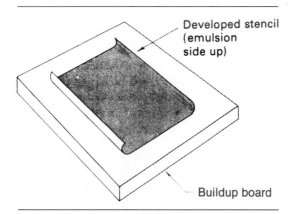

Developed stencil
(emulsion
side up)

Buildup board

Figure 14.24.   Placing the indirect stencil on a buildup board

RIGHT READING
SIDE

Figure 14.25.   Positioning the screen over the stencil

pressure—merely allow the weight of the frame to hold the screen in position. Excess moisture is removed from the stencil by blotting it through the screen with clean newsprint or inexpensive paper towels (figure 14.26). The function of blotting is to remove excess moisture and to "blot up" through the fibers the soft "top" of the emulsion. Lay the newsprint flat and gently wipe the newsprint with a soft, clean rag; *do not use pressure.* Keep changing the newsprint until it does not pick up moisture from the stencil. Excessive pressure during blotting pushes the fabric threads of the screen into the emulsion, which can cause pinholes or a ragged sawtooth edge during printing.

Drying
Indirect stencils should not be forced dry with hot or warm air. Rapid drying could result in poor adhesion or a warped stencil. To dry the emulsion properly, place the frame in a position so that air is allowed to flow over both of its sides—a gentle room air fan may be used. Spotty light and dark areas indicate that the stencil is drying. The emulsion is completely dry when the entire stencil area is a uniform color.

Removal of the Base Material
When the emulsion is dry, its clear support base can be peeled off (figure 14.27). After printing,

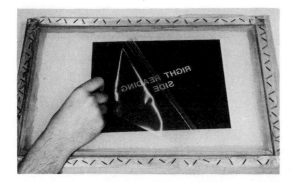

Figure 14.27. Peeling off the support material

all indirect photographic stencils can be removed from the screen fabric with a high-pressure, hot-water spray. For difficult materials, enzymes are available that will help to dissolve the old material. On metal or synthetic screens, bleach is commonly used for this purpose.

Direct Photographic Stencil Process

With the direct method of stencil preparation, a wet photographic emulsion is applied directly to the screen fabric by the printer. The entire screen is then exposed to a positive image, developed, and printed.

The main requirement of the direct process is some form of liquid, light-sensitive emulsion. All emulsions currently used fall into the following types of chemical formulations:

- A synthetic-based material, such as polyvinyl alcohol
- A gelatin-based chemical material
- A combination of synthetic and gelatin materials

Most printers use commercially prepared emulsions rather than prepare their own. Commercial emulsions are more economical, higher in quality, and can be formulated by the supplier to meet any printing requirements.

Commercial emulsions are available in two forms: presensitized and unsensitized liquids.

The five steps in preparing a **direct photographic stencil** are relatively simple:

1. Preparation of the sensitized emulsion
2. Application of the emulsion to the screen
3. Drying the emulsion
4. Exposure
5. Development

Preparation

Unsensitized, direct screen emulsions are provided by the manufacturer in two parts: a liquid unsensitized emulsion and a dry powder sensitizer. First, the dry powder sensitizer is dissolved in warm water according to the manufacturer's recommendations. The liquid sensitizer is then added to the dry powder sensitizer dissolved in water to create an active, sensitized emulsion. The emulsion may be stored in a closed amber or light-tight bottle, but it usually must be applied to the screen as soon as possible.

Application

The screen should be coated with the liquid emulsion in yellow or subdued light. One application technique is to pour a quantity of the emulsion on one edge of the bottom side of the frame rather than on the screen itself. With this technique the liquid does not seep rapidly through the screen mesh. With a round-edge scoop coater, squeegee the emulsion from the corner to the other end of the screen using smooth, continuous strokes (figure 14.28). Turn the frame over and immediately squeegee the inside of the screen until it is smooth. The quantity of liquid applied for the first coat depends on the length of the screen, but it is better to apply too much liquid and squeegee off the excess than it is to use too little liquid and not cover the screen totally.

Figure 14.28. **Using a scoop coater on the emulsion**

Figure 14.29. **Developing the image.** Gently spray both sides of the screen with warm water.

Expose the screen stencil material through the positive for the time determined from the test exposures.

Development
The stencil image is developed by first wetting both sides of the screen in warm (95°F to 105°F) water, then gently spraying both sides with warm water until the image areas are completely clear (figure 14.29). Allow the frame to drain and blot the emulsion dry with newsprint.

Masking the Stencil

The idea of a stencil is that ink passes through any open areas on the screen. It is necessary to block or mask the areas of the screen that are not covered by the stencil material and are not intended to print. There is generally a gap between the edge of the stencil and the screen frame that must be covered to prevent ink passage.

Preparing a Paper Mask

A paper **mask** works well for blocking nonimage areas in short runs. Cut a piece of Kraft pa-

Drying
Store the frame flat in a dark place. A circulating air fan can be used to hasten drying. When the first coat is dry, apply a second coat to the inside of the screen and allow it to dry. The thickness of the ink deposit can be controlled somewhat by the number of emulsion layers. If a thick ink deposit is desired, a third emulsion coating should be placed on the bottom side of the frame.

Exposure
Special contact frames must be used to hold the screen frame and film positive during exposure. Place the right-reading side of the transparent positive against the underside surface of the screen. The light must pass through the positive to expose the screen emulsion.

per (brown wrapping paper) slightly smaller than the inside dimensions of the frame. Lay the masking paper on the screen and trace the rough outline of the image area on the paper with a pencil. Remove the masking paper and cut out an area that is about 1 inch (2.54 cm) larger than the image extremes. Replace the masking paper on the screen and apply gummed tape around the edges of the frame. Then tape the edges of the masking paper to the stencil material. It is important that the tape be at least ¾ inch (1.91 cm) from the nearest image and in perfect contact with the solid stencil.

Preparing a Liquid Block-Out Mask

A second method of masking employs a liquid block-out mask which is a fluid (figure 14.30). These types of fluids are usually water based and are easy to use. Materials such as LePage's glue will work in this capacity, but specially formulated commercial products are inexpensive and work much better. Brush or scrape one coat of the fluid on the underside of the screen wherever the fabric is exposed but an image is not desired. Allow the fluid to dry and

Figure 14.30.   Using a liquid mask

then apply a second coat on the inside area of the screen.

It is often necessary to touch up any imperfections, such as pinholes, in the stencil. The liquid block-out is ideal for small corrections and should always be applied to the underside of the screen.

The processes of printing and cleaning the screen and stencil are discussed in detail in chapter 15.

Key Terms

screen printing	monofilament screens	step wedge
stencil	mechanical stretching	indirect photographic
hand-cut stencil	tooth	stencil
tusche-and-glue	indirect process	direct photographic stencil
photographic stencils	direct process	mask
multifilament screens	direct/indirect process	

Questions for Review

1. What is the basic concept of screen printing?

2. What are the three groups of stencil preparation methods?

3. How are screen fabrics classified?

4. Will a 6XX or a 14XX mesh count pass a coarser ink pigment?

5. Why must a tooth be produced on a monofilament fabric and not on a multifilament one?

6. Why should commercial household abrasive cleaners not be used to clean or degrease a screen?

7. What are the three basic steps in creating a hand-cut stencil?

8. What is the primary advantage of photographic stencils?

9. What are the three types of photographic stencils?

10. Briefly outline the six steps necessary to prepare an indirect photographic stencil.

11. Briefly outline the five steps necessary to prepare a direct photographic stencil.

12. What is the purpose of masking?

CHAPTER 15

Screen Printing

This illustration is a famous playing card called the "Knave of Bells" that dates from about A.D. 1500. There is some debate as to how the card was actually printed, but it was probably printed from a stencil. The "Knave" was part of a set of forty-eight playing cards found in the inner lining of a book cover that was printed and bound sometime around the turn of the sixteenth century. Paper was such a precious commodity then that discarded or inferior sheets were often used to stiffen book bindings. Many valuable early pieces of printing have been found in such hiding places.

As we understand the process today, the stenciled Knave card was made using a perforated metal plate. To create the stencil, many small holes were punched through the thin metal plate in the shape of the desired image. The "illuminator," as the stencil maker was called, positioned the plate over the paper and applied ink to the plate with a brush. The brush forced the ink through the small openings in the plate and onto the page. Several different colors were often used; a separate plate was used for each.

The "Knave of Bells." A printed playing card from about A.D. 1500.

No one knows exactly when playing cards were invented, but evidence of their existence is documented in a 1392 account book kept by the treasurer of King Charles VI of France, in which a notation was made on the purchase of three packs of cards for the king. Several scholars, however, have found references to "games of hazard," as card games were called, in French poetry as early as 1328.

The exact evolution of the printed card design is also difficult to trace. By 1550 printers had nearly universally adopted the four card suits we know today as symbols of the four classes of society. Hearts symbolized the clergy. Spades were a refinement of the Italian *spada*, a sword, and represented the nobility. Clubs meant the peasantry. Diamonds symbolized the citizens or burghers.

There are some experts who suggest that playing cards were the first printed product ever produced in Europe. Some even believe that the widespread use of games of hazard started an interest in learning for many uneducated peasants. There is little doubt that a demand was created for a printed product.

Objectives for Chapter 15

After completing this chapter, you will be able to:

■ Identify important considerations when selecting a squeegee and ink.

■ Explain basic screen printing techniques, including registration, on- and off-contact printing, printing, and clean up.

■ Recall multicolor printing techniques.

■ List methods of ink drying.

■ Recall methods of screen printing halftones.

■ Classify high-speed production screen printing presses.

■ Recognize special screen printing machine configurations.

Introduction

The basic process of screen printing has changed little in the last several hundred years. The standard printing device remains a stencil attached to a piece of fabric stretched over a wooden or metal frame. A flexible squeegee is used to force ink through the stencil opening. Even though the basic printing device has changed little, the printer's understanding of the variables that affect image quality has increased substantially.

The term **printing press** might sound strange when associated with the most basic screen printing frame, but the screen printing frame is a press in every sense—it has the four basic press units: feeding, registration, printing, and delivery. The receiver in screen printing (whether paper, metal, plastic, or even wood) must be fed and registered under the stencil. The ink must be transferred to the receiver. The printed product must be removed and stored for later distribution. Screen printing presses can range in complexity from an elementary homemade, hand-operated wooden frame (figure 15.1) to a sophisticated system that automatically inserts, registers, prints, and removes any receiving material, including cylindrical surfaces.

Figure 15.1. **Basic screen printing unit.** The wooden frame hinges on a particle baseboard. Courtesy of SUCO Learning Resources and R. Kampas.

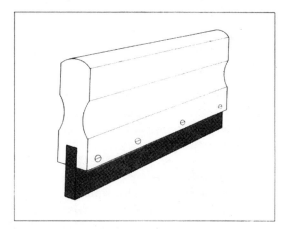

Figure 15.2. **Printer's squeegee**

Squeegee and Ink Considerations

Selecting the Proper Squeegee

The **squeegee** (figure 15.2) causes the image transfer to take place because it forces the ink through the stencil and the fabric openings onto the receiver. All squeegees have two parts: a handle and a blade. The handle can be any design that is comfortable for printers and meets their needs, but great care must be taken when selecting the squeegee blade. Four primary blade considerations must be examined prior to printing:

- Shape
- Chemical makeup
- Flexibility
- Length

Shape

The first blade consideration is blade shape. The blade shape generally determines the sharpness and thickness of ink deposit. There are six basic blade shapes (figure 15.3). A square blade (figure 15.3a) is the most common blade shape and is a good general purpose design that can be used to print on flat surfaces with standard poster inks. A double-bevel, flat-point blade (figure 15.3b) is good for working with ceramic materials such as glazes or slip. The double-bevel form (figure 15.3c) is used for printing on uneven surfaces or for placing a fine layer of ink on a surface when stenciling extremely fine line detail. The single-bevel blade (figure 15.3d) is generally used when printing on glass. The square-edge with rounded

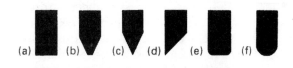

Figure 15.3. **Basic shapes of squeegee blades.** The six basic shapes are (a) square, (b) double bevel, flat point, (c) double bevel, (d) single bevel, (e) square edge with rounded corners, and (f) round edge.

corners shape (figure 15.3e) is generally used when screening light colors over dark backgrounds, and the round-edge design (figure 15.3f) works well when printing on fabrics. The round-edge design also has the advantage of forcing an extra-heavy amount of ink through the screen. Everyone but the special purpose printer will find the square form acceptable for almost every job.

Chemical Makeup

The chemical makeup of the squeegee blade is the second blade consideration. The base for some inks could actually dissolve the blade if the wrong type of blade were used. Most squeegee blades are cast from rubber or plastic. Blades that are designed for vinyl or acetate printing are water soluble and therefore cannot be used with a water-based pigment. Synthetic blades, such as polyurethane, retain their edges longer and resist abrasion better than do blades of any other material. They are significantly more expensive, however. A good general purpose squeegee blade is neoprene rubber. It can be used for vinyl, lacquer, oil, poster enamel, and ethocel inks. When selecting the chemical makeup of a blade, decide what type of ink will be used, identify the ink base, and determine which blade formulation is acceptable.

Flexibility

The third consideration for squeegee blade selection is flexibility. Flexibility is measured on a scale called Shore A ratings. As the number increases, so does hardness. Rubber hardness is measured in terms of **Shore durometer** readings. An average blade for general use has a 60 Shore A rating. Most squeegee manufacturers translate the value into the terms hard, medium, and soft. Soft blades (around 50 Shore A) deposit a fairly thick layer of ink. Hard blades (around 70 Shore A) deposit a sharp, thin ink layer. A medium squeegee blade (60 Shore A) meets most shop needs.

Length

The length of the squeegee is the fourth and final important consideration. As a rule, the blade should extend at least ½ inch (1.27 cm) beyond the limits of the stencil image, but it should be able to pass freely between the edges of the screen frame.

Squeegee Preparation

Whatever the shape, makeup, or hardness of the blade selected, the major factor controlling image quality is blade sharpness. Several types of commercial squeegee sharpeners are available that can be used to prepare any shape of blade edge (figure 15.4). Most sharpeners operate with a moving abrasive belt or drum. The blade is mounted in the sharpener with a series of clamps, and it passes against the cutting surface.

If a sharpening machine cannot be obtained, 6-inch and 8-inch (15-cm and 20-cm) widths of garnet cloth are suitable for sharpening square-edge blades. The cloth is mounted (generally with staples) on a hard, flat surface. The blade is held in a perfectly vertical position and is dragged back and forth over the abrasive cloth until a sharp edge forms.

Figure 15.4. Commercial squeegee sharpener.
Courtesy of Naz-Dar Company.

It is important that the squeegee be absolutely clean prior to printing. Any dry ink left on a blade from previous printing runs will contaminate the ink used with other printing jobs. This is especially important when a dark color is followed by a light color because the light color reveals impurities more readily.

Selecting the Proper Ink

The ink pigment and ink vehicle in screen printing must freely pass through screen fabric and create an image of acceptable density on the receiving surface. Screen inks are thinner than letterpress or lithographic inks, but thicker than inks used in gravure. (See chapter 16 for more about gravure.) Early screen inks were very similar to ordinary paint. The creation of new fabrics and stencil materials, the growth of printing on nontraditional materials (any material but paper), and the application of screen printing to specialized industrial needs (such as printed circuits) have resulted in the development of a wide variety of screen inks.

There are so many different materials intended for so many different applications in screen printing that both novice and experienced printers become confused easily. Choosing the appropriate ink becomes easier to understand if all elements of a particular job are examined in detail and several specific questions are answered.

Product Characteristics
The first area of concern should be the characteristics of the printed piece. What is the function of the final product? Will it be exposed to harsh weather conditions (as is a billboard)? Will it contact harsh chemicals (as does printing on a detergent bottle or even a cola container)? Should the image have a gloss finish or a flat finish? What is the surface of the image receiver? Will the ink have to dry by absorbing

into the material? Will it need to be heat set? Will it have to air dry?

Production Limitations
After considering the characteristics of the printed piece, the printer must address the limitations of the production situation. Ink manufacturers recommend a minimum **screen mesh count,** or screen opening, that can be used with each of their inks. If the screen mesh count of a screen is smaller than the recommended minimum, no ink will pass through the screen.

Any material that can be ground to a fine powder can be mixed with a liquid vehicle and used as a screen ink. The solvents for the stencil and for the ink must not be the same. For example, if a water-based ink is used with a water-based stencil, the ink and stencil rapidly become a puddle on the screen.

By making a list of both product and production limitations, it is possible to eliminate all but a narrow category of possible ink choices. More information about screen inks for specific applications is given in chapter 18.

Ink Preparation

Many manufacturers advertise that their inks are "ready to use directly from the can," but the printer usually has to prepare the ink before printing. **Ink viscosity** (resistance to flow) is very important in ink preparation. The goal is to keep the ink as dense as possible to form an acceptable printed image. At the same time, however, the ink must be thin enough to pass freely through the screen openings without clogging. The difficulty is that the required viscosity can be different for every job. The higher the screen mesh count, the thinner the ink must be. In very general terms, the ink should "flow like honey" from the ink knife. It should move slowly and smoothly and should flow immediately when the knife is tipped.

Many different additives can be mixed with screen inks to yield certain ink characteristics.

Ink viscosity can be decreased by adding a compatible thinner and/or reducer, for example. Adding a transparent base makes ink somewhat translucent. An extender base increases the quantity of usable ink without affecting density. A drier functions to hasten the drying of the ink on the receiver, but it can also increase the possibility of the ink drying in the screen fabric. A binder can be added to increase the adhesion of the ink to the paper or receiver. Individuals inexperienced with additives should always consult a screen ink supplier for information.

The Basic Screen Printing Process

The basic techniques for screen printing are discussed here in terms of a hand-operated, hinged-frame system. For this section it is assumed that the printing frame is held to a wooden or particleboard base with a pair of heavy-duty hinge clamps. The hinges can be either common butt hinges or special hinges purchased from a screen printing supplier.

The sequence of screen printing steps, as with any press system, is to feed, register, print, and deliver the paper. Because the simple screen system is hand fed and delivered, this section considers only registering the paper and printing the image. The processes of drying the image, cleaning the screen, and removing the stencil are also discussed.

Basic Registration Techniques

As with all printing systems, registration is placing the image in the same position on every press sheet. Recall from chapter 2 that three metal gauge pins are used on the tympan of a platen press to hold the press sheet in place. It is also possible to form "gauge pins" from a narrow strip of paper. These gauge pins

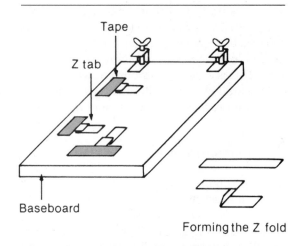

Forming the Z fold

Figure 15.5.   Making gauge pins. Three Z tabs taped in place on the baseboard serve as gauge pins used to register the press sheet.

hold the press sheet in register during screen printing. To create these gauge pins, cut three pieces of 20-pound to 40-pound paper ½ inch × 2 inches (1.3 cm × 5 cm) and make a simple Z-fold tab (figure 15.5). Tape the Z tabs to the baseboard under the screen frame.

Commercial printers use several methods to locate the image in the appropriate screen printing position. One simple method is to first place the original drawing or film positive used to produce the screen stencil so that it is right reading on a piece of the press sheet. Tape the original to the sheet so that the image is in the desired printing position. Place the sheet with the taped image on the baseboard and lower the screen frame into printing position over the sheet. Move the sheet until its taped image aligns with the stencil opening on the screen, then carefully hinge the screen up and out of the way. Without moving the press sheet, carefully insert the "gauge pins" and tape each one to the baseboard (figure 15.6). The pins should be positioned so that there are two pins on a long side of the press sheet and

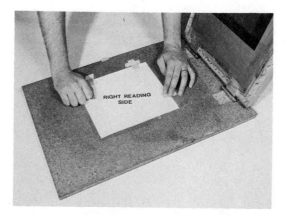

Figure 15.6. **Setting the image position.** The Z tabs are placed against the positioned stock and carefully taped in place.

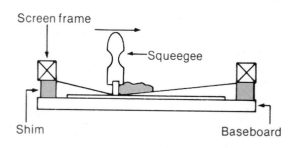

Figure 15.7. **Diagram of off-contact printing.** In off-contact printing, the screen touches the press sheet only when the image is transferred by the squeegee.

one pin on a short side. It is also important that the pins be placed as far from the image areas as possible. Remove the press sheet and tape the inside portion of the pins to the base. If every press sheet is seated against the inside of the three pins, the image will print in the same position on each sheet.

On-Contact and Off-Contact Printing

Two common printing methods are used for hinged-frame printing: on-contact and off-contact printing. With **on-contact printing,** the screen and stencil contact the press sheet throughout the image transfer process. With this method, the press sheet generally sticks to the screen. After the image is transferred, the frame must be hinged up and out of the way and the stock must be peeled away carefully. One method of preventing the press sheet from sticking is to place several pieces of thin, double-backed adhesive in nonimage areas on the baseboard. On-contact printing is the most common technique for small job shops or for short-run jobs that do not require extremely sharp impressions. However, off-contact print-

ing should always be done if possible to prevent the press sheet from sticking.

In **off-contact printing,** the screen and stencil are raised slightly (generally no more than ⅛ inch or 3.2 mm) from the press sheet by small shims, or spacing material, under the hinge and frame. With this technique the stencil touches the press sheet only when the squeegee passes over the screen. Once the image transfers across the squeegee line, the screen snaps back away from the receiver (figure 15.7). Off-contact printing helps keep the press sheet from sticking to the screen and usually prevents image smearing. It is often used to produce sharp impressions on smooth surfaces.

A vacuum frame base can be used with either on-contact or off-contact printing to help keep the press sheet from sticking to the screen. Vacuum bases are available as single units or as tables and are found on most semiautomatic sheet printing machines.

Printing the Stencil

Chapter 14 outlined several procedures for masking the nonimage portions of the screen. Before printing the stencil, however, two tasks remain. First, check to ensure that there are no pinholes or other unwanted openings in the stencil. Block any areas with the recommended block-out solution for the type of stencil being used. Second, seal off the inside edge of the stencil, between the fabric and the frame. Sealing can be done with any wide commercial tape (2-inch or 5-cm width tape is recommended). If the press run is exceptionally long or if special inks (such as water-based) or abrasive materials (such as ceramic glaze) are used, a plastic solvent-resistant, pressure-sensitive tape should be used. Otherwise, a water-moistened gummed tape will suffice.

Begin printing by positioning a press sheet on the baseboard in the registration system and lowering the screen frame into position. Pour a puddle of prepared ink away from the image at one end of the screen and in a line slightly longer than the width of the image (figure 15.8). Hold the squeegee at about a 60-degree angle to the screen surface and, pressing firmly, draw the puddle of ink across the stencil opening with one smooth motion (figure 15.9). It is important that the movement is uniform and does not stop until the squeegee is out of the image area. Make only one pass. Then remove the squeegee, raise the frame,

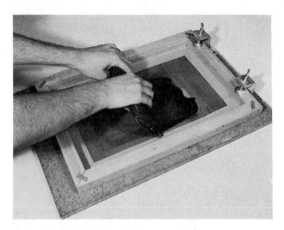

Figure 15.9. Distributing the ink

prop the screen away from the image surface, and remove the press sheet (figure 15.10).

Examine the printed image for correct position, ink uniformity, and clarity of detail. If necessary, readjust the registration pins for proper registration. If ink clogs or dries in the screen fabric it can cause the layers of ink on the image to be nonuniform or of a lower quality line detail. To correct clogging or drying, remove as much ink from the screen as

Figure 15.8. Adding ink to the screen

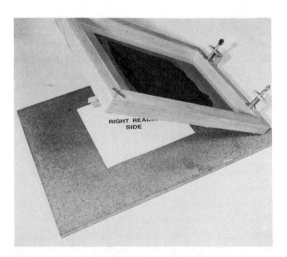

Figure 15.10. Removing the press sheet

possible and add thinner to the ink. Clean the clogged portions of the screen by gently wiping the underside of the stencil with a rag moistened with thinner. Then reink the screen and pull a second impression. Once an acceptable image is obtained, continue inserting a press sheet, passing the squeegee across the stencil, and removing the printed sheet until the job is completed.

Multicolor Printing

The primary concern of multicolor screen printing is the method of registration. It is important that the first color be placed accurately. If placement of the first printed image varies on the page, it will be impossible to register the second image to it.

A two-color screen printing job requires two separate stencils. Multicolor runs require careful planning of printing sequence and color overlaps to eliminate gaps. When opaque colors are used, the images must overlap by at least $\frac{1}{16}$ inch (1.6 mm). It is not necessary to overlap transparent colors except where a third color is desired.

Several techniques can be used to control accurate color fit. One technique is to register the first color using standard positioning methods, but to mark the first sheet as a proof. While the proof sheet is still held by the Z tabs, mark the position of the tabs with a pencil. Most press sheets are cut with some slight variation on the edges. If, for the second color, the Z tabs are placed in the same position as for the first color, the possibility of misregistration is lowered.

To position the second color over the first, mount a sheet of clear acetate over the baseboard and tape it from one edge so it can be hinged out of the way when necessary. With the acetate in place, swing the second stencil down into printing position and pull an impression. When the frame is removed, the second image position is defined on the acetate.

Slip the proof sheet from the first color under the acetate and line up both colors. Then carefully hinge the acetate out of the way and mount the register tabs on the baseboard in line with the edges of the proofsheet of the tab positions. The two colors should now fit for the second printing. Any number of additional colors may be registered with this technique.

Problems with registration are not always the operator's fault. Fabrics that are loosely stretched on the frame tend to cause problems with multicolor registration. Frame hinges can also become loose. If not taped securely, register tabs move out of position. Whatever the reason, when colors do not fit, all possible variables should be carefully examined.

Drying the Image

Most screen printing inks dry by absorption, aerial oxidation (air drying), a combination of both absorption and aerial oxidation, or by heat-setting action. Screen prints cannot be delivered from the press and stacked because all types of screen inks require some drying time. To reduce work and conserve production space, a drying rack is often used to receive press sheets (figure 15.11). Racks are available in a wide variety of sizes, and commercial models come equipped with spring systems attached to floating bars that swing each shelf down into position as needed.

Inks that dry by absorption into the press sheet or by aerial oxidation can generally be stacked and shipped within 30 minutes. It is possible to hasten drying time by passing the press sheet through a heat oven.

Heat-setting inks require an intense direct heat source. Some form of commercial curing or baking oven is generally used (figure 15.12). Most ovens heat to about 320°F, have forced air circulation and a temperature control device, and are equipped with a variable-speed, conveyer-belt feeding system.

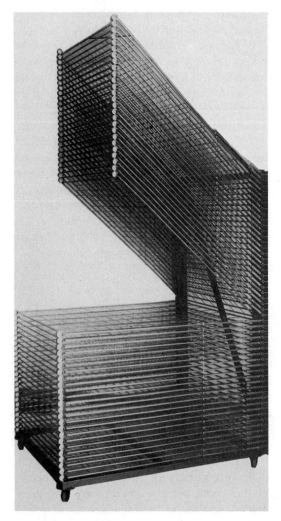

Figure 15.11.   Floating bar print drying rack.
Courtesy of Naz-Dar Company.

Cleaning the Screen

To clean the screen, first remove any large deposits of ink remaining on the screen and squeegee with an ink knife. It is generally wise to discard the ink from the screen surface and thereby avoid contaminating any fresh ink remaining in the can. Next, place ten to fifteen open sheets of newspaper on the baseboard and lower the screen into printing position. Place a quantity of compatible solvent on the squeegee side of the screen. It is important to dissolve all ink before any solvent is removed. If a rag were applied to the screen immediately, the solvent would be absorbed but no dissolving action would take place. Now, using your hand, rub the solvent into the entire surface of the screen. (Plastic gloves are practical during this process.) After all ink is dissolved, remove both the ink and the solvent from the screen with a dry cloth rag. Lift the screen and remove the several layers of newspaper. Repeat this operation until all ink has been removed. As a final step, moisten a clean rag with solvent and rub the underside of the screen to remove any remaining ink.

Commercial screen cleaning units (figure 15.13) also dissolve all ink and leave the screen perfectly clean. With these devices, the frame is placed on a washing stand, and a solvent spray is directed over it. The solvent drains back into a container where the ink and dirt settle or are filtered out, and the clear solvent is recirculated through the machine.

There is a tendency for novice printers to mix dissimilar solvents during the cleanup operation. Stencil material and printing inks are chosen so that their bases will not dissolve one another. If the stencil is water based, the ink is lacquer based, and water accidentally mixes with the ink, problems occur. The stencil may not wash away, but the ink will emulsify and hopelessly clog the screen. It is important that the printer have a clear understanding of the printing materials and their solvents before starting any cleanup.

Removing the Stencil

After all ink has been cleaned from the screen and any remaining ink solvent has evaporated, the stencil can be removed. One of the great advances in recent years is the development of a quality water-based stencil material. Whether

Figure 15.12. Commercial batch oven. A commercial batch oven is used to dry heat-setting inks.
Courtesy of Advance Process Supply Company, Chicago.

hand-cut or photographic, most water-based stencils are designed to be removed with a hot-water spray. With some stencils, a commercial enzyme is recommended to achieve removal.

To remove a stencil that requires an enzyme, wet both sides of the stencil and sprinkle on the enzyme. After letting the stencil and enzyme stand for 5 minutes (or whatever time is recommended by the manufacturer), spray the screen with hot water. It is necessary to

Figure 15.13. Commercial screen cleaning unit.
Courtesy of Advance Process Supply Company, Chicago.

neutralize the enzyme remaining on the wet screen by wiping the screen with a 5-percent acetic acid or white vinegar solution. After neutralizing, thoroughly rinse the screen with cold water and allow it to air dry.

If nylon, polyester, or stainless steel screens are used with water-based stencils, you can use a household chlorine bleach presoak in place of the commerical enzyme. One method is to wet both sides of the stencil with a sodium hypochlorite solution (bleach) and allow it to stand for 5 minutes. Then carefully rinse the bleach solution from the stencil (avoid splashing or contacting the eyes) and spray with hot water. This technique should *not* be used if a natural fiber, such as silk, is used.

Lacquer stencils must be removed with lacquer thinner. Lay several layers of newsprint on a flat surface and pour lacquer thinner on both sides of the stencil. Allow the thinner to sit on the stencil for several minutes before rubbing with a cloth. Lacquer thinner has a tendency to dry very rapidly, so several applications of the solution might be necessary before the screen is clean.

Troubleshooting Clogged Screens

A clean screen is the first requirement when preparing to print. A clogged screen should not be used because a stencil will not adhere to it well. If the stencil does adhere, the quality of the printed image will be very poor. In a learning situation where many different individuals use the same equipment, it is not always possible to identify what material is clogging a screen. It could be stencil emulsion, block-out material, ink, or even some foreign substance.

There are several steps to follow to clean a clogged screen when you do not know what is causing the problem. First, try using the household chlorine bleach mentioned in the preceding section (as long as the fabric is not silk) or a commercial enzyme (this should remove any water-based substance). Next, try the solvent for the ink that was used for the last printing. If the screen is still clogged, try scrubbing the area with lacquer thinner. Finally, try alcohol. It is important that the screen is dried thoroughly after each step. If the screen remains clogged after all of these attempts, discard the screen and restretch the frame.

Halftone Reproduction in Screen Printing

Screen printing halftone images has several advantages over relief or lithographic processes. First, it is ideal for short-run posters or illustrations and is less costly than any other method in terms of both time and materials. It can print extremely large image sizes as well. Finally, a wide range of inks can be used that have a brilliance, opacity, and texture unmatched by any other method.

There are, however, special considerations when screen printing halftones. Although 85-line and 110-line halftones are screened commonly in the printing industry, a small job shop without critical stencil preparation and print-

ing controls should stay with rather coarse halftone screen rulings (85 lines per inch or coarser) because the highlight and shadow dot structure must be carefully controlled in this process, and a film positive must be produced.

The reproducible halftone dot sizes of the final film positive in screen print should be 10 percent to 15 percent for highlights and 85 percent to 90 percent for shadows. Any dot size not within these ranges will probably not reproduce on the final printed sheet.

Methods of Halftone Preparation for Screen Printing

The basic challenge when preparing halftone images for screen printing is to work within the limits of the production facilities. Although a 65-line contact screen is readily available from printing suppliers, it is common only in those shops that prepare illustrations for newspaper production or in screen companies that specialize in halftone printing.

Basically four methods can be used to prepare film halftone positives in any printing company:

1. If a 65-line halftone screen is available, first make a film halftone negative to the reproduction size. Then make a contact film positive of the halftone negative.

2. Using an available halftone screen (such as 133-line screen), make a reduced halftone negative that can fit into a film enlarger (like that used to make continuous-tone prints). Then project through the negative in the enlarger onto a fresh piece of high-contrast film to make a film positive at the reproduction size.

3. Using the available halftone screen, make a same-size film halftone negative from the original. Then place the

negative on a back-lighted process camera copyboard and enlarge it to the required reproduction size on a fresh piece of high-contrast film.

4. Using an available diffusion transfer halftone screen (usually 100-line type), make a diffusion transfer opaque halftone positive the same size as the original. Then enlarge the positive on a process camera to the required reproduction size by using either a second set of diffusion transfer materials with a transparent receiver sheet or high-contrast film to make a film negative. Then contact print a film positive.

If the last three methods are used, it is necessary to be able to calculate percentage changes to make halftones that are the required screen rulings using available in-plant materials.

Assume, for example, that a 5 inch × 7 inch continuous-tone photograph must be printed as a 9 inch × 12 inch halftone reproduction with a 50-line ruling. The available screen is a 133-line negative grey contact screen. The printer decides to produce the final film positive by projection using an enlarger (method 2).

First, use the following equation to determine the percent enlargement (PE) of a 133-line ruling that is needed to obtain 50 lines per inch:

$$PE = \frac{\text{Available screen ruling}}{\text{desired screen ruling}} \times 100$$
$$= 133/50 \times 100$$
$$= 133 \times 2$$
$$= 266 \text{ percent}$$

In other words, it is necessary to enlarge a halftone with a ruling of 133 lines per inch 266 percent to obtain a 50-line ruling.

An enlarger is being used for this example, so it is necessary to determine the size of the first halftone negative. The easiest method of doing so is to refer to a proportion scale (re-

fer to figure 3.30). Set the wheel at 266 percent enlargement. Then read from the required size (9 inches × 12 inches) across the wheel to obtain the negative size to be placed in the enlarger. For this example, the first halftone negative must be reduced to 3⅜ inches × 4½ inches from a 5 inch × 7 inch original. Calculations for all four methods can be made in a similar manner.

Fabric Selection

When selecting fabric for screen printing halftone images, the screen mesh count is the major concern. In general, monofilament fabrics should be used with halftones. The specific mesh count depends on the halftone ruling of the film positive. The Ulano Company recommends multiplying the halftone ruling by 3.5 to 4.0 to obtain a usable screen mesh range. For example, if the halftone ruling is 60 lines per inch, any mesh count between 210 and 240 can be used (60 × 3.5 = 210, 60 × 4.0 = 240).

Whatever screen mesh count is used, the smallest halftone dot must attach to at least four fiber intersections (figure 15.14). For example, if a 133-line halftone stencil is attached to a number 12 fabric, which has approximately 125 threads to the inch, many individual

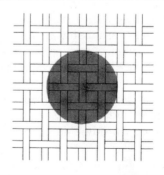

Figure 15.14. Halftone dot on screen printing fabric

dots would drop through the screen during the printing operation because there would be insufficient fabric support.

Moiré Patterns

A **moiré pattern** (an objectionable optical pattern discussed in chapter 9) may form when two screen patterns overlap (such as when a halftone image is placed on the fabric screen pattern). This is a problem particularly when the screen mesh count is too coarse for the halftone screen ruling. One way to avoid the moiré pattern is to place the clean, stretched screen over the film halftone positive on a light table before making the stencil. Rotate the positive under the screen until the moiré pattern disappears. Then mark the location or angle of the positive so that the stencil can be adhered in the same position.

Printing Considerations

Special inks designed for halftone reproduction are available from screen printing suppliers. Halftone ink is made from fine-ground pigment and can be purchased in either transparent or opaque versions. As with normal ink preparation, halftone ink should form a dense image on the receiving surface but it should not be so thick that it clogs the screen. If the ink is too thin, the halftone dots may bleed together on the press sheet, resulting in a loss of image detail in the shadow areas.

As mentioned earlier, a double-bevel squeegee blade (figure 15.3c) is recommended for halftone work. A sharp, square blade (figure 15.3a) can also be used, but the amount of pressure should be less than is applied typically for normal production runs.

When screen printing halftones, a vacuum base or off-contact printing will help prevent the press sheet from sticking to the screen and thereby diminish the possibility of a blurred image.

High-Speed Production Presses

The basic problem with any hand-operated, hinged-frame screen printing press is the small number of impressions that can be made per hour. Production is limited by how rapidly the printer can feed the press sheets, close the frame, position the squeegee, pull the impression, remove the squeegee, and deliver the printed sheets. Even the most skilled press operator has difficulty screen printing more than fifty impressions an hour with only a small stencil.

Low print output was no problem with the early, slow-drying inks because most printers could not store an output of several thousand wet prints an hour that required overnight drying. With the introduction of fast-drying inks, however, greater production speeds have become more important. High-speed screen printing presses can be classified as hand-operated, hand-fed, or hand-delivered; semi-automatic; or automatic units.

Lever-Action, Hand-Operated Presses

Figure 15.15 illustrates one type of lever-action screen printing press. The advantage of this press is that one operator can screen print images of nearly any size. The screen frame is counterbalanced over a vacuum frame that holds the press paper. With light pressure the frame swings down into position. The squeegee is attached to a lever that automatically springs up and out of contact with the screen. The operator grasps the lever handle, lowers both the screen and the squeegee, and, with a simple motion, drags the blade across the stencil.

Although this press is still hand operated, the action of lowering the screen, positioning the squeegee, and pulling the impression is shortened significantly. Large images are also

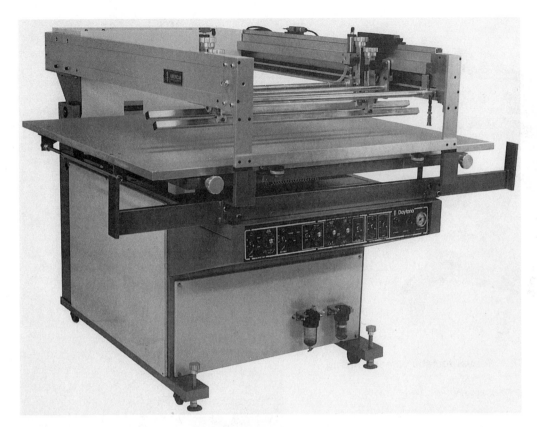

Figure 15.15. Lever-action screen printing unit.
Courtesy of Advance Process Supply Company, Chicago.

easy to handle with this device because the lever action ensures uniform pressure across the stencil.

Semiautomatic Presses

Semiautomatic screen printing presses (figure 15.16) are generally hand fed and delivered by the operator, but the actual image transfer is automatic. The operator first inserts and positions (registers) the press sheet. The machine then lowers the frame, draws the squeegee across the stencil, and raises the frame. Some semiautomatic devices have a 5-second to 30-second built-in time delay for the press sheets to feed. Others have a foot switch to activate

the squeegee that is controlled by the operator. As with lever-action presses, the speed of a semiautomatic press is limited by the speed of the operator.

Fully Automatic Presses

True high-speed screen printing is not achieved until the responsibility for feeding and removing each individual press sheet is taken from the operator and given to the press. The techniques for the automatic screen printing press are the same as for any automatic press, except that the screen printing press uses no rollers or cylinders. The image transfer concerns are the same as for the hand-operated

Figure 15.16.   Semiautomatic screen printing press.
Courtesy of Naz-Dar Company.

Figure 15.17.   Automatic screen printing press. This press is used to produce screen printed electronic circuits.
Courtesy of Electronic Products Division, E.I. Du Pont de Nemours and Company, Inc.

hinged system discussed earlier in this chapter, however.

One area of special importance in an automatic press is the delivery system. Because wet press sheets are removed from the press at a relatively high rate of speed, their handling becomes problematic. Devices are available that can be synchronized with any production press speed to deliver dry press sheets for stacking or packaging.

Special Machine Configurations

As touched upon earlier, screen printing has been applied to a wide variety of nontraditional materials and uses. One example is the production of printed circuits for the electronics industry (figure 15.17). Major machine designs have been developed since World War II to meet the special demands of the screen printing industry and its customers.

Screening Cylindrical Surfaces

One major area of growth has been the printing of labels directly on cylindrical or conical containers such as bottles, cans, and drinking cups.

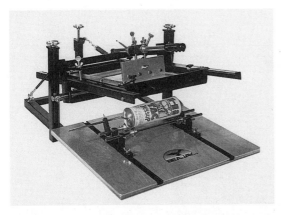

Figure 15.18. Hand-operated cylindrical screen printing press.
Courtesy of Naz-Dar Company.

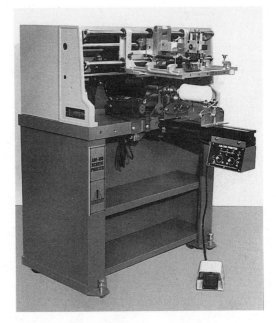

Figure 15.19. Automatic conical-shaped screen printing press.
Courtesy of Advance Process Supply Company, Chicago.

Whether automatic or hand operated (figure 15.18), all of these devices function according to the same basic principle. The familiar flat screen is always used as the stencil carrier. The cylindrical object to be printed is positioned beneath the screen and rests on ball bearings or some other system that allows the object to rotate. A squeegee is then lowered into contact with the screen and the cylindrical object and is locked into position. To transfer the image, the screen frame is moved along a track. The weight of the squeegee (which is stationary) pressing the screen against the cylindrical object rotates the object.

Figure 15.19 shows a fully automatic screen printing press that can feed, print, and deliver six thousand cone-shaped containers per hour. It operates with the same stationary squeegee and moving-screen idea.

Cylindrical Screens

There is a vast consumer market for continuously repeating images on long rolls of materials such as wallpaper or bolt fabrics. A single flat screen stencil was traditionally used to

meet this need. The stencil was prepared carefully so that the printer could step the image down the sheet. This method is still used with specially designed equipment, but it is slow and costly. Figure 15.20 shows a multicolor rotary screen printing press that is designed for this type of continuous web printing. In this press the stencil is carried by rigid screen mesh cylinders. Both the ink and squeegee ride inside the cylinders, which rotate as the line of material passes beneath them. With this approach a continuous multicolor image (up to sixteen colors with this model) can be placed on a roll of paper, plastic, or fabric at a rate of 240 feet a minute.

Carousel Units

A popular method of screening multicolor images on materials such as T-shirts is

Figure 15.20. Multi-color rotary screen printing press.
Courtesy of Naz-Dar Company.

wet-on-wet printing (figure 15.21). With this technique the individual pieces of material are mounted on **carousel carriers** that rotate under each different stencil color sequentially. The wet ink from the first color contacts the bottom of the second stencil, but because it touches in the same place each time, no blurring or loss of image detail occurs.

Registration is generally controlled with a pin system that positions each screen stencil accurately. Because the material is not moved until the entire printing cycle is complete, color fit should be perfect.

Some printers use automatic printing units that can be configured with the carousel design (figure 15.22).

Figure 15.21. Single-unit, multicolor, wet-on-wet screen printing press.
Courtesy of Naz-Dar Company.

Figure 15.22. **Automatic carousel printing system.**
Courtesy of Advance Process Supply Company, Chicago.

Key Terms

printing press	ink viscosity	moiré pattern
squeegee	on-contact printing	wet-on-wet printing
Shore durometer	off-contact printing	carousel carriers
screen mesh count		

Questions for Review

1. Why is the chemical makeup of the squeegee blade important?

2. Why must the solvent for the ink differ from the solvent for the stencil base?

3. What is the difference between on-contact and off-contact screen printing?

4. Briefly describe the techniques that can be used to control accurate color fit when doing multicolor screening.

5. How do most screen printing inks dry?

6. What are the highlight and shadow reproducible dot sizes when screening halftone images?

7. How can a moiré pattern be prevented when mounting a stencil with a halftone image?

8. What is the advantage of a lever-action, hand-operated screen printing press?

9. Briefly describe the operation of a semi-automatic screen press.

10. What is the advantage of a cylindrical screen?

11. What does the term "wet-on-wet printing" mean?

Gravure Printing

Anecdote to Chapter Sixteen

The history of gravure printing begins with the work of creative artists during the Italian Renaissance in the 1300s. Fine engravings and etchings were cut by hand into soft copper. The designs were cut away, leaving a channel, or sunken area, to hold the ink during printing. The term "intaglio", which we use today to describe a class of printing, is an Italian word meaning to print with a sunken pattern or design. Gravure is a type of industrial intaglio printing that is used for extremely long press runs.

Intaglio quickly gained widespread recognition as a rapid, high-quality printing process that could be put to many different uses. The French artist Jacques Callot developed his reputation by sketching the fighting on battlefields and then rushing back to his studio to print etchings of the scenes. He would sell the etchings only a few days after the battle. Callot is sometimes called the first photojournalist because of the speed with which he distributed copies of his sketches.

The first photographic intaglio prints were made by Joseph Nicephore Niépce in about 1814. Niépce, who called his process "heliog-

raphy," printed his products on a copperplate press. Fox Talbot refined Niépce's work and developed the first film negative in addition to working on heliography.

The person who is recognized as the inventor of modern gravure printing, however, is Karl Klif (born Klitsch). Klif began experimenting with photographic copper etching in 1875. By about 1879 he had refined the process and formally announced of his "heliogravure" process to the Vienna Photographic Society. Klif produced very high-quality reproduction for art collectors but gained little recognition outside Vienna because he wanted to keep his techniques secret. Klif eventually sold his "secret," but continued to refine the process until his death in 1926. He made the revolution-ary move from flat printing plates to printing from cylinders. He developed the first doctor blade, or squeegee, and even designed a method of printing color on a web press. Klif originated the term "rotogravure" for printing from a cylinder.

After Klif shared his secrets, others became interested in rotogravure and began

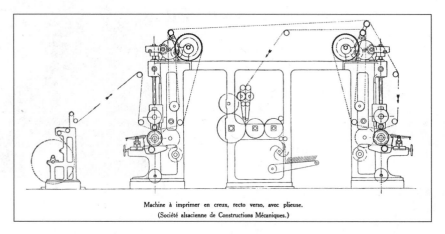

Machine à imprimer en creux, recto verso, avec plieuse.
(Société alsacienne de Constructions Mécaniques.)

An early patent design for a French rotogravure press

designing and building equipment for the process. By the beginning of this century, rotogravure had developed a relatively widespread reputation for fine reproductions. By 1920 huge presses with four or five color units were being used for gravure. Postcards, calendars, book illustrations, and even magazines were being printed in full color.

One of the major uses of gravure that began in the 1920s was the printing of the supplement section of the Sunday newspaper. The section carried human-interest stories, many advertisements, and lots of color photographs. The supplement section was, and continues to be, a favorite item that readers look forward to each week.

The supplement section and rotogravure printing gained such widespread public recognition that Irving Berlin wrote a Broadway play that used the two as a theme. Although Berlin was one of America's most famous songwriters, few remember that 1934 play called *As Thousands Cheer.* However, almost everyone remembers the play's opening song, called "Easter Parade." The most famous lines of the song mention both rotogravure printing and the Sunday supplement because the two terms had come to mean the same in the public's eye:

> *On the Avenue, Fifth Avenue, the photographers will snap us, and you'll find that you're in the rotogravure.*

Objectives for Chapter 16

After completing this chapter, you will be able to:

- Understand the organization of the gravure industry and the importance of professional associations in its growth.
- Recall the major methods of cylinder preparation, including diffusion etch, direct transfer, electromechanical, and laser cutting.

- Recognize the variables in gravure printing, including well formation, film positive quality, etching and plating tech-niques, cylinder balance, cylinder and doctor blade considerations, and impression rollers.
- Recall the major steps in cylinder construction and preparation.

■ Recall the major steps in placing an image on a cylinder by using the conventional gravure techniques.

■ Recognize the parts of a gravure press and recall cylinder, doctor blade, and impression roller functions.

Introduction

Recall from chapter 1 that intaglio is one of the five major printing processes (figure 16.1):

■ Relief forms an image from a raised surface.

■ Screen passes ink through openings in a stencil.

■ Lithography prints photochemically from a flat surface.

■ Electrostatic prints electromagnetically.

■ Intaglio transfers ink from a sunken surface.

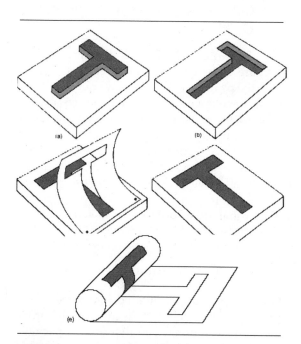

Figure 16.1. Five of the major printing processes. Relief printing (a), intaglio printing (b), screen printing (c), lithographic printing (d), and electrostatic printing (e).

Students new to the printing industry sometimes have difficulty visualizing how it is possible to print from a sunken or negative surface. As you will see in this chapter, preparing industrial intaglio plates is perhaps the most sophisticated and technically demanding of all current methods, yet they are the simplest to print on a high-speed press. The intaglio process also delivers the most significantly consistent, high-quality results.

Terms associated with intaglio include "etching," "engraving," "drypoint," and "collagraphy." Artists use these terms to describe images printed from lines cut into the surface of metal or plastic.

Industrial intaglio is called **gravure** printing, or **rotogravure.** *Roto* means "round." Therefore, rotogravure is printing from a cylinder. All industrial intaglio transfers an image from sunken areas cut into the surface of a cylinder (figure 16.2). Except for small proof presses, most industrial gravure presses are web fed (figure 16.3). As the plate cylinder turns, a continuous roll of paper, foil, or plastic passes through the press to receive the image. After printing, the roll is either rewound for shipment to the customer or cut into sheets at the end of the press by a device called a slitter.

The Gravure Industry

Gravure is a major printing process. Nearly twenty percent of all printing in this country is done by gravure. The gravure industry has

Figure 16.2.   A gravure press cylinder.
"Rotogravure" means printing from a cylinder.

Figure 16.3.   A web-fed gravure press. Almost all production gravure presses are web fed.
Courtesy of the Morrill Press.

enjoyed a steady growth rate and, with recent technical advances, will continue to gain a larger share of the printing market. Several important characteristics make gravure an ideal process for jobs requiring high quality and extremely long press runs:

- Gravure is the simplest of all printing systems, with the fastest press start up and the most direct press controls.
- Gravure's easy press control results in very little paper waste. Gravure has less than half the paper spoilage rate of lithography.
- Gravure press speeds are extremely high. The largest gravure presses can operate as rapidly as forty-five thousand impressions an hour.
- Gravure cylinders are especially hardy. Several million impressions from the same cylinder are common. Some printers report press runs as long as twenty million copies without the cylinder wearing out.
- Gravure gives the highest-quality image of the five major printing processes. It has a reputation for delivering excellent color and ink density, even on low-quality printing papers.

The only significant disadvantage of gravure is the length of time required to prepare the printing cylinder. New equipment has been developed to automate much of the process, but most cylinders are still produced specially by gravure engravers. Jobs with press runs of less than sixty thousand to seventy thousand impressions are generally considered ineffective uses of the gravure process. The cost of cylinder preparation is so much higher than other processes that some companies refuse jobs of less than one million copies.

Industry Organization

Gravure printing is divided into three broad product areas, each with its own special problems and solutions. The first area is **packaging printing.** This includes producing folding cartons, bags, boxes, gift wrappers, labels, and flexible materials that eventually form containers.

The second area is **publication printing.** Publication printing includes producing newspaper supplements, magazines, catalogs, and mass mailing advertisements. As mentioned in the chapter anecdote, gravure is ideally suited for the long press runs required for the Sunday newspaper supplement sections that are distributed on a national basis.

The third area of gravure printing is **specialty printing.** In this area gravure is used to print such materials as wallpaper, vinyl, floor coverings, and even textiles for both decoration and clothing fabrication.

Companies have found that they become more efficient and cost effective by limiting the jobs they accept to a specific product area.

The Gravure Association of America

One reason for the steady growth of gravure printing in the United States has been the cooperative efforts of gravure printers, suppliers, and manufacturers who focus through the **Gravure Association of America (GAA)**. GAA provides consultative assistance, publishes a wide range of technical materials related to all phases of gravure production, has worked to establish industry standards, supplies technical aids, and has a tradition of collegial efforts to educate printers and to disseminate information on gravure printing. Much of the information contained in this chapter was compiled through the courtesy and cooperation of the GAA. Individuals interested in using GAA's services or in becoming affiliated with the organization should write to the Gravure Association of America, 1200A Scottsville Road, Rochester, New York 14624.

Basic Gravure Concepts

Gravure is so radically different in both concept and technique from other printing processes that it is important to first review a number of key ideas. With these concepts in place we can move to descriptions of cylinder preparation and presswork.

Methods of Cylinder Preparation

There are four basic methods of gravure cylinder preparation:

- Diffusion etch
- Direct transfer
- Electromechanical process
- Laser cutting

Diffusion-Etch Process
In the **diffusion-etch process** (figure 16.4), a special mask is prepared by first exposing it through a special gravure screen and then through a film positive of the printing image onto a light-sensitive base. The mask is then applied to a copper gravure cylinder and is developed on the cylinder. After development, the mask is thick in the nonimage areas of the cylinder and very thin where the image will carry ink. The cylinder and mask are then placed in an acid bath. The acid bath penetrates the thin areas of the mask and eats or etches away the copper of the cylinder. The final step of diffusion etch is to remove the mask and apply a thin layer of chrome over the entire cylinder by an electroplating process. (See the Copper Plating and Polishing section of this chapter.) The purpose of the chrome is to extend the life of the surface areas.

Direct-Transfer Process
The second method of cylinder preparation is called **direct transfer.** The main difference between diffusion etch and direct transfer is the way in which the cylinder mask is exposed. In direct transfer, a light-sensitive mask is sprayed or applied over the cylinder surface. The mask is exposed by directing light through a halftone positive as it moves past the cylinder,

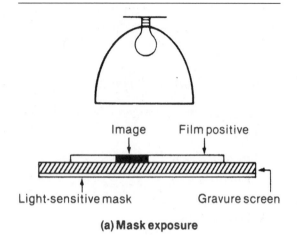

(a) **Mask exposure**

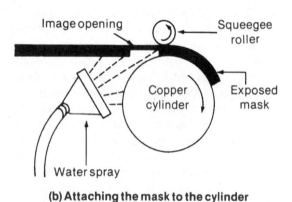

(b) **Attaching the mask to the cylinder**

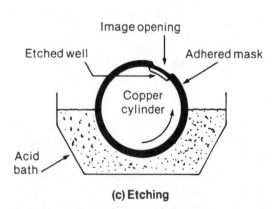

(c) **Etching**

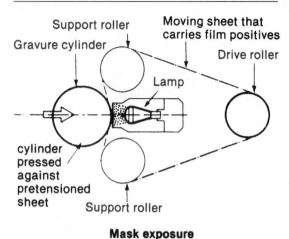

Mask exposure

Figure 16.5.   Cylinder preparation: Direct transfer. In the direct-transfer process, the light-sensitive mask is exposed by passing light through a halftone positive as it moves in contact with the rotating cylinder.
Courtesy of Southern Gravure Service.

which turns at the same rate that the positive moves (figure 16.5). The final steps of developing, etching, and chrome electroplating are the same as in the diffusion-etch technique.

Electromechanical Process
Another way of preparing a gravure cylinder is by the **electromechanical process.** In this process, a clean copper cylinder is mounted in a special engraving machine. Like a scanner used in color separation (see chapter 9), the original copy is read by a beam of light. The digitized information is then stored in a computer and is translated to the motion of a cutter head (figure 16.6). A special diamond stylus

Figure 16.4.   Cylinder preparation: Diffusion etch. The three main steps in the conventional gravure process are mask exposure (a), attaching the mask to the cylinder (b), and etching (c).

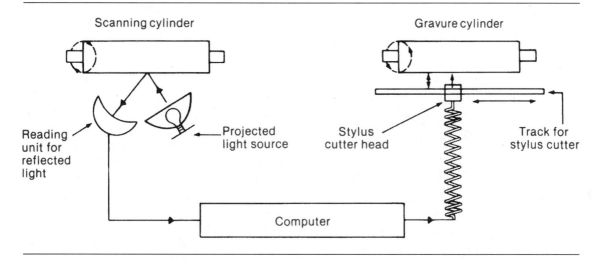

Scanning cylinder   Gravure cylinder

Reading unit for reflected light

Projected light source

Stylus cutter head

Track for stylus cutter

Computer

Figure 16.6.   Diagram of the electromechanical process. The cylinder is etched by using a diamond stylus in the electromechanical process.

cuts into the surface of the copper cylinder as the cylinder rotates. After cutting, the cylinder is chrome electroplated and is finally ready for the press.

Laser-Cutting Process

The fourth technique of gravure cylinder preparation is called **laser cutting.** In this process, a series of small holes, or wells, is etched chemically over the entire surface of a clean copper cylinder. The wells are then filled with a plastic material until the cylinder again has a smooth, uniform surface. Like the electromechanical method, the original copy is scanned by a beam of light. The laser cutting process, however, uses the narrow beam of a laser to blast away or remove parts of the plastic from individual wells rather than a diamond tool to cut away metal. In the final step of laser cutting, the cylinder can then be sprayed with a special electrolyte and electroplated with chrome.

Of the four cylinder preparation processes, diffusion etch is the oldest and still the most widely used in the industry. Recent advances with the laser process, and techniques still in the early research stages, point to changes in the near future that will revolutionize gravure cylinder preparation. Until then, however, the electromechanical technique is rapidly gaining widespread acceptance and use.

Well Formation

As mentioned earlier, gravure transfers ink from the small wells that are etched or cut into the surface of the cylinder (figure 16.7). On the press, the cylinder rotates through a fountain of ink. The ink is wiped from the surface of the cylinder by a doctor blade. The cup-like shape of each well holds ink in place as the cylinder turns past the doctor blade. The formation of perfect wells is the main goal of the gravure engraver. There are several important ideas to understand about gravure wells.

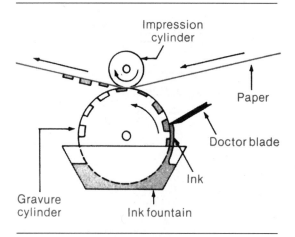

Figure 16.7.   Diagram of the gravure printing process. Etched wells in the printing cylinder pick up ink from the fountain. The excess ink is wiped from the surface of the cylinder by the doctor blade before the ink is applied to the press sheet.

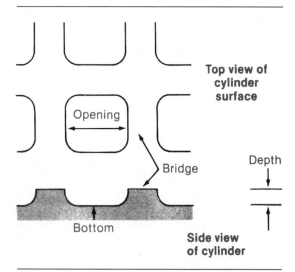

Figure 16.8.   Diagram of gravure cylinder wells. A gravure well has four variables—depth, bottom, opening, and bridge.

Every **gravure well** has four variables (figure 16.8):

- Depth
- Bottom
- Opening
- Bridge

The depth of the well is measured from the bottom of the well to the top surface of the cylinder. The opening is the distance across the well. The **bridge** is the surface of the cylinder between wells. The doctor blade rides against well bridges as it scrapes ink from the cylinder.

Within the diffusion-etch technique are two basic types of well design:

- Conventional gravure
- Lateral hard-dot process

In the **conventional gravure** design, every well on a cylinder has exactly the same opening size (figure 16.9a). The amount of ink to be transferred to the paper is controlled only by the depth of the well. When reproducing photographic material, a continuous-tone film positive, rather than a high-contrast halftone, is used to expose the mask.

The second major type of well design with diffusion etch is called the **lateral hard-dot process** (sometimes called **halftone gravure design**). Two separate film positives are used to expose the mask with the lateral hard-dot process. The first is a continuous-tone film positive, as with conventional gravure. A second exposure is then made with a halftone film positive that falls in the same position on the mask as that of the first exposure. The result is wells that vary in both opening size and depth (figure 16.9b).

The direct-transfer method of cylinder preparation produces yet another well design. A single halftone positive is used to expose the mask in this process. The dot formation in the

Uniform cell opening size
Varying depth of cells

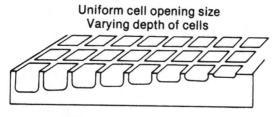

(a) Conventional gravure

Varying cell opening size
Varying depth of cells

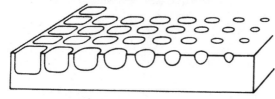

(b) Lateral hard dot

Varying cell opening size
Uniform depth of cells

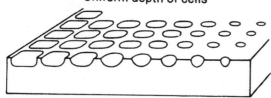

(c) Direct transfer

Figure 16.9. Three examples of gravure wells. (a) Conventional gravure wells vary in depth, but all have the same opening size. (b) Lateral hard-dot wells vary in both depth and opening. (c) Direct-contact wells vary in opening size, but all have the same depth.
Courtesy of the Southern Gravure Service.

halftone defines the opening size of each well (figure 16.9c). The depth of each well is the same, however.

Electromechanical well formation is a bit different from diffusion etch or direct transfer.

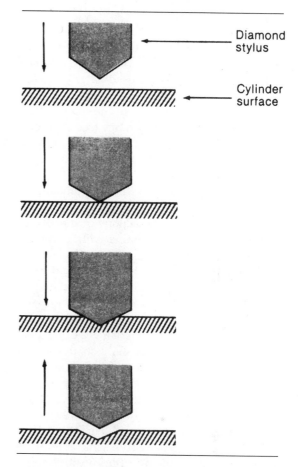

Figure 16.10. Cutting a cylinder surface. In the electromechanical engraving process, wells are cut in the cylinder as a diamond stylus moves into and out of the copper.

In the electromechanical process, each gravure well is created by the action of a diamond stylus as it pushes into the soft copper surface of the cylinder (figure 16.10). A direct relationship exists between the depth of the cut and the well opening size. As the stylus pushes deeper into the cylinder, it increases the opening of the well. This action influences the volume of ink that the well can carry. In photographs, shadow area wells are much deeper than highlight wells.

Film Positives

Most artwork is delivered to the gravure engraver in the form of film positives. The characteristics of film images used by gravure are somewhat different from those used in other printing methods, however. The main difference is the image density range (see chapter 7 for a review of densitometry). Wells are etched or cut in proportion to the density of the corresponding area on the film positive.

There is a minimum well depth that holds ink during the gravure printing process. If the well is too shallow, the actions of the doctor blade and the rapidly spinning cylinder can actually pull ink from the well. Film positives must therefore be prepared with a minimum density so that each well is deep enough to hold ink.

For continuous-tone images, the GAA recommends a density range of 0.30 to 1.65. This means that the highlight areas of the positive should have a transmission density of 0.30 and a shadow reading of 1.65. The difference between the two measurements produces a BDR of 1.35, which is acceptable to commercial photographers yet still exceeds the range of most halftone negatives used in lithography.

Line images, such as type, ink, or line borders, are also supplied in film positive form. Line image density should be near the 1.65 shadow area density of continuous-tone images. Film positives are often supplied to the engraver with both continuous-tone and line images on the same piece of film. The most common approach is to first prepare each type of image separately in negative form, and then to make several contact exposures on a new sheet of film to create one film positive.

Cylinder Construction and Preparation

The quality of the final gravure image depends first on the construction of the cylinder. Almost all cylinder cores are made from steel tubing. Some packaging printers prefer extruded, or shaped, aluminum cores because they are much lighter, less expensive, and easier to ship than steel. A few companies use solid copper cylinders, but steel remains the most popular core material.

A steel cylinder is used when printing with adhesives or other corrosive materials. In most gravure printing, however, a thin coating of copper is plated over the steel core of the cylinder to carry the image. Copper is easier to etch than steel and can be replaced easily when the job is finished.

Cylinder Design

There are five important parts to identify on a gravure cylinder (figure 16.11):

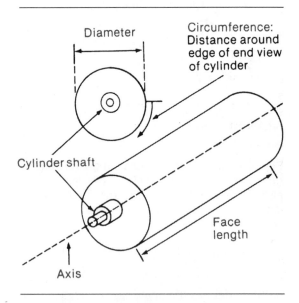

Figure 16.11. Parts of a gravure cylinder. The most commonly identified parts of a gravure cylinder are axis, shaft, diameter, circumference, and face length.

- Axis
- Shaft
- Diameter
- Circumference
- Face length

The axis is the invisible line that passes through the center of the length of the cylinder. The cylinder shaft is the bearing surface as the cylinder rotates in the press. If you look at the end view of a cylinder, the shaft appears as a circle. The diameter is the distance across the circle, through the center of the shaft. The circumference is the distance around the edge of the end view. The face length is the distance from one end of the cylinder to the other, along the length of the cylinder.

The face length of the cylinder limits the width of paper to be printed. The circumference limits the size of the image. One rotation of the cylinder around its circumference is called one **impression.** Continuous images can be etched on a cylinder without a seam so the design is repeated without a break. Wallpaper designs are commonly printed by gravure.

Gravure cylinders are built using many different sizes. The face length is always the same for each press to match the press sheet size but varies in diameter and circumference to closely match the cut-off size of the specific job. There are two basic cylinder designs (figure 16.12):

- Mandrel
- Integral shaft

A mandrel cylinder (sometimes called a sleeve or cone cylinder) is designed with a removable shaft. Most holes are tapered so that the shaft can be pressed into place and then removed easily.

In the integral shaft design, the shaft is mounted permanently on the cylinder. The cylinder is formed first, and then the shaft is ei-

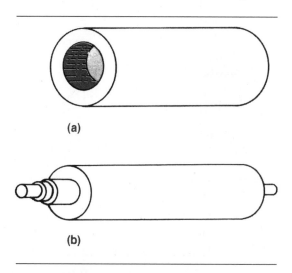

(a)

(b)

Figure 16.12. **Two forms of gravure cylinders.** There are two basic forms of cylinder construction—mandrel (a) and integral shaft (b).

ther pressed or shrunk into place. The shaft is attached permanently by welding and remains in place for the life of the cylinder.

Integral shaft cylinders are more expensive than mandrel cylinders but are generally considered to produce higher-quality images. This is because they produce greater support across the length of the cylinder during press runs than hollow mandrel cylinders.

Balancing the Cylinder

When a cylinder (or any round object) rotates at extremely high speeds, vibration can be a problem. That is why automobile tires must be carefully balanced before use to prevent undue wear or poor steering control. A major concern with gravure printing is vibration caused by an unbalanced cylinder (figure 16.13a). A great deal of vibration can bounce the cylinder against the doctor blade and result in a poor image. Vibration can also damage the press. There are two types of cylinder imbalance: static and dynamic.

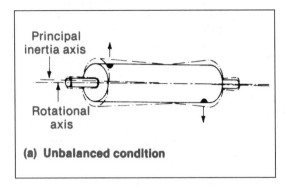

(a) Unbalanced condition

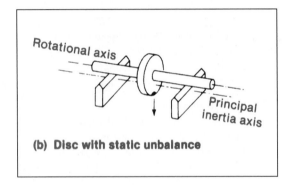

(b) Disc with static unbalance

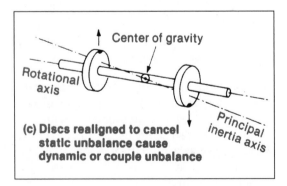

(c) Discs realigned to cancel static unbalance cause dynamic or couple unbalance

Figure 16.13. Examples of cylinder imbalance.
Courtesy of Gravure Association of America.

Static imbalance occurs when the cylinder is not perfectly round or has different densities within a cross section (figure 16.13b). Static imbalance can result from such defects as air holes, impurities in the steel core, or improper copper plating and polishing (see following section).

Dynamic imbalance occurs when the cylinder differs in density or balance from one end to the other (figure 16.13c). Dynamic imbalance is the greatest cause of cylinder vibration at high press speeds. Both static and dynamic imbalance can be corrected by either reducing or adding weight to each end of the cylinder.

Copper Plating and Polishing

Electroplating is the process of transferring and bonding very small bits (called **ions**) of one type of metal to another type of metal. This process takes place in a special liquid **plating bath.** The ions are transferred as an electrical current passes through the bath. The longer the current flows, the more new metal that is plated to the cylinder.

The first step in the gravure electroplating process is to clean the surface of the cylinder thoroughly. The cylinder is cleaned by brushing or rubbing it with special cleaning compounds and then rinsing it with a powerful stream of hot water (figure 16.14). Some plants use special cleaning machines for this purpose. The goal is to remove all spots of grease, rust, or dirt so that a perfect coating of copper can be applied over the entire cylinder surface. Cylinder areas that will not be plated, such as the ends, can be coated with asphaltum or other staging materials, which covers and protects its clean surface.

To electroplate a cylinder, the cylinder is suspended in a curved tank and rotated through the plating bath (figure 16.15). The electrical current is allowed to flow from the copper anode (the plating metal) through the inch (0.030 inch) is the common thickness range for the copper layer on a gravure cylinder.

A **newage gauge** is a device used to test the hardness of copper. Copper hardness is measured by pushing a diamond point into the copper surface. The diagonal length of the opening created by the diamond point is measured and then compared with the amount of force required to push the diamond into the copper. The result is expressed in diamond point hardness (D.P.H.). Most printers look for a D.P.H. between 93 and 122.

The last step in constructing a gravure cylinder is to bring the diameter (and circumference) of the cylinder to the desired size and at the same time create a perfect printing surface. The cylinder must not only be round and balanced perfectly, it must also be perfectly smooth and uniform across its length. If the cylinder is not uniform, the doctor blade will not be able to remove excess ink from the nonprinting surface (figure 16.16).

The newly plated cylinder is mounted in a lathe and prepared for final turning. Some plants use a diamond cutting tool to bring the cylinder into rough dimensions; they then use separate grinding stones to polish the cylinder's surface (figure 16.17). Other plants use specially designed precision machines that both cut and polish the cylinder at the same

Figure 16.14. Cleaning the cylinder surface. It is important to remove all spots of grease, rust, or dirt so that a perfect layer of copper can be applied to the cylinder surface.

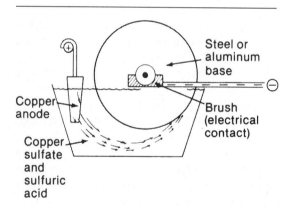

Figure 16.15. Diagram of the electroplating process. An electrical current passes from the copper anode through the plating solution to the steel or aluminum cylinder until the desired thickness of copper is plated on the cylinder.
Courtesy of Southern Gravure Service.

bath to the cylinder (base metal). Zinc sulfate, copper sulfate, or cyanide solutions are common plating-bath liquids. Six-thousandths of an inch (0.006 inch) to thirty-thousandths of an

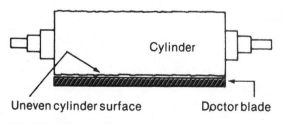

Figure 16.16. Diagram of a doctor blade against an uneven cylinder. If the cylinder is not uniform, the doctor blade will not be able to remove excess ink from the nonprinting surfaces.

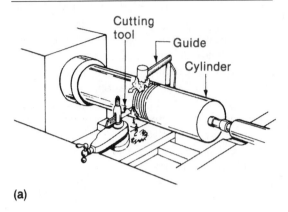

(a)

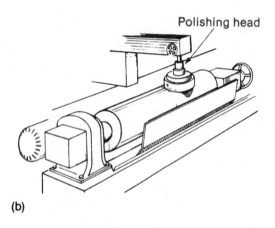

(b)

Figure 16.17.   Final turning of a plated cylinder. (a) The cylinder is first cut to rough dimensions. (b) Then it is ground or polished to final size. Courtesy of Southern Gravure Service.

time. With these machines, cylinders can be cut within one ten-thousandth of an inch (0.0001 inch) of the desired size and surface. After the final turning, the cylinder is ready for image etching.

Reusing Cylinders

Gravure cylinders can be reused many times. One way to reuse a cylinder is to cut away the old image on a lathe. This involves removing only two-thousandths to three-thousandths of an inch of cylinder surface. The cylinder is then replated with copper and recut or reground to its original diameter.

Another way to reuse a cylinder is to simply dissolve the cylinder's chrome coating (added as the final step in cylinder preparation to protect the soft copper on the press) and to then plate over the old image with new copper. The replating process fills the image areas above the original cylinder surface. Excess copper is then cut or ground away, and the cylinder is returned to the desired diameter size.

Ballard Shell Cylinders

The **ballard shell process** is a special technique used by some publication printers that allows easy removal of a copper layer after the cylinder has been printed. The cylinder is prepared in the usual manner, including copper plating, except that it is cut twelve-thousandths to fifteen-thousandths of an inch undersize in diameter. The undersized cylinder is coated with a special nickel separator solution and is returned to the copper plating bath. A second layer of copper is then plated onto the cylinder over the first layer. The cylinder is then cut or ground to the desired size, given an image etch, and printed.

The difference between most gravure cylinders and ballard shell cylinders is seen when the cylinder has been printed and is ready to receive another image. The second copper layer can be simply ripped off the ballard shell cylinder base. A knife is used to cut through the copper to the nickel separator layer, which allows the shell to be lifted away. The cylinder can then be cleaned, a new nickel separator solution can be applied, and another shell can be plated to receive the image.

Conventional Gravure

There are several different ways to prepare a gravure cylinder. Four techniques were described briefly at the beginning of this chapter (diffusion etch, direct transfer, electromechanical, and laser cutting). A detailed explanation of the steps for each method is beyond the scope of this chapter. It is valuable, however, to examine one technique—diffusion etch—as an example of methods used in the gravure industry.

While diffusion etch is not the most widely used process, it does allow easy understanding of all etching processes. Diffusion etch is still used in the industry, and the steps involved in its cylinder preparation are somewhat similar to those used in direct transfer. The following sections detail the procedures of diffusion etching a cylinder using conventional gravure with carbon tissue.

Cylinder Layout and Film Assembly

Most jobs arrive at the gravure printer in film format with a dummy showing final page position (see chapter 3 for a review of signature layout and use of a dummy). The first step in gravure printing is to lay out the cylinder and identify page or image positions.

Figure 16.18 shows the layout for the first of two cylinders that will be used to print a 2-color, 16-page advertisement. The face length of the cylinder is one dimension of the layout; the circumference of the cylinder is the other. The pages are identified by Roman numerals along the face length and by letters of the alphabet around the circumference. For example, position III-C is page 6 of the job. Page positions are determined by how the job will be folded and are always outlined in the job specifications. Remember that for this job a second cylinder will be used to print the other side of the paper. The web will then be cut and folded to form two separate rolls. The layout

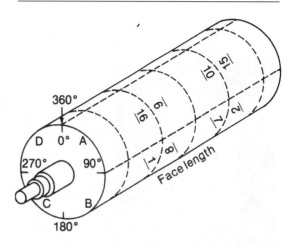

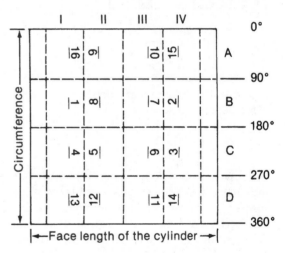

Figure 16.18. A 16-page cylinder layout

will be used as a guide for assembling the different pieces of film.

If the job arrives as film negatives, then the printer must prepare contact positives. To make film positives that fall into the correct positions on the cylinder, special carriers or cabs (cabriolets) are used. **Cabs** are special film masks that are punched and marked so they can be used as guides for the images (figure 16.19).

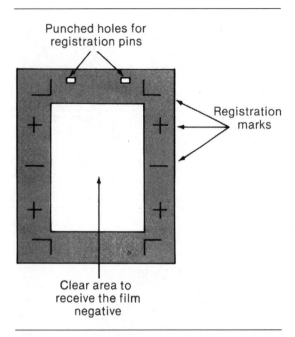

Punched holes for
registration pins

Registration
marks

Clear area to
receive the film
negative

Figure 16.19.   Diagram of a cab. A cab is used
to register the film negative.

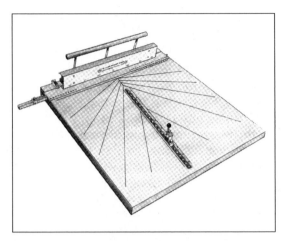

Figure 16.20.   A Berkey stripper punch. A two-
hole or three-hole punch is used to punch both the
cab and the unexposed film.

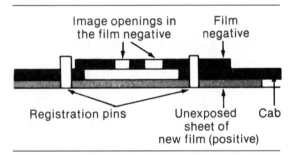

Image openings in   Film
the film negative   negative

Registration pins   Unexposed   Cab
sheet of
new film (positive)

**Figure 16.21.   Using a cab to make a film
positive.** The cab holds the film negative on
registration pins while the negative is contact
printed to a new sheet of unexposed film.

Each cab carries special registration
marks and has a clear, open area to receive the
film negative image. The negatives are first
stripped to the cab's registration marks and
are then contact printed to a new sheet of film.
The unexposed film is punched on the same
device used to punch the cab (figure 16.20).
When contact printing is done, both the cab
and the film are dropped onto registration
pins (figure 16.21). The processed film positive
then falls into place on register pins mounted
on a master plate.

The **master plate** is a frame with register
pins that hold the film positives in correct
printing position during exposure to the cylinder masking material. For color printing, each
set of separations is exposed to the cylinder
mask with the same master plate to ensure perfect color fit.

When the film positives are completed
and are positioned on the master plate, several additional positives are added before
exposure to the cylinder masking material.
Registration on many gravure presses is mon-
itored by special electronic eyes that sense
misfit and make press adjustments automatically. **Electronic-eye mark** film positives are
added to the master plate so that the marks

are etched into the cylinder out of the image area on the paper web.

Some jobs require blank pages. Where blank pages are required, pieces of burner film are added to the master plate. **Burner film** is transparent film that allows full passage of light to the cylinder mask. The light hardens the light-sensitive mask and prevents acid from reaching the copper cylinder. If acid does not reach the surface, the area is not etched and will not carry ink to the paper.

When all positives are positioned on the master plate, the job is ready for carbon printing.

Carbon Printing

Carbon printing is the process of transferring the positive image to the cylinder mask. The point of carbon printing is to create a resist that can be adhered to the cylinder. A **resist** is material that blocks or retards the action of the acid on the copper. There are two basic types of resist for diffusion etch: carbon tissue and rotofilm.

Carbon Tissue

Carbon tissue is a gelatin-based emulsion coated on a paper backing. This emulsion can be sensitized so that it "hardens" in proportion to the amount of light that strikes it. Carbon tissue must be made light sensitive by the engraver, however. Carbon tissue is sensitized when immersed in a 3-percent to 4-percent potassium bichromate solution. The tissue is placed in the solution, emulsion side up, for 3½ to 4 minutes. It is then squeegeed onto a plexiglass sheet to dry. The squeegeed tissue is dried under cool, circulating air for several hours before it is placed in storage for 8 to 10 hours to "cure," or set.

The sensitized carbon tissue is next placed emulsion side up on a vacuum frame for exposure. In conventional gravure, the carbon tissue receives two separate exposures. The first is a screen exposure, and the second is the image exposure.

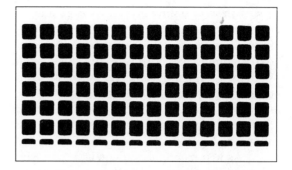

Figure 16.22. **A cross-line gravure screen.** A cross-line gravure screen is used to create the well openings in conventional gravure.

Recall that with conventional gravure the well openings on the cylinder are all the same size, and the wells vary only in depth (figure 16.9). A special cross-line gravure screen is used to create the outline of each well in conventional gravure (figure 16.22). A sharp screen pattern forms on the carbon tissue when an intense light is allowed to harden the outline of the well bridges (figure 16.23).

For most gravure work, printers use a 150-line screen (150 wells per inch). Gravure printers are also concerned with the ratio of opening to bridge dimensions. A ratio of 2½ to 1 (2½:1) or 3 to 1 (3:1) is common. This means that for each unit of well thickness there is 2½ or 3 units of opening.

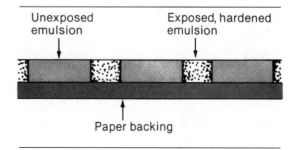

Figure 16.23. **Side view of carbon tissue after exposure to a cross-line screen**

Carbon printing is done by exposing the master plate (with the film positives in place) to the carbon tissue. Registration to the cylinder is commonly controlled by a lug system. Both the carbon tissue and the master plate are dropped over special lugs or pins on the vacuum frame. The punched carbon tissue can then be mounted on the cylinder with a corresponding lug system.

As just mentioned, the gelatin emulsion of the carbon tissue hardens in direct proportion to the amount of light that reaches it. The emulsion hardens first at the top of the gelatin layer. As light continues to reach the carbon tissue, the emulsion hardens down toward the paper backing of the tissue.

With line work, little light reaches the carbon tissue. As a result, the emulsion hardens only at the top gelatin layer. The varying densities of a continuous-tone photograph affect the emulsion differently. Highlight areas pass a great deal of light, so the hardened emulsion is very thick in those areas. Shadow areas pass little light, so the hardened emulsion is thin in those areas (figure 16.24). A highlight area on the positive with a density of 0.35 passes 50 percent of the light that strikes the film; the remaining 50 percent is absorbed by the image density. In the middle tones, an area with a density of 1.0 passes 10 percent of the light. At a density of 1.65 (a shadow area), only 2½ percent of the light reaches the carbon tissue.

Rotofilm

The second type of resist is called rotofilm and is manufactured by the DuPont corporation. Rotofilm has the same characteristics as carbon tissue but comes to the engraver presensitized and ready for use.

Tissue Laydown

The process of attaching the carbon tissue to the copper cylinder is called **tissue laydown.** The tissue can be laid down as a single piece of the same size as the cylinder. More commonly, however, tissue is applied to the cylinder in several separate pieces.

Before laydown the cylinder must be cleaned. Any traces of tarnish or grease prevent tissue adhesion. Most companies use a special laydown machine for this purpose (figure 16.25). The clean cylinder is placed in the machine and is positioned by a special control gauge. A fixed metal lug bar holds the carbon tissue in register with the cylinder. The emulsion side of the carbon tissue is against the cylinder (figure 16.25a). A layer of distilled water is then poured on the cylinder, and a rubber squeegee roller is brought into contact with the carbon tissue, against the cylinder (figure 16.25b). Next, the carbon tissue is cut from the lug bar, and distilled water is poured between the tissue and the cylinder as the rubber squeegee roller turns. The carbon tissue adheres to the cylinder after one rotation. If several pieces of tissue are to be applied to the cylinder, this operation is repeated for each piece. After all pieces of tissue are mounted, the paper backing of the tissue is soaked with cold water and then gently squeegeed by hand. The backing is then allowed to dry thoroughly (usually from 5 to 10 minutes with fan driers). This method is called **dry laydown.**

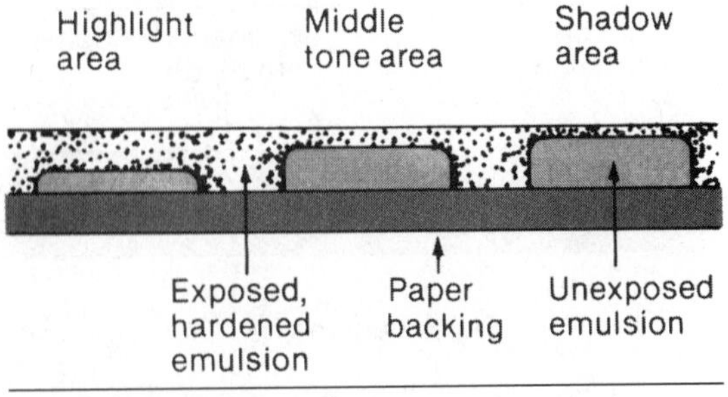

Figure 16.24.   Side view of carbon tissue after exposure to a continuous-tone film positive

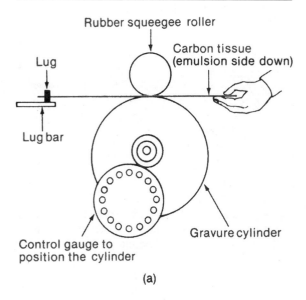

(a)

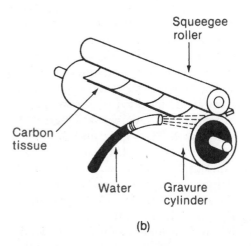

(b)

Figure 16.25. **Mounting the carbon tissue on the gravure cylinder.** A special laydown machine is used to mount the carbon tissue on the gravure cylinder.

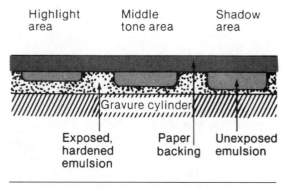

Figure 16.26. **Side view of carbon tissue attached to a gravure cylinder showing unexposed emulsion to be removed**

Development

When the paper backing of the carbon tissue is completely dry, development can begin. The first step in development is to swab the tissue with an alcohol solution. This solution rapidly soaks through the paper backing and begins to loosen it from the gelatin emulsion. The cylinder is then partially submerged in a water bath and slowly rotated so that all parts of the cylinder surface are kept uniformly wet. The water temperature gradually rises, so the paper backing loosens from the cylinder and can be pulled away.

The goal in development is to remove all portions of the unhardened gelatin emulsion (figure 16.26). Some engravers gently spray the cylinder as it turns in a warm-water bath. Others use an automatic system that changes the water in the bath using a low-pressure water spray located in the bottom of the tray.

Development is complete when no more gelatin can be removed and the surface is hard to the touch. The emulsion is fixed by first cooling the cylinder below room temperature and then pouring an alcohol solution over the surface. A soft rubber squeegee is then used to remove all alcohol from the cylinder, and the emulsion is finally allowed to dry.

Staging

Some areas of the cylinder often are not covered after laydown and development. The edges and ends of the cylinder must be protected from the action of the acid. Other areas must be also protected. When two or more pieces of tissue are applied to the cylinder, the area where the pieces meet often shows bare metal. If acid reaches the metal at this union, a line will be etched and will appear as an image on the press.

The process of covering bare metal or thin areas on the tissue is called **staging.** The most common staging material is asphaltum. **Asphaltum** is a tar-like, acid-resistant material. Using asphaltum, the engraver paints the unprotected areas of the cylinder by hand with a small brush or pen. After etching, the asphaltum can be dissolved with turpentine.

Etching

In etching, an acid bath penetrates through the resist to the copper (figure 16.27). When the acid reaches the surface of the cylinder, it dissolves a portion of the copper metal. The highlight areas of the resist are thick and therefore allow little acid to reach the cylinder. Correspondingly, highlight wells are shallow. The shadow areas of the resist are thin, however, and allow a great deal of acid to penetrate to the copper. As a result, shadow wells are deep.

Etching a cylinder is as much an art as it is a technical process. Conventional gravure typically involves five or six separate etching solutions, each of different acid strength. The acid used in the etching bath is perchloride of iron. The etching bath acid arrives at the engraver in large containers, usually at 48°

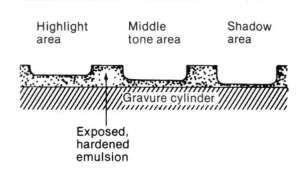

Figure 16.27.   Side view of carbon tissue attached to a gravure cylinder showing emulsion that the acid bath must penetrate

Baumé (pronounced "48 degrees bomb-a"). Recall that Baumé is a system of measuring the density (or specific gravity) of a liquid. Acid concentration, or strength, falls as the degrees of Baumé fall. A 48-degree solution, is much stronger than a 38-degree solution for example. For conventional gravure, separate etching solutions of 46 degree, 44 degree, 42 degree, 40 degree, 39 degree, and 37 degree Baumé are used commonly. The action of each bath penetrates the gelatin emulsion with a different degree of effectiveness. Figure 16.28 shows the action of the acid as it penetrates gradually through the carbon tissue to cut highlight, middle tones, and shadow wells. Some efforts have been made to automate this process, but successful cylinder etching still requires the practiced eye of a skilled engraver.

The last step in the etching process is to remove the carbon tissue and staging material. The cylinder is rotated through a hot acetic acid and saltwater bath. The action of the hot bath dissolves all traces of the carbon tissue layer. As mentioned before, the staging is dissolved with turpentine.

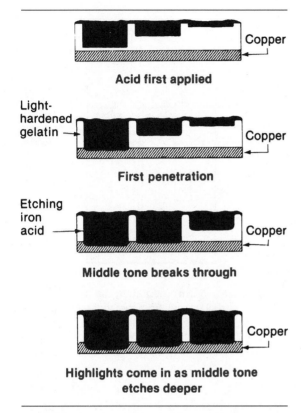

Figure 16.28. Stages of acid etch of a cylinder. The several different etching solutions penetrate through the gelatin emulsion gradually to form the wells.
Courtesy of Southern Gravure Service.

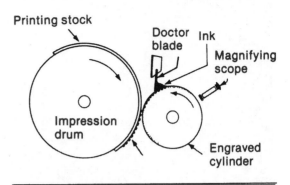

Figure 16.29. Diagram of a proof press. Special proof presses are used to duplicate the quality of the production press.
Courtesy of Southern Gravure Service.

Cylinder Proofing, Correction, and Chrome Plating

The final steps in gravure cylinder preparation with conventional gravure involve proofing, correction, and chrome plating.

Proofing
In the proofing step the cylinder is mounted in a special proof press that duplicates the quality of the production press (figure 16.29). Ink is applied to the press, and several proofs are pulled from the cylinder. Color proofs are always judged under special viewing lights—usually 5,000°K (see chapter 9 for a discussion of color viewing).

Correction
Several methods are used to correct defects in the cylinder or to improve image quality to meet the customer's approval. It is possible to hand tool on a cylinder using a special cutting tool. A skilled engraver can reduce contrast by using an abrasive to rub away well walls. It is also possible to burnish or cut new wells into the cylinder with tools called a graver and a roulette wheel.

Sometimes it is necessary to fill in etched wells with new copper and then re-etch an image. This is accomplished by spot plating. A **spot plater** is a machine that passes an electric current to the cylinder through a handheld electrode which is covered with cotton or gauze and then soaked in a plating solution. As the electrode is held against the cylinder, a small area of copper builds on the cylinder surface. Spot plating can be used only to correct small areas. Large area errors require an entire remake.

Figure 16.30.   Rollup of a gravure cylinder

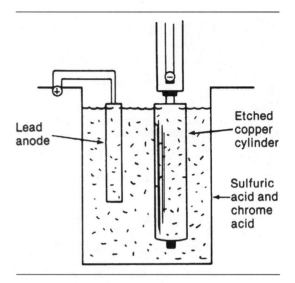

Figure 16.31.   Chromeplating the cylinder. An electric current passes from the anode through the chrome plating solution to the cylinder.
Courtesy of Southern Gravure Service.

Sometimes, however, the entire cylinder must be re-etched to increase overall well depth. A technique called **rollup** is used to cover the nonimage areas of the cylinder. A special brayer or inking roller is carefully rolled over the surface of the cylinder to apply a layer of rollup ink (figure 16.30). After rollup, the cylinder can be returned to the etching room or the engraver can apply an etch to select areas by using cotton soaked in acid.

Chrome Plating

After the press sheets have been approved by the customer, the cylinder is ready for chrome plating. Several different machines are used for chrome plating. All are designed to place a thin layer of chrome over the surface of the cylinder. Cylinders are chromed to extend run length.

In chrome plating the cylinder is first cleaned to remove all traces of ink or grease from the proofing operation. The edges of the cylinder are staged, or a special cover is applied to protect the cylinder shaft and face edge. The cylinder is then suspended in a solution of chrome and sulfuric acid (figure 16.31). Lead is commonly used as the anode. Electric current passes from the anode through the plating bath

and to the cylinder. By controlling both time and amperage, a layer of chrome can be deposited over the copper surface. Most chrome layers are between 0.0002 inch and 0.0007 inch thick. The desired thickness is determined by the type of screen and the depth of the well etch.

After all traces of the plating bath are washed away and the cylinder is dry, the cylinder is ready to be sent to the press room.

Gravure Press Work

Almost all gravure printing is done on web-fed presses (figure 16.3). Paper or some other material (called a substrate) feeds from large rolls to the printing unit through an intricate system of tension and registration controls (figure 16.32). The paper then passes between the image cylinder and an impression cylinder. Some companies use offset gravure, but most transfer the image directly from the cylinder. After

Figure 16.32. A printing unit of a web-fed press.
Courtesy of the Morrill Press.

Figure 16.34. Folding unit of a web press. Some jobs are cut into sheets and folded in line on the press.

the paper leaves the printing unit, it might pass through a set of driers to set the ink, or it might follow an intricate set of rollers to dry by aerial oxidation and absorption. When the paper enters the delivery unit of the press, it might be slit (figure 16.33), cut into sheets and folded (figure 16.34), or rewound onto a roll for shipment to the customer (figure 16.35).

Many of the common concerns in gravure web-press operation have been dis-cussed in previous chapters. Chapter 12 dealt with press design and operation, which apply to the basic procedures for any printing method, including gravure. Chapter 18 deals with ink and paper and discusses the special characteristics of gravure ink. Some concerns, however, are unique to gravure press operation. The two main concerns of cylinder and doctor blade adjustment and impression rollers are examined here to complement the information presented in other chapters.

Figure 16.33. Slitting the printed paper. Some jobs require that the web be slit into smaller rolls at the delivery end of the press.
Courtesy of the Morrill Press.

Figure 16.35. Rewinding printed paper. Some jobs are rewound onto a roll after printing.
Courtesy of the Morrill Press.

Cylinder and Doctor Blade Considerations

As has already discussed, the function of the doctor blade is to wipe ink from the surface of the plate cylinder, leaving ink in only the recessed wells. A great deal of research has been done on materials, angles, and designs for doctor blades.

Several different materials are used for blades. The goal is to minimize blade wear and reduce heat generated by the rubbing of the blade against the turning cylinder. Plastic, stainless steel, bronze, and several other metals have been used with success. The most common blade material, however, is Swedish blue spring steel. Blades are usually between 0.006 inch and 0.007 inch thick. The blades must be relatively thin to reduce wear on the cylinder, but strong enough to wipe away ink.

Blade angle is another important consideration. The angle between the blade and the cylinder is called the **counter** (figure 16.36). There is much debate about the proper counter for the best image quality. The "best" counter depends on the method used to prepare the cylinder. For example, with electromechanically engraved cylinders, image quality decreases as the counter increases. Most angles are set initially between 18 degrees and 20 degrees. After the blade is placed against the cylinder and production begins, however, the counter generally increases to around 45 degrees.

One way to set the blade angle is by using the reverse doctor principle. With this approach the doctor blade is set at a large enough angle to push the ink from the surface (figure 16.37).

Several different doctor blade designs are used by gravure printers (figure 16.38). The most popular are conventional and MDC/Ringier. Care must be taken to keep the conventional design sharp and uniform. Most

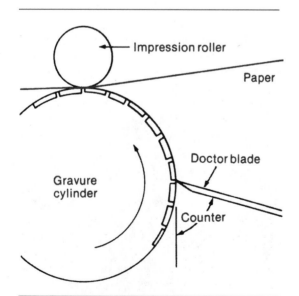

Figure 16.36.   Diagram showing the counter. The counter is the angle between the doctor blade and the cylinder surface.

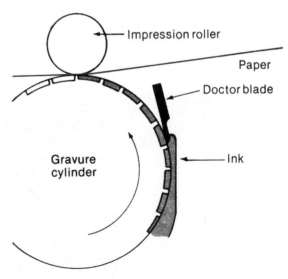

Figure 16.37.   Diagram showing a reverse doctor blade. A reverse doctor blade pushes ink from the cylinder surface.

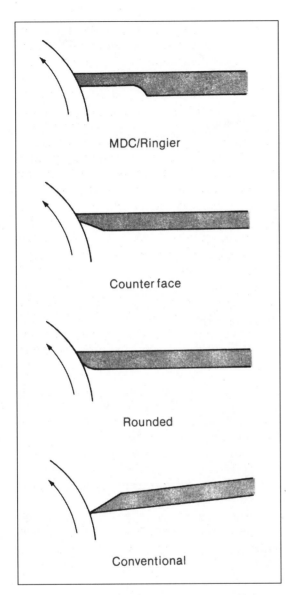

Figure 16.38.   Examples of different doctor blade designs

printers hone the blade by hand with a special stone and then polish it with a rouge or emery paper to get a flawless edge while the MDC/Ringier design tends to self-sharpen. The MDC/Ringier design has a longer working life

than the conventional form design and requires much less press downtime for blade cleaning and repair.

The action of the doctor blade against the cylinder is of special concern. The blade rides against the cylinder with pressure. Pressure is necessary so that the ink does not creep under the blade as the cylinder turns. The most common method of holding the blade against the surface is by air pressure. The blade fits into a holder, which is mounted in turn in a special pneumatic mechanism. Most printers use a pressure of 1¼ pounds per inch across the cylinder length.

Most doctor blades are not stationary, however. As the cylinder rotates, the blade oscillates, or moves back and forth, parallel to the cylinder. This oscillating action works to remove pieces of lint or dirt that might otherwise be trapped between the cylinder and the blade. Dirt can nick the blade. Nicks allow a narrow bead of ink to pass to the cylinder surface. Nicks are major defects that can ruin the image or scratch the surface of the cylinder.

A **prewipe blade** is commonly used on high-speed presses to skim excess ink from the cylinder (figure 16.39). This device prevents a large quantity of ink from reaching the doctor blade and ensures that the thin metal blade wipes the cylinder surface perfectly clean.

Impression Rollers

Use of an impression roller is the second main difference between gravure presses and other web-fed machines. The purpose of the impression roller is to push the paper against the gravure cylinder to transfer ink from the image wells (figure 16.7). The major considerations for impression rollers are coating and hardness, pressure, and electrostatic assist.

Coating and Hardness
Most impression rollers are formed from a steel core coated with rubber or a synthetic

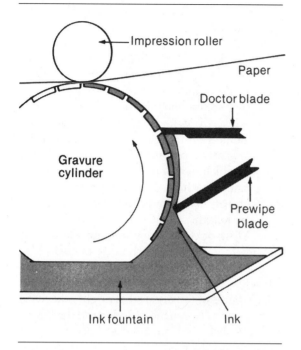

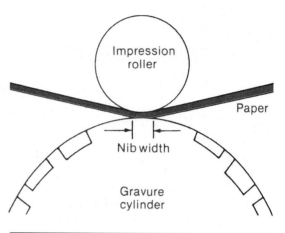

Figure 16.40. Diagram showing the nib width. The nib width is the area of the cylinder where the paper contacts the cylinder by the pressure of the impression roller.

Figure 16.39. Diagram of a gravure cylinder showing prewipe and doctor blades. Most presses use prewipe blades to skim most of the ink from the cylinder before the cylinder reaches the doctor blade.

material, such as DuPont's Neoprene. Rubber hardness is measured by a Shore durometer (discussed in chapter 15). Values are given in "Shore A" readings. Hardness increases as Shore A numbers get larger. Different types of paper or substrates require different degrees of hardness for the impression roller. Material such as cellophane might require 60 Shore A, but Kraft paper or chipboard might need 90 Shore A.

Pressure

As discussed earlier, ink transfers to the web by pressure of the impression roller. Pressure might vary from 50 pounds per linear inch (p.l.i.) to 200 p.l.i. More pressure does not always give better image quality, however. The amount of pressure the operator sets is determined by previous tests for the kind of paper being printed. Whatever setting is selected, it is critical that uniform pressure is applied over the entire length of the cylinder.

The area of contact between the impression roller and the cylinder is called the **nib width,** or flat (figure 16.40). The amount of nib width is determined by the hardness of the impression roller and the amount of pressure. The nib width is important because it is the area of image transfer to the paper or plastic web. The nib width is adjusted to give the best-quality image on the web stock.

Electrostatic Assist

A great advantage of the gravure process is that it allows high-quality images to be

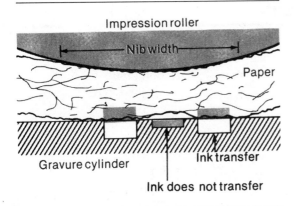

Figure 16.41. Diagram showing inking on defective paper. If defects in the paper prevent contact with the gravure cylinder, ink will not transfer.

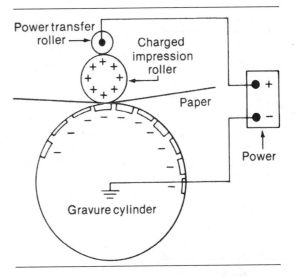

Figure 16.42. Diagram of electrostatic assist printing. Electrostatic assist printing charges the impression roller and the gravure cylinder so that the ink lifts electrostatically from the cylinder to the paper.

printed on low-grade papers. Problems do occur when the paper surface is coarse and imperfect, however. Ink transfers by direct contact. If a defect in the paper prevents that contact, then no image will transfer (figure 16.41). The Gravure Research Association (now part of the Gravure Association of America) designed and licensed a special device, called an **electrostatic assist,** to solve this problem and improve image transfer. With electrostatic assist printing, a power source is connected between the cylinder and the impression roller (figure 16.42). A conductive covering must be added to the impression roller, but the cover causes no special problems. An electric charge is created behind the web, which forms an electrostatic field

at the nib width. The charge pulls the ink around the edges of each well, which causes the ink to rise and transfer to the paper. Most presses are now equipped with electrostatic assist devices.

Gravure printing presses are sophisticated devices that have a wide range of controls to ensure high image quality. New presses are used that reach speeds as high as 3,000 feet per minute. This high speed, linked with outstanding image quality, makes gravure printing one of the major printing processes in this country.

Key Terms

gravure
rotogravure
packaging printing
publication printing
specialty printing
Gravure Association of
    America (GAA)
diffusion-etch process
direct transfer
electromechanical process
laser cutting
gravure well
bridge
conventional gravure

lateral hard-dot process
halftone gravure design
impression
static imbalance
dynamic imbalance
electroplating
ion
plating bath
newage gauge
ballard shell process
cab
master plate
electronic-eye mark
burner film

carbon printing
resist
carbon tissue
tissue laydown
dry laydown
staging
asphaltum
spot plater
rollup
counter
prewipe blade
nib width
electrostatic assist

Questions for Review

1. What are the main characteristics of roto-gravure printing?

2. List four characteristics of gravure that make it ideal for high-quality, long-run jobs.

3. What is the Gravure Association of America (GAA)?

4. List the four basic methods of gravure cylinder preparation.

5. What are the most commonly identified parts of a gravure cylinder?

6. What is the difference between static balance and dynamic balance?

7. What are the two basic forms of cylinder construction?

8. What is electroplating?

9. What is a newage gauge?

10. What is the ballard shell process?

11. What is the purpose of a cab in cylinder layout?

12. What is a master plate?

13. What is carbon printing?

14. What is a resist?

15. What is tissue laydown?

16. What is the purpose of staging?

17. Why is chrome plating done before printing a gravure cylinder?

18. What is the purpose of a doctor blade on a gravure press?

19. What is the difference between a conventional doctor blade design and a MDC/Ringier design?

20. What is the purpose of an impression roller in gravure press work?

21. What does "electrostatic assist" refer to in gravure press work?

22. What is the "nib width" on a gravure press?

Flexographic, Ink-Jet, and Digital Presses

Anecdote to Chapter Seventeen

All printing processes have been developed to meet a human need for information. Johann Gutenberg invented printing to meet Europe's increasing need for printed records in the late 1400s. His invention expanded the distribution of knowledge across all social classes. This expansion of knowledge quickly lead to an increasing demand for more printed material. For centuries inventors and printers tried to find ways to set type and print images faster and faster. However, it took more than four hundred years before truly revolutionary changes occurred—namely the Linotype machine and the rotary relief press in the late nineteenth century. But revolutions also create demand, so the inventors kept looking for methods of producing printed information faster and faster.

In the 1950s, when the commercial phototypesetter was introduced, many felt that the device could set type faster than would ever be necessary. Within a few short years, however, the phototypesetter was outstripped by the offset lithographic process, which came to full acceptance in the late 1960s. And so it has gone

throughout history. Each new technological innovation increases demand and leads to other, related innovations, which in turn produce more demand and spark the development of newer technologies.

The technological innovation that has probably had the greatest impact on the modern printing industry is the computer. Computers have made producing printed matter faster, easier, and more efficient than was ever thought possible. Printers use computers not only to set type but to control and to monitor almost every task in the printing plant. In addition, the computer has made a completely new type of printing, known as "on-demand" printing, possible. All traditional printing processes rely on a time-consuming and costly process that involves designing an image, generating camera-ready copy from which negatives are made, using the negatives to produce printing plates, and then using the plates to produce printed reproductions. The problem with this process is that producing the final copy requires a great deal of lead time. On-demand

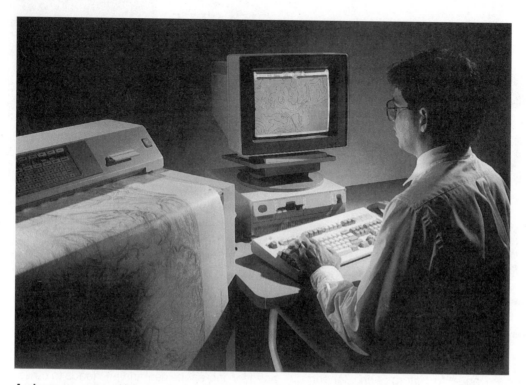

An image scanner. Using an image scanner to store graphics in computer memory can greatly reduce the lead time needed to produce printed matter.
Courtesy of Scangraphic.

printing, in which copy is reproduced directly from computer memory without negatives or plates, reduces the lead time needed for printed matter from months to minutes.

The invention of plastic materials is another innovation that has had a profound effect on printing. Plastics have greatly expanded the type of printing substrates. Before the development of plastics, printers were primarily called upon to print on paper. Printing presses, inks, plates, and all developments in printing centered around a paper substrate. The development of cellophane in the 1930s represented a major breakthrough in the packaging industry. When used for food packaging, this material would keep foods fresh far longer than paper wrappers. The material was also easy to use

because it would stretch and seal itself to the food surface and could be made clear so the customer could see the product inside the package. Above all, cellophane was inexpensive to produce, store, and handle. In all aspects of food packaging, cellophane provided the answer to the food processor's dreams. In all aspects, that is, except one—it was almost impossible to print on. Here, then, was a material that, in answering one need, created another. Aniline printing, which was introduced to this country in the early 1900s, rushed to meet this need. The aniline process, which today is known as flexography, provides the primary means for printing on plastic materials.

Will we ever have a printing process that can print on any material instantly? Probably not. As long as people can think, they will be creative. And as long as people create, they will produce a need for even more printing processes that will print at even greater speeds.

This cycle of innovation leading to innovation is what makes technology so interesting. It guarantees a future for us all, not only as printers, but as members of the human race.

Objectives for Chapter 17

After completing this chapter, you will be able to:

- Discuss the development of flexographic printing.

- Describe the major components of a flexographic press.

- Discuss the function of an anilox roll.

- Describe two-roll and three-roll flexographic inking systems.

- Explain how sheet and liquid photopolymer plates, and explain how rubber flexographic plates are made.

- Differentiate between a continuous spray printer and a drop-on-demand ink-jet printer.

- Discuss the major advantages of an ink-jet printer, and give an example of when an ink-jet printer would be used.

- Explain the term "direct digital press".

- Describe the operating principles of a digital press.

- Outline the advantages a digital press has over every traditional printing method.

- Discuss the future implications and applications of digital presses to both consumers and the printing industry.

Introduction

This chapter introduces three printing processes not discussed anywhere else in this text. They are contained in one chapter, rather than as stand-alone sections, because few academic programs have facilities or equipment that allow access to and experimentation with them. The introductory nature of descriptions would result in short chapters when contrasted with the rest of the book. *Printing Technology* 4/E cannot ignore these processes and still be termed "comprehensive"—the three processes are simply too important.

Flexography, the first process discussed here, has long been a significant relief process used in the package printing industry. Over the past decade flexography has become increasingly sophisticated. Millions of images are produced each year by this method.

Ink-jet printing, the second process, is a specialty printing process designed for relatively low-quality printing of unique images at exceptionally high speeds. Most Americans have received a envelope from Ed McMann announcing that they have just won $10 million. These envelopes are personalized by ink-jet printing. Students of the graphic arts must understand the ink-jet process because it is used extensively in direct-mail applications.

The third process discussed in this chapter is the digital press. First introduced in 1993, digital presses represent the second millennium revolution for the printing industry. In fact, the digital press printing process points to profound changes in the character, goals, and products of print. Digital presses reimage a plate cylinder with each rotation.

Flexographic Printing

Flexography, commonly referred to as flexographic or flexo printing, is a rotary relief printing process in which the image carrier is a flexible rubber or photopolymer plate with raised image areas. This process was first introduced in the early 1900s. At that time it was called **aniline printing** because the inks were made from synthetic, organic aniline dyes.

A variety of packaging products, including foil, tissue, paper, paperboard, corrugated board, and plastic film, can be printed with flexo. In fact, flexographic printing owes its wide acceptance in the packaging industry to the invention of cellophane, which became popular in the 1930s because it proved ideal for food packaging. Cellophane cannot be printed with the offset process. Although it can be printed on with gravure, the cost of gravure cylinder production is so high that only extremely long press runs make cellophane printing economical.

Ironically, the flexo process, which is ideal for printing on cellophane food packaging, got off to a slow start in commercial printing because of the mistaken belief that aniline dyes were poisonous and that they would contaminate food products. Even though the United States government approved the use of aniline inks for food packaging in 1946, the name "aniline printing" still caused many package printers and food processors to reject the process. To overcome this problem, the aniline printing industry formally changed the name of the process to "flexographic printing" in 1952. Since this name change, flexography has grown to the point where it currently represents about 17 percent of the commercial printing market.

Components of a Flexographic Press

A flexographic press consists of three major units: the infeed, printing, and outfeed units (figure 17.1). As we discuss these units, it should become apparent that one of the great-

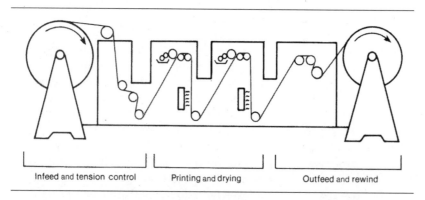

Figure 17.1. Schematic of a typical web-fed outfeed and rewind flexographic printing press

est benefits of flexography is simplicity, from infeed to delivery.

Infeed Unit

The majority of flexographic printing is done on roll-fed materials such as film, foil, and laminates used for food, medical, and sanitary packaging materials. Sheet-fed flexo is also possible, and is the only practical solution for printing thicker materials such as corrugated board. As with other web systems (see chapter 12), the flexo infeed system consists of a roll stand with some type of tensioning device. The roll stand typically operates in conjunction with a dancer roll and brake to control web tension.

Sheet-fed flexographic infeed units are not far different from those found on sheet-fed offset presses, except that a sheet-fed flexo infeed system must be designed to feed heavier stock than is generally fed through an offset press.

Printing Unit

The major advantage of flexographic printing lies in the printing unit, both in its simplicity and in its ability to deliver ink to a wide variety of substrates. Offset ink trains are designed to take relatively thick, viscous inks from an ink fountain and to spread them to thin consistencies by passing them through a number of distribution rollers and eventually to form rollers that ink the plate. Flexographic inks are much thinner than offset inks and require a much simpler inking system.

The heart of the flexo inking system is a roller with a cellular surface called the **anilox roll.** The process of manufacturing an anilox roll involves engraving a steel roller to form individual cells (from 10 to 550 cells per linear inch) on the roller surface. After the cells are formed on the steel roller, the roller is chrome plated or plasma coated with a ceramic material to protect it from corrosion and wear. The cells collect ink from the ink fountain and transfer it to the plate.

A great deal of research has gone into developing the structure, size, and number of cells needed for particular printing applications. Two cell structures are commonly used. Under magnification, the **pyramid cell** structure appears as a number of inverted pyramids with sharply sloping walls that form cells which are pointed at their bases (figure 17.2a). The **quadrangular cell** structure appears as four-sided cavities with relatively straight

a. Pyramid cell structure

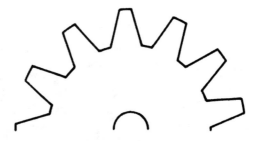

b. Quadrangular cell structure

Figure 17.2.   Cell structures. (a) The pyramid cell structure has cells with sharply pointed bases. (b) The quadrangular structure produces cells with flat bases.

walls that form cells which are relatively flat at their bases (figure 17.2b). The number, shape, and size of the cells required on the anilox roll depends on a variety of factors, including the type of ink to be used, the amount of ink to be transferred, the material to be printed on, the image to be printed, and whether the ink train is a three-roller or two-roller system.

Three-roller ink systems consist of an ink fountain roller, which is typically made of rubber, that passes ink to the anilox roll (figure 17.3). In these systems the fountain roller speed is kept constant but the anilox roll speed varies. As a result, the fountain roller not only passes ink to the anilox roll but it slips against it, wiping excess ink from the anilox roll. Therefore, ink metering is established in a three-roller ink system by controlling the rotating speed of the anilox roll.

Two-roller ink systems have no fountain roller. Instead, the anilox roll turns in the ink fountain directly and a steel doctor blade is used to remove excess ink from the anilox roll (figure 17.4). The doctor blade is positioned parallel to and set at a 30 degree angle to the surface of the anilox roll. The doctor blade arrangement provides more precise and consistent ink metering, but it tends to produce

more wear on the anilox roll than the three-roller system. This excess wear is compensated for to some extent by using quadrangular cells on the anilox rollers. Because quadrangular cells are square rather than pointed at their bases, they can tolerate more wear without significant reduction in cell capacity than can the pyramid-shaped cells used on three-roller systems (figure 17.5).

The plate cylinder is designed to hold the flexible flexographic plate through an adhesive. Unlike offset plates, flexographic plate size varies with the job to be printed. Generally, several repeat images are printed in succession from several plates mounted on the same cylinder. Thus, the size of the plate cylinder is chosen to match the repeated image size. That is, if the image to be printed is 6 inches, a 12-inch plate cylinder can be used to print two repeated images. However, a 10-inch plate cylinder could not be used to print a 6-inch job. Because the plate cylinder must be changed to match the plate, and the anilox roll must also match the job, flexo presses are designed so that the plate cylinder and ink train can be removed easily and installed as a unit in the press each time a new job is run.

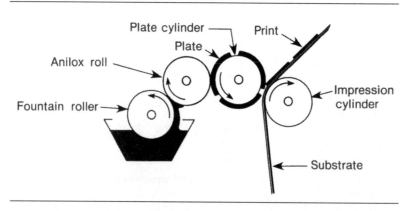

Figure 17.3.   Three-roller ink system

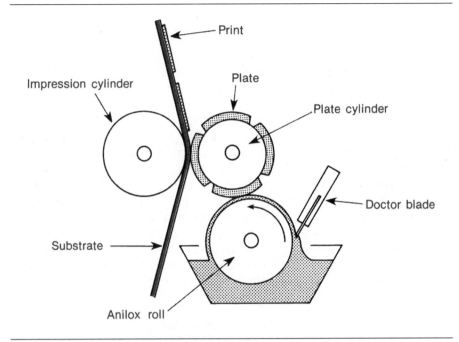

Figure 17.4.   Two-roller ink system

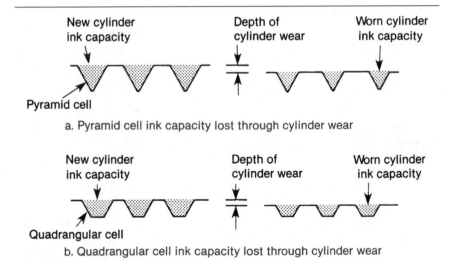

a. Pyramid cell ink capacity lost through cylinder wear

b. Quadrangular cell ink capacity lost through cylinder wear

Figure 17.5.   Comparison of cell capacity after cylinder wear. Because of their shape, the ink capacity of quadrangular cells, which are wider at their bases than pyramid cells, contain more ink in their bases and are less affected by cylinder wear at the cells' surface.

Many flexographic presses are configured with several printing units in a line so that four or more colors can be printed in one pass through the press. Drying units are located between each color head to dry the substrate before the next color is applied. Changing jobs on this type of flexographic press requires removing and replacing the printing units for each color. These replacements take time, but the lost time is compensated for because the new plates are mounted and proofed off press, which reduces on-press, make-ready time.

Pressure between the polished metal impression cylinder and the plate is adjusted to deliver what is termed a "kiss impression." Because the film and laminate materials often printed with flexo are thin, and because the plate and image areas are flexible, the lightest possible impression pressure needed to transfer the image must be used in flexography. If the pressure is too great, it causes the image to spread and impedes quality. Far too much impression damages the plate or the substrate being printed.

Outfeed Unit

Outfeed units vary considerably with the type of work being printed. Many outfeed units consist only of a rewinder, which rewinds the substrate into a roll for later processing. A rewinder might be used for foil-laminated, printed candy bar wrappers, for example. After rewinding, the roll of printed wrappers is sent from the flexo plant to the candy manufacturer. There the roll is remounted and fed into the manufacturing line where each wrapper is filled with a candy bar, sealed, and placed in a carton. Often flexo presses are designed to complement the manufacturing production line so that printing and packaging can be done as one continuous operation. Similarly, a sheet-fed flexo press for printing corrugated board may be configured to complement a converting machine that turns the printed board into folded cartons.

It is difficult to check for proper image register on substrates that are rewound for further processing. Stopping the press to check for register would destroy the image quality on the part of the web that was stopped in the printing unit(s). One approach to checking register on a moving web is to pass the web vertically before a large magnifying glass. The web is illuminated by a strobe light that flashes in time with the speed of the press. Synchronizing the strobe light with the press speed makes the image appear to be stationary in front of the magnifying glass. With this technique, the press operator is able to view register at web speed, and to make appropriate adjustments without shutting down the press.

Flexographic Plates

Flexographic plate composition must match to some extent the type of ink to be used and to the substrate to be printed. Both rubber and photopolymer plates are used.

Rubber Plates

Natural and synthetic **rubber plates** were first type of flexo plates developed, and they are still used for some applications. The process of producing a rubber plate is not far different from the process used to produce photoengravings used in the hot type letterpress process (figure 17.6). A sheet of metal alloy coated with a light-sensitive emulsion is first placed in a specially designed vacuum frame. The emulsion is not only light-sensitive, it is also an acid resist.

A negative is placed over the emulsion and light is passed through the negative. The acid resist hardens where light strikes the emulsion (image areas). During processing, the unhardened resist in the nonimage areas is washed away, leaving hardened resist only on the image areas. The metal alloy is then etched, which lowers the nonimage areas and leaves

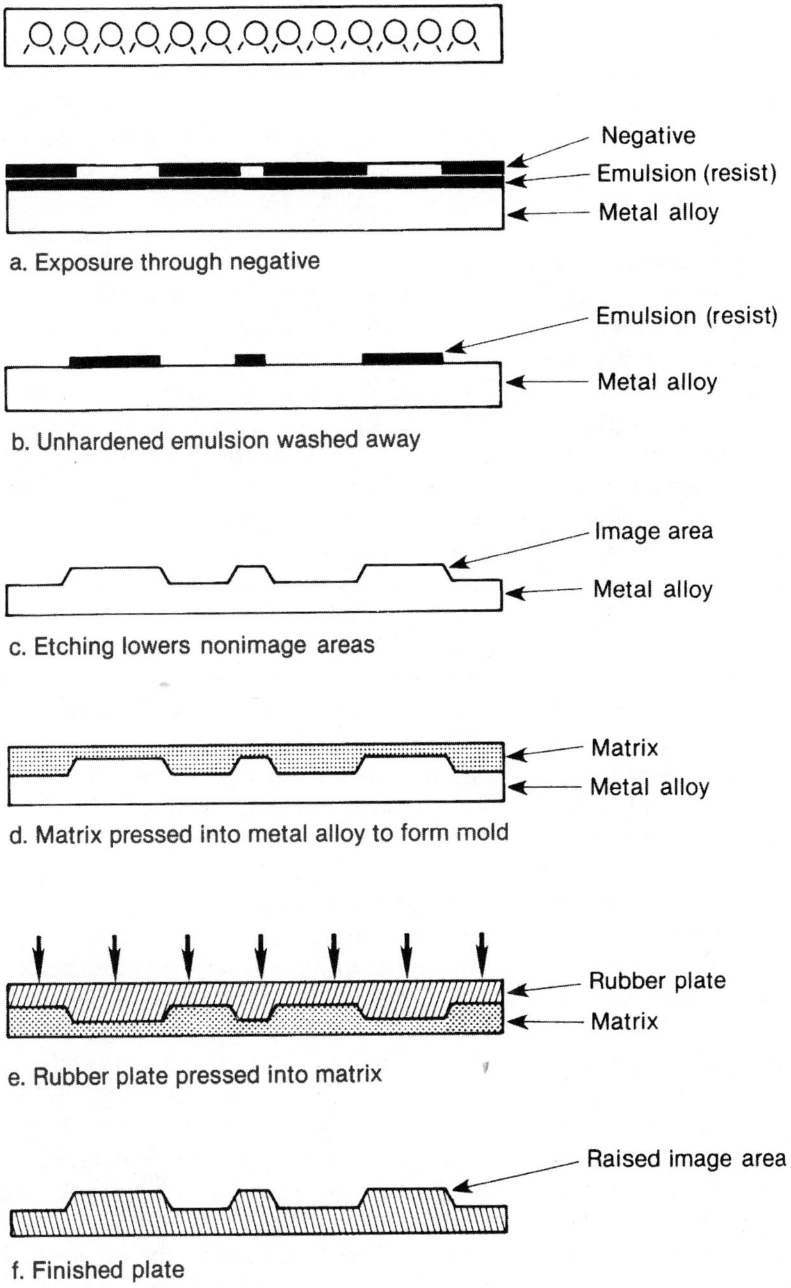

a. Exposure through negative

b. Unhardened emulsion washed away

c. Etching lowers nonimage areas

d. Matrix pressed into metal alloy to form mold

e. Rubber plate pressed into matrix

f. Finished plate

Figure 17.6. **Steps in producing a rubber plate**

the image areas raised. The remaining resist is washed off.

The completed engraving is then moved to a molding press where a matrix (mold) of the engraving is made by pressing matrix material against the engraving with controlled heat and pressure. The matrix material sinks into the metal engraving to form the mold. The rubber plate is made from the matrix by pressing a rubber sheet into the matrix, again under controlled heat and pressure. Preformed sheets for rubber plates are available in a variety of thicknesses. The thickness depends on the job to be printed and the press to be used.

The major disadvantage of rubber plates is that they are more costly to make than photopolymer plates. Also, because they are made from an engraving, any plate problems identified during proofing must be corrected by remaking the engraving, which further increases the expense of the process.

Photopolymer Plates

Photopolymer plates eliminate many of the disadvantages of rubber plates. These plates are made from light-sensitive polymers (plastics) that are hardened by ultraviolet light. Photopolymer plates are made from both sheet and liquid materials.

Sheet photopolymer plates are supplied in a variety of thicknesses for specific applications. These plates are cut to the required size and placed in an ultraviolet light exposure unit (figure 17.7). One side of the plate is completely exposed to ultraviolet light to harden or "cure" the base of the plate. The plate is then turned over, a negative of the job is mounted over the uncured side, and the plate is again exposed to ultraviolet light. This hardens the plate in the image areas. The plate is then processed to remove the unhardened photopolymer from the nonimage areas, which lowers the plate surface in these nonimage areas. After processing, the plate is dried and

given a postexposure dose of ultraviolet light to cure the whole plate.

Liquid photopolymer plates are made in a special ultraviolet light exposure unit. In this process, a clear plastic protective cover film is mounted over a negative transparency which is placed emulsion side up on the exposure unit (figure 17.8a). A layer of liquid photopolymer is then deposited by a motorized carriage over the transparency and cover film. The carriage deposits the liquid evenly over the cover film and controls the thickness of the deposit. While the carriage deposits the liquid, it also places a substrate sheet over the liquid (figure 17.8b).

The substrate sheet is specially coated on one side to bond with the liquid photopolymer and to serve as the back of the plate after exposure. Exposure is made first on the substrate side of plate. This exposure hardens a thin base layer of the liquid photopolymer and causes it to adhere to the plate substrate. A second exposure through the negative forms the image on the plate (figure 17.8c). As with sheet materials, the image areas are hardened by this exposure. The nonimage areas, however, remain liquid. Processing removes unwanted liquid in the nonimage areas to leave raised image areas. A postexposure is then made to cure the whole plate (figure 17.8d).

The **Cameron belt press** is a unique flexo press that uses liquid photopolymer plates. The Cameron press is used to produce a variety of publications such as softcover pocket books and coloring books. In the platemaking process, liquid photopolymer is coated on a belt of nylon. The length of the nylon belt is determined by the number of pages in the publication. All of the pages of the publication are exposed on the belt in the proper page imposition. One-half of the belt contains the odd-numbered pages, and the other one-half contains the even-numbered ("back up") pages. The web is first printed on one side from the half of the belt with the odd-numbered

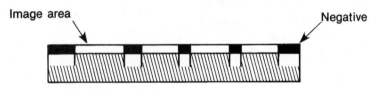
← Base
hardened
by exposure

a. Exposure of base side

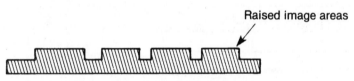

Image area   Negative

b. Exposure through negative

Raised image areas

c. Processing to remove unhardened photopolymer

d. Postexposure to cure plate

Figure 17.7. **Steps in producing a sheet polymer plate**

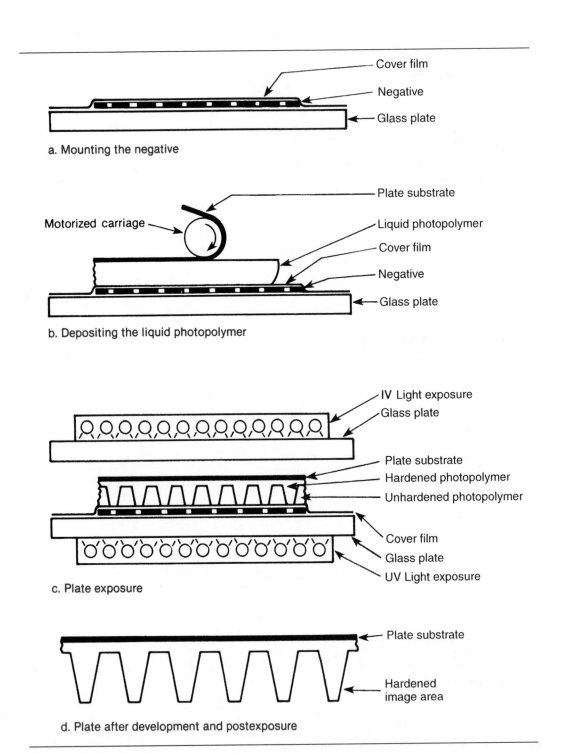

a. Mounting the negative

b. Depositing the liquid photopolymer

c. Plate exposure

d. Plate after development and postexposure

Figure 17.8.   **Steps in producing a liquid polymer plate** pages. Then it is turned over with a turn bar and is printed on the back side of the web by the other half of the belt with the even-numbered pages. Because the web runs continuously through the press, the entire book is printed in one pass. An in-line finishing operation folds, cuts, adds a preprinted cover, glues, and trims the book. The completed book is loaded into shipping boxes directly from the press outfeed section.

The Future of Flexography

For years flexography had the reputation of producing relatively low-quality printed images, suitable only for package printing on nontraditional substrates such as foil and corrugated board. With the developments in inks and plates that are taking place today, this reputation is rapidly changing to where flexography is now being used increasingly for halftone work, critical line work, and four-color printing on paper stock.

When compared to offset printing, flexographic printing offers two major advantages: long-run capabilities and relatively low waste during make-ready. Flexo can be used for press runs exceeding five million impressions. The flexible plate wears very little during a press run because of the low pressure used for impression. Also, all make-ready is done off press; this eliminates waste because the plate is proofed and produces quality copy after a few impressions once it is mounted on the press. Further, ink and water balance does not have to be achieved as it does in offset lithography. As a result, press start up is quicker and, once the ink metering system is adjusted, image quality remains constant throughout the press run. When compared to gravure, which can also be used for long press runs, flexographic printing offers low plate cost. Even if rubber plates, which require engraving, are used in the process, the cost of platemaking for flexog-

raphy is still only a fraction of the cost of producing a gravure cylinder.

One other reason the future of flexography is bright is because it is suitable for printing with water-based inks as well as solvent-based inks. Solvent-based inks have long been used for quality printing because they produce excellent color fidelity and dry quickly. These qualities make solvent-based inks extremely suitable for four-color process printing on coated papers. The major disadvantage of these inks, however, is that during drying the evaporating solvent pollutes the environment.

Over the last several years, the United States government has established environmental pollution guidelines that have forced many printers to install complex and expensive fume recovery systems. Water-based inks, which do not pollute the environment, eliminate this need. As a result, flexography is being used increasingly for color printing on a variety of papers, particularly for comic books and for medium-quality color inserts in newspaper printing. Several newspapers, including the *Pittsburgh Press*, the *Miami Herald*, and the *Providence Journal*, use the flexo process. As environmental controls become more stringent, and as research continues in flexographic plates, ink, and register systems, the move toward flexo will continue. Some researchers believe that flexo's share of the printing market will increase from its current 17 percent market share to well over 20 percent by the year 2000.

Ink-Jet Printing

Ink-jet printing produces an image by directing individual drops of ink from an orifice (opening) through a small air gap to a printing surface (figure 17.9). This process can be used to print on a variety of substrates, including corrugated board, plastics, fabric, and paper. The primary use for ink-jet printing in the

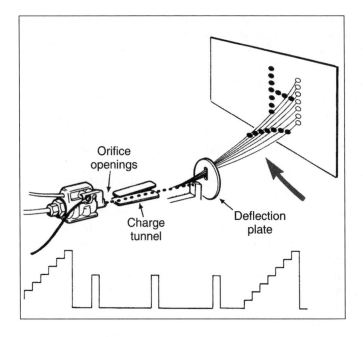

Figure 17.9.   Ink-jet printing

printing industry is in personalizing direct mail pieces. **Direct mail merging** is when a computer inserts a database of information into personalized printed pieces. Many people maintain that the current direct mail industry has been made possible largely through the development of ink-jet printing.

All ink-jet processes rely on computer input to form a dot matrix image that is made up of individual drops of ink. The major difference between ink-jet systems is whether the ink spray is "continuous" or "drop-on-demand."

Continuous-Spray Systems

In **continuous-spray systems**, each ink orifice sprays ink drops toward the printing surface continuously. When the ink drops leave the orifice, they are subjected to electric charges which vary in strength based on digitized computer information. The electric charges of var-

ious strengths deflect the ink drops from a straight path and move them in the appropriate directions to produce the desired dot matrix image. Drops not needed in the matrix are given a charge that deflects them into the ink recycling system.

The most commonly used continuous-spray ink-jet printing unit is the Videojet system (figure 17.10). The Videojet print head consists of an ink chamber that continuously emits a small stream of ink through a single ink orifice. When liquid ink is forced through a small orifice at high speed, it tends to break into a spray containing drops of various sizes. To control drop size and direction, the ink is given a frequency by a vibrating piezoelectric crystal. This frequency regulates the size, shape, and spacing of the emitted drops.

An alternative continuous-spray system is the Mead Dijit system (figure 17.11). The Dijit system provides an array of ink orifices in a single ink head. All of these orifices feed from the same ink chamber, which is given a fre-

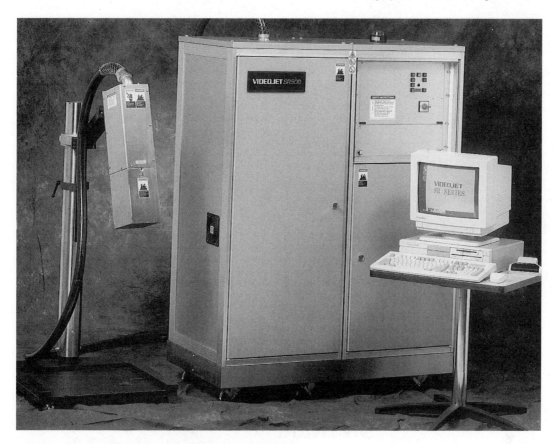

Figure 17.10.   A.B. Dick's Videojet printing system

quency by a crystal. Only the drops needed to form the image are charged when they leave the chamber. These drops travel in a relatively straight line from the orifice plate to strike the paper and form the image. Unwanted drops receive no charge and are deflected to the ink recycling system by a deflector ribbon. Because the group of ink orifices, called an "orifice array," is used with the Mead system (120 orifices per inch), characters can be printed many times faster than by a single-orifice system. Over 50,000 characters per second can be produced with an orifice array; only about 13,000 characters per second can be produced with a single-orifice system.

Drop-On-Demand Systems

In a **drop-on-demand,** or impulse, **system,** the printer produces a drop from the ink orifice only when the drop is needed to form the matrix image. The ink drops are given a frequency in a manner similar to that used for continuous drops. However, instead of being sprayed continuously, electrical impulses, which are based on digitized computer information, cause individual drops to be squeezed out of the ink orifice and propelled toward the printing surface. Drop-on-demand units have the advantage of being less complicated than continuous-spray systems because they do not require a dot

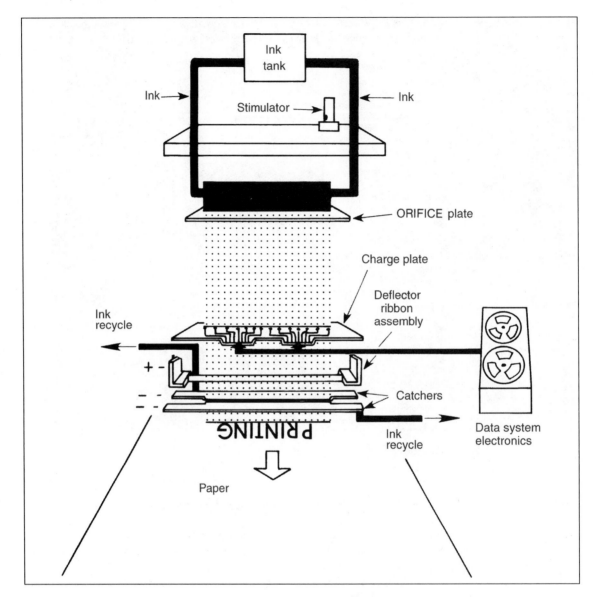

Figure 17.11.   Mead's Dijit printing process

deflection system to place needed dots or to remove unwanted drops. They are also more economical because ink is provided only where it is needed to form the image. The major disadvantage of this system is that it is much slower than a continuous-spray system.

System Evaluation

Disadvantages of Ink-Jet Printing

The major disadvantage of ink-jet printing is that images are printed in low resolution. In part, this low resolution is the result of the minimum size ink drop that can be produced at the ink orifice. Drop size affects the size of the matrix divisions that can be used to produce the image, and ultimately affects the number of dpi that make up the image. The highest-quality ink-jet printers currently available can provide images with resolutions around 300 dpi. In addition, there is a certain amount of drop misplacement during printing with all ink-jet systems. Misplaced ink drops further reduce the overall quality of the image. Finally, the inks used in ink-jet printing dry primarily by absorption, which tends to spread the individual dots that make up the image. The combination of all of these factors means that the image quality produced by ink-jet printing is not even close to the quality that can be produced by any of the major printing processes. However, in fairness to the process, we should point out that for most applications in which ink jet is used, high-quality imaging is not the primary concern.

Advantages of Ink-Jet Printing

The major advantage of ink-jet printing is the speed with which unique character images can be generated. This is the reason ink-jet printing is used so widely for addressing and producing variable information on repeat forms.

Ink-jet printers can be configured in line with web-fed presses and high-speed bindery equipment to address printed newspapers, magazines, catalogs, and other direct mail items automatically at web speeds. This eliminates the need for a separate addressing step in the direct mail operation. The publication leaves the press printed, bound, sorted in zip code order, addressed, and ready to deliver to the post office. Ink-jet printers are also used in manufacturing plants to print UPC bar codes and batch codes at assembly-line speeds on products such as cans, bottles, and boxes.

Ink-jet printers can also be stand-alone units that are moveable into nearly any production environment (figure 17.12). The "imagers" or ink units are connected to the "controller" which is managed by a microcomputer. The flexible connection between the two means that the imagers can be positioned to function within existing equipment configurations.

Another high-speed printing application for ink jet is in check-printing operations. Large corporations produce thousands of payroll checks every week. Each has a different name and dollar amount. Ink-jet printing is ideally suited to this application. Check blanks with the company name and bank identification information are preprinted as continuous, perforated rolls or sheets by offset printing. The variable information (name, address, and amount) is added by running the preprinted checks through an ink-jet printer.

One final advantage of ink-jet printing is that the process is nonimpact, which means the image carrier is not forced against the printing substrate. This feature makes it possible to print with ink jet on almost any surface, regardless of surface texture, shape, or pressure resistance. Ink-jet printing can place an image on a plastic container or bubble package (or even an egg yolk) as easily and as quickly as it can on paper, a textured surface such as sandpaper, or a curved surface such as a pill or capsule.

Figure 17.12.   An ink-jet imager. This ink-jet printer can be moved to adapt to nearly any production setup.
Courtesy of Videojet Systems International, Inc.

Direct Digital Presses

The conception that **Desktop publishing (DTP)** revolutionized publishing is largely a myth. While DTP did create a revolution in capability, ease of operation, and access to and control of image generation, it was only part of the printing production loop. Wonderful camera-ready images could be prepared by skillful operators using DTP. However, the copy still had to be photographed, stripped, plated, printed, and bound. This is hardly a revolution that gave publishing control from your workdesk.

As you saw in chapter 11, on-press, direct-to-plate technology is now used to move directly from the computer to the press to eliminate several time-consuming processing steps. This was still no revolution, however. To be cost effective, thousands of press sheets had to be printed.

In September 1993, the missing link in the printing revolution was announced to the printing community: the direct digital press.

The **direct digital press** "allows full-color pages to be printed directly or remotely from digital page data with the ability to vary the information at every cylinder revolution."[1] This means that electronically prepared images go directly to the press, eliminating mechanicals, film, and plates.

Development and Competition

Serious research and development on the commercial availability of the direct digital press began more than a decade ago. Revolutionary developments like this require vast human and

[1]Mr. Benny Landa, chairman and chief executive officer of Indigo America, Inc., Woburn, Massachusetts.

financial resources. A hundred years ago a similar investment was made to bring the Linotype machine to commercial reality.

The two direct digital press manufacturers are the result of independent, but parallel, research efforts. Xeikon, located in Belgium, has targeted the long-run, web-fed market. Indigo, developed in Israel, offers a sheet-fed press for short-run jobs (less than one thousand copies).

Press Configuration and Operation

The heart of the Indigo E-Print system (figure 17.13) is a Sun SPARCstation CPU. Data can be passed through the CPU from a variety of sources, such as tape, Ethernet, and optical disk, using industry-standard formats such as PostScript and Scitex. Because processing and printing are conducted simultaneously, one job can be printing while another is processing. The result is uninterrupted work flow.

Indigo describes the process as follows:

A new latent image is created on the image cylinder with each revolution while the Ink Color Switch injects a different color ink for each separation. After inking, the image is transferred to the blanket, and from blanket to paper. The paper is retained on the impression cylinder for multiple revolutions, one for each color. In duplex mode (perfecting), the trailing edge of the sheet is fed back onto the impression cylinder for printing and then fed to the Booklet Maker.

Figure 17.13. The E-Print 1000 digital press.
Courtesy of Indigo America, Inc.

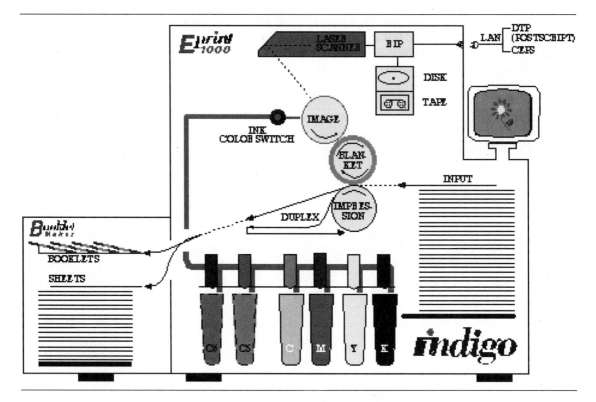

Figure 17.14.   Schematic of the E-Print 1000 digital press.
Courtesy of Indigo America, Inc.

Figure 17.14 shows a schematic of the basic system provided by Indigo.

The plate is digitally imaged or exposed by a patented laser diode module. Exposure takes place at 200 megabits a second. The exceptional characteristic of the plate is that it is reusable. The plate is made from an organic photosensitive base and is rated at tens of thousands of impressions before it must be replaced. In operation, the plate cylinder is charged electrostatically and exposed as it rotates at a constant speed of 4,000 revolutions per hour (66.7 rotations per minute). This translates to 8,000 **A4 sheets** or pages per hour (pph). The press runs **A3 sheets**, which are approximately 11 inches × 17 inches. Two A4 sheets, which are approximately 8½ inches ×

11 inches, can be cut from an A3 sheet. This nomenclature is based on a metric system of measurement, and is used widely nearly everywhere in the world except the in United States. Four-color work is run at 2,000 pph; duplex (both sides) color is run at 1,000 pph. Because this process is so rapid and is able to produce 1 or 1,000 copies, it is perfect for on-press proofing, in which the need for a separate proofing step is eliminated.

Next to the laser diodes in the Indigo E-Print system is the Ink Color Switch which applies ink. The plate is imaged, inked, and transfers the ink to the blanket in one revolution.

Little operator intervention is required during printing. It is possible, however, to adjust color by controlling brightness. The single-cylinder design, sequential printing on each sheet, and unique inking characteristics make registration nearly automatic and perfect.

The E-Print system has an optional Booklet Maker attachment. With this attachment, up to 100 folded, collated, stitched booklet pages can be delivered in the outfeed unit.

ElectroInk

The E-Print 1000 uses a patented liquid ink called "ElectroInk" rather than dry powder. This key element allows for elegantly simple press operation and delivery of exceptional color quality. ElectroInk contains polymer particles that average 1 to 2 microns in size. Powder toners use larger particles that cannot be as small (figure 17.15). If toner particles were 1 or 2 microns, they would act like thick smoke and float away.

When the ElectroInk film contacts paper it hardens instantly and peels from the blanket completely. This offers two major advantages. First, because the ink dries upon contact with the paper, **dimensional stability** is guaranteed. Most offset inks dry on the paper by absorption or aerial oxidation, which either introduces moisture into the sheet or leaves a wet ink layer (see chapter 18). When dimensional stability is assured more accurate color fit is possible.

The second primary advantage is that no residual ink remains on the blanket after each rotation. In contrast, conventional ink splits between the paper and blanket and leaves a residue. This means it is necessary to wash the unit before changing colors. The lack of residual ink also helps eliminate dot gain. Because unused ink does not build up on the blanket, halftone dot size is assured.

Total ink transfer is the primary reason it is possible to use only one cylinder set, yet print different colors, one after the other. The result is extremely sharp images (figure 17.16).

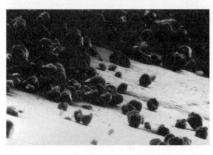

Figure 17.15. ElectroInk compared to powder toner (extremely magnified view).
Courtesy of Indigo America, Inc.

Figure 17.16. Enlarged view of digital press output compared to same image reproduced by xerography.
Courtesy of Indigo America, Inc.

Implications of Direct Digital Presses

Before Gutenberg, there was **demand-based publishing**. In demand-based publishing, if people wanted and could afford books they looked for ones to purchase or paid scribes to copy them. Gutenberg created **market-based publishing.** Gutenberg's invention created a situation where the printer decided what to print, prepared many copies, and then sought to convince the market it wanted the product.

For the past five hundred years there have been few opportunities for individuals to participate in a demand-based information environment. Someone else decided what to reproduce and distribute.

The introduction of DTP in 1984 was the first step toward individual control and access to focused information. The reality of a true digital press in 1993 took the next step toward those goals, and will, over the next decade, transform both the graphic arts industry and our daily lives.

Personalized Magazines and Other Information Pieces

Every home receives hundreds of pounds of magazines and newspapers each year. Much of this material goes unread. There are probably parts of the daily newspaper you do not read. Even special interest magazines, such as *Mac-World, Sports Illustrated,* or the *Worm Runner's Journal,* contain articles of little or no interest to the subscriber. All of these unread, and unwanted, pages come as part of a total package, clutter our homes, and must be discarded.

Digital presses can be used to personalize every publication that comes to your home. Advertisers that sell products in your interest areas can purchase advertising space in your exclusive magazine or newspaper.

In the office community database management can be used to create one-of-a-kind reports, reference manuals, and information books for every employee.

Elimination of Traditional Bookstores

Bookstores sell books. They are everywhere when you walk in the door. Book lovers revel in the environment. However, even the most ardent book lover does not need two hundred copies of the same book—one copy suffices.

Large bookstores are large because they need to shelve many copies of every title. If you do not come in and make a purchase then that storage space is wasted. Bookstores of the future may shelve only one sample copy of a work and print a fresh copy on a digital press when you have made your decision to purchase. Personalized information can be included in the copy in the process.

No Out-of-Print Books

Publishers only print and promote books that they can sell. If, after the first year of publication, the buying population of a book dwindles, then the publisher stops printing and promoting that book. The book then becomes "out of print," and is only available through libraries, used bookstores, or from a friend.

With digital presses a book will never go out of print. Computer archives can store digital information and anyone can order one or many copies of any book, no matter its current status.

Mass Marketing Replaced by Personalized Marketing

Mass marketing involves sending millions of pieces of mail to millions of individuals with the hope of selling an idea, service, or product to one or two percent of those individuals. Organizations like the Publisher's Clearinghouse have used ink-jet printing to customize direct mail solicitations with considerable success because individuals are more likely to open and read items that contain their names.

Indigo's founder, Benny Landa, offered an image of a customer who wishes to promote two or three dozen out of several thousand company products. However, there is no point to offering lawnmowers to apartment dwellers or diapers to pensioners. The smart company wants to customize individual color fliers so that each consumer sees only products he or she might actually buy. With a direct digital press, every consumer can receive a different catalog. It is now possible to deliver custom catalogs containing items the seller knows matches each buyer's personal interest.

In this example, the customer could program the digital press to deliver custom catalogs containing items it knows match your personal interests. Image databases could also be used to place your photograph next to the motorcycle, car, yacht, or pogo stick the customer wants you to buy.

Virtual Elimination of Warehousing
Traditional printing relies upon economies of scale. Companies order tens of thousands of copies of books, brochures, technical booklets, reference sheets, promotional items, and training manuals and store them for future use. The cost of warehouse space can be considerable, however.

All print storage space can be replaced by a digital press, computer memory, and a lot of blank paper. When a document is needed it can be simply ordered, printed, and delivered. Demand printing becomes a reality in this way.

Individual Access to Quality Color
Industry-based cost estimates place material costs for digital presses at less than 25> per 11 inch × 17 inch sheet. When equipment depreciation and overhead (see chapter 20) are factored in, a consumer price of $1.00 per page is possible. This price would apply whether 1 sheet or 1,000 sheets are purchased. With traditional printing, however, unit price goes down as the press run size goes up.

Anyone with a microcomputer and inexpensive software can afford to prepare and create professional-looking documents for personal use on a digital press—a personalized valentine for your favorite friend, full-color printed theme papers, copies of a family history booklet for your parents' anniversary, or your own book.

The direct digital press and demand-based printing will change your career and your life.

Key Terms

flexography	photopolymer plates	desktop publishing (DTP)
aniline printing	sheet photopolymer	direct digital press
anilox roll	liquid photopolymer	A4 sheets
pyramid cell	Cameron belt press	A3 sheets
quadrangular cell	ink-jet printing	dimensional stability
three-roller ink system	direct mail merging	demand-based publishing
two-roller ink system	continuous-spray system	market-based publishing
rubber plate	drop-on-demand system	

Questions for Review

1. What type of products are printed primarily with flexography?

2. What are the major components of a flexographic press?

3. What is the purpose of the anilox roll? Why does it have surface cells?

4. What is the difference between the pyramid cell structure and the quadrangular cell structure?

5. Why is the quadrangular cell structure used on ink systems that require a doctor blade?

6. How are rubber flexographic plates made?

7. Describe the processes for producing a sheet photopolymer plate and a liquid photopolymer plate.

8. Name two applications of ink-jet printing.

9. What is the difference between continuous-spray ink-jet printing and drop-on-demand ink-jet printing?

10. What are the advantages and disadvantages of ink-jet printing?

11. Explain the concept of a direct digital press.

12. Describe the basic operation of a digital press.

13. What advantages does a digital press have over traditional printing methods?

CHAPTER

Paper and Ink

Anecdote to Chapter Eighteen

Throughout the history of printing, the demand for paper has increased constantly. The paper industry has evolved to meet this growing demand. It is the craft of early paper-makers that allows us to hold Gutenberg's first Bible today, five hundred years after the sheets left his press.

The first paper-like material, called papyrus, was invented by the Egyptians about five thousand years ago. This "paper" was made from the papyrus plant, which grew along the banks of the Nile River. To make the paper the pith, or center of the plant, was first cut into strips. These strips were then glued together in thin, crosswise layers to form sheets. After pressing and drying, the sheets were ready to use. Papyrus sheets are still readable after more than five millennia.

The first truly modern paper was invented in China by Ts'si Lun in A.D. 105. Lun first shredded cloth fibers into a special hot-water solution. The resulting fiber solution was then poured into a frame covered with a loosely woven cloth screen. The water in the solution

drained through the cloth, leaving fine, interwoven fibers on the screen. The frame was then placed in the sun to dry. Any remaining water evaporated from the fibers, resulting in paper. Lun later created "laid papers" by immersing the frame in the fiber solution and gently raising the frame to the surface. This laid technique produced a better quality paper than did the earlier method. The laid process was used to produce all paper until around 1800.

The first automated process was developed in 1798 in the paper mill of M. Didot, member of a famous printing-publishing family, in Essonnes, France. Nicolas Louis Robert, a superintendent in Didot's mill, developed the idea of making paper by pouring the fiber solution onto a continuously moving wire belt. After the water drained through the belt, the paper was passed between felt-covered rollers. The machine worked very well and, with time for improvements, would have been a commercial success. However, the French Revolution, and several lawsuits with Didot, prevented Robert from reaching that goal.

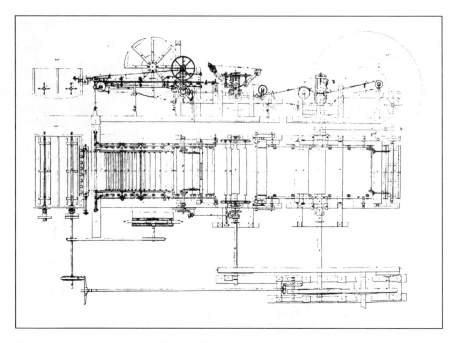

The patent drawing for the Fourdrinier papermaking machine

In 1801 an associate of the Didot family, John Gamble, joined the Fourdrinier brothers in a partnership to develop Robert's idea in England. By 1807 they had designed and constructed the first fully automated, continuous papermaking machine.

In this process the fiber solution, called "stuff," was deposited from a special box onto a finely woven copper wire belt. The belt moved both forward and side to side. The belt's copper web was 54 inches wide and 31 feet long. The full length of the machine, including driers, was almost 1000 feet. It took seven workers to operate and could produce a continuous roll of paper at the rate of more than 600 feet an hour.

The papermaking machine operated better than expected and created great excite-ment. At long last, here was a way to meet the ever growing demand for printing papers. Like so many other creative people, the men who perfected one of the greatest contributions to modern printing died in poverty. The Four-driniers lost a fortune attempting to market their device. Although by 1860 thousands of tons of paper were being produced on automated machines all over the world, none of the paper-making pioneers ever benefited financially from the effort.

While many refinements and improve-ments have been made, the basic design of the 1807 machine is still used today to produce all paper. The machine is called a Fourdrinier in honor of the brothers and the partnership that gave the world the supply of paper it needed.

Objectives for Chapter 18

After completing this chapter, you will be able to:

- Recall the basic papermaking process.
- Define six paper characteristics: bulk, opacity, finish, coated versus noncoated, reflectance, and grain.
- Classify paper into four common groups and recognize the characteristics of each.
- Recognize and define common paper terms such as ream, M weight, substance weight, and equivalent weight.

- Calculate press sheet cuts from standard paper sizes.
- List and define the properties of ink, including viscosity, tack, and drying time.
- List the common groups of ingredients of printing ink, including pigment, vehicle, and additives.
- Describe the characteristics of lithographic, screen printing, letterpress, flexographic, and gravure inks.
- Recognize the importance of color standards and accurate ink specifications.

Introduction

Two of the most important ingredients for the printing processes are ink and paper. Traditionally printing consisted of images set in dense black ink on white paper. For many years, the problems of creating the ink and paper were so troublesome and time consuming that no one bothered to use different colors.

Today, however, the printer and the printing customer are faced with another problem. There are so many different kinds of paper—with different colors, textures, finishes, thicknesses, and weights—that it is hard to choose among them. So many different kinds of ink, each formulated for a specific process, problem, or paper, are available in any color of the spectrum that the printer is hard-pressed to understand even a fraction of the possible choices.

The purpose of this chapter is to organize the information on paper and ink into an understandable form. It is divided into two sections. The first section deals with paper; the second section deals with ink. Each section classifies materials and examines ideas that are important for a novice printer to understand.

SECTION 1: PAPER

Introduction to Paper

The printed paper you are now reading and the sheets that form this book are made from cellulose fibers. Cellulose is the basic component of trees. By chopping wood into very small chips and then cooking them in a water mixture, the cellulose fibers can be released and used for papermaking. Wood fibers are filled with tree sap and bonding agents called **lignin**, which must be bleached or removed before making a sheet of printing paper. The brown sack you put your purchases in at the grocery store shows the color of unbleached wood fibers.

Historically, the bleaching process to remove lignin made papermaking among the most environmentally polluting industries in the world. Today, strict recycling of wastewater, efficient filtration devices, and water purification systems have drastically reduced environmental damage done by the industry.

Almost all industrial printing paper is made from a combination of softwoods (from Georgia and South Carolina) and hardwoods (from Canada). The different characteristics of these woods together produce strong, durable paper.

Although wood is the most common source of cellulose fibers for papermaking, any cellulose fibers can be used. Cotton was once used widely for this purpose in the United States. The primary fiber source was cotton rags. Even today we use the term "rag content" to describe the percentage of cotton fibers in a sheet of paper. Cotton does not have lignin and therefore does not require the use of intense acids in the bleaching process. Any trace of acid in paper reduces its permanency, causes brittleness, and can create "acid burns" in the paper years after production. In some areas of the United States, legal documents must be typed or printed on 100-percent rag paper by law to ensure that they will survive at least one hundred years. The sheets Gutenberg used to print his Bible in 1452 are still in good condition more than five hundred years later—they were made from linen rags, without acid.

One fascinating application of the fact that any cellulose-based material can be used to make paper is a current project by the Levi Straus company. The company is converting waste from the manufacture of blue jeans to produce a specialty paper popular with contemporary graphic designers. "Blue jean paper" is exceptionally strong, permanent, and distinctive, and it is also very printable.

Papermaking

Early papermaking involved first preparing a "slurry" that was made from cellulose fibers suspended in water. The slurry was as much as 95 percent water and 5 percent fibers. A fine meshed screen would then be dipped into the slurry. Water would fall through the screen, leaving interwoven fibers on the screen. The fibers would be dried and ironed to produce paper.

Papermaking technology was revolutionized by the invention of the Fourdrinier machine in the nineteenth century. Automatic papermaking vastly increased the supply of material for the growing printing industry.

The Fourdrinier follows the same basic techniques as the hand papermaking process just described (figure 18.1). The slurry is prepared in a large mixing vat. Dyes and chemical additives are mixed with the slurry to give different characteristics to the finished paper. The slurry is then piped to the machine and poured carefully onto a moving mesh screen. The screen both moves forward and jogs from side to side. The side-to-side movement shakes the majority of fibers so they are parallel and point in the direction of the belt's movement (figure 18.2). The direction of the fibers defines paper grain (see the following Paper Characteristics section). The side-to-side motion also hastens the fall of water through the screen.

Enough water has been removed from the slurry at the end of the belt so the fiber sheet can be lifted free. The web of new paper is then passed through a variety of rollers to impart different characteristics. Some rollers are heated to further remove moisture. Others polish the paper or add a "watermark," or design. Special textures such as a linen or parchment finish can even be embossed into the still soft sheet. Finally, the paper is wound onto a large roll for future use.

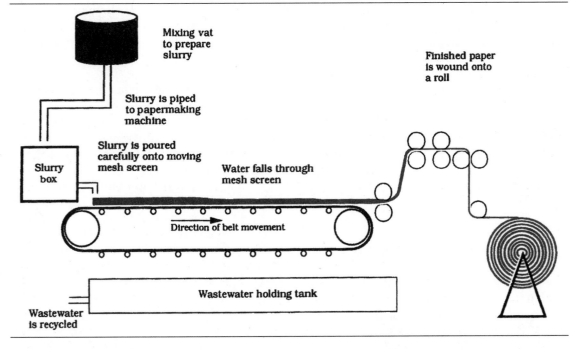

Figure 18.1.   Schematic of the Fourdrinier machine

Paper Characteristics

Papermaking technology can deliver a nearly unlimited array of characteristics for use by the printing industry. Some characteristics are natural consequences of the process; others are added intentionally or are controlled to meet customers' needs. This section reviews six primary paper characteristics (figure 18.3).

Grain

Paper **grain** results from cellulose fibers aligning in the direction of the continuous screen's movement in a papermaking machine. Grain is determined easily. To determine grain, dampen a small sheet of paper. The sheet curls parallel to the grain direction (figure 18.4).

Paper grain is an important issue on the offset press. Lithography introduces water to the printing process. However, most paper is not dimensionally stable, which means it changes size with changes in temperature and humidity (changes in the presence of moisture). The larger the sheet, the greater the change in size.

Also, paper does not change size uniformly with exposure to moisture. It changes more "with the grain" (parallel to the grain) than it does "against the grain" (perpendicular to the grain). Therefore, it is often important

Figure 18.2.   Magnified cross section of paper showing intertwined cellulose fibers

Bulk

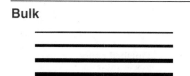

Refers to thickness of the sheet

Opacity

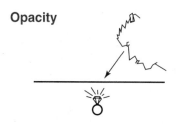

Refers to the ability to see (or rather, not see) through the sheet

Finish

Refers to the texture or surface of the sheet

Coated versus uncoated

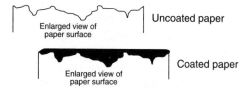

Uncoated paper

Enlarged view of paper surface

Coated paper

Enlarged view of paper surface

A clay-like material is used to fill the porous, irregular surface of the sheet

Reflectance

Refers to the ability of the sheet to reflect light

Figure 18.3.   Pictograms of five paper characteristics

with four-color printing to know the grain direction and feed the paper so it changes the least in size with repeated wettings. Papermakers identify grain direction for this reason (figure 18.5).

Grain long means that the grain is parallel to the long dimension of the sheet. **Grain short** means that the grain is parallel to the short dimension of the sheet. If the sheet is perfectly square, the paper carton or package indicates grain direction.

Grain is also important in the bindery. Paper folds easily with the grain, but it folds poorly against the grain. Try folding a sheet of paper in two right angle directions. One way gives a clean fold, the other breaks the grains and delivers a ragged edge. When folding thick sheets against the grain, it is often

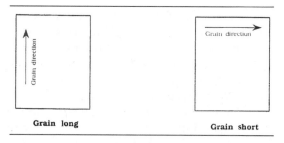

Figure 18.4.   Paper sheets curl parallel to the grain direction

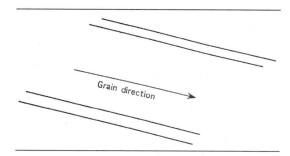

Grain long

Grain short

Figure 18.5.   Grain direction

necessary to **score**, or line indent, the sheet to get a clean fold. This adds another operation to the job and therefore increases cost.

Bulk

Bulk refers to the thickness of the sheet—not its weight. It is possible to have two sheets that weigh the same but have different thicknesses. Think of bulk as pumping air between the cellulose fibers. Add more air and the paper becomes thicker or bulkier.

Bulk is measured in "points." These points differ from the points used to measure type size, however. One point of bulk equals 1/1000th of an inch. Therefore, a 10-point paper is 0.010 inches thick ($10 \times 0.001 = 0.010$). Common bulks are 8, 10, and 11 points.

Opacity

Opacity refers to the ability of light to pass through a sheet, or it is the ability to see through a sheet. High opacity means it is difficult to see through the sheet. Low opacity means it is easy to see through the sheet.

When printing on both sides of a sheet of paper, high opacity is very important because we only want to see an image on one side. The image on the other side of the sheet should not interfere with readability. Hold your morning newspaper up to the light and try reading an article. You will see that most newsprint has low opacity.

Finish

In general, **finish** refers to the texture or surface of the sheet. Finish is usually applied after the wet paper leaves the moving wire screen on the Fourdrinier papermaking machine. Rollers, with patterns cut into the surface, can transfer nearly any finish to the wet material.

A smooth, hard surface is ideal for most industrial printing processes. Heated rollers can be used to achieve this type of surface. The terms "calendered" and "super calendered" are used to describe an exceptionally hard, smooth, and printable finish.

Coated versus Noncoated

A microscopic view of paper shows a surface that is filled with much irregularity (figure 18.2). The intertwined cellulose fibers create peaks and valleys—a lot like a moonscape. When ink is applied to a plain sheet of paper, several problems can occur:

- Ink can absorb into the paper like a sponge. This results in "dot gain" when printing halftones—the dot actually grows in size.
- There can appear to be density variation. Ink is thick in the valleys and thin over the peaks.
- The sheet can actually change size in the process of absorbing wet ink and then drying.

Calendering helps smooth the peaks and valleys of the paper. However, the ideal solution is to coat the paper surface with a clay-like material to create **coated paper.** The clay fills the valleys of the paper and produces a nearly flat, nonabsorbent surface. Ink then dries on the surface by aerial oxidation, not by absorption. This means that the dot size is reproduced from the plate and sheet stability is retained. Coated papers are ideal for multicolor printing.

Reflectance

The term **reflectance** describes the ability of a sheet of paper to reflect light. Remember that process color printing acts like a series of light filters. We see certain colors because light passes through the translucent ink and is then reflected. With four-color process work, the higher the reflectance of a sheet, the more vivid and accurate the color image.

Reflectance can be controlled by changing the degree of bleaching of the original cellulose fibers, adding chemicals to the slurry, calendering, and altering the coating formulation.

Recycled Paper

There has been increasing attention given to the issue of recycled paper. Concern is not focused on papermaking as a polluting process; that is generally under control. The real motivation behind recycling paper is America's diminishing landfill capacity. Nearly 41 percent of America's solid waste is paper and paperboard. The United States Environmental Protection Agency (EPA) estimates that unless drastic changes are made in paper recycling, the nation's landfills could close by the end of this century.

The response to this concern has been profound and substantive. Manufacturers and consumers have shifted their attention to this problem. The major issue is the use of preconsumer or postconsumer waste materials.

Preconsumer paper waste includes anything that was used to manufacture consumer products but was not actually sold. Examples are paper waste from making cartons or packages and portions cut from the edges of finished press sheets. Preconsumer paper waste also includes items from a wholesaler's unused inventory. These are generally out-of-date products that were never sold. **Postconsumer paper waste** products are generally considered anything that is sold to paper users that would normally end up in landfills.

Most recycling in this decade has been of preconsumer waste. Postconsumer paper recycling has been almost exclusively in the area of newsprint. However, newspapers are made from low-grade paper and represent only a small fraction of our total paper consumption.

Recycling Definitions

The EPA has created a number of definitions of materials within the recycling process. Three important definitions are mill broke, recovered materials, and wastepaper.

Mill Broke

Paper waste that is generated in the paper mill before completing the papermaking process is called **mill broke.** This includes slurry and cutoff from the continuous wire screen on the Fourdrinier machine. All of this material is generally returned to the pulping process and is excluded from the list of recovered materials.

Recovered Materials

Recovered materials is a broad category that includes used postconsumer materials from retailers, office buildings, and homes. Examples of recovered materials are old newspapers, magazines, mixed wastepaper, and general fibrous wastes that enter and are collected from municipal and solid waste facilities, wastes generated after the papermaking and printing processes, and materials from obsolete inventories. Also included in this category are fibrous by-products of harvesting, manufacturing, and woodcutting processes. The latter examples could include flax, straw, forest residues, waste rope, and fibers recovered from waste water.

Wastepaper

The **wastepaper** category is similar to the recovered materials category in that it includes postconsumer waste such as old newspapers, corrugated boxes, bindery trimmings, and paper from obsolete or out-dated copies of printed pieces in a company's inventories. However, wastepaper does not consider fibrous by-products of harvesting, manufacturing, or woodcutting processes.

Identifying Recycled or Recyclable Products

An absolute and universally accepted definition of "recycled paper product" has yet to emerge. Mill broke is not considered recycled material, but does a product have to be made from 100-percent wastepaper to be called "recycled"? In response to public and corporate interest, some products with as little as 10-percent postconsumer material are labeled "recycled" by the manufacturer. General EPA guidelines recommend a minimum of 50 percent wastepaper for printing and writing papers. However, these guidelines are not strictly followed.

The American Paper Institute has created symbols to assist consumers in identifying environmentally conscious products (figure 18.6). However, it is up to the manufacturer to determine if a product is recycled or recyclable. For example, Canada's EcoLogo symbol can only be used on paper products that contain more than 50 percent recycled paper and at least 10 percent postconsumer fiber.

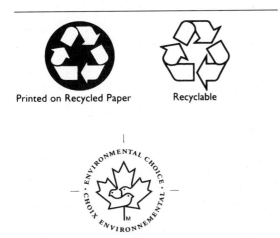

Printed on Recycled Paper   Recyclable

Figure 18. 6.   Environmental symbols. The top left symbol may be used in the United States on products and packages made from recycled paper. The top right image can be used in the United States on paper products that can be expected to be recycled. The EcoLogo (bottom) is used in Canada to indicate the paper meets requirements of the Office of Environmental Choice and the Canadian Standards Association.

Reclaiming Paper Materials

In order to be reused, paper must be returned to a clean, pure, cellulose fiber condition. The process of creating new paper from used paper involves de-inking, bleaching, and sludge disposal.

De-Inking

De-inking is a chemical and mechanical process that removes all additives from printed paper. These additives might include inks, fillers, clays, and metal materials such as foil, staples, or binders. There are two basic de-inking methods: washing and flotation.

The initial step for both de-inking methods is to chop the used paper into small pieces and blend them in a water mixture. The mixture is then filtered to remove metal and other impurities.

The washing de-inking method uses strong chemical detergents in a series of steps. It is much like the stages a washing machine follows in your home. The first bath contains the strongest chemicals. The mixture is then filtered and rinsed, and a weaker detergent is used for the next step. The sequence continues until the desired degree of cleanliness is reached.

The flotation de-inking method uses chemicals that cause inks and other noncellulose materials to float to the surface of the mixture. The undesirable materials are skimmed off while the mixture is stirred continually.

Some paper recycling companies use a combination of these two methods. Whatever method is used, the goal is to reduce the mixture to cellulose fibers suspended in a water slurry.

Bleaching

After the wastepaper is de-inked, it must be bleached because consumers want a bright, clean sheet of paper. Some papers are colored during the papermaking process. Ink on printed sheets that dry by absorption actually stains the cellulose fibers because it enters the fibers themselves. The de-inking process also tends to stain the fibers and discolors the water slurry mixture. Bleaching removes this stain and returns the cellulose to a pure white state.

The most effective bleaches are chlorine based. However, chlorine is a significant polluter. Discarding the chlorine could actually offset the benefits of recycling the paper. However, effective nonchlorine bleaches, such as sodium hydrosulphite, are being developed that reduce peripheral environmental impact.

Even though bleaching wastepaper is a major challenge, it should be recognized that virgin paper pulp must also be bleached to remove lignin. Most experts agree that bleaching de-inked fiber requires significantly fewer chemicals than bleaching virgin pulp.

Another solution to the bleaching waste challenge is to avoid bleaching all recycled fibers to pure white. Products such as newsletters, announcements, or newspapers that carry information with an extremely short use-life, do not have to be perfectly white.

Sludge Disposal

The by-product of the de-inking process is sludge. Sludge is composed of a variety of contaminants, fillers, and inks. Anything that is not cellulose fiber becomes sludge. Depending upon the type process, the type of paper, and the ink coverage, from 10 percent to 30 percent of wastepaper becomes sludge.

Under the EPA standards for ink manufacturing, air emissions, and water effluents, de-inking sludge is generally considered to be a nontoxic process. All sludge must be tested, however, and if a sample reaches a certain toxic level, it must be buried in a controlled landfill for hazardous materials.

Nontoxic sludge is disposed of in a variety of ways. Some sludge is placed in private or public landfills. Some manufacturers burn sludge to provide electrical power for the de-inking process. Others sell sludge as a raw material for other manufacturing processes, such

as making molded nursery pots. Polycoatings reclaimed from the sludge of polycoated paper can be used to make new polyethylene products. They are sometimes used to cover a sheet to protect it from moisture or to give an extremely glossy finish.

The move to recycle postconsumer, high-grade printing and writing paper depends upon two factors. The first is the paper industry's production capacity to de-ink and return fibers to a clean state. The second is consumer demand. Both factors must increase radically before recycled paper becomes standard.

Classifying Paper

There are literally thousands of different papers available to the designer and to the printer. Every different paper manufacturer creates its own list of names and labels of its proprietary lines or products. Such a list can be confusing and mystifying for both new and experienced professionals. That there is no universally accepted method to categorize all papers adds to the difficulty.

However, one workable way that is emerging is to classify all papers under one of the following five headings: book, writing, cover, bristol, and an "other" category (table 18.1).

Book paper is the most common type of paper found in the industry. It is used as a general purpose material for such things as catalogs, brochures, direct mail, and books. This classification includes "offset sheets" used in almost every plant in the country.

Writing paper is generally a high-quality material that was originally associated with correspondence and record keeping. Today it includes a wide range of qualities and uses such as stationery, inexpensive reproduction (such as for the ditto or mimeograph processes), and tracing or drawing.

Cover paper is commonly used for the outside covers of brochures or pamphlets and

Table 18.1.   One Way to Classify Types of Paper

Book Papers	**Bristol Papers**
Offset	Tag
Opaque	Index
Converting	Post card
Writing Papers	**Other**
Bond	Groundwood
Duplicator	(newsprint)
Mimeograph	Lightweights
Ledger	Special purpose
Tracing	
Cover Papers	
General purpose cover	
Duplex	

is generally thicker than both book and writing papers. Its common applications are booklets, manuals, directories, and announcements.

Bristol papers are stiff, heavy materials that are used widely for such things as business cards, programs, menus, file folders, and inexpensive booklet covers.

The "other" category is a holding bin for any paper that cannot be classified under the first four headings. Common examples are newsprint, lightweight materials such as onion-skin, and items that meet a special purpose such as no carbon required (NCR) paper.

Basis Weight

All papers within each category are further classified (and sold) according to weight. The system is called basis weight. **Basis weight** is the weight in pounds of one **ream** (500 sheets) of the basic sheet size of a particular paper type. Unfortunately, all paper types do not use the same basic sheet size to determine weight (figure 18.7). The basic sheet sizes of the four common paper classifications are:

- Book paper: 25 inches × 38 inches
- Writing paper: 17 inches × 22 inches
- Cover paper: 20 inches × 26 inches
- Bristol: 22½ inches × 28½ inches

Most papers are available in a variety of basis weights. For example, the most common weights for uncoated book papers are basis 40, 45, 50, 70, and 80. One ream of basis 40 book paper measures 25 inches by 38 inches and weighs 40 pounds. A basis 80 book paper has the same dimensions as 40 book paper, but one ream weighs 80 pounds. Within each category of paper (such as book paper), then, the greater

Book paper	Writing paper	Cover paper	Bristol paper
25"x 38"	17"x 22"	20"x 26"	22 ½" x 28 ½"

Figure 18.7.   Basic sheet sizes

the basis weight, the heavier the sheet. It is not possible, however, to make the same generalization between different categories of paper (such as comparing book paper to cover paper) because the sizes of the sheets being weighed are not the same.

M Weight

Sometimes basis weight is converted to **M weight,** which is the weight of 1,000 sheets (rather than 500 sheets) of the basic sheet size of a particular paper type. A paper's M weight

is twice its basis weight. The M weight is used merely as a convenience for paper calculation.

Regular Sizes

Although the basic size of book paper is 25 inches by 38 inches, other sizes are available to the printer. If the order is large enough, the printer can specify the required size to the manufacturer. In order to meet the needs of small jobs, local paper suppliers generally stock a variety of sizes within each paper type. These common sizes are called **regular sizes.** The left column in table 18.2

Table 18.2. Regular Sizes for Book Papers and Corresponding Equivalent M Weights

Basis Weights	40	45	50	60	70	80	90	100	120
Sizes (In Inches)	Equivalent M Weights (In Pounds)								
17 × 22	31	35	39	47	55	63	71	79	94
17½ × 22½	33	37	41	50	58	66	75	83	99
19 × 25	40	45	50	60	70	80	90	100	120
22½ × 29	55	62	69	82	96	110	124	137	165
22½ × 35	66	75	83	99	116	113	149	166	199
23 × 29	56	63	70	84	98	112	126	140	169
23 × 35	68	76	85	102	119	136	153	169	203
24 × 36	72	82	90	100	128	146	164	182	218
25 × 38	80	90	100	120	140	160	180	200	240
26 × 40	88	98	110	132	154	176	198	218	262
28 × 42	100	112	124	148	174	198	222	248	298
28 × 44	104	116	130	156	182	208	234	260	312
30½ × 41	106	118	132	158	184	210	236	264	316
32 × 44	118	134	148	178	208	238	266	296	356
33 × 44	122	138	152	184	214	244	276	306	366
35 × 45	132	150	166	198	232	266	298	332	398
35 × 46	136	152	170	204	238	272	306	338	406
36 × 48	146	164	182	218	254	292	328	364	436
38 × 50	160	180	200	240	280	320	360	400	480
38 × 52	166	188	208	250	292	332	374	416	500
41 × 54	186	210	234	280	326	372	420	466	560
41 × 61	210	236	264	316	368	422	474	526	632
42 × 58	206	230	256	308	358	410	462	512	616
44 × 64	238	266	296	356	414	474	534	592	712
44 × 66	244	276	306	366	428	490	550	612	734
46 × 69	268	300	334	400	468	534	602	668	802
52 × 76	332	374	416	500	582	666	748	832	998

shows some regular sizes for book papers. Regular sizes are also stocked in each of the common basis weights.

Equivalent Weights

As mentioned earlier, a paper's M weight is twice its basis weight. Printers and paper manufacturers use table 18.3 to determine **equivalent weights** for regular sizes of book papers. For example, locate the basic sheet size for book paper (25 inches × 38 inches) in table 18.3. Notice that the M weight for basis 40 is 80 pounds. One ream (500 sheets) weighs 40 pounds, so two reams (1,000 sheets) weigh 80 pounds. The M weight is 80 pounds. Now find the 38 inch × 50 inch regular sheet size (which is double the basic sheet size of 25 inches × 38 inches) and find the equivalent weight of 160 pounds. One thousand sheets of 38 inch ×

50 inch basis 40 book paper have an equivalent M weight of 160 pounds.

There are two general exceptions to this vocabulary of papers when dealing with the four main paper types. Some bristol and cover papers are described not in terms of weight but rather in terms of points (see the Paper Characteristics section earlier in this chapter). One point is 1 one-thousandth of an inch. Therefore, an 11-point bristol is 0.011 inch thick ($11 \times 0.001 = 0.011$). Common thicknesses or bulks are 8, 10, and 11 points. Most bristols and covers, however, are classified by the more common basis weight designation.

The second general exception deals with writing papers. Although in this category the term "substance weight" is used instead of "basis weight," but the terms mean the same thing. **Substance weight** is the weight in pounds of one ream of the basic sheet size (17 inch × 22 inch) of one particular type of writing paper.

Table 18.3.   Regular Sizes for Writing Papers and Corresponding Equivalent M Weights

	Substance Weights								
	13	16	20	24	28	32	36	40	44
Sizes (In Inches)	Equivalent M Weights (In Pounds)								
8½ × 11	6.50	8	10	12	Sizes and weights normally				
8½ × 14	8.25	10.18	12.72	15.26	used for business papers—				
11 × 27	13	16	20	24	often called "cut sizes"				
16 × 21	23	29	36	43	50	57	65	72	79
17 × 22	26	32	40	48	56	64	72	80	88
17		41	51	61	71	81	92	102	112
18 × 23	29	35	44	53	62	71	80	89	97
18 × 46	58	70	88	106	124	142	160	178	194
19 × 24	32	39	49	59	68	78	88	98	107
19 × 48	64	78	98	118	136	156	176	196	214
20 × 28	39	48	60	72	84	96	108	120	132
21 × 32	46	58	72	86	100	114	130	144	158
22 × 34	52	64	80	96	112	128	144	160	176
23 × 36	58	70	88	106	124	142	160	178	194
24 × 38	64	78	98	118	136	156	176	196	214
28 × 34	66	82	102	122	142	162	184	204	224
34 × 44	104	128	160	192	224	256	288	320	352

Table 18.3 shows some equivalent M weights of a list of regular sizes of writing papers.

When printers buy paper for a job, they order it from the supplier according to total pounds, type, and basis weight.

Determining Paper Needs

Even though paper is sold by the weight, when printers work on the press they deal with sheets, not pounds. Printers calculate the number of sheets needed to produce a job, and then deal with the paper merchant to determine weight and price.

Not every job uses regular size press sheets that are obtained easily from the paper supplier. Most printers stock only a few sizes of each paper type and then cut them to meet the needs of individual jobs. Others purchase the most efficient regular sizes to match the size of existing presses and gang several jobs together on a single press sheet. In either case, the printer is faced with the task of calculating the most efficient method of cutting smaller pieces from available stock sizes.

To illustrate the process, consider this example: A printer must cut a press sheet size of 8½ inches × 11 inches from a stock sheet that measures 28 inches × 34 inches. What is the maximum number of sheets that can be cut from the larger piece? Figure 18.8 shows the two common ways of solving the problem.

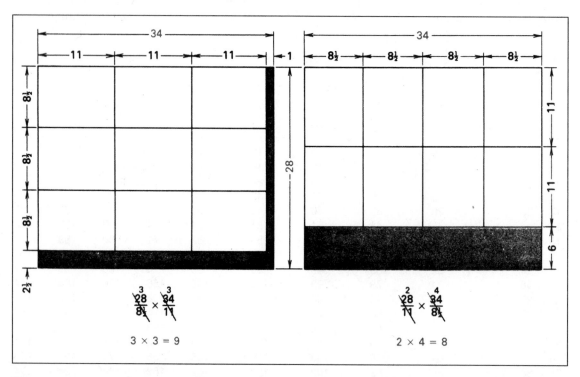

Figure 18.8.   Example for calculating the number of sheets to be cut from a stock sheet by dividing or by drawing

On the left side of the figure, the width and the length of the sheet are divided by the width and length of the press sheet, respectively. The two answers are then multiplied to show that 9 sheets can be cut this way. The same result can be obtained by simply drawing a picture of the stock sheet and blocking out the maximum number of press sheets.

On the right side of the figure, the width and length of the stock sheet are divided by the length and width of the press sheet, respectively. The two answers are then multiplied to show that 8 sheets can be cut this way. The printer, however, would probably cut the paper the first way to obtain 9 press sheets to gain the maximum number of press sheets from the stock sheet.

This procedure of dividing corresponding dimensions and then dividing alternating dimensions of the stock and press sheets is rather straightforward, but paper calculations are not always this simple. Drawing a picture of the calculations can make the process easier and often can show where additional gains in numbers of sheets can be made. Individuals new to paper calculations should both draw a diagram and work the math computations to ensure accuracy.

Diagrams are very important. Sometimes careful observation can increase efficiency and profits for a printing company. Drawing and working with the placement of press sheets on the stock sheet in figure 18.8 reveals that the stock sheet can actually be cut to obtain 10 sheets instead of 9 (figure 18.9). It is necessary, however, to tell the paper cutter the sequence of cuts.

Nonstandard Cuts

This process of manipulating the positions and order of cuts to gain an additional sheet is called making a **nonstandard cut** or a dutch cut. In an era when paper and other material can account for more than half the cost of a job,

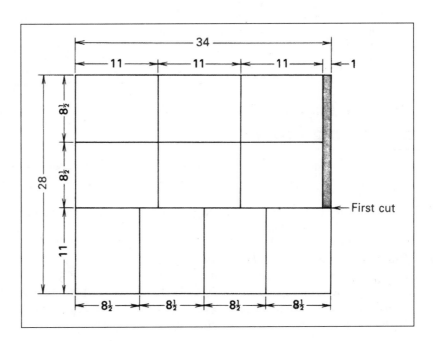

Figure 18.9. **Example of a nonstandard cut.** It is necessary to specify the sequence of cuts to be made by the paper cutter when a nonstandard sequence is to be followed.

a nonstandard cut can often mean the difference between profit and loss.

Spoilage

A very important consideration when calculating the paper needs of a specific job is spoilage. All printing processes require some start up to get the press feeding properly and the press sheets printing at proper ink density. This process is called **make-ready.** Rarely does a job not have some spoilage because of something as frustrating as a machine jam-up or as foolish as spilled coffee on a finished pile. It is necessary, then, to give the press or bindery operators more sheets than the job actually requires to allow for startup and printing problems. These extra sheets are called the **spoilage allowance**.

Table 18.4 shows a typical spoilage allowance chart that an estimator might use to calculate the average number of wasted sheets for different types of jobs. For example, if 5,000 copies that have two colors on one side are to be run on two-color equipment, the operator must begin the run with 5 percent more press sheets than the job requires or (5,000 × 0.05) + 5,000 = 5,250 press sheets.

Sample Paper Estimating Problem

To tie the ideas presented so far together, let us consider a sample problem of paper estimating.

A printer has been asked to bid on a job that requires 15,000 copies of a two-color poster to measure 9 inches × 12 inches. The printer has a basis 60 book paper in a 25 inch × 38 inch regular sheet size left over from a previous job. The printer has only a single-color lithographic press and wants to run the job in the 9 inch × 12 inch size. How many pounds of paper must be purchased to run the job?

How many press sheets must be given to the press operator?

The printer must deliver 15,000 sheets to the customer, plus a 6 percent spoilage allowance (4 percent for the first pass through the press plus 2 percent for the second pass) of 900 sheets. Most make-ready problems occur with the first pass, therefore the spoilage allowance is reduced for subsequent passes.

$$15,000 \times 0.06 = 900$$
$$15,000 + 900 = 15,900$$

1. A total of 15,900 press sheets must be given to the press operator to ensure the customer gets 15,000 good sheets.

2. How many basic sheets are needed in order to cut 15,900 press sheets (figure 18.10)?

If 8 press sheets can be cut from each stock sheet, then

$$15,900 \div 8 = 1987.5$$

Because partial sheets cannot be bought, however, we must always go to the next full sheet. The number of regular sheets then is 1,988.

3. How much does 1,988 sheets of basis 60, 25 inch x 38 inch book paper weigh in pounds?

Referring to table 18.2, the equivalent M weight is 120 pounds per 1,000 sheets.

We therefore need 1.988 M (1,000 sheets) or $1,988 \div 1,000 = 1.988$

$$120 \times 1.988 = 238.56$$

To bid the job, the printer must determine the purchase cost of 238.56 pounds of book paper, basis 60, measuring 25 inches × 38 inches.

Table 18.4. Paper Spoilage Allowances
(Percentages Represent Press Size Sheets, Not Impressions)

Lithographic	1,000	2,500	5,000	10,000	25,000 and over
Single-Color Equipment					
One color, one side	8%	6%	5%	4%	3%
One color, work-and-turn or work-and-tumble	13%	10%	8%	6%	5%
Each additional color (per side)	5%	4%	3%	2%	2%
Two-Color Equipment					
Two colors, one side	—	—	5%	4%	3%
Two colors, two sides or work-and-turn	—	—	8%	6%	5%
Each additional two colors (per side)	—	—	3%	2%	2%
Four-Color Equipment					
Four colors, one side only	—	—	—	6%	5%
Four colors, two sides or work-and-turn	—	—	—	8%	7%
Bindery Spoilage					
Folding, stitching, trimming	4%	3%	3%	2%	2%
Cutting, punching, or drilling	2%	2%	2%	2%	2%
Varnishing and gumming	7%	5%	4%	3%	3%

The figures above do not include waste sheets used to run up color, as it is assumed that waste stock is used for this purpose.

Use the next higher percentage for the following papers:
1. Coated papers when plant does not run coateds.
2. Papers that caliper 0.0025 and less
3. Difficult papers such as foil, cloth, and plastic.

Letterpress	1,000	2,500	5,000	10,000	25,000 and over
Single-Color Equipment					
One color, one side	7%	5%	4%	3%	3%
One color, two sides or work-and-turn	13%	9%	7%	5%	5%
Each additional color (per side)	6%	4%	3%	2%	2%
Two-Color Equipment					
Two colors, one side	—	—	4%	3%	2%
Two colors, two sides or work-and-turn	—	—	7%	5%	5%
Each additional two colors (per side)	—	—	3%	2%	2%
Four-Color Equipment					
Four colors, one side	—	—	—	6%	5%
Four colors, two sides or work-and-turn	—	—	—	8%	4%
Bindery Spoilage					
Folding, stitching, trimming	4%	3%	3%	2%	2%
Cutting, punching, or drilling	2%	2%	2%	2%	2%
Varnishing and gumming	7%	5%	4%	3%	3%

These paper spoilage allowance charts have been reproduced through the courtesy of the "Printing Industries of Metropolitan New York" and demonstrate how paper spoilage is calculated by printers belonging to this association.

Table 18.5.   A Sample Tear Sheet from a Paper Catalog

```
Adams Brilliant Book

   Shown in Sample Book number two.

   Processes-- Offset and Letterpress
   Color-- White
   Finish-- Vellum and Coral
   Packed-- Unsealed in Cartons
   Basic Size-- 25 x 38
                                    16     4     1    Less
                                    Ctns   Ctns  Ctn   Ctn

   --------------------------------------------------------

                             Per
   BA    Size, M Wt     G    Ctn        Per 1,000 sheets

   Vellum Finish
   50   17.5x22.5- 41M   L  3600    14.04  15.09  17.26  25.89
   50   23 x 35 -  85M   L  1800    29.11  31.28  35.79  53.68
   50   38 x 50 - 200M   L   800    68.50  73.60  84.20 126.30

   60   17.5x22.5- 40M   L  3200    17.13  18.40  21.05  31.58
   60   19 x 25 -  60M   L  2400    20.55  22.08  25.26  37.89
   60   23 x 29 -  84M   L  1800    28.77  30.91  35.36  53.05
   60   23 x 35 - 102M   L  1500    34.94  37.54  42.94  64.41
 → 60   25 x 38 - 120M   L  1200    41.10  44.16  50.52  75.78 ←

   70   17.5x22.5- 58M   L  2400    19.87  21.34  24.42  36.63
   70   19 x 25 -  70M   L  2000    23.98  25.76  29.47  44.21
   70   23 x 29 -  98M   L  1600    33.57  36.06  41.26  61.89
   70   23 x 35 - 119M   L  1200    40.76  43.79  50.10  75.15
   70   25 x 38 - 140M   L  1000    47.95  51.52  58.94  88.41
   70   35 x 45 - 232M   L   600    79.46  85.38  97.67 146.51

   80   23 x 35 - 136M   L  1100    46.58  50.05  57.26  85.88
   80   25 x 38 - 160M   L  1000    54.80  58.88  67.36 101.04
   80   35 x 45 - 266M   L   600    91.11  97.89 111.99 167.98

   Coral Finish
   70   17.5x22.5- 58M   L  2400    21.66  23.26  26.59  39.90
   70   19 x 25 -  70M   L  2000    26.15  28.07  32.10  48.16
   70   23 x 35 - 119M   L  1200    50.80  54.54  62.36  93.57
   70   25 x 38 - 140M   L  1000    52.29  56.14  65.19  97.64
```

The task of calculating paper needs can become more complex than in this example, but the basic procedures are always the same.

1. Determine the spoilage allowance and find the total number of press sheets to run the job.
2. Calculate the most efficient method of cutting the stock sheets and determine the required number of stock sheets.
3. Find the total weight by referring to the paper's equivalent M weight.

Determining the Price of Paper

It is sometimes necessary to refer to a manufacturer's or distributor's price schedule to estimate the cost of the paper for the job without contacting a salesperson. Table 18.5 shows a typical tearsheet from a price catalog. (The prices here are samples only and do not represent current paper costs.) It is important that the estimator have an understanding of price differences according to the quantity of paper

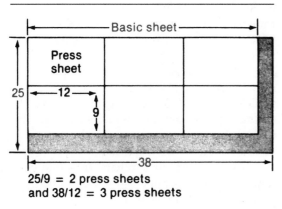

25/9 = 2 press sheets
and 38/12 = 3 press sheets

2 × 3 = 6

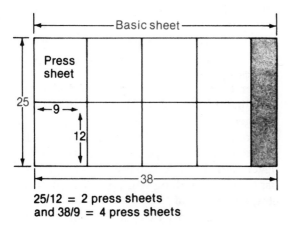

25/12 = 2 press sheets
and 38/9 = 4 press sheets

2 × 4 = 8

15,900 ÷ 8 = 1987.5
          = 1988 basic sheets

Figure 18.10. Calculations to determine the number of basic sheets needed to cut 15,900 press sheets

ordered. It is often economical to buy more paper than is needed for the specific job. Consider an example.

Assume that we need 1,100 sheets of 25″ × 38″ size for a job we are to print. The line from Table 18.5 that interests us most is:

	16 Ctns	4 Ctns	1 Ctn	less Ctn
25 × 38	41.10	44.16	50.52	75.78

Just as with most industrial or consumer products, the more we buy, the less the unit cost. If the supplier has to split open a carton to meet our needs, we pay more because of handling and the storage of the unused portion.

This is basis 60 paper, so the weight is 120 M (120 pounds per 1,000 sheets). There are 1,200 sheets per carton. We require 1,100, so we will figure the split-carton price. If the price is $75.78 per M, the cost per pound is $0.6315 ($75.78 divided by 120 pounds per M). The 1,100 sheets we need weigh 132 pounds (120 pounds per M x 1.1M). The cost of 1,100 sheets when purchased from a broken carton is $83.36 (132 pounds x $0.6315 per pound).

A quick glance at the carton price, however, shows that the price of an unbroken carton is over $30 less and we would get 100 more sheets if we bought a full box. The estimator must be aware of such price differentials and must spend time to calculate potential differences.

SECTION 2: INK

Ink forms the images you see as words and pictures in this book. Whatever the printing process, ink transfers to the paper in the shape of the lines on the image carrier.

Not all ink images, however, are transferred to paper. Although paper is the most common printing material, many other surfaces, such as metal foils, sheet laminates, plastics, and even wood veneers, are used. Because surfaces other than paper are also used to receive ink, they are given a special term. A **substrate** is any base material used in printing processes that receives an image transferred from a printing plate. The term "substrate" will be used throughout the rest of this chapter.

Properties of Ink

Three properties of ink that control the ease and quality of image transfer are viscosity, tack, and drying quality.

Viscosity

The term **viscosity** is used to describe the "body" of ink accurately. Some inks are thick and heavy (offset and letterpress inks), and some are fluid and light (flexographic and gravure inks). Viscosity, or resistance to flow, can be measured and is a term that is accepted universally in the printing industry.

Tack

Tack, or stickiness, is a property of ink that must be controlled in order to transfer images and deliver the sheet through the press. Tack can cause paper, especially coated paper, to adhere to the blanket of an offset press. Ink that is excessively tacky may also pick the surface of the paper and cause misfeeding. (Recall that "to pick" means to lift or tear small pieces of the paper's surface.) Tack increases when one color is printed over another. When printing multicolor and process color work, decrease the amount of tack on successive runs by adding a reducer. The first run should have the most tack. Each successive run should be printed with ink of less tack.

Drying Quality

The final, and extremely important, property of ink is its drying quality. There are two stages in the ink drying process. First, ink should **set** or stick to the paper instantly. When ink on the press sheet is set, it can be handled without smearing. If ink does not set when it is stacked in the delivery side of a press, the image will transfer to the bottom of the next sheet. This transfer of wet ink from sheet to sheet is called **set-off.**

The second stage in the drying process is called **hardening.** When ink has hardened, the vehicle (or solvent) has solidified completely on the paper surface and will not transfer. The time it takes for liquid ink to harden to a solid state is called the **drying time.**

Most natural or synthetic inks that contain a drying oil set and harden by a chemical process called **oxidation.** To oxidize is to combine with oxygen. When the oxygen of the air combines with the ink's drying oil, the vehicle of the ink changes from a liquid to a solid.

When an ink is printed on an absorbent substrate, drying results from a physical process called penetration. When ink dries by **penetration,** most of the vehicle of the ink absorbs into the substrate. The ink vehicle is not changed to a solid state in this drying process. As a result, inks that rely heavily on drying by penetration are not popular because the ink never hardens. Ink usually transfers to the hands when handling work printed with penetrating drying ink.

Some inks dry by **evaporation.** Resinous and other film-forming solutions in the ink vehicle pass off as vapor during the drying process. Drying by evaporation is much like drying by penetration. The volatile solutions disappear (by evaporating instead of penetrating), leaving an ink film on the surface of the substrate.

Ingredients in Ink

All printing inks are made from three basic ingredients: pigment, vehicle, and special additives. The **pigment** is the dry particles that give color to ink. The **vehicle** is the fluid that carries the pigment and causes it to adhere to the substrate. **Additives** are compounds that control ink characteristics such as tack, workability, and drying quality.

Pigments

The same basic pigments are used to produce all inks for the various printing processes. To some degree the pigment type determines whether the ink will be transparent or opaque. It also determines image permanency when exposed to various solvents such as water, oil, alcohol, and acid. Pigments are divided into four basic groups: black, white, inorganic color, and organic color pigments.

Black Pigments.

Black pigments are produced by burning natural gas and oil onto a collecting device. The by-products from the burning process are called "thermal" black and "furnace" black. Furnace black, the most popular pigment, is made from oil in a continuous furnace. Sometimes furnace black is combined with thermal black, which is made from natural gas. Each type of black pigment has unique properties. The pigments are used individually or mixed to produce the best pigment for the specified printing process.

White Pigments.

White pigments are subdivided into two groups: opaque pigments and transparent pigments. White ink containing "opaque" pigments (through which light cannot pass) is used when transferring an image to cover a substrate or when overprinting another color. Opaque whites are also used for mixing with other inks to lighten the color or hue.

"Transparent" white pigments (through which light can pass) are used to allow the background material or ink to be seen. Transparent whites are used to reduce the color strength of another ink, to produce a tint of another color, and to extend or add to some of the more costly materials in the ink's formula.

Transparent pigments are often referred to as "extenders" or "extender base."

Organic pigments.

Organic pigments are derived from living organisms. All organic pigments contain carbon and hydrogen, and most are made from petroleum; however, coal, wood, animal fats, and vegetable oils are also used in organic pigment manufacture. The major advantages organic pigments have over inorganic pigments is that organic pigments provide a wider selection of colors and tend to be richer in color, brighter, more transparent, and purer. These qualities are important, particularly for four-color process printing.

Inorganic Pigments

Inorganic pigments are chemical compounds that are typically formed by precipitation. When inorganic pigments are formed, chemical solutions are mixed together and a chemical reaction takes place that produces an insoluble pigment (one that cannot be broken into the primary chemicals from which it was formed). The insoluble pigment is then allowed to precipitate (settle) and is filtered out of the mixture and dried. Eventual pigment color is determined by the proportions of the chemicals in solution. Cadmium yellow, for example, may contain the chemical cadmium sulfide in a compound with zinc sulfide. Inks made with inorganic pigments are less expensive to produce than those made with organic pigments. Although inorganic inks have good opacity, they lack some of the positive qualities of organic pigment inks, such as transparency.

Vehicles

The printing process and drying system determine the vehicle used in the manufacturing process. As mentioned earlier, the vehicle of an ink is the liquid portion that holds and carries the pigment. The vehicle also provides workability and drying properties and binds the pigment to the substrate after the ink has dried.

Each vehicle used in the manufacture of ink has a slightly different composition. Non-drying vehicles used in newspaper and comic book production are made from penetrating oils such as petroleum and rosin. Resins are added to the oil base to control tack and flow.

Most letterpress and offset inks dry by oxidation. Linseed oil and litho varnish are the most widely used drying vehicles for these inks. The way in which the oil and varnish are "cooked" or prepared determines the viscosity of the final ink.

Gravure inks for paper consist of hydrocarbon solvents mixed with gums and resins. This combination causes rapid evaporation with or without heat. Naturally, the evaporation rate increases with the use of heat. Plastic, glassine, foil, and board inks are made with lacquer solvents and resins.

Alcohol and other fast-evaporating solvents that are combined with resins or gums are used to produce flexographic inks. Flexographic and gravure printing are capable of imaging many substrates. The substrate's surface characteristics determine the final ingredients of the vehicle.

Screen printing inks dry by evaporation and oxidation. Therefore, a solvent-resin vehicle is used in their manufacture.

Offset and letterpress "heat-set inks" are made from varnishes or soaps and hydrocarbon resins dissolved in petroleum solvents.

"Quick-setting inks" used for offset and letterpress consist of resin, oil, and solvent. During the drying process the solvent is absorbed by the substrate, leaving an ink film of resin and oil that dries by oxidation.

Additives

Additives are added to ink during the manufacturing process, and some are added in the press room to give the ink special characteristics. Additives can reduce ink if it is too stiff. They can make ink less tacky or shorten its drying time. Additives should not be used carelessly, however. Many inks are "ready to use" and in normal situations will image best as they are. When you use additives, be sure they are compatible with the ink's vehicle. The following list identifies major additives and describes their uses:

- *Reducers:* Varnishes, solvents, oils, or waxy or greasy compounds that reduce the tack or stickiness of ink. They also aid ink penetration and setting.
- *Driers:* Metallic salts added to inks to speed oxidation and drying of the oil vehicle. Cobalt, manganese, and lead are commonly used metallic salts. Cobalt is the most effective drier.
- *Binding varnish:* A viscous varnish used to toughen dried ink film. Can increase image sharpness, resist emulsification, eliminate chalking, and improve drying. Emulsification occurs in offset lithography when excessive fountain solution mixes with the ink. The result of emulsification is an ink that actually appears to break down and becomes greasy looking.
- *Waxes:* Usually cooked into the vehicle during the manufacturing process. Can be added to the ink later in the process. Paraffin wax, beeswax, carnauba wax, microcrystalline, ozokerite, and polyethylene are commonly used waxes. Wax helps prevent set-off and sheet sticking. Wax also "shortens" the ink — that is, it limits the ink's ability to stretch or web.
- *Antiskinning agents:* Prevent ink on ink rollers from forming a skin and drying on the press. If these agents are used excessively, the ink will not dry on the paper.
- *Cornstarch:* Can be used to add body to a thin ink. Also helps prevent set-off.

Calculating Ink Usage

A challenge for every printer when estimating the price of a job is to determine ink costs. For short-run jobs, ink expense is minimal and the cost is often ignored in final calculations. This approach is shortsighted, however, because ink costs then come out of profits.

Ink mileage charts are available for every ink type manufactured (table 18.6). They typically show the number of thousand square inches of area that can be covered by one pound of ink. Of course, coverage varies by printing process and type of paper or substrate. In practice, a ruler is used to measure area.

Figure 18.11 shows a layout for a job about to be printed. The order is for 50,000 final posters, printed in black on newsprint. It makes no difference when calculating ink coverage that the job will be run four-up (see chapter 4). Whether the job is ganged or run one final sheet at a time, the same number of ink inches will be printed.

Estimating the actual square inches of coverage is not an exact science. The inexact nature of this problem is compounded with the use of tints. Does a 10 inch × 10 inch area with a 50-percent tint count as 100 square inches of

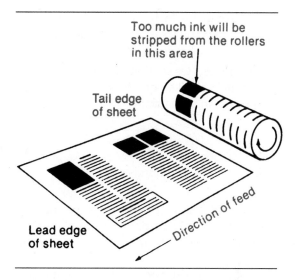

Figure 18.11. A job layout evaluated for ink coverage

coverage (10 × 10) or 50 square inches [(10 × 10) ÷2]? The answer is actually nearer 50 than 100. In any calculations, estimated coverage is determined by the experience of the craftperson.

Returning to figure 18.11, the estimator judged that the job covered 10 square ink inches per poster.

Table 18.6. Ink Mileage Chart

Grade of Stock	Black	Purple	Haven Blue	Sky Blue	Kelly Green	Yellow Lake	Opaque Orange	Fire Red	Antique Red	Opaque Base	White
Enamel	360	320	330	330	200	275	250	300	250	310	250
Litho coated	300	300	280	300	175	240	180	240	200	265	200
Label	240	250	250	220	155	190	160	190	165	195	165
Dull coated	205	200	200	205	120	160	130	170	140	190	140
Newsprint	150	155	150	140	160	110	140	130	105	110	104
Antique finish	135	120	130	120	140	95	115	110	90	95	90
Machine finish	180	170	180	170	180	100	140	130	125	120	120

The numbers indicate the approximate number of thousand square inches of area that one pound of offset litho ink will cover on a standard sheet-fed press.

10 square ink inches $\times$ 50,000 posters
= 500,000 square ink inches

From table 18.6 we see that this ink delivers approximately 150,000 square inches of coverage per pound on newsprint.

500,000 square ink inches $\div$
150,000 square inches of coverage per pound
= 3.3 pounds of ink

The job will require 3.3 pounds of ink, but the cost will probably be priced to an even four pounds because most ink is purchased by the even pound.

This procedure is simplified in many automated estimating systems or programs. The estimator is asked to classify the job as "light," "medium," or "heavy" ink coverage. The program then includes ink costs in its calculation based upon historical averages.

Ink Specification and Standards

It is generally ink that forms the images we read as words, the dots we see as pictures, or the lines we interpret as drawings. Sometimes, images are created by die-cutting or embossing—but most of the time it is ink. The ability to specify and match ink color is fundamental to communication between the designer and printer. This section introduces the language and system of specifying inks.

The PANTONE Matching System

The **PANTONE Matching System**® is a method nearly universally accepted for specifying and mixing colors. This system is often called the "PMS system," but that term is not legally associated with the Pantone Corporation.

It is unusual in this text to identify or refer by name to specific proprietary products or services. The PANTONE Matching System® is mentioned specifically in this chapter because of its profound, unique, and far-reaching impact and use. Table 18.7 summarizes the range of PANTONE products that are used by the printing industry.

Lawrence Herbert originated the PANTONE system in 1956 in an attempt to systematize what was then a chaotic, ill-defined, and unorganized approach to specifying printing ink colors. Every printer had individual color samples. If a customer changed printers, new color specifications were necessary. Herbert conceived of labelling colors by number and providing "swatch book" samples of standard colors (figure 18.12). Herbert's concept also included standard formulas to duplicate the sample colors on the printing press (figure 18.13). While the PANTONE system is today's common, accepted method of color specification, in 1956 it was a revolution.

Using the PANTONE system, artists and customers select any of the more than 500 hues from a swatch book. The printer can then mix the desired color by using the swatch number and referring to a formula guide. The formula guide gives the formula for making the color. It identifies the basic colors involved and indicates how much of each color to mix together. The ten basic colors in the PANTONE Matching System® are rhodamine red, purple, reflex blue, yellow, warm red, rubine red, process blue, green, black, and transparent white.

Today the PANTONE Matching System® is not only used for printing color control. It is applied in the fashion industry for fabric colors, in the interior design field for paint and textile colors, and in the computer field for specifying colors on color terminals across all computer-aided-design (CAD) applications.

Table 18.7. The PANTONE Matching System®

PANTONE Matching System 1000
International reference for selecting, specifying, and matching printed colors

PANTONE Color Formula Guide 1000
Displays corresponding printing ink formulas for each color

PANTONE Color Specifier 1000
Provides perforated tear-out chips that can be used for quality control

PANTONE Process Color System
Digitally created, provides more than 3,000 color effects, with process tint values

PANTONE Process Color Imaging Guide
Pairs a solid PANTONE Color beside its closest PANTONE process color simulation that can be achieved on a computer monitor, output device, or printing press

PANTONE Color Reference Guides
Displays metallics, pastels, black colors and effects, color tints, color and black combinations, two-color combinations, and PANTONE Colors for film and foil

PANTONE by Letraset Graphic Artists' Materials
Offers an array of markers, color papers, transfer materials, and transparent film that can be used by graphic designers to prepare compositions that reflect accurate PANTONE Colors

Figure 18.12. Swatch book samples. The PANTONE Matching System® provides color samples that can be used to identify, by number, an ink color desired for a printing job.

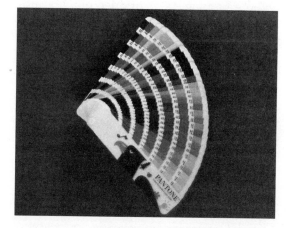

Figure 18.13. Color formula guide. The PANTONE Color Formula Guide 1000 provides corresponding ink formulas, or mixing directions, to duplicate the sample colors on the printing press.

Lithographic Inks

There are many ink formulations to serve lithographic printers. Table 18.8 charts various ink formulations for different presses and substrates. Lithographic inks are used on sheet-fed presses and on web-fed presses. A variety of ink vehicles are required because of the differences between sheet feeding and web feeding and because of the many substrates on which the printer must transfer images.

The viscosity of lithographic ink varies according to the vehicle and the pigment formulation. Some inks appear fluid, while others are stiff and viscous. An ink that appears stiff does not necessarily require an additive such as a reducer. Some inks are "thixotropic," which means they become stiff and heavy when left standing in their containers. Thixotropic ink is conditioned and milled by the ink train of the press before it reaches the printing unit. As a result, it is not as stiff and as heavy when it reaches the substrate as it was when it came from the can. The thixotropic phenomenon is typical in rubber-base ink formulations.

Rubber-Base Offset Ink

Rubber-base ink is a heavy formulation that gives quick setting and quick drying on both coated and uncoated paper. Rubber-base ink is a good all-purpose offset and letterpress ink; it can remain on the press for long periods without forming a skin of dried ink. It is also compatible with aquamatic or conventional dampening systems (see chapter 13).

Rubber-base ink can be left on the press and will stay usable overnight. After standing overnight, the ink on the rollers might appear to be setting or stiffening, however. To overcome this problem, leave a heavy ink film on the rollers by simply placing extra ink on the large oscillating roller and running the press. When restarting the press after the long shutdown, let the press idle. If the press is aquamatic, remove the dampening solution. If the press is overinked slightly, **sheet off** the excess ink by manually feeding scrap sheets of paper in and out of the ink train. The paper will collect the excess ink and bring the ink train to a normally inked condition.

Rubber-base ink works well with aquamatic dampening systems in which the ink and water travel on the same rollers because of its high tack and viscosity. When inking up the press, use just enough ink to cover the ink rollers and run low on the dampening solution. Then increase both ink and water to

Table 18.8.   Lithographic Inks and Substrates

Lithographic Inks	
Sheet-Fed Presses	**Web-Fed Presses**
Substrates	*Substrates*
Paper	Mostly paper
Foil	
Film	
Thin metal	
Ink Vehicle Class	*Ink Vehicle Class*
Oxidative—Natural or synthetic drying oils	Oxidative—Drying oil varnish
Penetrating—Soluble resins, hydrocarbon oils and solvents, drying and semidrying oils and varnishes	Penetrating—Hydrocarbons, oils and solvents, soluble resins
Quick Set—Hard soluble resin, hydrocarbon oils and solvents, minimal drying oils and plasticizers	Heat Set—Hydrocarbon solvents, hard soluble resins, drying oil varnishes, and plasticizers
UV Curing—High reactive, cross-linking proprietary systems that dry by UV radiation	UV Curing—Highly reactive, cross-linking proprietary systems that dry by UV radiation
Gloss—Drying oils, very hard resins, minimal hydrocarbon solvents	Thermal Curing—Dry by applying heat and using special cross-linking catalysts

achieve the desired density. Do not overink and/or overdampen. It is also important to keep the pH (acid content) of the fountain solution between 4.5 and 5.5. The pH factor keeps the nonimage area of the plate clean. Using additives with rubber-base inks is not recommended under normal conditions.

Nonporous Ink

Van Son's Tough Tex is an example of an ink with a nonporous formulated vehicle. Nonporous ink is suited for plastic-coated or metallic types of papers because it dries by oxidation rather than by absorption. It is important not to overdampen this ink. Because the substrate is nonporous, the fountain solution remains in the ink. Excessively dampened ink will not dry or set and will smear easily or set-off to the adjacent sheet. To prevent set-off, do not allow a large pile of paper to accumulate in the stacker and use small amounts of spray powder. An acid level of less than 4.5 will also retard drying. Ink additives are not recommended with this ink formulation.

Quick-Set Ink

Quick-setting, low-tack ink is formulated with the color and process printer in mind. Quick-set ink is usually available in a full range of process colors that will trap in any sequence. **Trapping** refers to the degree of ink transfer onto wet or dry ink films already on the substrate. Successful trapping depends on the relative tack and thickness of the ink films applied. Quick-set ink usually has very good drying qualities. It also produces accurate color and is scuff and rub resistant.

Additives for Lithographic Ink

The five ink characteristics that can be controlled with ink additives are tack, flow or lay, drying quality, body, and scuff resistance. The following list identifies major lithographic ink additives and describes their effects and uses:

- *Smooth lith:* A liquid that controls lay and set-off. Smooth lith also reduces tack, which prevents picking. Because smooth lith is a colorless solution, it does not change the hue of the ink. It also aids in the drying process. Use approximately one capful per pound of ink. If you are using small amounts of ink, add smooth lith with an eyedropper.

- *Reducing compound:* Cuts the tack of ink without changing its body. This compound is used to alter the ink's viscosity. About ½ ounce of reducer to each pound of ink is a starting recommendation (a heaping tablespoon is approximately ½ ounce).

- *#00, #0 Litho varnish:* A thin-bodied compound that reduces the ink's body rapidly. Use approximately ¼ ounce of varnish to each pound of ink (a teaspoon is about ¼ ounce).

- *#1 Litho varnish:* Reduces tack and body. It is used as a lay compound and prevents picking.

- *#2, #3, #4, and #5 Litho varnishes:* Increase ink flow without changing the ink's body. Use about ¼ ounce of varnish to each pound of ink.

- *Overprint varnish:* A gloss finish used to print over already printed ink. Also used as an additive to help prevent chalking on coated paper. When overprinting with varnish, use it directly from the can. When using overprint varnish as an additive to prevent chalking, add 1½ ounces to each pound of ink.

- *Cobalt drier, concentrated drier, and three-way drier:* Basic types of driers. Cobalt and some concentrated driers are recommended for jobs that will be cut or folded soon after printing. These driers should not be used for process colors or inks that will be overprinted. Some concentrated driers are rub proof. They are excellent for package printing where rough handling is anticipated. The ink's body can be built up with additives such as luster binding base, aqua varnish, and body gum.

- *Luster binding base:* Builds viscosity, gives ink a luster finish, and makes ink more water repellent. Mix about 1½ ounces of binding base to each pound of ink.

- *Aqua varnish:* Builds body and tack of ink. Works well for inks used in aquamatic types of presses. Aids the ink in repelling water and helps prevent emulsification (ink breakdown). Use approximately ¼ ounce of aqua varnish to each pound of ink.

- *Body gum:* A heavy varnish that increases the ink's body, tack, and water repellency. Use ¼ ounce of body gum for each pound of ink.

- *Gloss varnish and wax compound:* Increase the ink's resistance to scratching and scuffing. Gloss varnish gives ink a bright finish and helps prevent chalking on coated papers. Use about ½ to 2 ounces of gloss varnish to each pound of ink, depending on the ink's color strength. In addition to improving scratch resistance, wax compound also reduces tack and picking. It should not be used when ink is to be overprinted. This additive is good for package or label printing. Use about ¼ to 1 ounce of wax compound to each pound of ink.

Troubleshooting Lithographic Ink Problems

Many problems that occur on press are ink related. Set-off, scumming, slow drying, chalking, hickies, and scuffing are just a few. There is seldom one cause for each problem. Table 18.9 outlines common problems and their possible solutions.

Screen Printing Inks

Inks for screen printing are available in a rainbow of colors. Each type of screen printing ink has a binder suited to a specific class of substrate. Screen inks are formulated to be short and buttery for sharp squeegee transfer. These ink solvents should not evaporate rapidly. Rapid solvent evaporation would cause screen clogging during the printing process. Table 18.10 lists the many types of ink and substrates available to the screen printer.

Poster Ink

Inks whose end use is to produce point-of-purchase (PoP) displays, posters, wallpaper, outdoor billboards, greeting cards, and packaging materials are classified as poster inks. The following list identifies major poster inks and their uses:

- *Flat poster ink:* Recommended for printing on paper and board stocks. Dries by solvent evaporation in about 20 minutes or can be force dried with special driers in seconds. Produces a flat finish and is used for displays, posters, and wallpaper.

- *Satin poster ink and halftone colors:* Recommended for printing on paper and cardboard displays. Dries by solvent evaporation in about 20 to 30 minutes or can be force dried in seconds. Are used to print PoP displays, posters, outdoor billboards, greeting cards, and packaging materials. Standard colors are opaque; halftone colors are transparent.

- *Gloss poster inks:* Produce a hard gloss finish and are formulated for paper and

Table 18.9. Troubleshooting Lithographic Ink Problems

Problem	Cause	Cure
Set-off in delivery pile	Acid fountain solution	Test pH; keep between 4.5 and 5.5
	Overinking	Adjust fountain roller speed or fountain keys
	Not enough drier	Add three-way or cobalt drier
	Ink not penetrating paper	Add smooth lith or #00 varnish
	Too much paper in delivery pile	Remove small piles from press
	Paper pile being squeezed before ink sets	Handle with care
	Using wrong ink	Consult literature, manufacturer, or vendor
Scumming or tinting	Bad plate	Make a new one
	Overinking/underdampening	Adjust ink/water balance
	Incorrect pH	Keep pH between 4.5 and 5.5
	Too much drier	Change ink; use less drier
	Dirty molleton or dampening sleeve	Change cover or sleeve
	Soft ink	Add binding base, body gum, and aqua varnish
Slow ink drying	Incorrect pH—too acid	Test pH; keep between 4.5 and 5.5
	Bad ink/stock combination	Check with your paper or ink vendor
	Too little drier	Add drier
	Acid paper	Use different grade
Chalking	Too little drier	Add three-way or cobalt drier
	Wrong ink used	Overprint with varnish
	Ink vehicle penetrated too quickly	Add body gum or binding base
Hickies	Dust from cutting paper	Jog and wind paper before printing
	General dirt and dust	Clean, vacuum, and sweep press and press area
	Dried ink particles	Do not place drier or skinned ink into ink fountain
Scratching and scuffing	Overinked	Adjust ink fountain roller or keys
	Too little drier	Add drier concentrate or cobalt
	Wrong ink used	Overprint with varnish
	Ink not resistant enough	Add wax compound or scuff-proof drier

board stocks. Are used to print PoP displays, posters, greeting cards, corrugated displays, and packaging materials. Dry by evaporation in about 15 to 20 minutes or can be force dried in seconds.

■ *Economy poster inks:* Much like flat poster ink series but lack the outdoor durability of flat poster ink. Made for supermarket and chain store applications. Dry to a flat finish in about 20 to 30 minutes by evaporation or can be force dried in seconds.

■ *24-sheet poster ink:* Formulated mainly for outdoor use. Are waterproof and flexible and can withstand finishing processes such as die cutting, creasing, and folding. Recommended for poster, outdoor displays, sign cloth, and bumper stickers. Dry by evaporation in about 20 to 30 minutes or can be force dried.

Table 18.10.   Screen Printing Inks and Substrates

Ink Types	Substrates
Water soluble	Paper
Lacquer	Cardboard
Plastics	Textiles
Enamels	Wood
Metallic	Metals and foil
Ceramic	Glass
Electrical conducting	Lacquer-coated fabrics
Etching	Masonite
Luminescent	All plastics
Fluorescent	

Enamel Ink

Enamels are inks that flow to a smooth coat and usually dry to a glossy appearance slowly. Because enamels penetrate the substrate less than do poster inks and dry mainly by oxidation, their drying times are much longer. Enamel inks include gloss enamel (normal and fast dry), synthetic gloss enamel, and halftone enamel.

Gloss Enamel
Gloss enamels are used to image substrates such as wood, metal, glass, paper, cardboard, and fiber drums. They are also used as an adhesive base for flocking or beads in a variety of decorative products. Normal gloss enamels dry by oxidation and should be allowed to stand overnight. In addition to the substrates listed for gloss enamel, fast-dry gloss enamels are commonly used to image polyethylene bottles and lacquer-coated fabrics. This formulation will air dry in approximately 60 minutes or it can be cured (dry and usable) in about 5 minutes at 180°F (82°C).

Synthetic Gloss Enamels
Synthetic gloss enamels have high durability and are excellent outdoor inks. The synthetic vehicle adheres to a wide variety of surfaces.

These enamels are great for imaging metal, wood, masonite, glass, anodized aluminum, some types of plastics, novelty toys, synthetic decals, and packaging containers. They dry by oxidation in 4 to 6 hours or can be cured at 180°F (82°C) in about 30 minutes.

Halftone Enamels
Halftone enamels are formulated to give the special hues required for halftone process work. They are made to be durable under outdoor conditions. Halftone enamels are used on the same substrates as synthetic gloss enamels. Halftone vehicles dry to a satin finish (instead of a gloss finish) in 4 to 6 hours or can be cured in 30 minutes at 180°F (82°C). All halftone enamels are transparent inks.

Lacquer Ink

There are basically two types of lacquer inks:

- A general industrial lacquer ink that can produce a gloss or flat, hard finish with excellent adhesion to a wide variety of finishes
- A lacquer ink specifically formulated for making decals or printing on a specific substrate

Industrial Lacquer Ink
Industrial lacquer inks have numerous applications where chemical and abrasion resistance is important. They are used to image enamel, baked-urea or melamine-coated metal parts, and many polyester finishes. Because of their high opacity, lacquer inks are also popular for printing on dark-colored book cover stock. In addition, they are used to image lacquer and pyroxylin surfaces, many plastics (cellulose acetate, cellulose acetate butyrate, acrylics, nitrocellulose, ethyl cellulose) and many polyesters. Wood, paper, and foils can also be imaged with lacquers. Lacquer ink

dries by solvent evaporation in about 30 minutes or can be jet dried in seconds. It can be cured for 10 minutes at 250°F (93°C) for industrial applications.

Decal Lacquers

Decal lacquers are made for printing decalcomanias. **Decalcomania** is the process of transferring designs from a specially printed substrate to another surface. Decalcomanias can also be printed on any surface where a flexible lacquer ink is needed. Consult the manufacturer's literature on printing procedures. Decal lacquer dries by solvent evaporation in 1 to 2 hours.

Printing on Plastic

Because so many plastics are being manufactured, a complete line of special inks is needed by screen printers. Plastic materials are either thermoplastic or thermosetting. A **thermoplastic** material is one that can be reformed. A **thermosetting** plastic cannot be reformed once it has been formed and cured. Table 18.11 lists several thermoplastic and thermosetting materials and some of their uses. Inks used to print on plastic include acrylic lacquer, vinyl, mylar, and epoxy resin inks.

Acrylic Lacquer Inks

Acrylic lacquer inks are general purpose formulations for imaging thermoplastic substrates such as acrylics; cellulose butyrate; styrene; vinyl; and acrylontile, butadiene, and styrene (ABS). They are used to image vacuum-formed products; in fact, adhesion and gloss are improved by vacuum forming. Acrylic laquer inks dry by solvent evaporation in about 30 minutes, or they can be force dried.

Vinyl Inks

Vinyl inks are naturally formulated for both rigid and flexible vinyl substrates. These include novelties, inflatables, wall coverings, and book covers. They dry by evaporation in approximately 30 minutes, or they can be force dried. The ink vehicles can be formulated to produce a flat, fluorescent, or gloss finish. Gloss vinyl inks can be vacuum formed.

Mylar Inks

Mylar inks are formulated to image untreated mylar and other polyester films. They dry by solvent evaporation in about 30 minutes, or they can be force dried.

Epoxy Resin Inks

Epoxy resin inks are formulated for difficult-to-print surfaces such as phenolics, polyesters, melamines, silicones, and nonferrous metals and glass. Epoxy inks dry by a chemical process called **polymerization** and require a catalyst prior to use. Once the catalyst is added properly, the ink must stand for approximately 30 minutes. This period of time allows the catalyst to become part of the solution and to activate the polymerization process. The polymerization drying process takes approximately 2 to 3 hours and about 10 days for maximum adhesion and chemical resistance. The ink can be cured in 30 minutes at 180°F, in 10 minutes at 250°F, or in 4 minutes at 350°F. Epoxy inks that require no catalyst must be cured or baked and are not recommended for outdoor use. They are used on thermosetting plastic, glass, and ceramics. They dry to a flat finish and must be baked at 400°F for 3 minutes or at 350°F for 7 minutes. This type of epoxy ink is very suitable for nomenclature printing on circuit boards that must be soldered.

Resist Inks

Resist inks include alkali removable resist, solvent removable resist, vinyl plating resist, and solder resist inks.

Table 18.11.   Screen Printing Inks, Plastic Substrates, and Uses

Screen Printing Inks

Print on Thermoplastic Substrates	For End Use
Acrylontile, butadiene, and styrene (ABS)	Safety helmets, automotive componets, refrigerator parts, and radio cases
Acrylics	Outdoor signs
Cellulose acetate	Packaging, toys, book cover laminations, lampshades, and toothbrush handles
Cellulose acetate butyrate	Outdoor signs and packaging materials
Polyethylene	Cosmetic packaging
Polypropylene	Housewares, medicine cups, luggage, and toothpaste and bottle caps
Polystyrene	Construction, insulation, packaging, signs, displays, and refrigerator liners
Vinyl	PVC bottles, book covers, decorative tiles, and building components

Print on Thermosetting Substrates	
Melamine and urea	Cosmetic packaging and electrical components
Phenolics	Electronics and appliance industry (excellent insulators)

Alkali Removable Resist Inks
Alkali removable resist inks are ideal for print-and-etch boards. They are less expensive than solvent removable resist inks (see following) and can reproduce fine lines. They cure from between 250°F to 265°F (120°C to 130°C) in about 3 or 4 minutes. Air drying takes about 4 or 5 hours. Alkali removable ink can be removed from the print-and-etch board after etching with a 1-percent to 4-percent solution of sodium hydroxide.

Solvent Removable Resist Ink
Only black solvent removable resist ink is formulated for plating etch-resistant operations such as circuit boards or nameplates. It has excellent adhesion and printability and resists acids such as ferric chloride, ammonium persulphate, and other common etchants. Removable etch resist ink air dries in 30 minutes or can be dried in 5 minutes at 200°F (93°C).

Vinyl Plating Resist Inks
Vinyl plating resist inks are also formulated for plating or etch resist operations. They air dry in approximately 30 minutes or in 10 minutes at 200°F (93°C). They can be removed after etching with trichlorethylene or xylol.

Plating Resist Inks
Plating resist inks are formulated specifically for plating operations. These inks are recommended for long plating cycles. Curing takes about 30 minutes at 200°F (93°C). The resist can be removed from the substrate with trichlorethylene or xylol.

Solder Resist Ink
Solder resist inks are alkyd melamine formulations for printing on copper or copper-treated

coatings. Solder resist inks cure in 20 minutes at 250°F (140°C), in 10 minutes at 300°F (150°C), or in 5 minutes at 350°F (160°C).

Textile Ink

The three basic inks available to the textile printer are standard textile, plastisol, and dye inks.

Standard Textile Inks

Standard textile inks are formulated for cotton and other nonsynthetic fabrics. Ease of application makes these the most widely used inks for natural fabrics. They dry to a flat finish in about 45 minutes or can be cured in 5 minutes at 275°F (135°C).

Plastisol Inks

Plastisol textile inks are formulated for woven or knitted cotton and some synthetic fabrics. These inks can be printed directly onto the fabric or onto a coated release paper. When printing directly onto the fabric, cure for 3 minutes at 300°F (150°C). When printing onto release paper, cure for 1 1/2 to 2 minutes at 225° to 250°F (107° to 120°C). Images on release paper can be transferred to fabric with an iron or a heat transfer machine. Be sure to allow the release paper and fabric to cool before peeling away the paper backing.

Dye Inks

Dye textile inks are water-in-oil concentrated pigments that must be mixed with a clear extender. The proportions of water and oil in the mixture determine the color strength. These inks are used to image cotton, rayon, linen, some nylon, and other synthetic blends. Dye textile inks dry in 3 minutes at 300°F (150°C) and in 5 minutes at 250°F (120°C). Water-soluble stencil material cannot be used with dyes because of their water content. For best results use knife-cut lacquer or a direct emulsion when preparing the stencil.

Letterpress Inks

Letterpress was once the major printing process in the industry. Much of what is known about ink today was discovered for the letterpress process. Although letterpress is gradually being replaced by other processes, it is still used to produce newspapers, magazines, packaging, and some commercial printing.

Some letterpress inks are much like offset inks. They are viscous, tacky compositions that dry mainly by oxidation. Letterpress inks include job, quick-set, gloss, moisture-set, and rotary inks.

Job Ink

Job inks are standard items in most shops. They must be formulated to be compatible with a wide variety of presses and papers. By using additives, the characteristics of job inks can be altered to be short-bodied for platen press work, to flow well on faster automatic presses, or to set properly on different papers. In many shops, a rubber-base offset ink is a common job ink for both general printing on platen letterpresses and on small duplicator machines.

Quick-Set Ink

Quick-set inks are used when it is necessary to print another run or another color immediately or to subject the substrate to finishing operations. Quick-set inks are used mostly on coated papers and boards. The ink vehicle is a resin-oil combination that dries by a combination of oxidation, absorption, and coagulation. When printed, the oil penetrates the stock and leaves the heavy material on the surface to dry by oxidation and coagulation (thickening).

Gloss Ink

Gloss inks are made of synthetic resins (modified phenolic and alkyd) and drying oils that do not penetrate the substrate as other inks do. This resistance to penetration produces the ink's high gloss. Gloss ink combined with a paper that resists penetration produces the best ink finish. Because gloss ink does not penetrate the substrate rapidly, it must dry mainly by oxidation and coagulation.

Moisture-Set Ink

Moisture-set inks are used mainly in printing food packaging. Because they are free of odor, moisture-set inks are used to print wrappers, containers, cups, and packaging materials. The ink vehicle is a water-insoluble binder dissolved in a water-receptive solution. The ink sets as the water-insoluble binder adheres to the paper when the water-receptive solvent is exposed to humidity. Atmospheric humidity or moisture in the stock might be sufficient to cause setting on some substrates.

Rotary Ink

Rotary inks are used mainly to print newspapers, magazines, and books. These types of publications require different substrates. Book papers range from soft to hard and are coated or uncoated. Rotary inks for book printing flow well and are quick setting to be compatible with these substrates. Magazines are usually printed on coated or calendered paper, which often requires a quick-drying, heat-set ink. Heat-set inks are composed of synthetic resins dissolved in a hydrocarbon solvent. Presses using heat-set inks must be equipped

with a heating unit, cooling rollers, and an exhaust system.

Flexographic Ink

Flexography is a relief process much like rotary letterpress. This economical process is now printing a variety of substrates with a fast-drying, volatile ink. "Flexo printing" is used commonly to transfer an image to plastic films for laminating packaging, glassine, tissue, kraft, and many other paper stocks. It is also a popular process for printing wrapping paper, box coverings, folding cartons, and containers.

Flexographic ink is formulated with alcohols and/or esters and a variety of other solvents. Plasticizers and waxes are used to make the ink flexible and rub resistant. These volatile ingredients cause the ink to dry extremely rapidly by evaporation.

Water-base inks are also used to print paper, board, kraft, and corrugated substrates. There are many different water-base vehicles, including ammonia and casein. However, water-base inks are limited to absorbent stocks rather than nonabsorbent materials such as foil or plastic because they dry slowly and have low gloss. Water-base inks are popular because they are easy to use and are inexpensive.

Gravure Inks

Gravure printing uses two major kinds of ink: publications and packaging. Both inks are available in a full range of colors and properties. Publications ink basically consists of modified resins, pigments, and hydrocarbon solvents. Most packaging ink is formulated with nitrocellulose and various modifiers.

Because of the increased popularity of gravure printing on a variety of substrates, ink making and ink classification has become confusing. Many resins and solvents are used to make the gravure ink, and most are not compatible or cannot be mixed together. In order to know which solvents can be used with the inks purchased, a major ink supplier initiated the classification of various types of inks by using letters. In this system, all inks of a single type (a single letter) are compatible. Types of inks are identified by letters as follows:

- A-type inks are low-cost aliphatic hydrocarbons
- B-type inks use resins and aromatic hydrocarbons
- C-type inks are made up of modified nitrocellulose and an ester class of solvent

- D-type inks consist basically of a polyamide resin and alcohol
- E-type inks are based on binders thinned with alcohols
- T-type inks consist of modified chlorinated rubber reduced with aromatic hydrocarbons
- W-type inks use water and sometimes alcohol as a reducing solvent

This method of classification indicates which solvents should be used to obtain the proper viscosity. When you are mixing ink, examine the technical data sheets carefully because ink suppliers frequently use trade names rather than "type" classifications.

Key Terms

lignin	book paper	set-off
grain	writing paper	hardening
grain long	cover paper	drying time
grain short	basis weight	oxidation
score	ream	penetration
bulk	M weight	evaporation
opacity	regular sizes	pigment
finish	equivalent weight	vehicle
coated paper	substance weight	additives
reflectance	nonstandard cut	PANTONE Matching System®
preconsumer paper waste	make-ready	sheet off
postconsumer paper waste	spoilage allowance	trapping
mill broke	substrate	decalcomania
recovered materials	viscosity	thermoplastic
wastepaper	tack	thermosetting
de-inking	set	polymerization

Questions for Review

1. What is "grain"?
2. What is "bulk"?
3. What is "opacity"?
4. What is "reflectance"?
5. What is the purpose of deinking in the paper recycling process?
6. What are the five basic main paper types?
7. What is "basis weight"?
8. What is "M weight"?
9. Why is spoilage always considered when calculating paper needs?
10. Define the word "substrate."
11. Describe how the PANTONE Matching System® is used.
12. List at least four factors that slow the ink-drying process.
13. Define "polymerization."
14. Differentiate between an inorganic pigment and an organic ink pigment.

CHAPTER 19

Finishing Operations

Around A.D. 800, Charlemagne, the Frankish king who ruled from A.D. 742 to A.D. 814, ordered every abbot, bishop, and count to permanently employ a scribe who would reproduce books by hand and write in only roman letters. The books that the scribes lettered were to be bound and stored in special rooms called "scriptoriums," which later evolved into what we know today as libraries.

Binding the finished pages of the books was nearly as important as copying. It was felt that just as each page of a manuscript needed to be decorated, so too did the case that held the pages together. The more valuable works were often encased in bindings of precious metal such as gold and silver. These books were sculptured works of art. They were often so cumbersome that special lecterns were built just to hold them while they were being read. There is even a recorded instance when a reader accidently dropped a well-bound, sculptured book and was seriously injured. He almost had to have his leg amputated.

By the 1400s, bookbinding had grown into a profession with several special subdivisions. The person who sewed the pages and built the cover was called the "forwarder." The binding was then passed to a "finisher" who ornamented the cover. When a book was destined for a great deal of use, hog skin was frequently used as its binding. If it was to be a more expensive, carefully handled volume, calf or goat skin was often the binding choice. Large, inexpensive works were often bound in thin planks of wood.

The process of binding books remained a slow, specialized craft until the eighteenth century. The illustration shows one part of an industrial binding operation from around 1880. Several activities are taking place in this room. The women at the right are hand folding press sheets that will become signatures. Each is using an "ever-in-hand paper folder," which today we would call a bone knife, to crease each edge as a fold is made. The two rows of tables to the left hold the folded signatures, which are piled in the sequence they will appear in the

An industrial binding operation from around 1880

finished book. The women gather the book together as they walk down the rows, picking up one signature from each pile. After the signatures are gathered, three holes are punched through the edge of each one by the "stabbing-machine." The women seated in front of the large power wheel to the back are all involved with hand sewing the signatures together by passing thread through the punched holes. On the floor below, the sewed books are trimmed, glue is applied to the backs, and covers are put in place.

The bindery of 1880 may look a bit crude to us today, but it was a big step beyond the tedious book work of five hundred years before. The work that took months to complete in 1400 took only days in 1880. The same job can be done today in only a few minutes.

Objectives for Chapter 19

After completing this chapter, you will be able to:

- Define the term "finishing operations."
- List the steps in safely operating an industrial paper cutter and identify machine parts, safety steps, size adjustment, and actual cutting.

- Describe the basic folding devices and differentiate between knife folders and buckle folders.
- List and define the common assembling processes, including gathering, collating, and inserting.
- Describe and explain the advantages of in-line finishing.

▌ List and define the common binding processes, including adhesive binding, side binding, saddle binding, self covers, soft covers, and casebound covers.

▌ Describe several uses of demographic binding.

▌ Recall that finishing is not the final step in printing production, but is followed by packaging, shipping, and billing.

Introduction

Few printing jobs are delivered to the customer in the form in which they leave the printing press. Some work, such as simple business forms or posters, requires no additional handling other than boxing or wrapping. However, the vast majority of printed products require some sort of additional processing to meet the job requirements. The operations performed after the job has left the press are called **finishing.** Sometimes the term "post-press" is used.

A printer might do all the work on a complex book job through the press, and then hire another company to doing the binding. Because of the specialized nature of some finishing operations, and the high cost of equipment, some companies offer bindery services to other printers. Recall from chapter 1 these types of companies are called **trade shops**. Most organizations, however, have a small section in the plant that does common finishing operations.

Larger companies that handle repetitive types of jobs, such as book printing, might actually attach finishing equipment to the press to create a continuous operation. This is called **in-line finishing.**

The most common finishing operations are cutting, folding, assembling, and binding. Techniques such as embossing, perforating, scoring, and die cutting were discussed in chapter 2, and are also classified as finishing procedures. Finishing operations do not follow any certain order or sequence in a job and are not necessarily all performed on the same job

(although it is possible). The following sections examine some basic techniques within each of the four common operations. Because paper is the most widely used printing receiver, the discussions are restricted to devices and techniques used to finish paper materials.

Cutting

The Basic Cutting Device

The basic paper-cutting device used in the printing industry is called a **guillotine cutter,** or simply a paper cutter (figure 19.1). Guillotine cutters are manufactured in all sizes and degrees of sophistication. The size of the cutter is defined by the widest cut that it can make. Its sophistication is defined by the speed with which it can be set up and take a cut.

The bed of the guillotine cutter is a flat table that holds the paper pile. The back guide, or fence, is movable and is usually calibrated with some measurement system that tells the operator the distance of the guide from the cutter blade (figure 19.2). The side guides are stationary and are always at perfect right angles to the edge of the bed. The clamp is a metal bar that can be lowered into contact with the paper pile before a cut is made. Its purpose is to compress the pile to remove air and to keep the paper from shifting during the cut. The cutter blade itself is usually mounted up away from the operator's view and hands. When

Figure 19.1.   An industrial paper cutter.
Courtesy of AM International, Inc.

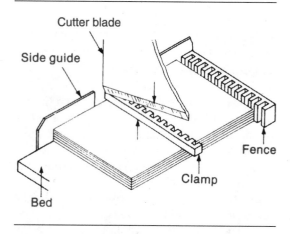

Figure 19.2.   Diagram of a guillotine cutter.
The blade of a guillotine cutter moves down and across to cut the paper pile.

activated, the blade moves down and across to cut the pile in one motion.

The simplest sort of guillotine cutter is called a **lever cutter.** The lever cutter obtains its power from the strength of its operator. The operator moves a long lever that is linked directly to the cutter blade. The most common cutting device is a power cutter, which automatically makes the cut at the operator's com-

mand. An electric motor, which operates a hydraulic pump, delivers the cutting action and the necessary power.

Moving paper onto and off of the bed of the guillotine cutter is the most fatiguing part of the paper cutter's job—one ream of paper can weigh 200 pounds and several tons of paper are usually cut in one day. Many devices are equipped with air film tables that work to reduce the operator's fatigue. With an air film table, the paper is supported by a blanket of air that escapes from small openings in the table. The air allows any size of paper pile to be moved easily over an almost frictionless surface (figure 19.3).

One of the most time-consuming actions when making a series of different cuts is resetting the fence, which controls the size of cut to be made. Automatic spacing devices can be programmed to "remember" the order and setting for as many as twenty different cuts. As the operator removes a pile, the machine readjusts the fence and is ready for the next cut by the time the new pile is in place. Some cutters can split the fence into three sections and then control each position independently so that three different lengths can be cut with one motion of the cutter blade.

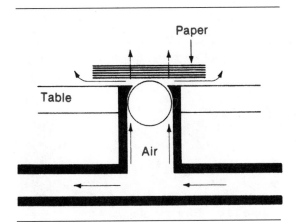

Figure 19.3. **Side view of an air film table.** A sketch of the side view of an air film table shows one of the table's small openings that releases air onto the table surface.

Cutting Safety

The guillotine cutter is named after the infamous "guillotine" that so efficiently removed heads in times past. Today's guillotine cutter is intended to cut only paper. Like its ancestor, however, the guillotine cutter will cut easily almost anything placed in its path.

Today's paper cutters require an operator to use both hands to activate the cutter blade. Early machines had no such safety feature. As a result, many operators lost fingers or hands. No cutting device is foolproof, so it should be a standard procedure to keep hands away from the blade and blade path at all times. It is also a wise practice never to place anything but paper on the bed of a cutter. A steel rule or paper gauge can damage the cutter by chipping the blade's cutting edge. This requires resharpening the blade.

Operating a Paper Cutter

Paper cutting is a critical operation. The time and effort that go into every job can be made useless by one sloppy cut. The fence and side guide of a paper cutter function similarly to the side guide and headstop of a printing press. If the pile is in contact with both guides on the cutter, the sheet will be cut square and to the proper length.

Every job delivered to the paper cutter should have a cutting layout attached to the pile (figure 19.4). The **cutting layout** is generally one sheet of the job that has been ruled to show the location and order of the cuts. Sequence may not seem important at first, but if the cutting layout is not followed faithfully, some part of the main sheet will be damaged and the job will have to be done over.

The first step in operating a paper cutter is to determine the length of the first cut from the cutting layout and adjust the fence to that dimension. Place a paper pile on the cutter table and seat it carefully against both the fence and the side guide. Activate whatever control system the machine uses and make the cut. Remove the scrap paper and pull the cut pile free. The scrap paper is generally compacted and

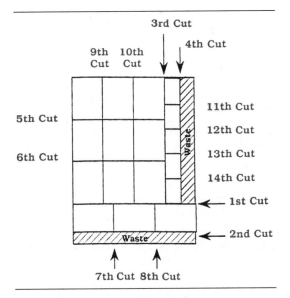

Figure 19.4. **Sample cutting diagram**

Figure 19.5. A typical packing device used to bind scrap into bales

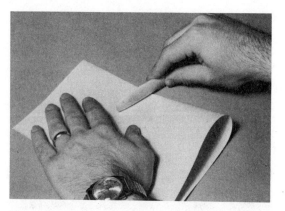

Figure 19.6. Example of a bone folder.
Courtesy of SUCO Learning Resources and R. Kampas.

sold back to the paper mill to be recycled (figure 19.5). This type of paper by-product would be considered preconsumer waste.

If the job is large and the cutter is not equipped with automatic spacing, the same cut would be repeated for the entire pile. Then the fence would be adjusted for the next cut, and the entire pile would be cut again. If automatic spacing is used, the cutter goes to the next cutting position at the operator's command.

Folding

The Basic Folding Devices

The most basic folding device is called a **bone folder.** Printers have used it for hundreds of years to do hand folding. The process is simple. The printer registers one edge of the sheet with the other and then slides the bone folder across the seam of the paper to make a smooth crease (figure 19.6). Bone folders are used today only for very small, limited-run jobs. Nearly all industrial folding is now done by high-speed machines. The two common industrial folding devices are knife folders and buckle folders.

Knife Folders

Knife folders operate by means of a thin knife blade that forces a sheet of paper between two rotating rollers. The action takes place in two steps. First the sheet is carried into the knife folder and comes to rest at a fold gauge (figure 19.7a). Just as in a press, the sheet is positioned by means of a moving side guide. Next the knife blade is lowered between the two rotating rollers until the knurled (ridged) surfaces of the rollers catch the sheet, crease it, and pass it out of the way so the next sheet can be moved into register (figure 19.7b). If sets of rollers and knives are stacked one over the other, many folds can be made on the same sheet as the piece travels from one level to the next.

Buckle Folders

Buckle folders also pass the sheet between two rotating rollers (figure 19.8). The sheet in this system, however, is directed a bit differently. Instead of a knife or some other object contacting the paper and causing the crease, the sheet is made to buckle or curve and passes of its own accord into the rollers. The sheet is passed between two folding plates by a drive roller until the sheet gauge is

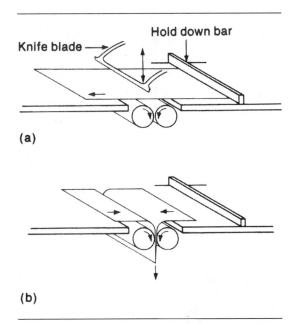

(a)

(b)

Figure 19.7.   Diagram of knife folder operation

reached. The gap between the folding plates is so slight that the paper can only pass through the opening between the rollers. As the sheet hits the sheet gauge, the drive roller continues to move the sheet, which buckles

directly over the folding rollers and passes through the two rollers to be creased and carried to the next level.

Sequence of Folds

Two important terms must be understood when discussing the sequence of folds. They are "right-angle folds" and "parallel folds." Figure 19.9a shows a traditional formal fold, called a **French fold,** that is frequently used in the production of greeting cards. To make a French fold, first fold a sheet across its length. Then make a second fold at a right angle to the first across the sheet's width. A French fold is a **right-angle fold** because it has at least one fold that is at a right angle to the others. Figure 19.9b illustrates an **accordion fold** that is commonly used in the preparation of road maps. An accordion fold can be made in a number of ways, but each fold is always parallel to every other crease. This is therefore called a **parallel fold.**

Ideally, all parallel folds should be made with the crease running in the same direction as (parallel to) the grain of the paper. Great stresses are involved with folding, and grain

Figure 19.8.   A buckle folder.
Courtesy of Baumfolder Corporation.

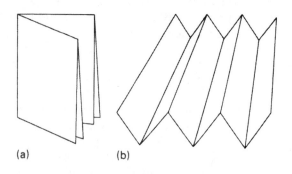

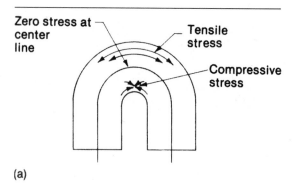

Figure 19.9.   Examples of French and accordion folds. A French fold (a) is often used for greeting cards. An accordion fold (b) is often used for road maps.

direction should be considered whenever possible (figure 19.10.)

Some folding products result from using either right-angle folds or parallel folds or a combination of the two. The sequence of folds is important and must be considered throughout the printing process.

The ideas of signature, work-and-turn imposition, and work-and-tumble imposition were discussed in chapter 10. When laying out for imposition, the order of folds in the bindery room dictates the position of each paper or form on the press sheet. Figure 19.11 shows four different ways that one sheet can be folded to produce a sixteen-page signature. It also shows the page layouts for one side of the sheet. If the job is laid out for one sequence of folds but another sequence is actually used, the final result will be unusable.

The sequence of folds is so important that the stripper always calls the bindery for a sample before starting to work on a job. The sample is a blank signature that has been folded on the piece of equipment and in the same sequence that will be used on the final press sheets. This blank signature is used to prepare the "dummy" which shows page

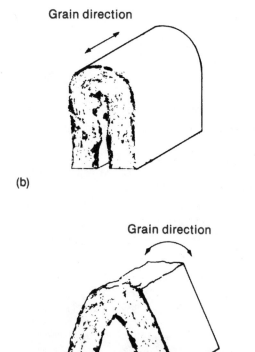

Figure 19.10.   Diagram showing areas of stress in folding (a). Fibers bend easily with the grain (b), but tend to break because of the stresses when folding against the grain (c).
Courtesy of Mead Paper.

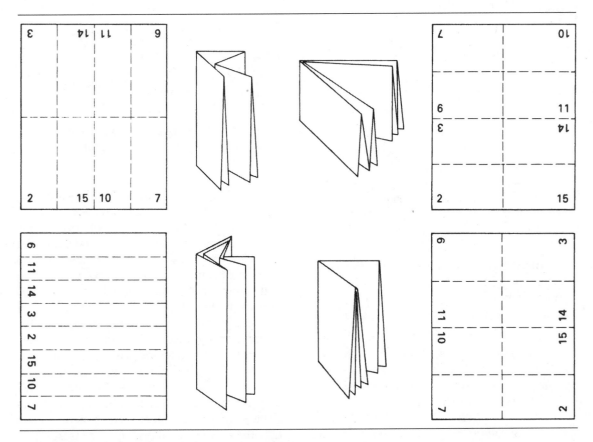

Figure 19.11. Four ways to fold a sixteen-page signature

number positions and head and foot orientation. If the stripper makes an error in imposition, then the entire job will have to be redone. It is critical to understand that planning on nearly every job starts at the bindery and moves back to prepress. It cannot happen any other way.

Assembling

Understanding Assembling Terms

Assembling is a term that is generally used to describe several similar operations that have the same final goal. Before a printed product can be bound, the separate pieces must be brought together into a single unit. For a hardback book, also called casebound, that unit might be made up of 10 16-page signatures; for a NCR forms job, the unit might be only two sheets. Whatever the size of the unit, assembling generally includes gathering, collating, and inserting.

Gathering is the process of assembling signatures by placing one next to the other (figure 19.12a). Gathering is commonly used to prepare books whose page thickness will be greater than ⅜ inch (0.95 cm).

Collating once meant checking the sequence of pages before a book was bound, but now it means gathering individual sheets instead of signatures.

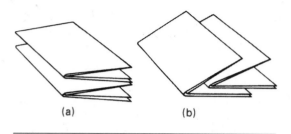

Figure 19.12.   Two ways of assembling signatures. (a) Gathered signatures are placed next to each other. (b) Inserted signatures are placed one within another.

Inserting is combining signatures by placing one within another (figure 19.12b). Inserting can be done for pieces whose final page thickness will be less than ½ inch (1.27 cm).

Basic Assembling Techniques

Assembling procedures are either manual, semiautomatic, or totally automatic.

Manual Assembly
Manual assembly is exactly what the term implies. Piles of sheets or signatures are laid out on a table, and workers pick up one piece from each stack and gather, collate, or insert them to form bindery units. Equipment is available that improves this process a bit by moving the piles on a circular table by a stationary worker. The process is still slow and clumsy, however. Manual assembly is reserved for either extremely small jobs or for work so poorly planned that it cannot be assembled in any other way. Nearly all contemporary industrial assembly is done with semiautomatic or automatic equipment.

Semiautomatic Assembly
Semiautomatic assembly machines require no human interaction except to pile the sheets or

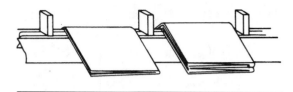

Figure 19.13.   Diagram of open signatures placed at saddlebars on a conveyor

signatures in the feeding units. In semiautomatic inserting, a moving chain passes in front of feeding stations. At each station an operator opens a signature and places it on the moving conveyor at "saddlebar" (figure 19.13). The number of stations at the machine is the same as the number of signatures making up the unit or book. By the time each saddlebar has moved past every station, an entire unit has been inserted or assembled and a saddle pin pushes the unit off the machine. The assembled unit can then be moved in line with a bindery unit for fastening or it can be stacked for storage and later binding. Little gathering or collating is done with semiautomatic equipment, but it uses the same general principle as inserting.

Automatic Assembly
Automatic assembling machines also use a conveyer device that moves past feeding stations. However, a machine instead of a person delivers the sheet or signature (figure 19.14). Almost all automatic systems are in line with bindery equipment so that assembly and fastening are accomplished at the same time.

Two designs of feeding mechanisms are used on automatic gathering devices (figure 19.15). Both designs allow for continuous loading of signatures because pieces are delivered from the bottom of the stack. With the swinging arm device, a vacuum sucker foot lowers one signature into position to be received by a gripper arm. The arm, with signature in hand, swings over the conveyer system and drops

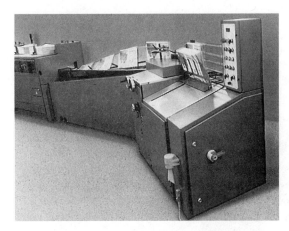

Figure 19.14. Automatic gathering during assembly.
Courtesy of Muller Martini Corporation.

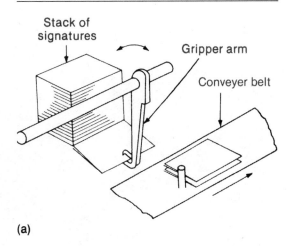

(a)

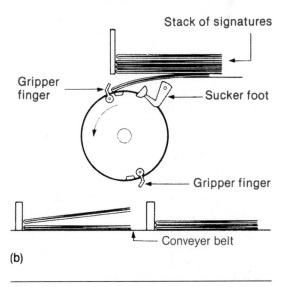

(b)

Figure 19.15. Two types of feeder mechanisms used on automatic gathering machines. (a) A swinging arm mechanism and suction action are used to move signatures onto a conveyer belt, or (b) a rotating wheel with gripper fingers does the same.

the piece into place on the belt. The rotary design uses the same suction system, but a rotating wheel with gripper fingers removes the signature and delivers it to the moving chain. With each rotation, the rotary device can gather two signatures and is therefore considered faster than the swinging arm mechanism.

Automatic collating equipment is similar in design to gathering machines, except that feeding is generally done from the top of the pile, as with most automatic printing presses. Even though the machine must be stopped to load the feeding units, the device is nearly as efficient as continuous devices because many single sheets can be placed in the same area that only a few large signatures would take up.

Automatic inserting devices also operate with a moving belt and receive individual units from a stack feeder (figure 19.16). Many automatic inserting units are part of a closed system of operations that extends from the composition room through plate preparation and press and past assembly to fastening, trimming, labeling for mailing, and even bundling of piles by zip code order. Magazines such as *Time* and *Newsweek*, with editions of

sometimes a million copies and little allowance for production time, require accurate planning, speed, accuracy, and a tightly controlled closed system of production.

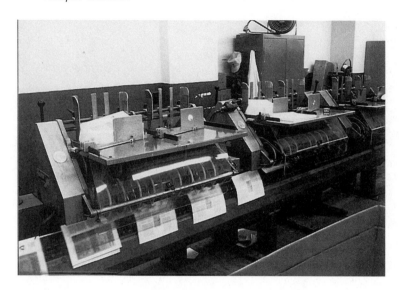

Figure 19.16.   Perfect binding machine

High-speed inserting is done by a combination of vacuum and grippers that removes the signature, opens it, and places it in the proper sequence with the other signatures in the job.

Binding

It is difficult to categorize neatly all the methods used by the printing industry to fasten the assembled unit into its final form. The type of cover used on a printed piece is often confused with the actual method of attaching the pages. Sheets or signatures can be fastened by using such techniques as adhesive, side, or saddle binding. The fastened pages can be covered with self-covers, soft covers, or casebound covers. The following sections describe the most common binding methods and covers.

Adhesive Binding

The simplest form of **adhesive binding,** called **padding,** is found on the edge of the common notepad. In the adhesive binding process, a pile of paper is clamped together in a press and a liquid glue is painted or brushed along one edge. The most common gluing material is applied cold and is water soluble while in a liquid state, but becomes insoluble in water after it dries. Individual sheets can be easily removed by puffing them away from the padding compound.

The popular "paperback" or "pocket book" is an example of an adhesive binding technique called **perfect binding** or **patent binding.** The perfect fastening process is generally completely automatic (figure 19.17). If signatures rather than individual sheets are combined, the folded edge is trimmed and roughened to provide a greater gripping surface. The liquid adhesive (generally hot) is then applied, and a gauze-like material called **crash** is sometimes embedded in the pasty spine to provide additional strength.

Adhesive binding offers many advantages in both book and magazine publishing. Not only is the process relatively fast and inexpensive, but it can be used to combine a number of different printing substrates in the same publication. In addition to the printed signatures used for most of the publication, special

Figure 19.17.   An automatic perfect fastening machine.
Courtesy of Muller Martini Corporation.

signatures or single pieces of paper, printed plastic sheets, and other printed substrates can be added to the publication. Paper of different thicknesses and different finishes may also be added without affecting the binding process.

Side Binding

A common office stapler is probably the most familiar device used for **side binding.** With this technique, the fastening device is passed through a pile at a right angle to the page surface. In addition to the wire staple, side binding can be accomplished by mechanical binding, looseleaf binding, or side-sewn binding.

Mechanical Binding

Mechanical binding is a process that is usually permanent and does not allow for adding sheets. One of the most common mechanical binders is a wire that resembles a spring coil. The wire runs through round holes that have been punched or drilled through the sheets and cover. The coil is generally inserted by hand into the first several holes of the book. Then the worker pushes the wire against a ro-

tating rubber wheel that spins the device on the rest of the way.

Looseleaf Binding

Looseleaf binding devices are considered permanent, but they allow for the removal and addition of pages. The casebound, three-ring binder is one popular looseleaf item, but they come in many other forms. An increasingly popular device is a plastic comb binder (figure 19.18). With this system, a special device is used to punch the holes, and another device expands the plastic clips so the pages can be inserted on the prongs of the clips. The binder can be opened later to add sheets or it can be removed completely and used to fasten another unit.

Side-Sewn Binding.

One pattern for side sewing a book is shown in figure 19.19. With hand sewing, the pile is first drilled (always an odd number of holes) and then clamped in place so the individual pages will not shift. A needle and thread is passed in and out of each hole from one end of the book to the other and then back again to the last hole, where the thread is tied. Automatic

Figure 19.18.   A hand-operated plastic punch and binder.

Courtesy of Plastic Binding Corporation.

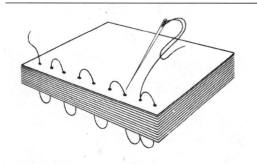

Figure 19.19.   Diagram of hand side sewing of a book

equipment has been designed that produces a side-sewn book rapidly and accurately, although with a different thread pattern than the hand technique (figure 19.20). The main drawback to side-sewn or wire-stapled side binding is that the book does not lie flat when open.

Saddle Binding

Saddle binding is the process of fastening one or more signatures along the folded or back-bone edge of the unit. The term comes from the fact that a signature held open at the fold resembles—with some imagination—the shape of a horse's saddle.

Popular news magazines are fastened by saddle wire stitching. With large editions, the stitching is done automatically in line with the inserting of signatures. Saddle wire stitching can also be done by hand with large staple machines. It can be performed semiautomatically: the operator merely places the signature over a

Figure 19.20.   An automatic side-sewing device.

Courtesy of Rosback Company.

support, the wire is driven through the edge, the wire is crimped, and the signature is delivered (figure 19.21). This method of wire fastening is generally restricted to thicknesses of less than ½ inch (1.27 cm).

Smyth sewing is commonly considered the highest-quality fastening technique in the world today. Sometimes called "center-fold sewing," the process produces a book that will lie nearly flat when open. Nearly all Smyth sewn books are produced on semiautomatic or completely automatic equipment. Semiautomatic devices require an operator to open each signature and place it on a conveyer belt that moves it to the sewing mechanism and combines it with the rest of the book. Automatic machines are usually in line with a gathering mechanism that delivers a single unit to the sewing device.

Self-Covers

Self-covers are produced from the same material as the body of the book and generally carry part of the message of the book. Newspapers and some news magazines have self-covers. No special techniques are required to assemble or attach the cover to the body of the work. Self-covers are generally restricted to the less expensive binding techniques, such as wire staple, side binding, or saddle fastening.

Soft Covers

Soft covers are made from paper or paper fiber material with greater substance than the material used for the body of the book. Soft covers rarely carry part of the message of the piece. They are intended to attract attention and to provide slight, temporary protection. Paperback books are one example of books with soft covers. Soft covers can be glued in place, as with perfect binding, or they can be attached by stitching or sewing. The covers are generally cut flush with the pages of the book.

Figure 19.21. A semi-automatic saddle-stitching device.
Courtesy of Rosback Company.

Casebound Covers

A **casebound cover** is a rigid cover that is generally associated with high-quality bookbinding. The covers are produced separately from the rest of the book and are formed from a thick fiber board glued to leather, cloth, or some form of moisture-resistant, impregnated paper (figure 19.22). A casebound cover extends over the edge of the body of the book by perhaps ⅛ inch (0.32 cm). This "turn-in" provides additional protection for the closed pages.

In order to casebind a book, several operations called "forwarding" are necessary. All forwarding can be completed on automatic equipment. First, the signatures are trimmed, generally by using a three-knife device that cuts the three open sides of the signature in a single motion (figure 19.23). The back or fastened edge of the book is then rounded. Rounding gives the book an attractive appearance and keeps the pages within the turn-in of the cover (figure 19.24). Next the edges of the signature are backed. The purpose of backing is to make the rounding operation permanent and to provide a ridge for the casebound cover. Backing is accomplished by clamping

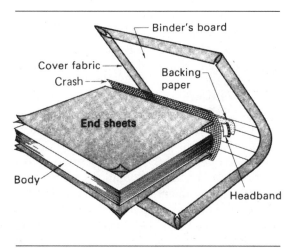

Figure 19.22.   The anatomy of a casebound book

the rounded book in place and mushrooming out the fastened edges of the signatures (figure 19.25). Next the book goes through a "lining-up" process, which consists of gluing a layer of crash and strips of paper called "backing paper" to the backed edges of the signatures. The crash and backing paper are later glued to

Figure 19.23.   A three-knife trimming machine.
Courtesy of Rosback Company.

Figure 19.24. **Rounded signatures of a book**

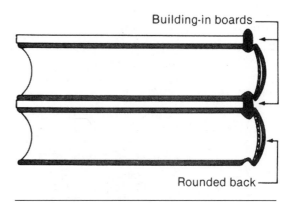

Figure 19.26. **Diagram of the use of traditional building-in boards**

the case and provide additional support for the book. A headband is a decorative tape that can be attached to the head and tail of the back of the book to give a pleasing appearance. The headband is not always attached, however.

The case itself is made from two pieces of thick binder's board glued to the covering cloth. The cloth can be printed before gluing to the board or it can be printed afterward by such processes as relief hot stamping or screen printing. The binder's board is cut so that it extends over the body of the book by at least ⅛ inch (0.32 cm) on each open edge and misses the backed ridge by the same distance. The cloth is cut large enough so that it covers one side of both boards completely and extends around the edges by at least ½ inch (1.27 cm) (see figure 19.22). The positions of the two boards on the cloth are critical and must be controlled carefully. Automatic equipment exists that cuts both the board and the cloth and joins the two pieces in their proper positions.

The final process of joining the forwarded book with the case is called "casing in." In this process, the two parts of the case are attached

by two sheets called **end sheets** (see figure 19.22). End sheets can be the outside leaves of the first and last signatures, or they can be special pieces that were joined to the pages during the assembling and fastening operations.

To case in a book, the end sheets are coated with glue, the case is positioned on the end sheets, and pressure is applied. The pressure must be maintained until the adhesive is dry. This was traditionally accomplished by stacking the books between special "building-in boards" (figure 19.26). This technique has been replaced gradually by special heat-setting adhesives that dry in a matter of seconds once the end sheets contact the case.

In-Line Finishing

Traditionally, the postpress operations of collating, gathering, binding, and finishing have been costly, labor-intensive operations handled by trade shops with specialized equipment. In-line finishing equipment links postpress operations directly to the press room. The sheet or web moves directly from the delivery end of the press into the binding unit.

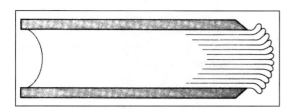

Figure 19.25. **Backing the edges of the signatures**

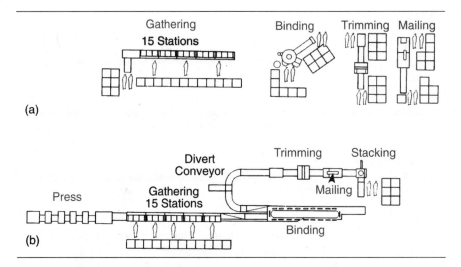

Figure 19.27. **Off-line finishing compared to in-line finishing.** An off-line finishing operation (a) may require as many as four operators and seventeen helpers to produce 2,000 to 4,000 finished units per hour. In contrast, an in-line operation (b), in which all finishing devices are connected and operate automatically, can require as few as three operators and eight helpers to produce 8,000 to 14,000 units per hour.

In-line finishing reduces the amount of labor required and speeds the finishing process. Figure 19.27 shows plant diagrams for both in-line and off-line finishing systems. The configuration in figure 19.27a illustrates an off-line design: The job is first printed, the press sheets are next moved physically to another room for assembly, then the sheets are moved to the trimming or other finishing operations, and finally they are carted to packaging or the mail room. The layout in figure 19.27b links all operations: As each individual form is printed and dried, it travels directly to an assembly unit, then to trimming, and leaves the system in boxes, ready for delivery (figure 19.28). With in-line operations a sheet of paper enters the system at one end and exits at the other as a finished product (figure 19.29).

Demographic Binding

The sophistication and intensity of competition for consumer attention has created a relatively new area of direct-mail and publication marketing. The term for this new area is **demographic binding.**

At the heart of many in-line finishing operations is a computer that not only controls the printing finishing equipment but contains information that personalizes each product element for a particular individual.

Say a manufacturer has a product that would appeal to the following very narrow part of the American population:

▪ Spanish speaking
▪ College-educated

Figure 19.28. In-line finishing system. This in-line finisher is designed to be rolled into place and set up at the outfeed side of the press. The machine can fold, cut, trim, glue, slit, score, perforate, and stack in one continuous operation. Additional folders can be added as modular units to produce multiple folds. Stacked items can be delivered directly to additional in-line equipment for further finishing and addressing.
Courtesy of Custom-Bilt Machinery, Inc.

▌ Interested in coin collecting

▌ Over 35 years of age

▌ Annual income above $40,000

These descriptors are called "demographics," which simply means characteristics of a population of people. There are companies that specialize in selling mailing lists across any number of demographic characteristics. With demographic binding, the computer can be used to link mailing information to a label or ink-jet printer that addresses each publication in zip code order.

Another application of demographic binding is selective assembly. Say a magazine has five signatures. The last signature could be designed so it to contains the same editorial content (articles or news pieces) as the original signature but different advertisements. In other words, the last signature might be printed in three different ways: one for the eastern part of the United States, one for the Mid-west, and another for the western portion of the country. During finishing, the computer then selectively assembles final copies based on address information. Thus, it is

Figure 19.29. In-line finishing. This is a six-color web offset press equipped with an in-line folder, trimmer, and stitcher. Note the computer console that controls the operation.
Courtesy of Rockwell Graphic Systems, Rockwell International Corporation.

possible for local advertisers to place ads in a national magazine such as *People* and have their information appear only in the magazines received by customers within their selling area. Magazines delivered to Chicago, for example, will contain advertisements for Chicago merchants; those magazines delivered to New York will advertise New York merchants.

Even greater personalization is possible. Surely every adult in America has received some form of sweepstake promotion announcing in print that he or she just won a million dollars. Ink-jet technology, and the new digital presses (see chapter 17), can merge demographic information directly in the printed piece—not just on a mailing label. Add further digital imaging technology to the mix (see chapters 5 and 9) and full-color pictures of the recipient on direct mail pieces will soon be commonplace.

Demographic binding meets advertisers' and publishers' demands for the illusion of personalized attention and, because products are addressed in zip code order, allows printed products to qualify for lower postal rates.

Packaging and Shipping

Those new to the printing industry think the finishing process is over after all finishing operations are completed. Even the term "finishing," on the surface suggests that everything is done. In reality, there are at least two more steps: packaging and shipping and sending the customer a bill. Billing is discussed in chapter 20.

The customer specifies the end use of a printed job. Some jobs must be packed in cartons for either shipping or storage. For example, *Printing Technology* is produced in sets of 10,000 units. The books are packed in cartons of 24 books and shipped to a distribution plant in Florence, KY. As orders arrive at the plant, labels are placed on the cartons and the cartons are shipped to a bookstore. For single-copy sales, a carton is opened and one book is placed in a mailing envelope. Most books, however, leave the bindery in boxes for later distribution and are not delivered to readers individually.

Magazines, on the other hand, leave the bindery individually addressed for consumer delivery. Some plants that specialize in magazine or periodical printing have direct links to mailing organizations, such as the United States Postal Service or alternative delivery companies. Pieces are addressed, sorted, given the appropriate indicia, and bagged according to geographic area. **Indicia** are similar to stamps in that they indicate that postage or delivery charges have been paid. They are printed on the piece directly and indicate an account number to which mailing is charged.

A very popular packaging method is shrink wrapping (figure 19.30). Individual items, or a set of several items, is inserted in a thin polymer film. The wrap is then cut, and the entire package is heated. The polymer is heat-sensitive and shrinks when warmed. The result is a strong, nearly weightless package.

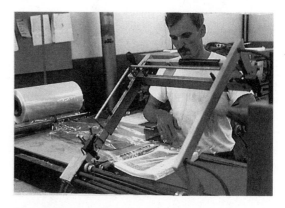

Figure 19.30.   Shrink wrapper

Key Terms

finishing	right-angle fold	crash
trade shop	accordion fold	side binding
in-line finishing	assembling	saddle binding
guillotine cutter	gathering	self-cover
lever cutter	collating	soft cover
bone folder	inserting	casebound cover
knife folder	adhesive binding	end sheets
buckle folder	padding	demographic binding
French fold	perfect binding	indicia
parallel fold	patent binding	

Questions for Review

1. What are the most common finishing operations?

2. How is the size of a guillotine paper cutter defined?

3. Differentiate between the operation of a knife folder and that of a buckle folder.

4. What do the terms "right-angle fold" and "parallel fold" mean?

5. What are the differences between gathering, collating, and inserting?

6. What does the term "perfect binding" mean?

7. Give three examples of side binding.

8. What is the process of saddle binding?

9. Explain the differences between self-covers, soft covers, and casebound covers.

10. What does the term "forwarding" describe?

11. Describe a typical in-line finishing operation.

12. What are some uses of demographic binding?

13. Why is finishing *not* the last step in the printing process?

CHAPTER

Estimating and Production Control

20

Anecdote to Chapter Twenty

Printing has made many contributions to our written and spoken language. Before printers, spelling and punctuation were inconsistent. When books were hand written by medieval scribes, words, sentences, and even paragraphs could be run together on the whim of the scribe. These words and sentences could become very difficult to read. Spaces between words, commas, periods, and other marks were invented by early printers to act as signals to the reader. There are many examples of printers' language in conversation today. Two examples are the terms "uppercase" and "lowercase" to describe capital letters and small letters in our alphabet respectively.

One of the early places to store pieces of foundry type was in a set of individual bins called a "news case" (see illustration). Two news cases were necessary to store a complete alphabet. There was one case for the minuscule, or small, letters and another for the majuscule, or capital, letters. In practice, the printer placed the case holding the capital letters above the case containing the small letters.

When the master printer wanted a certain letter, he would call out to his "devil" (a worker with less status than an apprentice) "Get me a *C* from the upper case." When he was trying to save time he would shout, "Get me an upper case *C*." This is how the terms "uppercase" and "lowercase" were born.

These terms have been accepted as the nicknames for the capital and small characters in our alphabet and are a direct result of the language of the early relief printers.

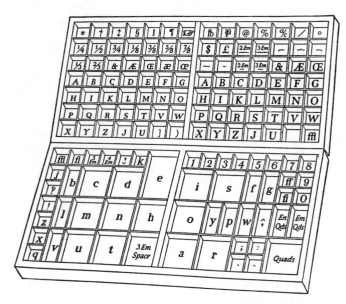

One of two news cases necessary to store a complete alphabet.
Courtesy of Mackenzie and Harris, Inc.

Objectives for Chapter 20

After completing this chapter, you will be able to:

▌ Explain how estimates are determined for the length of time required to complete a task and how to use a unit/time standards form.

▌ Explain how fixed costs are identified and determined in production costs.

▌ Outline the basic job estimating process.

▌ Discuss how a job work order is used to direct a job through scheduling and production control.

▌ Describe the major components of an automated data collection and information management system.

Introduction

Printing is an exciting industry. Few other enterprises attract such devotion, commitment, and enthusiasm from its participants. The expression "I've got printer's ink in my blood" expresses the special relationship between worker and craft. The printing craft—the process of translating ideas into physical forms that can be communicated to millions of other people—is so appealing that printers often lose sight of the true aim of their business. In America, the purpose of commercial organizations is to make profits.

What is "profit"? In the simplest terms, profit is the numeric difference between what it costs to perform a task or service and what the customer pays. However, as with most things in life, profit is usually not that simple. Sometimes it is difficult to anticipate all costs associated with a task.

Say you are hired by a neighbor to spend two days digging post holes for a new fence. You work 8 hours the first day and are paid $5 per hour. You have a $40 profit. Your neighbor then asks you to bring a spade the second day. You buy a spade for $19.20. At the end of the second day your profit is now only $40 − $19.20, or $20.80. Obviously, having to buy the spade decreased your profits. You now own the spade, however.

If you can find other jobs digging post holes with the spade, your profit will go up. Say you are able to obtain 10 days of work with another neighbor. You can spread out the cost of the spade over those 10 days ($19.20 ÷ 10 = $1.92). If you charge $1.92 of the spade against your profit for each day, then your "net profit" each day is $40 − $1.92, or $38.08.

What you have done is to amortize the cost of your spade over the entire digging job. If you had many more digging jobs, then the daily cost of the tool would go down, and your profit would continue to go up. **Amortization** is the process of distributing equipment costs across time periods or jobs. The term **depreciation** is often used with amortization interchangebly, but depreciation more accurately refers to annual decreasing value because of amortization.

The previous scenario is easy to understand. However, what if you had to buy a shovel on the third day of work, a special set of wire cutters on the fourth, replace worn gloves on the sixth, and buy a hammer on the eighth? The process of amortization and determining profit could then require more thought.

Managing a printing company profitably is even more complex than this. The company must earn a profit or it will go out of business.

This chapter introduces basic concepts in three key areas:

▪ Determining real printing costs
▪ Job estimating
▪ Production planning

Determining Real Printing Costs

There are three major **cost centers** in any manufacturing operation:

▪ Human labor
▪ Fixed costs (equipment and facilities)
▪ Raw materials

The most critical cost center is human labor. Included in this first category are all the people who work in the company—salespeople, estimators, accountants, managers, clerical staff—not just craftspeople.

Fixed costs include items for which there would be expenses whether the company printed 1 job or 10,000 jobs in a year. The physical space the organization occupies must be leased or provided for by monthly mortgage payments. The space must be heated or cooled, it must have lights, and it must have normal utilities. Most people think of presses as normal printing equipment, but literally hundreds of other tools, such as storage cabinets, telephones, computers, printers, desks, and wastebaskets, must all be in place and ready to use when an order arrives. Even if no job comes in the front door, the expenses for the equipment and facilities remain.

Raw materials are obvious needs. Ink and paper have been the foundation of printing for more than five hundred years. However, other supplies—chemicals, rags, razor blades, pencils, and even toilet paper—are part of running a company. Paper and ink cost estimates were introduced in detail in chapter 18. As a result this cost center is not discussed here.

It would be easy if a company could perform a job, measure the amount of time it took, and then bill the customer. Unfortunately, few orders come in with the direction "just bill me." Clients want to know the cost before the job is performed. This prediction is called a **job estimate** or a bid.

Therefore, every company must know how long it takes to perform a specific task. Without information on time and cost standards, it is impossible to predict the cost of a job accurately. A bid would be either so low that the company loses money or so high that a competitor gets the job.

Determining the Cost of Human Labor

A variety of techniques are used by the printing industry to determine labor standards. The complexity or simplicity of the procedures depends on the size and diversity of the business. A small "quick print" company that uses only one sheet size sold in units of one hundred will have one standard—a set amount of dollars per one hundred sheets. A large job shop, on the other hand, might need to determine labor standards for as many as one thousand different operations. Let us consider the procedures that a medium-sized job shop might use to determine labor costs. In this case "medium size" means from 30 to 50 employees and gross annual sales around $4 million.

Figure 20.1 shows a typical form used in any department of the plant to determine unit/time standards. The department supervisor maintains this form for each operation or piece of equipment. Some supervisors record every job; others select only a random sample of each week's work to be entered on the form. In either instance, an entry is simply the average time needed to complete a specified number of units for a specific operation.

The example in figure 20.1 is concerned with determining the average time to print 1,000 sheets of paper in the press section on a GTO press. On July 9, Mike Wick ran 5,000 sheets in 1.13 hours. The "unit quantity" in this case is 1,000 sheets, so Wick ran 5 units ($5,000 \div 1,000 = 5$). This run averaged 0.23 hours per unit (1.13 hours $\div$ 5 units = 0.23 hours per unit). The supervisor took a random sample of work on the GTO press for six dif-

ferent press operators across several shifts and several days and recorded them on the form. In each case the average time per unit (1,000 sheets), or the target unit quantity, was determined.

Industry has found it more convenient to record time in decimal units instead of hours, minutes, and seconds. It is far simpler to multiply $12.00 per hour times 1.13 rather than 1 hour, 7 minutes, and 48 seconds. The number *1.13* is a decimal equivalent of 1 hour, 7 minutes, and 48 seconds.

The arithmetic to determine a decimal equivalent is easy to follow:

1. Convert 48 seconds to minutes:

   48 seconds/60 seconds in one minute = 0.8 minutes

2. Convert minutes to hours:

   a. 7 minutes + 0.8 minutes = 7.8 minutes
   b. 7.8 minutes/60 minutes in an hour = 0.13 hours

3. Combine all units:

   1 hour + 0.13 hours (7 minutes and 48 seconds) = 1.13 hours

When the supervisor determined the labor standards sheet was full in figure 20.1, the "average hours per unit" column was totaled (2.39) and that total was divided by the number of entries (9) to give the standard time needed to print 1,000 sheets (0.27 hours).

When a request for an estimate comes in that calls for 7,500 sheets to be printed on the GTO, the estimator uses this labor standard to determine how long it will take to print the job:

7,500 sheets = 7.5 units (7,500 $\div$ 1,000)
7.5 units $\times$ 0.27 hours per unit = 2.025 hours

Standards Sheet

Thomas E. Schildgen & Associates, Inc.

Description		Department		Equipment		Unit Quantity
Labor		Press		GTO		1,000 sheets

Entry	Date	Employee	Units	Total Hours	Average Hours per Unit
1	7/9	Mike Wick	5	1.13	0.23
2	7/9	Will Romano	7	1.44	0.21
3	7/10	Joe Metcalf	2	0.88	0.44
4	7/10	Mike Wick	4	0.82	0.21
5	7/10	Bill Mulvey	10	2.1	0.21
6	7/11	Phil Age	5	0.98	0.20
7	7/11	Mike Wick	2	0.9	0.45
8	7/11	Doug Clayton	6	1.3	0.22
9	7/11	Will Romano	5	1.2	0.24

Total   2.39

Total (2.39) ÷ No. Entries (9) = 0.27

Standard for this Sample = | .27 hrs / M |

Figure 20.1.　**A typical unit/time standards form**

Multiply 2.025 by the hourly rate to get the press labor cost for the job.

This procedure can be duplicated in each department of the company. A master list can then be compiled for the estimator to use when preparing any job bid (figure 20.2). Some companies keep track of production standards continually and update their master lists weekly. Others merely spot-check their standards monthly or quarterly.

Computer-based management and estimating systems typically have applications that capture and update labor standards continually. When the press operator logs a job number into the press controls, the information is recorded in memory. When the job is done and logged off, the time is recorded in program memory automatically. These systems are discussed in greater detail later in this chapter.

Some printing companies keep no standards. They rely upon average industry standards provided through publications such as the *Franklin Printing Catalog*. These publications

Standard Labor per Unit Quantity *Thomas E. Schildgen & Associates, Inc.*		
Section	**Unit Quantity**	**Standard**

Composition	Body comp
	    100 m, 6-10 point
	Headlines
	    50 inches
		0.20 hour
		
		0.15 hour

Electronic	Disk conversion
	    variable
	Linotronic output
	    10 A4 pages
		variable
		
		0.80 hour

Stripping	Single color
	    12 x 19, one flat
	    19 x 24, one flat
	For each additional color
	    12 x 19, one flat
	    19 x 24, one flat
		
		0.25 hour
		0.48 hour
		
		0.34 hour
		0.58 hour

Plate	Plates, surface, one side 12 x 18 1/2, one flat For each additional burn	 0.30 hour 0.12 hour

Press, GTO	Single-color job
	    Make-ready
	    1,000 sheets
	Each additional color
	    Flat color, 1,000 sheets
	    Process color, 1,000 sheets
	Wash-up per additional color
		
		0.42 hour
		0.20 hour
		
		0.20 hour
		0.30 hour
		0.35 hour

Finishing	Single fold
	    11 x 17 or less, 1000 sheets
	Double fold
	    11 x 17 or less, 1000 sheets
		
		0.24 hour
		
		0.38 hour

Figure 20.2. **Part of a master list used by estimators to prepare job bids**

suggest what to charge for different types of jobs. However, without plant-specific performance standards no organization can truly know if it is maximizing profits or losing money on jobs.

Determining Fixed Costs

In any business there are expenses that are difficult to determine when completing a job estimate. How many paper clips should be charged to that job? What was the cost of the electricity used to operate the camera lights for five negatives? How much water was used to wash the press operators' hands at the end of the day, and what job should be charged? When considered individually these items are small. But when summed over the span of a year, they become significant. They are expenses that must somehow be included in the final charge for each job.

Per Hour Cost Factor Technique
One technique of distributing fixed costs across many jobs is to add a fixed factor to each productive hour spent on every job. Determinating that fixed amount is a bit involved, but it is a fairly accurate method of accounting for the difficult-to-measure expenses of any business. Much of the preparatory data collection needed here is also necessary for other techniques, such as adding an overhead factor to each job (see the following section).

Consider figure 20.3, a floor plan of Thomas E. Schildgen & Associates, Inc. This is a typical—although imaginary—medium-sized printing company. By reviewing previous years' bills, Schildgen determined the company has a fixed annual building cost of $17,040.

If this were a startup company, the figures needed to calculate this cost could be projected easily from the following documents and sources:

- Annual lease contract
- Maintenance contract with an outside organization
- An insurance agent who can provide an accurate estimate of annual insurance costs.
- City or town officials who know the building's exact assessed valuation and annual taxes

- Utility and telephone companies that provide base cost estimates

There are 15,600 square feet in the Schildgen building. To determine annual fixed costs per square foot, divide $17,040 by 15,600; it will cost Thomas E. Schildgen & Associates $1.09 per square foot each year to operate the building.

By measuring the square feet of every building section it is possible to assign a portion of fixed annual costs to each area of the building. Refer to the first three columns of table 20.1a. Each department is listed with its square feet (S.F.). To determine the figures for the "Fixed Building Costs by Dept." column, multiply the "S.F. by Dept." column and the "Fixed Cost per S.F."

Another cost that is difficult to apportion to each job is equipment expense (remember the spade story). Somehow the cost of the presses, platemakers, cameras, and all the other equipment must be paid for. Their combined cost is so great that no single job could cover it, however. Annual depreciation is arrived at by dividing the total cost for each piece of equipment by the number of years it should be productive. Table 20.2 shows annual depreciation for two units in the press department. The equipment manufacturers (and the Internal Revenue Service) have determined that with proper maintenance and service these two presses will each last 10 years. Their purchase prices are then divided by 10 to determine the annual cost that must be covered so that at the end of the life of each press a new press can be purchased.

The fourth column in table 20.1a lists equipment depreciation for each department. These figures were determined in the same manner as with the two presses in table 20.2. These amounts are then added to the fixed building cost in the third column. The resulting sums represent the amount that must be

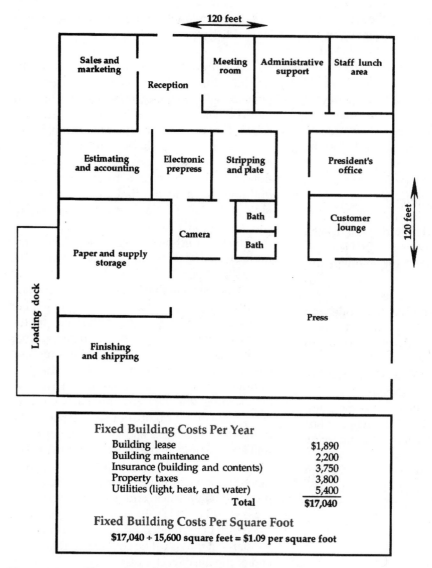

Figure 20.3.   **Floor plan of a typical printing company**

charged, throughout the entire year, for work done in each department (last column).

Table 20.1 shows two sets of numbers (a and b). We have just reviewed table 20.1a to determine the "Total Fixed Costs per Dept. per Year." The second table (table 20.1b) looks at determining an hourly charge. Notice that the

first column in table 20.1b duplicates the last column in table 20.1a.

In table 20.3 the total number of available productive hours per worker per year has been calculated. In table 20.4 the number from table 20.3 has been multiplied by the number of employees in each department to determine the

Table 20.1.   Determining Fixed Charges

(a)

Department	S.F. by Dept.	×	Fixed Cost per S.F.	=	Fixed Bldg. Costs by Dept.	=	Equipment Depreciation by Dept.	=	Total Fixed Costs per Dept. per Year
All administration	6100	×	$1.09	=	$ 6,649	+	$ 3,780	=	$10,429
Electronic Prepress	800	×	$1.09	=	$ 872	+	$10,840	=	$11,712
Stripping and plate	800	×	$1.09	=	$ 872	+	$ 860	=	$ 1,732
Camera	400	×	$1.09	=	$ 436	+	$ 1,180	=	$ 1,616
Press	6200	×	$1.09	=	$ 6,758	+	$ 6,592	=	$13,350
Fininshing and ship	1300	×	$1.09	=	$ 1,417	+	$ 3,890	=	$ 5,307
Totals	15600 S.F.				$17,004		$27,142		$44,146

(b)

Department	Total Fixed Costs per Dept. per Year	+	Total Prod. Hours per Year	=	Hourly Fixed Costs	+	Fixed Administrative Factor	=	Fixed Cost Factor per Prod. Hour
All administration	$10,429	+	11,520	=	$0.91				
Electronic Prepress	$11,712	+	9,600	=	$1.22	+	$0.18	=	$1.40
Stripping and plate	$ 1,732	+	3,840	=	$0.45	+	$0.18	=	$0.6
Camera	$ 1,616	+	3,840	=	$0.42	+	$0.18	=	$0.60
Press	$13,350	+	17,280	=	$0.77	+	$0.18	=	$0.95
Finishing and ship	$ 5,307	+	7,680	=	$0.69	+	$0.18	=	$0.87
Totals	$44,146		53,760						

total productive hours each year. Those figures have been transferred to the second column of table 20.1. If the "Total Fixed Costs per Dept. per Year" are divided by the "Total Productive Hours per Year," "Hourly Fixed Costs" have been determined (third column of table 20.1b).

A difficulty arises with the hourly fixed cost for the administrative department. It is

Table 20.2.   Depreciation, Press Section

	Purchase Price	Depreciation Life	Annual Depreciation
Press 1	$23,478	10	$2,348
Press 2	$42,440	10	$4,244
			$6,592

Table 20.3.   Productive Hours Per Year, Per Person

Total scheduled plant work hours
52 weeks × 40 hours/week = 2,080 hours

Paid, Nonproductive Time	Hours
2 weeks paid vacation	80
10 paid holidays	80
10 paid sick days	80
Company meetings	10
Total	250
Scheduled work hours	2,080
Nonproductive time	250
Total productive work hours	1,830

Table 20.4. Productive Work Hour Calculation

Department	Number of Employees	×	Productive Hours/Year	=	Total Productive Hours/Year
All administration	6	×	1,920	=	11,520
Electronic Prepress	5	×	1,920	=	9,600
Stripping and plate	2	×	1,920	=	3,840
Camera	2	×	1,920	=	3,840
Press	9	×	1,920	=	17,280
Finishing and ship	4	×	1,920	=	7,680
Totals	28				53,760

not possible to identify how much office time was devoted to each job. Also, time is spent estimating jobs that the company does not get, and that cost must be absorbed somewhere in the operation. Much office time is either nonproductive or is not associated with particular jobs.

To solve this problem, the fixed office cost is divided equally among all the other departments. In this case, $0.95 was divided by 5 (the number of remaining departments) to determine a fixed administrative factor. Therefore, $0.19 of "Fixed Administrative Factor" is added to the "Hourly Fixed Cost" for each department to determine a "Fixed Cost Factor per Prod. Hour" for each department of production (last column of table 20.1b). These amounts are then added to the base labor costs per department. In other words, if a finishing and stripping worker earns $9.37 per hour, for costing purposes the new charge becomes $10.28 ($9.37 + $0.91, which comes from the last column in table 20.1b). For a job that requires 10 hours of finishing and shipping work, the estimator will calculate costs in this area as 10 hours × $10.28 or $102.80.

Overhead Charge per Job Technique
Another technique to distribute fixed operating costs across many jobs is to determine a fix percentage charge. This is called **overhead.**

Refer to the upper right column in table 20.1a called "Total Fixed Costs per Dept. per Year." Look at the total, $44,146. This figure represents total building expenses and equipment depreciation for one year.

Say that the Schildgen company projected $2,250,000 in total sales for the coming year. Divide $44,146 by $2,250,000; the result is 0.0196. Convert 0.0196 to a percentage by multiplying by 100 to get 1.9%. Round this percentage for simplification and the figure becomes an even 2%. This is the overhead figure.

To determine the cost for a particular job, the estimator first determines and then sums all labor and material expenses. That total is then multiplied by 2%, the overhead figure. Say labor and materials sum to $2,210.00. Two percent of $2,210 is $44.20 ($2,210 × 0.02). The new estimate becomes $2,254.20 ($2,210.00 + $44.20).

As mentioned before, in America the purpose of commercial organizations is to make a profit. Schildgen should not submit a bid of $2,254.20 because it would yield no profit. That bid simply covers the cost of doing business and completing the work. The bid submitted should be higher. The last step in the estimating process, then, is to multiply the total estimated cost of the job by the target profit percentage. The target profit percentage varies from company to company. The estimated cost plus the profit amount becomes the job bid amount.

The previous discussion is only a brief introduction to costing techniques. In actual practice, the procedures are much more complex and involve a great number of other factors. Refer to the bibliography of this text for sources that provide more detailed coverage of this topic.

Job Estimating

Each company uses estimating procedures that work best for its type of organization. As mentioned previously, there are published pricing guides, such as the *Franklin Printing Catalog*, that give "average" costs for nearly all operations or products of a typical printing company. Computer-based applications are available that require the estimator to enter job specific information into a computer terminal. Estimated costs then display and can be printed in a variety of forms.

The Basic Estimating Process

Some companies prepare price schedules for items they work with frequently to avoid estimating every job. Whatever the method—computer application, pencil and paper, or published guide—certain procedures are always followed to obtain a final job estimate. There are eight basic steps for making any estimate. Some might expand or reduce the number of steps by combining or separating items, but the basic process is always the same.

1. Obtain accurate specifications.
2. Plan the job sequence.
3. Determine material needs and convert to standard units.
4. Determine time needed for each task.
5. Determine labor costs.
6. Determine fixed costs.
7. Sum costs and add profit.
8. Prepare formal bid contract.

When predicting the cost of a job, it is important to have all information about what the customer wants or expects. It is the job of the sales personnel to obtain all job specifications and to ensure that the company meets the job requirements within the final formal job estimate.

It is impossible to estimate printing costs without knowing how the job will be produced. It is necessary to outline the sequence of operations so time and material requirements can be determined easily. If an operation is forgotten or estimated incorrectly, the cost of that operation must come out of the profits. Customers will not pay more than the contracted bid price unless, of course, they contract for extra services after accepting the bid.

Once the sequence of operations has been determined, determining the quantities of materials needed for each task is simple. These quantities are then converted to unit amounts. The estimator can calculate the amount of time necessary to complete each operation from the standard units (see figure 20.2). Labor costs, which are usually paid on a per hour basis, are then determined for each operation. Fixed costs, or overhead, which are usually based on the time needed for each task, are then added. All of these figures are then summed, and a fixed percentage of profit is added to the total. This final sum is the proposed cost of the job.

As a last step, the estimator usually prepares a formal bid that acts as a binding contract for the company. The formal bid states that the company will print a specific job for the stated amount. The customer commonly has a fixed number of days to accept the bid before the contract offer becomes void.

A Sample Job Estimate

It is a valuable learning experience to follow through the procedures of estimating a sample job. Assume that a salesperson for a hypothetical company—Liedtke Graphics—has called on a company that would like to have an information brochure printed to explain the details of its training program to its employees. The company, Mark Sanders, Inc., would like to know how much the job will cost before Liedtke gets the job. Liedtke's salesperson records all of the important information about the job on a standard estimate request form (figure 20.4). Liedtke has found that this standard form is valuable in helping its sales personnel remember all important facts that might influence the job's final cost.

From figure 20.4 we see that the brochure is to be an 8-page, saddle-stitched booklet printed in one color on both sides of the page and trimmed to 8 inches × 10 inches. Sanders will supply composition on a Mac disk, four halftones, three line illustrations, and a dummy. Liedtke will print, fold, staple, trim, and shrink wrap the final product in units of 50. A proof will be prepared and approved by Sanders before printing. The job must be delivered to the Sanders corporate offices by August 10.

With all of this information, the salesperson returns to the office to calculate the job's cost. Before calculations are made, however, a decision must be made as to which press will be used because the press influences sheet size and how the job is stripped, folded, and stapled. If you are going to build a house and want to know how much it will cost, then the builder must be given detailed plans. Different presses, folds, or binding sequences produce different costs. In this case, a press was selected that allows a 17 inch × 22 inch sheet size. Figure 20.5 shows a folding order sketch and spoilage allowance calculations.

The seven steps in recording the job's costs are next recorded in the first three columns of the Liedtke Graphics standard estimate sheet (figure 20.6a). The list of steps is as follows:

1. Output the Mac disk copy to the Linotronic
2. Camera:
   - Shoot four halftones
   - Shoot three line illustrations
   - Shoot eight job pages
3. Stripping:
   - Strip the main job and cut mask flats
   - Strip in halftones and line art
4. Prepare proofs and deliver to the customer (two main flats, two mask flats)
5. Platemaking:
   - Burn plates (two main flats, two mask flats)
6. Press:
   - Make-ready
   - Print the job
7. Bindery:
   - Fold press sheets
   - Staple brochure
   - Trim
   - Shrink wrap

The next step is to determine the materials needed for each stage of production. Columns four through six on the job estimate sheet (figure 20.6a) identify the number of units of work and the total cost for each step. Refer to figure 20.2 to recall where these units came from. For example, the unit quantity for disk output from disk is 10 A4 pages (see chapter 18 for a review of A4 terminology). This job requires 8 pages, which translates to 0.8 units $(10 \div 8 = 0.8)$.

The cost per unit is obtained from the company's current price lists. The total material cost is determined by multiplying the number of units by the cost per unit. Notice that items for each cost center are totaled separately. For example, the total material expenses for camera is $77.00.

Liedtke Graphics

Request for Estimate

Client _Mark Sanders, Inc._   Date _7/12/9&_   Due _7/16/9&_

Address _1422 Main Street, Blacksburg, VA 24061_   File Number _10-346_

Contact _Gail_   Phone _703-954-1492_   Quantity _7,000_

Basic Description and Purpose _Employee Training Program Brochure_

Paper Specifications

		1	2	3	4			
Cover	Color	☐	☐	☐	☐	1/s ☐	2/s ☑
Text Stock _House 65# white offset_	Color	☑	☐	☐	☐	1/s ☐	2/s ☑
Other	Color	☐	☐	☐	☐	1/s ☐	2/s ☐
Other	Color	☐	☐	☐	☐	1/s ☐	2/s ☐

Ink Specifications

Color 1 _Black_

Color 2

Color 3

Color 4

			yes	no
No. Pages	**8**	Art Work Supplied	☑	☐
Self-cover	☑	Composition Supplied	☑	☐
Plus Cover	☐	Proof Required	☑	☐

Composition Details

Disk supplied, Linotronic output required

Dummy provided

Electronic Prepress

Disk _Mac_

Software _Microsoft Word 5.0_

Conversion

Camera

Square Finish _4_

Silhouette

Screen Tints

Line Illustrations _3_

Other

Bindery

Fold to _8 1/4 x 10 1/4_

Trim to _8 x 10_

Stitch ☐ Side

☑ Saddle

Collate ☐

Drill ☐

Other

Shipping

To _Corporate address - see above_

Via

Wrapping

☐ No Wrap

☐ Paper

☑ Shrink

Units _50_

Packing

☐ Cartons

☐ Skids

Special Instructions

Previous Bid Number

Reprint Likely _yes_

Required Delivery Date _8/10_

Previous Job Number _N/A_

Salesperson _Rachel Nicole_

Special Terms

Figure 20.4. Sample estimate request form

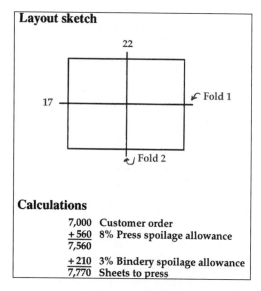

Layout sketch

Calculations

7,000	Customer order
+560	8% Press spoilage allowance
7,560	
+210	3% Bindery spoilage allowance
7,770	Sheets to press

Figure 20.5.   **Sample estimate calculations**

The labor necessary to complete each unit is also obtained from figure 20.2. For example, locate the stripping department. Notice the standard time for one single-color, 19 inch × 24 inch flat is 0.48 hour (or 29 minutes—0.48 hour × 60 minutes per hour = 29 minutes). Although the paper size for this job is 17 inches × 22 inches, the masking sheet size for the press is 19 inches × 24 inches. Refer to chapter 10 to recall why the masking sheet must be larger than the press sheet size.

On figure 20.6b, total labor units are obtained by multiplying the standard labor per unit and the number of units. The total labor cost for each production step can be found by multiplying the total number of labor units by the labor cost per hour. For the sake of simplicity, in this example we have assumed that all labor is paid at the rate of $10 per hour. It should be understood that in the printing industry the actual rate of pay depends on the type of job and the level of individual skill. The printing industry pays very competitive wages. We use $10 per hour here only to ease arithmetic.

Next the fixed operations cost must be determined. The fixed cost per hour for each department (from table 20.1) is recorded on the estimate sheet in column eleven of figure 20.6b. The total fixed cost is found by multiplying column eleven by column eight (total labor units).

For each step in the production sequence, the material, labor, and fixed costs are totaled and recorded in the last column of the estimate sheet. The total operation costs for each step are then summed and entered in the subtotal blank at the bottom of the page. Liedtke Graphics has set 12 percent as its desired rate of profit. Therefore, multiply 0.12 by the subtotal in the last column to obtain the actual dollar amount. This quantity is then added to the subtotal to find the total estimated cost of the job.

The final step is to prepare a formal bid contract to be sent to Sanders, the customer. In the contract letter used by Liedtke Graphics, the details of the job are again specified so that both parties understand the conditions, and the total price is given (figure 20.7). The actual estimate sheet is generally not sent to Sanders. It is retained by the printer to be used later if the job contract is received.

Production Planning

Before any job can go into production, it is necessary to carry the preliminary work done with the estimate a bit further. Jobs do not automatically flow through the shop. Every job requires continual planning, guidance, and follow-up. The following list outlines the typical steps involved in implementing printing production:

1. Prepare a production work order from the estimate request sheet and the estimate.

2. Determine in-house availability of materials and order if necessary.

Liedtke Graphics

Job Estimate Sheet

Client _____   Job _____   File Number _____
Salesperson _____   Estimator _____   Checker _____   Date _____

Sequence	Department	Description	No. of Units	Cost/Unit	Material Cost	Standard Labor Per Unit (hrs.)	Total Labor Units	Labor Cost/Hour	Total Labor Cost	Fixed Cost/Hour	Total Fixed Costs	Totals
		subtotals										

Sub-total (_____) x Profit (___) = _____

Sub-total _____
Profit _____
Total Job Cost _____

Figure 20.6.   Sample job estimate sheet (a)

Liedtke Graphics

Job Estimate Sheet

Client **Mark Sanders, Inc.** Job **Training Brochure** File Number **10-346**
Salesperson **Rachel Nicole** Estimator **Ron Todd** Checker **JMA** Date **7/14**

Sequence	Department	Description	No. of Units	Cost/Unit	Material Cost	Standard Labor Per Unit (hrs.)	Total Labor Units	Labor Cost/Hour	Total Labor Cost	Fixed Cost/Hour	Total Fixed Costs	Totals
1	Electronic	Lino output	0.8	$80.00	**$64.00**	0.80	0.64	$10.00	**$6.40**	$1.40	**$0.90**	**$71.30**
2	Camera	4 halftones	4	$8.00	$32.00	0.18	0.72	$10.00	$7.20	$0.60	$0.43	
		3 line shots	3	$3.00	$9.00	0.10	0.30	$10.00	$3.00	$0.60	$0.18	
		8, 8x10 line	8	$4.50	$36.00	0.12	0.96	$10.00	$9.60	$0.60	$0.58	
					$77.00				**$19.80**		**$1.19**	**$97.99**
3	Strip	2 flats/2mask flats	4	$2.30	$9.20	0.48	1.92	$10.00	$19.20	$0.63	$1.21	
		Windows & strip	7	$5.60	$39.20	0.12	0.84	$10.00	$8.40	$0.63	$0.53	
					$48.40				**$27.60**		**$1.74**	**$77.74**
4	Plate	Proof, 4 burns	2	$8.22	**$16.44**	0.42	0.84	$10.00	**$8.40**	$0.63	**$0.53**	**$25.37**
5	Plate	Plates, 4 burns	2	$17.34	**$34.68**	0.42	0.84	$10.00	**$8.40**	$0.63	**$0.53**	**$43.61**
6	Press	Make-ready	7.77		**$293.40**	0.42	0.42	$10.00	**$4.20**	$0.95	$0.40	
		Press run	7.77	n/a		0.20	1.55	$10.00	$15.54	$0.95	$1.47	
					$293.40				**$19.74**		**$1.87**	**$315.01**
7	Bindery	Fold	7.2	n/a		0.38	2.74	$10.00	$27.36	$0.87	$2.38	
		Staple	7.2	n/a		0.21	1.51	$10.00	$15.12	$0.87	$1.31	
		Trim	7.2	n/a		0.12	0.86	$10.00	$8.64	$0.87	$0.75	
		shrink Wrap	14	$2.00	$28.00	0.20	2.80	$10.00	$28.00	$0.87	$2.44	
					$28.00				**$79.12**		**$6.88**	**$114.00**
		subtotals			$561.92				$169.46		$13.64	

Sub-total **$745.02** x profit (**12%**) = 89.402

Sub-total **$745.02**
Profit 89.02
Total Job Cost **$ 834.04**

Figure 20.6. **Completed job estimate sheet (b)**

Liedtke Graphics

416 Apalogen Road
Blacksburg, Virginia 24055

July 16, 1996

Ms. Gail McMillan, President
Mark Sanders, Inc.
1422 Main Street
Blacksburg, VA 24061

Dear Ms. McMillan:

In reference to your request for a cost estimate for your employee training program brochure, we are pleased to submit the following information:

Quantity	7,000 10% overs or unders
Specifications	Eight pages, 8 inches x 10 inches, saddle stapled on the 10 side, single color (black), on our house 65-pound, white offset paper
Composition	Text provided on your Macintosh disk, which we will output. You will also provide four black-and-white photographs and three line illustrations.
Proof	We will provide a proof for your approval prior to producing the job.
Packaging	Shrink wrapped in units of 50 per package
Shipping	Delivered to your offices by August 10
Terms	Net thirty days
Cost	$835.15

A copy of printing industry trade customs is enclosed. These customs apply for all items not identified in this bid letter.

We look forward to your response and future business.

Sincerely,

J. Michael Adams
Sales Manager

Tel 703-954-1234 • Fax 703-954-5678 • e-mail adamsj@duvm.ocs.drexel.edu

Figure 20.7. **Sample bid letter**

3. Prepare a detailed job schedule.

4. Merge a detailed schedule into production control schedule.

5. Coordinate materials with the job's arrival in each department.

6. Put the job into production.

7. Check quality control and production as necessary.

8. Reschedule as necessary.

9. Remove the job from the production control schedule and send all records to accounting.

To follow through with the previous example, let us assume that the Sanders brochure that was bid in the previous section was awarded to Liedtke Graphics.

The Work Order

After Liedtke has accepted the bid and any legal contracts have been signed, the production manager takes control of the job. The first step is to transfer the information from the estimate request and the estimate sheet to a production work order or "job ticket" (figure 20.8). At this point the job is assigned a work order number. This is an internal reference used by the company to reference jobs. The **work order** is the road map that charts the job through all the production steps. It is used by the production control department to check on the progress of the job. It also notifies the accounting department to prepare an invoice. Each supervisor logs the time that the job arrives and the time it leaves the department on the work order. The work order can also serve as a means of updating the labor standards sheet (see figure 20.1).

At the same time that the work order is completed, inventory control staff must check to determine if all the required materials are on hand and are not reserved for another job. If the materials are in storage, they are reserved.

If the supplies are not available in house, they are ordered and information about the expected delivery date is sent to the people responsible for job scheduling.

Job Scheduling and Production Control

Job scheduling and production control is a problem of coordinating the most efficient combination of materials, machines, and time. This responsibility is typically assigned to the scheduling department, sometimes called production control. In small organizations this function may be only a part-time job for one individual. Large corporations, however, may have a dozen or more people assigned to the task full time.

A skillful production manager schedules jobs in a sequence that requires minimum machine changes. For example, if four jobs will be run on one press next Tuesday—two with black ink, one with yellow, and another with red—it is wise to schedule the yellow job first, then the red job, and then the two black. The lightest colors should be run first (which makes roller cleanup easier), and the two black runs should be paired together. Likewise, jobs with the same sheet sizes should be scheduled back to back.

The first step in the orderly scheduling of individual jobs is to prepare a detailed **job schedule** sheet (figure 20.9). Again, the operations are listed in sequence and the number of hours estimated in each section are identified. A sort of diagram of times is then laid out so the planner can get a visual impression of the required times and sequence. Hours from 1 to 8 are listed on the right portion of figure 20.9. These hours represent one shift. Notice that sequence number 5 nearly fills hour 7. As a result, sequence number 6 moves to the beginning of the next shift at hour 1.

Any job schedule is really only hypothetical. If the company had only one job, with each department waiting to perform its task,

Liedtke Graphics

Production Work Order

Customer   _Mark Sanders, Inc._   Phone   _954-1492_   Work Order No.   _S-1823_
Job Description   _Training Brochure_   Contact   _Gail McMillan_   Estimate File No.   _10-346_

Stock	Ink			
House 65# offset white	House Black	In date _7/30_	Fold Size _8¼ x 10¼_	Quantity _7,000_
		Out date	Final Trim _8 x 10_	To press _7,776_
		Proof date _8/4_	Bind _Saddle x x 10"_	Customer P.O. Order
		Due date _8/10_	Pack _Shrink - 50 ea_	Number: _5634_

Sequence	Department	Operation	Estimate Time	Time in	Time out	Actual	Remarks
1	Elec	Mac Disk — Microsoft Word File: "TRAINBRO"	0.64				Spell check
2	Camera	4 halftones - 56%	0.72				
		4 line - 100%	0.30				all detail critical
		8 Line output - 100%	0.96				
3	Strip	Cut Marks, strip art See attached Dummy for imposition & art	2.76				
4	Plate	Blueline proof Call Gail for approval	0.84				
5		Plate job	0.84				
6	Press	Run	1.97				
7	Bind	Fold	2.74				
		Staple	1.51				
		Trim	0.86				
		Wrap	2.80				carton as appropriate

Figure 20.8.   Sample production work order

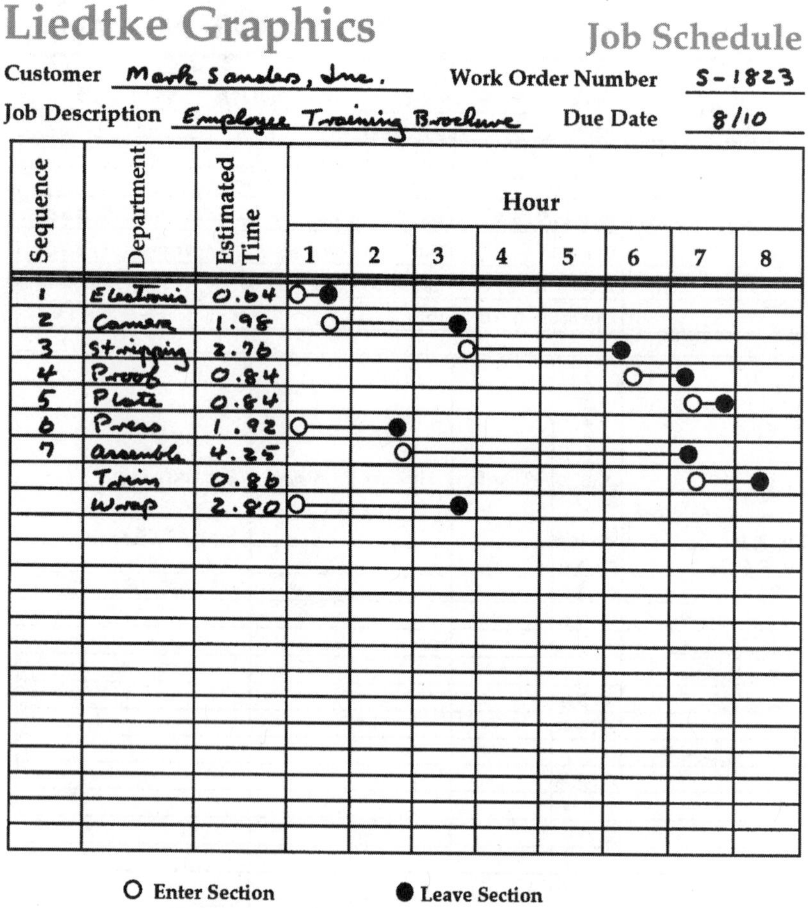

Liedtke Graphics

Job Schedule

Customer **Mark Sanders, Inc.** Work Order Number **S-1823**

Job Description **Employee Training Brochure** Due Date **8/10**

Sequence	Department	Estimated Time	Hour							
			1	2	3	4	5	6	7	8
1	Electronic	0.64	○—●							
2	Camera	1.98	○———		—●					
3	Stripping	2.76			○——			—●		
4	Proof	0.84						○—●		
5	Plate	0.84							○—●	
6	Press	1.92	○——	—●						
7	Assemble	4.25		○———					—●	
	Trim	0.86							○——	—●
	Wrap	2.80	○———		—●					

○ Enter Section   ● Leave Section

Figure 20.9. **Sample job schedule**

then the schedule would be real. However, this situation is not realistic. No company could survive with only one small job each day. In reality, each job must be merged with many others also flowing through the production sequence.

The frustration of production control is that jobs do not always conform to the estimated time. Perhaps the camera burns out a bulb, which must be replaced immediately. Paper might jam in the press, and 30 minutes are wasted removing the scrap. Materials might not arrive in the department on schedule, and

time is wasted checking on the delay. A delay at one point in the schedule is felt throughout the shop. It is therefore necessary to alter and adjust the flow of jobs continually to make up for time gains or losses.

The challenge of production control is to merge each individual job diagram into the overall shop schedule (figure 20.10). The goal is to match time blocks efficiently with available personnel; materials; and common sizes, colors, or types of jobs. The production manager prepares detailed production control schedules for each day's work well in advance. With a job

Liedtke Graphics   Production Schedule

Date **8/4**   Shift **Second**

Time	Electronic	Comp	Camera	Stripping	Plate	Press 17 x 22	Press 24 x 30	Bindery Assembly	Bindery Cutter	Bindery Packing
1600	↓									
1615	A-1819									
1630										
1645										
1700										
1715										
1730	S-1823									
1745										
1800	Break									
1815										
1830										
1845										
1900	M-1803		S-1823							
1915										
1930										
1945										
2000	Lunch									
2015										
2030										
2045				B-1916						
2100										
2115										
2130										
2145	K-1841									
2200										
2215	Break									
2230										
2245										
2300				S-1823						
2315										
2330										
2345										
2400										

Figure 20.10.   Sample production control sheet. The control sheet shows the job in this example sequenced across one workday.

scheduled as far as a week in advance, it is possible to coordinate the materials required in each department as the job flows through the shop.

Figure 20.10 is a quick overview of one production shift. Times in the left-hand column are listed on a 24-hour day basis. In this system *0800* is 8:00 a.m. and *1200* is noon. For p.m. numbers the time is added to *12*. For example, *1300* is 1:00 p.m. and *1630* translates to 4:30 p.m. This production schedule sheet shows the second shift for August 4. The shift starts at 4:00 p.m. and ends at midnight.

Figure 20.10 shows only a few jobs. Normally, the entire sheet would be filled with work in progress. To make understanding easier, this form has not been completed.

Notice that the Sanders job moves through production as other jobs are completed in each department. From figure 20.8 we know that S-1823 identifies the Sanders job. Job A-1819 is scheduled to be finished at 1730 in the electronic prepress department. The Sanders job is next in line. Similarly, the Sanders job should move into camera at 1900 and is scheduled to be done in that department at 2130. The next step for Sanders is stripping. However, the stripping department is already working on another job. The Sanders' brochure must wait until that job is finished.

If there are delays, the production manager must make adjustments. It is also the production manager's task to know the stage of each job at almost every moment in the day. When customers call and want to know how their material is progressing, it is important to be able to give them immediate and accurate answers. Information is critical. If there are problems, the department supervisor must inform production control immediately.

When the job has reached the last production step and is waiting to be picked up or is on its way to the customer, all records are sent through the production control office to the accounting or billing office. The job is removed from the production control schedule, and any materials that are to be stored, such as the original paste-up copy, negatives, or printing plates, are filed and new jobs enter the system. A bill is sent to the customer and payment is received.

Computer-Aided Management Tools

The development of computer-aided management tools is a natural outgrowth of the entrance of the computer into almost every phase of printing operations. For years, larger printing firms have been using computer-based **management information systems (MIS)** software to compare and assess business data. Until recently, however, true MIS systems have only been available to the largest printing firms capable of making considerable investments in computer hardware and software. Current developments in microcomputer technology and marked reductions in the price of microcomputer-based systems now make it possible for all but the smallest printers to take advantage of computer-aided production control.

Information Gathering

At the heart of any MIS system is the accurate and timely gathering of information. Traditionally, information on inventory, job status, operating costs, and other expenses related to a specific job was gathered at the end of a shift, a workday, or a work week. Such information proved valuable in assessing expenses and in isolating high-expense areas, but it was historical—all information was collected only after the job was printed. As a result, it was not useful for correcting problems as they occurred. **Automated data collection (ADC)** is a response to this problem. With ADC, data is collected through computer input as soon as it is known, rather than at the end of a specific time frame. This "real time" collection of data greatly enhances the plant's ability to assess the status of any particular operation and correct problems as they occur.

One example of ADC is the Shop-System™ offered by Covalent Systems Corporation (figure 20.11). All ADC/MIS systems contain a method of data entry, as well as software applications that process data and provide screen and/or printer display for operations monitoring and report generating.

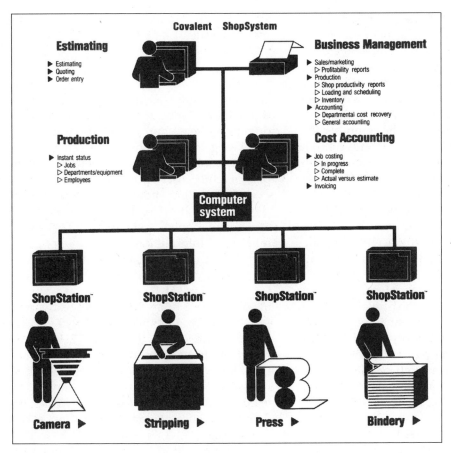

Figure 20.11.   Components of an ADC/MIS system.
Courtesy of Covalent Systems Corporation.

Data entry terminals are provided at all workstations where relevant data can be collected. Thus, input stations might be installed in the prepress areas for composition, customer-supplied disk conversion, camera, stripping, and assembling. They might also be installed in the press area and in the postpress areas for binding and finishing. Data is entered by the operator who is doing each specific task as the task is being done.

Entering data about every operation is accomplished in a variety of ways. One way is to have the person doing the operation simply keyboard information about the job while at the workstation terminal. Many systems use bar codes for information entry. With these systems, a bar code is attached to the job jacket containing the job. When operators receive the job jacket and start work on the job, they read the job information from the job jacket into the ADC/MIS system by moving a light pen pointer over the bar code on the job jacket. The bar code sends information identifying the job to a central computer.

Using this information, the central computer provides a screen menu that prompts the operator for additional job information. The menu might display a list of questions for the operator to answer. For example, the computer may ask questions about the start time, the type and amount of materials needed, and other job specifics. The operator would respond to these questions through the keyboard. These responses give the computer the data it needs for job tracking and control. When the job is complete, the bar code is again scanned to indicate that work on that particular job is finished at that work station.

Bar codes can also be used to identify supplies. Most paper, for example, is supplied directly from the manufacturer with bar code information. The ADC/MIS system can read this bar code information from the paper box or roll and relate it to the job information from the job jacket. In this way the printer can keep track of the type and amount of paper used for the job and the inventory conditions for that particular type of paper. The ADC/MIS system alerts plant management when inventory of that particular paper runs low so that paper orders can be placed before the paper is needed again.

The primary advantage of a computer-based ADC/MIS system is that whatever information is known about a particular job is available immediately. Thus, the customer service representative, in response to a customer's question, can look up the status of any printing job instantly on the computer screen and tell the customer how far the job has progressed through the plant, whether there have been any delays, and when the job will be delivered.

The ADC/MIS systems also greatly reduce the amount of paperwork to be done by workers at each individual workstation. With an ADC/MIS system, operators at each workstation must only enter data on the computer and check it on the screen rather than write all information out longhand on a form or on the job jacket. This makes data entry faster and more accurate.

Information Management

Job data entered about the job as it passes through the plant can also be compared to the original estimate and can be used to update estimating information so that estimates are more accurate and more closely reflect the plant's actual cost of producing the job.

Figure 20.12 shows a typical report that is generated by The Printers Management System by Hagen Systems, Inc. This report represents information about one press. It outlines activities across the first shift. Notice the time entries in the left column. The operator punched in at 8:00 a.m. Work on a 32-page brochure started at 9:15. Make-ready took 2.34 hours (from 9:15.32 to 11:36.20—do the arithmetic to affirm that 2.34 = 2 hours, 21 minutes). Each new operation is entered. Data from this day and workstation, along with all other data entry workstations, is entered into the company's database, which updates production standards for future job cost estimates.

Figure 20.13 shows a computer-generated estimate for a job. The estimator entered the specific job information. The application then referred to the production standards database and created a small spreadsheet of prices for three different quantities—10,000, 15,000, and 25,000. Examine the different columns for each quantity. Notice that the system kept the items that are independent of press run (film, proofs, and plates) constant. However, it has calculated incremental costs for items that increase expenses for press run length (paper, ink, and packing). The bottom of the form summarizes all of the information and provides projected value-added and profit information. This is an inter-

```
EMPLOYEE 601   CANDI HARRISON

07:18:38  1   * PUNCH IN *                                                                A   05
08:39:32  1   931047  16 PAGE PRODUCT CATALOG    602501 38° 2/C OFF/MAKEREADY   1.35    2      1.48    H   05
08:54:01  1                                      999990 NONCHRG/BREAK            .25                     H   05
12:06:20  1   931047  16 PAGE PRODUCT CATALOG    602502 38° 2/C OFF/RUN         3.20  25638  8011.88    H   05
12:06:20  1   * PUNCH OUT *                                                                B   05
12:35:00  1   * PUNCH IN *                                                                A   05
14:59:50  1   931047  16 PAGE PRODUCT CATALOG    602503 38° 2/C OFF/WASHUP      0.41    2      4.88    H   05
15:42:01  1                                      602902 38° 2/C OFF/MAINTENANCE 0.72    1      1.39    H   05
16:00:56  1   931008  BACK TO SCHOOL MAILER      602900 38° 2/C OFF/REWORK      2.55  19652  7706.67    H   05
16:00:48  1   * PUNCH OUT *                                                                B   05

                                                                               -----
                                                 TOTAL PAYROLL                  8.23
                                                 TOTAL HOURS                    8.23   CHRG % = 60.27
```

Figure 20.12.   Sample labor detail report.
Courtesy of Hagen Systems, Inc.

nal document that is not to be shared with the customer.

Hagen's system takes appropriate information from the estimate form and generates a formal bid or quotation letter (figure 20.14). Notice that the letter describes the job, identifies what the customer is to supply, and outlines a matrix of costs. For example, the cost of 10,000 sheets is $5,891.16. If the client decides to buy 11,000 sheets the cost would be $6,271.75 ($5,891.16 + $380.59 where $380.59 is the incremental charge for each additional thousand units). The task of generating all this information manually would require considerable time and estimator energy. Clearly, system like The Printers Management System provide the customer more information from which to make a purchase decision, ensures the printer greater accuracy, and saves everyone time.

In a manner similar to the way a bid letter is generated, the data captured in the estimating process can be moved into the production control phase once an order is given. Figure 20.15 shows a proposed production schedule for the company's 38-inch, two-color offset press.

In addition to information shown on a manual production schedule, ADC/MIS applications can provide a wealth of management information. Hagen's system offers eight clusters of reports and data points:

▮ Shop floor data collection
▮ Estimating and quotations
▮ Order entry and production forms
▮ Loading and scheduling
▮ Billing and receivables
▮ Inventory, shipping, and receiving
▮ Job tracking and job costing
▮ Production monitoring and management

The printing industry is more than just running a printing press or operating a process camera. Planning printing production does require a thorough understanding of production, but it also demands many skills beyond ink and image manipulation.

```
ESTIMATE NUMBER: 103                    ESTIMATE PRINT                         PAGE: 1
ESTIMATOR:     MIKE LEWIS        COMBINATION SUMMARY/DETAIL REPORT             DATE: 06-17-93
                                      HAGEN SYSTEMS, INC.                      TIME: 09:36

32 PAGE BROCHURE 2/2        JOHN SMITH              DATE OF REQUEST:  06-17-93
4 PAGE COVER 4/2           AMERICAN TESTING         DATE JOB REQUIRED:  07-20-93
SADDLESTITCH & CARTON PACK  2800 FIFTH AVE.     DATE ESTIMATE REQUIRED:  06-19-93
FOB OUR DOCK               MINNEAPOLIS MN 55455      PREVIOUS JOB NUMBER:
                                                     QUALITY LEVEL:  STANDARD
                           DAVE JOHNSON        CUSTOMER WILL SUPPLY:  CAMERA READY ART & MACINTOSH FILES
```

```
**********************************************      STOCK SHEET.: 23.0000 X 35.0000     QTY 1 UNIT $:   56.550
* SEGMENT-BODY                             *        DESCRIPTION.: 70# OFFSET            QTY 2 UNIT $:   56.550
* 32 PAGE BROCHURE 2/2                      *        U/M.........: CWT                   QTY 3 UNIT $:   56.550
**********************************************      BASIS WEIGHT: 70 POUNDS
8.5000 X 11.0000    2 COLORS SIDE 1  2 COLORS SIDE 2    # STOCK SHEETS  # PRESS SHEETS   SPOILAGE  # IMPRESSIONS
PRINT   2 SHEETS  16 PAGES  1 OUT    SHEETWISE      QUANTITY 1   21,898        21,898       1,898       43,796
PRESS SHEET: 23.0000 X 35.0000                      QUANTITY 2   32,703        32,703       2,703       65,406
PRESS  2  38" 2/C OFFSET                            QUANTITY 3   54,295        54,295       4,295      108,590
```

```
**********************************************      STOCK SHEET.: 25.0000 X 38.0000     QTY 1 UNIT $:   95.700
* SEGMENT-COVER                            *        DESCRIPTION.: 90# COVER             QTY 2 UNIT $:   95.700
* 4 PAGE COVER 4/2                         *        U/M.........: M                     QTY 3 UNIT $:   95.700
**********************************************      BASIS WEIGHT: 90 POUNDS
8.5000 X 11.0000    4 COLORS SIDE 1  2 COLORS SIDE 2    # STOCK SHEETS  # PRESS SHEETS   SPOILAGE  # IMPRESSIONS
PRINT   1 SHEET   4 PAGES  4 OUT     SHEETWISE      QUANTITY 1    2,896         2,896         396        5,792
PRESS SHEET: 25.0000 X 38.0000                      QUANTITY 2    4,237         4,237         487        8,474
PRESS  3  40" 4/C OFFSET                            QUANTITY 3    6,923         6,923         673       13,846
```

MAT'L TYPE OR CCC	DESCRIPTION	--QUANTITY 10,000-- UNITS	TOTAL $	--QUANTITY 15,000-- UNITS	TOTAL $	--QUANTITY 25,000-- UNITS	TOTAL $
PAPER	70# OFFSET	2597.79	1615.96	3879.61	2413.31	6441.10	4006.68
PAPER	90# COVER	2896.00	304.87	4237.00	446.03	6923.00	728.78
INK	BLACK + PMS 123	* 21.68	182.11	32.38	271.99	53.75	451.50
INK	BLACK + PMS 123	21.68	182.11	32.38	271.99	53.75	451.50
INK	4 COLOR PROCESS	5.34	41.65	7.81	60.92	12.76	99.53
INK	BLACK + PMS 123	2.83	23.77	4.13	34.69	6.75	56.70
FILM	MACINTOSH FILM OUTPUT	32.00	140.80	32.00	140.80	32.00	140.80
FILM	HALFTONES	4.00	15.18	4.00	15.18	4.00	15.18
FILM	LINESHOTS	4.00	9.90	4.00	9.90	4.00	9.90
FILM	SCANNER SEPARATIONS	2.00	17.93	2.00	17.93	2.00	17.93
PROOFS	BLUE LINE	4.00	15.40	4.00	15.40	4.00	15.40
PROOFS	MATCH PRINT	1.00	9.90	1.00	9.90	1.00	9.90
PROOFS	BLUE LINE	1.00	1.10	1.00	1.10	1.00	1.10
PLATES	STANDARD QUALITY PLATE	8.00	70.40	8.00	70.40	8.00	70.40
PLATES	STANDARD QUALITY PLATE	6.00	59.40	6.00	59.40	6.00	59.40
PACKING	LARGE CARTON - 80#	36.00	110.88	54.00	166.32	90.00	277.20
	TOTAL MATERIAL $		2801.36		4005.26		6411.90
183115	MACINTOSH/CONVERSION	2.13	130.36	2.13	130.36	2.13	130.36
183116	MACINTOSH/FILM OUTPUT	1.63	44.83	1.63	44.83	1.63	44.83
	TOTAL STUDIO $		175.19		175.19		175.19

Figure 20.13.   Sample estimate printout.

Courtesy of Hagen Systems, Inc.

```
ESTIMATE NUMBER: 103                    ESTIMATE PRINT                         PAGE: 2
ESTIMATOR:    MIKE LEWIS          COMBINATION SUMMARY/DETAIL REPORT            DATE: 06-17-93
                                       HAGEN SYSTEMS, INC.                     TIME: 09:37
```

MAT'L TYPE OR CCC	DESCRIPTION	--QUANTITY UNITS	10,000-- TOTAL $	--QUANTITY UNITS	15,000-- TOTAL $	--QUANTITY UNITS	25,000-- TOTAL $
201201	CAMERA/LINESHOT	0.25	11.00	0.25	11.00	0.25	11.00
201202	CAMERA/HALFTONES	0.45	19.80	0.45	19.80	0.45	19.80
204208	SCANNER/SEPARATIONS	2.00	220.00	2.00	220.00	2.00	220.00
301301	STRIPPING/ASSEMBLY	3.14	.120.89	3.14	120.89	3.14	120.89
302303	PROOFING/BLUE LINE	1.55	68.20	1.55	68.20	1.55	68.20
302305	PROOFING/MATCH PRINT	0.35	15.40	0.35	15.40	0.35	15.40
401401	PLATEMAKING/BURN PLATES	4.10	202.95	4.10	202.95	4.10	202.95
	TOTAL PREPRESS $		658.24		658.24		658.24
602501	38" 2/C OFFSET/MAKEREADY	1.85	101.75	1.85	101.75	1.85	101.75
602502	38" 2/C OFFSET/RUN	6.02	331.10	8.85	486.75	14.43	793.65
602503	38" 2/C OFFSET/WASH UP	0.40	22.00	0.40	22.00	0.40	22.00
604501	40" 4/C OFFSET/MAKEREADY	2.30	202.40	2.30	202.40	2.30	202.40
604502	40" 4/C OFFSET/RUN	0.87	76.56	1.25	110.00	1.98	174.24
604503	40" 4/C OFFSET/WASH UP	1.20	105.60	1.20	105.60	1.20	105.60
	TOTAL PRESS $		839.41		1028.50		1399.64
801501	CUTTER/SET UP	0.40	26.00	0.40	26.00	0.40	26.00
801502	CUTTER/RUN	2.56	166.40	3.56	231.40	5.72	371.80
802501	FOLDER/SET UP	1.40	49.00	1.40	49.00	1.40	49.00
802502	FOLDER/RUN	3.32	116.20	4.98	174.30	8.30	290.50
805501	STITCHER/TRIMMER/SET UP	0.65	26.00	0.65	26.00	0.65	26.00
805502	STITCHER/TRIMMER/RUN	1.28	51.50	1.93	77.25	3.21	128.75
	TOTAL BINDERY $		435.10		583.95		892.05

TOTAL MATERIAL $	2801.36		4005.26	6411.90
TOTAL LABOR $	2107.94		2445.88	3125.12
TOTAL $	4909.30		6451.14	9537.02
OVERALL MARKUP $	981.86		1290.23	1907.40
GRAND TOTAL $	5891.16		7741.37	11444.42
COST/M	589.12		516.09	457.78
ADD'L/M	380.59		377.08	374.36
GRAND TOTAL $	5891.16		7741.37	11444.42
MATERIAL COST	2514.14		3592.70	5748.54
VALUE ADDED	3377.02		4148.67	5695.88
VALUE ADDED %	57.32 %		53.59 %	49.76 %
LABOR COST	1945.98		2266.73	2912.23
PROFIT	1431.04		1881.94	2783.65
PROFIT %	24.29 %		24.31 %	24.32 %

```
953 -END- 5189
```

Figure 20.13. continued

✖ HAGEN

```
                              DATE : JUNE 19, 1993
                              EST #: 103




THANK YOU FOR THE OPPORTUNITY TO PRESENT THE
FOLLOWING QUOTATION:


    REQUESTED BY:  JOHN SMITH
    COMPANY NAME:  AMERICAN TESTING
                   2800 FIFTH AVE.
                   MINNEAPOLIS, MN 55455

    SALESPERSON:   DAVE JOHNSON

JOB DESCRIPTION:   32 PAGE BROCHURE 2/2
                   4 PAGE COVER 4/2
                   SADDLESTITCH & CARTON PACK
                   FOB OUR DOCK

CUST. TO SUPPLY:   CAMERA READY ART &
                   MACINTOSH TEXT FILES

                                          COLORS   COLORS
     FORM           PAPER DESCRIPTION      FRONT    BACK
     ------------   -------------------    ------   ------
     4 PAGE COVER   90# COVER                4        2
     32 PAGE BODY   70# OFFSET               2        2


          QUANTITY:        10,000       15,000      25,000

              COST:      5,891.16     7,741.37   11,444.42
      COST PER 1000:       589.12       516.09      457.78
COST PER ADDITIONAL 1000:  380.59       377.08      374.36


STANDARD TRADE CUSTOMS APPLY TO ALL QUOTES (SEE REVERSE).
PLEASE CONTACT YOUR SALES REPRESENTATIVE WITH ANY QUESTIONS
OR COMMENTS.  THANK YOU.
```

HAGEN SYSTEMS,INC.   6438 City West Parkway   Eden Prairie, MN 55344   (612) 944-6865

Figure 20.14.   Sample computer-generated bid letter.
Courtesy of Hagen Systems, Inc.

```
DAYS PER INTERVAL......: 1              SHOP LOAD/SCHEDULE               PAGE: 1
JOBS WITH NO HOURS.....: NO          CRITICAL ITEMS ONLY - NO           DATE: 06-29-93
CUSTOMER NAME/TIME.....: YES            HAGEN SYSTEMS, INC.             TIME: 15:22
COST CENTER RANGE......: 602 TO 602
```

DEPARTMENT: 6 SHEETFED PRESS

JOB CODE	CUSTOMER NAME/ JOB DESCRIPTION	HOURS PRIOR	07-12-93	07-13-93	07-14-93	07-15-93	07-16-93	07-17-93	07-18-93	07-19-93 COMPLETE	PROMISED TO DATE/TIME PRIORITY
	602 38" 2/C OFFSET										
	BATES ENGINEERING		4.28								07-23-93
881004	50 PAGE ANNUAL REPORT										2
	COPYWRITE		7.05								07-24-93
931007	ANNUAL REPORT										2
	THE L C SMITH ENGINEERING			4.61	8.00						07-25-93
931015	BOOKLET - 16PP + COVER 2/C										1
	AMERICAN TESTING				0.43	8.00					07-25-93
931034	32 PAGE BROCHURE 2/2										13:00 2
	AMERICAN TESTING					1.06					07-26-93
931029	LETTERHEADS - BLACK & PMS 805										12:00 1
	ABC DOORS						2.83				07-27-93
931016	COMPANY SPEC SHEET 8PP 2/C										1
	COPYWRITE						3.90				07-28-93
931025	FALL BROCHURE										1
	PHILLIPS BROTHERS, INC.						0.40			6.50	07-29-93
931027	16 PAGE PAMPHLET										H

```
          TOTAL COST CENTER LOAD    11.33    4.61    8.43    9.06    7.13
               AVAILABLE HOURS       8.00    8.00    8.00    8.00    8.00

          REMAINING TIME AVAILABLE  -3.33*   3.39   -0.43*  -1.06*   0.87          LOAD = 40.56
--------------------------------------------------------------------------------
           TOTAL DEPARTMENT LOAD    11.33    4.61    8.43    9.06    7.13
               AVAILABLE HOURS       8.00    8.00    8.00    8.00    8.00

          REMAINING TIME AVAILABLE  -3.33*   3.39   -0.43*  -1.06*   0.87          LOAD = 40.56
            TOTAL COMPANY LOAD      11.33    4.61    8.43    9.06    7.13
               AVAILABLE HOURS       8.00    8.00    8.00    8.00    8.00

          REMAINING TIME AVAILABLE  -3.33*   3.39   -0.43*  -1.06*   0.87          LOAD = 40.56

371 - END - 5348
```

Figure 20.15. Sample computer-generated production control sheet.

Courtesy of Hagen Systems, Inc.

Key Terms

amortization
depreciation
cost center
job estimate
Franklin Printing Catalog

overhead
work order
job scheduling and
  production control
job schedule

management of information
  systems (MIS)
automated data collection
  (ADC)

Questions for Review

1. What is the advantage of a uniform price schedule?

2. Why is reviewing the sequence of operations an important part of the estimating process?

3. What is the purpose of a production work order?

4. What is job scheduling?

5. What is a production control schedule?

6. Convert 4.70 hours to hours and minutes.

7. Explain why timely and accurate record keeping by production workers is important to accurate estimating.

8. What is a unit/time standards form?

9. Explain how fixed costs are identified and added to production costs.

10. List the eight steps of the estimating process.

11. What is the function of a work order?

12. What is the purpose of production scheduling?

13. List the major components of an ADC/MIS system.

CHAPTER

Customer-Defined Quality Management

21

Anecdote to Chapter Twenty-One

W. Edwards Deming is considered the father of the "quality movement." Born on a Wyoming homestead in 1900, Deming earned his undergraduate degree from the University of Wyoming and went on to complete a Ph.D. in Physics from Yale University in 1924.

During his undergraduate years Deming worked at General Electric's infamous Hawthorne plant in Chicago. More than forty-six thousand people worked at the plant to build telephone equipment. Of those, fifty-two hundred were assigned to the inspection department. Workers were paid by the unit and were docked for every piece that failed inspection. This experience influenced Dr. Deming's ideas about the failures of postproduction inspection. It was critically important to ensure consistency in manufacturing so every product would function as required. Without consistency there was no dependability.

While working for the Department of Agriculture in 1927 Deming met Walter A. Shewhart, a statistician for Bell Laboratories. Shewhart developed "statistical control," which later became the foundation for Deming's quality approach.

Statistical control examined random variation and established limits—highs and lows—that indicated when a process was out of control.

Deming's previous experience with sampling and quality control prompted the United States government to hire him to teach statistical control methods to World War II manufacturers. Following the war, however, Deming's ideas fell out of favor. Corporations felt his approach was unnecessary, expensive, and time consuming.

In 1949 Dr. Deming was asked to assist with Japan's redevelopment. His initial work involved sampling data for housing, employment, and food production and consumption.

Japanese industrial leaders began to listen to Deming's ideas and adopted his quality methods nearly universally. The Japanese government credits Deming with the model that transformed Japanese production. Japan's highest, most coveted industrial recognition award is now called the "Deming Medal."

Deming died in 1993. He never used the term "total quality management." Others developed the term and ascribed it to him.

Objectives for Chapter 21

After completing this chapter you will be able to:

- Define quality in terms of the customer's context or use, time requirement, and measure of success.

- Recall key terms, including "continuous quality improvement," "total quality management," and "total responsiveness management."

- Explain the meaning of the term "Kizan."

- Recall the purpose of ISO 9000 Standards Registration.

- Outline the motivation for customer-defined quality management.

- Define the customer in terms of external and internal clients.

- Recognize the cost of failure.

- Recognize the principles of customer-defined quality management.

- Outline a typical total quality management implementation process.

- Recognize four statistical process control tools, including histograms, Pareto charts, cause and effect charts, and control charts.

- Outline a six-step problem solving process.

- Recall three team roles, including leader, scribe, and timekeeper.

- Name several effective team behaviors.

Introduction

The term "quality" is meaningless. It carries no meaning for several reasons, but it is meaningless primarily because it is applied to every situation. Television and newspaper advertisements announce "if you are looking for true quality, then buy . . . " Soda containers are called "jumbo" rather than "large." Society's use of the superlative communicates nothing. When a word like "quality" is overused it loses definition.

Just what is a "quality printed product"? Consider two products:

Product 1. Will Romano is marketing manager for a medium-size manufacturing company that specializes in oil refinery pumps. The national distributors meeting is scheduled for 9:00 a.m. tomorrow. The company president has just announced a price reduction and wants the new information put in the briefing package that will be given to each of the 150 distributors at the meeting.

The briefing package is a thick, three-ring binder; one section of the binder contains the old price list. The cartons of binders are waiting at the hotel. At 4:00 p.m. Romano updates the price list on his computer and prints out the three-page list. He rushes to a local print shop and asks for 200 copies of each of the three pages.

Using an electrostatic copier, the printer copies the pages on the same paper used in the binder, drills three holes in all 600 sheets, and delivers the job to Romano while he waits. Rushing to the hotel, Romano's staff quickly replaces the old list with the new one. At 9:00 a.m. the meeting goes off without a hitch and no one notices any difference in the price section. The president is very pleased.

Product 2. Ray Davis is vice president of advertising for a nationally based travel agency. The agency wants to promote winter vacations in the Bahamas. The promotion vehicle will be a full-color brochure used as a direct mail piece to 300,000 high-income households.

Davis works with the agency's advertising department to design the piece. The final design involves four-color process photographs. Undercolor removal (UCR) is used to enhance the images. An 80-pound coated offset paper is the base. A separate varnish coat is added to each photo during printing to make the image appear to "jump off the page." The fold lines are prescored for especially crisp edges.

The entire production, from concept to product, takes three months and hundreds of hours, but meets the September 15 mail date target. The campaign is a huge success and Davis is given a free vacation in the Bahamas.

Does scenario 1 or 2 deliver a higher quality product? The answer is "yes." They are both high-quality printed products. They both have specific context, focused use, and time limits, and they were judged successful.

Defining Quality

Only these elements give meaning to the concept of quality.

Context or Use

The customer has a specific context for every job brought to the printer. That context might be a problem or a goal. The job might be critical to a company's continued success, or it might be only a small element of continuing operations. The purpose of the job might be to inform, persuade, sell, motivate, or entertain. Whatever the motivation of the job, the customer defines what is important and judges the printed product in that context.

Time

Every job has a time limit. It is a rare customer who says, "Print it when you get a chance." Nearly every job must meet a deadline that is defined by the customer. A price list delivered an hour late to an important meeting has no value. A brochure mailed a month outside a selling window is also worthless.

Measure of Successful Use

After the printed product is delivered and used it is evaluated. Did the national distributors find the new price list useful and effective in selling more oil pumps? Did individuals respond to the direct mail campaign and purchase vacation packages to the Bahamas? Every customer knows how to measure the success of the printed piece. If the intent was met then the product has great value; if the intent was not met then the product has no merit.

The point is this: Quality is a term that has different meaning for every printing job. Quality depends upon context, time, and the measure of successful use. Quality is defined by the customer, not by print materials, ink density, or elaborate technical preparations (figure 21.1).

Customer-Defined Quality

American industry has given attention to customer-defined quality over the last several decades. Several popular terms have emerged that describe the process of making each manufacturing or service step responsive to the customer's needs or expectations. At least three terms have emerged in the popular printing industry vocabulary:

- ■ **Continuous Quality Improvement (CQI)**
- ■ **Total Quality Management (TQM)**
- ■ **Total Responsiveness Management (TRM)**

This chapter is intended to provide an overview of the process of responding to customers' needs and expectations. Language is an important part of this process. The word "process," rather than "project," is used purposefully. "Process" is broad, ongoing, and denotes a permanent commitment. "Project" is a narrow, typically one-time event, and it is

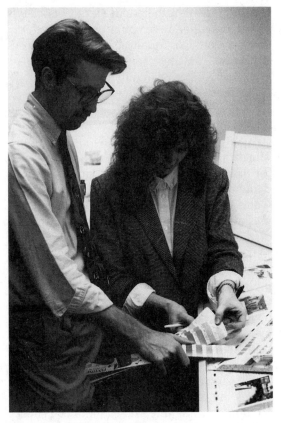

Figure 21.1.   The customer defines "quality". The definition of quality is based upon context, time, and the measure of successful use.

something that can be accomplished and then forgotten.

Although the concept of customer-defined quality was developed in the United States during World War II, the Japanese corporations used the term **Kizan** (pronounced "Key-Zan") to describe the continuous improvement effort. Kizan means that the capacity for improvement is endless. Incremental improvement is the key to success. The customer has more information than anyone. There is no limit to continually making small improvements and thereby improving customer satisfaction.

The drive for customer-defined quality is an attitude. It requires ongoing attention, absolute commitment, and specific behaviors. Continuous customer-defined improvement is a process. That process is transforming the American printing industry rapidly.

ISO 9000 Standards Registration

One measure of commitment to customer-defined quality is international **ISO 9000 standards registration.** The International Organization for Standardization (ISO) was founded in 1946 to establish international standards that would communicate clear, process-based operations. Its purpose is to facilitate the global exchange of products and services. Today ISO has more than ninety member countries. The American National Standards Institute (ANSI) is America's representative in ISO.

In 1987, ISO published five standards dealing with what it termed the "quality system":

- *ISO 9000*

    Quality Management and Quality Assurance Standards—Guidelines for Selection and Use

- *ISO 9001*

    Quality Systems—Model for Quality Assurance in Design/Development, Production, Installation, and Servicing

- *ISO 9002*

    Quality Systems—Model for Quality Assurance in Production and Installation

- *ISO 9003*

    Quality Systems—Model for Quality Assurance in Final Inspection and Test

- *ISO 9004*

    Quality Management and Quality System Elements—Guidelines

These standards outline expectations for the process, management structure, and materials that produce consistent and predictable products to specifications provided by a customer.

There are five steps in the ISO 9000 standards registration process:

1. Company commitment to pursue registration
2. Evaluate current organization and procedures against ISO standards
3. Develop a compliance plan that transforms all elements of the company and ensures that all appropriate ISO standards are met
4. Implement the compliance plan
5. Conduct a registration audit (typically, a third-party, ISO-certified auditor examines the plan and its conformance to specifications)

Of course, the company must continue the commitment and actions that will maintain registration.

For those manufacturing companies that market and deliver products globally, ISO registration is critical. Pharmaceuticals, aircraft, and machine tools are prime examples of these products. Few America-based printing companies supply printed work for consumption in Europe or Asia. However, many printers provide print support for organizations that are international players. If a corporation has earned ISO registration, then all suppliers to that organization must also conform to ISO standards.

Apart from the actual registration, ISO standards are one method the graphic arts industry is using to become more customer-defined quality oriented.

Motivation for a Customer-Defined Quality Orientation

The discussion of how and who defines quality can be viewed as academic in companies faced with the realities of day-to-day operation.

Even successful companies wonder why they should change what they are doing. A common response is "Printing is such a competitive business. There is so little time to spare. Why should I start a new project that will interfere with my job?"

It is exactly the competitive environment that motivates successful printers to embrace a customer-defined attitude.

Printing is a manufacturing process. However, it differs from almost all other manufacturing industries in that it produces custom-made products. Customers do not select four-color brochures for their product lines off of the rack in a department store. Print consumers place orders when they have needs that are specific to their organizations. There is perhaps a more direct relationship between the manufacturer and the customer in printing than in any other industry.

This close relationship, linked with a competitive environment, is moving successful printers to embrace a customer-defined attitude.

Technology Levels the Playing Field

This textbook is about print technology. Every chapter, except this one, deals with print organization, preparation, planning, prediction, or tools and materials. In reality, the equipment used by one company differs little from the equipment in another. Every company has access to the same paper, ink, film, and solvents that support the technology.

Progressive managers ask the question, then "Why does a customer chose my com-pany over my competitor to print a job?" The conclusion in nearly every case is not related to technology. The answer is in the attitude, commitment, and behaviors of individual employees as they perform each step in the process of delivering a final product. The understandings and efforts of individual employees to produce customer-defined quality establishes and maintains the reputation of any organization.

The accelerating technical sophistication of print tools have made this reality even more apparent. Companies face an endless, ever increasing array of new and better equipment to purchase. This sophistication forces companies to recognize that the only true difference in the product they offer is meeting or exceeding customer expectations.

Defining a Manufacturing Process

Figure 21.2 outlines a simple view of how products are manufactured. Raw materials first enter the system. In printing these are typically paper, ink, film, and chemicals. The raw materials are transformed by a process that involves skilled craftspeople, equipment, transformation techniques (such as stripping and platemaking), and the work facility. The result is a product.

Figure 21.3 shows a more traditional view of what actually happens during manufacture. The process takes place (materials → transformer → product). Customer service keeps the client informed as the process develops. At the end of the process the product is inspected. The question is asked, "Does the product meet specifications?" If the answer is

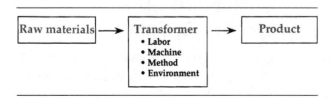

Figure 21.2.   Elements of a manufacturing process

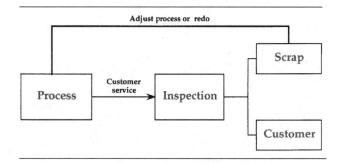

Figure 21.3. **The traditional production control system**

"yes," the product is delivered to the customer. If the answer is "no," the product is scrapped and redone.

Increasingly, companies are finding this approach flawed. It is good that defective or bad workmanship is discovered before it reaches the customer. However, two costs interfere with profits. The first is the cost of having a separate function that inspects the product. The second is the cost of waste associated with doing a job over. The cost of failure and the cost of preparing to catch failure are simply too high.

A more effective, productive view is shown in figure 21.4. It starts and ends with the customer. First, the customer defines expectations. The process and control of the process conform to those expectations. Every step is devoted to meeting job requirements. The customer also defines the control system. The key to this system is the skill, attitude, and attention of each employee in the company.

Some experts suggest that the traditional approach, which involves quality control after the process is finished, costs American business $60 billion a year. When this figure is translated to the printing industry, it means that a company might increase its annual profit by 4 to 10 percent.

Increased customer loyalty and increased profits mean continued job security. Moreover, nearly everyone who has been involved with a company that has moved to this new view of customer-defined quality feels an increased sense of self-worth, job satisfaction, and sense of purpose.

A New Definition of "Customer"

The traditional definition of "customer" is "someone who hires us to do a job." However, in this new environment, that definition has several meanings.

Differing Views of the Printing Process

This book presents a comprehensive view of printing production. A schematic of the production view of printing is presented in figure 21.5. It is a relatively accurate overview of the steps involved in the production of a printed job through most contemporary graphic arts companies.

However, not everyone has this same view. For example, figure 21.6 shows how the general manager or company president might see the printing process. This process begins with a job estimate. An estimate is produced and the client makes a decision. The company

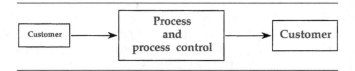

Figure 21.4. **A new control system model**

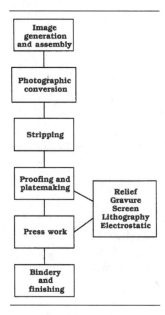

Figure 21.5. Work flow as viewed by production.
Courtesy of Gorelick & Associates.

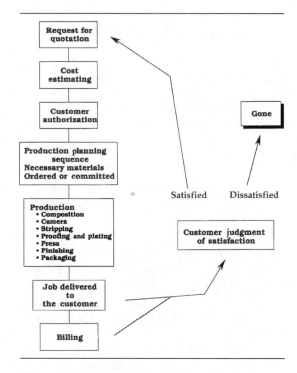

Figure 21.6. Work flow as viewed by the manager or company president.
Courtesy of Gorelick & Associates.

devotes significant resources to a sales force to bring new work to the organization. Once the customer gives authorization, production planning is the next step. Then the production steps take place. Next the job is delivered to the customer, and finally, a bill or invoice is sent. External to the process is the customer's evaluation. If the customer is satisfied, then another job might be given. If the customer is not satisfied, however, then no more work will appear.

Figure 21.7 shows yet another view of the printing process. This is how the customer sees the process. It differs radically from the two previous diagrams. The entire planning and production sequence is invisible. The customer is not concerned with how a job is produced. The client is concerned only with the product.

The customer is not impressed with technical equipment—only with the final product. It makes sense, then, that every printing company should be more concerned with its cus-

tomer's view of the process rather than with its equipment.

Defining Customers
It is critical that the last three figures are understood. Where you stand in the printing process influences how you see it. This understanding has developed several definitions of "customer."

The idea of internal and external customers has gained wide acceptance. External customers are obvious. They are the people who place the orders and use the printed products. External customers pay the invoices.

There is at least one other external customer. Say you are printing labels that will be glued to a prescription drug bottle. Information on the label can mean life or death to a pa-

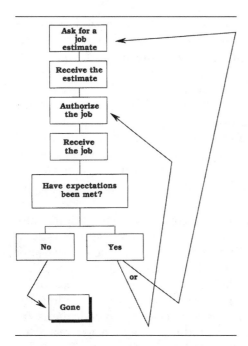

Figure 21.7.   Work flow as viewed by the customer.

Courtesy of Gorelick & Associates.

tient. Is the patient who takes the drug also your customer? The answer is "yes." End users also have a role in defining quality and must be considered.

The idea of customer-defined quality is made even more powerful when internal customers are defined and listened to. An internal customer is anyone who follows you in the manufacturing or service sequence.

Say a stripper is working on a complex multicolor job on the light table. The stripper's responsibility is to deliver a "quality" job to the platemaker, to the press room, to the bindery. The person at each next step is the stripper's internal customer. If the stripper makes a mistake on registration marks or trim lines, then it is highly probable that someone after will not be able to perform his or her job properly. The stripper has a responsibility to both the customer who ordered the job and to the partners who are producing it.

Everyone inside a company is both a supplier and customer to someone else. The accounting department cannot send invoices on time if their coworkers do not provide them with accurate, timely information. Therefore, people in the accounting department are customers. On the other hand, the president wants a weekly and monthly summary of accounts payable and accounts receivable. Accounting then becomes a supplier of information to the president.

This approach also makes the concept of customer-defined quality a bit more personal. A process photographer working in the darkroom might feel somewhat removed from the external customer. However, the photographer will deliver her product to the stripping department, where it will be tested on the press. If the photographer does not produce exactly what is required, she will learn rapidly of the extra effort needed by the stripping department to compensate. The photographer will learn to serve her internal customer.

The Cost of Failure

Yet another motivation for adopting a customer-defined quality management program is the cost of failure. Look again at figure 21.3. When a job is scrapped or redone the company must absorb the additional costs of materials and labor. Moreover, redoing a job bounces a new job out of sequence and delays profitable work.

Say a customer rejects a run of 10,000 four-color brochures because the registration is off. The company must redo the job. Consider the associated additional costs:

■ The job must be returned to the stripping department. Flats must be disassembled and restripped.

■ New plates must be made.

■ New paper, ink, and chemicals must be used.

- The production schedule must be interrupted and work in progress is delayed at every step in the process.
- Time to produce the job is more than doubled because each operation has to be repeated once.
- After the job is reworked, the jobs that were delayed may require overtime to complete.

After the job is redone, it is also highly probable the customer will take future work to some other company. Every salesperson knows it is far easier and less expense to keep an existing client than it is to solicit a new one. Failure has long-term implications.

By some estimates, the cost of failure represents 12 percent of all gross revenues and affects the printing industry's profit margin by 4 percent.

The Principles of Customer-Defined Quality Management

The anecdote for this chapter introduced W. Edwards Deming who is considered the founder of the world quality movement. Deming developed fourteen points as the foundation and guiding principles for his ideas. These fourteen points are fundamental understandings for any organization that wishes to implement customer-defined quality management:

- **Create consistency of purpose for improvement of product and service.**
  Deming says organizational purpose must change. Profit cannot be the goal. Profit is the result of a larger purpose—staying in business; providing jobs through innovation, research, and constant improvement; developing a reputation for exceptional customer satisfaction.
- **Adopt a new philosophy.**
  We can no longer accept poor workmanship, sullen service, and defective materials as the norm. This attitude prevents improved quality, productivity, customer satisfaction, and worker motivation. Deming speaks of the need for a new religion that rejects mistakes and negativism.
- **Cease to depend on postinspection to ensure quality.**
  American companies have traditionally relied upon product inspection as it comes off the production line—after the possibility of control or intervention. Failed results are either discarded or reworked. Quality must be built into the process using customer-based criteria. Inferior products should never reach the end of the line.
- **Cease awarding business on the basis of price.**
  Companies that buy supplies and products from the "low bidder" are not involved with the process. The new decision formula = customer-defined quality + perceived value + confidence in the supplier + delivery + price.
- **Improve constantly and forever the system of production and service.**
  Improvement is not an event—it is a continuous process. Production workers can only deliver a small portion of potential improvement. Management has the greatest responsibility. However, improvement must be a fundamental attitude shared by all.
- **Institute training.**
  Everyone must know his or her job. It is the company's responsibility to provide sufficient training and accurate instructions. If a job is not defined clearly it cannot be performed.

■ **Institute supervision.**

The function of supervision is problem solving, not worker watching or enforcement. The supervisor uses statistical tools to identify, evaluate, and control customer-based quality problems. The measure of successful supervision is not quantity.

■ **Drive out fear.**

Few employees ask questions out of fear—fear of ridicule, fear of job loss, fear of revealing they do not know a specific job task. The result is lack of attention to customer desires, economic loss to the company, and inferior or unacceptable products.

■ **Break down barriers between staff areas.**

Functional work areas often feel in competition with other departments or, at best, revel in placing blame for errors on other units. The entire organization must see itself as a team, seeking to anticipate and solve production problems that interfere with customer satisfaction.

■ **Eliminate slogans, exhortations, and posters for the workforce.**

These things do not work.

■ **Eliminate numerical quotas.**

Quotas look only to numbers, not process, product quality, or customer expectations. They are the surest way to ensure inefficiency, a cult of fear, increased costs, and product problems.

■ **Remove barriers to pride of workmanship.**

Individuals fundamentally want to do a good job. Some barriers are misguided supervisors, inexact directions, poor equipment and tools, and inferior or defective materials.

■ **Institute a vigorous program of education and retraining.**

A fundamental shift in philosophy, attitude, and behaviors requires education

and retraining. Everyone in the organization must embrace the philosophy, realign attitudes, and alter behaviors. The customer is the primary teacher.

■ **Take action to accomplish the transformation.**

Seminars, discussion groups, reading volumes on philosophy and new ideas, and even great resolve cause no change. Top leadership must develop and implement a comprehensive plan that will transform the entire organization.

Other Voices but Similar Principles

Deming is not the only individual who has added to the definition of customer-defined quality. Joseph M. Juran followed Deming to Japan and has had at least the same influence on industrial organizations there. In the United States two decades later Philip B. Crosby introduced the ideas of "zero defects" and "conformance to quality." Scores of others have added their voices to the process.

Books have been written by and about these individuals. Although there are differences between them, it is more important to recognize their similarities. Five concepts emerge as a common foundation for customer-defined quality management:

■ Commit to quality improvement throughout your entire organization.

■ Attack the system rather than the employee.

■ Strip down the work process to find and eliminate problems that prevent quality—whether production or service.

■ Identify your customer, internal or external, and satisfy that customer's requirements in the work process or in the finished product.

- Eliminate waste, instill pride and team-work, and create an atmosphere for continued and permanent quality improvement.

Some have referred to these ideas as "a blinding flash of the obvious."

The Typical TQM Process

Companies with a seemingly endless stream of problems, that are perhaps on the brink of failure, sometimes look to the TQM process as a solution. All experience, however, shows that TQM is not a solution to profound problems. The process is most effective when implemented in already strong organizations. It allows good companies to become better.

Immediate results are rarely found. Again, in reports from experienced companies, it takes 12 to 24 months before fundamental change takes place.

Organizations that have completed transformation to customer-defined quality management report four fundamental implementation steps: commitment, steering committee, training, and teams.

Commitment

The TQM process begins with a commitment at the highest level of the organization. Unless the president or CEO is actively committed and involved then the transformation process is doomed to failure.

This means that the top company officer is a partner with the entire organization in defining goals, helps outline and implement actions, does not interfere with team processes even if they appear to be taking too long, and does not allow a crisis to delay or prevent any meeting or scheduled activity. It also means the top company officer accepts the conclusions or recommendations of the team if there is a rational, information-based, problem-oriented solution.

Steering Committee

Action truly begins when a steering committee is formed. Employees from across the entire organization are invited to participate. The committee is commonly composed of six to eight individuals, including the president, managers and supervisors, production workers, and office or support staff. Members are chosen based upon a history of involvement with the company, openness to new ideas, evidence of wanting to do a good job, a commitment to the client, and a desire to improve the system.

The steering committee directs implementation of the transformation process. It identifies initial problems, develops an implementation plan, coordinates training, forms and charges teams, serves as a model, monitors progress, and supports and encourages everyone in the organization.

Logistically, the steering committee meets more frequently during the initial, proactive stage—perhaps several times a week—and moves into a responsive, supportive mode with less frequent meetings as the process gains momentum and acceptance.

In accepting a position on the steering committee, members also accept the responsibility to read, study, and learn about the process before the rest of the organization. Committe members must be prepared to answer questions and provide leadership. Both skills only come from knowledge and information.

Membership of the steering committee might change over time, but the committee as a body will continue forever as a functioning, critical part of the organization.

Training

Making a verbal commitment and forming a steering committee is only the beginning. Alone they are not sufficient to transform the organization. All participants must be given the tools to act.

Training includes at least the following elements:

- Belief in the company's commitment to the process
- Introduction to the vocabulary of customer-defined quality management
- Understanding that the process is based in precedence and success
- Successful team behaviors
- Decision making and problem-solving techniques
- Basic statistical methods
- An implementation model

Training might be delivered by the steering committee or by a firm outside of the company that specializes in such training.

Teams

The heart of the TQM process is the formation and action of individual teams. Teams might be cross-functional—that is, they may be made up of members from different departments in the company. Or, they might be all of the members of one department.

Whatever the composition, a team is charged with solving a problem. The team members follow a process (see next section). They gather information. They test solutions. They recommend action.

Most importantly, as both team members and individuals, employees are given license to change the way things have "always been done." They focus on internal and external customers. The following sections introduce basic statistical tools and the problem-solving process typically used by teams.

Statistical Process Control

A problem that cannot be quantified is difficult to solve. **Statistical process control (SPC)** describes the body of techniques that measure the elements of a manufacturing process that lend themselves to quantification. The goal of SPC is to describe numerically what is happening at any point in a process.

Detailed explanation of SPC is beyond the scope of this book. It is, however, possible to introduce a few basic tools used in SPC: histogram, Pareto chart, cause and effect chart, and control chart.

Histogram

A **histogram** shows the history of what has happened at one point in a process (figure 21.8). Histograms are frequency distributions. This means that they show how often an event takes place. Data is sorted into numerical categories that are usually presented in the form of a bar graph.

In figure 21.8 a company was concerned with how accurately the customer's job was delivered in terms of count. If an order was for 5,000 pieces, the company wanted to know how many were actually delivered. For one week a team counted the number of pieces for each job. Each count was then converted to a percentage.

If the order was for 6,000 pieces and 5,790 pieces were delivered, the job was 3.5 percent under what was specified on the order ($6000 - 5790 = 210; 210 \div 6000 = 0.035; 0.035 = 3.5$ percent). On a tally sheet, a tick mark was made under the "5% under" category. At the end of the week all marks under each category

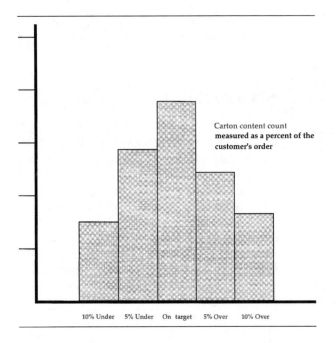

Carton content count **measured as a percent of the customer's order**

10% Under   5% Under   On target   5% Over   10% Over

Figure 21.8.   Example of a histogram. Contents of cartons were packed in the bindery. The number of final pieces for each job was measured against the customer's order, and the number was converted to a percentage. The graph plots individual results for many jobs across a defined time period.
Courtesy of Gorelick & Associates.

were summed and the results were displayed on a histograph.

Histograms cannot reveal what the process is going to do next, but it can report what has been done in the past. Knowing what has happened helps in understanding the process and is a first step toward controlling the process.

Pareto Charts

A **Pareto chart** is another form of frequency distribution (figure 21.9). Histograms typically examine variation in a focused part of the process, such as piece count accuracy, density consistency, or job readiness. Pareto charts generally look at frequency across a larger section of the process.

Figure 21.9 was created in response to a company's concern about the high number of nonchargeable or nonproductive hours on one press. For one week team members counted each time the press stopped and noted why.

This Pareto chart was created to display the count within each category in a bar chart. The categories are arranged from most frequent to least frequent.

The value of this type of chart is that it quickly shows what is the most vital or most important problem. It also shows items that are trivial and are not worth immediately addressing. Using figure 21.9 a team might quickly make the decision to find solutions for press control—density and fit or registration problems.

Cause and Effect

A **cause and effect chart** is a tool used to outline all elements of a process or problem (figure 21.10) It is sometimes call a "fishbone chart" because it looks somewhat like the skeleton of a large fish. Once a problem has been defined, a cause and effect chart can be used by the team to examine causes or potential causes.

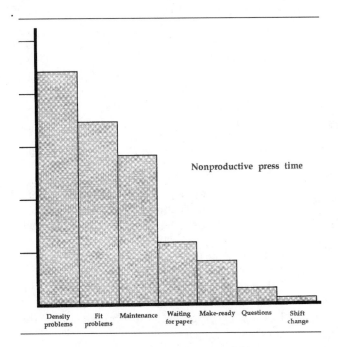

Nonproductive press time

Density problems | Fit problems | Maintenance | Waiting for paper | Make-ready | Questions | Shift change

Figure 21.9.   Example of a Pareto chart.
Courtesy of Gorelick & Associates.

All processes using this tool involve six elements. Consider how we might complete a cause and effect chart for operating an offset lithographic press:

■ **Environment**
   the press room
■ **Equipment**
   press   densitometer
   paper wedges   job proof
■ **Material**
   plates   paper
   ink   fountain solution
   solvent
■ **Measurement**
   density readings   sheet count
   registration marks
■ **Methods**
   make-ready   press run
■ **Operators**
   senior press operator   helper

Examining all details of a process allows a team to consider problem sources and how changes might be made.

Control Charts

A **control chart** is a visual tool used to examine variation in a repeating process (21.11). A control chart is based on the principle of random probability.

Random probability refers to the likelihood of an event happening. What is the probability of getting "heads" when you flip a coin? The answer is 50 percent because flipping a coin has an equal chance of landing on one side as it does on another. This idea also applies to rolling dice. What is the probability of rolling a 5 with one die? The answer is 1 out of 9 or 11.1 percent.

If you flipped a coin 100 times and it came up heads 75 times and tails 25 times, then you would suspect something was not right. Some

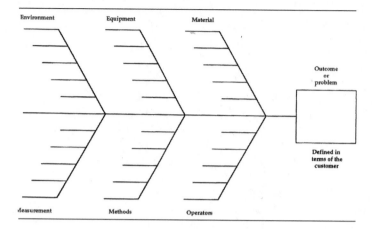

Figure 21.10.   Cause and effect or "fishbone" charts are used to define each element in a process

influence moved the process out of control—one side of the coin was weighted probably.

Control charts use this idea to examine whether something is "not right" about the process. Is some influence, outside of what we would normally expect, affecting the result? Control charts also establish normal limits of variation.

We might measure press ink density about every 100 sheets. Say we consistently read densities around 1.4—the range is from 1.28 to 1.52. Suddenly we read 1.12. We would expect variation a few points on either side of the average, but 1.12 is beyond what is expected normally. Something influenced the process. Clearly, the operator must intervene and remove or adjust the influence to get the density "back into control."

Control charts can be developed by teams to look at specific problem areas. How-ever, data is nearly always collected by the individual worker. In established TQM organizations, the operator is monitoring data continually. When the process goes out of control he or she is empowered to stop and adjust the process.

The example of measuring press density is a simple one. There are many formulas that can be used to create control charts for even the most complex processes. Individuals or teams interested in these more advanced tools should refer to a text on statistical process control.

The Problem-Solving Process

Teams deal with problems and process. Most teams use a six-step problem-solving process (figure 21.12).

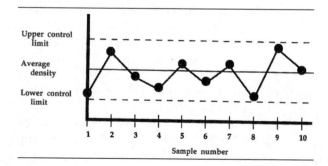

Figure 21.11.   A control chart plots samples against a band of normal or acceptable behavior

1. Identify the problem.

2. Define the problem.

3. Gather, quantify, and analyze the process path.

4. Establish root causes.

5. Solve the problem.

6. Confirm the results.

Figure 21.12.   The six problem-solving steps.
Courtesy of Gorelick & Associates.

Identify the Problem

The steering committee or the team itself usually identifies the problem. Awareness comes from external feedback—from the customer or one of the company's suppliers—and from internal sources—colleagues or personal observation.

External customers might complain that it takes too long to prepare an estimate, that density is always too low, that job orders are always short of the specified number, or that invoices do not arrive in a timely fashion.

Internal customers might complain that there are too many plate remakes, that paper is always late arriving at the press, that information flow to production planning is too slow, or that there is always a backlog in the camera department.

Teams must be able to write down the problem because if it cannot be written then it cannot be identified.

Define the Problem

There is a difference between identifying the problem and defining it. "The company is not making enough money" is an identifiable problem. However, that is not the definition of the problem. Perhaps there are not enough jobs

and the workforce is idle most of the time. Or perhaps estimates submitted to clients never cover actual job costs.

Recall the problem identified in figure 21.9—too much nonchargeable or nonproductive press time. Information from the Pareto chart suggests that the primary problem should be defined as lack of press control with density and registration.

In this step, the team must define the problem succinctly by answering the questions "what," "how," "why," and "when." Concrete definition leads to examining the process discussed in the next step.

Gather, Quantify, and Analyze the Process Path

Information must be collected and analyzed. The SPC tools, such as histograms or control charts, are used to describe the process. Decisions can only be made based upon data. A basic information set is the foundation for the next step—establishing causes.

Establish Root Causes

Cause and effect charts are put to good use at this point. Using the information that has been gathered, and a completed cause and effect chart, what are the possible root or basic causes of the problem?

The team might move back to the previous step and focus further data gathering and analysis upon one element, such as materials or method. Information is again the key.

Solve the Problem

At some point the team decides it has gathered enough information and has a possible solution to the problem. In practice, there might be several ideas that sum to a set of recommended changes.

Confirm the Results

The solutions must be tested. Again, information is collected and the process is examined. Has the problem disappeared? Is the process effectively back in control? If it is, then the team considers other problems or disbands. If it is not, then the process begins again with step two, defining the problem.

Group Processes

It should be apparent from the previous discussion that at the heart of this transformation process are employee teams. Success is measured in terms of individual team performance and accomplishments. The point is to empower individuals who control the system to make decisions about how to do their jobs better. If people take pride in meeting customers' expectations then the entire organization is transformed.

It is important to take a moment to discuss how groups or teams perform most effectively.

Teamwork Requirements

A team is a group of individuals who come together to solve a problem. Each individual can make a difference in the outcome of the problem. Everyone is accountable for performance. Everyone shares one mission or purpose.

To be successful, TQM teams must be well organized and well directed. Typically, teams meet once each week for 1 to 2 hours. With so little time, team meetings must be focused, efficient, and productive. To that end, most teams select individuals to fill several important roles:

■ **Leader**
Every meeting must have an agenda. The leader ensures that all discussion stays focused and on track. The leader also as-

signs tasks identified by the team that will take place outside the meeting.

■ **Scribe**
It is important that accurate records about what took place at each meeting are maintained. The scribe takes notes and writes a summary after the meeting. The minutes are read by the steering committee so members are informed of progress. The minutes are also used by the team to recall previous decisions and action.

■ **Timekeeper**
Time is critical. The team often decides to limit discussion on a specific agenda item. The timekeeper monitors progress and reminds the team where it is in the dialogue.

The team must make difficult decisions sometimes. Every member must emotionally and intellectually "buy into" the process that is taking place. If one member is disruptive or does not contribute to the process, then the team can ask the steering committee for a replacement.

Effective Team Behaviors

There is a wealth of information on effective team behaviors. Team training must be part of the education process developed and directed by the steering committee. Four key characteristics emerge as fundamental to team success:

■ **Full participation**
This means both physical and mental participation. The leader must be especially sensitive to drawing every member into discussion. Individuals must encourage each other by acknowledging each others' ideas and worth.

■ **Lack of dominance or peer pressure**
No one may be allowed to dominate the discussion, ideas, or process. Unless there is full participation, free exchange of ideas,

and the shared belief everyone was part of the solution, then nothing will change.

■ **Listening**
Sometimes individuals are so anxious to speak that they do not hear what others are saying. A good listening technique is for the leader to ask someone to summarize what someone else said. The exchange of ideas means everyone hears and considers.

■ **Concensus decisions**
This is the most difficult, but most powerful and effective, team behavior. Everyone should agree before action is taken. The behavior takes time. It involves give and take and negotiation. When this technique is achieved, however, everyone is committed.

Key Terms

Continuous Quality
  Improvement (CQI)
Total Quality Management
  (TQM)
Total Responsiveness
  Management (TRM)

Kizan
ISO 9000 standards
  registration
statistical process control
  (SPC)

histogram
Pareto chart
cause and effect chart
control chart

Questions for Review

1. Who was W. Edwards Deming and what was his role in customer-defined quality management?
2. How does the customer define quality in terms of context, time, and measure of success?
3. What does "Kizan" mean?
4. What is ISO 9000 standards registration?
5. Contrast how the customer and a press operator might view the printing process.
6. What is an internal customer?
7. Why did Deming urge the elimination of postinspection?

8. What are the five common concepts of customer-defined quality management?
9. What are the four typical TQM implementation steps?
10. What is the difference between a histogram and a Pareto chart?
11. What are the six steps in a problem-solving process?
12. What is the difference between "identifying a problem" and "defining a problem"?
13. What is the function of a team scribe?

Appendices
Calibrating and Using Graphic Arts Tools

APPENDIX A

Determining Proper Film Exposure

Proper exposure for all film images has always been important, but with the increasing use of film processors and rapid-access type films it is becoming even more critical. In the past, camera operators were able to compensate for improper exposure by adjusting development time or agitation. With film processors development time and agitation are controlled. Therefore, knowing the correct exposure is even more essential. There is only one correct exposure for any given type of film with a given type of copy. Most film manufacturers recommend a solid step 4 on the grey scale for normal copy. It is important to realize that, due to the characteristics of the original copy, the correct exposure may need to be adjusted. One such example would be fine line copy in which a solid step 3 is recommended. The development should stay the same and the exposure should change to produce a solid step 3. Once the copy has been evaluated and the exposure needs established, one must determine the proper exposure.

Determining the proper exposure is a systematic task and should never be approached by guessing or a hit-or-miss technique. To begin, it is important to review just what exposure is and what the basic elements are that affect exposure. **Exposure** is defined as the total quantity of light that strikes the film. The two key elements that control exposure are the length of time light is allowed to strike the film and the amount of light that is available. A simple analogy to explain this point would be filling a bathtub with water. If you want to fill the bathtub with 20 gallons of water and you turn the faucet on full, the bathtub will take 6 minutes to fill. If you were to install a second faucet on the other side of the bathtub and turn both faucets on full, the bathtub should take only half the time to fill because twice as much water is available. When dealing with process cameras or other exposure equipment, the exposure time is regulated by different devices (timers or integrators) and the amount of light is controlled by the light source (wattage and/or number of bulbs). The light source can be regulated further by either a controlled opening (such as an aperture f/stop) or a light intensity control box (changes the current to the bulb). The choice of these devices depends upon the exposure equipment being used, such as a process camera or a contact frame. The correct exposure is also determined differently depending upon the exposure equipment used. The following outlines the process for determining the proper exposure for both a process camera and a contact frame. There are many ways to determine the proper exposure times. What is described in this appendix is only one of a variety of successful techniques. This method is fast, accurate, and uses a minimal amount of film.

Basic Process Camera Exposure Test

It is always a good idea to include a grey scale when doing any work on a process camera whether you are processing film in a tray or in a film processor. Once you have used the grey scale to determine the proper exposure, it acts as a control device to assure quality and consistency. This testing method requires the use of a 12-step, reflection grey scale. When working with process camera photography, most film manufacturers recommend a solid step 4 with a standard amount of development. The true variable, and the problem at hand, is what exposure should be used. A good test exposure time to start with is two f/stops down from wide open at 15 seconds. In other words, if your camera has four f/stop openings (f/11, f/16, f/22, and f/32), begin with an exposure of f/16 at 15 seconds. There is no guarantee that this is the right f/stop or exposure time, but it will produce an image that can be adjusted according to the information outlined in the following paragraphs. If you are not putting your film through a film processor, it is important that you process the film in fresh chemistry and for precisely the length of time that the film manufacturer recommends; this is typically $2^1/_2$ or $2^3/_4$ minutes (if you are unsure, use $2^3/_4$ minutes). Once the film is processed you are ready to evaluate it and make compensations as needed according to a process referred to as **grey scale math.**

Grey scale math is based upon the laws of physics and how they relate to film emul-

sions. In simpler terms, it is based upon the fact that wherever light hits the film emulsion, the emulsion turns black after processing. The more light that strikes the film, the darker (denser) the emulsion becomes. If the light is adjusted in a controlled manner, we can predict the density change on the film. There are three key elements needed to predict and control the change when dealing with a process camera: a timer or integrator, a diaphragm control board (f/stop dial), and a grey scale. Figure 6.10 illustrates the relationship that each f/stop has to another. Looking again at that chart we can put this into a simple mathematical relationship. Whenever you move to a different f/stop above or below your original setting, you change the amount of light by a factor of 2. This means that if you were to start with f/22 and move to the next larger f/stop opening (f/16), you would let in exactly twice as much light. If you were to move to the next smaller f/stop opening (f/32), you would let in exactly half as much light. This relationship becomes even more important when it is recognized that a change of two steps on the grey scale equals to a factor of 2 as well. This means that if your test piece of film shows development to a solid step 2 and you want a step 4, you must increase your exposure by a factor of 2. This can be achieved by moving to the next larger f/stop opening as just mentioned or by doubling the exposure time. If the test works out to be a solid step 6, then you need to decrease your exposure time by a factor of 2 (cut the exposure in half). This can be done by either changing to the next smaller f/stop opening or by cutting the exposure time in half. This simple technique can be expanded to include changes in any number of steps on the grey scale. Figure A.1 goes into detail on the rules and procedures for using grey scale math. Figure A.2 illustrates two examples of working with grey scale math that could resemble the result of your initial test exposure.

The basic procedure for running an exposure test can be summarized in the following steps:

1. Determine an initial test exposure for the camera being used. Expose and process a piece of film according to the manufacturer's recommendations.

2. Evaluate the processed film and determine what step on the grey scale was reached using the test exposure.

3. Using the reference chart in this appendix (figure A.1), determine what adjustments should be made to the exposure time and/or f/stop. Reshoot the image.

4. Process and evaluate the second piece of film to see if the proper amount of exposure compensation was calculated. This piece of film must be developed exactly the same as the first test negative.

It is important to recognize that if any element in the exposure process changes, a new test may need to be run because the exposure time may have changed. This is true regardless of the exposure equipment (process camera or contact frame) being used. Some of the common elements that might affect the exposure are a new brand of chemical or film or a new batch of the same chemical or film, a different camera, new lights on the camera, or a change in the angle of the lights to the copyboard.

Because this method of testing can be done in under 5 minutes (once you are experienced) and uses as little as one-quarter of a sheet of 8 inch × 10 inch film, there is no reason to waste full sheets of film if you are not completely sure of the correct exposure for a box of film.

This procedure works just as well for duplicating film on the process camera. The only difference is what you want to see on the grey scale. If on line film you want a solid step 4, which means that you can see slightly through the 4 when the negative is on a light table, then you should see the opposite on duplicating film. The four should have a slight bit of grey. Regardless of the step you are trying to achieve, grey scale math works the same as long as you keep in mind that more light increases the amount of clear area on duplicating film. If step 7 was clear and you desired a clear step 4, you would move down 3 steps as illustrated in example B of figure A.2. Once again the important concept to remember when working with duplicating film is that light controls the quantity of clear area on the film—the more light, the more clear area. Grey scale math works equally well on duplicating film when approached from this perspective.

Contact Frame Exposure Test

Determining the proper exposure time in a contact frame follows the same rules of physics and light that we dealt with on the camera. Again in simple language, contact film (or fine film) becomes darker as the amount of light striking it increases; duplicating film does just the opposite—it becomes lighter with increased light. The key in contacting is determining the proper exposure to get the exact opposite of the original when working on contact film or the exact same reproduction when working on duplicating film. You must realize that no matter how good a reproduction may be, there is always some loss in the copy. There is a tremendous amount of exposure latitude when contacting, as compared to when exposing on the process camera. This cannot be interpreted as meaning that there is not a best exposure. If you hope to achieve the best possible reproduction, you must work in a systematic manner with an appropriate testing device. A contacting test target is available from most film manufacturers and, if used properly, can accurately establish the exposure time that will provide the best reproduction of the image for the film and processing methods you are using. The test target illustrated in figure A.3 has five identical images to allow you to make exposure step-offs to save film and time. Some test targets come only as single images. Once the correct exposure time has been established it is a good practice to make five duplicates and create your own test target with five identical images.

The test target is easy to use. The one shown in figure A.3 has seven areas; from left to right they are: clear, 2-percent dot, 5-percent dot, 50-percent dot, 95-percent dot, 98-percent dot, and solid black. Some versions have fewer dot percentages represented and, although it may be slightly harder to see the subtle changes in exposure, they can still produce very accurate results. To run a test, you expose the test image to a piece of film, stepping off in equal increments. (If you will be contacting emulsion-to-emulsion or emulsion-to-base, be sure to run your test the same way because there can be a difference.) Determining the increments depends on the light intensity and film used. It is best to work with final exposure times of between 10 and 20 seconds. Therefore, you should try to adjust the light intensity (either raise or lower the light or change voltage regulator if available) to produce an acceptable test with five 5-second step-offs (figure A.4). If in your initial test on contact film (or line film), it is too dark in all steps, decrease the intensity of the light. If you have an image that is not

even black on the film, increase the exposure. Because duplicating film is used a great deal in contacting work, keep in mind that these statements are reversed for duplicating film.

Once you obtain a test piece of film that has a range of exposures on it, look at the extreme dots. In the case of the test image shown here, these would be the 2-percent and the 98-percent dots. Decide which exposure best reproduced each as dot percentage (see figure A.5). As shown in this example the two areas reproduce best at different exposure times. The best overall reproduction is therefore halfway between the two.

If you are working with materials where a test target is not available, such as contacting through paper (the example shown in figure A.6 is diffusion transfer receiver paper contacted to line film), you can still do an exposure step-off.

Use as the "test target" an image on the same base material as the actual working material. This is best done with an image with fine detail, such as illustrated in figure A.6, or a halftone image. Follow the step-off procedures used for any exposure test. Several attempts may be necessary to determine the range of exposure needed to pass light through the base. As before, the key is to have a series of steps that can be compared with the original image. The best reproduction becomes the contact exposure time for that material and type of film.

APPENDIX B

Light Sources and Color Temperature

The radiation of light causes the chemical reaction on a sheet of film. As printers, we are concerned with the quantity and quality of light that creates that reaction. The sun is an ideal source of white light. For years it was the only light source printers used to produce photographic images. In line photography, huge rooms were set aside with large overhead windows and mirrors that could direct sunlight onto the movable cameras below. Quality photographs were produced—unless it rained, was cloudy, was at night, or was at the wrong time of year. It was difficult to control and predict the sun, so artificial light sources were developed. Although they were more controllable, these artificial devices were far from perfect. Improvements have been made, but the printer now is even more concerned about how to control the quality of light that reaches the film through the camera lens.

Light Sources

If we were to plot a graph of the relative intensity of natural white light across the visible spectrum, it would look something like figure B.1a. There would be nearly equal amounts of energy from all wavelengths of the spectrum. Contrast the natural white light curve with a similar distribution of energy emitted by a 40-watt, white tungsten lightbulb (figure B.1b). The artificial source is not made up of equal amounts of energy from the visible spectrum. Tungsten light is composed of much more red light than blue. This imbalance of radiation can cause significant problems for the line photographer if the sensitivity of the film does not match the emission of the light source.

Carbon arcs have been used as a light source for nearly every photographic application in the graphic arts industry. Light is generated by passing an electric current between two carbon rods, much as in the arc welding process. The electromagnetic emission of carbon arc light is continuous across the visible spectrum, but it is heavy in blue and violet light (figure B.1c). The quality of light is controlled by including metallic salts in the core of each carbon rod. This peaking of energy in the blue end is actually an advantage because the sensitivity of most printing films and plates is greatest in that area. However, carbon arcs have several disadvantages. Voltage changes can cause unstable variation in color temperature and light output. Noxious fumes are released and must be ventilated. A great deal of dirt is generated in an area that must be kept as clean as possible. A brief warm-up period is required (60 seconds) before peak intensity is reached. There is always a potential fire hazard because of the open carbon flame. Because of these limitations, carbon arcs find little application in modern printing operations.

Mercury vapor lamps operate by passing a current through a mercury gas in a quartz envelope. The vaporization and ionization of the gas generate light. The electromagnetic distribution is discontinuous across the visible spectrum (figure B.1d). There are massive peaks of emission in the blue-violet (b-v) and ultraviolet (u-v) regions, but radiation is practically nonexistent in all other areas. If images with colors other than b-v or u-v are photographed, it is very difficult to record a film image. This characteristic makes the light useless for color separation but causes no problems for blue-sensitive emulsions and platemaking. The lamps require a 2-minute to 3-minute warm-up time and are generally operated on a dual exposure system—a standby voltage and a full-intensity voltage. A shutter system is usually included to contain the light until an exposure is made. During the exposure the light is powered at full intensity and the shutter opens to allow the light to expose the plate. Once the lamp is extinguished, it has to cool down before it can be started again. However, additives to the mercury vapor can improve its light quality and significantly extend the lamp life.

Because of the 2-minute to 3-minute warm-up period for this type of light source, it is seldom, if ever, used for camera lights. To do so would require the extra expense of using a shutter over each camera fight.

Pulsed xenon lamps were first introduced in 1958. They were developed as an application of photographic electronic flash techniques. The lamp is formed by filling quartz tubing with low-pressure xenon gas. The xenon is charged and discharged at the rate of the power line frequency—120 times each second. Even though the lamp is pulsed, the frequency is such that the light appears continuous across the visible spectrum, with no radical peaks of emission (figure B.1e). Although lower in blue-violet output, the lamp has several overriding advantages for line photography. It reaches peak intensity instantly, has constant color temperature, has a spectral output very close to sunlight, is economical to operate, and is very clean. Pulsed xenon lamps are also used for platemaking. However, longer exposure times are required as compared to metal halide lamps of the same wattage.

The **metal halide lamp** is a recent development. It is basically a mercury lamp with metal halide additives. The electromagnetic emission peaks extremely high in the blue-violet area (figure B.1f). This output matches the maximum sensitivity of many printing materials. It has been applied successfully in platemaking, proofing, photofabrication, screen emulsion exposures, and gravure work.

It provides at least four times more **actinic output** (energy that activates or hardens light-sensitive coatings) than any other light source.

Color Temperature

Color temperature is a term used often by both printers and photographers but without accurate understanding. Light sources are often classified according to color temperature (table B.1), which makes people think that temperature is a primary concern for all photography—but it is not. Color temperature is not a concern in black-and-white process photography, but it is of paramount importance in color work, whether original photography or color separation.

Color temperature is a measure of the sum color effect of the visible light emitted by any source. The blue end of the visible spectrum is rated as having a higher color temperature than the red end. Color temperature is defined theoretically by heating a perfect radiator of energy or "black body." As the temperature increases, the color of the body changes. Each color of the visible spectrum is then assigned a temperature that corresponds to the temperature of the black body for that color. Color temperature is measured in degrees Kelvin ($°K$), which is derived by adding 273 to the temperature in degrees Centigrade ($°C$). Color temperature is not such an unusual idea. For centuries blacksmiths judged temperature visually by the color a piece of metal displayed as it was heated.

It is important to realize that color temperature describes only the visual appearance of a light source and does not necessarily describe its photographic effect. Both tungsten and fluorescent light sources might be rated at the same color temperature, but because they differ in spectral emissions, they might produce totally different results on a piece of film.

Most color films are balanced for a particular color temperature. In other words, they are designed to record images accurately under certain color conditions. If a film is rated around 5000°K, it should faithfully record color balance as viewed under natural sunlight. If film is rated around 3000°K, it is designed to be used under artificial incandescent light, as found in the average home.

Graphic arts films are rarely identified as being balanced for a particular color temperature. However, when working with color originals, the graphic arts photographer has to be certain that the reflected light that reaches the film is describing the color balance of the copy being reproduced faithfully. For that reason the industry has even adopted a color temperature standard for viewing and judging color proofing and printing (5000°K) to ensure consistent human color perception. Figure B.2 is an example of a standard viewing device. It ensures that each transparency viewed is illuminated with a light source used throughout the industry.

APPENDIX C

Finding Information Resources in the Graphic Arts

There is more information on print and the graphic arts than any single book, reference manual, or individual could hold. This book is intended to be a contemporary, comprehensive review of printing technology. However, because of its breadth, it is impossible to treat any single topic in exhaustive detail. In other words, behind every chapter or section is a vast array of information that was not discussed.

In some ways this appendix may be the most important portion of this entire book. There is an old Chinese saying: "Give a man a fish and he eats for a day; teach a man to fish and he eats for a lifetime." The purpose of this section is to outline the procedures and resources available to help you find information beyond what is covered in this book.

Strategy One

To begin any search, you must first get an idea of how much information is available on the topic. To do this, you need a quick overview. Any basic printing textbook (such as this one) is a good start. Read the chapter that contains your topic, and make notes on key terms. These key terms are called "descriptors." Also, work to gain a snapshot understanding of the issues or questions.

Use the index to determine if your key terms are used anywhere else in the text. See how they are used and if they appear in another context that might be related to the topic. Then review the bibliography. A bibliography is a list of books that describe a body of information. Each entry in a bibliography is called a "citation." A citation contains enough information to locate the work. Typical information is author's name, book title, publisher's name and city, and date of last publication. Some citations also include the number of pages in the text. Identify citations that appear appropriate to your topic.

Another way to find an overview of a subject is to use one of the encyclopedia-like books on printing. *The Lithographers Manual*, published by the Graphic Arts Technical Foundation, is one example. It is updated every five or six years and is a very technical treatment of every area of lithography. Another example is *The Gravure Industry*, published by the Gravure Association of America. Use the index to locate your descriptors. Then review the information in the book. Again, the purpose is to gain a good overview of issues and to identify other, more specific references.

Strategy Two

The next step is to locate the books described in your citations. Many printers have them in their personal libraries. Companies often purchase books on an ongoing basis from professional associations in order to maintain a reference collection.

Individuals seeking information do not typically have access to such resources. The best source is a public library. Large libraries purchase books across many topics. Good collections of printing books are typically held by better libraries. Another possibility might be the library of a university, community college, or technical institute with a program in printing. Even small libraries can be resources because they often have borrowing privileges from larger libraries. The system is called "interlibrary loans."

You can also locate additional information by looking in the library's card catalog. Many libraries have moved to electronic catalogues, but whether the catalog is paper or electronic, the problem is to link your key terms with the subject headings used by the library. Most large libraries use the same subject headings as the Library of Congress in Washington, D.C. Here are some useful headings from that system:

- Printing
  Used for general books about the whole industry
- Printing, practical
  Used for books that are about technical aspects
- Lithography
  Used for books concerned primarily with lithography for artists
- Offset Printing
  Used for books that are about technical aspects of industrial lithography
- Screen Process Printing
  Used for books that are about technical aspects of industrial screen printing
- Serigraphy
  Used for books about screen printing for artists

You might also find information under:

- Advertising Layout and Typography
- Book Industries and Trade
- Color Printing
- Color Separation
- Chromolithography
- Desktop Publishing
- Electrostatic Printing
- Flexography
- Handpress

- Intaglio Printing
- Map Printing
- Newspaper Layout and Typography
- Paper—Printing Properties
- Photolithography
- Printing Industry
- Proofreading
- Type and Type Founding
- Typesetting

If at any time you are having trouble finding what you need, be sure to ask a librarian for help. That is what librarians are there for.

Strategy Three

There are over two hundred magazines concerned with printing and the graphic arts in one form or another. Sitting down and thumbing through many issues of magazines is the most inefficient way to find information, however. An index is a list of all the articles in a number of different magazines or journals. All the titles of articles that relate to that same subject are grouped together with the name of the publication, date, and page number included for each one. Most indexes are compiled so that by looking in one book you will find everything under a subject heading that was published in a single year.

The *Business Periodicals Index* indexes *Graphic Arts Monthly* and *American Printer* (as well as a few other magazines concerned with publishing) and can lead you to some technical information quickly. Many indexes also include an "abstract." An abstract is a short summary of the article so you can tell whether it will help you without actually reading the entire article.

Most indexes are "on-line," meaning that they can be accessed and searched using a computer. Systems vary, but each library will provide instructions on use.

Strategy Four

In additional to using an index to find specific information, you can use the most common magazines to keep up with what is currently happening in your field. You should read the summaries at the front of each publication regularly and then read the complete articles if you have time. Some trade magazines are free. The following is a list of the most common printing trade publications. You may write or fax to ask for subscription information.

American Printer
20 N. Wacker Drive
Chicago, IL 60606–3298
Tel: 312–726–2802
Fax: 312–726–2574

Graphic Arts Monthly
249 W. 17th Street
New York, NY 10011
Tel: 800–637–6089
Fax: 212–463–6530

In-Plant Printer & Electronic Publisher
425 Huehl Road, Building 11
Northbrook, IL 60065–2319
Tel: 708–564–5940
Fax: 708–564–8361

Printing Impressions
401 North Broad Street
Philadelphia, PA 19108
Tel: 215–238–5300
Fax: 215–238–5457

Publishers Weekly
249 W. 17th Street
New York, NY 10011
Tel: 800–842–1669
Fax: 212–463–6631

Quick Printing
1680 SW Bayshore Boulevard
Port St. Lucie, FL 34984–3598
Tel: 407–879–6666
Fax: 407–879–7397

Step-By-Step Graphics
6000 N. Forest Park Drive
Peoria, IL 61614–3592
Tel: 309–688–2300
Fax: 309–688–3075

U & l c International Typeface Corporation
866 Second Avenue
New York, NY 10017
Tel: 212–371–0699
Fax: 212–752–4752

Computer Publishing Magazine
Pacific Magazine Group
513 Wilshire Boulevard, Suite 344
Santa Monica, CA 90401
Tel: 213–455–1414
Fax: 213–393–5222

Computer Pictures
Montage Publishing, Inc.
701 Westchester Avenue
White Plains, NY 10604
Tel: 914–328–9157
Fax: 914–328–9093

Pre-
The Magazine for Prepublishing & Prepress
8340 Mission Road, Suite 106
Prairie Village, KS 66206
Tel: 913–642–6611
Fax: 913–642–6676

Strategy Five

In addition to libraries and publications, technical and professional associations provide a good source of information on the graphic arts. There are associations associated with nearly every aspect of the industry. The following is only a partial list that focuses on national associations. Many states and most major cities also have local associations or clubs.

All of these associations provide information to people interested in the area of the industry represented by their membership. Many publish books, newsletters, and other educational materials. Most offer educational membership at a reduced cost to students and teachers in the graphic arts.

Association membership can be an important part of your career. Often the people you meet through an association remain friends for a lifetime, broaden your perspective, and increase your opportunities for advancement.

Gravure Association of America, Inc.
1200-A Scottsville Road
Rochester, NY 14624
Tel: 716–436–2150
Fax: 716–436–7689

National Printing Equipment Suppliers (NPES)
1899 Preston White Drive
Reston, VA 22091–4367
Tel: 703–264–7200
Fax: 703–620–0994

Screen Printing Association International
10015 Main Street
Fairfax, VA 22031
Tel: 703–385–1335
Fax: 703–273–0456
703–273–0469 Convention line

National Association of Quick Printers
401 North Michigan Avenue
Chicago, IL 60611
Tel: 312–644–6610
Fax: 312–321–6869

International Association of Printing House Craftsmen
7042 Brooklyn Boulevard
Minneapolis, MN 55429–1370
Tel: 800–466–4274
Fax: 800–733–4274

Education Council of the Graphic Arts Industry
1899 Preston White Drive
Reston, VA 22091–4367
Tel: 703–648–1768
Fax: 703–620–0994

Graphic Arts Technical Foundation
4615 Forbes Avenue
Pittsburgh, PA 15213–3796
Tel: 412–621–6941
Fax: 412–621–3049

International Prepress Association
7200 France Avenue, South
Edina, MN 55435–4302
Tel: 612–896–1808
Fax: 612–896–0181

Flexographic Technical Association/
Flexographic Technical Foundation
900 Marconi Avenue
Ronkonkima, NY 11779–7212
Tel: 516–737–6026
Fax: 516–737–6813

Research & Engineering Council of the Graphic Arts Industry
Box 639
Chadds Ford, PA 19317
Tel: 215–388–7394
Fax: 215–388–2708

Tag & Label Manufacturers Institute
1700 First Avenue, South
Iowa City, IA 52240
Tel: 319–337–8247
Fax: 319–337–8271

Printing Industries of America
100 Daingerfield Road
Alexandria, VA 22314
Tel: 703–519–8192
Fax: 703–548–3227

National Business Forms Association
433 East Monroe Avenue
Alexandria, VA 22301
Tel: 703–836–6232
Fax: 703–836–2241

National Newspaper Association
1627 K Street N.W.
Washington, DC 20006
Tel: 202–466–7200
Fax: 202–331–1403

National Paper Trade Association
111 Great Neck Road
Great Neck, NY 11021
Tel: 516–829–3070
Fax: 516–829–3074

Paper Industry Management Association
2400 East Oakto Street
Arlington Heights, IL 60005
Tel: 708–956–0250
Fax: 708–956–0520

Suburban Newspapers of America
401 North Michigan Avenue
Chicago, IL 60611–4267
Tel: 312–644–6610
Fax: 312–321–6869

Typographers International Association
84 Park Avenue
Flemington, NJ 08822
Tel: 908–782–4635
Fax: 908–782–4671

Newspaper Association of America
11600 Sunrise Valley Drive
Reston, VA 22091
Tel: 703–648–1000
Fax: 703–620–4557
     Newspaper in Education Department

American Paper Institute
260 Madison Avenue
New York, NY 10016
Tel: 212–340–0600
Fax: 212–689–2628

Direct Marketing Association
11 West 42nd Street
New York, NY 10036–8096
Tel: 212–768–7277
Fax: 212–768–4546

Engraved Stationery Manufacturers
     Association, Inc.
305 Plus Park Boulevard
Nashville, TN 37217
Tel: 615–366–1094
Fax: 615–366–4192

Fibre Box Association
2850 Golf Road
Rolling Meadows, IL 60008
Tel: 708–364–9600
Fax: 708–364–9639

International Press Association
222 South Jefferson, Suite 200
Chicago, IL 60661
Tel: 312–441–9017
Fax: 312–441–9019

Magazine Publishers Association
919 3rd Avenue
New York, NY 10022
Tel: 212–752–0055
Fax: 212–888–4217

APPENDIX D

Proofreading Exercise

The following is manuscript copy written for the anecdote for chapter 2. Notice that it has been proofread and marked for the typesetter. In this appendix you will find common proofreading marks and galley copy. Make a photocopy of the galley page, and use the most common proofreading marks to correct the errors in typesetting. A galley solution also is shown.

No ¶

The inventor of printing in the western world is generally considered to be Johann Gensfleisch zum Gutenberg, who was born in the city of Mainz, Germany, in 1397. The wealth of the Gutenberg family freed Johann for a life of leisure and pleasure, during which he developed an interest in technology, *em* primarily seal making and gold-smithing. In 1438 he started a business that produced mirrors in *religious* Strasbourg. By that time he was considered a master craftsmen in metalworking.

There is evidence that by 1444 he had returned to Mainz to set up a printing shop. As a goldsmith he had cut letters and symbols in precious metals or in reverse in wax to form a mold to cast jewelry. It is unknown exactly how the idea of casting individual letters for printing occurred to him. However, the concept of "mirror" images was obviously common knowledge. The casting process involved cutting l by hand in reverse on a piece of hard metal, then punching the letter shape into a soft copper mold to form a die called a matrix.

suitable Gutenberg next needed a metal to cast in the mold. He experimented with pewter hardened with large quantities of antimony, but the material shrank when it cooled and pulled away from the matrix. The letters formed were imperfect. His experience with lead in mirror manufacturing finally encouraged him to try a combination of lead, tin, and antimony. Gutenberg's original formula (5% tin, 12% antimony, and 83% lead) remains nearly unchanged today. Characters can *#this#* be perfectly cast with this alloy because it expands when it cools and forms an exact duplicate of the matrix cavity. Using his system, two workers could cast and dress (trim away excess material) twenty-five pieces of type an hour.

Gutenbergs most notable work, his forty-two-line bible (a Bible with forty-two lines to the page), was begun in 1452 and completed by 1455. Each page contained around 2,800 characters. Two pages were printed at the same time, so 5,600 pieces were needed to make each two-page printing. It was the common practice for the next two pages to be composed during the press run, so at least 11,200 letters were needed even to begin printing. Working a normal workday (twelve hours), two craftsmen took more than 37 workdays to prepare the initial type. At this rate of speed. over three years were needed to complete just two hundred copies of the Bible.

Much of modern printing comes to us from the craft of foundry type composition, developed by Johann Gutenberg and his workers more than five hundred years ago. Terms such as "form," "leading," "uppercase," "lowercase," "type size," "impression," and "make-ready" originated with Gutenberg. All printers today owed a debt to the hundreds of early craftsmen who followed Gutenberg in the tradition of hand-set foundry type and gave us both a language and an art.

Corrected Manuscript Copy

The inventor of printing in the Western world is generally considered to be Johann Gensfleisch zum Gutenberg, who was born in the city of Mainz, Germany, in 1397. The wealth of the Gutenberg family freed Johann for a life of leisure and pleasure, during which he developed an interest in technology—primarily seal making and goldsmithing. In 1438 he started a business that produced religious mirrors in Strasbourg. By that time he was considered a master craftsman in metalworking.

There is evidence that by 1444 he had returned to Mainz to set up a printing shop. As a goldsmith he had cut letters and symbols in precious metals or in reverse in wax to form a mold to cast jewelry. It is unknown exactly how the idea of casting individual letters for printing occurred to him. However, the concept of "mirror" images was obviously common knowledge. The casting process involved cutting a letter by hand in reverse on a piece of hard metal, then punching the letter shape into a soft copper mold to form a die, called a matrix.

Gutenberg next needed a suitable metal to cast in the mold. He experimented with pewter hardened with large quantities of antimony, but the material shrank when it cooled and pulled away from the matrix. The letters formed were imperfect. His experience with lead in mirror manufacturing finally encouraged him to try a combination of lead, tin, and antimony. Gutenberg's original formula (5% tin, 12% antimony, and 83% lead) remains nearly unchanged to this day. Characters can be perfectly cast with this alloy because it expands when it cools and forms an exact duplicate of the matrix cavity. Using his system, two workers could cast and dress (trim away excess material) twenty-five pieces of type an hour.

Gutenberg's most notable work, his forty-two-line Bible (a Bible with forty-two lines to the page), was begun in 1452 and completed by 1455. Each page contained around 2,800 characters. Two pages were printed at the same time, so 5,600 pieces of type were needed to make each two-page printing. It was the common practice for the next two pages to be composed during the press run, so at least 11,200 letters were needed even to begin printing. Working a normal workday (twelve hours), two craftsmen took more than thirty-seven workdays to prepare the initial type. At this rate of speed, more than three years were needed to complete just two hundred copies of the Bible.

Much of the language of modern printing comes to us from the craft of foundry type composition, developed by Johann Gutenberg and his workers more than five hundred years ago. Terms such as "form," "leading," "uppercase," "lowercase," "type size," "impression," and "makeready" originated with Gutenberg. All printers today owe a debt to the hundreds of early craftsmen who followed Gutenberg in the tradition of hand-set foundry type and gave us both a language and an art.

The Most Common Proofreading Marks

Size and Style of Type

	Direction	Corrected Result
lc	Lower Case letter	Lower case letter
lc	Set in LOWER CASE	Set in lower case
C	capital Letter	Capital Letter
caps	SET IN capitals	SET IN CAPITALS
ital	Set in italic type	Set in *italic* type
bf	Set in boldface type	Set in **boldface** type
sm caps	Set in Small Capitals	SET IN SMALL CAPITALS

Paragraphing

	Direction	Corrected Result
¶	Begin the paragraph at this point in the text	Begin the paragraph at this point in the text
no ¶	No paragraph.	No paragraph. Run in or run on.
run in	Run in or run on.	
flush	No indention	No indention
hang in	Hanging indention. This style	Hanging indention. This style should
one	should have all lines after the first	have all lines after the first
em	marked for the desired indentation.	marked for the desired indentation.

Insertion and Deletion

	Direction	Corrected Result
at	Insert matter omitted this point	Insert matter omitted at this point
	Delete or take out delete	Delete or take out
	Delete and close up	Delete and close up
e/	Correct latter or word marked	Correct letter or word marked
stet	Let it stand. All matter above dots	Let it stand. All matter above dots

Position

	Direction	Corrected Result
]	Move to right]	Move to right
[[	Move to left	Move to left
tr	Transposes pace	Transpose space
tr	Transpose enclosed in ring matter	Transpose matter enclosed in ring
tr	Transpose (order letters of or words)	Transpose (order of letters or words)
tr	Rearrange words of order numbers in	Rearrange in order of numbers
run over	Run over to next line. A two-letter/division should be avoided. *over*	Run over to the next line. A two letter division should be avoided.

run back Run back to preceding line. This div-
         ision should be avoided.

Run back to preceding line. This division should be avoided.

Spacing

Direction

⌒ Close up entirely; take out space

Insert space at the caret mark

⌣ Close up partly; leave some space

Corrected Result

Close up entirely; take out space

Insert space at the caret mark

Close up partly; leave some space

Special Symbols

Direction

EM Use an EM dash instead of hyphens

wo Write out the number ⑨

Corrected Result

Use an EM dash—instead of hyphens

Write out the number nine

Galley Copy

The inventor of printing in the Western world is generally considered to be Johann Gensfleisch zum Gutenberg, who was born in the city of Mainz, Germany, in 1397. The wealth of the Gutenberg family freed Johann for a life of leisure and pleasure, during which he developed an interest in technology—primarily seal making and goldsmithing.

\# In 1438 he started a business that produced religious mirrors in Strasbourg. By that time he was considered a master craftsman in metalworking.

There is evidence that by 1444 he had returned to Mainz to set up a printing shop. As a goldsmith he had cut letters and symbols in precious metals or in reverse in wax to form a mold to cast Jewelry. It is unknown exactly how the idea of casting individual letters for printing occurred to him. However, the concept of "mirror" images was obviously common knowledge. The casting process involved cutting a letter by hand in reverse on a piece of hard metal, then punching the letter shape into a soft copper mold to form a die, called a matrix.

Gutenberg next needed a suitable metal to cast in the mold. He experimented with pewter hardened with large quantities of antimony, but the material shrank when it cooled and pulled away from the matrix. The letters formed were imperfect. His experience with lead in mirror manufacturing finally encouraged him to try a combination of lead, tin, and antimony. Gutenberg's original formula (5% tin, 12% antimony, and 83% lead) remains nearly unchanged to this day. Characters can be perfectly cast with this alloy because it expands when it cools and forms an exact duplicate of the matrix cavity. Using his system, two workers could cast and dress (trim away excess material) twenty-five pieces of type an hour.

Gutenberg's most notable work, his forty-two-line Bible (a Bible with forty-two lines to the page), was begun in 1452 and completed by 1455. Each page contained around 2,800 characters. Two pages were printed at the same time, so 5,600 pieces of type were needed to make each two-page printing. It was the common practice for the next two pages to be composed during the press run, so at least 11,200 letters

were needed even to begin printing. Working a normal workday
(twelve hours), two craftsmen took more than thirtyseven workdays
dash to prepare the initial type. At this rate of speed, over three years were
needed to complete just two hundred copies of the Bible.

Much of the language ⌐f modern printing comes to us from the
craft of foundry type composition, developed by Johann Gutenberg
and his workers more than five hundred years ago. Terms such as
"form," "leading," "uppercase," "lowercase," "type size," "impression," and "makeready" originated with Gutenberg. All printers today
owe a debt to the hundreds of early craftsmen who followed Gutenberg in the tradition of hand-set foundry type and gave us both a language and an art.

Galley Copy (corrected)

The inventor of printing in the Western world is generally considered
to be Johann Gensfleisch zum Gutenberg, who was born in the city of
Mainz, Germany, in 1397. The wealth of the Gutenberg family freed
Johann for a life of leisure and pleasure, during which he developed
an interest in technology—primarily seal making and goldsmithing.
In 1438 he started a business that produced religious mirrors in Strasbourg. By that time he was considered a master craftsman in metalworking.

There is evidence that by 1444 he had returned to Mainz to set
up a printing shop. As a goldsmith he had cut letters and symbols in
precious metals or in reverse in wax to form a mold to cast jewelry. It
is unknown exactly how the idea of casting individual letters for
printing occurred to him. However, the concept of "mirror" images
was obviously common knowledge. The casting process involved cutting a letter by hand in reverse on a piece of hard metal, then punching the letter shape into a soft copper mold to form a die, called a
matrix.

Gutenberg next needed a suitable metal to cast in the mold. He
experimented with pewter hardened with large quantities of antimony, but the material shrank when it cooled and pulled away from
the matrix. The letters formed were imperfect. His experience with

lead in mirror manufacturing finally encouraged him to try a combination of lead, tin, and antimony. Gutenberg's original formula (5% tin, 12% antimony, and 83% lead) remains nearly unchanged to this day. Characters can be perfectly cast with this alloy because it expands when it cools and forms an exact duplicate of the matrix cavity. Using his system, two workers could cast and dress (trim away excess material) twenty-five pieces of type an hour.

Gutenberg's most notable work, his forty-two-line Bible (a Bible with forty-two lines to the page), was begun in 1452 and completed by 1455. Each page contained around 2,800 characters. Two pages were printed at the same time, so 5,600 pieces of type were needed to make each two-page printing. It was the common practice for the next two pages to be composed during the press run, so at least 11,200 letters were needed even to begin printing. Working a normal workday (twelve hours), two craftsmen took more than thirty-seven workdays to prepare the initial type. At this rate of speed, over three years were needed to complete just two hundred copies of the Bible.

Much of the language of modern printing comes to us from the craft of foundry type composition, developed by Johann Gutenberg and his workers more than five hundred years ago. Terms such as "form," "leading," "uppercase," "lowercase," "type size," "impression," and "makeready" originated with Gutenberg. All printers today owe a debt to the hundreds of early craftsmen who followed Gutenberg in the tradition of hand-set foundry type and gave us both a language and an art.

Glossary

Accordion fold. Several folds made parallel to each other.

Acetate sheet. Clear or frosted stable-base plastic material commonly used for overlays in paste-up.

Actinic light. Any light that exposes light-sensitive emulsions.

Actinic output. Energy that activates or hardens light-sensitive coatings; consists of shorter wavelengths of visible spectrum.

Additive primary colors. Colors that make up white light; red, blue, and green are the additive primary colors.

Additive plate. Presensitized lithographic plate on which ink-receptive coating must be added to exposed area during processing.

Additives. Compounds that control such ink characteristics as tack, workability, and drying time.

Adhesive binding. Glue fastening of printed sheets or signatures.

Agitation. Flow of solution back and forth over film during chemical processing.

Alphanumeric code. A unique code made of numbers and letters for all uppercase and lowercase letters, numbers, as well as some common punctuation and symbols.

Amortization. The process of distributing equipment costs across time periods or jobs.

Aniline printing. An early term for flexography. See *Flexography*.

Anilox roll. An inking roller on a flexographic press with a cellular surface.

Antihalation dye. Dye that is generally coated on back of most transparent-based film to absorb light that passes through emulsion and base during exposure.

Aperture. Opening through which light passes in the lens of a camera.

Ascender. Any portion of a letter that extends above the x-height.

ASCII (pronounced "As-Key"). An alphanumeric code used in telecommunication.

Asphaltum. Tar-like material used as an acid resist in gravure printing.

Assembling. Finishing operations that bring all elements of a printing job together into final form; common assembling operations are gathering, collating, and inserting.

Back-lighted copyboard. Equipment in some process cameras for photographing transparent copy; light is projected through the back of the copyboard and the camera lens to the new film.

Balance. Equilibrium of the visual images on a sheet.

Ballard shell process. Special technique used by many gravure publication printers for easy removal of copper layer after cylinder has been printed.

Basic density range (BDR). Range of detail produced from halftone screen by main exposure.

Basic exposure. Camera aperture and shutter speed combination that produces a quality film image of normal line copy with standardized chemical processing.

Basic sheet size. Basis from which all paper weights are determined by the manufacturer; differs for each of the four paper classifications: book paper (25 inches × 38 inches), writing paper (17 inches × 22 inches), cover paper (20 inches × 26 inches), and Bristol paper (22 inches × 28 inches).

Basis weight. Weight in pounds of one ream (500 sheets) of the basic sheet size of a particular paper type.

Baumé. Density scale used by Antoine Baumé, a French chemist, in graduating his hydrometers.

Bimetal plate. Plate manufactured with two dissimilar metals; one forms the ink-receptive image and the other forms the solution-receptive area.

Bit. A binary digit, either a *0* or a *1*.

Blanket cylinder. Part of a rotary press that transfers the image from the plate cylinder to the press sheet.

Bleed. Extension of a printing design over the edge of a sheet.

Blueline flat method. Special method of preparing a flat as part of one multiflat registration system; blueline flat carries all important detail, including register marks.

Blueprint paper. Inexpensive photomechanical proofing material; is exposed through the flat on a platemaker, developed in water, fixed in photographic hypo, and then washed to remove fixer stains.

Blue-sensitive material. Photographic material that reacts to the blue part of white-light exposure.

Body-height. Distance from the base line to the top of a lowercase letter *x* in a given font; varies depending on alphabet design; also known as "x-height."

Bone folder. Most common type of hand folding device; consists of a long, narrow blade of bone or plastic.

Book paper. Most common type of paper found in the printing industry; available in a wide range of grades and noted for easy printability.

Bridge. Surface of a gravure cylinder between wells.

Bristol paper. Stiff, heavy material used for business cards, programs, file folders, inexpensive booklet covers, and the like.

Brownline. Inexpensive photomechanical proofing material; is exposed through the flat on a platemaker, developed in water, fixed in photographic hypo, and then washed in water to remove fixer stains; the longer the exposure, the more intense the brownline image.

Buckle folder. Paper-folding machine that operates by forcing a sheet between two rollers and causing it to curve.

Bump exposure. No-screen image exposure made through the lens; used to change contrast by compressing the screen range.

Burner film. Piece of transparent film that allows full passage of light to the cylinder when preparing a gravure mask.

Burnisher. Tool used to apply pressure to a small surface; usually has a long handle and a hard, smooth ball or point.

Cab. Special film mask used in gravure printing; is punched and marked to be used as a guide for stripping negatives prior to making a gravure cylinder.

Calendering. Papermaking process that passes paper between rollers to smooth or polish the paper surface.

California job case. Most popular case for holding foundry type; contains all characters in a single drawer.

Camera-ready copy. Finished paste-up used to create the images of the final job.

Cameron belt press. Web-fed printing machine used in book production; prints from rubber plates imposed on a flexible belt; designed to mass produce an entire book rapidly.

Carbon arcs. Rods whose electromagnetic emission is heavy in blue and violet light; were used commonly as a light source for the graphic arts industry.

Carbon printing. Process of transferring the positive image to the cylinder mask in conventional gravure.

Carbon tissue. Gelatin-based material coated on a paper backing and used in gravure printing.

Carousel carrier. Multicolor screen printing equipment that holds individual screen frames, one for each color; rotates around a central axis and moves each screen into position sequentially over the object to be printed.

Cause and effect chart. A tool used to outline all elements of a process or problem.

Casebound cover. Rigid cover generally associated with high-quality bookbinding.

Center lines. Lines drawn on a paste-up in light-blue pencil to represent the center of each dimension of the illustration board.

Chain gripper delivery. Press delivery unit technique in which sheets are pulled onto the delivery stack by a mechanical system.

Characteristic curve. Visual interpretation of a light-sensitive material's exposure/density relationship.

Chase. Metal frame used to hold forms during relief platemaking or printing.

Chaser lockup. Method of arranging furniture around a relief form when the form is not a standard dimension.

Checking for lift. Procedure that checks all elements within a locked chase; determines whether the elements are fixed tightly in position and will not move or fall out during handling or printing.

Clip art. Art supplied in camera-ready form; copyright given with purchase; available from a number of companies that specialize in providing art to printers.

Closed shop. Shop that requires craftspeople to join a union to maintain employment.

Coated paper. Paper with an added layer of pigment bonded to the original paper fiber surface to smooth the rough surface texture.

Cold type composition. Preparation of any printing form intended to be reproduced photographically.

Collating. Finishing operation in which individual printed sheets are assembled into the correct sequence.

Collodion. Viscous solution of cellulose nitrates, ether, and alcohol used to coat photographic plates.

Colloid. Any substance in a certain state of fine division.

Color sensitivity. Chemical change response of a particular silver halide emulsion to an area of the visible electromagnetic spectrum.

Color temperature. Measure of the sum color effect of the visible light emitted by any source.

Combing wheel. Type of sheet separator.

Commercial printing. Type of printing in which nearly any sort of printing job is accepted.

Common edge method. Method of multiflat registration in which two edges of each flat are positioned in line with each other; if the edges are lined up with corresponding edges of the plate, the images should be in correct positions.

Complementary flats. Two or more flats stripped so that each can be exposed singly to a plate but still have each image appear in correct position on the final printed sheet.

Composing stick. Instrument in which foundry type is assembled in lines for printing.

Composition. Process of assembling symbols (whether letters or drawings) in the position defined on the rough layout during image design.

Comprehensive. Artist's rendering that attempts to duplicate the appearance of the final product.

Contact printing. Process of exposing a sheet of light-sensitive material by passing light through a previously prepared piece of film.

Control chart. A visual tool used to examine variation in a repeating process.

Continuous Quality Improvement (CQI). Process of making each manufacturing or service step responsive to the customer's needs or expectations.

Continuous sheet-feeding system. A press that adds sheets to the feeding system without stopping the press in the middle of a run.

Continuous-tone photograph or copy. Image created from many different tones or shades and reproduced through photography.

Continuous-tone photography. Process of recording images of differing density on pieces of film; continuous-tone negatives show varying shades of grey or different hues of color.

Contrast. Noticeable difference between adjacent parts in tone and color.

Control strip. Piece of film used in automatic film processing to gauge the activity level of solutions in the machine; several times a day the photographer sends a pre-exposed control strip through the machine and then examines the processed piece to determine whether machine adjustments need to be made.

Conventional gravure. Method of preparing gravure cylinders that delivers well openings of the same opening size.

Copy. Words to be included on the rough layout; final paste-up; or, in some situations, the final press sheet.

Copyboard. Part of a process camera that opens to hold material to be photographed (the copy) during exposure.

Copy density range (CDR). Difference between the lightest highlight and the darkest shadow of a photograph or continuous-tone copy.

Counter. In gravure printing, angle between the doctor blade and the cylinder; in relief printing, sunken area just below the printing surface of foundry type.

Counting keyboard. Operator-controlled keyboard that requires end-of-line decisions as copy is being typed.

Cover paper. Relatively thick paper commonly used for outside covers of brochures or pamphlets.

Crash. Gauze-like material that is sometimes embedded in the perfect binding adhesive to increase strength.

Creasing. Process of crushing paper grain with a hardened steel strip to create a straight line for folding.

Cathode ray tube (CRT) character generation. Third-generation typesetting system that generates images by using a computer coupled with a cathode ray tube.

Ctn weight. Weight in pounds of one carton (ctn) of paper.

Cursor. A term used to describe a blinking line or rectangle on a computer screen that marks the next point of data entry.

Curvilinear type generation. A computer image generation technique that produces letters and symbols by a complex mathematic expression rather than by a series of points.

Cutting layout. Drawing that shows how a pile of paper is to be cut by the paper cutter.

Cylinder line. Area of a printing plate that marks the portion of masking sheet used to clamp the plate to the plate cylinder; always marked on the flat before stripping pieces of film.

Dampening sleeves. Thin fiber tubes that are slightly larger in diameter than the water form roller when dry; when moistened, they shrink to form a seamless cover.

Dark printer. One of the halftones used to make a duotone; usually printed with the use of black or another dark color; often contains the lower middle tones to shadow detail of the continuous-tone original.

Darkroom camera. Type of process camera designed to be used under the safelight of a darkroom; can be either vertical or horizontal.

Dead form. Any form that has been printed and is waiting to be remelted or distributed (if hot type).

Decalcomania. Process of transferring designs from a specially printed substrate to another surface; products are sometimes called "decals."

Deep-etch plate. Offset plate with the emulsion bonded into the base metal.

Default parameters. Parameters supplied by the computer when the operator fails to provide them.

Delivery unit. Unit on a printing press that moves the printed sheet from the printing unit to a pile or roll.

Demon letters. In foundry type composition, lowercase *p*, *d*, *q*, and *b*.

Densitometry. Measurement of transmitted or reflected light with precision instruments expressed in numbers.

Density. Ability of a photographic image to absorb or transmit light.

Depreciation. Financial technique of spreading the cost of major purchases, such as equipment or a building, over several years.

Descender. Any portion of a letter that extends below the base line.

Design. Process of creating images and page layouts for printing production.

Desktop publishing (DTP). A term used to describe a process of preparing full-page images on a microcomputer; generally intended to circumvent traditional composition and page makeup processes.

Developer. Chemical bath used to make the image on a light-sensitive emulsion visible and useful to the printer; some developers are used in the darkroom to process line film; others are used in proofing, platemaking, stencil preparation in screen printing, and some areas of masking in gravure.

Developer adjacency effect. Underdevelopment caused by chemical exhaustion of small, lightly exposed areas when surrounded by large, heavily exposed areas.

Diagonal line method. Technique to determine size changes of copy.

Diaphragm. Device that adjusts the aperture, or opening size, in the camera lens.

Diazo paper. Light-sensitive material developed by exposing to ammonia fumes; also, a material used in one of the proofing processes.

Die cutting. Finished technique used to cut paper to shape.

Diffusion-etch process. Process used in gravure printing to transfer an image to a gravure cylinder; involves the preparation of a photomechanical mask that is applied to the clean cylinder; acid is used to eat through the varying depths of the mask into the cylinder metal.

Diffusion transfer. Photographic process that produces quality opaque positives from positive originals.

Direct image nonphotographic surface plate. Short-run surface plate designed to accept images placed on its surface with a special crayon, pencil, pen, typewriter ribbon, and the like.

Direct image photographic plate. Short- to medium-run surface plate exposed and processed in a special camera and processor unit; used mainly in quick print area of printing industry.

Direct/indirect process. Method of photographic, screen printing stencil preparation in which stencil emulsion is applied to clean screen from precoated base sheet; when dry, the base is removed and the stencil is exposed and developed directly on fabric; see also *Photographic stencils.*

Direct process. Method of photographic, screen printing stencil preparation in which stencil emulsion is applied wet to screen fabric, dried, and then exposed and developed; see also *Photographic stencils.*

Direct screen color separation. Color separation method that produces a color-separated halftone negative in a single step.

Direct transfer. Process used in gravure printing to transfer an image to a gravure cylinder by applying a light-sensitive mask to the clean cylinder; light is passed through a halftone positive as it moves in contact with the rotating cylinder; acid is used to eat through the varying depths of the mask into the cylinder metal after the mask has been developed.

Dominance. Design characteristic that describes the most visually striking portion of a design.

Dot area meter. Transmission or reflection densitometer designed to display actual dot sizes.

Dot etching. Chemical process used to change dot sizes on halftone negatives and positives.

Dot-for-dot registration. Process of passing a sheet through the press twice and fitting halftone dots over each other on the second pass.

Double dot black duotone. Reproduction of a continuous-tone original made by printing two halftones, both with black ink; its purpose, when compared with a halftone, is to improve quality in tone reproduction.

Drafting board. Hard, flat surface with at least one perfectly straight edge that is used to hold the board during paste-up.

Dressing the press. Process of placing standard packing on the platen of a press.

Drying time. Time it takes for something to dry or for liquid ink to harden.

Dry offset. Printing process that combines relief and offset technology; in dry offset, a right-reading relief plate prints onto an intermediate blanket cylinder and produces a wrong-reading image, and the wrong-reading image is then transferred to paper as a right-reading image.

Dry transfer. Cold type method of producing camera-ready images in which pressure-sensitive material carries a carbon-based image on a special transparent sheet; the image is transferred to the paste-up by rubbing the face of the sheet.

Ductor rollers. Any press roller that moves ink or water from the fountain to the distribution rollers.

Dummy. Blank sheet of paper folded in the same manner as the final job and marked with page numbers and heads; when unfolded, can be used to show page and copy positions during paste-up or imposition.

Duotone. Reproduction of a continuous-tone image that consists of two halftones printed in register; adds color and quality to the image.

Duplicate plates. Relief plates made from a (master) form that was not intended to be used as a printing surface.

Duplicating film. A film designed to produce either duplicate film negatives from original negatives or duplicate film positives from original positives.

Duplicator. Any offset lithographic machine that makes copies and can feed a maximum sheet size of 11 inches by 17 inches.

Dynamic imbalance. Defect in the cylinder balance on a press such that the cylinder differs in density or balance from one end to the other.

EBCDIC (pronounced "Ebsee-dick"). An alphanumeric code used in telecommunication.

Electric-eye mark. Mark added to the gravure cylinder as an image to be read by special electronic eyes to monitor registration.

Electromechanical engraving. Method of producing a relief plate by cutting an image into a material with a device that is electrically controlled.

Electromechanical process. Technique used in gravure printing to place an image on a gravure cylinder by cutting into the metal surface of the cylinder with a diamond stylus.

Electroplating. Process of transferring very small bits (called ions) of one type of metal to another type of metal.

Electrostatic assist. Device licensed by the Gravure Association of America that pulls ink from the cylinder wells in gravure printing by using an electronic charge.

Electrostatic transfer plate. Transfer plate produced by electrical charges that cause a resin powder to form on the image area; the powder is then fused and forms the ink-receptive area of the plate.

Electrotypes. High-quality duplicate relief plates made by producing a mold from an original form; the final printing plate, which is made from silver and copper or nickel, is then produced in the mold by an electrochemical exchange.

Embossing. Finishing operation that produces a relief image by pressing paper between special dies.

Em quad. Basic unit of type composition; physical size varies with the size of type being set (for 12-point type, an em quad measures 12 points × 12 points; for 36-point type, it measures 36 points × 36 points).

Emulsified.   Condition in which something has become paste-like from contact with a highly acidic substance.

Emulsion.   Coating over a base material that carries the light-sensitive chemicals in photography; the emulsions in mechanical masking film and hand-cut stencil material are not light sensitive.

En quad.   Unit of type composition whose physical size varies with the size of type being set; two en quads placed together equal the size of the em quad for that size of type.

End sheets.   The two inside sheets that hold the casebound cover to the body of the book.

Equivalent weight.   Weight, in points, of one ream of regular size paper; see *Regular sizes*.

Etch resist.   See *Staging solution*.

Evaporation.   Conversion that occurs when a liquid combines with oxygen in the air and passes from the solution as a vapor.

Exacto knife.   Commercial cutting tool with interchangeable blades.

Excess density.   Density difference after the basic density range of the screen is subtracted from the copy density range (CDR).

Fake color.   One-color reproduction printed on a colored sheet.

Fake duotone.   Halftone printed over a block of colored tint or a solid block of color.

Feathering.   Tendency of ink on a rough, porous surface to spread.

Feeding unit.   A unit on a printing press that moves paper (or some other substrata) from a pile or roll to the registration unit.

File.   A term used in computer storage to describe information contained in a distinct area.

Fillet.   Internal curve that is part of a character in alphabet design.

Filmboard.   Part of a process camera that opens to hold the film during exposure; a vacuum base usually holds the film firmly in place.

Film speed.   Number assigned to light-sensitive materials that indicates sensitivity to light; large numbers (like 400) indicate high sensitivity; low numbers (like 6 or 12) indicate low sensitivity.

Final layout.   See *Mechanical*.

Finish.   Texture of paper.

Finishing.   Operations performed after the job has left the press; common finishing operations are cutting, folding, binding, and packaging.

Fit.   Relationship of images both to the paper and, if multicolors, to each other; often confused with the term "registration," which refers to position of the press sheet in the press.

Fixing bath.   Acid solution that removes all unexposed emulsion in film processing; the third step in processing which follows the developer and stop-bath; also called fixer.

Flare.   Exposure problem caused by uncontrolled reflection of stray light passing through the camera's lens.

Flash exposure.   Nonimage exposure made on the film through a halftone screen; regulates detail in the shadow area.

Flat.   Assembled masking sheet with attached pieces of film; the product of the stripping operation.

Flat bed cylinder press.   Press designed so that the sheet rolls into contact with the type form as a cylinder moves across the press.

Flat color. Ink the printer purchases or mixes to order for a specific job.

Flexography. A rotary relief printing process in which the image carrier is a flexible rubber or photopolymer plate.

Floppy disk. A magnetic storage system usually used in micro- and minicomputers.

Focal length. Distance from center of lens to filmboard when lens is focused at infinity.

Focusing. Process of adjusting the lens so light reflected from the object or copy is sharp and clear on the film.

Fold lines. Lines drawn on a paste-up in light-blue pencil that represent where the final job is to be folded; small black lines are sometimes drawn at the edge of the sheet to be printed and used as guides for the bindery.

Font. Collection of all the characters of the alphabet of one size and series.

Form. Grouping of symbols, letters, numbers, and spaces that make up a job or a complete segment of a job (such as one page set to be printed in a book).

Formal balance. Design characteristic in which images of identical weight are placed on each side of an invisible center line.

Form rollers. Any press rollers that contact the plate.

Fountain. Unit that holds a pool of ink and controls the amount of ink passed to the inking unit on a press.

Four-color process printing. Technique using cyan, magenta, yellow, and black process inks to reproduce images as they would appear in a color photograph.

Franklin Printing Catalog. Privately published pricing guide for printers to use to determine average costs for nearly all operations or products.

French fold. Traditional paper fold made by first creasing and folding a sheet along its length and then making a second fold at a right angle to the first, across the width.

Frisket. Sheet of paper placed between two grippers to hold a press sheet while an impression is made; the form prints through an opening made in the frisket.

f/stop system. Mathematically based way of measuring aperture size in the lens of a camera; f/stop numbers predict the amount of light that passes through any lens; moving from one f/stop number to another either doubles or halves the amount of light.

Furniture. Any line-spacing material that is thicker or larger than 24 points; used primarily in relief printing.

Furniture-within-furniture technique. Method of arranging furniture around a relief form when the form is of standard furniture dimension.

Galley. Sheet-metal tray used to store hot type.

Galley camera. Type of process camera used in a normally lighted room; film is carried to the camera in a light-tight case, the exposure is made, and the case is carried to the darkroom for processing.

Galley proof. Proof taken from a hot type form on a device called a galley proof press.

Gathering. Finishing operation that involves assembling signatures by placing one next to the other.

Gauge pins. Mechanical fingers that hold sheets in position on the tympan of a platen press.

Glaze. Buildup on rubber rollers or blanket that prevents proper adhesion and distribution of ink.

Graining. Mechanical or chemical process of roughing a plate's surface; ensures quality emulsion adhesion and aids in holding solution in the nonimage area during the press run.

Grain long. Condition in which the majority of paper fibers run parallel to the long dimension of the sheet.

Grain short. Condition in which the majority of paper fibers run parallel to the short dimension of the sheet.

Graphic images. Images formed from lines.

Gravity delivery. Process in which sheets simply fall into place on the press delivery stack.

Gravure. Industrial intaglio printing in which an image is transferred from a sunken surface.

Gravure well. Sunken portion of a gravure cylinder that holds ink during printing.

Grey-scale image. Continuous-tone picture of shades of grey used by graphic arts photographers to gauge exposure and development during chemical processing; also known as "step tablet" or "step wedge."

Grippers. Mechanical fingers that pull a sheet through the printing unit of a press.

Gripper margin. Area of paper held by mechanical fingers that pull the sheet through the printing unit of the press.

Guillotine cutter. Device used to trim paper sheets; has a long-handled knife hinged to a large preprinted board which can be used to accurately measure the size of each cut.

Halftone gravure design. See *Lateral hard-dot-process.*

Halftone or conversion. Process of breaking continuous-tone images into high-contrast dots of varying shapes and sizes so they can be reproduced on a printing press.

Hand-cut stencil. Screen printing stencil prepared by removing the printing image areas manually from base or support material.

Hanger sheets. Major part of the packing on a platen press.

Hard disk. A magnetic storage system used for computer data storage.

Hardening. Stage in ink drying when vehicle has solidified completely on paper surface and will not transfer.

Headstop. Mechanical gate that stops the paper on the registration unit of a press just before the gripper fingers pull the sheet through the printing unit.

Hickey. Defect on the press sheet caused by small particles of ink or paper attached to the plate or blanket.

Highlight area. Lighter parts of a continuous-tone image or its halftone reproduction.

Histogram. A visual frequency distribution that shows the history of what has happened at one point in a process. Data is sorted into numerical categories that are usually presented in the form of a bar graph.

Holding lines. Small red or black marks made on a paste-up to serve as guides for mounting halftone negatives in the stripping operation; are carried as an image on the film and are covered prior to platemaking.

Horizontal process camera. Type of darkroom camera that has a long, stationary bed; film end is usually in the darkroom, and lights and lens protrude through a wall into a normally lighted room.

Hot type composition. Preparation of any printing form used to transfer multiple images from a raised surface; examples include Linotype, Ludlow type, foundry type, and wooden type.

Hypo. Fixing bath of sodium thiosulfate.

Illustration board. Smooth, thick paper material used in paste-up to hold all job elements.

Image assembly. Second step in the printing process; involves bringing all pieces of a job into final form as it will appear on the product delivered to the customer.

Image carrier preparation. Fourth step in the printing process; involves photographically recording the image to be reproduced on an image carrier (or plate).

Image conversion. Third step in the printing process; involves creating a transparent film image of a job from the image assembly step.

Image design. First step in the printing process; involves conceptual creation of a job and approval by the customer.

Image guidelines. Lines used in paste-up to position artwork and composition on illustration board; are drawn in light-blue pencil and are not reproduced as a film image.

Image transfer. Fifth step in the printing process; involves transfer of the image onto the final job material (often paper).

Imposing stone. Metal surface on which letterpress forms are arranged and locked into a chase or metal frame.

Imposition. Placement of images in position so they will be in desired locations on the final printed sheet.

Impression. Single sheet of paper passed through a printing press; is measured by one rotation of the plate cylinder.

Impression cylinder. Part of a rotary press that presses the press sheet against the blanket cylinder.

Incident light. Light that illuminates, strikes, or falls on a surface.

India ink. Special type of very black ink used for high-quality layout.

Indirect process. Method of photographic, screen printing stencil preparation in which stencil is exposed and developed on a support base and then mounted on the screen; see also *Photographic stencils.*

Indirect relief. Process that involves transferring ink immediately from a relief form to a rubber-covered cylinder and then onto the paper; often called dry offset printing.

Indirect screen color separation. Color separation method that first produces a continuous-tone separation negative; requires additional steps to produce color-separated halftone negatives.

Informal balance. Design characteristic in which images are placed on a page so that their visual weights balance on each side of an invisible center line.

Ink-jet printing. A printing process that produces an image by directing individual drops of ink from an opening, through a small air gap, and to a printing surface.

Ink proofs. Press sheets printed on special proof presses using the ink and paper of the final job; are extremely expensive and usually reserved only for high-quality or long-run jobs.

Ink train. Area from ink fountain to ink form rollers.

Ink viscosity. Measure of ink's resistance to flow.

In-plant printing. Any operation that is owned by and serves the needs of a single company or corporation.

Input.   A computer term used to describe entering information (data) into computer memory.

Inserting.   Finishing operation that involves placing one signature within another.

Instant image proof paper.   Proofing material that creates an image when exposed to light; does not require special equipment or chemicals.

Intaglio printing.   Transferring an image from a sunken surface.

Intelligent Character Recognition (ICR). Similar to Optical Character Recognition (OCR), except that ICR has the ability to learn new fonts and new symbols.

ISO 9000 standards registration.   Established by the International Organization for Standardization (ISO) establishes international standards to communicate clear process-based operations and facilitate the global exchange of products and services; ISO 9000 registration is one measure of commitment to customer-defined quality.

Job estimate.   Document submitted to printing customers that specifies the cost of producing a particular job.

Job schedule.   Schedule prepared for each printing job as it passes through each production step; shows how long each step should take and the order of its movement through the shop.

Job scheduling and production control.   Section of most printing companies that directs the movement of every printing job through the plant.

Justification.   Technique of setting straight composition in which the first and last letters of each line of type fall in vertical columns.

Kizan.   A Japanese term that describes the never ending effort for incremental improvement and customer satisfaction.

Knife folder.   Paper-folding machine that operates using a thin knife blade to force a sheet of paper between two rotating rollers.

Laser cutting.   Process used in gravure printing to transfer an image to a gravure cylinder by means of a laser that cuts small wells into a plastic surface on the cylinder; the finished plastic surface is then chrome plated.

Latent image.   Invisible change made in film emulsion by exposure to light; development makes latent image visible to the human eye.

Lateral hard-dot process.   Type of well design used in gravure printing in which a cylinder is exposed by using two separate film positives: continuous-tone and halftone.

Lateral reverse.   Changing a right-reading sheet of film to a wrong-reading one.

Lead.   Thin line-spacing material used in hot type composition; is lower than type high and is generally 2 points thick.

Lead edge.   Portion of a sheet that enters the printing press first; for sheet-fed automatic presses, the gripper margin is the lead edge.

Lens.   Element of a camera through which light passes and is focused on the film.

Letterpress.   Process that prints from a raised or relief surface.

Lever cutter.   Hand-operated guillotine paper cutter.

Ligature.   Two or more connected letters on the same type body.

Light integrator.   Means of controlling film exposure by measuring the quantity of light that passes through the lens using a photoelectric cell.

Light printer. One of the halftones used to make a duotone; is usually printed with a light-colored ink and often contains the highlight to upper-middle tones of the continuous-tone original.

Light table. Special device with a frosted glass surface and a light that projects up through the glass for viewing and working with film negatives and positives.

Line photography. Process of recording high-contrast images on pieces of film; line negatives are either clear in the image areas or solid black in the nonimage areas.

Line art. Any image made only from lines, such as type and clear inked drawings.

Linen tester. Magnifying glass used for visual inspection.

Lithography. Transfer of an image from a flat surface by chemistry.

Live form. Any form waiting to be printed.

Lockup. Process of holding a relief form in a frame or chase.

Logo. Unique design created to cause visual recognition of a product, service, or company.

Logotype. Two or more letters not connected but still cast on the same type body in relief printing.

Lowercase. Letters in the alphabet that are not capitals.

Magnetic tape. Tape that stores keystrokes by recording electrical impulses; is faster and more practical than storing information on paper tape.

Main exposure. Image exposure made through the lens and a halftone screen; records detail from the highlights or white parts of a photograph to the upper-middle tones; also called a highlight or detail exposure.

Make-ready. All preparation from mounting the image carrier (plate, cylinder, type-form, stencil) on the press to obtain an acceptable image on the press sheet.

Mask. Any material that blocks the passage of light; is used in paste-up, stripping, and platemaking; is generally cut by hand and positioned over an image; photomechanical masks used in color separation are produced in the darkroom.

Masking. Continuous-tone photographic image that is used mainly to correct color and compress tonal range of a color original in process color photography.

Masking sheets. Special pieces of paper or plastic that block the passage of actinic light; are used most commonly in the stripping operation.

Master flat. In multiflat registration, the flat with the most detail.

Master plate. In gravure printing, a frame with register pins that hold the film positives in correct printing position during exposure to the cylinder masking material.

Mechanical. Board holding all elements of composition and artwork that meet job specifications and are of sufficient quality to be reproduced photographically; also called a "paste-up," "final layout," or "camera-ready copy."

Mechanical line-up table. Special piece of equipment used in the stripping operation; comes equipped with roller carriages, micrometer adjustments, and attachments for ruling or scribing parallel or perpendicular lines.

Medium. Channel of communication; mass media are radio, television, newspapers, and magazines.

Mercury vapor lamp. Popular light source for the graphic arts industry that operates when current passes through a mercury gas in a quartz envelope; a mercury vapor lamp emits massive peaks in the blue-violet and ultraviolet regions of the visible spectrum.

Metal halide lamp. Recent development in light sources for the graphic arts; a metal halide lamp is a mercury lamp with a metal halide additive and is rich in blue-violet emissions.

Microcomputer. A small, general purpose computer with the ability to accept a wide variety of software and additional components to increase power; much smaller and less powerful than a mainframe and not dedicated like a minicomputer; also called a "personal computer" or a "PC."

Middle tone area. Intermediate tones between highlights and shadows.

Minicomputer. A small, dedicated computer usually used for only one task; smaller and less powerful than a mainframe computer.

Moiré pattern. Undesirable image produced when two different or randomly positioned screen patterns (or dots) overprint.

Molleton covers. Thin cloth tubes that slip over water form rollers.

Monofilament screens. Fabrics made from threads composed of a single fiber strand, such as nylon.

Multifilament screens. Fabrics made from threads composed of many different fibers, such as silk.

M weight. Weight of 1,000 sheets of paper rather than of a ream (500 sheets).

Mylar sheet. Clear or frosted stable-base plastic material commonly used for overlays in paste-up.

Negative-acting plate. Plate formulated to produce a positive image from a flat containing negatives.

Newage gauge. Gauge used to test hardness of copper.

News case. Container formerly used to store foundry type; upper case held capital letters and lower case held small characters.

Nib width. Area of contact between impression roller and plate (or image) cylinder on any rotary press.

Noncounting keyboard. Keyboard that can capture operator keystrokes without end-of-line decisions.

Nonstandard cut. In paper cutting, manipulation of positions and order of cuts to gain an additional sheet; always produces press sheets with different grain direction.

Occasional. One of the six type styles; includes all typefaces that do not fit one of the other five styles; also known as "novelty," "decorative," and "other typeface."

Optical character recognition (OCR) system. Optical scanning device that converts, stores, and/or outputs composition from special typewritten information.

Off-contact printing. Screen printing in which screen and stencil are slightly raised from printing material; stencil touches stock only while squeegee passes over screen.

Offset press. Press design in which an image is transferred from a plate to a rubber blanket that moves the image to the press sheet; offset principle allows plates to be right reading and generally gives a better-quality image than do direct transfers.

Offset lithographic press. Any machine that can feed sheets larger than 11 inches × 17 inches.

Offset paper. Paper intended for use on an offset lithographic press; surface is generally smooth and somewhat resistant to moisture.

On-contact printing. Screen printing in which screen and stencil contact material throughout ink transfer.

Opaque. Liquid used to "paint out" pinholes on film negatives; also used as adjective meaning "not transparent or translucent under normal viewing."

Opaque color proofs. Proofs used to check multicolor jobs by adhering, exposing, and developing each successive color emulsion on a special solid-base sheet.

Open shop. Shop that does not require craftspeople to join a union to maintain employment.

Optical center. Point on a sheet that the human eye looks to first and perceives as the center; is slightly above true, or mathematical, center.

Orthochromatic material. Photographic material that is sensitive to all wavelengths of the visible spectrum except red.

Oscillating distribution rollers. Press rollers in ink and water systems that cause distribution by both rotation and movement back and forth.

Overcoating. Protective coating placed on most transparent-based film to protect film emulsion from grease and dirt.

Overhead. Cost of operating a business without considering cost of materials or labor; typically includes cost of maintaining work space and equipment depreciation.

Overlay. Sheet of packing added under tympan sheet during make-ready; composed of built-up and cut-out areas to increase or decrease pressure on final press sheet.

Overlay sheet. Sheet often used in paste-up to carry images for a second color; clear or frosted plastic overlay sheet is hinged over the first color and carries artwork and composition for the second.

Oxidation. Process of combining with oxygen; in aerial oxidation, a solution or ink combines with oxygen in the air to evaporate.

Packing. On hand-fed platen presses, material used to control overall impression; top packing sheet holds gauge pins that receive press sheet during image transfer.

Padding. Simplest form of adhesive binding and an inexpensive way of gluing individual sheets together to form notepads.

Panchromatic material. Photographic material that is sensitive to all visible wavelengths of light and some invisible wavelengths.

Pantone Matching System®. Widely accepted method for specifying and mixing colors from a numbering system listed in a swatch book.

Paper lines. Lines drawn on paste-up board to show final size of printed piece after it is trimmed; are measured from center lines and are usually drawn in light-blue pencil.

Paper tape. Continuous band of paper (about 1 inch wide) that stores keystrokes when punched; punched holes can then be read by other machines to output characters.

Pareto chart.   Another form of frequency distribution that displays categories from the most to least frequent.

Paste-up.   See *Mechanical.*

Patent binding.   See *Perfect binding.*

Penetration.   Drying of ink by absorption into a substrate (usually paper).

Perfect binding.   Common adhesive binding technique to glue signatures into a book, usually a paperback; also known as "patent binding."

Perfecting press.   Press that prints on both sides of the stock (paper) as it passes through the press.

Perforating.   Finishing operation in which slits are cut into stock so a portion can be torn away.

Photoelectric densitometer.   Instrument that produces density readings by means of a cell or vacuum tube whose electrical properties are modified by the action of light.

Photoengraving.   Relief form made by photochemical process; after being exposed through laterally reversed negative, non-image portion of plate is acid etched, allowing image area to stand out in relief.

Photographic stencils.   Screen printing stencils produced using a thick, light-sensitive, gelatin-based emulsion that is exposed and developed either on a supporting film or directly on the screen itself; the three types of stencils include direct, indirect, and direct/indirect stencils.

Photomechanical proofs.   Proofs that use light-sensitive emulsions to check image position and quality of stripped flats; are usually exposed through the flat on a standard platemaking device.

Photopolymer plates.   Plates formed by bonding a light-reactive polymer plastic to a film or metal base; polymer emulsion hardens upon ultraviolet exposure and unexposed areas are washed away to leave image area in relief.

Photostat.   Photographic copy of a portion of a paste-up; images are sometimes enlarged or reduced and then positioned on the board as a photostat; also called "stat."

Phototypesetting.   Cold type composition process that creates images by projecting light through a negative and a lens and from mirrors onto light-sensitive material.

pH scale.   Measure of a liquid's acidity; numeric scale is from 0 (very acid) to 14 (very alkaline, or a base); midpoint, 7, is considered neutral.

Pica.   Unit of measurement used by printers to measure linear dimensions; 6 picas equal approximately 1 inch; 1 pica is divided into 12 points.

Picking.   Offset press problem identified by small particles of paper torn from each press sheet and fed back into the inking system.

Pigment.   Dry particles that give color to printing ink.

Pilefeeding.   Method of stacking paper in feeder end of press and then operating press so that individual sheets are moved from top of pile to registration unit.

Pinholes.   Small openings in film emulsion that pass light; are caused by dust in the air during camera exposure, a dirty copyboard, or, sometimes, acidic action in the fixing bath; must be painted out with opaque in the stripping operation.

Pixel. A dot or picture element in a computer scanned image; also one element in computer image resolution.

Plate cylinder. Part of a rotary press that holds the printing form or plate.

Platemaker. Any machine with an intensive light source and some system to hold the flat against the printing plate; light source is used to expose the film image on the plate; most platemakers use a vacuum board with a glass cover to hold the flat and plate.

Platemaking sink. Area used to hand process printing plates; usually has a hard, flat surface to hold the plate and a water source to rinse the plate.

Platen press. Traditional design used almost exclusively for relief printing; type form is locked into place and moves into contact with a hard, flat surface (called a platen) that holds the paper.

Plates. Thin, flexible aluminum sheets for lithographic printing; can be purchased uncoated and then sensitized at the printing plant or obtained presensitized and ready for exposure and processing; specific characteristics vary depending on end use.

Plating bath. Solution used for electroplating.

Point. Unit of measurement used by printers to measure type size and leading (space between lines); 12 points equal 1 pica; 72 points equal 1 inch.

Polymerization. Chemical process for drying epoxy inks.

Positive-acting plate. Plate formulated to produce a positive image from a flat containing positives.

Posterization. High-contrast reproduction of a continuous-tone image; usually consists of two, three, or four tones and is reproduced in one, two, or three colors.

Prepress. Prepress is a new term that describes the revolutionary technological changes that have transformed traditional copy preparation steps prior to reaching the printing press. In general, it refers to computer applications of full-page composition, color separation, and color proofing.

Preprinted paste-up sheets. Sheets commonly prepared for jobs of a common size and layout specifications; are printed with blue lines to help paste-up artist position composition and artwork.

Prepunched tab strip method. Strips of film punched with holes and used to hold flat in place over pins attached to light table.

Pressboard. Hard, heavy sheet used as packing material when dressing a platen press.

Prewipe blade. Blade sometimes used in gravure printing to skim excess ink from cylinder.

Primary plates. Relief plates intended for use as printing surfaces; capable of producing duplicate plates.

Printing. The process of manufacturing multiple copies of graphic images.

Printing processes. Relief, intaglio, screen, and lithographic printing.

Process camera. Large device used by graphic arts photographers to record film images; can enlarge or reduce images from the copy's original size and can be used to expose all types of film.

Process color. Use of ink with a translucent base that allows for creation of many colors by overprinting only four (cyan, magenta, yellow, and black).

Process color photography. Photographic reproduction of color originals by manipulation of light, filters, film, and chemistry.

Proof. Sample print of a job yet to be printed.

Proofing. Process of testing final stripped images from flat on inexpensive photosensitive material to check image position and quality.

Proportion. Design characteristic concerned with size relationships of both sheet size and image placement.

Proportionally spaced composition. Composition made up of characters that occupy horizontal space in proportion to their size.

Proportion scale. Device used to determine percentage of enlargement or reduction for piece of copy.

Publishing. Category of printing services that prepare and distribute materials such as books, magazines, and newspapers.

Pulsed xenon lamp. Recently developed light source for the graphic arts; xenon lamps are made by filling quartz tubing with low-pressure xenon gas; output is similar to sunlight.

Punch and register pin method. Method of multiflat registration in which holes are punched in the tail of the flat or in strips of scrap film taped to the flat; the punched holes fit over metal pins taped to light table surface and cause the flat to fall in correct position.

Quadding out. Filling a line of type with spacing material after all characters have been set in a composing stick.

Quality printing. Has different meaning for every printing job; judgment of quality depends upon context, time, and the measure of successful use.

Quick. Early term for a skilled compositor (especially foundry type composition).

Quick printing. Printing operation characterized by rapid service, small organizational size, and limited format of printed product.

Quoins. Metal devices that hold or lock relief forms into chase.

Rapid access. A process of preparing a film image using an emulsion and developer that allows for wide latitude in skill to produce an acceptable film image.

Ream. Five hundred sheets of paper.

Reflectance. Measure of ability of a surface or material to reflect light.

Reflection densitometer. Meter that measures light reflected from a surface.

Register marks. Targets applied to the paste-up board and used in stripping, platemaking, and on the press to ensure that multicolor images fit together in perfect register.

Registration unit. Unit on a printing press that ensures that sheets are held in the same position each time an impression is made.

Reglets. Thin pieces of wood used to fill small spaces and protect larger furniture from quoin damage during lockup.

Regular sizes. Sizes other than basic sheet size in which paper is commonly cut and stocked by paper suppliers.

Related industries. Category of printing services that includes raw material manufacturers (ink, paper, plates, chemicals), manufacturers of equipment, and suppliers that distribute goods or services to printers.

Relief printing. Transferring an image from a raised surface.

Reproduction proof. Proof taken from hot type composition; can be reproduced photographically.

Resist. Material that blocks or retards the action of some chemical.

Resolution. Used to describe the smoothness of the edges of an image output by a computer.

Retouching pencil. Special pencil used by retouch artists to add detail or repair continuous-tone images.

Reverse. Technique of creating an image by using an open area in the midst of another ink image.

Right-angle fold. Any fold that is at a 90-degree angle from one or more other folds.

Right reading. Visual organization of copy (or film) from left to right so that it can be read normally; see *Wrong reading.*

Rollup. Technique used to cover an area on a gravure cylinder for re-etching.

Roman. One of the six type styles; is characterized by variation in stroke and by use of serifs.

Rotary press. Press formed from two cylinders, one holding the type form and the other acting as an impression cylinder to push the stock against the form; as the cylinders rotate, a sheet is inserted so an image is placed on the piece.

Rotating distribution rollers. Press rollers in ink and water systems that cause distribution by rolling against each other; see *Oscillating distribution rollers.*

Rotogravure. Printing by the gravure process from a round cylinder.

Rough layout. Detailed expansion of thumbnail sketch that carries all printing information necessary for any printer to produce final reproduction.

Saddle binding. Technique of fastening one or more signatures along the folded or backbone edge of a unit.

Safelight. Fixture used in the darkroom that allows the photographer to see, but not expose, film; color and intensity of safelight vary with type of film used.

Sans serif. One of the six type styles; is characterized by vertical letter stress, uniform strokes, and absence of serifs.

Scoring. Finishing operation that creases paper so it can be folded easily.

Screen mesh count. Measure of the number of openings per unit measure.

Screen printing. Transferring an image by allowing ink to pass through an opening or stencil.

Screen ruling. Number of dots per inch produced by a halftone screen or a screen tint.

Screen tint. Solid line screen capable of producing evenly spaced dots and of representing tone values of 3 percent to 97 percent in various fine rulings.

Script. One of the six type styles; is characterized by a design that attempts to duplicate feeling of free-form handwriting.

Scumming. Offset press condition in which nonimage areas of the plate accept ink.

Self-cover. Cover produced from the same material as the body of the book.

Sensitivity guide. Transparent grey scale often stripped into a flat to be used as a means of gauging plate exposure; also used in one method of direct color separation.

Sensitometer. An instrument that exposes a step tablet or grey scale onto light-sensitive materials.

Series. Variations within a family of type; common series are bold, extra bold, condensed, thin, expanded, and italic.

Serifs.   One of three variables in alphabet design; refers to small strokes that project from top or bottom of main character strokes.

Set.   Ability of ink to stick to paper; properly set ink can be handled without smearing.

Set-off.   Transfer of excess ink from one sheet to another when press is overinked.

Set width.   Distance across nick or belly side of foundry type.

Shadow area.   Darker parts of a continuous-tone image or its halftone reproduction.

Shaft.   Center support of a press cylinder.

Sheet-fed press.   Press that prints on individual pieces of paper rather than on paper from a roll.

Sheet off.   Process of removing excess ink from ink rollers by carefully hand rolling a sheet of paper through the ink system and then removing it.

Sheet separators.   Elements used in the press feeder unit to ensure that only one sheet is fed into the registration unit at a time.

Sheetwise imposition.   Arrangement in which a single printing plate is used to print on one side of a sheet to produce one printed product with each pass through the press.

Shore durometer.   Device to measure rubber hardness in units called "durometers"; the lower the rating, the softer the rubber.

Short-stop.   See *Stop-bath.*

Shutter.   Mechanism that controls the passage of light through the camera lens by opening and closing the aperture.

Shutter speed.   Length of time the camera lens allows light to pass to the film; is adjusted by use of a shutter.

Side binding.   Technique of fastening pages or signatures by passing the fastening device through the pile at a right angle to the page surface.

Signature imposition.   Process of passing a single sheet through the press and then folding and trimming it to form a portion of a book or magazine.

Single-edge razor blade.   Tool used to cut and trim materials during paste-up.

Slipsnake.   Fine, abrasive stone or hard rubber eraser used to remove images from plates.

Slug.   Thick line-spacing material used in hot type composition; is lower than type high and is generally 6 points thick.

Slur.   Condition in which an image is inconsistent in density and appears to be unsharp or bluffed; is usually caused by platen press roller condition or adjustment.

Snap fitter and dowel method.   Method of multiflat registration in which adhesive dowels are attached to the light table surface; plastic snap fitters that fit over the dowels are stripped into the tail of the flat; exact image position can be controlled because the flats always fall in the same position on the dowels.

Soft cover.   Book cover made from paper or paper fiber material with greater substance than that used for the body of the book but with much less substance than binder's board.

Software.   Instructions that direct a computer to perform specific tasks.

Special purpose printing.   Printing operation that accepts orders for only one type of product, such as forms work, legal printing, or labels.

Spectral highlight.   White portion of a photograph with no detail, such as bright, shiny reflection from a metal object.

Spoilage allowance. Extra sheets delivered to the press to allow for inevitable waste and to ensure that required number of products are delivered to the customer.

Spot plater. Machine used to build up the metal in small areas on a gravure cylinder.

Square serif. One of the six type styles; is characterized by uniform strokes and serif shapes without fillets or rounds.

Squeegee. Device used to force ink through the stencil opening in screen printing; also used in platemaking.

Stable-base jig. Exposed piece of stable-base film containing register marks; has a density between 0.7 and 1.0; used as a carrier for color transparencies during color separation process.

Stable-base sheet. Sheet that does not change size with changes in temperature.

Staging. Process of covering bare metal in gravure printing.

Staging solution. Solution used as a resist in the etching process; prevents dots or tones from being etched.

Stain. Black liquid used by retouch artists to add detail on continuous-tone images.

Standing form. Form that is never destroyed, melted, or distributed so that it can be reprinted.

Stat. See *Photostat.*

Static eliminator. Piece of copper tinsel mounted in delivery unit to remove static electric charge that makes it difficult to stack individual sheets of paper.

Static imbalance. Defect in cylinder balance on a press that occurs when a cylinder is not perfectly round or has different densities within a cross section.

Stencil. Type of mask that passes ink in the image areas and blocks ink passage in nonimage areas.

Step-and-repeat platemaking. Method of making identical multiple plate images on a single printing plate with one master negative; special machines move the negative to the required position, expose it, and then move it to the next location.

Step tablet. See *Grey scale.*

Step wedge. See *Grey scale.*

Stereotyping. Process of producing a duplicate relief plate by casting molten metal into a mold (or mat) made from an original lockup.

Stone proof. Proof taken from a form in hot type composition without using a machine.

Stop-bath. Slightly acidic solution used to halt development in film processing; is sometimes called the "short-stop."

Straight composition. Composition in which the first and last letters of each line of type line up in vertical columns; also known as justified composition.

Stream feeder. Press element that overlaps sheets on the registration table; allows registration unit to operate at a slower rate than the printing unit and gives better image fit.

Stress. One of three variables in alphabet design; refers to distribution of visual "heaviness" or "slant" of the character.

Strike-on composition. Cold type method of producing images by striking a carrier sheet with a raised character through an ink or carbon ribbon.

Stripping. Process of assembling pieces of film containing images that will be carried on the same printing plate and securing them on a masking sheet that will hold them in their appropriate printing positions during the platemaking process.

Stroke.   One of three variables in alphabet design; refers to thickness of lines that actually form each character.

Subjective balance.   Design characteristic in which images are placed on white space in such a way as to create a feeling of stability.

Substance weight.   Weight in pounds of one ream of the basic sheet size (17 inches × 22 inches) of one particular type of writing paper.

Substrate.   Any base material used in printing processes to receive an image transferred from a printing plate; common substrates are paper, foil, fabric, and plastic sheet.

Subtractive plate.   Presensitized lithographic plate with ink-receptive coating applied by the manufacturer; nonimage area is removed during processing.

Subtractive primary colors.   Colors formed when any two additive primary colors of light are mixed; subtractive colors are yellow, magenta, and cyan; yellow is the additive mixture of red and green light; magenta is the additive mixture of red and blue light; cyan is the additive mixture of blue and green light.

Successive sheet-feeding system.   Most common form of press-feeding system; feeding unit picks up one sheet each time the printing unit prints one impression.

Sucker feet.   Elements used in the press feeding unit to pick up individual sheets and place them in the registration unit.

Surprint.   Technique of printing one image over another.

Tack.   Characteristic of ink that allows it to stick to the substrate (usually paper).

Telecommunication.   A method of sending data from one computer to another over telephone lines or by satellite.

Text.   One of the six type styles; is characterized by a design that attempts to recreate the feeling of medieval scribes.

Thermoplastic.   Condition in which a material is capable of being heated and reformed after hardening and curing.

Thermosetting.   Condition in which a material is not capable of being reformed after hardening and curing.

Three-cylinder principle.   Most common configuration for most offset lithographic presses; the three cylinders are plate, blanket, and impression.

Thumbnail sketch.   Small, quick pencil renderings that show size relationships of type, line drawings, and white space; the first step in the design process.

Tinting.   Offset press problem identified by slight discoloration over entire nonimage area, almost like a sprayed mist.

Tones.   Values of white, black, or color.

Tooth.   Roughening of the threads of monofilament screen fabrics to increase the stencil's ability to hold on to the fabric; is applied prior to mounting a stencil.

Total Quality Management (TQM).   Process of making each manufacturing or service step responsive to the customer's needs or expectations.

Trade shops.   Printing operation that provides services only to other printers.

Transfer lithographic plate.   Plate formed from a light-sensitive coating on an intermediate carrier; after exposure, an image is transferred from the intermediate carrier to the printing plate.

Transmission densitometer.   Meter that measures light passing through a material.

Transmittance. Measure of the ability of a material to pass light.

Transparent-based image. Any image carried on a base that passes light; transparent-based sheets can be seen through.

Transparent color proofs. Proofs used to check multicolor jobs; each color is carried on a transparent plastic sheet, and all sheets are positioned over each other to give the illusion of the final multicolor job.

Trapping. Ability of one ink to cover another.

Triangle. Instrument used to draw right-angle lines with a T-square; is also available in a variety of angles, such as 30 degrees, 45 degrees, and 60 degrees.

Trim lines. Lines often added to a paste-up in black india ink so they will reproduce on the final job; are used to guide paper cutter in trimming the paper pile.

T-square. Instrument used to draw parallel lines.

Tusche. Lithographic drawing or painting material of the same nature as lithographic ink.

Tusche-and-glue. Artist's method of preparing a screen printing stencil by drawing directly on the screen fabric with lithographic tusche and then blocking out nonimage areas with a water-based glue material.

Two-cylinder principle. Offset lithographic duplicator configuration that combines the plate and impression functions to form a main cylinder with twice the circumference of a separate blanket cylinder.

Tympan sheet. Top oil-treated packing sheet that holds the gauge pins; often referred to as a "drawsheet."

Typeface. Alphabet design used in a printing job.

Type family. Unique combination of stroke, stress, and serif created and named by a typographer; is generally made up of many different series.

Type-high. Distance from the face to the feet of hot type; for English-speaking countries, type high is 0.918 inch.

Type-high gauge. Device that measures 0.918, or type high; is used to accurately adjust relief press form rollers to touch the form evenly.

Type specifications. Directions written on rough layout that informs compositor about alphabet style, series, size, and amount of leading or space between lines.

Type style. Grouping of alphabet designs; the six main type styles are roman, sans serif, square serif, text, script, and occasional.

Typographer. Craftsperson who designs typefaces.

Uncoated paper. Paper is made up merely of raw interlocking paper fibers; see *Coated paper.*

Underlay. Piece of tissue or paper pasted under the form in areas light in impression.

Unity. Design characteristic concerned with how all elements of a job fit together as a whole.

Uppercase. Capital letters in the alphabet.

Vectoring. A computer image generation technique that produces letters and symbols by drawing straight lines between points on the symbol's outline.

Vehicle. Fluid that carries ink pigment and causes printing ink to adhere to paper or some other substrate.

Velox. Prescreened halftone print used to mount on a paste-up board; looks like a regular photographic print but has been broken into small dots for reproduction.

Vertical process camera. Type of darkroom camera that is contained entirely in the darkroom; is a self-contained unit that takes up little space because the film-board, lens, and copyboard are parallel to each other in a vertical line.

Vignetted screen pattern. Pattern made up of gradually tapering density and found in halftone screens; produces the variety of dots found in a typical halftone reproduction.

Viscosity. See *Ink viscosity*.

Visual densitometer. Instrument that helps the operator to measure density by visual comparison.

Wax coater. Device used to place a thin layer of wax over the back of a piece of artwork or composition so that the copy can be repositioned any number of times.

Web-fed press. Press that prints on a roll of paper.

Wedge spectrogram. Visual representation of a film's reaction to light across the visible spectrum.

Wet-on-wet printing. Printing of one color directly over another without waiting for the ink to dry.

Window. Clear, open area on a piece of film created on the paste-up by mounting a sheet of black or red material in the desired window location.

Wipe-on metal surface plate. Pregrained metal surface plate coated at the printing plant with a diazo type of emulsion.

Work-and-tumble imposition. Printing on both sides of a sheet, with the tail becoming the lead edge for the second color by turning the pile for the second pass through the press.

Work-and-turn imposition. Printing on both sides of a sheet, with the same lead edge for both passes through the press.

Work order. Production control device that carries all information about a particular printing job as it passes through each step of manufacturing.

Writing paper. High-quality paper originally associated with correspondence and record keeping; is considered the finest classification of paper, except for some specialty items.

Wrong reading. Backward visual organization of copy (or film) from right to left; see *Right reading*.

WYSIWYG (pronounced "Wizzy-wig"). "What you see is what you get."

x-height. Distance from the base line to the top of a lowercase letter *x* in a given font; varies depending on the particular design; also known as "body-height."

Zeroing. Setting or calibrating a densitometer to a known value.

Bibliography

Abe, T.; Dove, D. B.; and Heinzl, J. *Printing Technologies for Images, Gray Scale, & Color.* Bellingham, WA: SPIE, International Society for Optical Engineering, 1991.

Adams, J. Michael. *Graphic Arts Processes.* Teaneck, NJ: National Association of Printers & Lithographers, 1994.

Adams, J. Michael.; Faux, David D.; and Rieber, Lloyd J. *Printing Technology 4/E.* Albany, NY: Delmar Publishers, 1994.

Aldrich-Ruenzel, Nancy (Ed.). *Designer's Guide to Print Production: A Step-by-Step Publishing Book.* New York, NY: Watson-Guptill Publications, Inc., 1990.

Aldrich-Ruenzel, Nancy (Ed.). *Designer's Guide to Typography: A Step-by-Step Publishing Book.* New York, NY: Watson-Guptill Publications, Inc., 1991.

Ames, Steven E. *Elements of Newspaper Design.* Westport, CT: Greenwood Publishing Group, Inc., 1989.

Apicella, Vincent; Pomeranz, Joanna; and Wiatt, Nancy. *The Concise Guide to Type Identification.* Blue Ridge Summit, PA: TAB Books, 1990.

Baker, Kim. *Professional Publishing with QuarkXpress for the Macintosh: High-Level Design & Power.* New York, NY: Random House, Inc., 1993.

Banister, Manly. *Practical Lithographic Printmaking.* New York, NY: Dover Publications, Inc., 1987.

Banks, W. H. (Ed.). *Advances in Printing Science & Technology.* Elkins Park, PA: Franklin Book Co., Inc.

Banzhaf, Robert A. *Screen Process Printing.* Westerville, OH: Glencoe, 1983.

Barnard, Michael. *Introduction to Print Buying.* New York, NY: Van Nostrand Reinhold, 1991.

Baudin, Fernand. *How Typography Works: And Why It Is Important.* Blue Ridge Summit, PA: TAB Books, 1989.

Beach, Mark and Cowden, Steve (Illustrator). *Graphically Speaking: An Illustrated Guide to the Working Language of Design & Printing.* Manzanita, OR: Coast to Coast Books, 1992.

Beach, Mark; Shepro, Steve; and Russon, Ken. *Getting It Printed: How to Work with Printers & Graphic Arts Services to Assure Quality, Stay on Schedule & Control Cost.* Manzanita, OR: Coast to Coast Books, 1986.

Beechick, Al. *Resource Manual for Typesetting with Your Computer.* Pollock Pines, CA: Arrow Press, 1986.

Benton, Randi and Balcer, Mary S. *The Official Print Shop Handbook: Ideas, Tips & Designs for Home, School & Professional Use.* Foreword by Doug Carlston. New York, NY: Bantam Books, Inc., 1987.

Bivins, Thomas H. and Ryan, William E. *How to Produce Creative Publications: Traditional Techniques & Computer Applications.* Lincolnwood, IL: NTC Pub Group, 1992.

The Blueprint Dictionary of Printing & Publishing. New York, NY: Van Nostrand Reinhold, 1991.

Blum, Mike. *Understanding & Evaluating Desktop Publishing Systems: A How To Guide from Graphic Services Publications.* Arroyo Grande, CA: Graphic Services Publications, 1992.

Bold, Mary (Ed.). *Publishing in the Classroom: Sourcebook for the Teacher as Publishing Consultant.* Arlington, TX: Bold Productions, 1992.

Book, Albert C. *Fundamentals of Copy & Layout: A Manual.* Lincolnwood, IL: NTC Pub Group, 1990.

Borowsky, Irvin J. *Opportunities in Printing Careers.* Lincolnwood, IL: NTC Pub Group, 1991.

Brady, Philip. *Using Type Right.* Cincinnati, OH: North Light Books, 1988.

Bridgewater, Peter and Woods, Gerald. *Halftone Effects: A Complete Visual Guide to Enhancing & Transforming Halftone Images.* San Francisco, CA: Chronicle Books, 1993.

Brier, David (Ed.). *Typographic Design.* New York, NY: Madison Square Press, 1992.

Bringhurst, Robert. *Elements of Typographic Style.* Point Roberts, WA: Hartley & Marks, Inc., 1992.

Bristow, Nicholas. *Screenprinting: Design & Technique.* North Pomfret, VT: Trafalgar Square, 1991.

Busche, Don and Keefe, Nick. *Desktop Publishing Using PageMaker on the IBM-PC.* Englewood Cliffs, NJ: Prentice Hall, 1991.

Byers, Steve. *Linotype Type Library.* New York, NY: Bantam Books, Inc., 1993.

Carter, Rob; Meggs, Phil; and Day, Benjamin R., II. *Typographic Design: Form & Communication.* New York, NY: Van Nostrand Reinhold, 1985.

Chapman, Gillean. *Making Books: A Step-by-Step Guide to Your Own Publishing.* Boston, MA: Houghton Mifflin, 1992.

Clarke, Joe. *Control Without Confusion: Trouble Shooting Screen Printed Process Color.* Cincinnati, OH: Signs of the Times Publishing Co., 1987.

Clifton, Merritt. *The Samisdat Method: A Do-It-Yourself Guide to Offset Printing.* Shushan, NY: Samisdat, 1990.

Cogoli. *Photo Offset Fundamentals.* New York, NY: Macmillan Publishing Co., 1986.

Collier, David. *Collier's Rules for Desktop Design & Typography.* Redding, MA: Addison-Wesley Publishing Co., 1991.

Collier, David and Cotton, Bob. *Basic Desktop Design & Layout.* Cincinnati, OH: North Light Books, 1989.

Collin, P. H. *Dictionary of Printing & Publishing.* Kinderhook, NY: i.b.d., Ltd., 1989.

Cost Study on Web Presses. Teaneck, NJ: National Association of Printers and Lithographers, 1990.

Craig, James. *Production for the Graphic Designer.* New York, NY: Watson-Guptill, Inc., 1990.

Crouse, David B. and Schneider, Robert J., Jr. *Web Offset Press Operating.* Pittsburgh, PA: Graphic Arts Technical Foundation, 1989.

Current, Ira. *Photographic Color Printing: Theory & Technique.* Stoneham, MA: Focal Pr, 1987.

Curtin, Dennis P. *Desktop Publishing with WordPerfect 5.1–5.25 Bk-Disk Package.* Englewood Cliffs, NJ: Prentice Hall, 1991.

Day, David. *Trouble with Fonts: The Font Answer Book.* Carmel, IN: Alpha Books, 1993.

Deaton, Donald B. (Ed.). *Glossary of Printing Terms.* Research Triangle Park, NC: AATCC, 1991.

Dennis, Ervin A. *Lithographic Technology.* New York, NY: Macmillan Publishing Co., 1980.

Dennis, Ervin A. *Lithographic Technology.* New York, NY: Macmillan Publishing Co., 1986.

Desktop Publishing: Design Basics. New York, NY: Van Nostrand Reinhold, 1991.

Destree, Thomas M. (Ed.). *Lithographers Manual.* Pittsburgh, PA: Graphic Arts Technical Foundation, 1994.

Duff, Jon M. *Introduction to Desktop Publishing.* Englewood Cliffs, NJ: Prentice Hall, 1989.

Durbin, Harold. *Interactive Page Layout Comparison Charts, 1992.* Easton, PA: Durbin Assocs., 1992.

Eakins, Jan. *Desktop Publishing! Using Page-Maker 3.0-IBM Ps-2 Version with DeskDisc.* New York, NY: McGraw-Hill, Inc., 1990.

Easy Way to Tone B&W Prints. Kingston, NY: Embee Pr., 1988.

Eckhardt, Robert. *Publish Tips & Techniques.* New York, NY: Bantam Books, 1991.

Eckstein, Helene W. *Color in the 21st Century: A Practical Guide for Graphic Designers, Photographers, Printers, Separators, & Anyone Involved in Color Printing.* New York, NY: Watson-Guptill Publications, Inc., 1991.

Eldred, Nelson R.; Scarlett, Terry; and Stevenson, Deborah L. (Ed.); O'Toole, Mary A. (Illustrator) *What the Printer Should Know about Ink.* Introduction by Thomas M. Destree. Pittsburgh, PA: Graphic Arts Technical Foundation, 1990.

Field, Gary G. and Destree, Thomas M. (Ed.); O'Toole, Mary A. (Illustrator). *Tone & Color Correction.* Pittsburgh, PA: Graphic Arts Technical Foundation, 1991.

Field, Gary G. and Mertz, Ann (Ed.). *Color Scanning & Imaging Systems.* Pittsburgh, PA: Graphic Arts Technical Foundation, 1990.

Flick, Ernest W. *Printing Ink Formulations.* Park Ridge, NJ: Noyes, 1985.

Gaynor, J. (Ed.). *Hard Copy & Printing Materials, Media, & Processes.* Bellingham, WA: SPIE, International Society for Optical Engineering, 1990.

Geis, A. John and Stevenson, Deborah L. (Ed.); O'Toole, Mary A. (Illustrator). *Printing Plant Layout & Facility Design Handbook.* Pittsburgh, PA: Graphic Arts Technical Foundation, 1991.

Geist, A. John; Addy, Paul L.; and Destree, Thomas M. (Ed.). *Materials Handling for the Printer.* Pittsburgh, PA: Graphic Arts Technical Foundation, 1993.

Glossary of Reprography & Non-Impact Printing Terms for the Paper & Printing Industries: Technical Association of Pulp and Paper Industries. 1990.

Glover, Gary. *Clip Art Scanning & Enhancement.* Blue Ridge Summit, PA: TAB Books, 1993.

Green, Merrill. *A Practical Guide to Screen Printing.* Chicago, IL: The Advance Group, 1984.

Groff, Pamela; Jorgensen, George; Lavi, Abraham; and Mooney, Dillon. *Lithographic Press Operator's Handbook.* Pittsburgh, PA: Graphic Arts Technical Foundation, 1988.

Hargrave, Sally and Berkemeyer, Kathy M. (Ed.). *Desktop Publishing with WordPerfect.* Addison, IL: FlipTrack OneOnOne Computer Training, 1990.

Hart, Thomas L. and Everhart, Nancy. *Instant Pagemaker Handbook.* Englewood, CO: Libraries Unlimited, Inc., 1992.

Herod, Thomas D. and Trainor, Diane (Ed.). *Environmental Compliance in the Printing Industry.* Woodstock, VT: Compliance Technologies, 1991.

Hird, Kenneth. *Introduction to Photo-Offset Lithography.* New York, NY: Bennett Publishing Co., 1981.

Holman, R. and Oldring, P. (Ed.). *UV & EB Curing Formulations for Printing Inks, Coatings & Paint.* Port Washington, NY: Scholium International, Inc., 1988.

Holt, Roger W. and Millman, Jack H. *A Methodology for Measurement of Publications Quality.* Redding, MA: Addison-Wesley Publishing Co., 1992.

Hulburt, Allen. *Layout.* New York, NY: Watson-Guptill Publications, Inc., 1989.

Hunt, Larry. *Larry Hunt's Keys to Successful Quick Printing.* Burnham Ln, FL: Larry Hunt, 1988.

Japan Typography Staff. *Applied Typography.* Carson, CA: Books Nippan, 1993.

Jinno, Yoh. *Color Communication: How to Get the Most Out of Printers.* Chestnut Ridge, NY: Jinno International, 1989.

Jinno, Yoh. *Creative Process Color Chart.* Chestnut Ridge, NY: Jinno International, 1990.

Jinno, Yoh. *Printing Production Workbook.* Chestnut Ridge, NY: Jinno International, 1990.

Johnson, Jerome L. *Principles of Nonimpact Printing.* Irvine, CA: Palatino Press, 1992.

Johnson, Lois M.; Stinnett, Hester; and Naples, Marie (Ed.); Denick, David and Johnson, Lois M. (Photographers). *Water-Based Inks: A Screenprinting Manual for Studio & Classroom.* Philadelphia, PA: University of Arts Press, 1990.

Kagy, Frederick, D. and Adams, J. Michael. *Graphic Arts Photography.* Albany, NY: Delmar Publishers, 1983.

Karsnitz, John R. *Graphic Arts Technology.* Albany, NY: Delmar Publishers, 1984.

Karsnitz, John. *Graphic Communication Technology.* Albany, NY: Delmar Publishers, 1992.

Kieper, Michael L. *The Illustrated Handbook of Desktop Publishing & Typesetting.* Blue Ridge Summit, PA: Tab Books, 1987.

King, Jean. *Designer's Guide to PostScript Text Type.* New York, NY: Van Nostrand Reinhold, 1993.

Kleper, Michael L. *The Illustrated Dictionary of Typographic Communication.* Rochester, NY: Technical & Educational Center of the Graphic Arts, Rochester Institute of Technology, 1983.

Kleper, Michael L. *The Illustrated Dictionary of Typographic Communication.* Pittsford, NY: Graphic Dimensions, 1983.

Kosloff, Albert. *Photographic Screen Printing.* Cincinnati, OH: Signs of the Times Publishing Co., 1987.

Krasucki, Cheryl A. *The Art of Professional Typography—Mac Style.* Norfolk, VA: TypograMac Publishing, 1990.

LaBuz, Ronald. *Typography & Typesetting.* New York, NY: Van Nostrand Reinhold, 1987.

Lampe, Harold C. *Paper Complaint Handbook.* Alexandria, VA: Printing Industries of America, Inc., 1988.

Lawson, Alexander S. *Anatomy of a Typeface.* Boston, MA: David R. Godine Publisher, Inc., 1990.

Leach, Robert. *The Printing Ink Manual.* New York, NY: Van Nostrand Reinhold, 1988.

Magee, Babette. *Screen Printing Primer.* Pittsburgh, PA: Graphic Arts Technical Foundation, 1985.

Mantus, Roberta. *Design Guidelines for Desktop Publishing.* Albany, NY: Delmar Publishers, 1992.

McMurtrie, Douglas C. *The Book: Story of Printing & Bookmaking.* New York, NY: Dorset Press, 1990.

Misanchuk, Earl R. *Preparing Instructional Text: Document Design Using Desktop Publishing.* Englewood Cliffs, NJ: Educational Technology Publications, Inc., 1992.

Molla, Rafiqul K. *Electronic Color Separation.* Introduction by Michael Bruno. Charleston, WV: R.K. Printing & Publishing Co., 1988.

Morgenstern, Steve. *No-Sweat Desktop Publishing: A Guide from Home Office Computing Magazine.* New York, NY: AMACOM, 1992.

Mort, J. *The Anatomy of Xerography: Its Invention & Evolution.* Jefferson, NC: McFarland & Co., Inc., Publishers, 1989.

Mott, W. S. *Printing Four Color Process on a Duplicator or Small Press: A How to Guide from Graphic Services Publications.* Arroyo Grande, CA: Graphic Services Publications, 1992.

Mulvihill, Donna C. *Flexography Primer.* Pittsburgh, PA: Graphic Arts Technical Foundation, 1985.

Munro, Kathy. *Bringing Typesetting In-House.* New York, NY: Van Nostrand Reinhold, 1991.

Myers, R. and Harris, M. *Aspects of Printing.* Detroit, MI: Omnigraphics, Inc., 1988.

Nothmann, Gerhard A. and Destree, Thomas M. (Ed.); O'Toole, Mary A. (Illustrator). *Nonimpact Printing.* Pittsburgh, PA: Graphic Arts Technical Foundation, 1989.

Offset Printing Communication Guide System Series. Chestnut Ridge, NY: Jinno International, 1990.

Pantone Book of Color. Moonachie, NJ: Pantone Inc., 1992.

Pantone Color Formula Guide 1000. Moonachie, NJ: Pantone Inc., 1992.

Pantone Color Tint Selector 1000. Moonachie, NJ: Pantone Inc., 1992.

Pantone Library of Color. Moonachie, NJ: Pantone Inc., 1992.

Pantone Process Color Imaging Guide 1000. Moonachie, NJ: Pantone Inc., 1992.

Perfect, Christopher. *The Complete Typographer.* Englewood Cliffs, NJ: Prentice Hall, 1992.

Perfect, Christopher and Rookledge, Gordon. *Rookledge's International Typefinder.* Preface by Adrian Frutiger. Wakefield, RI: Moyer Bell, 1991.

Phil's Photo Staff (Ed.). *A Typeface Sourcebook.* Rockport, MA: Rockport Publishers, 1990.

Pickens, Judy E. *The Copy-to-Press Handbook: Preparing Words & Art for Print.* New York, NY: John Wiley & Sons, Inc., 1985.

Plate Mounting on the Offset Press. Pittsburgh, PA: Graphic Arts Technical Foundation, 1985.

Pocket Glossary of Printing, Binding & Paper Terms. New York, NY: Van Nostrand Reinhold, 1991.

The Print & Production Manual Practical Kit. New York, NY: Van Nostrand Reinhold, 1991.

The Print & Production Manual. New York, NY: Van Nostrand Reinhold, 1991.

Print's Best Letterheads & Business Cards, 1990. Portland, OR: R.C. Publications, 1990.

Printing with a Small Lithographic Offset Press. Pittsburgh, PA: Graphic Arts Technical Foundation, 1985.

Prust, Z. A. *Photo-Offset Lithography.* South Holland, IL: Goodheart-Wilcox Co., 1977.

Richardson, Kristin K. (Ed.). *Total Quality Management in the Printing & Publishing Industry.* Alexandria, VA: Graphic Communications Association, 1992.

Richmond, Wendy. *Design & Technology.* New York, NY: Van Nostrand Reinhold, 1990.

Rimmer, Steve. *Graphic File Toolkit: Converting & Using Graphic Files.* Redding, MA: Addison-Wesley Publishing Co., 1992.

Ritchie, Ward. *The Mystique of Printing: A Half Century of Books Designed by Ward Ritchie.* Foreword by Lawrence C. Powell. Sacramento, CA: California State Library Foundation, 1984.

Romano, Frank. *The Typencyclopedia: A User's Guide to Better Typography.* New Providence, NJ: Bowker R.R.A. Reed Reference Publishing Company, 1984.

Rosen, Arnold. *Desktop Publishing: Applications & Exercises.* Fort Worth, TX: Dryden Pr, 1988.

Rosen, Ben. *Digital Type Specimens: The Designer's Computer Type Book.* New York, NY: Van Nostrand Reinhold, 1990.

Rosen, Ben. *Type & Typography: The Designer's Type Book.* New York, NY: Van Nostrand Reinhold, 1989.

Ross, Shirley. *Learning to Print: Level Two.* Los Angeles, CA: Price Stern Sloan, Inc., 1992.

Rudman, Jack. *Offset Lithography.* Syosset, NY: National Learning Corp., 1991.

Ruggles, Philip K. *Printing Estimating.* Albany, NY: Delmar Publishers, 1994.

Safe Handling of Materials in the Printing Industry. Lanham, MD: UNIPUB, Division of Kraus Limited, 1988.

Saltman, David and Forsythe, Nina. *Lithography Primer.* Pittsburgh, PA: Graphic Arts Technical Foundation, 1986.

Sassoon, Rosemary. *Computers & Typography.* Allentown, PA: Cromland, Inc., 1993.

Scaling Copy. Pittsburgh, PA: Graphic Arts Technical Foundation, 1985.

Schneider, Robert J., Jr. (Ed.). *Solving Sheetfed Offset Press Problems.* Pittsburgh, PA: Graphic Arts Technical Foundation, 1993.

Schneider, Robert J., Jr. (Ed.) and O'Toole, Alice (Illustrator). *Solving Web Offset Press Problems.* Introduction by Thomas M. Destree. Pittsburgh, PA: Graphic Arts Technical Foundation, 1990.

Schneider, Robert J., Jr. *Aligning & Adjusting Cylinders on the Sheetfed Offset Press.*

Pittsburgh, PA: Graphic Arts Technical Foundation, 1990.

Schneider, Robert J., Jr. *Direct-Screen Color Separation Instructor's Guide.* Pittsburgh, PA: Graphic Arts Technical Foundation, 1989.

Schneider, Robert J., Jr. *Direct-Screen Color Separation.* Pittsburgh, PA: Graphic Arts Technical Foundation, 1989.

Schneider, Robert J., Jr. *Make Ready on the Sheetfed Offset Press.* Pittsburgh, PA: Graphic Arts Technical Foundation, 1990.

Schneider, Robert J., Jr. *Operating the Dampening System on a Sheetfed Offset Press.* Pittsburgh, PA: Graphic Arts Technical Foundation, 1990.

Schneider, Robert J., Jr. *Operating the Inking System on the Sheetfed Offset Press.* Pittsburgh, PA: Graphic Arts Technical Foundation, 1990.

Schneider, Robert J., Jr. *Paper Estimating.* Pittsburgh, PA: Graphic Arts Technical Foundation, 1990.

Schneider, Robert. *Layout Preparation & Markup.* Pittsburgh, PA: Graphic Arts Technical Foundation, 1987.

Screen Printing. Pittsburgh, PA: Graphic Arts Technical Foundation, 1988.

Seidman, Michael. *From Printout to Published.* New York, NY: Carroll & Graf Publishers, 1992.

Sharma, M. K. (Ed.). *Surface Phenomena & Additives in Water-Based Coatings & Printing Technology.* New York, NY: Plenum Publishing Corp., 1992.

Sharma, M. K. and Micale, F. J. (Ed.). *Surface Phenomena & Fine Particles in Water-Based Coatings & Printing Technology.* New York, NY: Plenum Publishing Corp., 1990.

Shushan, Ronnie and Wright, Don (Ed.). *Desktop Publishing by Design: Aldus PageMaker Edition.* Redmond, WA: Microsoft Park, 1991.

Silver, Gerald A. *Professional Printing Estimating.* Encino, CA: Editorial Enterprises, 1991.

Smith, Keith A. *Structure of the Visual Book.* Buffalo, NY: Sigma Foundation, Inc., 1993.

Smith, Robert C. *Basic Graphic Design.* Englewood Cliffs, NJ: Prentice-Hall, 1992.

Sosinsky, Barrie. *Beyond the Desktop: Tools & Technology for Computer Publishing.* New York, NY: Bantam Books, Inc., 1991.

Southworth, Miles F. *Color Separation Techniques.* Livonia, NY: Graphic Arts Publishing, Inc., 1989.

Southworth, Miles. *Pocket Guide to Color Reproduction Communication & Control.* 3rd ed., Livonia, NY: Graphic Arts Publishing, Inc., 1989.

Spring, Michael B. *Electronic Printing & Publishing.* New York, NY: Marcel Dekker, Inc., 1991.

Stephens, John. *Screen Process Printing: A Practical Guide.* New York, NY: Van Nostrand Reinhold, 1991.

Stone, Bernard and Eckstein, Arthur. *Preparing Art for Printing.* New York, NY: Van Nostrand Reinhold, 1983.

Stone, Sumner and Wu, Brian. *On Stone: The Art & Use of Typography on the Personal Computer.* San Francisco, CA: Chronicle Books, 1991.

Stopke, Judy; Staley, Chip; and McClaran, Jeanne L. (Ed.). *An Eye for Type.* Ann Arbor, MI: Promotional Perspectives, Inc., 1992.

Sutton, James and Bartram, Alan. *Typefaces for Books.* Franklin, NY: New Amsterdam Books, 1990.

Swerdlow, Robert M. *The Step-By-Step Guide to Photo-Offset Lithography.* Englewood Cliffs, NJ: Prentice Hall, 1982.

Swerdlow, Robert M. *The Step-by-Step Guide to Screen Process Printing.* Englewood Cliffs, NJ: Prentice Hall, 1985.

Swiftwater, George A. *Small Press Publishing Techniques: Desktop (Word) Publishing.* Round Rock, TX: Homer W. Parker, 1989.

Test Images for Printing. Compiled by Pamela Groff and Frank Kanonik. Pittsburgh, PA: Graphic Arts Technical Foundation, 1990.

Van Milligen, Jane and Gray, Bill. *Tips on Layout & Design.* Blue Ridge Summit, PA: TAB Books, 1992.

Virkus, Robert. *Quark Prepress: Desktop Production for Graphics Professionals.* New York, NY: John Wiley & Sons, Inc., 1993.

Waste & Spoilage in the Printing Industry: Web Press Edition. Teaneck, NJ: National Association of Printers and Lithographers, 1987.

Webb, Richard C. *Screen Printing Production Management.* Cincinnati, OH: Signs of the Times Publishing Co., 1989.

West, Suzanne. *Working with Style.* New York, NY: Watson-Guptill Publications, Inc., 1990.

Westerfield, Wiley. *Desktop Publishing Teletypesetting: A Resource Guide to Electronic Publishing.* San Diego, CA: Westerfield Enterprises, Inc., 1987.

White, Alex. *How to Spec Type.* Introduction by Jan White. New York, NY: Watson-Guptill Publications, Inc., 1987.

White, Jan V. *Color for the Electronic Age.* New York, NY: Watson-Guptill Publications, Inc., 1990.

Wilkinson, Judith. *Designing & Producing Artwork.* New York, NY: Intermediate Technology Development Group of North America, 1985.

Wilkinson, Judith. *Planning the Project.* New York, NY: Intermediate Technology Development Group of North America, 1985.

Wilkinson, Judith. *Printing Processes.* New York, NY: Intermediate Technology Development Group of North America, 1985.

Will-Harris, Daniel. *Desktop Publishing with Style: A Complete Guide to Design Techniques & New Technology for the IBM PC & Compati-* bles. Introduction by Peter A. McWilliams. South Bend, IN: And Books, 1987.

Williams, Roger L. *Paper & Ink Relationships.* Introduction by David G. Vequist. Nappanee, IN: Practical Printing Management, 1986.

Williams, Thomas A. *How to Save Money on Printing.* Plantation, FL: Venture Pr., 1991.

Worcester, Robert L. and Pugsley, Anna (Illustrator). *In Print: How to Plan, Purchase, & Produce Print.* Bloomingdale, IL: Media Assocs. International, Inc., 1989.

Selected Bibliography
Customer-Defined Quality Management

Barker, Joel A. *Future Edge: Discovering the New Rules of Success.* New York: Morrow, 1992.

Bennis, Warren. *On Becoming a Leader.* Redding, MA: Addison-Wesley, 1990.

Bennis, Warren. *Why Leaders Can't Lead: The Unconscious Conspiracy Continues.* San Francisco: Jossey-Bass, 1990.

Butman, John. *Flying Fox: A Business Adventure in Teams and Teamwork.* New York: American Management Association, 1993.

Byham, William C. with Cox, Jeff. *Zapp! The Lightning of Empowerment.* New York: Fawcett Columbine, 1988.

Cocheu, Ted. *Making Quality Happen: How Training Can Turn Strategy into Real Improvement.* San Francisco: Jossey-Bass, 1993.

Cribbin, James J. *Leadership: Strategies for Organizational Effectiveness.* New York: AMACOM, 1984.

Crosby, Philip B. *Quality is Free: The Art of Making Quality Certain.* New York: McGraw-Hill, 1979.

Crosby, Philip B. *The Art of Getting Your Own Sweet Way.* New York: McGraw-Hill, 2nd ed. 1981.

Crosby, Philip B. *Quality Without Tears: The Art of Hassle-Free Management.* New York: McGraw-Hill, 1984.

Deming, W. Edwards. *Out of Crisis*. Cambridge, MA.: MIT Center for Advanced Engineering Study, c1986.

Deming, W. Edwards. *Quality, Productivity and Competitive Position*. Cambridge, MA.: MIT Center for Advanced Engineering Study, c1982.

Denton, D. Keith. *Quality Service*. Houston: Gulf Publishing Company, 1989.

Drucker, Peter F. *Managing for the Future: The Nineteen Nineties & Beyond*. New York: NAL-Dutton, 1992.

Drucker, Peter F. *Managing in Turbulent Times*. New York: Harper-Collins, 1985.

Guest, Robert H. et al. *Organizational Change Through Effective Leadership* (2nd ed.). Englewood Cliffs, NJ: Prentice-Hall, 1986.

Griffiths, David N. *Implementing Quality: With a Customer Focus*. Milwaukee: American Society for Quality Control, 1990.

Juran, Joseph M. *The Corporate Director*. New York, American Management Association, 1966.

Juran, Joseph M. *Juran on Planning for Quality*. New York: Free Press; London: Collier Macmillan, c1987.

Juran, Joseph M. *Juran on Quality by Design: The New Steps for Planning Quality into Goods and Services*. New York: Free Press; Toronto: Maxwell Macmillan Canada; New York: Maxwell Macmillan International, c1992.

Juran, Joseph M. *Juran's Quality Control Handbook*. New York: McGraw-Hill, c1988.

Juran, Joseph M. *Quality Planning and Analysis, from Product Development through Usage*. New York: McGraw-Hill, 1970.

Juran, Joseph M. *Juran on Planning for Quality*. New York: Free Press, 1987.

McLagan, Patricia and O'Brien, Michael. *Designshop: Customer-Focused Instructional Design*. San Diego: Pfeiffer & Co., 1992.

Pascale, Richard T. *Managing on the Edge: How the Smartest Companies Use Conflict to Stay Ahead*. New York: Touchtone Books, Simon & Schuster Trade, 1992.

Peters, Thomas J. *In Search of Excellence: Lessons from America's Best-Run Companies*. New York: Harper & Row, c1982.

Peters, Thomas J. *Liberation Management: Necessary Disorganization for the Nanosecond Nineties*. New York: A.A. Knopf, 1992.

Peters, Thomas J. *A Passion for Excellence: The Leadership Difference*. New York: Random House, c1985.

Peters, Thomas J. *Thriving on Chaos: Handbook for a Management Revolution*. New York: Knopf; Distributed by Random House, 1987.

Peters, Thomas J. and Waterman, Robert H., Jr. *In Search of Excellence*. New York: Warner Books, 1993.

Prichett, Price and Pound, Ron. *Team Reconstruction: High Velocity Moves for Repairing Work Groups Rocked by Change*. Dallas, TX: Prichett Assoc., 1992.

Quinn, Robert E. et al. *Becoming a Master Manager: A Competency Framework*. Thompson, Michael P. and McGrath, Michael R. (Ed.) New York: Wiley, 1990.

Reid, Peter C. *Well Made in America: Lessons from Harley-Davidson on Being the Best*. New York: McGraw-Hill, 1992.

Ryan, Kathleen D. and Oestreich, Daniel K. *Driving Fear Out of the Workplace: How to Overcome the Invisible Barriers to Quality, Productivity, & Innovation*. San Francisco: Jossey-Bass, 1993.

Wellins, Richard S. et al. *Empowered Teams: Creating Self-Directed Work Groups That Improve Quality, Productivity, & Participation*. San Francisco: Jossey-Bass, 1991.

Zemke, Ron and Bell, Chip R. *Service Wisdom: Creating & Maintaining the Customer Service Edge*. Minneapolis: Lakewood Publications, 1989.

Zemke, Ron and Schaff, Dick. *Service Edge: One Hundred One Companies That Profit from Customer Care*. New York: NAL-Dutton, 1990.

Index